septe

24 training contract application deadline:
freshfields bruckhaus deringer (penultimate year law undergrads)

31 training contract application deadline:
allen & overy (law students)
arnold & porter
brabners
bristows (for september interviews)
cadwalader, wickersham & taft
clyde & co
field fisher waterhouse
herbert smith
hewitson becke + shaw
keoghs
laytons
leboeuf, lamb, greene & macrae
lester aldridge
lovells
mayer, brown & platt
prettys
shadbolt & co
sheridans
taylor vinters
theodore goddard
wedlake bell

1 training contract application deadline:
fenners

3 training contract application deadline:
ince & co

30 training contract application deadline:
cleary, gottlieb, steen & hamilton
cumberland ellis peirs
hodge jones & allen
taylor walton
travers smith braithwaite

1 training contract application deadline:
hill dickinson

30 training contract application deadline:
gouldens

31 training contract application deadline:
sinclair roche & temperley
teacher stern selby

The Law Society's Guide to Good Practice requires law firms not to interview students for training contracts before 1st September in the final year of undergraduate study. For the full regulations see www.lawsoc.org.uk

---

"I was attracted to Shoosmiths because of its reputation for outstanding training. I knew that it would be a marvellous opportunity to gain valuable experience in a commercial environment"

Zoe Wright, Second year trainee.

july

1 training contract application deadline:
sidley austin brown & wood

24 training contract application deadline:
freshfields bruckhaus deringer (final year undergrads/grads)

26 training contract application deadline:
addleshaw booth
radcliffes

28 training contract application deadline:
baker & mckenzie (law)

29 training contract application deadline:
olswang

30 training contract application deadline:
henmans

31 training contract application deadline:
ashurst morris crisp
berwin leighton paisner
bevan ashford
bird & bird
blake lapthorn
bond pearce
browne jacobson
campbell hooper
capsticks
cobbetts
coffin mew & clover
coudert brothers
cripps harries hall
d j freeman
davies arnold cooper
dickinson dees
dla
eversheds
farrer & co
finers stephens innocent
forbes
goodman derrick
halliwell landau
hammond suddards edge
harbottle & lewis
holman fenwick & willan
howes percival
hugh james ford simey
irwin mitchell
klegal
knight & sons
lawrence graham
le brasseur j tickle
lee bolton & lee
lewis silkin
macfarlanes
manches
martineau johnson
masons
mccormicks
mcdermott, will & emery
mishcon de reya
morgan cole
nabarro nathanson
nicholson graham & jones
osborne clarke
pinsent curtis biddle
pritchard englefield
reed smith warner cranston
richards butler
russell jones & walker
salans hertzfeld & heilbronn hrk
shearman & sterling
shoosmiths
sj berwin
stephenson harwood
thomson snell & passmore
walker morris
ward hadaway
watson, farley & williams
weightmans
weil, gotshal & manges
white & case
withers
wragge & co

august

1 training contract application deadline:
payne hicks beach
trowers & hamlins

2 training contract application deadline:
davies wallis foyster
denton wilde sapte
may, may & merrimans

3 training contract application deadline:
norton rose

9 training contract application deadline:
burges salmon
pannone & partners
taylor joynson garrett

10 training contract application deadline:
tarlo lyons

11 training contract application deadline:
russell-cooke

15 training contract application deadline:
mills & reeve
penningtons
rowe & maw
speechly bircham

16 training contract application deadline:
dechert
reynolds porter chamberlain
simmons & simmons
tlt solicitors

21 training contract application deadline:
wiggin & co

april

1 vacation scheme application deadline:
hill dickinson

30 training contract application deadline:
rickerby watterson
(for 2003)

vacation scheme application deadline:
fenners
knight & sons (summer)
morgan cole
penningtons (summer)
taylor walton

may

31 training contract application deadline:
charles russell

june

1 training contract application deadline:
boyes turner

30 training contract application deadline:
edwards geldard

shoosmiths
SOLICITORS

Interested?
www.shoosmiths.co.uk

The Lakes, Bedford Road, Northampton NN4 7SH
Tel: 01604 543 223 Fax: 01604 543 543 Email: joinus@shoosmiths.co.uk www.shoosmiths.co.uk
Offices in Northampton, Solent, Basingstoke, Reading, Milton Keynes, Banbury, Nottingham.

calendar of events

february

2 vacation scheme application deadline:
norton rose (summer)

6 nottingham university law fair

8 vacation scheme application deadline:
clifford chance
garretts (andersen legal)
slaughter and may
withers

13 sheffield university law fair

14 vacation scheme application deadline:
freshfields bruckhaus deringer
holman fenwick & willan
speechly bircham
weil, gotshal & manges

chambers student guide essay competition deadline

15 vacation scheme application deadline:
ince & co
lovells (easter and summer)
masons
penningtons (easter)
stephenson harwood

18 training contract application deadline:
baker & mckenzie (non-law)

22 vacation scheme application deadline:
burges salmon
simmons & simmons
taylor joynson garrett

23 vacation scheme application deadline:
addleshaw booth

28 training contract application deadline:
allen & overy (cpe candidates)

vacation scheme application deadline:
berwin leighton paisner
bird & bird
bristows (easter and summer)
capsticks
d j freeman
dechert
dickinson dees
dla
edwards geldard
field fisher waterhouse
gouldens (easter and summer)
hammond suddards edge
klegal
knight & sons (easter)
macfarlanes
martineau johnson
mills & reeve
nabarro nathanson
pinsent curtis biddle
reynolds porter chamberlain
richards butler
rowe & maw
shoosmiths
sinclair roche & temperley
theodore goddard
walker morris
wedlake bell
white & case

march

1 vacation scheme application deadline:
irwin mitchell
olswang
trowers & hamlins

8 vacation scheme application deadline:
pannone & partners

10 vacation scheme application deadline:
nicholson graham jones

15 vacation scheme application deadline:
arnold & porter
denton wilde sapte

16 vacation scheme application deadline:
shadbolt & co

29 vacation scheme application deadline:
mishcon de reya
radcliffes

31 training contract application deadline:
davenport lyons
mace & jones (fe)

31 vacation scheme application deadline:
bond pearce
halliwell landau
laytons
lester aldridge
reed smith warren cranston
taylor vinters
watson, farley &

student guide

2001

november

1 city university law fair

2 vacation scheme application deadline:
clifford chance (christmas)

3 vacation scheme application deadline:
norton rose (christmas)

6 bristol university law fair

7 bristol university law fair (continued)

8 manchester university law fair

13 leicester university law fair

14 uea law fair

16 vacation scheme application deadline:
bristows (christmas)
lovells (christmas)

19 leeds university law fair

20 liverpool university law fair

21 queen's university belfast law fair

22 reading university law fair
southampton university law fair

23 vacation scheme application deadline:
herbert smith (christmas)

24 oxford university law fair

26 newcastle university law fair

27 durham university law fair
warwick university law fair

28 birmingham university law fair
queen mary university of london law fair

29 cambridge university law event

30 cambridge university law event (continued)

december

3 university college london law fair

4 university college london law fair (continued)

31 training contract application deadline:
dmh (for 2003)

2002

january

1 vacation scheme application deadline:
mccormicks

21 king's college law fair

22 king's college london law fair (continued)

25 vacation scheme application deadline:
ashurst morris

29 exeter university law fair

31 training contract application deadline:
bristows (for february interviews)

vacation scheme application deadline:
allen & overy
baker & mckenzie
dmh
eversheds
farrer & co
herbert smith (summer)
lawrence graham
manches
osborne clarke
sj berwin
wragge & co

"I learnt a lot during my time at Shoosmiths; Lawyers don't have to be stuffy and unapproachable, they don't have to work 20 hour days to be successful and they are just as human as the rest of us!"

Rachael Parman, Summer Placement Student 2001.

Published by Chambers and Partners Publishing
(a division of Orbach & Chambers Ltd)
Saville House, 23 Long Lane, London EC1A 9HL
Tel: (020) 7606 1300 Fax: (020) 7600 3191
email: info@ChambersandPartners.co.uk
www.ChambersandPartners.com

Our thanks to the many students, trainees, pupils, solicitors, barristers, graduate recruitment personnel and careers officers who assisted us in our research. Also to Chambers and Partners recruitment team for their knowledge and assistance and to the researchers of the Chambers Guide to the Legal Profession 2001-2002 and Chambers Global 2001-2002 from which all firm rankings are drawn.

Copyright © 2001 Michael Chambers and
Orbach & Chambers Ltd
ISBN: 0 85514-304-5

Publisher: Michael Chambers
Managing Editor: Fiona Boxall
Editor: Matthew Butt
True Picture Editor: Anna Williams
Writers: James Lloyd, Greg Lascelles, Juliette Seddon
Database Manager: Derek Wright
A-Z Team: Nicola Cowan, Alex Ballantine, Laura Gladwin
Production: Laurie Griggs
Business Development Manager: Brad D. Sirott
Business Development Team: Richard Ramsay, Neil Murphy, Sam Nicholls, Janis Witicki

Printed by: Polestar Wheatons Limited

CONTENTS

starting out

how to choose what you want to do – where you want to do it and how to get it

choices

contacts
useful numbers, addresses and websites to get you started **6**

solicitor or barrister?
we help you make that all important first decision **8**

funding
how to get funding for CPE/PgDL, LPC and BVC including awards and scholarships from the Inns of Court **12**

academic and vocational education
we give you the lowdown on the LPC, CPE/PgDL and BVC **16**

solicitors section

solicitors timetable
what to do and when to do it **20**

vacation schemes
these can play a vital part in getting a training contract – don't miss out **22**

vacation schemes table
fancy spending your Christmas, Easter or summer vacations with a top law firm? Who to apply to and when **24**

the city lpc
what's all the fuss about? Who are the gang of eight law firms behind it and which colleges offer it? **28**

vocational course providers – the inside story
what law school graduates really thought about their law schools. Plus the Law Society's assesment grades **30**

applications and selection
making sense of application forms and how to avoid being a pushover during group excercises **35**

selection table
open days and interviews – who does what and how many training contracts are they offering? **38**

what the top firms are looking for
which buttons you should be aiming to press **45**

what you are looking for – salaries table
the hard cash plus details of sponsorships and other benefits available **48**

paralegal questions
answers to the most commonly asked questions **62**

paralegal salaries table **64**

barristers section

barristers timetable
what to do and when to do it **66**

the bar system
an introduction to the sometimes mystifying world of the Bar **67**

pupillage – how to get it
during the bad old days it was hit and miss – has it improved under OLPAS? **70**

practice areas at the bar
chancery, commercial, common law, criminal, family, public law – which one's for you? **72**

www.ChambersandPartners.com

specialist practice areas

what you should know about the main areas of law and a guide to who does them best. Information about the top firms hot off the press from the *Chambers Guide to the Legal Profession 2001-2002*. Banking, corporate, crime, employment, environmental, EU, family, intellectual property, IT, litigation, media, personal injury, private client, projects, property, public interest law, shipping, sports, tax **81**

qualifying in other jurisdictions

New York and Australian Bar courses – how to do them, where and why. Plus qualifying as a Scottish solicitor **182**

overseas lawyers

qualifying in the UK from abroad **184**

the true picture

introduction
still want to go through with it but not sure which firms to apply to? Put down that firm brochure and get the true picture here. We interviewed hundreds of trainees and newly qualified solicitors at our top 100 firms and asked them to tell us about their training contracts in their own words... and they did! They were remarkably frank with us **186**

the true picture top 100 firms table
it's the biggest True Picture we've ever done! **188**

the true picture 100
as ever we don't pull any punches. Totally unvetted by the law firms, we tell it like it is. Don't pick a firm without looking here first **191**

international firms – international locations
it's all gone global – we take a look at the top international players and where they operate **396**

prospects for newly qualifieds
it seems a long time away, but you should be thinking about it now – where are the best job prospects in private practice, in-house and elsewhere? **399**

A-Zs

every phone number, address and e-mail you need to make your applications. Plus loads of really useful facts and figures on the top law firms. All in simple easy to follow A-Z format

universities and law schools A-Z	**403**
solicitors A-Z	**419**
barristers A-Z	**566**

STARTING OUT

contacts	6
solicitor or barrister?	8
funding	12
academic and vocational education	16
solicitors timetable	20
vacation schemes	22
vacation schemes table	24
the city lpc	28
vocational course providers	30
applications and selection	35
selection table	38
what the top firms are looking for	45
what you are looking for (money)	48
paralegal questions	62
paralegal salaries	64
the bar system	67
pupillage – how to get it	70
practice areas at the bar	72

CONTACTS

The Law Society:	114 Chancery Lane, London WC2A 1PL Tel: 020 7242 1222 www.lawsoc.org
Trainee Solicitors Group:	The Law Society 114 Chancery Lane, London WC2A 1PL Tel: 020 7320 5794 E-mail: info@tsg.org www.tsg.org.uk
The Bar Council:	3 Bedford Row, London WC1R 4DB Tel: 020 7242 0082 www.barcouncil.org
Education and Training Department:	2/3 Cursitor Street, London EC4A 1NE Tel: 020 7440 4000 www.lawzone.co.uk/barcouncil
Gray's Inn, Education Department:	8 South Square. Gray's Inn, London WC1R 5EU Tel: 020 7458 7900 www.graysinn.org.uk
Inner Temple, Education & Training Department:	Treasurer's Office, Inner Temple, London EC4Y 7HL Tel: 020 7797 8250 www.innertemple.org.uk
Lincoln's Inn, Students' Department:	Treasury Office, Lincoln's Inn, London WC2A 3TL Tel: 020 7405 0138 www.lincolnsinn.org.uk
Middle Temple, Students' Department:	Treasury Office, Middle Temple, London EC4Y 9AT Tel: 0207 427 4800 www.middletemple.org.uk
Career Development Loans:	Freepost, Warrington WA4 6FB Tel: (freephone) 0800 585505 www.lifelonglearning.co.uk/cdl
Government Legal Service:	Lawyers' Management Unit, Queen Anne's Chambers, 28 Broadway, London SW1H 9JS Tel: 020 7210 3184 E-mail:pbeecroft@gls.gsi.gov.uk www.civil-service.gov.uk/jobs
Crown Prosecution Service:	50 Ludgate Hill, London EC4M 7EX Tel: 020 7796 8500 www.cps.gov.uk

CONTACTS

Institute of Chartered Secretaries and Administrators:	16 Park Crescent, London W1B 1AH Tel: 020 7580 4741 www.icsa.org.uk
The Institute of Legal Executives:	Kempston Manor, Kempston, Bedfordshire MK42 7AB Tel: 01234 841000 E-mail: info@ilex.org.uk www.ilex.org.uk
Chartered Institute of Patent Agents:	Staple Inn Buildings, High Holborn, London WC1V 7PZ Tel: 020 7405 9450 E-mail mail@cipa.org.uk www.cipa.org.uk
Institute of Trade Mark Attorneys:	Canterbury House, 2-6 Sydenham Road, Croydon, Surrey CR0 9XE Tel: 020 8686 2052 www.itma.org.uk
Free Representation Unit:	Fourth Floor, Peer House, 8-14 Verulam Street, London WC1X 8LZ Tel: 020 7831 0692 www.fru.org.uk
The Law Commission:	Conquest House, 37-38 John Street, Theobalds Road, London WC1N 2BQ Tel: 020 7453 1220 E-mail secretary.lawcomm@gtnet.gov.uk www.lawcom.gov.uk
Citizens Advice Bureaux:	Head Office, Myddleton House, 115-123 Pentonville Road, London N1 9LZ Tel: 020 7833 2181 www.nacab.org.uk (Information on local branches and how to volunteer.)
CPE Central Applications Board:	P.O. Box No. 84, Guildford, Surrey GU3 1YX Tel: 01483 451080 www.lawcabs.ac.uk
LPC Central Applications Board:	P.O. Box No. 84, Guildford, Surrey GU3 1YX Tel: 01483 301282 www.lawcabs.ac.uk
Legal Services Commission	Head office, 85 Gray's Inn Road, London WC1X 8TX Tel: 020 7759 0000 www.legalservices.gov.uk

solicitor or barrister? we help you decide...

What do you want from a career in the law? Depending on the type of lawyer you become, you could be working in the City of London assisting plcs with their acquisitions and investments, you could be working for a small specialist firm dealing with intellectual property law or you might be standing up in court, prosecuting or defending those accused of crimes. In reality 'the law' is a huge umbrella covering a vast array of diverse careers. Your choice of career will depend on where your skills lie and, just as importantly, what interests you. If you have no enthusiasm for the area you plan to move into then you are simply not going to make it or enjoy it. The first choice you need to make is between the two branches of the profession.

barristers

Over the last fifteen years the old divisions between barrister and solicitor have begun to break down, increasing competition at the Bar. Most large firms now provide advocacy training since solicitors have gained rights of audience in all but the highest courts. Increasingly, this means that solicitors will be handling cases themselves from beginning to end, without instructing a barrister to handle the advocacy. In today's legal profession it is wrong to picture only barristers speaking in court with solicitors simply handling client contact and preparing the paperwork.

Despite these changes, barristers continue to provide two traditional services: giving second opinions on matters of law to solicitors and appearing in court as specialist advocates. The Bar maintains a strong reputation in both areas which is unlikely to be eroded in the immediate future, despite the best efforts of solicitor advocates and the continual deregulation of the legal profession. There is no doubt, however, that competition from solicitors is tough.

If you do choose the bar, do not assume that you will be pontificating in front of a judge every day. The amount of court work you will see varies between practice areas. Some commercial barristers might be in court only once a month at most. If you want to specialise in business law at the Bar, you should be aware that judges will be unimpressed by you wasting their time with 'Rumpole of the Bailey' impressions. You'll need to develop a style of advocacy which is not only sophisticated and persuasive, but also efficient, clear and concise.

Your choice of practice area will have significant bearing upon your financial well-being. Commercial and Chancery barristers fare much better than their colleagues who pursue some of the more advocacy based practice areas, like family, crime and common law. Top commercial and Chancery sets offer up to £40,000 a year during pupillage. The equivalent remuneration for those who opt for common law, crime and family is around £15,000 a year max. and often significantly less. A proportion of this will be tax-free. Obviously, this rises significantly if you gain tenancy and build up your practice. Note that we use 'if' rather than 'when'.

The road to a career at the Bar is considerably riskier and more expensive than the alternative route to practising as a solicitor. Chambers do not, as a rule, sponsor students during vocational education, although a small number are prepared to advance around £5,000 for the Bar Vocational Course (BVC) year. As BVC fees are now pushing over the £8,500 mark with living costs on top, qualifying can be an expensive business. The Inns of Court distribute around £2 million a year in scholarships for those studying the BVC but for those who are not funded and do not gain a scholarship, the only means of funding available is a bank loan. It is estimated that the average level of debt by the end of pupillage is some £25,000. This is even higher for those who need to sit the Common Professional Exam (CPE).

Before you start your vocational education you will need to apply to chambers for pupillage. Only around twenty five percent of those who commence the BVC will be successful in obtaining pupillage first time around.

The Bar Council has recently required that all pupillages commencing in 2003 be funded by at least a £5,000 grant from chambers during the first (non-practising) six months with guaranteed earnings of a further £5,000 in the second (practising) six. Whilst this will go some way towards removing the abject poverty suffered by some pupils, it is still below the Law Society's minimum wage for trainee solicitors.

> Your performance over the duration of your pupillage will be instrumental as to whether or not you gain tenancy.

Following pupillage you will need to make the final cut – being accepted as a tenant in chambers. This decision is normally taken by a vote involving all members of chambers. Your performance over the duration of your pupillage will be instrumental as to whether or not you gain tenancy. For those who don't make it, an uncertain future awaits. Many pupils nowadays recognise the need to complete a third six months, continuing as a practising pupil, 'squatting' in chambers and picking up as much work as possible whilst looking for tenancy elsewhere. Some even hang on to undertake a fourth six months before in the most part calling it a day.

Even if you do secure tenancy, your worries are not over yet. As a self-employed practitioner, you must pay rent on your office space in chambers and organise income tax and VAT returns for yourself. You only see your hard earned cash when the client coughs up. Some will prove better than others at paying promptly. To cap things off, the taxman is not concerned about your problems and will demand prompt payment whether or not you have received the money from your client.

If you have not been warned before then take this as the first in a long line of warnings. The young Bar is feeling the pinch with dwindling fees, increased competition from solicitors and fewer cases reaching court. Of those graduates who commence the BVC, only one in three will have a lasting career at the Bar. You must be prepared for rejection along the way. Most graduates preparing to take the BVC have reconciled themselves to the fact that to have a serious stab at a career at the Bar, they must be prepared to take a gamble. On the plus side, if things do not go quite according to plan, do remember that the BVC is a valuable qualification whether you practice at the Bar or not. It will not be a wasted year whatever happens.

Many non-lawyers assume that clever solicitors become barristers if they are very good at their work. Seeing your solicitor friends simmer with rage when people ask them if they will become a barrister one day is some small consolation for the fact that they are earning a shed load during their training contract whilst you are eating beans on toast during pupillage.

If you are happy to take the financial and professional risk and want to be self-employed and entirely responsible for your own actions, victories and defeats, then a career at the Bar may just be for you.

solicitors

So you want to be a solicitor. Deciding which firm to train at is one of the most important decisions you will make. This choice will determine the types of client and areas of practice to which you'll become exposed. We have profiled the 100 leading firms in the True Picture section of this book, giving you a taster of life inside these firms before you commit yourself. What follows here is a rough guide as to the sort of firm which might suit you and the kind of work you can expect to receive when you get there.

city

For those interested in a career at a City law firm, it's good news. Despite a dip in the recruitment market this year, there remain excellent prospects upon qualification. This year the top 10 City firms will offer around 1,000 training contracts between them, representing around 20% of the total training contracts registered with the Law Society. The work of the biggest firms is almost entirely focused around business law, although some firms retain specialisms in family law and private client work. The hours are long and the money is exceptionally good. Interested?

Right at the top of the tree sit the magic circle firms; Allen & Overy, Clifford Chance, Freshfields Bruckhaus Deringer, Linklaters, and Slaughter and May. These firms are perceived to be in a league of their own in international business law and the training you receive will make you a highly valued commodity upon qualification. Snapping at their heels are a number of other top tier international practices. There is barely any difference between the training offered by the magic circle and firms such as Ashurst Morris Crisp, Herbert Smith, Lovells and the rest of the top tier. You'll be exposed to high profile deals and challenging work. You should expect to be pushed hard and, at times, be prepared to give 110%. If you are working against a deadline on a deal then you will be expected to stay until it is finished. This can mean working through the night and coming in at weekends from time to time.

> The hours are long and the money is exceptionally good. Interested?

To get into one of the top firms you will need a consistently good academic record, from A Levels through to your second year exam results or final degree classification. Unfortunately for some, this means going right to the back of the queue if you failed to gain at least a 2:1. degree. Recruitment personnel in City firms are also keen to ensure that prospective trainees possess commercial awareness. This doesn't mean that you have to read the FT every day throughout your degree, indeed, the managing partner of an expanding US firm's London office said he would be *"rather scared to hear of a student who had done!"* It is about understanding what businesses want, how they work and what lawyers can do to help them. You need to show that you have an interest in law, an interest in business and an interest in the firm you are going to.

If you are thinking of applying, perhaps the best way to get your foot in the door and experience first-hand what life is like at one of your target firms is to undertake a vacation placement. These last for a few weeks, provide an invaluable insight into the life you are letting yourself in for and will give you valuable experience to draw upon when you turn up for interview.

regions

Whilst the City of London is the heart of the big ticket blue chip deal, there is more to life than just an EC post code.

Firms such as Wragge & Co, Burges Salmon and Osborne Clarke – to name but a few – bear many similarities to the top London firms. The top regional firms boast global reach, top notch clients, and big name partners. Some firms aim to be the direct competitors of the top London firms and may even have London offices, while others focus on building up a regional practice.

Regional firms can be every bit as difficult to get into as City firms. In some cases you are statistically better off applying to a magic circle firm as the ratio of vacancies to applications can be much better at the biggest practices. It is not a good idea to apply to a regional firm because you think that it will be easier to get into having been refused by the magic circle. The firm will be aware of this strategy already and is unlikely to be impressed by it.

Speaking to trainees and recruitment personnel at the top regional practices, we found that these firms are looking for exactly the same abilities and experience as the top City firms. If you have a connection with the region this often helps. If you are applying to join a firm in Bristol and have studied and lived in London all your life, be prepared to be asked why you want to move to the area. The last thing firms want is to spend a fortune on training only for their newly qualifieds to swan off to jobs in the City.

Salaries are lower outside London, in some cases significantly so, but the cost of living is much more reasonable than in the capital. You will also benefit from less frantic hours than the largest City practices. Provincial firms have a reputation for (generally) being a bit friendlier, a bit calmer and a bit more human than the City. As you will see in the True Picture section, however, it is all about finding a firm which has an atmosphere to suit you.

high street

High Street practice ranges from long-established firms in large town centres, some with over ten partners, to sole practitioners working above shops in the suburbs. These practices can be found throughout the country.

You will deal with publicly funded clients, individuals funding themselves and local businesses. Staple work for a high street lawyer will include: landlord and tenant, personal injury, employment, family, wills and probate and criminal. There is also a good deal of conveyancing work as well as small-scale share purchases and sales.

High street firms are increasingly likely to have an additional specialism in small ticket commercial work for local businesses. Over the last few years this more labour intensive but higher value work has brought considerable dividends for high street practitioners.

Be prepared to earn considerably less than your friends in commercial firms. It may well mean that as a trainee you will be paid at the Law Society's minimum wage level – £12,000 for the provinces and £13,600 for inner London. In addition to lower wages, the hours, whilst nowhere near as long as large, commercial practices can be unsociable, especially if you work visiting police sations and court on the duty solicitor register. You will find, however, that you will be handling clients and real work very early on in your training. High street solicitors also have an opportunity to see how the law actually affects individuals and the community they practice in.

High street recruitment varies significantly between practices, with the largest firms taking on two to three trainees a year and smaller firms recruiting as and when additional fee earners are needed. Unlike the larger commercial practices, they may not recruit two years in advance.

funding

Legal education is not cheap. The less profitable the area you are hoping to move into, the more you will have to fund your own way through vocational education. City firms are only too happy to crack out the chequebook and fund their trainees all the way through law school. If your social conscience has driven you to human rights law at the Bar, however, then you will need to meet many of the costs yourself by borrowing the money.

Banks recognise the CPE, LPC and BVC as being worthwhile investments in their customers' futures and are normally happy to advance around £10,000 a year in recognition of this. Typically, such loans will be at a low rate of interest (normally 1% over base rate) and repayments can be delayed until after qualification.

> Banks recognise the CPE, LPC and BVC as being worthwhile investments in their customers' futures.

Students studying in London should note that they are entitled to a 30% discount on tubes and buses. This is obtained by a special photo-card. You will need to speak to the registry at law school or your Inn of Court who will give you a stamped form which can be used to get your photo-card. The discount applies to full-time students only, but also covers pupil barristers.

solicitors

CPE fees come in at around £5,000 a year whilst the LPC can cost £7,500. The first trick in off-setting this cost is to try and get someone else to pay for it!

If you have a training contract with a large commercial practice, there's a good chance that your firm will give you a grant, fund your LPC fees and hopefully, if necessary, your CPE fees too. We provide full details of what the top firms will pay on pages 50 to 63. Not all firms will pay for your education, and not all students are able to acquire training contracts before commencing vocational education.

If you don't manage to find a training contract and still have your heart set upon becoming a solicitor, you will probably be able to borrow some of the cash you need from the bank.

Both the CPE and the LPC are recognised as full-time courses of higher education and, accordingly, you cannot actively seek employment whilst studying. Sadly this means that you will not be eligible to claim Job Seekers' Allowance. The law schools clearly prefer students not to juggle full time courses with part time employment. Despite heavily advising against part-time work, the reality is that some students simply do not have the luxury of heeding this advice. Most institutions provide the option of studying vocational courses part-time, with lectures held during the evenings and the occasional weekend. This allows students to combine study with full-time employment or family commitments. Part-time courses take two years to complete.

In the absence of law firm sponsorship for vocational education, determined students should be able to make ends meet through a combination of bank loans, holiday work and frugal living.

barristers

Barristers face a tough time in making their way through vocational education. Chambers will not fund the BVC or the CPE. A very limited number of chambers are, however, prepared to advance around £5,000 to students on the BVC. Check whether this might apply to you through OLPAS.

The situation becomes bleaker with the measly awards made to the majority of pupils. This situation will improve slightly with the introduction of the minimum wage for pupil barristers in 2003. With state benefits notable by their absence, the two main means of funding the Bar Vocational Course are bank loans and scholarships. Oh and having rich parents is always handy.

scholarships

The Inns of Court distribute over £2 million in financial assistance to BVC students every year. Some Inns will have a cursory means test to assess students' needs, others will not. The table at the end of this section outlines what is provided by each Inn. You can only apply for scholarships from one Inn. If you attempt to apply to more than one, you won't get diddly.

getting a scholarship

The procedure will vary from Inn to Inn. The most common procedure, however, is a simple application form which, once submitted, will be used to draw up a short list for interview. Gray's Inn requires you to have achieved at least a 2:1 in your degree to be considered for an award. The other Inns will consider applications from anyone with at least a 2:2.

The Inns do not seem to have a hard and fast policy on whether or not your means are taken into account. There will be questions about your finances and you will need to make a declaration of income on the application form, but certainly no exhaustive investigation is made. Scholarships would seem to be provided on merit first, with means as a secondary consideration.

Make sure that your application is as impressive as possible. Being short-listed for interview is half the battle. If you are short-listed your chances of receiving an award are good. The interview will normally be with three to five lawyers from the Inn. They might be QCs or even judges. The Under Treasurer will usually sit in on the interview with some trustees; they will not be involved in the questioning of candidates or in the final decision.

The panel are looking for academic ability, likelihood of making a superb advocate and, importantly, commitment to the Bar. The last thing they want is to give several thousand pounds to someone who will then drop out of the BVC and join the circus.

It is very unlikely that you will be tested on substantive legal matters, although you should definitely be ready to discuss topical legal issues or to talk through an area of law that interests you. In addition to this, expect to be quizzed on what area of law you want to go into, why you are interested in that area and what skills you can bring to the Bar.

If you have a good CV, knowledge of topical legal issues and know why you want to be a barrister you should do well.

Full details of what all the Inns are offering can be found on the next page.

TABLE OF AWARDS AND SCHOLARSHIPS FOR BARRISTERS

NAME OF INN	TOTAL FUNDS AVAILABLE	CPE/BVC AWARDS	PUPILLAGE AWARDS	CONTACT DETAILS
Inner Temple	£765,000	For CPE: £12,500 x 1 £10,000 x 5 £70,000 in bursaries For BVC: £17,500 x 1 £20,000 x 1 £15,000 x 1 £12,500 x 4 £10,000 x 20	£280,000 in bursaries £160 x 50 for admissions/call fees £15,000 disability grants One at £14,000 One at approx £4,000	Rachel Jenkins Tel: 020 7797 8210 Fax: 020 77797 8212 rjenkins@innertemple.org.uk
Middle Temple	£620,000	For CPE: 20-30 of between £1000 and £8000 For BVC: £1,000 - £15,000 x 80 -100	Approx 25 awards of between £500 and £5,000	Students Department Tel: 020 7427 4800 student_enquiries@middletemple.org.uk
Gray's Inn	c £600k+	For CPE: £46,500 split into separate awards For BVC: £15,000 x 3 £12,500 x 12 £10,000 x 6 £5,000 x 22 £3,000 x 19 £85 Admission Fees x 25 Up to £10,000	£59,800 split between various awards £15,500 split between various awards for the 1st year of practice	Miss Louise Rouse PA to Deputy Under Treasurer (Students) Tel: 020 7458 7900 louise.rouse@graysinn.org.uk
Lincoln's Inn	£758,000	For CPE: Up to 15 scholarships of up to £8,000 Up to 100 awards for admission, call and dining For BVC: Up to 40 scholarships of between £8,000 and £15,000 each Up to 40 bursaries of up to £6,000 each	2 Awards of approx £8,000 each 15 Rooms in Self Contained Flats (7 at £5,500, 8 at £4,350) Up to 10 scholarships of £3,000 £3,000 for a place at European Court for a young barrister £3,000 for a place at European Court of Human Rights 2 x £5,000 for a stage in Brussels	Judith Fox Tel: 020 7405 0138 judith.fox@lincolnsinn.org.uk

All figures are accurate at the time of going to press

Professions

Do you need to finance your way through the CPE, LPC or BVC ?

Do you have a Relationship Bank Manager who understands the Legal Profession and can advise you on the options available ?

We are a specialist Branch, whose client base is completely legal. To discuss our Professional Trainee Loan Scheme, please write to:

Law Courts, Temple Bar Legal Centre
PO Box 11052
217 Strand
London WC2R 1AR

or contact Ash Khan, Business Manager.
Telephone: 020 7664 9166

Remember to mention the Chambers Student Guide

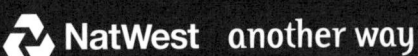

Written quotations available on request. National Westminster Bank Plc. Registered Office: 135 Bishopsgate, London EC2M 3UR. Registered Number 929027 England

academic and vocational education

making the most of your time at university

Kick-starting your legal career can be tough and the sooner you start planning your campaign the better. This needn't be an all consuming obsession throughout your degree, but it helps to bear in mind where you want to be in four years time and how you can give yourself a head start. If you want to move into business law then you should start keeping an eye on the financial news so you have a basic grounding in your subject before you attend interviews. It is much easier to pick up a sense of commercial awareness by paying attention to relevant stories over a few years than trying to memorise fifteen back issues of the FT the night before your interview.

During your time at university there will be plenty of opportunities to get a feel for City practice and even to make contacts at the top firms. Law firms put on presentations and organise careers evenings to woo the best students. These events are normally open to all students, not just those studying law. Information will be distributed in law departments and by student law societies. Another excellent way to absorb information is to attend the law fairs and pupillage fairs which are held around the country and attended by all the top firms (for details see in the calendar inside the cover at the front of this guide).

> "I wish I had done more at university."

If you want to move into criminal or human rights law, you will need to show more than a working knowledge of The Bill and membership of Amnesty International. Get involved in human rights campaigns, volunteer at a local Citizens Advice Bureau or take on some Free Representation Unit work. Details for these organisations are in the contacts section (see pages 6 and 7). Chambers and law firms do value such practical experience. Some of the top human rights chambers and criminal law firms see this sort of experience and commitment as being just as important as academic qualifications.

When filling in application forms, many students suddenly find they draw a blank on what to write in the sections asking about activities and interests, positions of responsibility held and achievements whilst at university. There are endless opportunities to get involved in student activities; be they sporting, cultural, social or political. Such experience looks good on an application form and will make your application more rounded and impressive. Many graduates complain "I wish I had done more at university." If it is not too late, don't become one of them.

You should also expect to set some time aside in the holidays to undertake mini pupillages and vacation placements. Some students still think that having a non-law degree is a significant drawback. They are wrong. As long as you can show that you are committed to a legal career there should be no discrimination. Increasingly, firms and chambers appreciate students from a variety of degree backgrounds. One magic circle firm takes up to 50% non-law graduates per intake. Science and language degrees are particularly well regarded. Language skills are appreciated by all firms, indeed some are specific about their language requirements. Pritchard Englefield for example, looks for *"a second European language"* and prefers German and French.

It is essential that you put yourself in as strong a position as possible whilst you are still at university. You will be applying for and will hopefully receive a training contract before you have finished your degree.

vocational education

Having completed your degree you need to study for a further year if you have a degree in law or two years if you studied another subject. Legal education can be a little confusing at times. If you don't know your CPE from your LPC then read on.

common professional examination (CPE) or postgraduate diploma in law (pgDL)

The Common Professional Examination is so called because both barristers and solicitors undertake the same course. It is a conversion course, which is designed to put you on a level footing with people who did a law degree. The course lasts for one year if you study full-time and certain institutions will allow you to study part-time over two years. The cost of the full time course varies between institutions but fees tend to be around £5,000.

Starting off with a few weeks introduction to the English Legal System, the CPE goes on to cover all the areas undergraduate law students were sweating over as they scurried past the union bar to the library. These will include:
- contract and tort
- equity and trusts
- land law
- criminal law
- constitutional and administrative law
- european union law

The CPE is an intensive course with a very different feel to undergraduate study. You must be self-motivated and hard working if you want to succeed. The College of Law schedules around 10 hours of lectures and tutorials a week and students are expected to spend the rest of their time in private study, preparing for class and undertaking research. You should be aware that the CPE is the first part of your legal career. It is quite possible that the firm providing your training contract will cover your fees. It will not be impressed if you fail!

Once you have completed the CPE, you will need to move on to the LPC for solicitors or the BVC for barristers.

legal practice course (LPC)

City, commercial or conventional?

At the moment the LPC is at a crossroads. Following years of criticism from the legal profession, certain course providers have set up a new course which has been termed the City LPC. The College of Law has set up its own specialised course for commercial practice in response. This is referred to as the Commercial LPC. A full explanation of the new courses is provided on page 29.

The LPC aims to provide students with the skills they will need to survive as a solicitor in practice. There is an emphasis on practical skills that are applied in the real world. The course is a long way away from undergraduate legal study, which has its focus on theory and academic legal issues. The Inns of Court School of Law (ICSL) sets around 14 hours of classes a week for students and expects about 18 hours of private study to be undertaken in addition.

The LPC will vary slightly depending upon where you study as different course providers design their own courses. Broadly, however, its content is divided into compulsory subjects, legal skills and electives.

The **compulsory subjects** cover the knowledge areas deemed fundamental to practice as a solicitor. They will certainly include: litigation, conveyancing and business law.

Legal skills are the practical skills that you will need on a day to day basis as a solicitor. For example: interviewing skills, drafting contracts, advocacy and IT.

During the **electives**, you will choose two or three subjects from a wide range of choices. The electives that you choose will obviously be tailored to the kind

of practice that you hope to move into. Electives offered at the College of Law include:
- acquisitions and group structures, commercial law (commercial contracts, competition law, intellectual property) corporate finance, commercial litigation.
- commercial property, media and entertainment law, employment law and practice, personal injury and clinical negligence, litigation, family law and practice, welfare benefits and immigration law, private client: wills, trusts and estate planning.

the bar vocational course

The BVC is the vocational course necessary to practise at the Bar. Upon completion of the course you are called to the Bar. Before you can practise, however, you will need to undertake a one-year pupillage. The BVC is the most expensive course, with fees set at around £8,500.

The BVC is a practical course which aims to provide students with the skills required to practise at the Bar and the specific knowledge necessary to undertake court work, for example: rules of evidence and civil and criminal procedure.

Inns of Court School of Law (ICSL) timetables around 14 hours of lectures for students a week and expects about 20 hours of private study in addition to this.

Wherever you study, the components taught will be divided into three broad areas:

Practical skills are taught by a variety of methods including role play, videoed assessments, tutorials and lectures. The skills you will acquire over the course of your study include:
- advocacy
- negotiation
- drafting
- legal research
- opinion writing
- conference skills

Knowledge areas are mostly taught in lectures and tutorials and then assessed by Multiple Choice Tests (M.C.T.). You will cover: civil litigation, criminal litigation, sentencing and evidence.

You will choose two **electives** to study in addition to the above compulsory areas. As with the LPC, you should obviously ensure that the electives you choose are relevant to the area that you hope to practise in. ICSL currently offers the following electives:
- advanced civil litigation
- employment law in practice
- family law in practice
- landlord and tenant law in practice
- sale of goods and consumer credit law in practice
- company law in practice
- european community competition law
- free representation unit work

SOLICITORS

SOLICITORS TIMETABLE

LAW STUDENTS • Penultimate year

October 2001- February 2002:	Compile information about law firms. Obtain firm brochures. Attend presentations and law fairs on campus.
January - March 2002*:	Apply for open days and vacation schemes.
Spring - Summer 2002**:	Attend vacation schemes. Apply to law firms for training contracts for 2004. Apply for a place on the LPC.

LAW STUDENTS • Final year

September - December 2002:	Attend interviews for training contracts for 2004.

LAW STUDENTS • Post Graduation

September 2003:	Commence LPC.
July 2004:	Finish LPC.
September 2004:	Commence training contract (first intake).
March 2005:	Commence training contract (second intake).
September 2006:	Qualify as a solicitor (first intake).
March 2007:	Qualify as a solicitor (second intake).

* It is important to check closing dates for each firm as these will vary. Many close in January or February. Some firms will only accept applications for vacation schemes from penultimate year students whether law or non-law. See pages 20-25 for further information.

** It is important to check closing dates for each firm. Many firms will not accept applications after the summer. A few firms accept applications into the Autumn or even into the following year. Some firms require very early applications from non-law graduates. See pages 39-46 for further information.

*** Some firms may interview earlier or later than these dates.

SOLICITORS TIMETABLE

NON-LAW STUDENTS • Penultimate year (2001/2002)

October 2001 - February 2002:	Compile information about law firms. Obtain firm brochures. Attend presentations and law fairs on campus.
January - March 2002*:	Apply for open days and vacation schemes.
June - August 2002:	Attend vacation schemes.

NON-LAW STUDENTS • Final year (2001/2002)

October 2001 - February 2002:	Compile information about law firms. Obtain firm brochures. Attend presentations and law fairs on campus. Apply for training contracts to those firms with unusually early closing dates.
November 2001:	Apply for a place on the CPE course.
January - March 2002*:	Apply for open days and vacation schemes.
January - Autumn 2002**:	Apply to law firms for training contracts for 2005.
September - December 2002***:	Attend interviews for training contracts for 2005.

NON-LAW STUDENTS • Post Graduation

June - August 2002:	Attend vacation schemes and interviews for training contracts for 2004. Apply for a place on the LPC if your CPE institution does not guarantee you a place.
September 2002:	Commence CPE.
July 2003:	Finish CPE.
September 2003:	Commence LPC.
July 2004:	Finish LPC.
September 2004:	Commence training contract (first intake).
March 2005:	Commence training contract (second intake).
September 2006:	Qualify as a solicitor (first intake).
March 2007:	Qualify as a solicitor (second intake).

vacation schemes

If you want to get a head start on your application, undertaking work experience at a firm is the best way to go about it. Vacation schemes are held over the summer months, last for a few weeks and are reasonably well paid. Firms run these schemes to get a closer look at students who will be applying for training contracts and to allow applicants to get a feel for the law and specifically their firm. It is competitive to get on a scheme, especially at the top firms. In the past we have spoken to trainees and students who were disorganised and missed the deadlines set for applications. If you want to undertake a scheme, make sure your application is in early.

But what's all the fuss about? Why bother? A vacation scheme is an excellent way of improving your chances of getting a training contract. A trainee at one firm told us: *"The summer vacation schemes are the main source of recruitment here."* Law Society guidelines state that no interviews may take place or offers of training contracts be made until 1st September in the final year of undergraduate study, so don't expect an offer on the spot during the scheme. Sometimes a formal interview is just that though; a mere formality.

> A vacation scheme is an excellent way of improving your chances of getting a training contract.

the experience

"It was fairly stressful" one successful student told us. She said, *"everyone was watching you, taking notes."* So is it a legal Big Brother? Less so than you might think. To have secured the place, students will already have beaten most of the competition and impressed the firm on paper. In many cases they will have been successful in an interview equally as tough as a training contract interview. The time spent with the firm ought to be an enjoyable few weeks, learning about what the firm does, whether or not you like the people – whether or not the chemistry is right. Think of it as a very long interview. Try to impress, don't make a fool of yourself. Frankly, as long as you're sensible, keen and likeable you can't go wrong. There's only so much you can get out of one interview, *"whereas if you're working for two weeks you get a much better idea in terms of internal structure and friendliness."*

Many students will be checking out a number of different firms. So it's a hard sell. *"It was certainly a busy week, full of meals and theatre trips as we were wined and dined whilst they tried to sell the firm to us."* A summer spent hopping from one scheme to another could also leave you loaded. Some firms pay up to £250 per week.

Some firms take vacation schemes much more seriously than others. *"At Garretts they'd arranged lots of things, like taking us on City tours including the London Exchange and they arranged social things."* Our True Picture interviewees often speak of how the trainee social scene at their firm picks up during the vac student 'season' and the party budget goes through the roof. But remember, the aim is to impress. It's not always an accurate measure of the training experience. But you'll have ample opportunity to get to know people at the firm and find out how they work and what they work on. It may be a chance for you to find out whether the law suits you. That should be of greater concern to you than how many trips or nights out are laid on. In fact some firms, such as Freshfields, have stopped putting on the 'glamour' trips round the London financial institutions and try to give their summer students more 'real' work.

Whilst you are trying to convince the firm that you are right for them, you also need to establish whether the firm is right for you *"It was like viewing a house. I got an idea of what people at the firm were like, not just in a brochure or at interview but up close in their working environment. I did two schemes and by the time I had finished I knew the kind of environment in which I would fit in and had decided which of the two firms was for me."* It is crucial that you pay attention throughout the time you are at the firm. Everyone will be on their best behaviour because the vac students are there. You will need to peer underneath the surface to get an insight into what the firm is really like.

Some firms really make the effort to keep students occupied. *"At Eversheds we were supporting or shadowing for 60% of the time and the other 40% was either talks given by people from the firm or group discussions and exercises. There were a couple of social events as well."* Others score E for effort. *"The firm that I was at I didn't like at all, so I didn't apply to them. I was put in a room on my own and just given the odd file to read. It was terrible. People didn't even come and talk to you. I had a miserable time. I went to complain to the personnel officer and she wasn't prepared to listen."* Another student at one of the largest firms was turned off by its scheme *"I felt like I was just passing through, there was no real work to get my teeth into and again and again I would be standing in a lift with fifteen people whose names I did not know feeling like a spare part. I was left thinking if this is what training here is like then I don't want to come here."*

making the most of it

If you're not getting much out of a vacation scheme feel free to talk to personnel. Maybe the department you're in is too busy or particularly quiet. If there's a particular type of work you want to experience, ask the firm if you can spend time in that department. *"If it's well organised, it will give you a good chance not only to take in the environment but also to meet people.... Speak to people, that is the most important thing."*

It's not just the lawyers you'll get to talk to. Plenty of students pool information. One shared an experience of a visit to a magic circle firm, where a trainee showed her round. *"She burst into tears and said don't come here, it's horrible."* Sure, you should take such reports with a pinch of salt. Perhaps she hated being a lawyer. Perhaps she would have been happier at a small firm. Perhaps she was having a bad day. Use your own judgement; it's going to be your career. On the other side, a trainee who doubted whether or not she wanted to be a solicitor gave some words of encouragement. *"I didn't enjoy studying law but thought I'd give it try. I really enjoyed it...my vacation scheme inspired me."*

Whilst vacation schemes are important, there is much more to your application than showing that you trudged around firm after firm throughout the summer. It might suggest a certain lack of initiative if the only items of interest on your CV or application form are vacation schemes. Firms differ on the importance they attach to schemes. A trainee at Slaughter and May told us *"I didn't do a vacation scheme. Slaughters assume you have an interest in law already, it is better to be an interesting person. Slaughters take the view that vacation schemes are for people who want to see what corporate work is like."* One firm went further *"to be honest we are more interested in applicants who have used their initiative and got some alternative experience through involvement in industry or travel. The schemes are mainly there so the firm can get a close look at you, and you can have a close look at the firm, they don't really make you a better applicant as such."* On the other hand, some firms almost require a scheme to be completed. Bond Pearce, for example, describes their summer programme as *"an integral part of the recruitment process"* and draw trainees attention to this at the top of their application form. If your heart is set on a certain firm, make sure you know their policy on vac schemes. The bottom line is that whilst a scheme will put you ahead at that specific firm, it is unlikely to count for much elsewhere.

VACATION SCHEMES TABLE

FIRM NAME	NUMBER OF PLACES	DURATION	REMUNERATION	2002 DEADLINE
Addleshaw Booth & Co	40	2 weeks	£150 p.w.	23 February 2002
Allen & Overy	90	3 weeks	£250 p.w.	31 January 2002
Arnold & Porter	Places available	Not known	Not known	15 March 2002
Ashurst Morris Crisp	30 non-law students 70 law students	2 weeks Easter 3 weeks summer	£250 p.w.	25 January 2002
Baker & McKenzie	30	3 weeks	£250 p.w.	31 January 2002
Berwin Leighton Paisner	180 places on the Open Days 60 summer placements	1 week	Not known	28 February 2002 for open day – could lead to placement in summer
Bevan Ashford	80	Not known	Not known	Not known
Bird & Bird	12	3 weeks	£185 p.w.	February 2002
Bond Pearce	Places available	Not known	Not known	31 March 2002
Bristows	36	Summer - 2 weeks, Christmas/Easter - 1 week	£200 p.w.	Christmas 16 November 2001 Easter/summer 28 February 2002
Burges Salmon	32	2 weeks	£150 p.w.	22 February 2002
Capsticks	Places available	2 weeks	Not known	28 February 2002
Clarkes	Places available for 2003 on application	Not known	Not known	Not known
Clifford Chance	Places available	Approx. 2 weeks Christmas, Easter and summer	£240 p.w.	2 November 2001 for Christmas scheme; 8 February 2002 for other schemes
Clyde & Co	2 legal training days – summer vacation placements available	2 weeks		28 February 2002
CMS Cameron McKenna	55	2 weeks	£200 p.w.	Not known
Cobbetts	18	Not known	Not known	Not known
Coffin Mew & Clover	Places available	1 week	Not known	Not known
Davenport Lyons	14	2 weeks	£175 p.w.	None fixed
Dechert	16 plus open days (20-30 places for law, 20-30 places for non-law	2 weeks	no less than £225 p.w.	28 February 2002
Denton Wilde Sapte	80-90	Information week/open day	Not known	15 March 2002
Dickinson Dees	36	1 week	£125 p.w.	28 February 2002
D J Freeman	18	3 weeks	£150 p.w.	28 February 2002

Schemes take place in the summer unless otherwise indicated

VACATION SCHEMES TABLE

FIRM NAME	NUMBER OF PLACES	DURATION	REMUNERATION	2002 DEADLINE
DLA	200	1 week	£200 p.w. (London), £150 p.w. (Regions), £140 p.w. (Scotland)	28 February 2002
DMH	Limited number, priority given to trainee interviewees and Sussex University	1-2 weeks	£100 p.w. plus expenses	31 January 2002
Eversheds	150	2 weeks	Regional variations	31 January 2002
Farrer & Co	18	2 weeks Easter, 3 weeks summer	£210 p.w.	31 January 2002
Fenners	10	2 weeks	Competitive rates	30 April 2002
Field Fisher Waterhouse	Places available	Not known	Not known	28 February 2002
Freshfields Bruckhaus Deringer	100	2 weeks	£450	14 February 2002, but apply as quickly as possible
Garretts (Andersen Legal)	60	3 weeks	£250 p.w.	8 February 2002
Gouldens	56	2 weeks	£250 p.w.	28 February Easter (non law) summer (law) 13 October Christmas (non law)
Halliwell Landau	24	2 weeks	£100 p.w.	31 March 2002
Hammond Suddards Edge	60	3 weeks	£230 p.w. (London), £180 p.w. (Regions)	28 February 2002
Herbert Smith	115	2 weeks	Not known	Friday 23 November 2001 for Christmas scheme Thursday 31 January 2002 for Easter and summer scheme
Hewitson Becke + Shaw	A few available	1-2 weeks	Not known	Not known
Hill Dickinson	Places available	1 week	None	1 April 2002
Holman Fenwick & Willan	12	2 weeks	£250 p.w.	14 February 2002
Howes Percival	Limited number available	Not known	Not known	Not known

Schemes take place in the summer unless otherwise indicated

VACATION SCHEMES TABLE

FIRM NAME	NUMBER OF PLACES	DURATION	REMUN-ERATION	2002 DEADLINE
Hugh James Ford Simey	Places available	Not known	Not known	Not known
Ince & Co	16	2 weeks	£250 p.w.	15 February 2002
Irwin Mitchell	30	2 weeks	£75 p.w.	1 March 2002
KLegal	12	5 weeks	£250 p.w.	28 February 2002
Knight & Sons	Places available	Not known	Not known	31 October 2001 – Christmas 28 February 2002 – Easter 30 April 2002 – summer
Lawrence Graham	40	2 weeks	£225 p.w.	31 January 2002
Laytons	6	1 week	Not known	31st March 2002
Lester Aldridge	8	2 weeks	£60 p.w.	March 2002
Linklaters	120	Not known	£250 p.w.	Not known
Lovells	90	Not known	Not known	Christmas – 16 November 2001 Easter and summer – 15 February 2002
Macfarlanes	40	2 weeks	£250 p.w.	28 February 2002 but applications considered and places offered from the beginning of January 2002
Manches	24	1 week	£175 p.w.	31 January 2002
Masons	41	2 weeks	Not known	15 Feb 2002
McCormicks	Places available	Not known	Not known	1 January 2002
Mills & Reeve	Places available	2 weeks	Not known	1 March 2002
Mishcon de Reya	12	3 weeks	£150 p.w.	29 March 2002
Morgan Cole	Places available	1 week	Not known	30 April 2002
Nabarro Nathanson	60	3 weeks	Not known	28 February 2002
Nicholson Graham & Jones	8	2 weeks	£210 p.w.	10 March 2002
Norton Rose	60	3 weeks (summer), 2 weeks (Christmas)	£250 p.w.	2 February 2002 – summer 3 November 2001 – Christmas
Olswang	45	2 weeks	£250 p.w.	1st March 2002
Osborne Clarke	35-40	Easter or summer placements for 1-2 weeks	£150-£200 p.w.	31 January 2002
Pannone & Partners	50	1 week	None	8 March 2002

Schemes take place in the summer unless otherwise indicated

VACATION SCHEMES TABLE

FIRM NAME	NUMBER OF PLACES	DURATION	REMUN-ERATION	2002 DEADLINE
Penningtons	60 on London open days at Easter. Some summer vacation places out of London	Not known	Expenses	Open days – 15 February 2002 Summer schemes – 30 April 2002
Pinsent Curtis Biddle	140	1 week	Not known	28 February 2002
Radcliffes	10	2 weeks	£130 p.w.	29 March 2002
Reed Smith Warner Cranston	12	2 weeks	£400	31 March 2002
Reynolds Porter Chamberlain	12	2 weeks	£200 p.w.	28 February 2002
Richards Butler	20	Not known	£200 p.w.	28 February 2002
Rowe & Maw	25	2 weeks	£200 p.w.	28 February 2002
Shadbolt & Co	6	2 weeks	£170 p.w.	6 March 2002
Shoosmiths	30	2 weeks	£120 p.w.	28th February 2002
Simmons & Simmons	40-50	2-4 weeks	£225 p.w.	22 February 2002
Sinclair Roche & Temperley	10-12	2 weeks	TBA	28 February 2002, subject to availability
SJ Berwin	60	2 weeks	£225 p.w.	31 January 2002
Slaughter and May	60 for penultimate year (of first degree) students only	2 weeks	£250 p.w.	8 February 2002
Speechly Bircham	10	3 weeks	£250 p.w.	14 February 2002
Stephenson Harwood	21	2 weeks	£200 p.w.	15 February 2002
Taylor Joynson Garrett	30	2 weeks	£200 p.w.	22 February 2002
Taylor Vinters	Places available	1 week	Not known	31 March 2002
Taylor Walton	4	up to 4 weeks	Agreed with applicant	30 April 2002
Theodore Goddard	20	2 weeks	£200 p.w.	28 February 2002
TLT Solicitors	6	Not known	Not known	Not known
Trowers & Hamlins	25-30	2 weeks	£175 p.w.	1 March 2002
Walker Morris	45	1 week	£120 p.w.	28 February 2002
Ward Hadaway	Places available	1 week	Not known	Not known
Watson, Farley & Williams	30	2 weeks	£200 p.w.	31 March 2002
Wedlake Bell	6	3 weeks in July	£150 p.w.	28 February 2002
Weil, Gotshal & Manges	12	Not known	Not known	14 February 2002
White & Case	30	2 weeks	£250 p.w.	28 February 2002
Withers	26	2 weeks	Not known	8 February 2002
Wragge & Co	60	1 week Easter 2 weeks summer	£170 p.w.	31 January 2002

Schemes take place in the summer unless otherwise indicated

the city lpc

The recent introduction of LPC courses geared towards the reality of practice in the City is one of the most significant changes in legal education since the origination of the LPC in 1993. If you are considering applying for a place on the LPC next year, it is important that you consider the implications of the new course and where you want to end up practising.

Since its creation, the LPC has been the subject of extensive criticism. The loudest grumbles have come from the big City law firms and specifically eight of the largest firms. Together they instigated the establishment of the City LPC. These firms: Allen & Overy, Clifford Chance, Freshfields Bruckhaus Deringer, Herbert Smith, Linklaters, Lovells, Norton Rose, and Slaughter and May spend around £8 million a year on LPC fees between them. They have helped develop a new course which they feel will be of greater relevance to students intending to pursue a career in a City law firm.

To further confuse things, the Law Society has actually banned the use of the phrase 'City LPC', saying that there is only one LPC course in the Law Society's eyes and it will be referred to as the LPC, regardless of what electives are offered. To simplify things, however, we will continue to refer to the new LPC supported by the big eight as the 'City LPC '. We will refer to the College of Law's new course as the 'Commercial LPC'.

The Law Society ratified the new City LPC course on 29 January 2001 and it is now offered at BPP Law School (London), Nottingham Law School and the Oxford Institute of Legal Practice. The notable omission from this list is The College of Law. Clearly rattled by being passed over to teach the City LPC, The College of Law set up its own special LPC course aimed at meeting the needs of practice in the City. This course, the Commercial LPC, has also been ratified by the Law Society and the College will start teaching it in the academic year commencing in September 2001.

> "Students will no longer be able to tread water for a year."

Peter Jones, Dean and Chief Executive of Nottingham Law School, explained that someone starting the City LPC will notice that it is *"mostly oriented towards the commercial"* and that they *"were concentrating a lot more on the law contained in transactions."* There will be more emphasis put on preparation for tutorials and a greater reliance on original source materials. Significantly, students will no longer be able to take their manuals into exams. This was the case with the old LSF (Law Society Finals) which pre-dated the LPC. Regardless of which subjects you elect to do in the second part of the course, if you go to Nottingham, Oxford or BPP you'll notice more of a 'City' slant in the first, compulsory part of the course. There will be less emphasis on oral skills. Peter Jones admitted that the course will be more intense. *"Students will no longer be able to tread water for a year."*

So how do you decide between the City LPC, the Commercial LPC or a conventianal LPC? In reality this should not cause much head scratching for the majority of students, as many applicants will have secured a training contract before they commence the LPC. If your sponsoring firm doesn't reveal a clear preference, look at the course providers' prospectuses and work out which syllabus would suit you best.

The eight firms that initiated the City LPC reserve places at the chosen three schools for their prospective trainees, so if you are heading to one of the big eight this will be taken care of for you. A word of warning though – You can't guarantee undertaking the City LPC in London as only BPP is offering the course in the capital. The London option is often over subscribed and your firm may put you into a ballot to decide who gets a London

> "I am not prepared to preside over a law college that is devoted to serving the needs of an exclusive few at the expense of the many."

place. Another problem comes where law schools guarantee places on their LPC course to their own CPE students. If you are not going to one of the big eight firms and you have not done the CPE at BPP it is going to be more difficult to get a place on the BPP LPC. Phew! While BPP deny that this is going to be a problem, it is hard to imagine how there will be room for all candidates who are otherwise perfectly well qualified.

There has been considerable debate and controversy over these developments in vocational education, with fears that the creation of the City LPC heralds a two tier system of legal education. Nigel Savage, Chief Executive of the College of Law, has attacked the course. *"I am not prepared to preside over a law college that is devoted to serving the needs of an exclusive few at the expense of the many."* A cynic might regard this as sour grapes. After all, the College of Law tendered unsuccessfully for the City LPC. But these fears can't be ignored. The Lord Chief Justice, Lord Woolf also weighed in to the debate, expressing a fear that the City LPC might lead to élitism, which could damage the profession as a whole.

If the views of the trainees who talked to us about their experiences of the LPC are of any worth (and we certainly think that they are) then legal education needed a kick up the behind. Anything that helps to make the LPC year more relevant to the reality of practice is to be applauded. Next year we will report on students' first impressions of the new courses.

vocational course providers – the inside story

Whilst researching the True Picture we spoke to hundreds of law school graduates. We asked them where they had studied for the LPC and how well they thought their law school had run the course. In this section we report on the institutions about which we received sufficient representative comment. The Law Society undertakes a rigorous assessment of all law schools offering vocational education. Its findings, which are based upon in depth visits to the course providers, can be found on its own website : www.lawsoc.org (Qualifying as a solicitor – LPC course format). We have also incorporated some of these findings in this report.

Nottingham Law School

facts
number of lpc students pa: 504
law society rating: excellent
city lpc: yes

Nottingham has always been rated highly by law firms, students and the Law Society, which consistently awards an 'excellent' rating to the school. In recognition of this track record, Nottingham was picked by the big eight firms to be one of the schools to offer the City LPC.

The school was praised for the quality of most of its facilities, the social life and teaching standards. The Nottingham LPC has always been commercially orientated, even before the City LPC components were introduced. Study here and you'll find that most of your peers will be off to commercial practice at one of the big City firms. Career guidance and support was also singled out for praise.

We were told that the course kicks in pretty quickly and students need to ensure that they *"hit the ground running."* The workload will settle down over the year, but it has a very steep incline at the start. Some students seemed to think that they were worked a little bit harder than students at other law schools. There seems no need to worry, however, as nobody suggested that the course was beyond them.

The most critical comment we received related to facilities. *"There were a few problems when everyone needed to get work in at the same time as there was a bit of a shortage of computers."*

Socially, Nottingham was praised to the hilt. Some sources were slightly concerned when they arrived in *"a rather forboding concrete jungle,"* but once they had delved a bit deeper they found the town to be *"welcoming and fun, a great place to live and socialise in."*

The College of Law

facts
number of lpc students pa: see individual branches
law society rating: see individual branches.
city lpc: no: offers own 'commercial lpc' course

For years it was literally the only law school. The College of Law has had an eventful time over the last couple of years. Overlooked by the 'Group of Eight' Law firms for the City LPC, it has responded assertively by setting up its own rival City practice-oriented course, the 'Commercial LPC.' Its second innovation is the opening of the brand-spanking-new COL in Birmingham. The COL tells us that students can expect good IT, library and teaching facilities plus a Legal Advice Clinic where students can gain practical experience. Just eight minutes from the legal heart of Birmingham, expect oodles of attention from leading local firms. Its location in the up-and-coming Jewellery Quarter means that Birmingham's thriving night life is on the doorstep. This year's interviewees were the first students to experience the long-awaited refurbishment of the Store Street branch which is the first stop on our tour.

london - store street

number of lpc students pa: 1392
law society rating: very good

The Store Street branch was set up as the London replacement for the Chancery Lane and Lancaster Gate branches. After only 10 years or so the site became a victim of its own popularity, as numbers seemed to grow too rapidly for the facilities to cope. It takes almost twice as many full-time LPC students as the next biggest provider (Guildford).

There was no clear consensus amongst students about the Store Street experience. Some didn't like it at all, but many told us they enjoyed it and, just like your granny used to tell you, *"it really is what you make of it!"* One positive point, which came across very strongly, was the quality of the teaching materials. *"The manuals are even more useful to me now that I am in practice. I keep them in a box under my desk and still use them frequently."*

For years students bemoaned the tired and cramped facilities, however, after a substantial refurbishment programme this problem has now been remedied. Interviewees praised the improved building which now provides *"excellent facilities and equipment."* Despite the makeover, Store Street is still compared to an educational factory. *"They really turn over a huge number of students – they just polish you up and boot you out again."* Another problem we heard about was the ratio of tutors to students, which sometimes meant work was handed back late. *"The staff were always nice, always helpful but dreadful about getting results out on time. When they were supposed to be out at 4pm you'd still be waiting round at 7pm. They never made concessions on the deadlines for getting work in though."*

Opinion was divided over the quality of the social life at Store Street. Some enjoyed studying in the heart of London and thrived upon it. *"I made loads of friends at Store Street and we are still in touch now."* The social life just seemed to pass others by. *"London is such a big place, with so many distractions, everyone just melted away after class."*

chester

number of lpc students pa: 656
law society rating: good

Set in the 14 acre grounds of Christleton Hall, COL's Chester outpost seemed to be a particularly attractive choice for those who are not drawn to practice in the City. COL Chester normally scatters a high proportion of its alumni around law firms in the North West. *"Don't apply to Chester if you intend practising in the City and hope to have an LPC reunion."*

Several students commented on the useful revision sessions the college runs at the beginning of the course. These cover land law and contract law. *"I took a gap year between university and the LPC. I was terrified that they would assume I knew everything from my degree but I hadn't really looked at land law since I walked out of my first year exams."*

As for the town itself, Chester received a big thumbs up from students who found it a friendly and fun place to live. You will see a fair bit of your fellow students as *"everyone goes to the same parties."* Regular outings are organised to Cream in Liverpool, so there's something else to do if you get bored of trying to spot the cast of Hollyoaks around town.

guildford

number of lpc students pa: 800
law society rating: very good

Just like the Marmite ad, you either love or hate COL Guildford. Some students had a whale of a time and went as far as to say that doing the LPC at Guildford was *"better than university."* Others found the student community to have *"a few too many rugby playing and jolly hockey sticks types."* Our sources reported that most students seemed to be straight out of uni and attended Oxbridge or the top red bricks.

Teaching materials were again popular amongst all the trainees we spoke to and the Guildford careers service was singled out for extensive praise. It offers comprehensive advice on CVs, applications and interviews, which are conducted during the summer before the course begins.

The course is taught in an old country mansion located just outside the centre of Guildford. The town seems to have reinvented itself over the last few years, and in the evenings the centre is *"pretty much back to back bars. You wouldn't have thought it but it is a great place to go out in."*

york

number of lpc students pa: 572
law society rating: very good

Set in an old junior school and its playgrounds, you will really be able to relive the fun of your old school trips to the Jorvik Viking Museum.

Any criticism from students who studied at York was directed at the course itself rather than the college. *"The LPC is pants!"* one trainee said categorically. But others said they had a ball, juggling Woolf reforms with drafting and negotiation skills. None the less, all the staff, from personal tutors through to the librarian, were found to be extremely friendly and helpful and teaching standards were deemed to be more than satisfactory.

York itself gets the thumbs up all round. As one person put it (presumably a southerner), there's *"a Coronation Street communal atmosphere."* *"I thought York was a perfect place. It's such a nice city."*

The social life is *"great."* Students are thought to be mainly from the north or graduates of northern universities. It's small enough that people at least recognise each other. There's *"plenty going on if you wanted to put yourself about."* *"Everyone lived in the same area and went to the same pubs, there was inter-class football and netball"* and *"you got to meet lots of people."* There are plenty of organised social events in addition to sports, including visits to Tetleys Brewery and the racecourse next door.

With accommodation available from only £35 per week, students can afford a *"good standard of living."*

Oxford Institute of Legal Practice

facts
number of lpc students pa: 168
law society rating: very good
city lpc: yes

A coalition between Oxford University and Oxford Brookes University, the Oxford Institute has had a busy few years. Last year the Law Society demoted the course from an 'excellent' rating to a paltry 'good.' This year, they have clawed back up to 'very good.' Oxford is also one of the schools picked by the big eight to offer the City LPC.

On the face of it, Brookes and Oxford University make unlikely bedfellows and there seemed to be a few problems with LPC students not always having access to all the facilities the two universities had promised. On the positive side, interviewees were very enthusiastic about the programme of external lectures and guest speakers, which *"really helped bring the course to life."*

In terms of the location, unsurprisingly students *"loved the place."* After all, Oxford was made for students. There's a social committee on the LPC course, but *"most of the organising and money was spent on the Law School Ball."* Apart from that *"everyone got to know each other well because it was quite a small place and everyone socialised together."* And there were always the social events organised by the rowing club. We'll say no more!

It's not cheap to live in Oxford though; accommodation costs around £60-65 a week.

BPP

facts
number of lpc students pa: 432
law society rating: very good
city lpc: yes

Located right in the heart of legal London, BPP is your only choice in London if you are going to one of the big eight firms who will require you to undertake the City LPC. Be warned, you are not going to be the only person to find the bright lights of London irresistible, and most students will have to go into a ballot to get their place at BPP.

Students appreciate the central location, which is certainly *"really convenient if you are attending interviews or need to speak to someone at your firm."* The old problem of cramped facilities mentioned by some students, will vanish althogether this year as BPP has moved into larger, newly refurbished premises.

It is in the quality of teaching that BPP impresses most. Once again, we got the impression that most of the academic staff were prepared to go that extra mile for their students, especially as nerves became frayed around exam time.

Socially the place is a good bet. Despite the fact that many people live at home to save money, *"there is still a community feeling. I belonged there and made four or five good friends for life."* Students go out on Wednesday and Friday nights and a committee organises quiz nights and a summer ball.

University of the West of England

facts
number of lpc students pa: 220-240
law society rating: excellent
city lpc: no

We received overwhelmingly positive comments about the LPC at UWE. Trainees said they would *"recommend the course to anyone"* and the college passed the Law Society's inspection with flying colours on everything from organisation, to teaching, facilities and atmosphere. UWE is one of only three institutions to receive a Law Society 'excellent' rating.

Outside of lectures, *"the social life was excellent and everyone was very keen to arrange things."* You socialise with your group, but it's *"not at all cliquey,"* and even *"the lecturers will pitch up in the pub."* The course director came in for particular praise. *"He hosts parties every year for students and lecturers."*

Bristol is an ideal city for students, with ample centrally-located accommodation at reasonable prices and the delights of the West Country on your doorstep.

Cardiff Law School

facts
number of lpc students pa: 160
law society rating: excellent
city lpc: no

Cardiff Law School scooped up an 'excellent' rating with former students as well as the Law Society. Those on the LPC and BVC courses have access to *"excellent new library and IT facilities"* and because lectures and tutorials (in groups of 16) are staggered throughout the day (not just mornings or just afternoons) students were not competing with each other for resources.

Lecturers are praised for *"knowing everyone by name"* and staff in general are *"wonderful."* A personal tutor system works well and one source reported that she'd been able to attend a different tutor group when the timetable clashed with unavoidable commitments. The practical skills training is useful and covers the usual interviewing and negotiating techniques. And at the end of the day you'll leave Cardiff with some *"pretty handy manuals"* to keep under your desk.

Students come from all over the UK, but many are graduates of Cardiff Uni or are local to the city. Many of the students go on to train with Welsh firms, but certainly not all. Few students come to the Law School without a training contract lined up for the following year. The social scene was described as *"brilliant"* and many of those arriving to start the LPC are already familiar with *"Cardiff's great night life."*

University of Sheffield

facts
number of lpc students pa: 120
law society rating: very good
city lpc: no

Sheffield came out well in this year's trainee interviews. Our sources praised the intimate and friendly atmosphere. *"There are never more than about 120 students on the course so we are taught in small groups of around 15 per tutorial."* This makes it more *"personal."* The numbers also allow for more inter-group socialising than is the norm: *"I socialised an enormous amount."* Many people on the course are heading for firms in the north such as DLA, Nabarros etc.

Staffordshire University Law School

facts
number of lpc students pa: 100
law society rating: very good
city lpc: no

The majority of students hail from the locality and head for Midland firms. The Staffs LPC offers 100 places, with three classes further subdivided into tutor groups. With a maximum of 10 students per group, *"the small numbers mean you get to know each others and the staff quickly."* The course fees are far cheaper than COL.*" Staffordshire also offers pretty good value for money."* There shouldn't be too much fighting over computers either, with a ratio of *"two students per computer."*

The only drawback seemed to come after hours. Perhaps because so many students had been based in the area for so long, options for all night rave ups with your fellow students are limited. *"The social life is not too clever. Most students would tend to go home afterwards to their halls of residence and flats or parental homes."*

VOCATIONAL COURSE PROVIDERS: LAW SOCIETY'S ASSESSMENT GRADES

Provider	Grade	Provider	Grade
Anglia Polytechnic University	Good	University of Central Lancashire	Very Good
University of Central England	Good	Leeds Metropolitan University	Satisfactory
Bournemouth University	Good	Liverpool John Moores University	Good
BPP Law School	Very Good	London Guildhall University	Good
University of Bristol	Good	Manchester Metropolitan University	Good
Cardiff Law School	Excellent	University of Northumbria at Newcastle	Good
College of Law Chester	Good	Nottingham Trent University	Excellent
College of Law Guildford	Good	Oxford Institute of Legal Practice	Very Good
College of Law Store Street	Very Good	University of Sheffield	Very Good
College of Law York	Very Good	Southbank/University of North London	Good
De Montfort University	Good	Staffordshire University	Very Good
University of Exeter	Good	Thames Valley University	Good
University of Glamorgan	Good	University of the West of England	Excellent
University of Hertfordshire	Good	University of Westminster	Very Good
University of Huddersfield	Good	University of Wolverhampton	Good
Inns of Court School of Law	Good		

applications and selection

Just over a decade ago a third year student at Birmingham University did a summer placement with a top five City firm. She liked the firm and they liked her. Without a single interview or assessment they offered her a job. In 1990, this was not particularly unusual.

Now, however, it's a different story. Students applying for training contracts are likely to face an assault course of group exercises, written tests and day-long assessments before they secure a job. The purpose of this section is to provide a few pointers direct from leading recruiters, to help guide you through the process.

making the application - some basic pointers

Application procedures vary between firms. The vast majority will work to a timetable for applications and interviews. Make sure that you don't miss the boat! The application deadlines for all the top firms can be found on the calendar, inside the front cover of this guide. Some firms, notably Slaughter and May, recruit all year round. You may need to fill in an application form or alternatively, the firm might simply request a CV and covering letter. Many forms are available online.

When filling in application forms, first and foremost ensure that you answer all the questions and that you answer them fully. Whilst this might sound obvious, one gripe we continually hear from graduate recruitment officers is that students continue to make basic mistakes every year. It does not say much about your analytical skills if you appear to be unable to understand an application form.

Crossed out sentences or forms caked in Tipp-Ex are another big turn off. Deborah Dalgleish, Head of UK graduate recruitment at Freshfields Bruckhaus Deringer told us, *"In a job where attention to detail is so important, what does it say about you if you couldn't be bothered to think about what you wanted to say beforehand to avoid making mistakes?"*

If you have a query whilst filling in your application, it is perfectly acceptable to call graduate recruitment at the firm and ask for clarification. But obviously you can't expect them to fill the form in for you!

Some firms will attempt to make life a little easier for applicants by simply requiring a CV and covering letter, thus removing the need to fill in a specific and detailed application form. Make sure that you include all relevant information in your CV. Andrew Hearn, graduate recruitment partner at London firm Dechert, points out that *"if you have something important to say, make sure it is in the application and not just in your covering letter."* Not all selection panel members will see your covering letter.

> A typical assessment day consists of one or two written tests, at least one group exercise, one or two interviews and perhaps a presentation to a group of partners.

assessment days

Getting a good night's sleep is an old interview cliché but has never been more important than now, with the new approach to graduate selection. An assessment day means just that. A whole day. You are continuously assessed from the moment you stutter your name at reception through spilling pasta down your front at the buffet lunch to the point where you wander out of the office at 5pm. The time when you could drink three cups of coffee, chat to a partner for half an hour and then fall asleep on the train home, smug in the knowledge you had got the job, are long gone.

A typical assessment day consists of one or two written tests, at least one group exercise, one or two interviews and perhaps a presentation to a group of partners. Firms place varying degrees of emphasis on the different elements. For some the interview is crucial, while for others group exercises are of primary importance. If it is possible to find out in advance (from current trainees perhaps) then this might be advantageous.

group exercises

One student told us of her *"nightmarish"* experience at a large City firm. She and three others were given a group exercise where they had to imagine they were stranded in the desert. They were given fifteen items to rank in order of importance to their survival. The exercise lasted half an hour and a recruitment officer closely observed the whole process. What she found particularly difficult was the awkward behaviour of everyone in the group. Nobody seemed to know what was expected of them and the individuals ranged from being over-assertive to quiet and difficult.

A very different group exercise at another City firm involved a more business-like situation. Twelve candidates were divided into two groups and asked to advise on the purchase of two factories. One had union problems, but solid financial backing, the other had a different set of problems. Again, the group was observed and again our student found the experience quite *"tense."* She must have performed well though because she was offered a job. When asked why she thought she was successful at one firm and not at the other, she said it had a lot to do with the nature of the group. She felt more comfortable with the second set of people and also with the task. So, it was partly down to chance.

However, she also felt more prepared second time round and realised it was better just to be herself. What can a candidate in their first selection round learn from this?

> "It's important not to be a pushover – say something."

The most obvious answer is to be yourself and you'll find the right firm for you. Bob Llewellin, training director with Burges Salmon, says *"It's important not to be a pushover – say something. But it doesn't help to be bombastic."* If your arguments aren't accepted by the group don't worry – you might have been asked to argue an unwinnable case. Firms are looking to see how good a team player you are, whether you listen to other people's ideas, whether you can compromise, and whether you keep an eye on key factors, such as time and budget.

You should also remember that firms are looking for all kinds of people – the more measured, thoughtful type as well as the outgoing team leader. Though these events always bring out the actor in people, it won't help to reinvent your personality for the occasion. One (successful) candidate said *"I was told in the interview afterwards that the assessors had been impressed that I had noticed time was running out when the others were still arguing over who should be spokesperson."*

written tests

These tend to fall into two types. Firstly, there are the reasoning/personality tests, usually presented in multiple choice format. Though often a minimum standard is set, below which candidates must not fall, you will not get the job simply on the basis of your mental agility. On many assessment days the tests will be marked and returned to the assessors before you leave or even before your interview. As you cannot prepare for these tests, the best advice is to stay calm, work quickly but effectively and keep an eye on the clock.

There is often a second, scenario-based written exercise. Candidates may be asked to note the issues and propose some solutions in a particular situation. You may be asked to put the answer in a particular form (ie. letter, fax, report). Other things you may be asked to do include advising on documents or rewriting something into 'plain English.'

Although spotting potential legal issues is sometimes an important part of the 'situation' exercises, the assessors will not want a detailed analysis of the case law, stuffed full of quotes from Lord Denning. Instead they want sensible, practical, often business-aware comments on the problem. So non-law students need not worry about their lack of legal knowledge. Nobody will expect you to have learnt contract law before the assessment.

presentations

Two candidates at a City law firm were put together and asked to prepare a joint presentation to be given to a partner. To our source the task did not seem that difficult. After all the scenario was quite fun and the other candidate easy to get on with. It was only whilst doing the presentation that he realised that the other candidate would not let him get a word in. She even covered his areas in her speech. Yet halfway through her speech it became obvious from his expression that the partner was not impressed by her attitude to her co-presenter. Result: she did not get an offer and he did. She had failed to realise that a key point of assessment days is not just to assess your mental agility or oratory skills but how well you work with others.

a friendly chat?

If the day involves a session with trainees, be careful, particularly if it is one-to-one. They are not just there to answer your questions. They will be asked for feedback on you (do not believe them if they say otherwise) and will often be your harshest critics. So don't look at it as a chance to slag off your interviewer or confess that you don't really want to be a lawyer, but your parents have forced you into it.

Lunch can also be a particularly stressful affair. Trying to eat tagliatelle with a fork, whilst simultaneously drinking a glass of wine and making small talk with a senior partner can be more taxing than any reasoning test. Remember: red wine on the carpet will not go down well.

The selection and recruitment process is in many firms a polished, highly professional procedure and the City firms, in particular, waste no time in letting successful and unsuccessful applicants know their fate. In many cases, candidates hear that day, especially if the firm wants them. With the benefit of hindsight, most of our interviewees said they enjoyed their assessments and *"the day will almost certainly end with a drinks party."* Don't relax too much – you're being assessed there too!

SELECTION TABLE

FIRM NAME	METHOD OF APPLICATION	SELECTION PROCESS	DEGREE CLASS	CONTRACTS	APPLICA-TIONS
Addleshaw Booth & Co	Application form	Assessment day. Interview	2:1	40	2,000
Allen & Overy	Application form & online	Interview	2:1	120	4,000
Arnold & Porter	Application form	Interviews	2:1	4-6	–
Ashurst Morris Crisp	Online application form	Interviews with 1 assistant followed by interview with 2 partners	2:1	50	3,500
Baker & McKenzie	Letter & application form	Candidates to give a short oral & written presentation, interview with 2 partners, meeting with a trainee	2:1	30	2,000
Berwin Leighton Paisner	Application form	Assessment day and partner interview	2:1	35	2,000
Bevan Ashford	Application form & covering letter	Not known	2:1	25	–
Bird & Bird	Application form	Assessment mornings	2:1	17	1,500
Blake Lapthorn	Application form (on website) & CV	Interview with partners, including giving a presentation plus group exercise	2.1	5	750
Bond Pearce	Application form & CV + photograph	Interviews & vacation placement scheme	–	10-15	500
Boyes Turner	Letter & CV	2 interviews & 1 week work placement	2:2	3/4	2,200
BP Collins	Handwritten covering letter & CV	Screening interview & selection half day	–	–	–
Brabners	Application form	Open day & interview	2:1 or higher	–	–
Bristows	Application form	2 individual interviews	2.1 (preferred)	10	2,000
Browne Jacobson	CV & covering letter	Not known	2:1	8	1,500
Burges Salmon	Application form	Not known	2:1	20-25	1,000
Cadwalader, Wickersham & Taft	CV & covering letter	2 interviews	2:1	4-6	500
Campbell Hooper	CV with covering letter	Interviews	2:1	3-4	c.1000
Capsticks	Application form	Encouraged to participate in summer placement scheme. Final selection is by interview with the Training Principal and other partners	2:1 or above	6-8	c.200
Charles Russell	Handwritten letter & application form	Assessment days including interview & other exercises	2:1	10-12	2,000

SELECTION TABLE

FIRM NAME	METHOD OF APPLICATION	SELECTION PROCESS	DEGREE CLASS	CONTRACTS	APPLICA-TIONS
Clarks	Application form (from brochure or website)	Open day/interview plus second interview (with limited written tests)	usually 2:1 or above (but will consider lower grade subject to explanation)	5-6	500-600
Cleary, Gottlieb, Steen & Hamilton	Letter & CV	2 interviews	2:1	up to 4	–
Clifford Chance	Application form preferably apply online	Assessment day comprising an interview with a partner & senior solicitor, a group exercise and a verbal reasoning test	2:1	130	2,000
Clyde & Co	Application form & covering letter	Individual interview with HR, followed by interview with 2 partners	2:1	20	3,000+
CMS Cameron McKenna	Application form	Two-stage selection procedure. Initial interview followed by assessment centre.	2:1	80	1,500
Cobbetts	Application form (available on request/via Internet)	Half-day assessments	2:1	10	700
Coffin Mew & Clover	CV & covering letter	Interview	2:1 (save in exceptional circumstances)	4-5	400+
Coudert Brothers	Letter & CV	2 interviews with partners	2:1	4	–
Cripps Harries Hall	Handwritten letter & application form available online	1 interview with Managing Partner & Head of Human Resources	2:1	8	Up to 750
Cumberland Ellis Peirs	Handwritten letter & covering CV (adding reference to 'Chambers')	2 interviews with partners	2:1	1 or 2	500
Davenport Lyons	Letter & CV	Interviews	2:1	5	1,500
Davies Arnold Cooper	Application form	Open day & interviews	2:1 capability	5	1,000
Davies Wallis Foyster	Handwritten letter & CV or application form	Two-stage interview/selection process	2:1 in any subject preferred	8	c.1,000
Dechert	Letter & application form	Written exercise & interviews with partners and associates	2:1 (or capability of attaining a 2:1)	20	Over 1,000
Denton Wilde Sapte	Application form	First interview; selection test; second interview	2:1	50	2,500
Dickinson Dees	Application form & letter	Interview & in-tray exercise	2:1	15	700

SELECTION TABLE

FIRM NAME	METHOD OF APPLICATION	SELECTION PROCESS	DEGREE CLASS	CONTRACTS	APPLICATIONS
D J Freeman	Application form	Interview	2:1	12-15	600
DLA	Application form	Interviews and assessment afternoon	2:1	80+	2,000
DMH	CV & covering letter	Not known	2:1	4-6	350-450
Edwards Geldard	Application form	Interview	2:1 desirable	12	400
Eversheds	Application form to be returned to London office, specifying the region you wish to work in	Selection days include group & written exercises, presentations & interview	2:1	125	3,000
Farrer & Co	Application form & covering letter	Interviews with graduate recruitment manager & partners	2:1	6	1,500
Fenners	Handwritten letter & CV	2 interviews with partners.	2:1	4	400
Field Fisher Waterhouse	Application form & covering letter	Interview	2:1	10-12	2,000
Finers Stephens Innocent	CV & covering letter	Two interviews, each with two partners usually including one of the Training Partners	2:1	3-6	1,500
Foot Anstey Sargent	Handwritten letter & CV, or online	Interview & assessment day	–	4	–
Forbes	Handwritten letter & CV	Interview with partners	2:1	3	350
Forsters	Application form	First interview with HR Manager & Graduate Recruitment Partner; second interview with two partners	–	–	–
Freshfields Bruckhaus Deringer	Application form	1 interview with 2 partners & written test	2:1	100	c.2,500
Garretts (Andersen Legal)	Application form	1 hour interview in London, second interview held in regional office of choice	2:1	40	2,000
Goodman Derrick	CV & covering letter	2 interviews	2:1	3/4	1000
Gouldens	Letter & CV	2 interviews with partners	2.1	20	2,000
Halliwell Landau	CV & application form	Open days or summer placements	2:1	10	1000
Hammond Suddards Edge	Application form	2 interviews	2:1	45	1,500
Harbottle & Lewis	CV & letter	Interview	2:1	4	800
Henmans	Handwritten letter & CV	Interview with HR Manager & partners	–	3	500
Herbert Smith	Application form	Interview	2:1	100	1,750

SELECTION TABLE

FIRM NAME	METHOD OF APPLICATION	SELECTION PROCESS	DEGREE CLASS	CONTRACTS	APPLICATIONS
Hewitson Becke + Shaw	Application form	Interview	2:1	15	1,400
Hill Dickinson	CV & letter with photograph	Assessment day	–	–	–
Hodge Jones & Allen	By application form only one year in advance	Interview and selection tests	2:1 degree preferred	–	–
Holman Fenwick & Willan	Handwritten letter and typed CV	2 interviews with partners & written exercise	2:1	8	1,200
Howes Percival	Letter, CV and application form	Assessment centres including second interview with training principal & partner	2:1	6	300
Hugh James Ford Simey	Application form	Assessment Day	2:2	7	350
Ince & Co	Typed/handwritten letter and CV	Interview with HR professional plus interview with 2 partners & a written test	2:1	12	2000
Irwin Mitchell	Application form	Assessment centres and interview. Successful candidates are invited to second interview with 2 partners	–	15	1,000
Keoghs	Apply by sending a covering letter & CV	2-stage interview	2:1	3 in Bolton, 1 in Coventry	800
KLegal	Online application form	2 interviews + assessment exercises	2:1	30	c.750
Knight & Sons	Handwritten application supported by CV	Not known	2:1	3-4	–
Lawrence Graham	Application form	Interview	2:1	18	1,000
Laytons	Application form	2 interviews	1 or 2:1	8	2,000
LeBoeuf, Lamb, Greene & Mac Rae	CV & covering letter	2 interviews	–	4	1000
Le Brasseur J Tickle	Letter & CV	2 interviews	–	3	1,500
Lee Bolton & Lee	Letter & CV	Panel interview	2:1	2	800
Lester Aldridge	Letter, CV & application form	Interview by a panel of partners	2:1	5	300
Lewis Silkin	Application form	Assessment day, including an interview with 2 partners & an analytical exercise	2:1	6	1,000
Linklaters	Application form	2 Interviews (same day)	2:1	150	2,500
Lovells	Application form	Assessment day: critical thinking test, group exercise, interview	2:1	80	1,500
Mace & Jones	Covering letter & typed CV	Interview with partners	2:1	8	1,500

SELECTION TABLE

FIRM NAME	METHOD OF APPLICATION	SELECTION PROCESS	DEGREE CLASS	CONTRACTS	APPLICATIONS
Macfarlanes	Application form & letter	Assessment day	2:1	25	1,500
Manches	Application form	Individual interview with 2 partners. Possible 2nd interview & assessments	2:1	7-8	1,000
Martineau Johnson	Online application form	Assessment centre - half day	2:1	14	500
Masons	Application form	Assessment day followed by an interview	2:1	32	2,000
May, May & Merrimans	Letter & CV	Interview	2:1	1	200
Mayer, Brown & Platt	Application form	Two interviews with partners, associates & often a current trainee	High 2:1	2	600
McCormicks	Application form	Selection day and interview with Training Partner	2:1	4	1,000
McDermott, Will & Emery	Application form	Not known	–	–	–
Mills & Reeve	Application form	Normally one day assessment centre	2:1	25-30	Approx 500
Mishcon de Reya	Application form	Not known	2:1	8	800+
Morgan Cole	Application form	Assessment centre and interview	Preferably 2:1	–	–
Nabarro Nathanson	Application form	Interview & assessment day	2:1	30	1,500
Nicholson Graham & Jones	Application form	Interview & assessment	2:1	10	1,000
Norton Rose	Application form	Interview and group exercise	2:1	80-90	2,500+
Olswang	CV & covering letter	Business case scenario, interview, psychometric test	2:1	Up to 25	Up to 3,000+
Osborne Clarke	Application form, available online	Individual interviews, group exercises, selection testing	2:1 preferred	30-35	1,000-1,200
Pannone & Partners	Application form & CV	Individual interview. Second interview comprises a tour of the firm & informal lunch	2:2	8	500
Payne Hicks Beach	Handwritten letter & CV	Interview	2:1	2	1,000
Penningtons	Handwritten letter, CV & application form	1 interview with a partner & director of studies	2:1	10/11	2,000
Pinsent Curtis Biddle	Application form	Assessment centre including interview	2:1	30+	4000
Prettys	Handwritten application letter & CV	Not known	2:1 preferred in law or other relevant subject. Good A Levels	4-5	–

SELECTION TABLE

FIRM NAME	METHOD OF APPLICATION	SELECTION PROCESS	DEGREE CLASS	CONTRACTS	APPLICATIONS
Pritchard Englefield	Application form	1 interview	Generally 2:1	3-4	300-400
Radcliffes	CV & covering letter or EAF	2 Interviews with partners	2:1	4	1,016
Reed Smith Warner Cranston	Application form & covering letter	Assessment day: 2 interviews, aptitude test & presentation	2:1	4	1,000
Reynolds Porter Chamberlain	Handwritten covering letter & application form	Assessment Days held in September	2.1	10	600
Richards Butler	Online application form	Selection exercise & interview	2:1	20	2000
Rickerby Watterson	Application form & CV	Interview & assessment day	2:1	3-4	200
Rowe & Maw	Application form	Selection workshops including an interview, a business exercise & a group exercise	2:1	25	1,000
Russell-Cooke	CV & covering letter	First & second interviews.	2:1	4	500
Russell Jones & Walker	Application form	Not known	2:1	10	800
Salans Hertzfeld & Heilbronn HRK	Handwritten Letter & CV	2 interviews with partners	2:1	3 or 4	500+
Shadbolt & Co	Handwritten letter & CV	Interviews	2:1	6	200
Shearman & Sterling	Application form	Interviews	2:1	6	–
Sheridans	Letter & CV	2 interviews	2:1	2-3	700
Shoosmiths	Application form	Assessment centre - half day	2:1	10	2,000
Sidley Austin Brown & Wood	Covering letter & application form	Interview(s)	2:1	6-8	500
Simmons & Simmons	Application form, CV & covering letter	Assessment day: document exercise, interview & written exercise	2:1	50-60	2,700
Sinclair Roche & Temperley	Application form	Interview	2:1	6-8	1,000
SJ Berwin	Letter & CV	Interview (early September)	2:1	35	3,000
Slaughter and May	Covering letter & CV	Interview	Good 2:1 ability	Approx 85	3,000
Speechly Bircham	Application form	Interview	2:1	5	1,000
Steele & Co	Handwritten letter & CV	Interview	2:1	6	300-400
Stephenson Harwood	Application form only	Interview with 2 partners	2:1	18	–
Tarlo Lyons	Application form, available online	2 Interviews with partners & skills assessment	2:1	3	500

SELECTION TABLE

FIRM NAME	METHOD OF APPLICATION	SELECTION PROCESS	DEGREE CLASS	CONTRACTS	APPLICATIONS
Taylor Joynson Garrett	Application form	2 interviews, 1 with a partner	2:1	25	1,600
Taylor Vinters	Application form	Interview with one partner & the HR Manager	2:2	5	300
Taylor Walton	CV & covering letter	2 interviews with opportunity to meet other partners	2:1 or above	–	–
Teacher Stern Selby	Letter & application form	2 interviews	2:1 (not absolute)	6	1,000
Theodore Goddard	Application form	Initial interview followed by second interview	2:1+	20	3000
Thomson Snell & Passmore	Handwritten letter & application form available online	2 interviews	2:1	4	Approx. 500
TLT Solicitors	Application form	Assessment Day	–	8	1000
Travers Smith Braithwaite	Handwritten letter & CV	Interviews	2:1	25	1,600
Trowers & Hamlins	Letter, application form and CV	Interview(s), essay & practical test	2:1+	12-15	1,600
Walker Morris	Application form	Telephone & face to face interviews	2:1	15	Approx. 600
Ward Hadaway	Application form & handwritten letter	Interview	2:1	10	400
Watson, Farley & Williams	Handwritten letter & application form	Interview & assessment	2:1 ideally	12	1,000
Wedlake Bell	CV & covering letter	Interview	2:1	4 or 6	800
Weightmans	Application form	Not known	–	–	–
Weil, Gotshal & Manges	Application form	Not knwon	2:1	10	–
White & Case	Application form, CV & covering letter	Interview	2:1	20-25	1,500
Wiggin & Co	Letter & CV	2 interviews	2:1	3	1,700
Withers	Application form & covering letter	2 interviews	2:1	12	1,500
Wragge & Co	Application form & online	Telephone interview & Assessment Day	2:1	25	1,000

what the top firms are looking for

The obvious – great academics, communication skills, a well organised approach and attention to detail are all important. In a nutshell, firms want to know if you are right for the law and if the law is right for you. We spoke to hundreds of trainees whilst researching the True Picture section and to graduate recruitment officers themselves to get an indication of which buttons you should be aiming to press.

languages
Language skills will always stand you in good stead. They put you at a clear advantage where the firm has overseas offices and also where it has existing business with the particular countries which speak your second language. Coudert Brothers says *"In view of the international nature of the firm's work and clients, language skills are an advantage."* Pritchard Englefield is more specific. *"Normally only high academic achievers with a second European language (especially German and French) are considered."* Prettys indicates that *"languages are valued - you will have a real opportunity to use them"*

law or non-law degree?
As a rule, a non-law degree is no drawback. Most firms are very positive towards non-law graduates. Clyde & Co confirms. *"Non-law graduates are welcome, especially those with modern languages or science degrees."* Macfarlanes seeks candidates from *"Any degree discipline."* These firms are not alone. A few, however, indicate that a law degree is required. For example, Cleary, Gottlieb, Steen & Hamilton states that it wants *"at least a 2.1 law degree from a top UK university."* This, however, is because the firm requires trainees to sit the New York Bar Exam, which can only be taken if you have a degree in law. The majority of top firms will put their money where their mouth is and fund the CPE for applicants who do not have a law degree.

class of degree
This is usually critical. A 2:1 or better will almost always be a requirement of the commercial firms. There are one or two exceptions, but such firms receive many hundreds of applications from candidates with a 2:1 or better. Their policy is not an indication that they prefer to take those with a 2:2, just that they are prepared to be open minded about the result. Pritchard Englefield confirms that *"exceptional subsequent education or experience"* can sometimes make up for a 2:2.

your university
It's the old school tie phenomenon. The better regarded your university, the greater your chances of securing the training contract that you want. It is as simple as that. The top City firms still have an Oxbridge bias, although this has begun to change over the last couple of years. After Oxford and Cambridge, there is a pecking order of other preferred institutions with the old established universities (Bristol, Durham, the more established London Colleges etc.) at the top. Regional firms tend to have a greater affinity with universities in their region (whether new or old). Some firms claim not to actively discriminate against newer universities and whilst researching the True Picture, we spoke to plenty of successful trainees with degrees from new universities. Firms generally take all your qualifications into account. Good A Levels will be an advantage. If you chose to study at a new university close to home for financial reasons, make sure that you point this out in your application.

local connections
These definitely count for something at many regional firms. The reason why firms look for local ties (family or an education in the area) is that on

qualification, they want to retain their young lawyers, not see them drawn to London or other big cities such as Bristol or Leeds. Forbes in Blackburn seeks *"high calibre recruits with strong local connections..."* Knight & Sons (Manchester and Newcastle-under-Lyme) requests *"trainees who will stay on once they have qualified."* Pannone & Partners looks for those with *"a connection with the North West."* The True Picture section highlights other firms looking to recruit locally.

> Remember, some firms will not be right for you, just as you will not be right for them.

previous careers

The True Picture flags a number of firms that seem to have woken up to the fact that those with first careers often make great lawyers. They already know what work is all about. Many bring client contacts with them and a number find themselves on a fast track through to partnership. The following industry sectors and careers are particularly popular: shipping, insurance, pharmaceuticals, medical professionals, engineers, surveyors, accountants, IT and the armed forces. Here's what some of the law firms said on the matter. Addleshaw Booth & Co welcomes applications *"from mature students who may be considering a change of direction."* Beale and Company: *"... experience or an interest in construction, insurance and IT will assist."* Davies Arnold Cooper: *"Welcomes applications from all age groups and backgrounds."* Richards Butler says that *"Candidates from diverse backgrounds are welcome, including mature students with commercial experience and management skills"* and Holman Fenwick & Willan welcomes those with *"a scientific or maritime background."*

personality

You should definitely have one. Each firm knows what it's after. Many firms ask for *"creative problem solvers,"* others request those with a sense of humour, others enthusiasm. Not every firm has a particular type in mind and there are firms that stress that they look for a range of different characters. North East firm Dickinson Dees simply wants those *"able to fit into a team."* Firms can't always give a blueprint for exactly what they are looking for, but by reading the True Picture profiles you should get a feel for the firms you are most likely to fit into. Remember, some firms will not be right for you, just as you will not be right for them.

commercial awareness

They all seem to be after it, but do not expect Sir John Harvey-Jones to turn up on their doorstep! Deborah Dalgleish, head of UK graduate recruitment at Freshfields Bruckhaus Deringer told us *"We are not necessarily looking for someone who has commercial awareness as such. We don't expect it. Applicants aren't experienced enough. What we need to see is evidence that they have the ability to develop commercial awareness. This might be indicated by an applicant who has operated outside their comfort zone, pushed themselves or taken a sensible calculated risk."* This kind of experience could be gained during part-time employment, during a gap year, or at university. Slaughter and May *"does not expect applicants to know much of commercial life."* The firm expects you to have been busy with academic work. There are some clear messages from the firms in their own literature. Hodge Jones & Allen, for example, states that candidates should have *"a proven commitment to and/or experience of working in Legal Aid/Advice sectors."* Sometimes it's more vague. Farrer & Co says those who *"break the mould – as shown by their initiative for organisation, leadership, exploration, or enterprise – are far more likely to get an interview than the erudite, but otherwise unimpressive student."*

travel

At last! Travel is now seen as a positive advantage. It shows that you have a bit of spirit and the recruiters assume that you will have benefited from time abroad, especially if you had to organise things for yourself whilst you were out of the country. Baker & McKenzie says *"The firm encourages their trainees to take time out before commencing their training contract, whether just to travel or undertake further studies."* Hill Taylor Dickinson also confirms that previous travel experience is taken into account. Osborne Clarke says that *"...time spent travelling [is] viewed positively."*

team spirit

Most firms like to see that applicants can demonstrate an ability to work with others. Some place a very high priority on team working and, for these firms, you must be able to demonstrate appropriate characteristics and experience. Insurance firms in particular value team working. A popular question on application forms and at interview could be along the lines of. 'Describe a situation where you had to work effectively as a member of a team…' So start thinking now.

interests

To get a firm interested in you, it's of real importance that you demonstrate that there's a little bit more to you than the next candidate. The firm looks to how you spend your free time, whether you are a person who interacts or remains a loner. Eversheds tells us that it wants *"candidates that appear to mix well with others, take part in team events, get involved in projects that necessitate dealing with people at all levels. Interests don't have to run to the exotic or unusual, down-to-earth and unstuffy but not dull is what we are looking for."*

involvement

When firms are selecting candidates to invite to interview, they will be trying to find applicants with more to offer than just a decent law degree. One obvious opportunity to make your application stand out from the crowd is involvement in activities at university. This will need to be more than just membership of a society. Experience running activities or setting up societies will help to indicate that you have the spark which suggests you will get on at the top firms. You need to be able to assess your skills and experience and present the information in the most positive and relevant fashion. Andrew Hearn, graduate recruitment partner at Dechert, said on this point *"Everyone socialises with friends; not everyone has pursued that particular hobby or filled that particular role at university."* Remember, nobody is trying to trip you up with these questions Deborah Dalgleish, told us how firms are unimpressed by applicants who don't seem to have gone out and obtained this kind of experience *"We are interested in applicants who might have a wide range of different experiences. We don't prescribe anything specific. Applicants who have not been involved in anything, especially at university, aren't doing themselves any favours."*

the right balance

Find the right pitch between selling yourself to the firm and going over the top. Andrew Hearn gives the example of an applicant who, when asked if he had any questions of his own for the panel, dashed off the poser *"How do you see the twin forces of globalisation and information technology shaping the future of your firm."* Not necessarily the most relevant of questions for a potential trainee solicitor! Andrew also stresses the need to be polite to everyone you meet at the firm. One promising applicant was crossed off the list after he was rude and arrogant to an administrator who was taking him to the interview room. Firms understand that you might be nervous. They do not expect you to be rude.

SALARIES TABLE

FIRM NAME	FIRST YEAR	SECOND YEAR	SPONSORSHIP/ AWARDS	OTHER BENEFITS	QUALIFICATION SALARY
Addleshaw Booth & Co	£18,000-18,500 Manchester & Leeds £22,000-22,500 London	£19,000-19,500 Manchester & Leeds £23,500-24,000 London	CPE & LPC fees are paid, plus a maintenance award of £4,000	Corporate gym membership, season ticket loan	£29,000 Manchester & Leeds £40,000 London
Allen & Overy	£28,000	£32,000	CPE & LPC fees & £5,000 maintenance p.a. (£4,500 outside London, Oxford and Guildford)	Private healthcare scheme, private medical insurance, season ticket loans, subsidised restaurant, gym membership, 'cybercafe', 6 weeks unpaid leave on qualification	£48,000
Arnold & Porter	Minimum £28,000	Not known	Sponsorship for CPE & LPC	Private health insurance, season ticket loan, life assurance	£59,000
Ashurst Morris Crisp	£28,000-29,000	£31,000-32,000	CPE & LPC funding, plus £5,000 maintenance allowance p.a. (£4,500 outside London & Guildford). LPC Distinction award £500. Lang. tuition bursaries	Private health insurance, pension, life assurance, interest-free season ticket loan, gym membership, 25 days holiday p.a. during training	£48,000
Baker & McKenzie	£28,000	£32,000	CPE: Fees plus £5,000 maintenance. LPC: Fees plus £5,000 maintenance	Permanent health, life, & private medical insurance, group personal pension plan, gym membership, luncheon vouchers, interest-free season ticket loan	£50,000-52,000
Berwin Leighton Paisner	£28,000	£32,000	CPE/PgDL & LPC fees paid plus £4,500 maintenance p.a.	Flexible benefits package including permanent health insurance, private medical insurance, subsidised conveyancing & gym 25 days holiday p.a.	£48,000
SJ Berwin	£28,000	£32,000	CPE & LPC fees paid plus £4,000 maintenance p.a. (£4,500 in London)	Corporate sports membership, free lunch, health insurance	£50,000
Bevan Ashford	Not available	Not available	Available for LPC & in some cases CPE	Not known	£42,000 (London)
Bird & Bird	£25,000	£27,000	LPC & CPE fees paid plus a yearly grant of £3,500	BUPA, season ticket loan, subsidised sports club membership, life cover, PHI	£43,000
Blake Lapthorn	£15,000	£17,000	LPC: Fees up to £6,000 & bursary of £4,000	Not known	£28,000

SALARIES TABLE

FIRM NAME	FIRST YEAR	SECOND YEAR	SPONSORSHIP/ AWARDS	OTHER BENEFITS	QUALIFICATION SALARY
Bond Pearce	Depending on location up to £16,250	Not known	LPC: Financial assistance	Not known	Depending on location up to £28,000
Boyes Turner	£17,000	£18,000	LPC: Loan of £3,000	Firm pension scheme	£26,000
BP Collins	£15,500	£16,500	50% LPC costs payable on start of contract	Not known	Not known
Brabners	£16,000	Not known	May be available for LPC	Not known	£28,000
Bristows	£26,000	£28,000	CPE & LPC fees plus £5,000 maintenance grant for each	Excellent career prospects, a competitive package, firm pension scheme, life assurance & health insurance	£43,000
Browne Jacobson	£18,000		CPE & LPC		Regional variations
Burges Salmon	£20,000	£21,000	CPE & LPC fees plus maintenance of £4,500 (LPC students) or £5,000 (students of CPE & LPC)	Annual bonus & pension scheme	£34,000
Cadwalader, Wickersham & Taft	£30,000	£33,600	CPE: Fees plus £4,500 maintenance LPC: Fees plus £4,500 maintenance	Permanent health insurance, season ticket loan, BUPA (dental/health) & life assurance	£65,000
Campbell Hooper	£21,000-22,000	£23,000-24,500	LPC & CPE fees paid	Private medical & permanent health insurance, pension scheme, life assurance, & season ticket loan	Not known
Capsticks	£23,000	£25,000	Scholarship contributions to CPE & LPC courses	Bonus scheme, pension, PHI, death in service cover, interest-free season ticket loan	£36,000
Charles Russell	£26,500	£29,000	CPE & LPC fees paid and annual maintenance of £4,000 (under review)	BUPA immediately, PHI & life assurance after six months service, 25 days holiday	£43,500
Clarks	£17,000	£18,500	Not known	Pension, free conveyancing	Not known
Cleary, Gottlieb, Steen & Hamilton	£33,000	£39,000	LPC: Fees paid plus £4,500 maintenance award	Pension, health insurance, long-term disability insurance, health club, employee assistance programme	Salary varies from office to office

STARTING OUT WHAT YOU ARE LOOKING FOR

49

SALARIES TABLE

FIRM NAME	FIRST YEAR	SECOND YEAR	SPONSORSHIP/ AWARDS	OTHER BENEFITS	QUALIFICATION SALARY
Clifford Chance	£28,500	£32,000	CPE & LPC fees paid & £5,000 maintenance for London, Guildford & Oxford, £4,500 payable elsewhere. Prize for first class degrees & distinction in LPC	Interest free loan, private health insurance, subsidised restaurant, fitness centre, life assurance, personal health assurance, occupational health service	£50,000
Clyde & Co	£24,000	£27,000	CPE & LPC: Fees paid if no local authority funding, plus maintenance grant	Subsidised sports club, interest-free ticket loan, staff restaurant & weekly free bar (London); monthly staff lunch & monthly free bar (Guildford)	£46,000
CMS Cameron McKenna	£28,000	£32,000	CPE & LPC: Fees paid plus £5,000 maintenance in London, Guildford & Oxford, £4,500 elsewhere	The firm financially supports trainees who wish to learn or improve a foreign language	£50,000
Cobbetts	Competitive rate	Reviewed each year	CPE & LPC grant	Social club and LA Fitness pool and gym	Not available
Coffin Mew & Clover	Competitive market rate	Competitive market rate	CPE & LPC funding available by discussion	Not known	£23,500
Coudert Brothers	£25,000 Subject to review	£28,000 Subject to review	CPE & LPC: Fees paid plus £4,000 maintenance for each	Pension, health insurance, subsidised gym membership, season ticket loan	£50,000
Cripps Harries Hall	£15,500	£17,000	Discretionary LPC funding. 50% interest-free loan, 50% bursary	Not known	£28,000
Cumberland Ellis Peirs	£17,500 (plus £500 every 6 months)	Not known	None	Season ticket loan, luncheon vouchers	£25,000
Davenport Lyons	£24,500	£25,500	The firm does not generally offer financial assistance other than in exceptional circumstances	Season ticket loans, client introduction bonuses, contribution to gym membership, discretionary bonuses, 23 days holiday	£40,000
Davies Arnold Cooper	Not known	Not known	CPE & LPC: Grants covering course & examination fees	Discretionary interest-free loans for maintenance are available	Not available
Davies Wallis Foyster	£16,000	Not known	LPC funding for tuition fees	Life assurance, pension scheme	Not known

SALARIES TABLE

FIRM NAME	FIRST YEAR	SECOND YEAR	SPONSORSHIP/ AWARDS	OTHER BENEFITS	QUALIFICATION SALARY
Dechert	£28,000	£32,000 (to be reviewed in Sept 2002)	CPE/PgDL & LPC fees paid plus £4,500 maintenance p.a. (where local authority grants unavailable)	Free permanent health & life assurance, subsidised membership of local gym & interest-free season ticket loans	c.£50,000 (to be reviewed July 2002)
Denton Wilde Sapte	£27,000-28,000	£30,000-31,000	CPE & LPC: Fees paid plus maintenance grant (less any local authority funding)	Holiday entitlement commences at 23 days, meal away from home allowance, private health cover, season ticket loan, subsidised sports club membership, permanent health insurance, death in service cover	£48,000
Dickinson Dees	£18,000	£19,500	CPE/LPC fees paid & £4,000 interest-free loan	Not known	£30,000
D J Freeman	£25,000-26,000	£27,000-28,000	CPE & LPC funding	Subsidised meals in staff restaurant, BUPA after three months & a variety of social/sporting events.	£46,000
DLA	£28,000 (London) £20,000 (regions) £16,000 (Scotland)	£31,000 (London) £22,000 (regions) £18,000 (Scotland)	Payment of full fees for the CPE & LPC plus a maintenance grant in both years	Contributory pension scheme, health insurance, life assurance, 25 days holiday, good sports & social facilities, car scheme & Lifeworks concierge service	£47,000 (London) £33,000 (Birmingham) £32,000 (regions) £30,000 (Scotland)
DMH	£16,000	£18,000	Not known	Not known	£27,500
Edwards Geldard	£14,000	£15,200	£5,000 towards the LPC & £2,000 towards the CPE	Life assurance at three times salary, 20 days holiday entitlement p.a.	Under review
Eversheds	Regional variations London £27,500	Regional variations London £30,500	CPE/LPC fees & maintenance grants	Not known	Regional variations London £48,000
Farrer & Co	£24,000	£26,000	CPE: Fees paid plus £4,000 maintenance LPC: Fees paid plus £4,000 maintenance	Health & life insurance subsidised gym membership, season ticket loan	£37,000
Fenners	Market for City	Market for City	CPE & LPC funding to be discussed with candidates	Health insurance, season ticket loan	Market for City

SALARIES TABLE

FIRM NAME	FIRST YEAR	SECOND YEAR	SPONSORSHIP/ AWARDS	OTHER BENEFITS	QUALIFICATION SALARY
Field Fisher Waterhouse	£25,000	£28,000	Tuition fees & maintenance grant paid for CPE and LPC	25 days annual holiday, season ticket loans, health insurance, private medical healthcare	£44,000
Finers Stephens Innocent	Highly competitive	Highly competitive	Contribution of £3,000 towards LPC course fees	20 days holiday, private medical insurance, life insurance, long term disability insurance, subsidised gym membership, season ticket loan	Highly competitive
Foot Anstey Sargent	Not available	Not available	Not known	Not known	£26,500
Forbes	£12,000	Not known	Not known	Not known	Highly competitive
Forsters	£23,500	£25,500	None	22 days holiday p.a. season ticket loan, permanent health insurance, life insurance, subsidised gym membership	£40,000
Freshfields Bruckhaus Deringer	£28,000	£32,000	CPE & LPC fees paid & £5,000 maintenance p.a. for those studying in London and Oxford and £4,500 p.a. for those studying elsewhere	Life assurance, permanent health insurance, group personal pension; interest-free loan for season ticket, free membership of the firm's private medical insurance scheme, subsidised staff restaurant, gym	£50,000
Garretts (Andersen Legal)	£28,500 (London)	Not known	CPE & LPC fees paid plus £4,500-£5,000 grant p.a.	Flexible benefits package including BUPA & holiday allowance. Also subsidised gym membership & S.T.L.	£48,000
Goodman Derrick	£20,500	£21,750	LPC fees plus maintenance grant	Medical health insurance, season ticket loan, pension scheme	£35,000
Gouldens	£32,000	£36,000	CPE & LPC fees paid & £5,000 maintenance p.a.	BUPA, season ticket loan, subsidised sports club membership, group life cover	£55,000
Halliwell Landau	£18,000	£19,000	CPE & LPC fees will be paid in full	A subsidised gym membership is available	£26,000-28,000

SALARIES TABLE

FIRM NAME	FIRST YEAR	SECOND YEAR	SPONSORSHIP/ AWARDS	OTHER BENEFITS	QUALIFICATION SALARY
Hammond Suddards Edge	£20,500	£23,000	CPE & LPC fees paid plus maintenance grant of £4,500 p.a.	Subsidised accommodation in all locations. Flexible benefits scheme with a range of options	London £47,000 Other £33,000-34,000
Harbottle & Lewis	£22,500	£24,000	LPC: Fees paid, plus interest-free loans towards maintenance	Lunch provided, season ticket loan	£40,000
Henmans	£14,000	£15,100	Not known	Not known	£24,000
Herbert Smith	£28,500	£32,000	CPE & LPC fees paid plus £4,500 maintenance p.a. (£4,000 outside London)	Profit share, permanent health & private medical insurance, season ticket loan, life assurance, gym, group personal accident insurance & matched contributory pension scheme	£50,000
Hewitson Becke + Shaw	£17,000	£18,000	None	Not known	Under review
Hill Dickinson	£16,500	£18,000	LPC funding	Not known	Not known
Hodge Jones & Allen	Not known	Not known	Not known	Pension, life assurance, permanent health insurance, social events	Not known
Holman Fenwick & Willan	1st six months £25,000 2nd six months TBA	3rd six months TBA 4th six months TBA	CPE: Fees paid plus £5,000 maintenance LPC: Fees paid plus £5,000 maintenance	Private medical insurance, permanent health & accident insurance, subsidised gym membership, season ticket loan	£44,000
Howes Percival	£16,500	£17,750	Discretionary LPC funding available to candidates	Contributory pension scheme, private health insurance	£30,000
Hugh James Ford Simey	Competitive & reviewed annually	Competitive & reviewed annually	Not known	Company pension scheme	Continually under review
Ince & Co	£25,000	£28,000	LPC fees, £4,000 grant (London), £3,500 elsewhere. Discretionary sponsorship for CPE	STL, corporate health cover, PHI, contributory pension scheme.	£47,000
Irwin Mitchell	£16,500	£18,500	CPE & LPC: Fees plus £3,000 maintenance	Not known	Varies
Keoghs	Currently under review (in excess of Law Society minimum)	Not known	Not known	Not known	£24,500

STARTING OUT WHAT YOU ARE LOOKING FOR

SALARIES TABLE

FIRM NAME	FIRST YEAR	SECOND YEAR	SPONSORSHIP/ AWARDS	OTHER BENEFITS	QUALIFICATION SALARY
KLegal	£28,000	£32,000	CPE: Fees paid plus maintenance of £4,500 LPC: Fees paid plus maintenance of £4,500	Non-contributory pension, life assurance, free lunch, Flextra, 25 days holiday	£45,000
Knight & Sons	Above Law society minimum with a review each six months	Not known	Interest free loans may be available but are strictly subject to individual negotiation	Subsidised gym membership	Not known
Lawrence Graham	£28,000	£32,000	CPE: Fees plus £3,750 maintenance grant LPC: Fees plus £3,750 maintenance grant	Season ticket loan, on-site gym	£48,000
Laytons	Market rate	Market rate	CPE & LPC funding	Not known	Market rate
LeBoeuf, Lamb, Greene & MacRae	£28,000	£32,000	The firm's policy is currently under review. Please ask about this at interview	Private medical insurance, season ticket loan, subsidised restaurant	£50,000
Le Brasseur J Tickle	£19,000 (London) £14,750 (Leeds)	£21,000 (London) £15,500 (Leeds)	Not known	Not known	(London) £32,500 (Leeds) £25,000
Lee Bolton & Lee	£18,500	£19,500	A contribution towards LPC funding	Season ticket loan, non-guaranteed bonus	£29,000
Lester Aldridge	£16,500	£18,000	Discretionary	Life assurance and pension schemes	£29,000
Lewis Silkin	£25,000	£26,500	Full fees paid for LPC	Life assurance, critical illness cover, health insurance, season ticket loan, group pension plan	£40-42,000
Linklaters	£28,500	£32,000	CPE & LPC fees are paid in full. Maintenance grant of £4,500-£5,000 per annum. Language bursaries are also offered upon completion of the LPC	PPP medical insurance, life assurance, pension, season ticket loan, in-house gym & corporate membership of Holmes Place, in-house dentist, doctor and physio, 24 hour subsidised restaurant	£48,000 + bonus
Lovells	£28,000	£32,000	CPE & LPC: Fees plus a maintenance grant of £5,000 for London, Guildford & Oxford & £4,500 elsewhere. £500 bonus on joining the firm; £500 prize for a First Class degree; £250 for a distinction in the LPC	PPP medical insurance, life assurance, PHI, season ticket loan, corporate membership of Holmes Place, staff restaurant, financial planning, in-house dentist, doctor and physio, discount at local retailers	£50,000

SALARIES TABLE

FIRM NAME	FIRST YEAR	SECOND YEAR	SPONSORSHIP/ AWARDS	OTHER BENEFITS	QUALIFICATION SALARY
Mace & Jones	£13,000	£13,500	Not known	Not known	Negotiable
Macfarlanes	£28,000	£32,000	CPE & LPC: Fees paid in full plus a £5,000 maintenance allowance for courses studied in London, Guildford & Oxford & £4,500 elsewhere. Prizes for those gaining distinction or commendation for the LPC	21 working days holiday p.a. (rising to 26 days upon qualification), interest-free season ticket loan, pension, permanent health & private medical insurance, subsidised conveyancing, subsidised health club/ gym membership, subsidised restaurant, subscription to the City of London Law Society or the Trainee Solicitors Group	£50,000
Manches	£23,100 (London)	£25,900 (London)	CPE & LPC: Tuition fees plus maintenance	Season ticket loan, BUPA after 6 months, permanent health insurance, life insurance, pension after 6 months	£39,000 (London)
Martineau Johnson	£18,000	£19,500	CPE: Discretionary loan LPC: Grant for fees & maintenance of £3,000	Pension, private health, life assurance, permanent health insurance, interest-free travel loans, critical illness cover, Denplan, Birmingham Hospital Saturday Fund, gym membership, domestic conveyancing, will drafting, training & subscription fees	£33,000
Masons	(Under review) No less than £25,000	(Under review) No less than £28,000	Fees paid for CPE & LPC courses plus maintenance grant (under review)	Life assurance, private health care, subsidised restaurant & season ticket loan (London)	(Under review) No less than £42,000
May, May & Merrimans	Competitive	Not known with similar size/type firms	Discretionary loans for LPC	Not known	Not known
Mayer, Brown & Platt	£30,000	£35,000	100% funding for CPE & LPC plus maintenance grant.	Private medical insur, season ticket loan, life assurance (4 x basic salary), long term disability insurance, critical illness & pension	£54,000
McCormicks	Highly competitive	Highly competitive	Not known	Not known	Highly competitive

SALARIES TABLE

FIRM NAME	FIRST YEAR	SECOND YEAR	SPONSORSHIP/ AWARDS	OTHER BENEFITS	QUALIFICATION SALARY
McDermott, Will & Emery	£29,000	Not known	CPE and LPC funding & maintenance grant; Tuition for relevant courses	Private medical and dental insurance, life assurance, permanent health insurance, non-contributory pension, interest-free season ticket loan, gym membership	£60,000
Mills & Reeve	£17,000	£18,000	LPC fees & maintenance grant for LPC year. Funding for the CPE is discretionary	Life assurance at two times pensionable salary, a contributory pension scheme & 25 days holiday	£30,000-31,000
Mishcon de Reya	£24,000	£26,000	CPE & LPC funding with bursary	Medical cover, subsidised gym membership, season ticket loan, permanent health insurance, life assurance & pension	£36,000
Morgan Cole	Competitive for the London, Thames Valley & South Wales regions	Not known	Full funding for CPE/ PgDL and LPC fees, plus a contribution towards maintenance	Not known	Not known
Nabarro Nathanson	London/Reading £28,000 Sheffield £20,000	London/Reading £32,000 Sheffield £22,000	Full fees paid for CPE & LPC plus a maintenance grant of £5,000 for London & Guildford, £4,500 elsewhere	Private medical insurance, 25 days holiday p.a., season ticket loan, subsidised restaurant & corporate gym membership	£48,000 (London)
Nicholson Graham & Jones	£25,000	£28,000	CPE & LPC fees paid in full plus £4,000 maintenance	Life assurance, season ticket loan, subsidised gym membership, BUPA, 25 days holiday a year	£40,000
Norton Rose	£28,500	£32,000	£1,000 travel scholarship, £800 loan on arrival, 4 weeks unpaid leave on qualification	Life assurance (25+), private health insurance (optional), season ticket loan, subsidised gym membership	£50,000
Olswang	£26,500	Not known	Not known	After six months: pension contributions, medical cover, life cover, dental scheme, season ticket loan, subsidised gym membership. After 12 months: private health insurance	£46,000

SALARIES TABLE

FIRM NAME	FIRST YEAR	SECOND YEAR	SPONSORSHIP/ AWARDS	OTHER BENEFITS	QUALIFICATION SALARY
Osborne Clarke	£25,000 London & Thames Valley, £19,000 Bristol	Not known	CPE & LPC fees & maintenance grant paid (some conditions apply)	21 days holiday, employer's pension contributions, private healthcare cover, season ticket loan, permanent health insurance, group life assurance cover	£34,000 Bristol, £47,500 London
Pannone & Partners	£16,500	£18,500	Not known	Not known	£27,000
Payne Hicks Beach	£22,000	£24,500	Fees for the CPE & LPC are paid	Season ticket loan, life assurance 4 x salary, permanent health insurance	£42,000
Penningtons	£23,000 (London)	£25,000 (London)	LPC funding is available. Awards are given for commendation or distinction in LPC	Subsidised sports & social club, life assurance, private medical, season ticket loan	£38,000 (London)
Pinsent Curtis Biddle	£28,000	£30,000	CPE & LPC: Fees paid plus maintenance of £2,500 for CPE & £4,500 for LPC	None	Approx £48,000
Prettys	Above Law Society guidelines	Not known	Discretionary	Not known	Not known
Pritchard Englefield	£19,000	£19,250	£2,000	Not known	Approx £30,000
Radcliffes	£20,000	£21,500	Not known	Health insurance, season ticket loan, life assurance, PHI	£37,000
Reed Smith Warner Cranston	£26,500	£30,000	CPE/LPC fees & maintenance grant plus interest-free loan	BUPA, IFSTL, life assurance, permanent health insurance, pension contributions (after qualifying period)	£47,000
Reynolds Porter Chamberlain	£25,000	£27,000	CPE: Fees paid plus £4,000 maintenance LPC: Fees paid plus £4,000 maintenance	4 weeks holiday, bonus schemes, private medical insurance, income protection benefits, season ticket loan, subsidised gym membership, active social calendar	£45,000
Richards Butler	£25,000	£28,000	CPE & LPC fees & maintenance paid	Performance related bonus, life insurance, BUPA, interest-free season ticket loan, subsidised staff restaurant, staff conveyancing allowance	£48,000 plus bonus

SALARIES TABLE

FIRM NAME	FIRST YEAR	SECOND YEAR	SPONSORSHIP/ AWARDS	OTHER BENEFITS	QUALIFICATION SALARY
Rickerby Watterson	£15,000	£16,000	Not known	Non-contrib pension, life assurance, 24 days holiday	£25,000
Rowe & Maw	Not known	Not known	CPE & LPC fees paid & £4,000 (£4,500 for London/Guildford) maintenance p.a.	Interest free season ticket loan, subsidised membership of sports clubs, private health scheme	£48,000
Russell-Cooke	£19,500	£21,000	Not known	Not known	Market
Russell Jones & Walker	£19,500-20,750	£21,250-22,500	LPC: Interest-free loan provided to assist with fees	Season ticket loan, pension, private healthcare or gym membership, group life assurance, all subject to qualifying periods	c.£32,000 (London)
Salans Hertzfeld & Heilbronn HRK	£22,500	£23,500	LPC tuition fees paid	Private healthcare, pension, season ticket loan	Variable
Shadbolt & Co	£21,000	£25,000	LPC partly payable when trainee commences work. PSC fees payable	Permanent health insurance, death in service, preferential rates on private medical care, annual bonus & season ticket loan	£35,000
Shearman & Sterling	£30,000	£34,000	Sponsorship for CPE & LPC courses, plus a maintenance grant of £4,500	Not known	£55,000
Sheridans	£20,000	£22,000	LPC sponsorship is available	Life assurance	£34,000
Shoosmiths	£16,000	£17,250	£10,000 - split between fees and maintenance	Life assurance, pension after 3 months, various staff discounts on a range of products and services	Market rate
Sidley Austin Brown & Wood	£27,000	£30,000	CPE & LPC: Fees & maintenance	Healthcare, disability cover, life assurance contribution to gym membership, interest-free season ticket loan	£75,520
Simmons & Simmons	£28,000	£32,000	(In the absence of local authority funding) LPC & PgDL/CPE fees are paid. Maintenance of £5,000 (London, Oxford or Guildford) or £4,500 elsewhere	Season ticket loan, fitness loan, group travel insurance, group accident insurance, death in service, medical cover, staff restaurant	£50,000

SALARIES TABLE

FIRM NAME	FIRST YEAR	SECOND YEAR	SPONSORSHIP/ AWARDS	OTHER BENEFITS	QUALIFICATION SALARY
Sinclair Roche & Temperley	£25,000	£26,000	CPE & LPC fees paid plus £4,500 maintenance p.a.	Private health cover, pension scheme, discretionary bonus, PHI, accident insurance, subsidised sports club membership	£43,000-45,500
Slaughter and May	£29,000	£32,500	CPE and LPC fees & maintenance grants; some grants are available for postgraduate work	BUPA, STL, pension scheme, subsidised membership of health club, 24 hour accident cover	£50,000
Speechly Bircham	£26,000-27,000	£28,000-29,000	CPE & LPC: Fees plus maintenance of £4,000 (£4,500 in London & Guildford) p.a.	Season ticket loan, private medical insurance, life assurance.	£45,000
Steele & Co	Not known	Not known	Not known	Pension, accident insurance, legal services, interest free season ticket loan, gym membership loan	Not known
Stephenson Harwood	£26,000	£29,000	£7,400 fees paid for CPE and LPC and £4,700 maintenance p.a.	Subsidised membership of health clubs, private health insurance, BUPA membership, season ticket loan and 25 days paid holiday per year	£48,000
Tarlo Lyons	£23,000 on average	£26,000 on average	LPC fees paid	Discretionary bonus, membership of a private health scheme, pension plan & subsidised membership of a health club	£42,000+
Taylor Joynson Garrett	£24,000	£27,000	CPE & LPC: Fees paid plus £4,000 maintenance p.a.	Private medical care, permanent health insurance, STL, subsidised staff restaurant, non-contributory pension scheme on qualifying	£41,000 (2000 figure)
Taylor Vinters	£15,500	£17,100	Not known	Benefits include private medical insurance, life insurance and pension	£31,500
Teacher Stern Selby	£22,000	Not known	CPE funding: None LPC funding: Unlikely	Not known	£33,000

STARTING OUT WHAT YOU ARE LOOKING FOR

SALARIES TABLE

FIRM NAME	FIRST YEAR	SECOND YEAR	SPONSORSHIP/ AWARDS	OTHER BENEFITS	QUALIFICATION SALARY
Theodore Goddard	£27,500	£30,000	CPE & LPC fees paid in full. £4,200 maintenance paid for London & South East, £3,750 elsewhere	Pension, profit-related bonus, permanent health insurance, private medical insurance, subsidised health & fitnesss club membership & firm restaurant	£48,000
Thomson Snell & Passmore	£15,000	£16,000	Grant & interest-free loan available for LPC	Not known	£24,000
TLT Solicitors	Not known	Not known	See TLT's website	Subsidised health insurance, subsidised sports & health club facility, pension	Market rate
Travers Smith Braithwaite	£28,000	£32,000	LPC & CPE fees paid & between £4,500 & £5,000 maintenance p.a.	Private health insurance, permanent sickness cover, life assurance cover, season ticket loans, refreshment credit, subsidised sports club membership	£50,000
Trowers & Hamlins	£24,000	£26,000	CPE & LPC fees paid & £4,000-4,250 maintenance p.a.	Season ticket loan, private health care after six months service, Employee Assistance Programme & discretionary bonus, death in service	£40,000
Walker Morris	£17,250	£18,500	PgDL & LPC fees and maintenance of £4,000 (both PgDL & LPC) or £3,500 (LPC only)	Not known	£31,000
Ward Hadaway	£16,000	£17,000	LPC fees paid plus £2,000 interest-free loan	23 days holiday (26 days after 5 years service), death in service insurance, pension	Minimum £27,500
Watson, Farley & Williams	£25,000	£28,000	CPE & LPC fees paid & £4,500 maintenance p.a. (£4,000 outside London)	Life assurance, PHI, BUPA, STL, pension, subsidised gym membership	Not less than £48,500
Wedlake Bell	Not known	Not known	LPC & CPE fees paid where local authority grant not available.	During training contract: pension. On qualification: pension, life assurance, medical insurance, PHI, subsidised gym membership & travel loans	Not known

SALARIES TABLE

FIRM NAME	FIRST YEAR	SECOND YEAR	SPONSORSHIP/ AWARDS	OTHER BENEFITS	QUALIFICATION SALARY
Weil, Gotshal & Manges	£35,000	£37,000	The firm will pay tuition fees & a maintenance allowance for CPE & LPC	Pension, permanent health insurance, private health cover, life assurance, subsidised gym membership, season ticket loan	£60,000
White & Case	£33,000, rising by £1,000 every six months	Not known	CPE & LPC fees paid & £4,500 maintenance p.a. Prizes for commendation & distinction in the LPC	BUPA, gym membership contribution, life insurance, pension scheme, permanent health scheme, season ticket loan, bonus scheme	£57,500
Wiggin & Co	£21,900	£27,000	CPE & LPC fees & £3,000 maintenance p.a.	Life assurance, private health cover, pension scheme, permanent health insurance	£36,700
Withers	£26,500	£29,000	CPE/PgDL & LPC fees & £4,500 maintenance p.a. Cash prize for distinction or commendation in the CPE/PgDL &/or LPC	Interest free season ticket loan, private medical insurance, life assurance, social events, subsidised cafe facilities	TBA
Wragge & Co	£21,000	£24,000	Tuition fees for CPE & LPC & maintenance grant of £4,500 for each year of study, £1,000 interest free loan, prize for 1st class degree & LPC distinction	Pension scheme, life assurance, 23 days holiday p.a., travel schemes, sports & social club, permanent health insurance, independent financial adviser, Christmas gift & access to private medical insurance at corporate rates	£33,000

STARTING OUT WHAT YOU ARE LOOKING FOR

paralegal questions

Paralegals work as extra fee earners within firms. A qualified solicitor's time can be expensive and it is often more cost effective for certain types of work to be completed by a paralegal.

Many paralegals will have a law degree or the CPE/PgDL or even the LPC, and will have some practical legal experience. However, it is not essential to have all the above. Whether you are looking at career paralegal work or want temporary work to gain experience and earn some money, you probably have a few questions. Chambers and Partners Recruitment's paralegal guru, Rebecca Saxby, gave us the following pointers.

how can agencies help me?
At Chambers and Partners Recruitment, we work with many of the top City law firms, high street practices and in-house legal departments. We assist them in recruiting paralegals for temporary vacancies, short-term contracts and permanent positions. We will spend time with you discussing your requirements over the telephone or invite you to come and meet us.

We have a number of positions available at any one time and regularly have new roles that we will consider you for and discuss with you. These vary enormously in terms of practice area and experience required. Generally, the candidates we register have six months practical legal experience and have completed legal education.

if I have no practical legal experience, how can I go about getting some?
It can be difficult for us to assist you in finding a permanent role if you do not have any practical legal experience. The paralegal market is very competitive, but any additional experience or assets, such as fluency at business level in a foreign language or particularly impressive IT skills, could make you attractive to firms.

Undertaking vacation schemes, applying directly to law firms or working for a company that assists large firms on litigation cases will all provide you with the kind of experience which will help us to place you quickly.

can I work as a paralegal if I have not completed my LPC/BVC?
You can. It may prevent you from applying for certain roles, however, if you have some previous practical legal experience and your academic results to date are impressive, you will be able to secure work. It can work in your favour if you are pursuing career paralegal work, as firms will not be concerned about you hassling them for a training contract or leaving to train elsewhere.

if I undertake a number of short term contracts in order to gain different work experiences, will this look unprofessional on my CV?
Not at all. If the roles you have taken are short-term and you have stayed for the duration of the contract, this will not be regarded negatively. It is perfectly acceptable to move between assignments on a regular basis, especially as many paralegal opportunities are short-term contracts.

can you get me a training contract?
As an agency we cannot assist you with finding a training contract; you must apply directly to law firms.

can I apply for paralegal work to a firm that I have also applied to for a training contract?

The two applications are separate and treated as such; therefore you can apply to the same firm for paralegal work.

I am a qualified solicitor. I'd like to change specialisation. can I take a paralegal role to assist in my transition?

This is an option, however, in practice this is not usually feasible. There are a number of reasons why; firms would perceive you to be over-qualified for the role and may question your ability as a solicitor if you are applying for a paralegal post. Additionally, the paralegal market is so competitive that firms will already have a wide choice of paralegals with relevant experience to fill any vacancy.

what could I expect from a career as a paralegal?

There are some interesting long-term roles for those who decide they do not want to qualify as a solicitor. We place candidates in managerial roles within paralegal departments, in professional support and know-how roles and as contract managers and legal assistants, particularly within in-house legal departments. All of these can be very rewarding and will pay a good salary.

I am legally qualified overseas and cannot work as a solicitor/barrister in this country. Could I work as a paralegal?

Many firms and companies are more than happy to consider candidates with overseas qualifications; again, experience is the most important prerequisite.

Paralegal work is the obvious choice if you are here for a short period of time or if you require employment before undertaking the Qualified Lawyers Transfer Test (QLTT).

what is the difference between a paralegal and a legal executive?

Quite often the two terms are interchanged. Paralegals usually have some practical legal experience and may or may not have completed the LPC, CPE, or a law degree.

Legal Executives will be members or fellows of The Institute of Legal Executives (ILEX) and will study for the Institute's exams while gaining experience working in a solicitor's office or in-house legal department. If you would like any more information on Legal Executives, please call our Legal Executive Consultant, Milo O' Connor on 020 7606 8844 or refer to www.ilex.org.uk

LONDON PARALEGAL SALARIES TABLE

NUMBER OF PARTNERS	UP TO 6 MONTHS EXPERIENCE	6 MONTHS TO 2 YEARS EXPERIENCE	2 OR MORE YEARS EXPERIENCE
150+	£18,000 to £19,500	£18,750 to £20,625	£21,875 to £24,000
75-149	£17,000 to £18,062	£18,156 to £19,500	£19,000 to £23,125
45-74	£15,700 to £18,141	£19,250 to £23,875	£21,625 to £27,500
20-44	£17,500 to £20,000	£18,000 to £20,500	£24,375 to £28,125
1-19	£15,250 to £18,250	£18,000 to £19,750	£18,750 to £23,000
US Firms	£19,450 to £23,000	£23,125 to £26,000	£26,000 to £30,500

REGIONAL PARALEGAL SALARIES TABLE

LOCATION	UP TO 6 MONTHS EXPERIENCE	6 MONTHS TO 2 YEARS EXPERIENCE	2 OR MORE YEARS EXPERIENCE
South East	£13,750 to £18,125	£15,117 to £19,875	£17,642 to £24,375
South West/Wales	£13,575 to £15,500	£14,812 to £17,562	£15,594 to £18,875
Midlands	£10,000 to £14,875	£13,787 to £16,062	£14,875 to £21,290
North	£12,000 to £14,483	£13,625 to £17,875	£16,220 to £20,500

These tables are drawn up each year from the paralegal salary survey conducted by Chambers and Partners Recruitment. Paid overtime and bonuses have not been taken into account in these figures.

BARRISTERS

TIMETABLE FOR TRAINING AS A BARRISTER

SECOND YEAR LAW STUDENTS AND THIRD YEAR NON-LAW STUDENTS

Autumn Term:	Compile information about sets of chambers. Obtain chambers' literature. Attend law fairs on campus. Look into funding possibilities for the CPE and/or BVC.
Spring Term:	Apply for mini-pupillages and other work experience. Apply for the CPE before February closing date if necessary. Attend law fairs on campus.
Summer Term:	Obtain application details for BVC from CACH (Centralised Applications Clearing House). Find out about pupillage applications. Attend pupillage fairs.

You will be able to apply to certain chambers under the 'year early' system. Check through OLPAS to see which chambers are offering pupillage two years in advance. The application timetable is the same as below.

FINAL YEAR LAW STUDENTS AND STUDENTS ON THE CPE

Autumn Term:	Apply for BVC. Sort out funding if possible. Research the Inns of Court and join one. Make further pupillage enquiries. Apply to your Inn for scholarships.
Spring and Summer Terms:	Attend pupillage fair in London. Make OLPAS (Online Pupillage Application System) and non-OLPAS pupillage applications.* Application deadline for OLPAS summer season is the end of April; offers may be made from the beginning of August.**

BVC STUDENTS

Autumn Term:	OLPAS autumn season. Closing date at the end of September, offers may be made from the beginning of November.**

* Non OLPAS chambers 'can't' make offers before the above dates, but not all chambers play by the rules. Check the OLPAS website – www.olpas.co.uk – for up to the minute information on deadlines for non OLPAS chambers and precise dates for the 2002 season.

** All offers of pupillage must remain open for 14 days. Bear in mind that you will probably need to decide on any summer season offers before you have even entered the autumn season.

the bar system

barcode

brief: document by which a solicitor instructs a barrister in court

chambers: the offices occupied by a barrister or group of barristers; the collective name for the barristers practising from that set of chambers

clerk: administrator/manager for barristers who organises diaries, payment of fees etc

counsel: barrister; or barristers collectively

junior: a barrister who is not a QC, however senior in age or experience (a 'senior junior')

OLPAS: Online Pupillage Application System. The web-based system used to apply for pupillage.

CACH: Central Applications Clearing House. The process used for applying to and receiving offers from Bar Vocational Course providers.

pupil master/mistress: barrister who supervises the training of a pupil in chambers

set: set of chambers

silk: a Queen's Council (QC), so called because s/he is entitled to wear silk robes

tenant: a barrister who is a member of chambers

an introduction

The majority of barristers in England and Wales are in independent practice as tenants of sets of chambers. Essentially, they are self-employed, running individual practices within a support network of other barristers, clerked by increasingly commercial and professional managers. The London Bar is the largest, but nationally the six court circuits are served by chambers throughout the country.

Members of the 'employed bar' work in industry and finance and for a range of government bodies from the Crown Prosecution Service to the armed forces.

Each set of chambers will have its own reputation and specialist practice areas. The following sections of the book expand on just some of these practice areas. When applying to chambers through OLPAS or to sets that take direct applications, it is essential to select those that specialise in the practice area to which you are best suited. Consider carefully whether you have an interest and an aptitude for its practice area before applying to a niche set. The choice of pupillage is one of the most significant career decisions you will make – so get it right.

Mini pupillages are a great way of gauging which sort of practice you are most in tune with and the opportunity to work for one or more sets for a few weeks can really make a difference. It will ensure that you move forward to the next stage of training with your eyes wide open and a feeling of greater confidence in what can, at first, be an unfamiliar world. Per Laleng of 42 Castle Street in Liverpool told us that *"the deep division between the theory and practice isn't emphasised enough at university or Bar School. You're really ignorant in the early stages of training and you start to pick up the secret language and understand things during pupillage. Students could help themselves by going out and gaining experience doing mini pupillages. Try to decide quite early which area to specialise in and make sure you really want to do it."* Do not, however, waste too much time by completing mini pupillage after mini pupillage. The purpose of minis is to clarify whether the Bar is for you and which practice area you hope to move into. If you know what you want to do and have completed two or three mini pupillages, there is not a great deal to be gained by applying for more, unless a chambers which you are especially interested in requires an assessed mini pupillage to be completed.

time at the bar?

Is there still a need for two branches of the profession and are solicitors really a threat to the Bar? The Bar is staring at two very significant issues at the moment, each posing at the least a challenge to the profession and at worst a threat to the livelihood of individual barristers. First, the increase in solicitor advocates who can take a case through from start to finish without recourse to the Bar. The Access to Justice Act 1999 contains the latest in a series of measures which have had the effect of removing the exclusivity of the Bar's rights of audience in most courts. Increasingly during the research for the Chambers Guide to the Legal Profession, the response to questions as to which barristers are instructed by leading solicitors brings the response *"We don't really use counsel, we do the advocacy ourselves."* Then consider the impact on court procedure and case management brought about by the Woolf reforms. The overriding theme of the changes to civil litigation procedures is the requirement to keep costs to a reasonable minimum and to use all means to avoid trial. Solicitors now think twice about instructing counsel for advice, and may completely avoid using them for advocacy.

The government is also pushing to ensure 'value for money' in criminal justice. With the recent creation of the Criminal Defence Service and the abolition of the Legal Aid Board, publicly funded defence work is now entirely handled by firms of solicitors who hold a franchise to undertake criminal defence work from the Criminal Defence Service. If counsel is required in such cases they will be instructed as before by solicitors, but counsel's fee will be paid by the solicitor not the Legal Aid Board. As a result more solicitor advocates will handle simple cases themselves from beginning to end. This inevitably means a drying up of some of the work previously available to the young Bar. With the proposed mode of trial bill likely to increase the use of the Magistrates Court, the problem is especially acute for those intent on criminal practice. None the less, speaking to pupil barristers in their second (practising) six, the long-predicted demise of the criminal Bar has, as yet, failed to materialise. Pupils told us that they are still reasonably busy during their second six. Being busy and actually receiving your fees, however, are two different things!

It's a long, tough and winding road to make it through the first few years of practice. The journey is an expensive and often precarious one, but once there the professional and financial rewards have the potential to be huge. If you have strength of character and a tenacious, independent nature; if you can marshal your thoughts and present concise and clear advice with confidence; if you can hold the attention of all and be persuasive in your argument then this may be the career for you.

the inns of court

The Bar of England and Wales comprises four Inns of Court – Inner Temple, Middle Temple, Lincoln's Inn and Gray's Inn. Physically, they are Oxbridge-like oases of gardens, squares, staircases, cobbles and chapels around the Royal Courts of Justice in London. Historically, all barristers would have lived and worked within one or other of these Inns. Practically, only the Inns have the power to make new barristers. Students who successfully complete the Bar Vocational Course are 'called to the Bar' by them.

In order to qualify as a barrister you must join an Inn before the end of June in the year that you start your BVC. Choice of Inn is completely personal and does not dictate the subsequent choice of chambers. Most people choose their Inn for practical or social reasons. All provide broadly the same services: a library, lunching and dining facilities, a collegiate support network, common rooms, training, social activities and beautiful gardens in the centre of London. Importantly, they also provide the opportunity to network with qualified barristers in your chosen area of practice. However, for many students the first role of the Inn is as a funding body for the BVC. See pages 12 to 14.

"At the time," one young tenant told us, *" I based my decision as to the choice of Inn solely on the likelihood of getting an award. But now I wish I had taken other factors, such as the quality of their advocacy training, into account. Some Inns are definitely better than others for*

training." With tuition fees alone ranging between £7,000-9,000, finding some sort of scholarship or award is a must for many Bar hopefuls. Many chambers currently do not fund their pupils and aside from the potential to earn small amounts during the second six of pupillage, times can be extraordinarily lean for a couple of years. The Inns of Court do, however, provide over £2 million in bursaries and scholarships. Students, nonetheless clearly require an additional source of funds.

dining

One of the peculiarities of qualifying as a barrister is the requirement to dine in hall at your Inn. Dining is divided between education dinners (includes lectures and talks), domus dinners (when students and seniors dine together) and social dinners (such as Grand Night or nights when students may bring guests). Most students are at best ambivalent about the whole question of dining, feeling it is an old-fashioned and daunting process. Daunting because part of the process is for barristers to pick on new faces and challenge them to make a speech or raise a toast for example. However, it does give students a chance to meet and talk with other prospective pupils and with the barristers and judges themselves. It is also a chance to become acquainted with a number of old traditions and customs of the Inn. One pupil who recently left Bar School advises; *"You have to do it, so make the most of it."*

Some pupils and junior tenants feel there is still an 'ivory tower' feel to the Bar and that nepotism is still a factor. As with any profession, you will come across individuals of all types and views. Your choice of set will be the most crucial factor in determining the cultural environment in which you will find yourself. Some sets are more 'pc' than others; some more set in their ways. The most prominent cultural influence was that of educational background. Whilst an Oxbridge degree is not a guaranteed passport to acceptance by the Bar, it is still believed by many to be of great assistance.

qualifying

In order to practice, you must complete pupilage. This is an apprenticeship in chambers consisting normally of two six month slots called 'sixes.' Adding a third six is becoming increasingly common, allowing for a second bite at the cherry of tenancy (a permanent place within chambers). First and second sixes can be served at two different chambers. Indeed, with the prior consent of the Bar Council's Joint Regulations Commitee (JRC), there are several options open to pupils during their second six, including:

- working with a solicitor or other practising lawyer in an EU country for three months
- undertaking a 'stage' in the legal departments of the European Commission in Brussels or Luxembourg or a placement at the European Commission in London for 5 months
- working with a registered pupil master in the employed Bar
- marshalling with a judge of the High Court or a Circuit Judge for up to six weeks
- working with a solicitor or other professional person whose work is relevant to the practice of your pupil master for up to four weeks
- the JRC may approve other training in appropriate circumstances.

Pupils are assigned to a pupilmaster/mistress who they shadow during the first six. Performance assessment is on-going and the pupil becomes introduced to 'real work' via the practice of the master or mistress. As time goes by, other members of chambers will seek the pupil's assistance, thus adding to their workload. *"You're being assessed the whole time,"* Claire Weir of Blackstone Chambers told us. *"It's a fairly impressive year - you learn so much. However, it can be stressful."* As you progress through the second six, more opportunities arise to take on cases and earn fees for yourself, although this is unlikely to be a significant amount.

However, the harsh fact is that completing pupillage is absolutely no guarantee of tenancy.

pupillage – how to get it

During the bad old days (pre 1996) applying for pupillage was a rather hit and miss affair. With no centralised application system, students would have to crack out the scribbling board and crayon and dash out over a hundred letters in their best copperplate, in the hope that one of their speculative applications might be successful. Horror stories abound of chambers receiving nearly one thousand applications, then using such indiscriminate selection procedures as chucking out half of the applications at random.

In response to these problems, the Bar Council introduced the Pupillage Applications Clearing House (PACH) in 1996.

down in old ol'paso

This has now been superceeded by a new system fit for the twenty first century. It is known as OLPAS, which stands for Online Pupillage Application System. OLPAS has three important differences to the old system. First of all, it is online. All applications to participating chambers must be entered through the OLPAS website (www.olpas.co.uk). Importantly, OLPAS runs over two 'seasons'– the summer season, which has an April deadline for applications with offers made in July and an autumn season with an October deadline. Finally, all chambers are required to abide by a common timetable, with all pupillage vacancies advertised on the OLPAS website, whether the chambers is participating in OLPAS or not. Those who opt out retain their own application forms.

Speaking to students who have recently applied through OLPAS, reactions have been reasonably positive. The new system is much more user friendly than the old floppy disk system used under PACH and which is still used for making applications to BVC course providers.

However, there are early indications that the system has not achieved all that it set out to. The Bar Council does not have legal powers to force chambers to abide by the common timetable. Sure enough, this has led to several chambers, including top Chancery sets, Wilberforce Chambers and Serle Court, breaking from the pack. These sets offer huge pupillage awards in a rather blatant attempt to snap up the best candidates, requiring them to accept their pupillage offer before the OLPAS season has even begun. Some rival chambers have reacted angrily to this and unless something can be done to prevent such behaviour in the future application seasons, OLPAS may fare no better than its predecessor.

olpas top tips

- Whilst you will only be able to apply to 24 chambers a year through OLPAS, you can apply to an unlimited number of non-OLPAS chambers. Unless you are supremely confident of your OLPAS applications, take advantage of this opportunity.
- OLPAS allows text to be cut and pasted into the online form. Print out the form from the website and take your time tweaking the application off line. Using your PC also gives you the opportunity to use spell check on your form. Use it!
- Don't worry about the system being complex. It is as easy as using an internet mail account or a search engine.
- Once you have submitted your application you can't change anything apart from your contact details and exam results. Check for errors exhaustively before you submit the form.

funding

Following the introduction of the national minimum wage there has been litigation on the issue of pupillage funding. In the past there was no requirement for a pupillage to be funded. A test case decided that those over the age of 24 must receive remuneration at the level of the national minimum wage. The Court of Appeal, however, overruled this judgment and held that there was no need to fund pupillage, as the primary purpose of such a position was training and pupillage could not, therefore, constitute gainful employment. In response to the debate over this issue, the Bar Council has now introduced a requirement that all pupils must be paid at least £10,000 a year with £5,000 by way of a grant in the first (non-practising) six months and guaranteed earnings of £5,000 in the second (practising) six months. This policy will apply to pupillages commencing in 2003.

This is obviously good news for prospective pupils, although it may result in a decrease in the number of pupillages available.

> Don't be disheartened if your first few interviews don't go quite according to plan. You will get much better with practice.

interviews

Even being short-listed for interview is an incredibly competitive process at the Bar. The nature of the interview and selection process varies quite significantly between chambers. The best (and most obvious) advice is to be as well prepared as possible. Read the legal press and The Times on Tuesday so that you can develop your opinions on current or controversial topics in the area of law that you are looking to move into.

Many chambers will set you exercises. These could be a simple legal problem, a topical issue to discuss or a general proposition to argue. An example of the latter, given by top human rights set Doughty Street Chambers is; "Do you agree with the proposition Women and children first?" You might receive the exercise shortly before your interview begins or a few days in advance. Make sure you prepare as well as you possibly can. If you are giving an oral answer then expect the panel to come back at you. Don't panic if they present an argument or a case you have not heard before or did not anticipate. An important part of the interview is testing your ability to think on your feet. Stay calm and stick to your guns. The panel are neither looking for, nor do they expect, ready packaged barristers. Many chambers will hold two rounds of interviews, whittling applicants down to a handful of hopefuls before making the final cut. Going through the selection process is a stressful and exhausting marathon. You need to be thick-skinned and have the ability to deal with the inevitable disappointments as you make your way through the process. Don't be disheartened if your first few interviews don't go quite according to plan. You will get much better with practice.

It is important not to be so over-zealous in your efforts to impress with your advocacy skills that you seem arrogant. Chambers are looking for someone who wants to learn during pupillage. During our research we heard a painful story about a student who sat down before the panel, crossed his legs and offered the opening gambit: "So, what do you want to know." They ripped him to shreds. Whilst this is an extreme example, bear in mind the need to balance your assertiveness and confidence with respect and a willingness to learn.

Chambers are looking for people who will fit in. They do not want robotic legal brains. Show your human side, conversational skills and (obviously in limited doses) sense of humour if you can. It doesn't matter how well you did in your degree, if the interview panel don't think you will get on at their workplace, they won't offer you pupillage.

practice areas at the bar

chancery

If you don't already know anything about Chancery work then you're missing out on a fascinating area. Take the time to investigate further. Some find a rewarding career within the Chancery Division of the High Court. The meat of the work will require complex problem solving together with the application of hard legal principles and a rigorous examination of facts.

Chancery barristers are a different breed to their common law and commercial brothers and sisters. Facts are always crucial, but in Chancery there is a definite emphasis on the application of the law and its principles. Members of the Chancery Bar are sometimes described as 'lawyers' lawyers.' The tools of their trade are legal principles and arguments. The skill in Chancery work is applying these tools to real situations.

As with other sections of the Bar, sets are becoming increasingly specialised, sophisticated and commercial in the way they interact with solicitors and the business world. Typically, you remain a generalist for the first few years. You then aim to develop a reputation for specific expertise. This is what makes you particularly attractive to your clients. Barristers at the premier end of the Chancery Bar have a reputation for being quite expensive and maybe a 'cut above.' This is an area in which only the highest quality of advice is viable.

Chancery work comes in two flavours, most often referred to as 'traditional' (trusts, probate, real property, charities, mortgages, partnerships) and 'commercial'(company cases, shareholdings, banking, pensions, financial services, insolvency, media and IP, professional negligence). The division between traditional and commercial Chancery is vanishing in that most sets will now do both types of work.

There are some fine brains at the Chancery Bar and it has a reputation for producing highly respected QCs and judges. But don't labour under the illusion that it's all paperwork and lofty academia. Rupert Reed, a tenant at Wilberforce Chambers, told us how real and relevant Chancery work felt. *"After six months at the Commercial Bar, focused largely on dry reinsurance matters, I switched to the Chancery Bar to complete my pupillage. There is enormous human interest in contentious probate work and even corporate work, involving shareholder disputes in small companies for example."*

You'll have plenty of opportunity to spend time in court developing your advocacy style although you should be aware that the volume of court work tends to be higher in other practice areas. As a junior led by seniors you'll be introduced to the specialist work of your set. You'll probably cut your teeth on County Court landlord and tenant actions, winding up applications and insolvency cases, allowing you to hone those courtroom skills. After a few years you may find that you have ended up with a fascinating overseas practice. The offshore tax havens provide plenty of high value work for Chancery barristers. Rupert Reed has already gained a fair share of overseas experience. He has been called to the Cayman Bar for a case in the Grand Court, travelled regularly to Switzerland and has acted in cases to be heard in Hong Kong, Bermuda and the Channel Islands.

skills needed

You need to be pretty bright to succeed within the Chancery Bar. More importantly, you must be an excellent communicator. Solicitors will sometimes come to you with extremely complex and puzzling cases. These must be pulled apart and analysed. You must adore research and get a buzz from getting to the crux of often very interesting and intellectual questions. You then need to be able to interpret and communicate these conceptual ideas to your client and feel confident in your findings.

You can tell pretty quickly when someone's right for the Chancery Bar. Brian Green QC at Wilberforce Chambers says *"It's a spark of inventiveness and imagination; a light behind the eyes that singles someone out. It takes more than being persuasive on paper, you need to have life in the way you communicate."*

TRADITIONAL CHANCERY • London (leading sets)

1. Wilberforce Chambers
2. 5 Stone Buildings
3. Maitland Chambers
   3 New Square
   New Square Chambers
   10 Old Square

COMMERCIAL CHANCERY • London (leading sets)

1. Maitland Chambers
2. Serle Court
   4 Stone Buildings
   Wilberforce Chambers
3. 9 Old Square
   3-4 South Square
   11 Stone Buildings
4. New Square Chambers
   24 Old Buildings
   3 Stone Buildings

Within each band, sets are listed alphabetically.
Source: Chambers Guide to the Legal Profession 2001-2002

commercial

The work handled by the Commercial Bar will cover a broad range of business disputes and problems, for a variety of industry sectors. A barrister may be asked to advise on the breakdown of a contract between a supplier and its customer or on a dispute between a record company and its artist. There are as many different types of case as there are different types of business relationship. There are more opportunities to get a variety of work at the Commercial Bar than you might think.

Barristers and whole sets may develop a niche area in work such as shipping, banking or construction, for example. Increasingly, specialisation is seen as the way forward by some, whilst for others a more general practice can be maintained in one of the top league of commercial sets. There is certainly an overlap of work between the Chancery Bar and the Commercial Bar, but that merely reflects the fact that commercial work is an umbrella term and not a rigidly defined practice area.

Commercial work, in its purest sense, is dealt with by the Commercial Court or one of the County Court Business Courts. However, a large amount of work is also heard by the High Court (both Queen's Bench and Chancery Divisions) or dealt with by way of arbitration. Alternative Dispute Resolution is an increasingly common way to conclude business disputes and at the same time allow for the possibility of the commercial relationship continuing without the damage inflicted upon it by full-blown litigation.

type of work

Instructions are generally paper- and fact-intensive. They may involve huge sums of money. There may be multiple parties. In a construction case any number of contractors, subcontractors, suppliers or professionals could have contributed to a defect in a building or a delay in its completion. With the increase in globalisation commercial barristers are advising increasingly on cross-border issues. This includes EU/competition, international public and trade law and conflicts of laws.

Do you have business acumen? You'll certainly need it to feel comfortable advising lay clients in conference, such as the reinsurance head of department who comes to you with a highly complex point, or the shipping company that wants your opinion on how an international trade treaty impacts on its liability in a certain dispute.

Prepare yourself for a career which is mainly advisory. You won't be on your feet in court every day like a criminal advocate, for example. However, there is likely to be a steady flow of arbitrations and County Court hearings during the first few years. In any case, as one pupil in a leading construction set notes, even drafting pleadings in the early stages of your career can be exciting *"when you have a case looming and, as a pupil, it's one of the few times when you are on the cusp of litigation. Although you don't have the fear of having to stand up in court, you know that the stuff you're drafting is going to be used."* In terms of the big high profile cases, initially you can aspire to a role as second or third junior. Although this is unlikely to provide many opportunities for oral advocacy, it will certainly allow you to be a vital member of the team. You will, however, gain valuable advocacy experience in interlocutory applications and through deployment in a range of tribunals.

skills needed

"It's a fiercely practical area of the law," states Deepak Nambisan, tenant at Fountain Court. *"Often it's less about black letter law and more about being a business adviser. You're always trying to gear towards the business solution. You need an eye for detail and to be fully on top of the facts."*

As so much of the contact with your clients will be by way of written advice, you need to be a skilled paper advocate. You need to absorb yourself in the world of commerce and have a genuine interest in it. If you become specialised (and many believe that this is essential) the requirement to be steeped in your particular niche is paramount. Some previous industry experience could be the thing that marks you out from the rest of the pack. Competition for pupillage at the Commercial Bar is fought out by some of the very best candidates. You will need to prove you have what it takes.

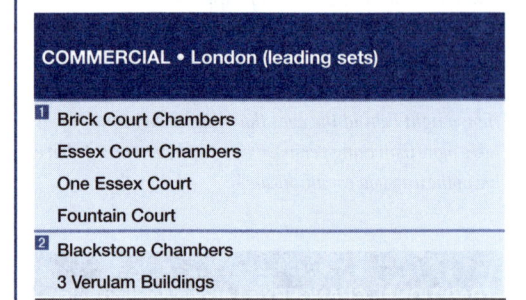

COMMERCIAL • London (leading sets)
[1] Brick Court Chambers
Essex Court Chambers
One Essex Court
Fountain Court
[2] Blackstone Chambers
3 Verulam Buildings

Within each band, sets are listed alphabetically.
Source: Chambers Guide to the Legal Profession 2001-2002

common law

The body of common law has developed through precedents set in previous cases rather than from statutes. The majority of these cases are dealt with in the Queen's Bench Division (QBD) of the High Court and the County Courts. Most cases turn on tort and contract claims. However, the work handled by the Common Law Bar is very broadly based and its edges blur into both Chancery and commercial law.

Certain factors have reduced the volume of instructions currently available to junior barristers. Solicitor advocates are definitely on the increase. Coupled with legal aid cutbacks and the growth in ADR and mediation, this has cut down the number of available cases. The Woolf reforms have certainly changed the adversarial nature of claims and many preliminary hearings simply no longer take place. Competition for the sort of work that juniors cut their teeth on is fierce and rumours circulate about brief fees tumbling to uneconomic levels.

type of work

Many common law sets offer a mix of other types of work such as crime, family or personal injury. This mix forms a significant part of the junior's common law caseload. In the early years, much of the work will involve drafting pleadings and attending hearings. These could be on anything ranging from RTA's and consumer credit debts to criminal hearings at the magistrates court and arbitrations, employment tribunals and family cases. The more general the profile of the set, the more general your experience. The opportunities for advocacy are fewer than at a specialist criminal set but greater than with a Chancery or commercial set. Your workload will be a blend of drafting, advice and court work.

skills needed

You'll need to be a quick learner and have a good short-term memory for facts and the law. This is particularly true during the initial stages of your tenancy when your practice will probably leap-frog between many different types of case. Perseverance is essential if you are to get to the stage where routine matters become familiar and straightforward and you can, perhaps, begin to specialise in a chosen area. If work really is scarce in the early years you'll have to be impressive to justify your next instruction and part of that boils down to personality and how well you interact with your client. *"Clearly we look for someone who's pretty bright,"* said Practice Director Joanna Poulton at 9 Gough Square *"but personality is the key. You've almost got to have a sixth sense about people. The Common Law Bar needs people who can get on with clients, be prepared to listen but not get taken in."*

You'll probably be doing a mixture of written advice and presentation in court. There will be less client contact than in criminal law, but probably more than in commercial or Chancery practice, so you'll need good people skills and an ability to adapt to a range of clients. As Philip Naughton QC points out. *"This area involves many different types of litigant, so the demeanor of the barrister is very important."*

criminal

Criminal law and specifically criminal advocacy is portrayed in a pretty glamorous light on TV, in films and in literature. Is the reality of life as a criminal advocate as dramatic and exciting? In terms of the buzz you can get from the work, the sense of being involved in something of key social importance and utility and the adrenaline levels, then yes, it probably is. When you speak to a criminal barrister, there's a genuine feeling that this is a really challenging and rewarding area of the law. We suspect that you probably already know if you want to be a criminal advocate – its almost a calling, not a career choice.

On the whole, the Criminal Bar fears no shortage of work. Whilst that may be a sad indictment of our society, it is encouraging for those in the early stages of a career. Despite talk of an assault on traditional Bar work from solicitor advocates and the Crown Prosecution Service, there is still plenty of work keeping the junior Bar busy. In fact, many juniors would say that, given direct access to clients, they could do without solicitors and their practices would be thriving.

type of work

The first year or so will be a continual round of Magistrates' Court appearances on minor matters like motoring offences, committals to the Crown Court, sentencing, pleas in mitigation and directions hearings. This, however, is where you'll learn to develop court skills, confidence and client handling techniques. With just a little time you'll progress to trials themselves, initially on smaller crimes such as common assault and the taking of motor vehicles, then graduating to ABH, robbery, indecent assault, and possession of drugs with intent to supply. You may get the opportunity to be a junior working with more senior members of chambers on white collar crime, kidnapping, rape or murder for example.

During your first six in pupillage you'll shadow

your pupil master or mistress and see first hand how a criminal advocate operates. The seriousness of the crimes you'll be involved with will be a taste of what is to come in the long-term future. It's a time to observe how an experienced barrister interacts with all the other participants in the case; the instructing solicitor, the defendant, the prosecution barrister, the witnesses, the judge and the jury. You'll be of assistance in researching points of law and helping to prepare skeleton arguments. But be prepared for mundane work too – photocopying and running around for other members of chambers. Many chambers will also send you out to court with juniors to give you a more immediate experience of the work you'll be handling following pupillage.

Almost immediately after pupillage you may apply to be included on the CPS List, which will enable you to receive instructions to prosecute as well as defend private clients. There will be opportunities to appear in the Crown Court on sentencing and pre-trial review and gradually you will move towards your own trials in that venue. Some juniors also advise on Criminal Injuries Compensation and do voluntary work for legal advice centres or organisations such as Victim Support, the Free Representation Unit and Justice.

The Criminal Bar is no different to any other area of the law in that the volume of work available to you (and potential earnings) in the early years depend on the reputation and fortunes of your chambers. Some barristers at less well known sets pointed out the unpredictability of Criminal Bar work. You may be kept busy for weeks and then suddenly have nothing for days on end. At the leading sets, however, it is not uncommon for you to be in court almost every day and in any set you must be prepared for action at any time and often on no notice.

skills needed

The work of a criminal barrister centres on people. Those who commit crimes, the victims and witnesses of those crimes, the juries that must reach verdicts and the professionals who administer justice. You need to be a good judge of character and to exercise good judgement yourself. You will be in the spotlight and it's important that you enjoy this. You will be responsible for your victories and for your defeats, so a balanced outlook will assist. As an advocate, your audience includes lay members of the public and you must speak their language and not just that of the other lawyers.

As a junior you will be asked to do unappealing work. You will often be required to travel a great deal with papers you have had little or no time to prepare. You may find that when you get to the trial your witnesses are not there.

One junior tenant related the time her train ticket to a hearing cost more than the brief fee. *"You just have to grin and bear it - you need the experience."* It's hard work, so stamina is essential. Instructions will often come to you on short notice so you'll need to be flexible and quick thinking. In court too, you need to think quickly on your feet; you can't just turn round to the judge and ask him for half an hour to figure out how to deal with a witness's response to a question in your cross-examination.

The job requires immense sensitivity at times, especially in cases of child sex abuse and rape. It is vital that you take great care with some witnesses. At the same time you do need to be thick-skinned in order to deal with sometimes rather unpleasant clients or defendants who have committed serious crimes. You don't have to be a hard person but sometimes you have to be tough in court. Tough, yet appealing. Jury skills are vital. A winning smile, a cheeky turn of phrase, and a sensitive approach with witnesses are all invaluable. If you're popular with juries and get a good success rate, you will never be short of good work.

Benjamin Squirrel of 2 Tudor Street has some hard words for those thinking of going to the Criminal Bar. *"The Criminal Bar is an insecure and fickle profession. Competition is intense. Success does not only depend on ability. It depends upon self-promotion, practical awareness and luck. If you can combine this with genuine skill as an advocate then you should succeed."

CRIMINAL • London (leading sets)

- 2 Bedford Row (formerly 3 Hare Court)
- Doughty Street Chambers
- 6 King's Bench Walk
- Hollis Whiteman Chambers
- 3 Raymond Buildings
- 18 Red Lion Court

Within each band, sets are listed alphabetically.
Source: Chambers Guide to the Legal Profession 2001-2002

family

The popular image of family law is of feuding couples and desperately bitter child custody battles. It is certainly a demanding practice area for a barrister, who will only be involved in the most complex or combative cases.

In truth, a large amount of court time in England & Wales is allotted to divorce, separation, adoption, child residence and contact orders, financial provision and domestic violence. Family barristers cut their teeth on simple County Court matters. They then progress over time to more complex matters, which might be heard in the Family Division of the High Court. Some practitioners see this area of the law as a market for legal services that won't shrink. People will always end up in messy matrimonial and family situations that need sorting out in court. But in the last ten years or so, there has been an increase in the profile of mediation between parties to attempt to resolve disputes in a more efficient and less unsettling fashion.

At one stage the Family Bar was worried. It seemed that a wave of mediation and a surge of new solicitor advocates would lead to a sharp downturn in the amount of work available. But work for the Bar appears to have continued unabated. One senior barrister told us that *"the Family Law Bar definitely has a future because there will always be family disputes and people who want to go to court. There are surprisingly few specialist solicitors. Most don't have the time to take cases all the way to court."*

type of work

Typically in pupillage and in the early period of tenancy your caseload will include a lot of private law children work. At first this will be minor appointments, directions hearings and time-tabling. Soon you'll begin to receive more substantive work, including final hearings. The ancillary relief work (financial arrangements between the parties) can be more complex and it takes a little longer to become proficient at it. To do well on the financial side it helps to have a flair for things like pensions and shares and to have grounding in the basics of trusts and property. After a few years of experience, and having built up a reputation amongst instructing solicitors, a barrister will often find herself or himself specialising, whether in the field of work relating to children, their custody, access and adoption or in matrimonial finance following marriage breakdown. The two specialisms draw on very different skills, but some barristers build up excellent reputations in both.

Whilst conflict is often deeply embedded in a case, the law requires an attempt at resolution through mediation. A tough adversarial approach is generally not appropriate and practitioners need to focus on client contact and genuine discussion. They must bear in mind that at the heart of child cases is the paramount consideration of the child's best interests.

skills needed

Sometimes it can feel as if everyone involved is in a no win situation, particularly where children are concerned. The talented barrister will sift through the facts of a case and find something worthwhile rather than merely assuming that there is little prospect of any sensible solution. The ability to maintain an even keel when dealing with distressing matters and to remain positive towards clients is essential. A genuine empathy for your lay client and his or her position is a must; no solicitor would wish to instruct a barrister who seems aloof or disinterested in the specifics of the client's case. At the same time, it is not the barrister's role to issue soothing words and paper handkerchiefs.

Mark Saunders, a tenant at specialist family law set Queen Elizabeth Building, feels that you must really know which facet of family law interests you before embarking on your career. *"You don't need to be a tree-hugging cardigan-wearing philanthropist to become a family barrister…many people imagine family as being all about care or child cases. Most of my practice is ancillary relief. You must undertake a few mini pupilages to get a feel for the area you want to move into."* Mark did not feel that the Family Bar was that different from other areas of practice but pointed out the human dimension of the work. *"You can read the instructions or the brief but the case really comes alive when you meet the client. One of the most interesting features of the work is getting to know the client and seeing the person behind the facts."*

Perhaps the thing to remember is that in family cases the ruling made or the settlement reached can have a massive impact on each of the human lives touched by it. As a consequence, it is vital that the barrister recognises the appropriate course of action in each case and works with the solicitor in managing the case from an early stage.

FAMILY • London (leading sets)

1
One King's Bench Walk
1 Mitre Court Buildings
Queen Elizabeth Building

2
29 Bedford Row Chambers

3
One Garden Court Family Law Chambers
4 Paper Buildings

4
14 Gray's Inn Square
Renaissance Chambers

Within each band, sets are listed alphabetically.
Source: Chambers Guide to the Legal Profession 2001-2002

public law

Public bodies operate within statutory constraints. Their decisions may be challenged. Have they considered the relevant facts in reaching decisions? Have the officers acted strictly in accordance with the correct procedure? Did the body or officer have the authority to make the decision in the first place? Will they reveal to you how and why they have made a decision? If these questions interest you and you are passionate about principles of justice and the advancement of the law, then read on.

A decision made by a publicly accountable body is subject to question by an affected party. For example, the decision of the Home Office to deny a non-national the right to remain in the country, or the decision of a Local Planning Authority to refuse permission for an out of town supermarket. One of the most recent high profile and contentious public law cases concerned the separation of the conjoined twins Jodie and Mary.

The new Human Rights Act has made a huge impact upon numerous areas of law. Practitioners are seeing an increasing amount of work dealing with issues thrown up by the Act. Indeed, Matrix Chambers was formed largely to tackle different areas of law which are affected by the HRA and international law. The HRA will continue to have a significant impact upon all areas of law but most notably it is public law which will find itself at the cutting edge.

type of work

A public law barrister will receive instructions to act on a case by case basis. Those building up a Local Authority clientele, for example, may find themselves acting for a number of different departments on a range of work, often leaning heavily towards decisions concerning planning, housing or environmental matters and education, health and children.

By far the most common public law matter is the judicial review of an immigration decision. About half of the Administrative Court comprises immigration cases. This work is likely to feature prominently in a junior barrister's practice.

Not all public law sets limit themselves to this practice area. Many combine the work with general common law, competition or employment. Additionally, many sets that do not hold themselves out as specialist public law sets carry out judicial review work.

Public Inquiries are raised where an event is deemed to be of great significance to society as a whole. The Bloody Sunday Inquiry, the Paddington Rail-Crash Inquiry and the inquiry following the death of Stephen Lawrence are examples of the very different types of issues under scrutiny.

Pupillage at a public law set will often consist of drafting opinions and shadowing your pupilmaster, with some advocacy in the second six such as applying for urgent injunctions. As applications for judicial review are heard in the High Court, it is not usual for the most junior barristers to provide advocacy in this area, but after a few years you should have a highly interesting practice with a good balance of advice and advocacy.

skills needed

It's all about understanding red tape and wanting to battle through it for your client. You have to really care about the development of the fundamental laws by which we live. But remember that the work doesn't necessarily involve close contact with your lay client. In many cases the client does not attend the hearing in person at all.

You must develop a comprehensive knowledge of administrative and constitutional law and be familiar with the inner workings of central and local government generally. Familiarity with EU and international law is increasingly important.

The courts deal with such a high volume of cases that you need to develop an efficient style of advocacy. This is not an area in which long and dramatic performances are well received. You'll have to learn how to cut to the chase and deliver the pertinent information, draw on the relevant case law or statutory regulations and present your arguments promptly. An inquiring and analytical mind is essential.

PUBLIC LAW • London (leading sets)
[1] Blackstone Chambers
[2] 4 Breams Buildings
Matrix Chambers
[3] 39 Essex Street
11 King's Bench Walk Chambers
[4] Brick Court Chambers
Doughty Street Chambers
Two Garden Court
2-3 Gray's Inn
4-5 Gray's Inn Square

Within each band, sets are listed alphabetically.
Source: Chambers Guide to the Legal Profession 2001-2002

COMING SOON TO A PC NEAR YOU, THE VIRTUAL RECRUITMENT FAIR.

LET THE LAW FIRMS COME TO YOU, CALL 01423 875222 TO GET YOUR FREE CD.

2020Law gives you the opportunity to visit the major law firms who are hunting the best talent.

No more ploughing through brochures or leaflets, no lengthy and time consuming visits to recruitment fairs. All you need is a PC and your free 2020Law CD-Rom.

2020Law transports you to a virtual building. Every floor houses a different firm and a new career opportunity – using your web browser will allow you to go on line to get more information or make a direct application.

Your future at your fingertips

Email: **contact@2020law.com**   Web: **www.2020law.com**

2020 TWENTY TWENTY LAW

SPECIALIST PRACTICE AREAS

- banking 82
- corporate 87
- crime 94
- employment 98
- environmental 103
- EU 107
- family 111
- IP 116
- IT 120
- litigation 124
- media 130
- personal injury 136
- private client 145
- projects 153
- property 159
- public interest 165
- shipping 172
- sports 176
- tax 180
- qualifying in other jurisdictions 182

banking

In modern parlance 'banking' covers basic commercial loan agreements, constituted by contracts between borrowers and lenders, together with capital markets work. This covers the issuance of debt or equity securities and related areas such as securitisation, repackaging and structured finance, plus the whole range of derivatives products. A banking lawyer's work might vary from the preparation, negotiation and drafting of a syndicated loan agreement – considered 'pure' banking – to the structuring of a foreign exchange currency or interest rate swap. Increasingly, banking work involves tax efficient deal structures, requiring the setting up of special purpose companies in jurisdictions which have sympathetic tax regimes, such as the Cayman Islands.

Banking lawyers in 'straight' banking work will be responsible for drafting all the major terms of loan contracts including the taking of security, events of default and the covenants. Basically, they are concerned with the documentation of lending money, and arranging its signing and completion. In capital markets work they will often actually assist with the structuring of the commercial terms of a deal and advise on whether a proposed transaction breaches any securities laws. A typical capital markets transaction might involve a company raising several million sterling via an issue of a bond sold into say Europe or a public offering of equity. The proceeds are then swapped into dollars and perhaps used for an acquisition. In this way banking obviously overlaps with corporate finance work, particularly M&A. Banking lawyers should have a broad knowledge of these areas. This area of practice is now completely global and much of the work is international.

Banking is strictly regulated, though not prohibitively so. Financial services regulation now employs ever greater numbers of compliance lawyers. As credit risk departments and capital adequacy requirements become increasingly important so does their advisory role. In London they will primarily be concerned to ensure compliance with the Financial Services Authority which regulates the UK market.

type of work

Top level banking and capital markets work is highly polarised and concentrated in the world financial centres. *"You get to work in a handful of glamorous cities like New York, Hong Kong and Paris."* said one senior banking lawyer. Within the UK, there is a chasm between work done by the inner core of top City specialists, such as **Allen & Overy**, **Clifford Chance**, **Linklaters** and **Freshfields Bruckhaus Deringer**, and other firms. The complexity and value of the transactions are greater at the larger City firms, whose clients tend to be international merchant and investment banks. There are also prominent and reputable national firms based in the northern financial centres such as **Addleshaw Booth & Co** and **DLA**.

At the leading City firms with strong banking practices – such as **Allen & Overy** and **Clifford Chance** – deals are cutting edge and clients are prestigious. Reflecting the global nature of the practices themselves, top City banking deals can span continents and cover the front pages of the Financial Times. Stephen Lucas at **Clifford Chance** believes that this creates a *"culture of high level support and a great degree of sophistication."* Modern technology and the use of precedents frequently means a time-critical deal can be pulled off quickly instead of having to reinvent the wheel every time.

Regional firms with well-developed banking practices see a very different type of work. Their client base may consist of smaller retail banks or building societies. As Richard Papworth from **Addleshaw Booth & Co** in Leeds explains, *"the real-*

ity is that you won't see a huge number of multi-billion pound international financings. However the quality of the work can be high and young lawyers have a lot of opportunities to get actively involved."

Banking involves less 'pure law' than other practice areas – "there is more emphasis on the preparation of contracts and the financial side of things than on legality – the satisfaction tends to come from the delivery and completion of projects, seeing something through from start to finish." The work is dominated by transactions but there is a fast turnaround. This can be an attractive feature to those with short attention spans; "you don't get bogged down in things which go on for years. You see things through relatively quickly."

Although perceived as a niche area, banking overlaps with many other disciplines. Invariably lawyers will be involved in financing a range of things – property, corporate acquisitions or a power project for example. Stephen Lucas from **Clifford Chance** described this spread – "*you are very often managing a transaction involving a number of different specialisms. You become the focus for that because you represent the deliverer or the recipient of the finance so you have to manage a large team.*" Banking is not a support department. It occupies a frontal position facing the clients – the providers of the money.

Among the more complex structured banking transactions, you will touch on a cross-section of almost all basic legal knowledge and will need to know how these areas work. Stephen Lucas describes how it involves a peripheral knowledge of many other areas – "*If a company wants to buy another publicly listed company but doesn't have the money to do so, it borrows from banks, it will secure that borrowing on its assets and on the assets of the target company – its shares, its intellectual property and real estate. When the financing and the loan agreement are underway, you need to understand the corporate regime that will allow company A to buy company B because that is what you're funding. Although you're not documenting that corporate sale purchase agreement you*

need to understand the way it works, because it has to tie in with the financing."

Banking law is definitely placed at the glamorous end of the profession. Prestigious high finance deals and international travel are common. "*The banking lawyer is always more glamorous than his tax counterpart!*" said one categorically. Another lawyer enjoyed the travel and exposure to other cultures.

"*I've been able to travel to Moscow and other exotic cities taking advantage of several working opportunities!*" However it is also hard work and you should enter banking law for the right reasons. One lawyer loved his area but was understated and philosophical. "*Some people will say there is nothing glamorous about international travel, hotels or getting on the front page of the FT. Sometimes you're exhausted.*"

There are certain macho stereotypes associated with banking lawyers. The practitioners interviewed were keen to stress that these are unfair caricatures of a small minority. Like the banking profession itself, lawyers are frequently outgoing and dynamic and sometimes exhibit a certain bravado. Salary rewards are high, however, and the 'work hard, play hard' maxim is never far from the norm.

a day in the life of....

On a day to day level, banking lawyers operate in small transaction management teams spanning the range of seniority. It is a meeting intensive environment involving a lot of documentation, managing several supporting aspects of the transaction such as the availability of funding. There is a high premium placed on technical ability and judgement. At **Addleshaw Booth & Co**, juniors would be permitted to handle the documentation for a straightforward bank or building society loan from very early on. More complex transactions require additional experience and supervision but this is an area of law where early responsibility is common. "*I love doing what I do,*" said one young lawyer enthusiastically, "*sealing big transactions and negotiating contracts. Banking law is the pivot which allows you do that.*"

Newly qualified banking lawyers will usually see a good deal of the work – mainly because they will be given a lot of drafting and asked to attend a lot of meetings. This has its rewards: *"the interaction with the business world is excellent – banking law gives such a good understanding of financial markets."* On a new deal, banking lawyers will assist on structuring issues, give advice and work on the completion of a deal, culminating in the drafting and signing of a loan agreement. One young lawyer summed up the appeal: *"I really enjoy the big deals"* and contact with *"very on the ball clients!"*

The lifestyle implications for banking lawyers can be tough and days rarely predictable. One lawyer humorously confirmed its commonly held reputation for long and strenuous hours – *"banking could certainly be recognised as being at the stickier end of quality of life,"* but the pay-off can be huge. *"There is so much adrenalin in deal completion."* The demands are intensive because of the cyclical nature of transactional management – peaks and troughs rather than core repeat business is the norm. A normal 50 hour week can easily rise to 75 or 100 hours as a deal nears completion. Working into the early hours is not uncommon, even in the early stages of a career. However, banking lawyers universally speak of the buzz of completing a deal – a major motivational force.

Dedication is a fundamental requirement as transactions vary from the very simple to very complicated ones. Some keep you in the office from 9-6 pm, some keep you there from 9-6 am and you can gravitate towards the type of complexity and deal that suits you – often dependent on the firm or its specialist area.

skills needed

Strong practical intelligence…analytical skills…keen interest and understanding of business and international finance…the ability to dedicate to the task, to see it through to completion…commitment…sense of humour…diligence, accuracy and care…the capacity to do routine work in the early stages of your career….

career options

Many young lawyers at City firms view banking law as an ideal platform for the financial markets with the potential to open up future doors. There is frequently an overlap and fluidity with the banking world itself. It is relatively common for lawyers with a couple of years PQE to move to an investment banking or corporate finance role. With slightly more legal experience, movement to an in-house legal position within a bank is another common option. However, Stephen Lucas from **Clifford Chance** warns against making the wrong career move – *"If you want to become a banker, become a banker not a lawyer. It's really that simple. Don't spend time at university studying law, CPE, LPC, articles etc. – you'd be a four year qualified banker by the same stage. However, if you want to be a banking lawyer, but decide it's not for you, there is ample opportunity soon after qualification to move into banking."* This is a big-money world. Salary levels in all related areas are similarly placed, if not even higher. Even at very junior levels, secondments to international banks are made available by most firms and can provide a taster of things to come.

LEADING FIRMS

BANKING • London

1 Allen & Overy
Clifford Chance
2 Linklaters
3 Freshfields Bruckhaus Deringer
Norton Rose
4 Ashurst Morris Crisp
Lovells
Slaughter and May
5 Denton Wilde Sapte
Herbert Smith
Shearman & Sterling
6 Baker & McKenzie
Berwin Leighton Paisner
CMS Cameron McKenna
DLA
Gouldens
Macfarlanes
Simmons & Simmons
SJ Berwin
Taylor Joynson Garrett
Theodore Goddard
Travers Smith Braithwaite
Watson, Farley & Williams
White & Case

BANKING • Wales

1 Eversheds Cardiff
2 Edwards Geldard Cardiff
Morgan Cole Cardiff

BANKING • The South & South West

1 Burges Salmon Bristol
Osborne Clarke Bristol
2 Bond Pearce Bristol, Southampton
3 CMS Cameron McKenna Bristol
4 Blake Lapthorn Fareham

BANKING • Midlands

1 Eversheds Birmingham, Nottingham
Pinsent Curtis Biddle Birmingham
2 Wragge & Co Birmingham
3 DLA Birmingham
Gateley Wareing Birmingham
Martineau Johnson Birmingham
4 Browne Jacobson Nottingham

BANKING • East Anglia

1 Eversheds Cambridge, Ipswich, Norwich
2 Mills & Reeve Cambridge, Norwich

Within each band, firms are listed alphabetically.
Source: Chambers and Partners Guide to the Legal Profession 2001-2002

LEADING FIRMS continued

BANKING • North West

1. **DLA** Liverpool, Manchester
   Eversheds Manchester
2. **Halliwell Landau** Manchester
3. **Addleshaw Booth & Co** Manchester
4. **Chaffe Street** Manchester
   Cobbetts Manchester
   Davies Wallis Foyster Liverpool, Manchester
   Hammond Suddards Edge Manchester
5. **Kuit Steinart Levy** Manchester

Within each band, firms are listed alphabetically.
Source: Chambers and Partners Guide to the Legal Profession 2001-2002

BANKING • North East

1. **Dickinson Dees** Newcastle upon Tyne
2. **Eversheds** Newcastle upon Tyne
   Ward Hadaway Newcastle upon Tyne
3. **Robert Muckle** Newcastle upon Tyne

BANKING • Yorkshire

1. **Addleshaw Booth & Co** Leeds
2. **Hammond Suddards Edge** Leeds
3. **DLA** Leeds
   Pinsent Curtis Biddle Leeds
4. **Eversheds** Leeds
   Walker Morris Leeds

corporate law

All commercial law firms are keen to be involved in corporate work. Transactions in this area command large fees and receive coverage in the national and regional press. Experienced corporate lawyers are much in demand and are among the highest paid in the profession, earning seven figure salaries in some instances.

The core of corporate work relates to mergers and acquisitions (M&A) and corporate restructurings. Requiring large amounts of capital, this type of work is often interdependent with finance (banking and capital markets work) and thus often comes under the umbrella name of corporate finance. Companies fund their acquisitions by a variety of means. They may restructure, disposing of certain assets not considered essential to their core business in order to raise capital. If they are privately held, they may decide to raise finance by 'going public.' This involves an offering of their shares to the public (an equity offering), including institutional investors like pension funds, on any of the public stock exchanges such as the London or New York Stock Exchanges. If they are already public companies, they may make a rights issue (offer of new shares). They may also raise money via debt. This may take the form of loans from the 'market' (bonds) or from banks or other specific financial institutions (see banking). Finance is often raised by a combination of these methods for a complex high value deal.

Other areas of corporate practice are joint ventures and buy-outs. Buy-outs can be simply the present management raising capital to take control of their company (an MBO). Buy-out companies like 3i often fund this type of deal. Often the buy-out company will itself pinpoint the deal and take a controlling interest in the target. These sorts of deals can involve the buy-out company borrowing a large amount of capital proportionate to its underlying value, hence the term 'leveraged buy-outs.' Companies can bring in other buy-out companies to spread the risk and the values of the buy-outs can be as large as any public take-over. **Ashurst Morris Crisp** for example, advised Cinven and Citicorp Venture Capital on the £825m acquisition of William Hill. Joint ventures can be structured in the form of a partnership through the formation of a new company or under a contractual arrangement. These can be as huge as the £800m HMV Media Group joint venture (advised by **Rowe & Maw**) which includes the HMV, Dillons and Waterstones music and book retail outlets.

type of work

Corporate work depends on the size and location of the firm. Large City firms act for listed companies on the stock exchange, and deal with household names such as BT, BP and Tesco. Smaller City and regional firms tend to advise leading regional private companies and a handful of FTSE 250 companies.

The distinction between stock exchange and private company work is more than just the size of the company. Private companies' M&A work is amicable because the deal can only proceed if all parties agree to it, whereas stock market companies can be subject to hostile take-overs.

Lawyers advising on private company acquisitions will help draft the sale and purchase agreements, arrange the financing for the deal and carry out a process known as 'due diligence.' The sale, purchase and financing negotiations are usually carried out between company board members and lawyers. Trainees are not expected to take a lead role in negotiating the agreement, although they may be asked to attend the meetings. A private company sale takes about a month to complete. Whereas a trainee can expect to be involved in one or two deals at a time, newly qualifieds can expect to be working on several at once under the supervision of different partners.

Trainees and students on work experience tend to carry out due diligence work – a time consuming but necessary task to ensure honesty between a purchaser (known as a bidder) and a company being purchased (known as a target). If a target claims to be the largest widget manufacturer in the country, then it could be the trainee's job to check this is true. Trainees will also be expected to check that the target is not involved in outstanding litigation and does not have damaging 'change of control' clauses, which could harm profitability after a takeover.

Stock exchange deals are different. Private companies have few shareholders (owners). Stock exchange-registered companies can have millions. This makes them vulnerable to hostile takeover bids from rival companies who can buy shares and thereby obtain a controlling stake.

To help public companies combat this threat, the London Stock Exchange has developed a detailed takeover code to govern both friendly and hostile M&A activity. The code sets a strict timetable for companies to make and respond to potential bidders and sets out detailed guidelines for the treatment of shareholders. Lawyers advising these companies know this code inside out, and will explain what company directors should be doing at every stage of a potential acquisition. If a merger or acquisition is agreed, corporate lawyers will advise on the formation of the new or modified company and any required financing.

a day in the life...

The hours a trainee is expected to work depends on the type of deal and the individual managers. A partner in a medium-sized London firm said trainees could expect to work an average of five-and-a-half days a week. Working three 20 hour days in a row may be unusual, but should not be dismissed out of hand. In public company takeover work strict timetables under the yellow and blue books must be adhered to. This often results in 'all-nighters' to ensure that all the due diligence exercise is watertight and that all the necessary final agreements and documentation are prepared according to the timetables. Private company work can be equally time pressured with the client pushing for the best deal in the shortest time.

However, trainees and newly qualifieds who excel in company work seem to thrive in pressured situations where the need to have an eye for detail is paramount.

Because corporate work is often a whole new world for trainees, they can find it takes time to adjust. But Mark Rawlinson, corporate partner with **Freshfields Bruckhaus Deringer**, would urge trainees not to be put off in their first few months. *"I hated my first six months in the corporate department and found it difficult,"* says Rawlinson." *But a senior property lawyer who had been a captain in the marines said to me that I'd make a good corporate lawyer, so I went back and tried it again. After the first 18 months, it began to get more interesting. The trouble is as a trainee everything moves at 100mph and there's such a lot to take in."*

skills needed...

....not for the fainthearted...ability to work long hours under extreme pressure...media-friendliness...you enjoy seeing the deals you do in the newspapers and meeting high quality, high profile people on deals where there's a lot of money at stake...good presentation skills...ability to think on your feet...decisiveness...confidence, tact and clear communication skills...a good eye for detail... patience and understanding....

career options

Currently the corporate world is contracting, particularly noticably in IT/e-commerce, an area which had previously benefited many smaller City firms and those in the regions. Although the work undertaken by the regional firms is often of a lower value, it can still involve tricky cross-border negotiations. At the smaller end of the market, transactions tend to focus on private equity financing, AIM (Alternative Investment Market) or Ofex flotations, often following the specialisms of the firms. Watch out also for the growing influence of US law firms acting out of their London office. Whilst at the moment only a small number of these firms (e.g **Weil Gotshal & Manges**, **Shearman & Sterling**) are running deals without the support of their big brothers across the pond, the ability to leverage US style relationships with major investment banks should not be overlooked.

The reward for working in a large commercial department of a smaller firm (both in the regions and in London) is often involvement in a client's affairs at an earlier stage. These larger regional firms also provide the opportunity, like their City counterparts, for qualified lawyers to be seconded to major clients. **Osborne Clarke** has had a corporate lawyer at South Western Electricity plc for example.

A sound grounding in corporate finance makes an excellent springboard for working in industry. Many lawyers move in-house to major companies at an early stage of their careers, tempted by salaries comparable with private practice, but more predictable hours.

Moves in-house do occur at partner level, but they are less common.

Another popular move among young corporate finance lawyers is to join the banking world, either as an in-house lawyer or as a corporate finance executive or analyst. This is a chance to move from 'lawyer' to 'client.' Those who have made the transition seem to enjoy the dynamic pace of life and are glad to have shed the advisory role. Such moves generally occur early on, but high profile moves of senior partners to investment banks is not uncommon.

Becoming a company secretary and advising board members on their internal legal compliance procedures is an alternative route. This position is suitable for senior lawyers with a general range of company and commercial skills and salaries can be in excess of £100,000.

Although an in-house career is increasingly common for corporate lawyers, the majority of lawyers are happy working in private practice. Nigel Boardman originally trained at **Slaughters** in 1973 and has remained in the corporate department – apart from a two year break working for a major bank – ever since. If you enjoy corporate work, it seems you are reluctant to leave the lifestyle behind.

LEADING FIRMS

CORPORATE FINANCE: LARGER DEALS • London

1 Freshfields Bruckhaus Deringer
Linklaters
Slaughter and May

2 Allen & Overy
Clifford Chance
Herbert Smith

3 Ashurst Morris Crisp

4 Lovells
Norton Rose

5 Macfarlanes
Simmons & Simmons

Within each band, firms are listed alphabetically.
Source: Chambers and Partners Guide to the Legal Profession 2001-2002

CORPORATE FINANCE: MEDIUM DEALS • London

1 CMS Cameron McKenna
Travers Smith Braithwaite

2 Denton Wilde Sapte
Gouldens
Rowe & Maw
SJ Berwin
Weil, Gotshal & Manges

3 Berwin Leighton Paisner
Olswang

4 Baker & McKenzie
Hammond Suddards Edge
Nabarro Nathanson
Taylor Joynson Garrett
Theodore Goddard

5 Bird & Bird
Dechert
DLA
Osborne Clarke
Pinsent Curtis Biddle

LEADING FIRMS continued

CORPORATE FINANCE: SMALLER DEALS • London

1
- DJ Freeman
- Eversheds
- Lawrence Graham
- Stephenson Harwood

2
- Field Fisher Waterhouse
- Memery Crystal
- Reed Smith Warner Cranston
- Richards Butler

3
- Harbottle & Lewis
- Lewis Silkin
- Nicholson Graham & Jones

4
- Coudert Brothers
- Hobson Audley
- Sinclair Roche & Temperley
- Watson, Farley & Williams
- Wedlake Bell

5
- Fox Williams
- Howard Kennedy
- Manches
- Marriott Harrison

6
- Beachcroft Wansbroughs
- Charles Russell
- Laytons
- Middleton Potts
- Steptoe & Johnson Rakisons

Within each band, firms are listed alphabetically.
Source: Chambers and Partners Guide to the Legal Profession 2001-2002

CORPORATE FINANCE • East Anglia

1
- Eversheds Ipswich, Norwich
- Mills & Reeve Cambridge, Norwich

2
- Garretts Cambridge
- Hewitson Becke + Shaw Cambridge
- Taylor Vinters Cambridge

3
- Birketts Ipswich
- Prettys Ipswich

4
- Greene & Greene Bury St Edmunds
- Greenwoods Peterborough
- Steele & Co Norwich

CORPORATE FINANCE • Midlands

1
- Wragge & Co Birmingham

2
- Eversheds Birmingham
- Pinsent Curtis Biddle Birmingham

3
- Browne Jacobson Nottingham
- DLA Birmingham
- Gateley Wareing Birmingham, Nottingham
- Hammond Suddards Edge Birmingham
- Martineau Johnson Birmingham

4
- Freethcartwright Nottingham
- Lee Crowder Birmingham
- Shoosmiths Northampton, Nottingham

5
- Edwards Geldard Nottingham
- Garretts Birmingham
- George Green Cradley Heath
- Harvey Ingram Owston Leicester
- Hewitson Becke + Shaw Northampton
- Howes Percival Northampton

LEADING FIRMS continued

CORPORATE FINANCE • North East

1. **Dickinson Dees** Newcastle upon Tyne
2. **Eversheds** Newcastle upon Tyne
   Ward Hadaway Newcastle upon Tyne
3. **Robert Muckle** Newcastle upon Tyne
4. **Watson Burton** Newcastle upon Tyne

CORPORATE FINANCE • North West

1. **Addleshaw Booth & Co** Manchester
2. **DLA** Liverpool, Manchester
   Eversheds Manchester
3. **Halliwell Landau** Manchester
4. **Brabners** Liverpool
   Chaffe Street Manchester
   Hammond Suddards Edge Manchester
5. **Cobbetts** Manchester
   Davies Wallis Foyster Liverpool, Manchester
6. **Kuit Steinart Levy** Manchester
   Pannone & Partners Manchester
   Wacks Caller Manchester

Within each band, firms are listed alphabetically.
Source: Chambers and Partners Guide to the Legal Profession 2001-2002

CORPORATE FINANCE • South West

1. **Burges Salmon** Bristol
   Osborne Clarke Bristol
2. **TLT Solicitors** Bristol
3. **Bevan Ashford** Bristol, Exeter
   Bond Pearce Exeter, Plymouth
4. **Bretherton Price Elgoods** Cheltenham
   Charles Russell Cheltenham
   CMS Cameron McKenna Bristol
   Foot Anstey Sargent Exeter, Plymouth
   Laytons Bristol
   Lyons Davidson Bristol
   Michelmores Exeter
   Stephens & Scown Exeter, St Austell, Truro
   Veale Wasbrough Bristol
5. **Clark Holt** Swindon

CORPORATE FINANCE • Thames Valley

1. **Osborne Clarke** Reading
2. **Manches** Oxford
3. **Clarks** Reading
   Kimbells Milton Keynes
   Nabarro Nathanson Reading
   Pitmans Reading
4. **Brobeck Hale and Dorr** Oxford
5. **BP Collins** Gerrards Cross
   Garretts Reading
   Shoosmiths Reading

LEADING FIRMS continued

CORPORATE FINANCE • The South

1 **Blake Lapthorn** Fareham, Portsmouth, Southampton
Bond Pearce Southampton
2 **Shadbolt & Co** Reigate
Stevens & Bolton Guildford
3 **asb law** Crawley
Clyde & Co Guildford
Cripps Harries Hall Tunbridge Wells
Mundays Esher
Paris Smith & Randall Southampton
Rawlison Butler Crawley
Shoosmiths Fareham
Thomas Eggar Church Adams Chichester, Horsham, Reigate, Worthing
Thomson Snell & Passmore Tunbridge Wells
4 **Brachers** Maidstone
DMH Brighton, Crawley
Lester Aldridge Bournemouth, Southampton

CORPORATE FINANCE • Yorkshire

1 **Addleshaw Booth & Co** Leeds
2 **Eversheds** Leeds
Hammond Suddards Edge Leeds
3 **DLA** Leeds, Sheffield
4 **Pinsent Curtis Biddle** Leeds
Walker Morris Leeds
5 **Irwin Mitchell** Leeds, Sheffield
Lupton Fawcett Leeds
Read Hind Stewart Leeds
Rollits Hull
6 **Andrew M Jackson & Co** Hull
Gordons Cranswick Solicitors Bradford, Leeds
Gosschalks Hull

Within each band, firms are listed alphabetically.
Source: Chambers and Partners Guide to the Legal Profession 2001-2002

CORPORATE FINANCE • Wales

1 **Morgan Cole** Cardiff
2 **Edwards Geldard** Cardiff
3 **Eversheds** Cardiff
4 **Berry Smith** Cardiff
M and A Solicitors Cardiff
5 **MLM** Cardiff

crime

General criminal lawyers act for defendants in Magistrates' Courts, Crown Courts and courts martial. Whatever the seriousness of the charge, the basic process is the same. The difference is in the detail. Less serious offences are dealt with in the Magistrates' Courts, with the accused usually represented by a solicitor. More serious cases are tried in the Crown Courts. Though solicitors can now take exams to enable them to work as advocates in the Crown Courts, most still prefer to use a barrister.

In addition to expertise in criminal law and procedure, lawyers need to be familiar with mental health, immigration and extradition issues. This chapter deals mainly with general criminal law.

type of work

It's hard work but it can be fun. Unlike in many legal careers, you are not office-bound, and there are plenty of opportunities for advocacy. Dealing with criminal clients can often be challenging, but is not as hard as you might think. *"Major criminals can be very, very interesting people"* says Gerry McManus of Manchester firm **Burton Copeland**. *"A lot of them have a number of problems; drugs, drink, health and psychiatric problems"* says Mark Studdert, partner in Camden practice **Hodge, Jones & Allen** *"but in the general scheme of things they are easy people to deal with, because they are unwilling participants in the system and want the case to go away as soon as possible."*

The immediacy of the work is another plus, and criminal lawyers are often able to see the fruits of their advice and work within a relatively short time. This is particularly true for lawyers who are accredited to work as duty solicitors at magistrates' courts. Their role is to provide advocacy for those who cannot afford representation. Clients often have no idea of how the process works and are very grateful for their intervention, which can often lead to immediate results. Because the work is date driven, cases have a quick turnover, and even murder cases are dealt with in under a year. *"There is a lovely rhythm to criminal work"* says Girish Thanki, partner with niche firm **Thanki Novy Taube**. *"You finish it, you bill it, you get the money within a couple of months. Whether you're upbeat because you got the desired result or annoyed because you failed to, it's all over quickly and things are moving on."*

This last year has left criminal practice in flux. The introduction of the Human Rights Act, the restructuring of publicly funded defence work and proposals to curb the right to trail by jury have turned criminal practice inside out. By far the biggest issue facing criminal defence lawyers has been the block contracting of criminal legal services. On 1 April 2001, the Legal Aid Board was abolished and replaced by the Legal Services Commission. Criminal defence work is now undertaken only by franchised firms, which can demonstrate their ability to handle the work. There is no limit upon the number of firms entitled to hold a franchise but it is hard for small high street firms to compete with larger rivals who have the resources to corner the market. There has been unease in the profession with concerns that everything will be done with an eye to costs, reducing the system to a conveyor belt. These worries are compounded by the ongoing debate over trial mode. The government is still keen to push ahead with plans carried over from the last Parliament to make a number of hybrid offences (triable by Magistrate or jury at the defendant's discretion) summary (tried only in the magistrates court). Civil liberties arguments aside, trials in the Magistrates' Court, without juries are cheaper.

The precise effects of the Human Rights Act are uncertain as yet, but all courts will have to take its provisions into account in all cases. With specific articles dealing with, amongst others, the right to privacy, the right to a fair trial and freedom of expression, this will mean extra tools in the hands of the defence lawyer at every stage of the criminal process.

All this change makes it a very interesting time to become a criminal lawyer. As Mark Studdert, points out: *"There have been major pieces of legislation every year that I've been in practice. Not only changing specific laws, but also the whole procedural approach. You are very much at the cutting edge of legislative changes, and of how society is dealing with its problems."*

a day in the life...

Criminal lawyers lead a hectic life, particularly in small practices, where administrative pressures are greater. You might get into the office at 8.30 am, having already spent some of the night at the police station as duty solicitor. At 9.30 am, it's off to the magistrates' court for procedural and remand hearings, or a plea in mitigation. Lunch is on the hoof. The afternoon is spent interviewing clients and conferring with counsel. There is still paperwork to deal with and you could be back in the police station tonight. When at last you get home, you'll have to spend some of your 'free' time preparing for the next day's court hearing.

As a criminal trainee you will be thrown in at the deep end, with your own caseload and appearances in the magistrates' courts from day one. One of the most important elements of your training will be attending police station interviews or listening to tapes of them. You will also get to assist senior lawyers and barristers in more serious assault, rape and murder cases, and may get to sit through major trials. This breadth of opportunity and responsibility is one of the main attractions of the training.

skills needed

....an eye for fine detail...strong understanding of the law...ability to be sharp and resolute on your feet...finely honed social skills...flair...imagination ...client-handling skills..."Those with prior experience in psychology or counselling usually make excellent criminal lawyers"...empathy...good organisational, administrative and IT skills...you'll need to love your work and be 100% committed to it...ability to work without reward....

career options

At the moment most high street practices handle criminal work, though, as explained above, this may change with increasing specialisation. For those seeking a good general criminal practice, Greg Powell of **Powell Spencer & Partners** has a tip. *"Ask a senior probation officer, social worker or the Citizens Advice Bureau which firms they have a good relationship with."*

Specialist criminal firms offer high profile criminal and civil rights work. However, training contracts in these firms are scarce as some are unable to offer experience in all areas of law required by the Law Society. Advancement for assistants may be slow as they usually have a small number of partners.

Aspiring criminal lawyers often have a preference for Legal Aid work. Many firms specialising in family and child care also have criminal departments, enabling trainees to handle the full range of Legal Aid work during training. In terms of quality, such firms are often regarded as highly as specialist criminal practices. The Crown Prosecution Service does not take trainees but recruits qualified solicitors.

LEADING FIRMS

CRIME • London

[1]
- Bindman & Partners
- Birnberg Peirce & Partners
- Edward Fail Bradshaw & Waterson
- Hodge Jones & Allen
- Kingsley Napley
- Saunders & Co
- Simons Muirhead & Burton
- Taylor Nichol

[2]
- Edwards Duthie
- Fisher Meredith
- Hallinan, Blackburn, Gittings & Nott
- Henry Milner & Co
- Hickman & Rose
- Powell Spencer & Partners
- Russell Jones & Walker
- Russell-Cooke
- Thanki Novy Taube
- TV Edwards
- Whitelock & Storr

[3]
- Alistair Meldrum & Co
- Andrew Keenan & Co
- Christian Fisher
- Claude Hornby & Cox
- Dundons
- Iliffes Booth Bennett
- Joy Merriam & Co
- McCormacks
- Reynolds Dawson
- Tuckers & Co
- Venters & Co
- Victor Lissack & Roscoe

CRIME • South West

[1]
- Bobbetts Mackan Bristol
- Douglas & Partners Bristol

[2]
- John Boyle and Co Redruth
- Stephens & Scown Exeter
- Stones Exeter

[3]
- Crosse & Crosse Exeter
- Parlby Calder Plymouth
- Wolferstans Plymouth

CRIME • Midlands

[1]
- Fletchers Nottingham
- Glaisyers Birmingham
- Nelsons Nottingham
- The Johnson Partnership Nottingham
- The Smith Partnership Derby

[2]
- Banners Jones Middleton Chesterfield
- Barrie Ward & Julian Griffiths Nottingham
- Bate Edmond Snape Coventry
- Brethertons Rugby
- Elliot Mather Chesterfield
- Jonas Roy Bloom Birmingham
- Kieran & Co Worcester
- Parker & Grego Birmingham
- Purcell Parker Birmingham
- Tyndallwoods Birmingham
- Varley Hadley Siddall Nottingham
- Woodford-Robinson Northampton

Within each band, firms are listed alphabetically.
Source: Chambers and Partners Guide to the Legal Profession 2001-2002

LEADING FIRMS continued

CRIME • Wales

1 **Graham Evans & Partners** Swansea
Huttons Cardiff
Martyn Prowel Solicitors Cardiff
Spiro Grech Co Cardiff
2 **Colin Jones** Barry
Gamlins Rhyl
Robertsons Cardiff

CRIME • East Anglia

1 **Belmores** Norwich
Cole & Co Norwich
Copleys Huntingdon
Hunt & Coombs Peterborough
Overbury Steward Eaton & Woolsey Norwich
2 **David Charnley & Co** Romford
Gepp & Sons Chelmsford, Colchester
Gotelee & Goldsmith Ipswich
Hatch Brenner Norwich
Lucas & Wyllys Great Yarmouth
Thomson Webb Corfield Cambridge
Twitchen Musters & Kelly Southend-on-Sea

Within each band, firms are listed alphabetically.
Source: Chambers and Partners Guide to the Legal Profession 2001-2002

CRIME • North West

1 **Burton Copeland** Manchester, Liverpool
2 **Betesh Fox & Co** Manchester
Jones Maidment Wilson Manchester
Maidments Manchester
Tuckers Manchester
3 **Brian Koffman & Co** Manchester
Cunninghams Manchester
Draycott Browne Manchester
Forbes Blackburn
Garstangs Bolton
RM Broudie & Co Liverpool
Russell & Russell Bolton
4 **Cobleys** Salford
Farleys Blackburn
Jackson & Canter Liverpool
Kristina Harrison Solicitors Salford
Linskills Solicitors Liverpool
The Berkson Globe Partnership Liverpool

CRIME • North East

1 **David Gray & Company** Newcastle upon Tyne
Grahame Stowe, Bateson Leeds
Henry Hyams & Co Leeds
Irwin Mitchell Sheffield
Sugaré & Co Leeds
The Max Gold Partnership Hull
2 **Howells** Sheffield
Levi & Co Leeds
Williamsons Hull

employment law

If you are fascinated by human nature, curious about the internal workings of corporate Britain and want to be involved in cases provoking legislative and social changes affecting everyone who has ever had a job, then you should think about employment law.

The work of an employment lawyer is a rich and varied mix of advisory, pre-emptive, contractual and litigious work. Contentious work may be in an employment tribunal, County Courts or the High Court. Some employment cases, which start in the employment tribunal, become test cases appealed to the higher courts. They may end up in the Court of Appeal, House of Lords or even the European Court of Justice. In tribunals employees ('applicants') may claim for redundancy pay, unfair and wrongful dismissal, sex, race and disability discrimination against their employers ('respondents'). Claims for breach of contract may also be made in the High Court or County Courts depending on the value of the claim.

Specialist employment teams are divided along partisan lines. The 'fat cat' firms (City firms with a corporate client base and high charge-out rates) work for employers and highly-paid senior executives. The 'right on' firms act mainly for Trade Union clients and other individuals. They sometimes have allied practices in defendant personal injury.

Almost every high street practice, Citizens Advice Bureau and law centre purports to give employment advice to individuals. In fact, the practice area is now so law-intensive that even specialists have a hard time keeping up with almost weekly changes from the European and domestic courts.

type of work

Employment law guru Janet Gaymer is the senior partner of **Simmons & Simmons**, which has the leading London employment team. The firm acts primarily for employers although it does handle cases for senior executives and individuals with particularly complex cases. Janet spent much of her time building relationships with clients and developing an understanding of their businesses. *"Long-term client relationships are hugely important,"* she states, *"because so much of employment law is a question of industrial relations, communications and strategy planning."* Advice may be one part of a highly politicised industrial relations problem. *"I have to maintain an apolitical detachment to a certain degree. You may be acting for a right-wing newspaper and a Labour-controlled local authority at the same time. Of course you're conscious that the instructions you're receiving may be coloured, but this does not affect the advice you give."*

Lawyers acting for trade unions are often ideologically motivated. A lawyer may find himself representing thousands of union members in their campaigns to change working practices or the law on, say, pension rights for part-time workers.

Employment, or labour law, is by its nature highly politicised, regulating as it does the power struggle between workers and employers. Dr John McMullen, national head of employment law at Pinsent Curtis Biddle emphasises this. *"It's one of the few subjects that can combine topical issues of politics, industrial relations and people alongside the intellectual disciplines studied at university."*

Employment lawyers see themselves as somewhat different from corporate lawyers although they find themselves working closely with them on transactions, with employment advice commonly being a vital ingredient. The hours are usually not so relentless. Chris Goodwill, an employment partner at Clifford Chance, says *"I'm glad you asked me and not my wife. The hours are absolutely fine and I've never missed a play or a film or a dinner or a Leeds match because of work (can I uncross my fingers now?)"* More seriously, he points out *"The worst thing about an employment lawyer's hours is not so much the number of them, but the unpredictability of when they might have to be put in."*

a day in the life of...

8.30am: arrive in office nursing hangover and facing pile of urgent paperwork. First draft Notice of Appearance in Employment Tribunal proceedings, setting out employer's side of story in 'drunken sacking' unfair dismissal case. Make and inhale large cup of strong coffee. Consider recent instructions to draft contract of employment for senior executive.

Next turn (slightly depressed) to considering implications of Transfer of Undertakings Regs on business sale being handled by corporate colleagues. Corporate partner in charge thinks himself rather an expert on TUPE and has written detailed note on his understanding of position; i.e. TUPE does not apply. Tactfully but firmly (in view of junior position and partner's greater ego) break it to him that TUPE does apply. All seller's employees will transfer to purchaser of company. Draft letter of advice to client about potential redundancies. Client will panic. Advise how best to break news and consult with employees while avoiding major public relations disaster.

Receive any number of phone calls from clients' personnel managers throughout day. What do fiendish Working Time Regulations say about paid holiday? Appropriateness or otherwise of taking disciplinary action against employee in love triangle with two colleagues. Love triangle not problem. Threatening colleagues outside work is.

8.30pm: Leave office having prepared submissions for tribunal. No need to instruct counsel so will do own advocacy, not just sit behind barrister and fall asleep. If witnesses perform well, satisfaction of seeing evidence hit home, expertly followed up by (own) strong submissions on law. If not, rise manfully to challenge of pulling things round in closing speech or, (last resort) settling with applicant.

skills needed

...need to like and be interested in people......sensitivity....sense of humour....versatility....flexibility....practicality....ability to assimilate quick changes in strategy and advice....detailed knowledge of relevant statutes and case-law.

Dr John McMullen Points out *"The law is so fast moving that continuous education and development is vital for the employment law practitioner. Added to this, with dimensions of European law, discrimination, human rights, strikes and industrial action and dismissal disputes, no day is boring."*

Employment lawyers need good people skills. Hilary O'Connor, employment partner at S J Berwin, says *"There is a lot of law so a good memory is useful. In some cases the legal solution to a problem is not the cheapest or quickest solution for the client so you need good business judgment and good instincts to know which one to choose. It is very people orientated so patience, empathy and the ability to inspire confidence is essential. If you are interested in human nature and what makes people tick you will be in your element."* But it's not all about being warm and cuddly. Chris Goodwill thinks that you have to be versatile in your approach to the work. *"An employment lawyer needs to be one part lawyer, one part agony aunt and one part hit man!"*

career options

First of all you may wish to choose between acting for applicants or respondents. The largest commercial firms act primarily for respondents or employers. Smaller, more affordable firms act for primarily individual employees or applicants. Some firms act for both. There are options to go in-house, increasingly larger companies are beginning to include specialist employment lawyers within the legal team but these are mainly limited to those with huge workforces. It is more likely that a move in-house would combine employment law with perhaps general commercial litigation.

Towards the top end of the professional scale,

SPECIALIST PRACTICE AREAS — EMPLOYMENT LAW

lawyers may apply to chair employment tribunals; many partners in leading employment practices combine their practice with part-time tribunal chairs.

Remaining in private practice seems to be the popular choice among the lawyers we interviewed and they expressed confidence in the choice of employment law as a career. Like most litigation, the volume of work increases in times of recession.

LEADING FIRMS

EMPLOYMENT • The South

1. **DMH** Crawley
2. **Blake Lapthorn** Portsmouth
3. **Cripps Harries Hall** Tunbridge Wells
   Rawlison Butler Crawley
4. **asb law** Crawley
   Bond Pearce Southampton
   Brachers Maidstone
   Paris Smith & Randall Southampton
   Thomson Snell & Passmore Tunbridge Wells
5. **Clarkson Wright & Jakes** Orpington
   Pattinson & Brewer Chatham
   Stevens & Bolton Guildford

EMPLOYMENT • South West

1. **Bevan Ashford** Bristol
   Bond Pearce Plymouth
   Burges Salmon Bristol
   Osborne Clarke Bristol
2. **Pattinson & Brewer** Bristol
   Thompsons Bristol
   Thring Townsend Bath
3. **Burroughs Day** Bristol
   Michelmores Exeter
   Stephens & Scown Exeter
   TLT Solicitors Bristol
   Veale Wasbrough Bristol

EMPLOYMENT • Thames Valley

1. **Clarks** Reading
2. **Henmans** Oxford
   Morgan Cole Oxford, Reading
   Underwoods Hemel Hempstead
3. **Osborne Clarke** Reading
   Pitmans Reading

EMPLOYMENT • Wales

1. **Eversheds** Cardiff
2. **Morgan Cole** Cardiff, Swansea
3. **Edwards Geldard** Cardiff
   Hugh James Ford Simey Cardiff
4. **Palser Grossman** Cardiff Bay

Within each band, firms are listed alphabetically.
Source: Chambers and Partners Guide to the Legal Profession 2001-2002

LEADING FIRMS continued

EMPLOYMENT • Midlands

1. **Eversheds** Birmingham, Nottingham
   Wragge & Co Birmingham
2. **Hammond Suddards Edge** Birmingham
   Pinsent Curtis Biddle Birmingham
3. **DLA** Birmingham
   Higgs & Sons Brierley Hill
   Martineau Johnson Birmingham
4. **Browne Jacobson** Nottingham
   Freethcartwright Nottingham
   Shakespeares Birmingham
   Shoosmiths Nottingham
5. **Mills & Reeve** Birmingham

EMPLOYMENT • East Anglia

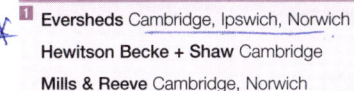

1. **Eversheds** Cambridge, Ipswich, Norwich
   Hewitson Becke + Shaw Cambridge
   Mills & Reeve Cambridge, Norwich
2. **Steele & Co** Norwich
3. **Greenwoods** Peterborough
   Taylor Vinters Cambridge
4. **Prettys** Ipswich

EMPLOYMENT • Yorkshire

1. **Pinsent Curtis Biddle** Leeds
2. **Hammond Suddards Edge** Leeds
3. **Addleshaw Booth & Co** Leeds
   DLA Leeds, Sheffield
4. **Eversheds** Leeds
   Ford & Warren Leeds
   Read Hind Stewart Leeds
   Rollits Hull
   Walker Morris Leeds
5. **Irwin Mitchell** Sheffield
   Nabarro Nathanson Sheffield

EMPLOYMENT • North East

1. **Dickinson Dees** Newcastle upon Tyne
   Eversheds Newcastle upon Tyne
   Short Richardson & Forth Newcastle upon Tyne
   Thompsons Newcastle upon Tyne
2. **Crutes** Newcastle upon Tyne
   Jacksons Stockton on Tees
   Samuel Phillips & Co Newcastle upon Tyne
   Ward Hadaway Newcastle upon Tyne

Within each band, firms are listed alphabetically.
Source: Chambers and Partners Guide to the Legal Profession 2001-2002

LEADING FIRMS *continued*

EMPLOYMENT • North West

1. **Addleshaw Booth & Co** Manchester
   DLA Liverpool, Manchester
   Eversheds Manchester
   Hammond Suddards Edge Manchester
2. **Mace & Jones** Liverpool, Manchester
   Whittles Manchester
3. **Cobbetts** Manchester
   Thompsons Liverpool, Manchester
4. **Davies Wallis Foyster** Liverpool, Manchester
   Pannone & Partners Manchester
5. **Halliwell Landau** Manchester
   Weightmans Liverpool, Manchester

EMPLOYMENT: MAINLY APPLICANT • LONDON

1. **Pattinson & Brewer**
2. **Russell Jones & Walker**
   Thompsons
3. **Bindman & Partners**
   Rowley Ashworth
4. **Lawfords**
5. **Irwin Mitchell**

Within each band, firms are listed alphabetically.
Source: Chambers and Partners Guide to the Legal Profession 2001-2002

EMPLOYMENT: MAINLY RESPONDENT • London

1. **Simmons & Simmons**
2. **Baker & McKenzie**
3. **Allen & Overy**
   Eversheds
   Fox Williams
   Lewis Silkin
   Lovells
   Rowe & Maw
4. **Herbert Smith**
5. **Beachcroft Wansbroughs**
   Charles Russell
   Clifford Chance
   CMS Cameron McKenna
   Dechert
   Denton Wilde Sapte
   Linklaters
   McDermott, Will & Emery
   Olswang
   Slaughter and May
   Stephenson Harwood
6. **Archon**
   Berwin Leighton Paisner
   Boodle Hatfield
   Doyle Clayton
   Farrer & Co
   Freshfields Bruckhaus Deringer
   Hammond Suddards Edge
   Macfarlanes
   Nabarro Nathanson
   Norton Rose
   Osborne Clarke
   Salans Hertzfeld & Heilbronn HRK
   Speechly Bircham
   Theodore Goddard
   Travers Smith Braithwaite

environmental law

Don't assume that to be an environmental lawyer you must be a fully paid up member of Greenpeace and passionate about saving the planet. There certainly are careers for the passionate and crusading, but these are unlikely to be in private practice as a solicitor. Most environmental lawyers are instructed by corporate clients. Their role is primarily damage limitation and pre-emptive advice, the avoidance of damaging negative publicity and defence from prosecution when mistakes are made. It also includes considerable involvement in transactional work, ensuring that environmental liability arising out of corporate acquisitions and disposals is fully apportioned and understood. A small minority of lawyers act for the Environment Agency, environmental pressure groups and private individuals.

type of work

The caseload of an environmental lawyer will be split between contentious and non-contentious matters. Unusually for commercial firms, contentious work may involve criminal law, such as defending clients from criminal prosecution for breach of regulations. On the civil side it may involve tortious claims ('toxic torts') from those who suffer loss as a result of environmental impact as well as disputes as to liability following a mishap. On transactional work the environmental lawyers have a vital input where there is a sale or purchase of a business or land, drafting contractual provisions for the allocation of risk. There is also 'stand alone' work; advice to clients, perhaps on the likely extent of their obligations following a change in the law or the introduction of new EC Regulations. This may cover issues such as waste, pollution control, water abstraction and nature conservation.

Most environmental litigators have wider practices. A number are commercial litigators with experience of environmental defence work, others do a mix of contentious and non-contentious work. Chris Papanicolaou, partner at **Gouldens**, says that there is plenty of scope for getting involved in defending clients against prosecution by the regulatory authorities. He has seen an upturn in the numbers of prosecutions since the authorities really began to flex their muscles a couple of years ago. *"In the Magistrates Court I might find myself running an argument on abuse of process. Or I might argue that the regulator has interpreted the law incorrectly."* He points out that if there are still arguments being run over the 1954 Landlord and Tenant Act then it's going to take years before the environmental legislation of 1990/91 and onwards is interpreted properly. This means a lot of argument in court.

This is a key point. The fact that the area of law is relatively new means a substantial amount of research and interpretation to be carried out. A trainee can really come into his or her own in their environmental law seat, given that they might, almost by accident, become the most expert person in the team on a new piece of legislation or EC Directive. Chris Papanicolaou told us that this was how his career in environmental law took off. *"In 1989 the Environmental Protection Bill came out. I was the one who read it and did the report for the senior partner."* Ross Fairley, senior associate at **Allen & Overy**, agrees. *"There's far more of a role to play for a trainee in advising on the law because the area is so new. I think the appeal is that someone can come in and, if a piece of legislation is in development, their views can be as valid as people who have been in the area for five or six years."*

Many specialists approach non-contentious work from a property or planning base. The government recently introduced its contaminated land regime which is set to provide increased opportunities to offer environmental-related advice, particularly for property based lawyers.

Others at the largest firms may be kept more than busy in a support role to the corporate lawyers. Environmental insurance is another niche, and there are firms such as **Leigh, Day & Co** who have cornered the market for claimants in multi-party environmental tort litigation.

skills needed

"You have to be a jack of all trades"...versatility...a sound knowledge of how business and corporate structures work...an interest in environmental matters...a basic knowledge of science...research, interpretation and presentation skills...ability to work as part of a team.

career options

A decade ago solicitors suddenly saw environmental law as a new emerging practice area and got pretty excited about it. A generation of new partners, now in their thirties, have firmly established themselves from their roots as original pioneers and vanguards of environmental law. Commercial reality has tempered that excitement and lawyers now understand that it is not the growth area that everyone perceived it to be. Only the large London firms and a few large regional firms can offer specialism in environmental law. However, if you are lucky enough to become a specialist you will gain experience fast and be much in demand.

The local authority route is an alternative to starting out in private practice. A training contract with a L.A. may put you into contact with regulatory work, environment-related planning issues, waste management and air pollution cases and a role in advising the L.A. of its own liability in relation to property and business activities.

In-house positions are few and far between. Whilst it might be more common in the US for a company to have a lawyer responsible for environmental/health and safety issues, over here an in-house lawyer is more likely to have a general corporate counsel role. Paul Kelly at Northumbria Water, for example, deals with environmental law matters, commercial contracts, civil and criminal litigation as well as water and drainage law. Certain environmental pressure groups such as Greenpeace have their own lawyers.

The Department for Environment, Food and Rural Affairs employs over 80 lawyers, generally recruited from within the Government Legal Service but with a small number coming from private practice. There are opportunities for trainees on GLS funded schemes in the Department. Chris Muttukumaru, the department's director of legal services, points out that the variety of work available for lawyers in the department allows for a flexible career. Work covers litigation, the drafting of subordinate legislation, preparation of bills, straight advisory work and contract drafting. He stresses that someone with a real interest in the way government operates would be best suited for such a role.

Another career option is with the Environment Agency for England and Wales. The Agency has responsibility for protecting and enhancing the environment through the regulation of the most potentially polluting corporate activities. It also protects water resources, flood defence and fisheries. The legal workload is diverse and includes the prosecution of environmental crime, civil litigation, the maintenance of the Thames Barrier and regulating the disposal of radioactive waste. Peter Kellett of the Agency's Head Office legal staff observes *"The work is stimulating, highly politicised and vital. Our goal is firm but fair regulation to safeguard the environment for current and future generations."* The Agency employs 56 solicitors and two trainees, seven barristers and five legal executives who work from eight regional offices and a head office in Bristol. Opportunities exist for further progression into management. Vacancies are generally advertised in the legal press. Anyone interested should contact the regional solicitor in the relevant office.

LEADING FIRMS

ENVIRONMENT • London

1 Allen & Overy
Freshfields Bruckhaus Deringer
2 CMS Cameron McKenna
Simmons & Simmons
3 Ashurst Morris Crisp
Barlow Lyde & Gilbert
Denton Wilde Sapte
Leigh, Day & Co
Linklaters
Slaughter and May
4 Berwin Leighton Paisner
Clifford Chance
Herbert Smith
Lawrence Graham
Lovells
Nabarro Nathanson
Norton Rose
Rowe & Maw
SJ Berwin
5 Gouldens
Hammond Suddards Edge
Nicholson Graham & Jones
Stephenson Harwood
Theodore Goddard
Trowers & Hamlins

ENVIRONMENT • The South

1 Blake Lapthorn Portsmouth, Southampton
Bond Pearce Southampton
Brachers Maidstone
DMH Brighton
2 Fynn & Partners Bournemouth
Stevens & Bolton Guildford

ENVIRONMENT • South West

1 Bond Pearce Plymouth
Burges Salmon Bristol
Osborne Clarke Bristol
2 Bevan Ashford Bristol
Clarke Willmott & Clarke Bristol, Taunton
3 Stephens & Scown Exeter
Veale Wasbrough Bristol

ENVIRONMENT • Wales

1 Edwards Geldard Cardiff
Eversheds Cardiff
Morgan Cole Cardiff

Within each band, firms are listed alphabetically.
Source: Chambers and Partners Guide to the Legal Profession 2001-2002

LEADING FIRMS continued

ENVIRONMENT • Midlands

1. **Pinsent Curtis Biddle** Birmingham
   Wragge & Co Birmingham
2. **Eversheds** Birmingham
3. **Hammond Suddards Edge** Birmingham
4. **Kent Jones and Done** Stoke-on-Trent

ENVIRONMENT • North East

1. **Eversheds** Leeds
2. **Nabarro Nathanson** Sheffield
3. **Addleshaw Booth & Co** Leeds
   DLA Sheffield
4. **Dickinson Dees** Newcastle upon Tyne
   Hammond Suddards Edge Leeds
   Pinsent Curtis Biddle Leeds

ENVIRONMENT • East Anglia

1. **Mills & Reeve** Cambridge, Norwich
   Richard Buxton Cambridge
2. **Eversheds** Norwich
   Hewitson Becke + Shaw Cambridge

ENVIRONMENT • North West

1. **DLA** Manchester
   Eversheds Manchester
   Leigh, Day & Co Manchester
2. **Addleshaw Booth & Co** Manchester
   Hammond Suddards Edge Manchester
   Masons Manchester
   Wake Dyne Lawton Chester

Within each band, firms are listed alphabetically.
Source: Chambers and Partners Guide to the Legal Profession 2001-2002

european union/competition

Covers both domestic and EU competition law and non-competition EU law. Many firms handle work spanning all these departments although most have particular strengths. The practice is mainly about the implications of EU Articles 81 and 82 . These contain the prohibitions on anti-competitive agreements and the abuse of a dominant market position.

Merger control and clearance is a major area of activity within the competition sphere – the regulation of both UK and European mergers which may have a bearing on competition in member state countries. Domestic competition law brings practitioners into close contact with regulatory bodies such as the Office of Fair Trading and the Department of Trade and Industry. Non-competition EU law covers the general principles of EU law and specialist areas such as the anti-discrimination provisions of the EU treaty.

The volume of work generated by the EU is huge. It is now so pervasive that almost any practice area has to consider the impact of European law.

type of work

All areas within competition are growing fast – it is a fairly specialised field in its own right and few junior lawyers would expect to sub-specialise initially. A senior lawyer from a reputable regional firm outlined the broad flavour of the work. *"Many of the regional and smaller City firms try and deal with most things. Our main areas are merger control, UK competition law (Competition Act), EU Articles 81 and 82, state aids, sectorial regimes such as gas and telecoms and also public procurement."*

Ralph Cohen from City firm **SJ Berwin & Co** described the spread at his practice. *"It could involve dealing with merger clearances, acting as general counsel and reviewing all forms of agreement with respect to competition laws, assisting companies in getting deals approved by regulators and explaining to clients why they are required to be competitive."*

Slaughter and May has a heavily M&A-related practice. Much of its work concerns obtaining approval in the relevant jurisdiction for the merger to take place. There is also significant stand-alone monopoly work – investigation of those companies that are alleged to have abused their market power. Michael Rowe, one of the firm's young competition lawyers, believes the proportion of work in these areas tends to reflect the client base of the firm. *"Many of our clients are number one or two in their market, so monopoly and merger work frequently surfaces."*

There are areas of competition where smaller niche firms tend to predominate. These include anti-competitive agreements, anti-trust measures and compliance agreements, review of industrial agreements and licence and supply agreements.

There is an increasingly significant regulatory aspect to competition work which exhibits different characteristics and involves a sizeable level of contact with officialdom in the EU cities. *"You have to be prepared to talk to officials!"* says Ros Kellaway from **Eversheds**. The amount of regulatory involvement will depend on the firm – some large City firms have made a specialisation out of it. One regional lawyer describes its growth – *"Ten years ago no-one knew anything about regulation, now there are people in top City firms who do nothing but telecoms regulation."*

Competition work can fall under both contentious and non-contentious umbrellas. The emphasis is usually on providing strategic and preventative advice to avoid recourse to litigation. One lawyer stressed the importance of these services. *"Although litigation is increasing, contentious work is a small part, probably under 10% of our business. In a sense, if you get to court you've been defeated."*

EU/competition law demands a greater knowledge of how markets operate than other corporate practice areas. Michael Rowe says. *"I actually spend a lesser proportion of my time researching black letter law or doing things that are strictly legal. I focus more time on reading into markets, developing an understanding of how markets operate, of how competition operates within those markets."* Ralph Cohen makes a similar point. *"It's unlike usual commercial practice in that the objective being sought is very different. There is no deal-making, it's all about commercial transactions complying with the regulators."*

One senior partner believes it is technically more exacting. *"As a corporate lawyer you need a lot of skills but you don't need to be quite as intellectually rigorous as you do in an area like competition. It is quite complex."* Ros Kellaway stresses that it is "qualitatively different" to other practice areas because it is fundamentally about how markets work and the economics of these arrangements. *"It is very different to a straightforward legal understanding. You have to understand a very different body of law, a different legal order – the final analysis is an economic market analysis."*

There is major exposure to power and politics in the work of a competition lawyer and you will be immersed in industries that have their own sensitivities. The work involves the exercise of advocacy skills, either in written form when putting together a brief or arguing a case – the aim being to tell a story that is credible and persuasive when appearing before the regulators.

Within competition law, client contact and meetings are frequently undertaken. Although it is a specialist area of law, positions of autonomy and greater responsibility are soon awarded with ability.

a day in the life...

"The workload might include assisting with a merger filing, analysing products and businesses, advising on drafting agreements and attending an OFT meeting with a partner." Juniors are often involved when instructed on a new case and are required to research the background to the market, absorb information and become an expert very quickly – *"the ability to see the wood from the trees is important,"* says Ralph Cohen.

Most competition firms have a Brussels office (*"it would be difficult to function successfully without one,"*) and are keen to send junior lawyers on placements there. Although some UK firms do the majority of active work on-site domestically, presence in Belgium is useful for *"keeping eyes and ears open"* and maintaining close contacts with the politicians and power-brokers! Anti-dumping and trade law is still one area of competition which remains very heavily Brussels-driven.

The transnational nature of competition law brings with it a high degree of glamour, frequent travel and prestigious clients. Overseas trips and high-profile cases are common. According to one lawyer, *"we certainly to and fro a lot more, not just to Brussels but all over, you do pick up a fairly international clientele."* The highlight for her is *"working in an area of law that it is very rapidly developing. You open the paper every day and there are two or three stories that are of crucial relevance to something you're working on. Its a very immediate area – so it can be glamorous!"*

Michael Rowe is pleased with his career choice and supports this view: *"there are so many options – you're more likely to travel, you're more likely to get a greater degree of responsibility at an earlier stage in your career. But as with any other practice area, there will be times when you're in the office late and you're churning out something that has to be done. At those moments, it feels very unglamorous!"*

Lifestyle-wise *"You don't have to sell your soul to being here 24 hours a day,"* said one lawyer. The hours can be cyclical in that they are governed by the number of transactions that are in the office at any one time, however they are becoming more regular as new areas of competition open up. Another competition expert believes the specialist areas give you more control over your life. *"It is better in that it is far less meeting driven than corporate, you're more in control of your own destiny. There is flexibility to take time out during the day and make it up later."*

skills needed

...adaptability...a broad understanding...an interest in business and markets and how competition functions...strong technical skills...clear analytical mind...top-level academic credentials...attention to detail, thoroughness...good mediation and lobbying skills...persuasiveness...effective communication skills...decisiveness...linguistic ability...enthusiasm...

career options

At the bottom end, EU/competition can be competitive and difficult to break into – more so perhaps than other areas of law, but there are still opportunities to be had. Ros Kellaway says the irony is, *"that although there are enormous volumes of work generated by the EU, there are still relatively few practices with large departments and only a small number of niche practices."* She receives a large number of unsolicited CVs from students keen to break into this area of practice but only some have the right mix of ability and practical experience. Don't be put off. The number of active firms and size of competition departments are set to carry on growing – this is very much an upwardly moving area of law. High academic credentials, technical and communication skills top the requirement list. Failing to qualify into an EU department, Ros Kellaway offers some alternative entry routes. *"The best method is to enter a mainstream corporate department and work towards specialisation or go for employment which is hugely dominated by an EU dimension."*

Competition is a specialist area but there are a reasonable number of options available as more companies take on in-house competition lawyers. The skills you develop in industry analysis and understanding of markets could well be employed in a broader business context. There is not a huge transference or movement out of private practice to in-house or mainstream business at the moment although success in this practice area certainly provides great potential for it.

LEADING FIRMS

EUROPEAN UNION/COMPETITION • London

1 Freshfields Bruckhaus Deringer
Herbert Smith
Linklaters
Slaughter and May
2 Allen & Overy
Lovells
3 Ashurst Morris Crisp
Denton Wilde Sapte
Simmons & Simmons
SJ Berwin
4 Baker & McKenzie
Clifford Chance
Norton Rose
5 Bristows
CMS Cameron McKenna
Eversheds
Richards Butler
Theodore Goddard

EUROPEAN UNION/COMPETITION• Midlands

1 Pinsent Curtis Biddle Birmingham
Wragge & Co Birmingham
2 Eversheds Birmingham

EUROPEAN UNION/COMPETITION • The North

1 Addleshaw Booth & Co Leeds, Manchester
Eversheds Leeds, Manchester, Newcastle upon Tyne
2 Pinsent Curtis Biddle Leeds
3 Dickinson Dees Newcastle upon Tyne

EUROPEAN UNION/COMPETITION• South West

1 Burges Salmon Bristol
2 Bond Pearce Plymouth

EUROPEAN UNION/COMPETITION • Wales

1 Edwards Geldard Cardiff
Eversheds Cardiff
Morgan Cole Cardiff

Within each band, firms are listed alphabetically.
Source: Chambers and Partners Guide to the Legal Profession 2001-2002

family law

Family law includes the law relating to divorce and any resulting financial settlements, domestic violence and child law. It also covers the growing area of the breakdown of unmarried relationships ('cohabitation'). Child law includes private issues relating to children (such as residence, parental contact, surrogacy and adoption) and public law work (where children are taken into care by local authorities or otherwise have contact with social services). While many lawyers practise in all of these areas, the increasing specialisation of the profession means that there is a growing divide between those who do largely financial/matrimonial and some private child work, and those who specialise in children and public law work. The division is often dependent on where the firm is situated, with high street and specialist legal aid firms doing the majority of public law work.

Of course all family lawyers require an up to date knowledge of family law, but there is more to the practice than that. Those working on the financial side also require an understanding of property, tax, trusts and pensions. Those on the public law side may need a grounding in criminal law, welfare law, education law and mental health issues.

type of work

Divorce is one of the most stressful life events. One of the tasks of a family lawyer is to offer support through it. Their clients are often emotional, bitter and oblivious to logical argument and the lawyer must be able to circumvent this emotion delicately. They must assist the client to articulate their true concerns, and to ensure that they can see the bigger picture. Clients range from 'high net worth' individuals with substantial property and assets to people with very little money, but a painful parental contact battle to fight. The well-known London firms acting for wealthy and often high-profile clients must also learn how to deal with the media interest in their cases. **Manches** for example represented Paloma Picasso in her high profile divorce case last year.

High income matrimonial work often involves complex commercial, financial and tax problems, often with an international aspect. *"An element of my work is looking at balance sheets, trust documents, pension funds and property transfers,"* says Richard Sax of **Manches**. A typical day may include meeting a new client who wishes to divorce her wealthy Italian husband and is worried about gaining custody of her children and calling the Cayman Islands to sort out another client's tax problem. For **Withers** partner Mark Harper, the most interesting cases are those involving competing jurisdictions, which may make the finances harder to sort out on divorce, or may mean that a divorce cannot be obtained in another jurisdiction.

Public childcare work can be the most disturbing type of family law. It comes into play when a local authority has concerns about the welfare of a child and applies to the court to have the child taken into care. Childcare lawyers will thus represent either the parents, the local authority or the guardian appointed by the court to look after the child's interests. Parents in these cases often have a history of violence, alcoholism or mental illness while the children themselves could have the same problems and could also be victims of mental, physical or sexual abuse. Philip Kidd of Exeter firm **Tozers** once had to interview two children with armed police standing by because the father was looking for them with a gun. Acting for children, he says, requires particular skill. *"You have to remember you're acting for a vulnerable human being,"* says Kidd, *"My youngest child client was just seven days old, and the rest range from toddlers to teenagers. I see older children more often to check whether they continue to give the same* *instructions as their guardians. You can get into close relationships with them – but not too close, obviously, because you walk away at the end of the case."*

Most newly-qualified solicitors specialising in childcare will start by representing parents. At the moment you need to be at least three years' qualified (and have experience doing childcare work) before you can get on the Law Society's Children Panel, from which most representatives for children are selected.

a day in the life...

West End Firm: As a trainee in a West End family department, your job will involve taking notes in client interviews, drafting documents, researching points of law and court work. The court work can vary from preparing bundles, to running to court to lodge documents in time, to attending court with counsel. In addition you will usually have a structured training programme, plenty of supervision and support and earn a reasonable salary.

High Street Firm: Family work in a small or high street practice often involves both divorce and childcare work. A typical day will be very different from a day spent at **Withers**, **Manches** or **Mishcon de Reya**. In a high street practice you are more likely to be thrown in at the deep end and given more responsibility early on. Your first client of the morning may walk in off the street with her children, having fled from her violent husband. She needs an emergency loan, temporary accommodation and an injunction to prevent her husband from attacking her and her children. Your second client has a first appointment to discuss his potential divorce. The first interview is often a challenge. *"The impact of the emotional consequence of a marriage breakdown is huge,"* comments Peter Jones, of Leeds firm **Jones Myers Gordon**, *"I've had clients in front of me who have been in physical shock when their spouse has walked out. You need a lot of patience, you need a lot of understanding, but you still need to move them foward."* The afternoon may involve assisting counsel on your own.

skills needed

Matrimonial…understanding of human weakness…ability to be non-judgmental…sympathy and objectivity…non-confrontational skills…"the ability to negotiate from strength but without making it litigious"…listening skills…commercial acumen…numeracy

Childcare work…humanity…a fair amount of medical knowledge…conversance with the legal aid system…determination…level-headedness…counselling skills…ability to separate any emotional response from your professionalism

career options

In the prestigious London firms, and in some large regional outfits, trainees may be able to do a family seat as part of their training. The work will generally be for wealthy private clients and will focus on divorce and financial disputes. In the high street, work will be a mixture of private and legal aid cases. Some high street family departments are mixed with conveyancing or criminal departments, so you will receive a grounding in several areas. There will be the opportunity to handle childcare work from day one.

There is no typical career path into family law, and some lawyers come to it after working for several years in City firms. However, because it is such an emotional and demanding field, most family lawyers have been committed to it from very early on in their careers. According to Mark Harper, it certainly helps to have gained some prior experience in counselling or dealing with people. *"If you've only studied law through books, it can be quite overwhelming dealing with all this raw emotion."*

Many family lawyers derive their vocation from the cutting edge element of much of the work and the pace of legislative change. As Peter Jones puts it, "Its developments attempt to reflect, perhaps faster than most areas of law, the change of views of society." At present the main issues under the microscope are no-fault divorce, pension sharing and the rights of co-habitees and gay and lesbian couples. "The next five years are not going to be complacent" says Jones. "It stops you from being bored."

The alternatives to private practice are limited, but qualified lawyers can work in-house for local authorities and charities such as the NSPCC. In rare cases, those with good advocacy skills might go to the Bar, but this is preferably done at an early stage in their career. Family lawyers occasionally move into mediation or social work, but the remuneration in these fields is poor and the pressure can be just as great as in private practice.

LEADING FIRMS

FAMILY/MATRIMONIAL • The South

1 Lester Aldridge Bournemouth

2 Brachers Maidstone
Paris Smith & Randall Southampton
Thomson Snell & Passmore Tunbridge Wells

3 Blake Lapthorn Portsmouth
Coffin Mew & Clover Portsmouth
Cripps Harries Hall Tunbridge Wells
DMH Brighton
Horsey Lightly Newbury
Max Barford & Co Tunbridge Wells

FAMILY/MATRIMONIAL • Thames Valley

1 Blandy & Blandy Reading
Manches Oxford

2 Darbys Oxford
Henmans Oxford
Morgan Cole Oxford

3 Boodle Hatfield Oxford

4 Iliffes Booth Bennett Uxbridge
Linnells Oxford

FAMILY/MATRIMONIAL • South West

1 Burges Salmon Bristol
Foot Anstey Sargent Plymouth
Gill Akaster Plymouth
TLT Solicitors Bristol
Tozers Exeter, Plymouth, Torquay
Wolferstans Plymouth

2 Clarke Willmott & Clarke Bristol, Taunton
Stephens & Scown Exeter

3 Hooper & Wollen Torquay
Ian Downing Family Law Practice Plymouth

4 Stone King Bath
Stones Exeter
Woollcombe Beer Watts Newton Abbot

5 David Brain & Co St Austell
Hartnell & Co Exeter
Hugh James Ford Simey Exeter
Veale Wasbrough Bristol
Withy King Bath

Within each band, firms are listed alphabetically.
Source: Chambers and Partners Guide to the Legal Profession 2001-2002

SPECIALIST PRACTICE AREAS FAMILY LAW

LEADING FIRMS continued

FAMILY/MATRIMONIAL • London

1 Manches
Withers
2 Alexiou Fisher Philipps
Charles Russell
Hughes Fowler Carruthers
Levison Meltzer Pigott
Miles Preston & Co
Sears Tooth
3 Bindman & Partners
Clintons
Collyer-Bristow
Dawson Cornwell
Goodman Ray
Kingsley Napley
Mishcon de Reya
Payne Hicks Beach
4 Cawdery Kaye Fireman & Taylor
Farrer & Co
Gordon Dadds
Hodge Jones & Allen
International Family Law Chambers
Reynolds Porter Chamberlain
The Family Law Consortium
5 Anthony Gold
Barnett Sampson
Dawson & Co
Fisher Meredith
Forsters
Russell-Cooke
Stephenson Harwood

FAMILY/MATRIMONIAL • Wales

1 Hugh James Ford Simey Cardiff
Larby Williams Cardiff
Nicol, Denvir & Purnell Cardiff
2 Martyn Prowel Solicitors Cardiff
3 Granville-West Newbridge
Harding Evans Newport
Leo Abse & Cohen Cardiff
Robertsons Cardiff
Wendy Hopkins & Co Cardiff

FAMILY/MATRIMONIAL • Midlands

1 Blair Allison & Co Birmingham
Challinors Lyon Clark West Bromwich
Nelsons Nottingham
Rupert Bear Murray Davies Nottingham
Tyndallwoods Birmingham
2 Freethcartwright Nottingham
Hadens Walsall
Lanyon Bowdler Shrewsbury
Wace Morgan Shrewsbury
Young & Lee Birmingham
3 Blythe Liggins Leamington Spa
Varley Hibbs Coventry

Within each band, firms are listed alphabetically.
Source: Chambers and Partners Guide to the Legal Profession 2001-2002

LEADING FIRMS continued

FAMILY/MATRIMONIAL • East Anglia

1 **Mills & Reeve** Cambridge, Norwich

2 **Greenwoods** Peterborough
Hunt & Coombs Peterborough
Silver Fitzgerald Cambridge

3 **Buckle Mellows** Peterborough
Eversheds Cambridge
Miller Sands Cambridge

4 **Cozens-Hardy & Jewson** Norwich
Fosters Norwich
Hatch Brenner Norwich
Leonard Gray Chelmsford
Rudlings & Wakelam Thetford
Ward Gethin King's Lynn

FAMILY/MATRIMONIAL • North West

1 **Pannone & Partners** Manchester

2 **Cuff Roberts** Liverpool
Farleys Blackburn
Laytons Manchester

3 **Cobbetts** Manchester
Green & Co Manchester
Jones Maidment Wilson Manchester
Mace & Jones Knutsford
Stephensons Leigh

4 **Addleshaw Booth & Co** Manchester
Burnetts Carlisle
Morecroft Urquhart Liverpool
Rowlands Manchester

FAMILY/MATRIMONIAL • Yorkshire

1 **Addleshaw Booth & Co** Leeds

2 **Grahame Stowe, Bateson** Leeds
Irwin Mitchell Sheffield
Jones Myers Gordon Leeds

3 **Andrew M Jackson & Co** Hull
Gordons Cranswick Solicitors Bradford
Zermansky & Partners Leeds

4 **Chivers Walsh Smith & Irvine & Co** Bradford
Crombie Wilkinson York
Kirbys Harrogate

FAMILY/MATRIMONIAL • North East

1 **Dickinson Dees** Newcastle upon Tyne

2 **Sinton & Co** Newcastle upon Tyne

3 **Hay & Kilner** Newcastle upon Tyne
Mincoffs Newcastle upon Tyne
Samuel Phillips & Co Newcastle upon Tyne
Ward Hadaway Newcastle upon Tyne

4 **Askews** Redcar
Jacksons Stockton on Tees

Within each band, firms are listed alphabetically.
Source: Chambers and Partners Guide to the Legal Profession 2001-2002

intellectual property

Intellectual property lawyers divide the field into two broad areas: patent work (hard IP) i.e. the protection of inventions and processes; and non-patent work (soft IP) i.e. trade marks, design rights, copyright, passing off, anti-counterfeiting and confidential information. Hard IP has links with product liability work. Both types of IP overlap with IT (information technology), telecommunications, broadcasting and internet work. Outside London, there are hot spots for IP lawyers, such as the Thames Valley with its concentration of IT companies and 'Silicon Fen' which has grown up in the Cambridge area, (focusing on the hi-tech and biotech companies that have spun out of the university.)

type of work

IP clients include manufacturers and suppliers of hi-tech and engineering products, leading brand owners, teaching hospitals, universities, scientific institutions and media clients (including broadcasters, newspapers, publishers and artists). IP work can be contentious or non-contentious. Disputes usually revolve around an allegation of infringement of one or more intangible property rights existing in an invention, a literary/artistic work, a trade mark or a product.

"*You'll be instrumental in defending a leading brand and fighting off competitors in the market place,*" says Vanessa Marsland, an IP partner at **Clifford Chance**. "*One of my clients is Kimberley Clark which owns the Andrex brand of toilet paper. Last year their competitor, Fort Sterling, started packaging its rival Nouvelle eco-toilet paper with the message that softness was guaranteed. If customers disagreed, they could exchange the product for a packet of Andrex. Kimberley Clark felt the offer was confusing, and that people might believe that Nouvelle was endorsed by Andrex.*" **Clifford Chance** carried out a number of street surveys to see if people really were confused. "*I've got an interesting job,*" Marsland jokes, "*I show people packets of toilet paper.*" But she won the case.

Richard Kempner, a partner in the Leeds office of **Addleshaw Booth & Co**, handled the supermarket 'look-alike' case, defending Asda, makers of Puffin biscuits, against United Biscuits, makers of Penguin chocolate biscuits. United claimed that Asda was passing off the Puffin as the Penguin, and that the Puffin name and picture breached its Penguin trade marks. The case ended in a draw. Asda won on trade mark infringement, but United Biscuits won on passing off, forcing Asda to alter its packaging.

Asima Khan, an IP solicitor with **Addleshaw Booth & Co**, worked on the Puffin-Penguin case as a trainee. "*IP lets you see the corporate side of work but in a more interesting way,*" she says. "*I was surprised there was such high-profile work outside London. Before starting my IP seat, I helped produce market research questionnaires which were part of Asda's defence. At the beginning of my IP seat, I attended the closing speeches of the case at the Royal Courts of Justice. It was so exciting playing a part in a case like that.*"

Internet IP law is a fledgling area of work, constantly throwing up new issues. **Clifford Chance**'s Vanessa Marsland is involved in a variety of cases concerning trade mark infringement on the internet. Many cases, she says, involve complex international issues. "*If you're trading globally on the internet and infringe someone else's rights, are you guilty of infringement all over the world or just in the country where you're physically located?*"

Few students know much about IP when they begin their training contracts, which is why many large firms with an IP specialism send trainees on a course in Bristol run by the Intellectual Property Lawyers' Association. The residential course counts as half an MA and is taught by partners from major IP firms.

a day in the life...

An IP lawyer's day might begin with an early morning hearing in the Patents Court. Your client, a French company, has brought an action for patent infringement. The other side's applying to strike it out on a technical ground. They fail. By mid-morning, you're on the phone to the client to tell them the good news and discuss possible options for a settlement. When you get back to the office, there's a message waiting for you from an American biotech company. They're forming a joint venture with a multi-national pharmaceutical company, and want you to draft various licensing agreements. They have to be finished within 48 hours. You've been working at it for an hour when the phone rings. It's one of your most important clients. They have evidence that their goods are being counterfeited, and want to know what steps they can take to protect their trade marks. You advise them to commence proceedings immediately, and apply the next day for an order preventing the other side from destroying evidence. You get on the phone to counsel's clerk and say you'll need one of his top barristers the next morning. Then you spend the rest of the evening taking evidence from your client and preparing the affidavit in support of the next day's application. You get home late, slump into bed and wake up in the middle of the night worrying about those licensing agreements. There's another long day ahead of you tomorrow . . .

skills needed

Patent law...a basic understanding of science (at least science A-levels)...an aptitude for technical matters and concepts...good organisational skills ...the ability to draft documents with precision.

General IP...curiosity for things artistic and technological...the ability to deal wth quirky and eccentric characters...an interest in the internet and consumer trends.

career options

Many established IP lawyers began their careers as litigators or general commercial lawyers and only started to specialise as they saw niche areas opening up. Constantly developing technology keeps this field moving and there are ever-increasing opportunities to specialise in IP from early on in your career. If you choose the right firm, you'll probably be able to do at least one IP seat during training.

IP knowledge is equally valuable outside private practice. Manufacturing, pharmaceutical and research companies employ patent specialists and there are in-house legal teams at Proctor & Gamble, Reckitt & Benckiser and Unilever. Non-patent lawyers find their way into the media world: all major publishers and television companies have in-house IP lawyers.

Alternatives to strictly legal practice include more general business/management posts within the organisations mentioned above. Many broadcasting companies now employ lawyers in positions such as Head of Business and Legal Affairs. Additionally firms of trademark agents and patent attorneys are often keen to recruit those with a legal training.

LEADING FIRMS

INTELLECTUAL PROPERTY: GENERAL • London

1
- Bird & Bird
- Bristows
- Taylor Joynson Garrett

2
- Linklaters
- Simmons & Simmons

3
- Baker & McKenzie
- Clifford Chance
- Eversheds
- Herbert Smith
- Lovells
- Wragge & Co

4
- Allen & Overy
- Denton Wilde Sapte
- Olswang
- Slaughter and May
- Willoughby & Partners

5
- Arnander Irvine & Zietman
- Ashurst Morris Crisp
- Field Fisher Waterhouse
- Freshfields Bruckhaus Deringer
- Gouldens
- Roiter Zucker
- Rowe & Maw

6
- Briffa
- CMS Cameron McKenna
- Dechert
- H2O (Henry Hepworth Organisation)
- Hammond Suddards Edge
- Norton Rose
- SJ Berwin

Within each band, firms are listed alphabetically.
Source: Chambers and Partners Guide to the Legal Profession 2001-2002

INTELLECTUAL PROPERTY: PATENT • London

1
- Bird & Bird
- Bristows

2
- Linklaters
- Simmons & Simmons
- Taylor Joynson Garrett

3
- Herbert Smith
- Lovells
- Wragge & Co incorporating Needham & Grant

4
- Baker & McKenzie
- Clifford Chance
- Eversheds

5
- Allen & Overy
- Roiter Zucker

6
- Stringer Saul

INTELLECTUAL PROPERTY • The South

1 Lochners Technology Solicitors Godalming
2 DMH Brighton
3 Lester Aldridge Bournemouth

INTELLECTUAL PROPERTY • Thames Valley

1 The Law Offices of Marcus J O'Leary Bracknell
Willoughby & Partners Oxford
2 Garretts Reading
Nabarro Nathanson Reading
3 Manches Oxford
Osborne Clarke Reading

LEADING FIRMS continued

INTELLECTUAL PROPERTY • South West

1 Osborne Clarke Bristol
2 Bevan Ashford Bristol
3 Beachcroft Wansbroughs Bristol
Burges Salmon Bristol
Humphreys & Co Bristol
4 Laytons Bristol

INTELLECTUAL PROPERTY • Wales

1 Edwards Geldard Cardiff
2 Eversheds Cardiff
Morgan Cole Cardiff

INTELLECTUAL PROPERTY • Midlands

1 Wragge & Co incorporating Needham & Co Birmingham
2 Martineau Johnson Birmingham
3 Pinsent Curtis Biddle Birmingham
4 Browne Jacobson Nottingham
Eversheds Birmingham, Nottingham
Shoosmiths Northampton
5 Freethcartwright Nottingham
Hammond Suddards Edge Birmingham

Within each band, firms are listed alphabetically.
Source: Chambers and Partners Guide to the Legal Profession 2001-2002

INTELLECTUAL PROPERTY • East Anglia

1 Mills & Reeve Cambridge, Norwich
2 Eversheds Cambridge, Ipswich, Norwich
3 Hewitson Becke + Shaw Cambridge
4 Greenwoods Peterborough
Taylor Vinters Cambridge

INTELLECTUAL PROPERTY • North West

1 Addleshaw Booth & Co Manchester
Halliwell Landau Manchester
2 Hill Dickinson Stockport
3 DLA Liverpool, Manchester
Eversheds Manchester
Hammond Suddards Edge Manchester
Philip Conn & Co Manchester
4 Kuit Steinart Levy Manchester
Lawson Coppock & Hart Manchester
Taylors Blackburn

INTELLECTUAL PROPERTY • North East

1 Addleshaw Booth & Co Leeds
2 DLA Leeds, Sheffield
Pinsent Curtis Biddle Leeds
3 Eversheds Leeds
Hammond Suddards Edge Leeds
Walker Morris Leeds
4 Irwin Mitchell Leeds
Lupton Fawcett Leeds
5 Dickinson Dees Newcastle upon Tyne

IT, e-commerce & telecoms

The boundaries between IT, telecoms, IP, broadcasting, e-commerce and digital media are growing ever more blurred as 'convergence' issues tighten their grip over the broader communications industry. With IP enjoying a section in its own right and broadcasting covered under media, this section will focus on IT, e-commerce and telecommunications law. IT work (including e-commerce) consists principally of outsourcing (where outside IT specialists are brought in to set up and run a company's computer systems), systems development, IT contract drafting and on-line/internet advice. Telecoms largely revolves around proffering advice on the regulatory statutes which govern telecommunications companies and are designed to protect the interests of consumers and licensing matters, such as the 3G mobile phone licenses recently issued by the government to telecommunications companies. Competition law is also of ever growing importance in the telecoms field, as mega-mergers bring monopoly issues to the forefront.

The transactional side of telecoms, differs little from standard M&A work, though a certain knowledge of regulatory matters is of course necessary.

Digital media is an increasingly important aspect of media law which relates to information disseminated in a digitised format. This is a heavily internet-oriented practice area sometimes dubbed 'multimedia.' A dynamic new area of practice, with both regulatory and transactional aspects, digital media is at the very forefront of 'convergence' issues. Most digital media lawyers originally hailed from an IP/copyright background, though others started out in telecommunications (principally on the regulatory side) and data protection. Clients are very varied, including internet service providers, internet industry bodies, software developers, games designers and banks providing online services.

a day in the life...

A typical day for an IT lawyer might include advising on a new software development contract, reading through a system integration contract, advising on an internet issue and popping down to court for a hearing on a major system. **Osborne Clarke**'s Paul Gardner specialises in computer games. He is currently advising a games publisher on what copyright allows you to depict in terms of club strips in football games and several games console manufacturers on how close to the Sony games console they can design their products.

For internet and communications lawyer David Naylor of US firm **Weil Gotschal & Manges** there is no such thing as a 'typical day.' A week's work might consist of advising internet and communications start-ups on all aspects of internet law from content liability to online contracting, through to advising more mature internet companies on building business networks across Europe, and acting for telecoms companies on UK and EU commercial and regulatory matters. He would be in frequent contact with the firm's US and Brussels offices in relation to cross-border work for US and EU clients and collaborating with the corporate department on funding issues and acquisitions in commercial internet deals. Foreign travel is not as frequent as you might think, as London is a major hub for the telecoms industry anyhow and *"our office is so phenomenally busy."*

skills needed

IT/e-commerce...ability to be a "deal-maker"...an excellent understanding of "hard" regulatory matters...a good grasp of the commercial world...ability to keep up to speed...sensitivity to the needs of artists...a willingness to "roll up your sleeves"...real mental dexterity...gut feel for the issues...feel challenged and thrilled by change....

Telecoms...general grounding in corporate... some industry knowledge...background in economics...comfort with technical language or jargon ...innovative...knowledge of competition law....

Digital media...basic understanding of copyright matters...up to date understanding of new media, both technically and as an industry...flexibility to clients' needs...a "sensible approach to risk"....

LEADING FIRMS

INFORMATION TECHNOLOGY • London

1
- Baker & McKenzie
- Bird & Bird
- Clifford Chance

2
- Allen & Overy
- Lovells
- Masons
- Olswang
- Osborne Clarke
- Taylor Joynson Garrett

3
- Denton Wilde Sapte
- Field Fisher Waterhouse
- Tarlo Lyons

4
- Bristows
- Freshfields Bruckhaus Deringer
- Herbert Smith
- Kemp Little LLP
- Linklaters
- Rowe & Maw
- Slaughter and May

5
- Ashurst Morris Crisp
- Berwin Leighton Paisner
- Brobeck Hale and Dorr
- CMS Cameron McKenna
- D J Freeman
- Nabarro Nathanson
- Shaw Pittman
- Simmons & Simmons
- Theodore Goddard

INFORMATION TECHNOLOGY • The South

1
- DMH Brighton

2
- Bond Pearce Southampton
- Clyde & Co Guildford
- Lester Aldridge Bournemouth

INFORMATION TECHNOLOGY • South West

1
- Osborne Clarke Bristol

2
- Bevan Ashford Bristol
- Burges Salmon Bristol

3
- Beachcroft Wansbroughs Bristol
- Foot Anstey Sargent Plymouth
- Laytons Bristol

INFORMATION TECHNOLOGY • Thames Valley

1
- Nabarro Nathanson Reading
- The Law Offices of Marcus J O'Leary Bracknell

2
- Garretts Reading
- Manches Oxford
- Osborne Clarke Reading

3
- Clark Holt Swindon
- Willoughby & Partners Oxford

4
- Boyes Turner Reading

Within each band, firms are listed alphabetically.
Source: Chambers and Partners Guide to the Legal Profession 2001-2002

SPECIALIST PRACTICE AREAS — IT, E-COMMERCE & TELECOMS

LEADING FIRMS continued

INFORMATION TECHNOLOGY • Wales

1. **Edwards Geldard** Cardiff
2. **Eversheds** Cardiff
   Morgan Cole Cardiff

INFORMATION TECHNOLOGY • Midlands & East Anglia

1. **Eversheds** Birmingham, Nottingham
   Wragge & Co Birmingham
2. **Hewitson Becke + Shaw** Cambridge, Northampton
   Pinsent Curtis Biddle Birmingham

INFORMATION TECHNOLOGY • The North

1. **Masons** Leeds, Manchester
2. **Addleshaw Booth & Co** Leeds, Manchester
   Eversheds Leeds
3. **Halliwell Landau** Manchester
   Pinsent Curtis Biddle Leeds
4. **Hammond Suddards Edge** Leeds, Manchester
   Irwin Mitchell Leeds

TELECOMMUNICATIONS • London

1. **Bird & Bird**
   Clifford Chance
2. **Allen & Overy**
   Linklaters
   Olswang
3. **Baker & McKenzie**
   Denton Wilde Sapte
4. **Ashurst Morris Crisp**
   Field Fisher Waterhouse
   Freshfields Bruckhaus Deringer
   Simmons & Simmons
   Taylor Joynson Garrett
5. **Charles Russell**
   Norton Rose
   Osborne Clarke
   Rowe & Maw
   Steptoe & Johnson Rakisons

TELECOMMUNICATIONS • The Regions

1. **Eversheds** Leeds

Within each band, firms are listed alphabetically.
Source: Chambers and Partners Guide to the Legal Profession 2001-2002

LEADING FIRMS *continued*

E-COMMERCE • London

1 Bird & Bird
Olswang

2 Baker & McKenzie
Clifford Chance
Denton Wilde Sapte
Field Fisher Waterhouse

3 Kemp Little LLP
Osborne Clarke
Taylor Joynson Garrett

4 Harbottle & Lewis

5 Brobeck Hale and Dorr
Herbert Smith
Masons
Tarlo Lyons

6 Allen & Overy
Ashurst Morris Crisp
Berwin Leighton Paisner
Bristows
Linklaters
Lovells
SJ Berwin
The Simkins Partnership
Theodore Goddard

E-COMMERCE • The Regions

1 Osborne Clarke Reading

2 Addleshaw Booth & Co Manchester
Garretts Reading
Nabarro Nathanson Reading
Wragge & Co Birmingham

3 Halliwell Landau Manchester
The Law Offices of Marcus J O'Leary Bracknell

Within each band, firms are listed alphabetically.
Source: Chambers and Partners Guide to the Legal Profession 2001-2002

litigation

Litigation lawyers – or litigators – act for clients involved in disputes. There are three ways in which disputes can be pursued. The first, litigation itself, involves recourse to the courts. This can be an expensive and time-consuming process. For this reason, contracts often provide for disputes between the parties to be referred to the second method, binding arbitration, normally by an expert in the field. Unlike court proceedings, arbitrations are confidential. They are particularly common in the shipping, insurance and construction industries. Alternative Dispute Resolution (ADR) is a cheaper alternative to both litigation and arbitration. Although it can take various forms, ADR often involves structured negotiations between the parties directed by an independent mediator. This form of ADR is known as mediation. There are other less common forms such as neutral evaluation, expert determination and conciliation. The parties retain the right to litigate if they find it impossible to reach an agreement.

If you think that contentious work is all about court-room drama, think again. Many disputes settle before commencement of proceedings. If proceedings are commenced, the odds are that the case will never reach trial. Parties to commercial litigation are not, as a rule, interested in having their 'day in court' although there may be matters of principle which need to be determined. The emphasis, therefore, is on reaching a commercial settlement. *"If you can keep your clients out of court, they will love you much more than if you get them into a scrap,"* says Neil Fagan, leading litigation partner at **Lovells**. *"Most of our work involves trying to stop people litigating."*

type of work

General commercial litigators handle a variety of business disputes. Most cases will be contractual – everything from a dispute over the sale of a multi-million pound business, to an argument over the meaning of a term in a photocopier maintenance contract. They might also deal with negligence claims by companies against their professional advisors. Some litigators specialise in certain industry sectors – for example, construction, shipping, insurance, property or media. But most of the litigator's skills are common to all areas of commercial litigation, according to Christopher Style of **Linklaters**. *"The procedure in running a court action or an arbitration, and the skill in negotiating an agreement is the same, whether you're talking about a dispute between the manufacturers of widgets or between accountants, stockbrokers or bankers,"* he says.

Litigation is a process. Once a case has been commenced, it follows a pre-determined course laid down by the rules of court – statement of case, disclosure of documents, various procedural applications and, in a small number of cases, trial. In a major case, this process can take several years. The mutual disclosure of relevant documents can be a particularly protracted and expensive affair, although new rules which came into force in April 1999 were designed to limit this.

Managing the process is the litigator's primary role. This requires not only a mastery of the rules of court, but also a keen appreciation of tactics. If you're acting for a defendant, for example, you might ask the claimant for more information about its claim by means of a request for further information. Obtaining the information might not be your primary aim. You might know perfectly well the main thrust of the claim. But your request may expose weaknesses in the claimant's case. It also has a nuisance value, forcing the claimant to spend time and money in providing you with further information. If you're lucky, the request may persuade the claimant to settle a case. Disclosure can also be used as a tactical ruse, with parties taking advantage of their disclosure obligations to swamp their opponents with largely irrelevant documents. The Woolf reforms to the civil justice system, implemented in April 1999 have reduced the scope for such tactical games by simplifying procedures.

The range of the litigator's work has increased over the last few years, thanks largely to the extension of High Court rights of audience to solicitors. Although solicitors could always draft statements of case – the formal documents setting out the claimant's claim and the defendant's response – and act as advocates in High Court procedural hearings, they rarely did so. Instead, such work was normally referred to barristers. This is now changing. There hasn't been a flood of solicitor-advocates into the High Court. But the possibility of a career as an advocate, together with potential costs savings for the client, is encouraging solicitors to keep more work in-house. This phenomenon is particularly marked in the large City firms. **Herbert Smith** and **Lovells** for example have advocacy policies where solicitor advocates are used in all cases other than major hearings or full trials. The Woolf reforms are thought to have accelerated this trend since they put a greater emphasis on written advocacy and have introduced the preliminary hearing – the case-management conference – which must be dealt with by the solicitors with the day-to-day handling of the case.

a day in the life...

As a trainee, a proportion of your time will be spent researching points of law and procedure. Depending on your firm, specialist group you sit in and timing, you could be involved on one massive case with an important role in running the organisation of all the documents to be disclosed. Or you could be running a caseload of small County Court cases in which you may be making small applications before a District Judge. In a large City firm, a qualified litigator may sometimes work on no more than two or three big cases at a time. The caseload will probably be more varied in smaller litigation departments.

Paul Williams, a 5-year qualified litigator at **Lovells**, says his days can be quite varied. You might start your day preparing for a procedural hearing in the Commercial Court at which you will be the advocate, arriving at court to find you are opposed by an experienced barrister instructed by the other side. (The firm has a policy of instructing counsel only in limited circumstances and litigators are encouraged to undertake as much advocacy as possible.) After a discussion outside the court with the other party's counsel, you reach agreement on a number of points but there is one matter on which you cannot agree. Your opponent insists that his client is entitled to ask your client to produce certain documents. You disagree.

You enter court and the judge asks a number of questions about the conduct of the proceedings. You have to explain the reasons for delays in taking certain procedural steps. However, after some argument the judge agrees with you and refuses to order your client to produce the documents. After the judge has given directions dealing with the disclosure of documents and witness statements, the hearing ends. You look at your watch to see that the hearing has lasted over an hour, although it only felt like a few minutes.

You rush back to the office, listen to a number of voicemail messages from clients and other lawyers, check your e-mails, then see you have received a fax from a client requesting an urgent response. You are already running late for lunch with another client but have to stay to deal with the enquiry. After twenty minutes or so you arrive at the restaurant where the client and your supervising partner are having lunch to celebrate a successful mediation in which you were involved. The client, an insurer, is pleased because the mediation resulted in the settlement of a £7m claim for less than £1m and avoided the time and expense of a trial. *"Mediation is a cost-effective and constructive way of resolving commercial* disputes," says Williams *"and clients favour it because they are fully involved in the process, unlike a trial, where the lawyers control what happens."*

Back to the office after lunch for a meeting with a witness. You are preparing his witness statement. It is hard work because his recollection of events is poor. This is not surprising because the events in question happened over five years ago. This is not uncommon in litigation. Luckily you are able to use the firm's document database to locate a letter written by the witness which jogs his memory. *"Computer databasing of documents is the way forward in litigation,"* says Williams. *"It allows you to view images of documents on screen, and searches for documents which would have taken hours now take a matter of seconds. Trainees who would previously have carried out manual searches can do something more productive."*

Finally it is time for a conference call with clients in the USA. Due to the time difference the call is arranged for 6pm. You and your supervising partner update the clients on procedural matters. The client wants to discuss strategy and the possibility of bringing other parties into existing litigation. After discussing this you raise the question of mediation. The client, a US insurer, has participated in numerous mediations and expects you to be familiar with the mediation process. Luckily your recent mediation experience allows you to discuss the different approaches to mediation in the UK and the USA. The client is clearly impressed by your experience. By 7.30pm the conference call is over. The client has asked for a letter of advice. You consider whether to start this now but decide instead to write it first thing the next morning when you can approach the matter fresh. Your department is having drinks at the local wine bar and, after a busy day, you are only too glad to join them at 8pm.

skills needed

....drive...commercial-mindedness...grasp of tactics...natural toughness...competitiveness..."You need to like to win"...the ability to assimilate information quickly and see the big picture..."The best litigators are those with strong commercial awareness and an ability to think laterally around the immediate dispute"...strong negotiating skills... "Verve and panache"...a hard edge..."Charm takes you a long way but clients and opponents need to know that you can bite."

career options

All commercial practices in London and the provinces have litigation departments. Law Society rules require that all trainees do a contentious element in their training contract. **Herbert Smith** has the leading general commercial litigation practice in the City, followed by **Freshfields Bruckhaus Deringer**, **Clifford Chance** and **Lovells**. Among the specialist industry sectors, Masons leads the field in construction litigation. The insurance and shipping firms such as **Barlow Lyde & Gilbert**, **Clyde & Co**, **Ince & Co** and **Davies Arnold Cooper** are strong, not only in insurance litigation, but also in professional negligence work and shipping litigation.

In-house opportunities are less common than for corporate lawyers. Banks, insurance, construction and shipping companies sometimes employ specialist litigators. Only the very largest in-house departments need general commercial litigators.

LEADING FIRMS

LITIGATION: GENERAL COMMERCIAL (FEWER THAN 40 LITIGATORS) • London

1
- Baker & McKenzie
- SJ Berwin
- Stephenson Harwood

2
- Clyde & Co
- Gouldens

3
- D J Freeman
- Dechert
- Eversheds
- Nabarro Nathanson
- Nicholson Graham & Jones

4
- Berwin Leighton Paisner
- Lawrence Graham
- Macfarlanes
- Reynolds Porter Chamberlain
- Rowe & Maw
- Taylor Joynson Garrett
- Travers Smith Braithwaite

5
- Hammond Suddards Edge
- Mishcon de Reya
- Theodore Goddard

6
- Charles Russell
- Ince & Co
- Lane & Partners
- Lewis Silkin
- Masons
- Memery Crystal
- Pinsent Curtis Biddle
- Reed Smith Warner Cranston
- White & Case

Within each band, firms are listed alphabetically.
Source: Chambers and Partners Guide to the Legal Profession 2001-2002

LITIGATION: GENERAL COMMERCIAL (40+ LITIGATORS) • London

1
- Herbert Smith

2
- Clifford Chance
- Freshfields Bruckhaus Deringer
- Lovells

3
- Allen & Overy
- Linklaters

4
- Ashurst Morris Crisp
- Norton Rose
- Slaughter and May

5
- Simmons & Simmons

6
- Barlow Lyde & Gilbert
- CMS Cameron McKenna
- Denton Wilde Sapte
- Richards Butler

LITIGATION: GENERAL COMMERCIAL • The South

1
- Blake Lapthorn Fareham

2
- Bond Pearce Southampton
- Cripps Harries Hall Tunbridge Wells
- DMH Brighton
- Thomas Eggar Church Adams Chichester

3
- asb law Crawley
- Brachers Maidstone
- Clyde & Co Guildford
- Stevens & Bolton Guildford
- Thomson Snell & Passmore Tunbridge Wells

4
- Barlows Surrey
- Lester Aldridge Bournemouth
- Paris Smith & Randall Southampton

LEADING FIRMS continued

LITIGATION: GENERAL COMMERCIAL • Thames Valley

1
- Clarks Reading
- Morgan Cole Oxford, Reading

2
- Boyes Turner Reading
- Nabarro Nathanson Reading
- Shoosmiths Reading

3
- Garretts Reading

LITIGATION: GENERAL COMMERCIAL • South West

1
- Burges Salmon Bristol
- Osborne Clarke Bristol

2
- Beachcroft Wansbroughs Bristol
- Bevan Ashford Bristol
- Bond Pearce Bristol, Exeter, Plymouth
- TLT Solicitors Bristol
- Veale Wasbrough Bristol

3
- Clarke Willmott & Clarke Bristol
- Foot Anstey Sargent Exeter, Plymouth
- Laytons Bristol

LITIGATION: GENERAL COMMERCIAL • Wales

1
- Edwards Geldard Cardiff
- Eversheds Cardiff
- Hugh James Ford Simey Cardiff
- Morgan Cole Cardiff, Swansea

2
- Palser Grossman Cardiff Bay

LITIGATION: GENERAL COMMERCIAL • Midlands

1
- Pinsent Curtis Biddle Birmingham
- Wragge & Co Birmingham

2
- Eversheds Birmingham, Nottingham

3
- Browne Jacobson Nottingham
- DLA Birmingham
- Hammond Suddards Edge Birmingham
- Martineau Johnson Birmingham

4
- Freethcartwright Nottingham
- Gateley Wareing Birmingham
- Lee Crowder Birmingham

5
- Bell Lax Litigation Birmingham
- Shakespeares Birmingham
- Shoosmiths Northampton

6
- Kent Jones and Done Stoke-on-Trent
- Moran & Co Tamworth
- The Wilkes Partnership Birmingham

LITIGATION: GENERAL COMMERCIAL • East Anglia

1
- Eversheds Cambridge, Ipswich, Norwich
- Mills & Reeve Cambridge, Norwich

2
- Hewitson Becke + Shaw Cambridge
- Taylor Vinters Cambridge

3
- Birketts Ipswich
- Greenwoods Peterborough
- Prettys Ipswich

Within each band, firms are listed alphabetically.
Source: Chambers and Partners Guide to the Legal Profession 2001-2002

LEADING FIRMS continued

LITIGATION: GENERAL COMMERCIAL • North West

1 **DLA** Liverpool, Manchester
Eversheds Manchester
2 **Addleshaw Booth & Co** Manchester
Cobbetts Manchester
Hammond Suddards Edge Manchester
3 **Halliwell Landau** Manchester
4 **Berg & Co** Manchester
Brabners Liverpool, Preston
Davies Wallis Foyster Liverpool, Manchester
Hill Dickinson Liverpool
5 **Kershaw Abbott** Manchester
Pannone & Partners Manchester
Wacks Caller Manchester
6 **Chaffe Street** Manchester
Cuff Roberts Liverpool
Mace & Jones Liverpool, Manchester
Rowe Cohen Manchester

Within each band, firms are listed alphabetically.
Source: Chambers and Partners Guide to the Legal Profession 2001-2002

LITIGATION: GENERAL COMMERCIAL • Yorkshire

1 **Addleshaw Booth & Co** Leeds
DLA Leeds, Sheffield
Eversheds Leeds
Hammond Suddards Edge Leeds
Walker Morris Leeds
2 **Irwin Mitchell** Sheffield
Pinsent Curtis Biddle Leeds
3 **Lupton Fawcett** Leeds
Rollits Hull
4 **Andrew M Jackson & Co** Hull
Gordons Cranswick Solicitors Bradford, Leeds
Keeble Hawson Leeds
5 **Brooke North** Leeds
Ford & Warren Leeds
Gosschalks Hull
Read Hind Stewart Leeds

LITIGATION: GENERAL COMMERCIAL • North East

1 **Dickinson Dees** Newcastle upon Tyne
Ward Hadaway Newcastle upon Tyne
2 **Eversheds** Newcastle upon Tyne
3 **Watson Burton** Newcastle upon Tyne
4 **Hay & Kilner** Newcastle upon Tyne
5 **Robert Muckle** Newcastle upon Tyne

SPECIALIST PRACTICE AREAS — LITIGATION

media

We have divided this chapter into three categories: Advertising and Marketing, Defamation and Entertainment law. Entertainment is further subdivided into Film and Broadcasting, Music, Theatre and Publishing. According to Nigel Bennett, partner in the Film & Television Department at leading media firm **The Simkins Partnership**, students should ask themselves one fundamental question. Do you want to be in the world of money or the world of ideas? If you want the former then join a big City firm. If you want something more flexible and less institutionalised, then entertainment law may just be for you.

area of law

advertising & marketing: Firms with advertising and marketing clients specialise in both 'pure' and general advertising law. 'Pure' advertising law is copy clearance for ad agencies, marketing, PR, advertisers and other media clients. It requires a knowledge of broadcasting and publishing self regulatory codes, such as the Advertising Standards Authority code and the Independent Television Commission code, as well as statutes such as the Obscene Publications Act. An understanding of defamation and intellectual property law is also required.

General advertising law means advising your advertising client base on commercial contracts with suppliers, clients and the rest of the media, employment issues, corporate transactions and litigation. It is more likely that having gone to a firm with a client base in this industry you will tend to specialise one way or the other. The complete all-rounder is a rare creature.

'Talent contracts' are a specialism in themselves and require a depth of industry knowledge to do well. This is where an advertising lawyer acts on behalf of an ad agency client to negotiate a contract for the 'talent' to appear in a magazine, radio or TV ad. Clients will deal with the more routine ones themselves, but lawyers get called in for the bigger stars when the contracts become more complex.

"*It's not a document intensive area of law,*" said Dominic Farnsworth, an assistant at **Lewis Silkin**, specialising in pure advertising advice to a number of agencies. "*It's more of a mind game. You simply don't have the time to do hours of research....it's fast in and fast out. That keeps it fresh and fun.*"

a day in the life....

Dominic tells us, "*at 2pm I might get a call from an agency with a legal problem for an ad with a 5pm print deadline. They need immediate and robust copy clearance advice. The key legal risks that I have to assess are trademark and copyright infringement, passing off issues, defamation, regulatory codes, whether or not any consents are required from personalities, whether the ad is misleading and whether or not there are comparative advertising considerations. You've got to think really fast to identify the problems.*" He then has to find a way to minimise these. Any letter of advice has to be written with the agency's own clients in mind as his advice will normally be passed on to the advertiser as well and needs to be diplomatically presented.

skills needed

...a fast, practical and commercial mind... an understanding of and sensitivity to the industry...quick turnaround time...readiness to innovate...detailed knowledge of copyright law....

defamation: One of the most high-profile and arguably most 'glamorous' areas of legal practice. A person can be defamed by written word, which is libel, or by spoken word, which is slander. The majority of actions taken are for libel. On the contentious side, lawyers act for either individuals or companies (claimants) seeking to sue publishers or broadcasters for damaging their reputation or for the individuals or companies being sued (defendants). On the non-contentious side, work includes pre-publication or pre-broadcast advice to authors, editors and TV companies.

Defamation is a fascinating field of law to work in, hinging as it does on questions of personal honour and the right to freedom of expression. Clients can range from high profile politicians or popstars to unknown businessmen. A libel lawyer will therefore gain experience of people from all walks of life and numerous different professions. Client contact is likely to begin at a much more junior level than in the corporate sector. Many see it as 'critical to career progression' to build up personal links to clients and in-house lawyers as quickly as possible. A typical day might involve a client meeting – hearing a claimant's story for the first time and giving advice on the best course of action; planning how to run an action; making an application to court on a procedural matter; persuading a reluctant witness to give evidence in court and possibly investigating an obstruse point of law. Many people think libel is all about trials, but in fact most libel lawyers have only one or two full trials per year. Trainees will probably spend more time in court than qualified solicitors, because they are encouraged to shadow barristers on short hearings and they may also undertake advocacy themselves. Libel lawyer Katherine Rimell of **Theodore Goddard** sees it as *"a very interesting career, especially as it relates to freedom of expression. And it certainly has its glamorous moments!"*

Unlike most areas of law, principles or public image often matter more than money. This means that clients may insist on taking a case to court for reasons of personal 'honour' even where they have a near hopeless case. *"Principles are awfully expensive,"* said Rupert Grey of **Farrer & Co**, *"but they drive the whole game."*

skills needed
...people skills...ability to understand what makes people tick...an interest in language (many are English graduates or former journalists) and current affairs...a keen understanding of human nature...flexibility...sensitivity...understanding of psychology....sharp, analytical mind...creative approach...working knowledge of copyright, confidentiality, contempt of court and the relevant industry codes of practice....

entertainment: We divide entertainment law into Film and Broadcasting, Music, Theatre and Publishing. Clients range from film studios and television production companies to theatre groups and individual artists. Work varies from the financing of West End productions to clearance and classification advice for the British Board of Film Classification. Equally, clients of all types will need contract, employment and litigation advice. Key to almost everything is an understanding of commercial law and intellectual property and how these apply to the entertainment industry.

According to Nigel Bennett of **The Simkins Partnership**, the entertainment lawyer often fulfills a traditional role as a general commercial advisor, as well as providing technical legal services. *"You are providing solutions to a whole range of problems. Someone may require a co-producer in Spain. Another client may wish to buy the film rights to John Le Carré's latest novel. Another may ask you to find the finance for a project. You have a broader brief. It is fascinating work."*

As opposed to a lot of City work, entertainment law is not mainly a matter of standard form procedures. In the early stage of your career you must learn quickly how the industry works. Clients value experience and want lawyers who have done it before. You play a prominent role and are much more than a small cog in a huge corporate wheel.

You therefore need the confidence to stand up and be counted.

SPECIALIST PRACTICE AREAS   MEDIA

film & broadcasting: According to Nigel Bennett, from a lawyer's point of view, you can look at a film or a television programme as any other commercial product. First you have to develop the product, then you have to finance it, then you have to produce it and then you have to sell it. All of these elements require legal advice of one kind or another. The work can be roughly summarised as a combination of commercial contract law (with an element of banking and secured lending) and the law of copyright. The film lawyer would normally see the process through from start to finish.

music: Clients come from all sectors of the music industry including record labels, production companies, managers and the artists themselves. Some firms lean more towards acting for talent, others to the record labels. Central to the work of each type of practice is contract work. High profile litigation sometimes arises when there is a dispute over contract terms or ownership of rights in compositions. Sometimes when band members split with each other or with their management, as happened with the Spice Girls and Robbie Williams, lawyers find that they are brought in to fight their client's corner in the process of sorting out who is entitled to what. Whether specialising in contentious or non-contentious work, music lawyers have to be fully versed in all aspects of copyright as well as contract law. Specialist music firms may also advise on the incorporation and development of new record labels and joint venture agreements between larger and smaller labels.

theatre: There are a few practitioners in London who thrive off the theatrical world. Some work with broader media firms, others attract clients by virtue of their own reputation. Clients include theatre and opera companies, producers, theatrical agents and actors. Theatre lawyers will spend a lot of time in contract negotiations for their clients. Relationships between the constituent parties to a new production all need to be established and regulated through these contracts. A lawyer will usually find himself involved from the inception of the idea for a production right through to the opening curtain and beyond. Increasingly, lawyers will become involved in arrangements for the funding of a new production.

publishing: Work in this sector includes contractual, licensing, copyright and libel work for publishing houses. Most of this work is carried out in-house or by libel lawyers, so there are only a few London firms who can be said to specialise in publishing law. As with libel, an interest in language and literature is an obvious requirement.

skills needed

…social skills…same outlook and language as clients…understanding of the way creative people work…understanding of the industry…a thorough working knowledge of contract and copyright law…communication skills…creativity in problem solving…be prepared to immerse yourself in the business…commercial aptitude…patience…methodical nature…inquisitiveness….

career options

Increasingly there is crossover between private practice and working in-house for media and entertainment organisations. Lawyers transfer between the two more readily than they did a few years ago. Money is generally perceived to be better in-house and the hours are considered more favourable – you do not need to go out looking for new clients, for example. However, one should remember that in recessionary times, in-house counsel are normally the first to go as their legal work can quite easily be outsourced.

Michael Griffiths works for the legal department of Paramount Home Entertainment International, having initially been in private practice. His colleagues have come from a variety of places, both specialist media firms and general commercial firms. Mike's workload is very varied and all manner of things land on his desk. In addition to the film work, the company requires its lawyers to give them a range of advice, just like any other large organisation.

Working in-house can have distinct advantages over private practice. A lack of stiffness and formality is characteristic of the entertainment industry generally and Mike says that this translates through to his working environment. Casual dress, less hierarchy and involvement in a fair degree of non-legal business management tasks can make for a refreshing contrast to the usual experience of a commercial lawyer. Just after we interviewed him Mike was going to the screening of a film for two hours. Just part of the job!

LEADING FIRMS

ADVERTISING & MARKETING • London

1
- Lewis Silkin
- Macfarlanes
- Osborne Clarke

2
- The Simkins Partnership

3
- Hammond Suddards Edge
- Theodore Goddard

4
- Lawrence Graham
- Rowe & Maw
- Taylor Joynson Garrett

5
- Baker & McKenzie
- Clifford Chance
- CMS Cameron McKenna
- Field Fisher Waterhouse
- Olswang
- Townleys

6
- Harrison Curtis
- Lovells

Within each band, firms are listed alphabetically.
Source: Chambers and Partners Guide to the Legal Profession 2001-2002

DEFAMATION • London

1
- Olswang

2
- DJ Freeman
- Davenport Lyons
- Farrer & Co
- Peter Carter-Ruck and Partners
- Schilling & Lom and Partners
- Theodore Goddard

3
- David Price Solicitors & Advocates
- Reynolds Porter Chamberlain

4
- Goodman Derrick
- H2O (Henry Hepworth Organisation)
- Lovells
- Pinsent Curtis Biddle
- Russell Jones & Walker
- Simons Muirhead & Burton
- Wiggin & Co

5
- Bindman & Partners
- Charles Russell
- Clifford Chance
- Swepstone Walsh

6
- Finers Stephens Innocent
- Harbottle & Lewis
- Lewis Silkin
- Mishcon de Reya

SPECIALIST PRACTICE AREAS

MEDIA

133

SPECIALIST PRACTICE AREAS — MEDIA

LEADING FIRMS continued

DEFAMATION • The Regions

1. Foot Anstey Sargent Exeter
   Wiggin & Co Cheltenham
2. Cobbetts Manchester
3. Brabners Liverpool
   Pannone & Partners Manchester
   Wragge & Co Birmingham

MEDIA & ENTERTAINMENT: BROADCASTING • London

1. Denton Wilde Sapte
   Olswang
2. Ashurst Morris Crisp
   Clifford Chance
3. Goodman Derrick
   Richards Butler
   Wiggin & Co
4. Field Fisher Waterhouse
5. DJ Freeman
   Davenport Lyons
   Harbottle & Lewis
   SJ Berwin
   The Simkins Partnership
6. Allen & Overy
   Herbert Smith
   Lovells
   Travers Smith Braithwaite

Within each band, firms are listed alphabetically.
Source: Chambers and Partners Guide to the Legal Profession 2001-2002

MEDIA & ENTERTAINMENT: FILM & TV PRODUCTION • London

1. Olswang
2. Harbottle & Lewis
   Lee & Thompson
3. Davenport Lyons
   SJ Berwin
   The Simkins Partnership
   Theodore Goddard
4. Harrison Curtis
   Richards Butler
   Schilling & Lom and Partners
5. Denton Wilde Sapte

MEDIA & ENTERTAINMENT: MUSIC • London

1. Russells
2. Clintons
   Lee & Thompson
3. Sheridans
4. Bray & Krais
   Mishcon de Reya
   Statham Gill Davies
   The Simkins Partnership
   Theodore Goddard
5. Davenport Lyons
   Denton Wilde Sapte
   Eversheds
   Hamlins
   Harbottle & Lewis
   Harrison Curtis
   Searles
   Spraggon Stennett Brabyn

LEADING FIRMS continued

MEDIA & ENTERTAINMENT: PUBLISHING • London

1. Denton Wilde Sapte
2. Taylor Joynson Garrett
3. Finers Stephens Innocent
   H2O (Henry Hepworth Organisation)
   Harbottle & Lewis
   Lovells
   The Simkins Partnership

MEDIA & ENTERTAINMENT: THEATRE • London

1. Clintons
   Tarlo Lyons
2. Campbell Hooper
   The Simkins Partnership
3. Harrison Curtis
4. Bates, Wells & Braithwaite
   Harbottle & Lewis
   Theodore Goddard

Within each band, firms are listed alphabetically.
Source: Chambers and Partners Guide to the Legal Profession 2001-2002

MEDIA & ENTERTAINMENT • The South

1. Manches Oxford
   Wiggin & Co Cheltenham

MEDIA & ENTERTAINMENT • Wales

1. Morgan Cole Cardiff, Swansea

MEDIA & ENTERTAINMENT • Midlands

1. Hammond Suddards Edge Birmingham
   Kent Jones and Done Stoke-on-Trent

MEDIA & ENTERTAINMENT • The North

1. McCormicks Leeds
2. Eversheds Leeds, Manchester
   Lea & Company Stockport
3. Ramsbottom & Co Blackburn

SPECIALIST PRACTICE AREAS

MEDIA

personal injury & clinical negligence

As related areas of practice, personal injury and clinical negligence work are often undertaken in the same department or sometimes by specialist firms. Claimant firms are instructed by private individuals, legal expenses insurers and trade unions. Clients of defendant firms include private individuals, health authorities, hospitals, trusts, insurance companies, public bodies and self-insuring companies. Firms acting for both claimants and defendants are on the decrease, mainly as a result of major insurers shrinking their panels of firms which represent them.

Personal injury cases range from simple "slip and trip" cases (such as falling over uneven paving stones) to fatal accidents, major disaster litigation (the Paddington Rail crash) and complex group ("multi-party") actions, often in the environmental or industrial disease context. Examples of these include the asbestos-related disease actions brought on behalf of the South African miners, the tobacco litigation and the Gulf War Syndrome cases.

Clinical negligence actions include those arising from treatment of medical conditions or injuries. Among the most complex and serious cases which carry the highest potential amount of compensation are those arising from birth, such as brain-damaged babies.

type of work

PI and clinical negligence lawyers spend the majority of their time gathering information from clients as evidence to support their cases, obtaining expert evidence, researching the technicalities of their cases and generally preparing for litigation. Pre-litigation advice includes advising the client on the strength of their case, and if it is strong enough to take forward, taking the client through aspects of funding the case and general case strategy. Only a very small percentage of cases reach trial as most settlements are reached out of court to avoid unecessary costs - an imperative objective under the recent reforms to the legal system (commonly referred to as 'the Woolf reforms').

personal injury: Road traffic accident ("RTA") claims are generally routine in nature ('high volume, low value claims') but are the staple diet of many high street and general practices. The most efficient practices will have dedicated IT resources to deal with the substantial amount of standard documentation and paperwork generated by this type of work. Other claimant firms which are more specialist in nature have lawyers with expertise in a variety of niche areas. **Leigh, Day & Co** specialises in multi-party actions with an environmental aspect such as asbestos-related diseases work and gas poisonings. They also have expertise in aviation disasters and horse-riding accidents. **Russell Jones & Walker** handle deafness cases, for example, representing police officers deafened by motorcycle and gunfire noise, and an office worker deafened by a faulty fire alarm. They also have a special unit for victims of sexual assault.

Defendant firms are often instructed by insurers, but they require as much specialist knowledge as their claimant counterparts. *"Shortly after qualifying I bought myself a Teach Yourself Anatomy book and read it from cover to cover,"* says Steve Daykin, head of defendant PI at **Nabarro Nathanson** in Sheffield. He is has been defending British Coal in the 'Vibration White Finger' (a condition where vibrating machinery causes fingers to turn white and go numb) litigation in the Court of Appeal, and in a group respiratory disease claim. He obviously needs to be fully aware of the medical conditions allegedly suffered by the claimants.

This type of work takes lawyers from the factory floor to the coal mine, from the scene of an accident to the hospital, and from the home to the sports field. They become mini-experts in a number of activities. Terry Lee, partner with **Evill & Coleman**, had to learn the ins and outs of the rules of rugby as well as draw on his knowledge of head and spinal injuries, when he represented the rugby player, Ben Smolden, in his ground-breaking action against two rugby referees. Smolden sustained severe injuries during a match and one of the referees was held liable for those injuries.

clinical negligence: Like PI, clinical negligence work ranges from simple injuries to actions worth millions of pounds in damages. The more complex cases require an in-depth knowledge of medical technicalities. Katie Hay, a consultant with the defendant firm, **Capsticks**, explains that the doctors and experts can tell you much of what you need to know, but that with most specialist cases, "*you just have to sit down and learn it for yourself.*"

Hay defended Merton, Sutton and Wandsworth Health Authority in an action brought by a patient who became pregnant after she had supposedly been sterilised. Following detailed gynaecological, histological and video evidence, it was established that the doctor who performed the sterilisation had not been at fault. The lawyers knew as much about the medical complications as the doctors by the end of the trial.

An awareness of mental as well as physical illness is often required by the lawyers. Specialist claimant firm, **Pritchard Englefield**, acted for Mr and Mrs Tredget in their test case against Bexley Health Authority, which established that a father who witnessed the mismanaged birth of his son (who died shortly afterwards) could recover damages for his own psychological injury.

Magi Young, partner with claimant firm, **Parlett Kent**, recently achieved a settlement of £1.2 million for a psychiatric patient who managed to take an overdose while under one-to-one observation. For 12 hours, the hospital failed to realise that she had lapsed into a coma.

These cases are at the top end of the scale and a trainee or recently qualified solicitor would obviously play only a junior role in such matters. Nevertheless, this role could still involve liaising with clients and doctors. As a trainee with Parlett Kent points out: "*I already have a lot of client contact, and give advice and support on the 'phone, as well as taking witness statements and attending consultations with counsel.*" He also undertakes advocacy for his firm and sometimes finds himself up against a partner on the other side.

Clinical negligence and PI are intense and absorbing fields and require hard work and long hours just to keep up to speed with advances in medicine and technology. According to Steve Daykin, those at the top of the profession routinely work a 60-70 hour week.

skills needed

...an interest in medical issues...knowledge of anatomy and medical conditions...understanding of how the NHS works...awareness of the professional relationships between doctors, nurses, managers and patients...non-squeamish nature...good communication skills...sensitive and sympathetic approach...great strength of character...empathy...tact and sensitivity...assertiveness...confidence, tenacity and common sense...emotional commitment and dedication...

career options

Magi Young has always acted for claimants. She trained in a small legal aid practice where she tackled personal injury, clinical negligence, mental health, housing, immigration, crime and family law. She then moved to Pannone Napier (now **Pannone & Partners**), where she immediately specialised in personal injury and clinical negligence and became a partner after four years. She has been a partner with **Parlett Kent** for the past eight years and recently set up a branch of the firm in Exeter.

After training with **Robert Muckle**, Steve Daykin joined British Coal as an assistant solicitor to experience the public sector. In 1986, he became British Coal's area solicitor for the north east and was in charge of 20 lawyers. In 1990, **Nabarro Nathanson** took over part of British Coal's legal department and Daykin moved to join the firm. He now heads their PI department. He had this to say of his field: *"You talk to commercial lawyers who think their jobs are more demanding because they earn more money, but acting for defendants in PI is a hell of a challenge and no less intellectually demanding."*

There are very few in-house options for lawyers in this field. When pressed, Steve Daykin suggested that there may be openings for defendant solicitors with health authorities and the Post Office, but commented that *"such opportunities are getting rarer all the time, with the majority of work being referred to specialist practices."* Magi Young knows of no in-house lawyers in this field and stressed that as it is such a demanding and highly-focused area, *"It is only for those whose commitment is total and career changes on the inside are extremely rare."* Katie Hay agrees: *"This is a popular area of law as it involves commercial decision-making in a human context. Those who succeed in breaking into it tend to be here to stay."*

Their advice is to make focused applications to specialist firms, because the trend within private practice is towards increasing specialisation in a small number of niche firms.

Finally, some breaking news for those eyeing up practice within a clinical negligence firm. As part of the government's aim to cut back on the cost of litigation, the National Health Service Litigation Authority is set to take over all NHS medical negligence claims. The NHSLA is serviced by 16 firms which sit on a panel who will effectively be handed a monopoly upon all NHS defendant work. It is too early to predict exactly what impact this will have upon the market, however, it would be safe to say that those firms on the panel will see a doubling of their medical negligence workload, whilst those who are not will be frozen out of this lucrative area completely - and might begin to feel the pinch.

LEADING FIRMS

CLINICAL NEGLIGENCE: MAINLY CLAIMANT • London

1 Leigh, Day & Co
2 Bindman & Partners
   Kingsley Napley
   Parlett Kent
3 Alexander Harris
   Charles Russell
   Evill and Coleman
   Field Fisher Waterhouse

CLINICAL NEGLIGENCE: MAINLY CLAIMANT • The South

1 Blake Lapthorn Portsmouth
2 Thomson Snell & Passmore Tunbridge Wells
3 Penningtons Godalming
   Wynne Baxter Brighton

CLINICAL NEGLIGENCE: MAINLY CLAIMANT • Thames Valley

1 Boyes Turner Reading
2 Osborne Morris & Morgan Leighton Buzzard
3 Harris & Cartwright Slough

Within each band, firms are listed alphabetically.
Source: Chambers and Partners Guide to the Legal Profession 2001-2002

CLINICAL NEGLIGENCE: MAINLY CLAIMANT • South West

1 Barcan Woodward Bristol
   Preston Goldburn Falmouth
2 John Hodge & Co Weston-super-Mare
   Over Taylor Biggs Exeter
   Russell Jones & Walker Bristol
   Withy King Bath
   Wolferstans Plymouth
3 Woollcombe Beer Watts Newton Abbot

CLINICAL NEGLIGENCE: MAINLY CLAIMANT • Wales

1 Huttons Cardiff
2 Edwards Geldard Cardiff
   Hugh James Ford Simey Cardiff
   John Collins & Partners with Edward Harris Swansea
   Russell Jones & Walker Cardiff

CLINICAL NEGLIGENCE: MAINLY CLAIMANT • Midlands

1 Freethcartwright Nottingham
   Irwin Mitchell Birmingham
2 Anthony Collins Solicitors Birmingham
3 Challinors Lyon Clark Birmingham

SPECIALIST PRACTICE AREAS — PERSONAL INJURY & CLINICAL NEGLIGENCE

LEADING FIRMS continued

CLINICAL NEGLIGENCE: MAINLY CLAIMANT • East Anglia

1. Cunningham John Thetford
2. Gadsby Wicks Chelmsford
3. Morgan Jones & Pett Great Yarmouth

   Prettys Ipswich

   Scrivenger Seabrook St Neots

CLINICAL NEGLIGENCE: MAINLY CLAIMANT • North West

1. Pannone & Partners Manchester
2. Alexander Harris Altrincham
3. Jones Maidment Wilson Manchester

   Leigh, Day & Co Manchester

   Linder Myers Manchester

CLINICAL NEGLIGENCE: MAINLY CLAIMANT • Yorkshire

1. Irwin Mitchell Sheffield
2. Heptonstalls Goole

CLINICAL NEGLIGENCE: MAINLY CLAIMANT • North East

1. Peter Maughan & Co Gateshead
2. Hay & Kilner Newcastle upon Tyne
3. Samuel Phillips & Co Newcastle upon Tyne

CLINICAL NEGLIGENCE: MAINLY DEFENDANT • London

1. Capsticks
2. Hempsons
3. Vizard Oldham

CLINICAL NEGLIGENCE: MAINLY DEFENDANT • The South

1. Beachcroft Wansbroughs Winchester
2. Brachers Maidstone

CLINICAL NEGLIGENCE: MAINLY DEFENDANT • South West

1. Bevan Ashford Bristol
2. Beachcroft Wansbroughs Bristol

CLINICAL NEGLIGENCE: MAINLY DEFENDANT • Midlands

1. Bevan Ashford Birmingham

   Browne Jacobson Birmingham, Nottingham

CLINICAL NEGLIGENCE: MAINLY DEFENDANT • East Anglia

1. Kennedys Newmarket

Within each band, firms are listed alphabetically.
Source: Chambers and Partners Guide to the Legal Profession 2001-2002

LEADING FIRMS continued

CLINICAL NEGLIGENCE: MAINLY DEFENDANT • North West

1. **Hempsons** Manchester
2. **Hill Dickinson** Liverpool
3. **George Davies** Manchester

CLINICAL NEGLIGENCE: MAINLY DEFENDANT • Yorkshire

1. **Hempsons** Harrogate

CLINICAL NEGLIGENCE: MAINLY DEFENDANT • North East

1. **Eversheds** Newcastle upon Tyne
2. **Ward Hadaway** Newcastle upon Tyne

Within each band, firms are listed alphabetically.
Source: Chambers and Partners Guide to the Legal Profession 2001-2002

PERSONAL INJURY: MAINLY CLAIMANT • London

1. **Leigh, Day & Co**
   Russell Jones & Walker
   Thompsons
2. **Evill and Coleman**
   Irwin Mitchell
   Pattinson & Brewer
3. **Anthony Gold**
   Field Fisher Waterhouse
   Hodge Jones & Allen
   Rowley Ashworth
   Stewarts
4. **Bolt Burdon**
   Levenes
   OH Parsons & Partners

PERSONAL INJURY: MAINLY CLAIMANT • The South

1. **Lamport Bassitt** Southampton
   Shoosmiths Basingstoke
2. **Amery-Parkes** Basingstoke
   George Ide, Phillips Chichester
   Thomson Snell & Passmore Tunbridge Wells
3. **Blake Lapthorn** Portsmouth
   Moore & Blatch Southampton
   Pattinson & Brewer Chatham
   Warner Goodman & Streat Fareham

SPECIALIST PRACTICE AREAS

PERSONAL INJURY & CLINICAL NEGLIGENCE

LEADING FIRMS continued

PERSONAL INJURY: MAINLY CLAIMANT • Thames Valley

1. **Osborne Morris & Morgan** Leighton Buzzard
2. **Boyes Turner** Reading
   Fennemores Milton Keynes
   Harris & Cartwright Slough
3. **Henmans** Oxford

PERSONAL INJURY: MAINLY CLAIMANT • South West

1. **Bond Pearce** Plymouth, Bristol
   Lyons Davidson Bristol
   Russell Jones & Walker Bristol
   Veale Wasbrough Bristol
2. **Rowley Ashworth** Exeter
   Thompsons Bristol
   Wolferstans Plymouth
3. **David Gist Solicitors** Bristol
4. **Bobbetts Mackan** Bristol

PERSONAL INJURY: MAINLY CLAIMANT • Wales

1. **Hugh James Ford Simey** Merthyr Tydfil
2. **Leo Abse & Cohen** Cardiff
   Thompsons Cardiff
3. **Loosemores** Cardiff
   Smith Llewelyn Partnership Swansea

Within each band, firms are listed alphabetically.
Source: Chambers and Partners Guide to the Legal Profession 2001-2002

PERSONAL INJURY: MAINLY CLAIMANT • Midlands

1. **Irwin Mitchell** Birmingham
   Rowley Ashworth Birmingham
   Russell Jones & Walker Birmingham
   Thompsons Birmingham
2. **Barratt Goff & Tomlinson** Nottingham
   Freethcartwright Nottingham
   Nelsons Nottingham

PERSONAL INJURY: MAINLY CLAIMANT • East Anglia

1. **Cunningham John** Thetford
2. **Morgan Jones & Pett** Great Yarmouth
   Taylor Vinters Cambridge
3. **Edwards Duthie** Ilford
   Leathes Prior Norwich

PERSONAL INJURY: MAINLY CLAIMANT • North West

1. **Pannone & Partners** Manchester
2. **John Pickering & Partners** Oldham
   Leigh, Day & Co Manchester
   Russell Jones & Walker Manchester
   Thompsons Liverpool
3. **Donns Solicitors** Manchester
   Whittles Manchester
4. **Hugh Potter & Company,** Manchester
   Linder Myers Manchester

LEADING FIRMS continued

PERSONAL INJURY: MAINLY CLAIMANT • Yorkshire

1. Irwin Mitchell Leeds, Sheffield
2. Morrish & Co Leeds
   Pattinson & Brewer York
   Rowley Ashworth Leeds
   Russell Jones & Walker Leeds, Sheffield
3. Hamers Hull

PERSONAL INJURY: MAINLY CLAIMANT • North East

1. Thompsons Newcastle upon Tyne
2. Browell Smith & Co Newcastle upon Tyne
   Marrons Newcastle upon Tyne
3. Hay & Kilner Newcastle upon Tyne
   Russell Jones & Walker Newcastle upon Tyne
4. Beecham Peacock Newcastle upon Tyne

PERSONAL INJURY: MAINLY DEFENDANT • London

1. Barlow Lyde & Gilbert
   Beachcroft Wansbroughs
   Berrymans Lace Mawer
2. Kennedys
   Vizards, Staples & Bannisters
3. Badhams
   Davies Arnold Cooper
   Hextall Erskine
   Watmores

PERSONAL INJURY: MAINLY DEFENDANT • The South

1. Beachcroft Wansbroughs Winchester
   Berrymans Lace Mawer Southampton
   Bond Pearce Southampton
   Ensor Byfield Southampton
2. AE Wyeth & Co Dartford
   Davies Lavery Maidstone
   Keoghs Southampton
   Palser Grossman Southampton

PERSONAL INJURY: MAINLY DEFENDANT • Thames Valley

1. Morgan Cole Reading
2. Henmans Oxford

PERSONAL INJURY: MAINLY DEFENDANT • South West

1. Beachcroft Wansbroughs Bristol
2. Bond Pearce Bristol, Plymouth
   Cartwrights Insurance Partners Bristol
3. Bevan Ashford Bristol
   Hugh James Ford Simey Exeter
   Palser Grossman Bristol
   Veitch Penny Exeter

Within each band, firms are listed alphabetically.
Source: Chambers and Partners Guide to the Legal Profession 2001-2002

LEADING FIRMS continued

PERSONAL INJURY: MAINLY DEFENDANT • Wales

1
- Hugh James Ford Simey Cardiff
- Morgan Cole Cardiff
- Palser Grossman Cardiff Bay

2
- Dolmans Cardiff

PERSONAL INJURY: MAINLY DEFENDANT • Midlands

1
- Beachcroft Wansbroughs Birmingham
- Browne Jacobson Nottingham

2
- Buller Jeffries Birmingham

3
- Everatt & Company Evesham
- Weightmans Birmingham

4
- Chapman Everatt Wolverhampton
- Keoghs Coventry

PERSONAL INJURY: MAINLY DEFENDANT • East Anglia

1
- Eversheds Ipswich
- Mills & Reeve Norwich

2
- Edwards Duthie Ilford
- Greenwoods Peterborough
- Kennedys Brentwood
- Merricks Ipswich
- Prettys Ipswich

PERSONAL INJURY: MAINLY DEFENDANT • North West

1
- James Chapman & Co Manchester
- Keoghs Bolton
- Weightmans Liverpool, Manchester

2
- Beachcroft Wansbroughs Manchester
- Berrymans Lace Mawer Liverpool, Manchester
- Halliwell Landau Manchester
- Hill Dickinson Liverpool, Manchester

PERSONAL INJURY: MAINLY DEFENDANT • Yorkshire

1
- Beachcroft Wansbroughs Leeds

2
- DLA Bradford, Leeds, Sheffield

3
- Irwin Mitchell Sheffield
- Nabarro Nathanson Sheffield

4
- Keeble Hawson Leeds, Sheffield
- Praxis Partners Leeds

PERSONAL INJURY: MAINLY DEFENDANT • North East

1
- Eversheds Newcastle upon Tyne
- Hay & Kilner Newcastle upon Tyne
- Sinton & Co Newcastle upon Tyne

2
- Crutes Newcastle upon Tyne
- Jacksons Stockton on Tees

Within each band, firms are listed alphabetically.
Source: Chambers and Partners Guide to the Legal Profession 2001-2002

private client

'Private clients' are private individuals as opposed to corporate entities. The definition of 'private client' work really depends on what sort of firm you're thinking of applying to. In a commercial practice, the term generally refers to advice on tax and trusts to high net worth individuals who are prepared to pay hundreds of pounds an hour for top specialist advice and personal service. For a high street firm it could mean any member of the public, wealthy or otherwise and would include advice on divorce, conveyancing and drawing up wills. In this chapter we refer to the work carried out in commercial firms.

Private client work has become synonymous with certain services provided to individuals. These include trusts, tax and probate advice and associated services connected with the acquisition, disposal and management of personal assets.

Solicitors who have developed a niche in trust law may find that their expertise is sought after by charitable organisations and so need an understanding of the rules governing charities. Work is generally purely advisory and non-contentious although litigation is always a possibility.

type of work

trusts and personal tax: Any solicitor must respect client confidentiality. With private clients the reasons for doing so are more acutely apparent. The solicitor is often drawn into a very detailed examination of a client's family life and finances. The solicitor has to respect the client's privacy whilst maintaining impartiality and giving the best possible practical advice. The solicitor must also hear the most private details of family circumstances and finances with understanding but without judgment.

David Long, partner at City firm **Charles Russell**, sees UK trusts law as a very portable product internationally. He is confident that firms will find their private client lawyers becoming more in demand in the future by foreign clients. *"The beauty of our English language is that it is world-wide, and English corporate and commercial law is world-wide, ranking with New York law as the dominant law. Trusts and the tax planning work is also an important invisible export. The trust is a wonderfully flexible tool for planning."* Surprisingly, Andrew Young of **Lawrence Graham** sees the trust as a fashionable tool for the internationally wealthy. *"Rich people in foreign countries know their friends have trusts so they want one too. It is the ultimate fashion accessory for the seriously rich."*

Trusts are a very popular way of holding assets and avoiding tax (rather than evading tax, which is illegal) often by holding funds in off-shore jurisdictions. Trusts allow family members access to funds whilst also allowing the donor a degree of control over the manner in which the funds are accessed.

The creation of trusts in other jurisdictions often means that the lawyer will have to spend time ensuring that his client understands the system of law behind the setting up of a trust. David Long told us, *"In the off-shore world you get a culture clash between people brought up in Napoleonic Code countries which have certain heirship rights for children which don't fit at all well with our common law system. So you get rich men in Italy or Spain taking their money to the Bahamas or Bermuda and creating trusts. Then you may have litigation in the original country to determine whether the trust works to defeat the interest of the children who would otherwise have inherited."* A lawyer must be very careful to appraise the client of all the possible foreign law implications.

As well as handling off-shore trusts in conjunction with overseas lawyers and trust companies, private client lawyers find that they advise an increasing number of overseas clients seeking to invest in the UK. Off-shore and private banks may also need advice about their clients' UK interests.

A private client lawyer will be consulted on a range of different issues from immigration and employment questions through to share transactions and property deals. The most experienced individuals have the breadth of experience to give an answer to these diverse questions. However, in a large multi-service law firm there is plenty of opportunity to turn to the expertise of colleagues.

Says David Long: "*Some private clients get very close to you and don't do anything major without asking or discussing it with you. You are often a trustee or executor looking after their money for the next generation and that's tremendous. It's very flattering to be asked to be a trustee.*" He likes the fact that aside from having some money the clients are all very diverse. "*I would not wish my practice to have only rich farmers or aristocrats or businessmen. I like the variety because human beings are so different all the time. That's the beauty of it! And you do get to know them quite well when you're advising them on this sort of thing.*"

charities: A related area of practice is charities law, where clients range from well known national charities to low profile local private charitable trusts. Work consists of charity registration and reorganisation, Charity Commission investigations, the development of trading subsidiaries and advising charitable clients on any other issues necessary such as tax, trust or property matters. Many firms, especially the smaller ones, frequently specialise in advising particular types of charity, for example religious or environmental charities.

skills needed

...good all round legal skills...good 'bedside manner'...facilitation skills...flexibility...enormous tolerance....strong grounding in trusts and tax...innovative yet well-organised thinker...ability to see the bigger picture...

career options

Training at an established private client firm such as **Withers, Farrers** and **Boodle Hatfield** will give the best possible start. City firms such as **Allen & Overy** and **Macfarlanes** have continued to offer these services to their clients, allowing trainees to combine private client work with a corporate training. Following the 90's trend for hiving off private client departments from large corporate practices, very recently firms are recognising the value of private client lawyers to service the new breed of 'e-trepreneurs.'

In-house opportunities are limited although some off-shore trust companies and private banks do have in house legal advisers. For those who fancy working abroad, banks in the Bahamas, Cayman Islands and Jersey may employ lawyers in advisory or risk control positions.

For charities specialists there is less scope in terms of law firms specialising in this area, but with the opportunity to make strong contacts with clients there is always the possibility of moving into a more general role within the industry.

LEADING FIRMS

AGRICULTURE • London

1. **Farrer & Co**
   Macfarlanes
   Withers
2. **Currey & Co**
   Dawson & Co
   Lee & Pembertons
3. **Boodle Hatfield**
   Payne Hicks Beach

AGRICULTURE • The South

1. **Brachers** Maidstone
2. **White & Bowker** Winchester
3. **Cripps Harries Hall** Tunbridge Wells
   Thomas Eggar Church Adams Chichester
4. **Knights** Tunbridge Wells
   Penningtons Godalming

AGRICULTURE • Thames Valley

1. **Henmans** Oxford
2. **Pryce Collard Chamberlain** Abingdon
   Stanley Tee Bishop's Stortford

AGRICULTURE • South West

1. **Burges Salmon** Bristol
2. **Wilsons** Salisbury
3. **Clarke Willmott & Clarke** Taunton
   Stephens & Scown Exeter
4. **Bevan Ashford** Bristol
   Thring Townsend Bath
5. **Battens (with Poole & Co)** Yeovil
   Bond Pearce Plymouth
   Osborne Clarke Bristol
6. **Pardoes** Bridgwater
   Porter Dodson Yeovil

AGRICULTURE • Wales

1. **John Collins & Partners with Edward Harris & Son** Swansea
   Margraves Llandrindod Wells
2. **Gabb & Co** Abergavenny
   Morgan Cole Cardiff

Within each band, firms are listed alphabetically.
Source: Chambers and Partners Guide to the Legal Profession 2001-2002

LEADING FIRMS continued

AGRICULTURE • Midlands

1 Arnold Thomson Towcester
Wright Hassall Leamington Spa
2 Hewitson Becke + Shaw Northampton
Martineau Johnson Birmingham
3 Knight & Sons Newcastle-under-Lyme
Manby & Steward Wolverhampton
4 Gwynnes Wellington
Lanyon Bowdler Shrewsbury
Lodders Stratford-upon-Avon
Morton Fisher Worcester

AGRICULTURE • East Anglia

1 Mills & Reeve Norwich
Roythorne & Co Spalding
2 Barker Gotelee Ipswich
Birketts Ipswich
Taylor Vinters Cambridge
3 Eversheds Norwich
Hewitson Becke + Shaw Cambridge
4 Ashton Graham Bury St Edmunds, Ipswich
Howes Percival Norwich
Prettys Ipswich
5 Wilkin Chapman Louth

AGRICULTURE • North West

1 Cartmell Shepherd Carlisle
2 Oglethorpe Sturton & Gillibrand Lancaster
Walker Smith & Way Chester
3 Birch Cullimore Chester
Hibbert Durrad Davies Nantwich
Mason & Moore Dutton Chester
Napthen Houghton Craven Preston

AGRICULTURE • Yorkshire

1 Rollits Hull
Wrigleys Leeds
2 Addleshaw Booth & Co Leeds
3 Andrew M Jackson & Co Hull
Grays York
Stamp Jackson and Procter Hull

AGRICULTURE • North East

1 Dickinson Dees Newcastle upon Tyne
2 Ward Hadaway Newcastle upon Tyne
3 Latimer Hinks Darlington
4 Jacksons Stockton on Tees

Within each band, firms are listed alphabetically.
Source: Chambers and Partners Guide to the Legal Profession 2001-2002

LEADING FIRMS continued

CHARITIES • London

1 Bates, Wells & Braithwaite
2 Farrer & Co
3 Withers
4 Allen & Overy
Berwin Leighton Paisner
Bircham Dyson Bell
Charles Russell
Claricoat Phillips
Harbottle & Lewis
Nabarro Nathanson
Sinclair Taylor & Martin
Trowers & Hamlins
5 Lawrence Graham
Lee Bolton & Lee
Macfarlanes
Radcliffes
Winckworth Sherwood
6 Field Fisher Waterhouse
Herbert Smith
Linklaters
Vizard Oldham

CHARITIES • The South

1 Blake Lapthorn Portsmouth
Thomas Eggar Church Adams Chichester
Thomson Snell & Passmore Tunbridge Wells
2 Barlows Surrey
Cripps Harries Hall Tunbridge Wells
Griffith Smith Brighton
Lester Aldridge Bournemouth

CHARITIES • Thames Valley

1 Manches Oxford
Nabarro Nathanson Reading
Winckworth Sherwood Oxford
2 BrookStreet Des Roches Witney
3 Henmans Oxford
Iliffes Booth Bennett Uxbridge
Linnells Oxford

CHARITIES • South West & Wales

1 Stone King Bath
2 Bond Pearce Exeter
Burges Salmon Bristol
Osborne Clarke Bristol
3 Thring Townsend Bath
Tozers Exeter
Veale Wasbrough Bristol
Wilsons Salisbury
4 Clarke Willmott & Clarke Taunton
Edwards Geldard Cardiff
Michelmores Exeter
Parker Bullen Salisbury
Rickerby Watterson Cheltenham

Within each band, firms are listed alphabetically.
Source: Chambers and Partners Guide to the Legal Profession 2001-2002

LEADING FIRMS continued

CHARITIES • Midlands

[1] **Anthony Collins Solicitors** Birmingham
Martineau Johnson Birmingham
Wragge & Co Birmingham

[2] **Gateley Wareing** Birmingham
Hewitson Becke + Shaw Northampton
Lee Crowder Birmingham
Shakespeares Birmingham

CHARITIES • East Anglia

[1] **Cozens-Hardy & Jewson** Norwich
Mills & Reeve Norwich
Taylor Vinters Cambridge

[2] **Eversheds** Cambridge, Norwich
Greenwoods Peterborough
Hewitson Becke + Shaw Cambridge
Leathes Prior Norwich

CHARITIES • North West

[1] **Birch Cullimore** Chester
Brabners Liverpool

[2] **Oswald Goodier & Co** Preston

[3] **Halliwell Landau** Manchester
Pannone & Partners Manchester

Within each band, firms are listed alphabetically.
Source: Chambers and Partners Guide to the Legal Profession 2001-2002

CHARITIES • North East

[1] **Wrigleys** Leeds

[2] **Addleshaw Booth & Co** Leeds
Grays York

[3] **Dickinson Dees** Newcastle upon Tyne
Irwin Mitchell Sheffield

[4] **Eversheds** Newcastle upon Tyne
Keeble Hawson Sheffield
McCormicks Leeds

TRUSTS & PERSONAL TAX • The South

[1] **Cripps Harries Hall** Tunbridge Wells
Thomas Eggar Church Adams Chichester

[2] **Adams & Remers** Lewes
Stevens & Bolton Guildford
Thomson Snell & Passmore Tunbridge Wells
White & Bowker Winchester

[3] **Blake Lapthorn** Portsmouth
Moore & Blatch Lymington
Mundays Esher
Paris Smith & Randall Southampton
Penningtons Godalming

[4] **Brachers** Maidstone
Charles Russell Guildford
DMH Brighton
Lester Aldridge Bournemouth

[5] **Barlows** Surrey
Buss Murton Tunbridge Wells
George Ide, Phillips Chichester
Griffith Smith Brighton
Whitehead Monckton Maidstone

LEADING FIRMS continued

TRUSTS & PERSONAL TAX • London

1
- Allen & Overy
- Macfarlanes
- Withers

2
- Lawrence Graham

3
- Boodle Hatfield
- Charles Russell
- Currey & Co
- Payne Hicks Beach

4
- Bircham Dyson Bell
- Farrer & Co
- Forsters
- Nicholson Graham & Jones
- Speechly Bircham
- Taylor Joynson Garrett

5
- Baker & McKenzie
- Hunters
- Linklaters
- Radcliffes
- Rooks Rider
- Simmons & Simmons
- Wedlake Bell

6
- Berwin Leighton Paisner
- Dawson & Co
- Lee & Pembertons
- Maxwell Batley
- May, May & Merrimans
- Trowers & Hamlins
- Witham Weld

Within each band, firms are listed alphabetically.
Source: Chambers and Partners Guide to the Legal Profession 2001-2002

TRUSTS & PERSONAL TAX • Thames Valley

1
- Boodle Hatfield Oxford

2
- Blandy & Blandy Reading
- Henmans Oxford

3
- Boyes Turner Reading
- Iliffes Booth Bennett Uxbridge

4
- BP Collins Gerrards Cross
- Pictons Hemel Hempstead

5
- Clarks Reading
- Matthew Arnold & Baldwin Watford
- Stanley Tee Bishop's Stortford

TRUSTS & PERSONAL TAX • South West

1
- Burges Salmon Bristol
- Osborne Clarke Bristol
- Wiggin & Co Cheltenham
- Wilsons Salisbury

2
- Bond Pearce Plymouth
- Charles Russell Cheltenham
- Foot Anstey Sargent Plymouth

3
- Clarke Willmott & Clarke Taunton
- Hooper & Wollen Torquay

4
- Coodes St Austell
- Meade-King Bristol
- Michelmores Exeter
- TLT Solicitors Bristol
- Veale Wasbrough Bristol

5
- Rickerby Watterson Cheltenham
- Stephens & Scown Exeter
- Stones Exeter
- Woollcombe Beer Watts Newton Abbot

SPECIALIST PRACTICE AREAS — PRIVATE CLIENT

LEADING FIRMS continued

TRUSTS & PERSONAL TAX • Midlands

1 Martineau Johnson Birmingham
2 Browne Jacobson Nottingham
　Hewitson Becke + Shaw Northampton
　Lee Crowder Birmingham
　Lodders Stratford-upon-Avon
　Wragge & Co Birmingham
3 Higgs & Sons Brierley Hill
　Pinsent Curtis Biddle Birmingham
4 Freethcartwright Nottingham
　Gateley Wareing Birmingham
　Shakespeares Birmingham
　The Wilkes Partnership Birmingham
　Willcox Lane Clutterbuck Birmingham

TRUSTS & PERSONAL TAX • East Anglia

1 Mills & Reeve Norwich
2 Hewitson Becke + Shaw Cambridge
3 Greene & Greene Bury St Edmunds
　Howes Percival Norwich
　Roythorne & Co Spalding
　Taylor Vinters Cambridge
4 Ashton Graham Bury St Edmunds
　Cozens-Hardy & Jewson Norwich
　Hood Vores & Allwood Dereham
　Prettys Ipswich
　Ward Gethin King's Lynn
　Willcox & Lewis Norwich

Within each band, firms are listed alphabetically.
Source: Chambers and Partners Guide to the Legal Profession 2001-2002

TRUSTS & PERSONAL TAX • Wales

1 Edwards Geldard Cardiff
2 Hugh James Ford Simey Cardiff
3 Margraves Llandrindod Wells

TRUSTS & PERSONAL TAX • North West

1 Brabners Liverpool
　Halliwell Landau Manchester
2 Addleshaw Booth & Co Manchester
　Birch Cullimore Chester
　Cuff Roberts Liverpool
3 Cobbetts Manchester
　Davies Wallis Foyster Liverpool
　Pannone & Partners Manchester

TRUSTS & PERSONAL TAX • North East

1 Dickinson Dees Newcastle upon Tyne
　Wrigleys Leeds
2 Addleshaw Booth & Co Leeds
　Pinsent Curtis Biddle Leeds
3 Andrew M Jackson & Co Hull
　Brooke North Leeds
　Grays York
　Irwin Mitchell Sheffield
　Lupton Fawcett Leeds
　Rollits Hull
　Ward Hadaway Newcastle upon Tyne
4 Gordons Cranswick Solicitors Bradford, Leeds
　Walker Morris Leeds

SPECIALIST PRACTICE AREAS — PRIVATE CLIENT

projects

project finance: The structuring, financing, construction and operation of infrastructure developments such as roads, power stations, bridges and telecommunications networks – is now considered a 'sexy' area for many of the UK's leading law firms. Several of these now have stand-alone project groups. Certainly, the high profile, international nature of the work attracts many of the most talented lawyers in the UK and overseas. Projects are located throughout the world and projects lawyers hail from every major jurisdiction. However, the major projects are dominated by a few City firms and the largest US practices.

PFI/PPP: In the UK, the Private Finance Initiative (PFI), a part of the Public Private Partnerships (PPP) introduced under the Conservative Government and relaunched by Labour, has provided an important source of work. The objective of PFI is to introduce private funding and management into areas which were previously the domain of government, such as the building and operation of roads and hospitals. Through PFI, many smaller London firms and regional practices have become involved in projects work for the first time. That said, it is the City firms who are at the forefront of a current trend towards exporting the principle of PFI to governments abroad.

energy: Some energy projects fall within the heading 'Project Finance' – e.g. the development of the Manah power plant in Oman – but 'energy' is a much wider field. Examples of general energy work include **CMS Cameron McKenna** advising several Indian states on the restructuring and privatisation of their electricity boards and **Lovells** conducting specialist international joint venture work on production-sharing contracts to secure exploration rights in North Africa and Russia.

construction: The physical building of infrastructure projects is only a small, if vital, part of project finance. Similarly, for most construction departments, project finance developments are only one of several sources of work. There are two aspects to construction work: developing the contractual arrangements prior to building work starting (negotiating the contracts between the employer, the contractor, sub-contractors, architects, engineers, surveyors, interior designers, etc.) and litigating when it all goes horribly wrong. Most construction practices do both contentious and non-contentious work.

type of work

Projects vary from telecoms links in Tanzania, oil pipelines in the Caucasus and Sahel, power projects in China and India, port developments in Yemen and Oman, toll roads in Israel and gold mines in Indonesia, to PFI hospital projects in Greenwich and sewage plants in Birmingham. The exact nature of the work depends on the type, size and location of the project. However, almost all the major infrastructure projects in which regional firms are involved will be PFI projects of one sort or another. In addition to PFI and PPP other common acronyms include BOO (build, own and operate), BOOT (build, own, operate, transfer) and DBFO (design, build, finance, operate) to name but a few.

Projects work also varies depending on the type of client a firm is acting for. There are a number of parties in a project finance development. There is the project company – usually a special purpose company established to build, own and operate (hence BOO) the power station or whatever the project is. Often the project company is a joint venture between a number of project sponsors who contribute equity to part-fund the project. Project sponsors could include the manufacturer of the gas turbines to be installed in the power station, the construction company that will erect the plant, and the power company that will buy the electricity produced. The company could also be partially owned by a government body or banks.

The project promoter is the organisation that commissions the project. It could be an NHS Trust that wants a new hospital built, or a host government which thinks a privately financed motorway would be a great idea. Funders provide the finance to build the project. Funders include banks, guarantors, export credit agencies, governments, and international funding agencies and they operate in consortiums and individually. Other categories of client are the contractors, operators, and so on. Each party requires its own legal representation.

A common feature of most major projects is the tender process. A public authority or major corporation (the procurer) will invite interested parties (bidders) to tender on the design, building, financing and operation (i.e. DBFO) of a project. At the end of this tender process – which can last up to two years – the winning company or consortium will be selected to manage the project. This company will then have to secure the finance, obtain the necessary planning permission and agree construction, service and employment contracts. Lawyers advising on any of these contracts must understand the big picture. They have to see how changing one contractual term will have a knock-on effect throughout the entire transaction.

Charles Robson, a partner in **Lovells**' projects department, acted for the banks in one of the PFI's flagship hospital projects, the £300m Norfolk and Norwich. "*A commercial deal was struck between the project company and the NHS Trust. In the deal, the Trust promised to pay for the delivery of a new building and the services within it.*" says Robson. "*There were two main parts to our role. We assessed how the principal parties had apportioned the risk in the project, and advised the bank on any amendments to their documents.*" This function can sometimes include a renegotiation of the deal. The firm's other primary role was drafting the credit agreement between the project company and the banks, and the security documentation that supports it.

International transactions are generally larger, more complex and can appear more glamorous. Jeremy Gewirtz of **Linklaters** recently advised the project sponsors financing an LNG tanker to transport gas from Muscat to the Dhabol power station in Maharashtra, India. Though the tanker financing was stand alone, it was also intimately linked to the complex and high profile Dhabol Power Project. The most complex issue involved the co-ordination of arrangements between the lenders to the tanker project and the lenders to Dhabol.

skills needed

...be prepared to travel overseas several times a year or even live abroad for a time...all-round commercial awareness...patience...resilience...tact and diplomacy...strong client skills...broad general legal knowledge...

career options

Lawyers used to specialise in major projects after gaining several years' experience in a relevant discipline. Whilst a lot of people continue to enter projects work via this route, many take a more direct approach. It is now possible to specialise in projects work on qualification.

Nearly all international projects are governed (to varying degrees) by English law or New York law, so experience in this field is internationally marketable. American law firms in particular are recruiting experienced English lawyers, which has forced up salaries to make international projects work one of the highest paid specialisms in the legal world

LEADING FIRMS

CONSTRUCTION • London

1 Masons
2 CMS Cameron McKenna
Rowe & Maw
Shadbolt & Co
3 Berwin Leighton Paisner
Fenwick Elliott
Herbert Smith
Linklaters
4 Clifford Chance
Freshfields Bruckhaus Deringer
Lovells
Nicholson Graham & Jones
Norton Rose
Taylor Joynson Garrett
5 Allen & Overy
Ashurst Morris Crisp
Denton Wilde Sapte
Hammond Suddards Edge
Simmons & Simmons
Trowers & Hamlins
Winward Fearon
6 Baker & McKenzie
Beale and Company
Berrymans Lace Mawer
Campbell Hooper
Corbett & Co
Davies Arnold Cooper
Glovers
Kennedys
Macfarlanes
SJ Berwin
Wedlake Bell

CONSTRUCTION • The South

1 Shadbolt & Co Reigate
2 Cripps Harries Hall Tunbridge Wells
3 Blake Lapthorn Portsmouth

CONSTRUCTION • Thames Valley

1 Clarks Reading
Linnells Oxford
Morgan Cole Oxford

CONSTRUCTION • South West

1 Masons Bristol
2 Bevan Ashford Bristol, Exeter
3 Beachcroft Wansbroughs Bristol
Laytons Bristol
4 Burges Salmon Bristol
Osborne Clarke Bristol
5 Bond Pearce Plymouth
Veale Wasbrough Bristol

CONSTRUCTION • Wales

1 Morgan Cole Cardiff, Swansea
2 Eversheds Cardiff
Hugh James Ford Simey Cardiff

Within each band, firms are listed alphabetically.
Source: Chambers and Partners Guide to the Legal Profession 2001-2002

LEADING FIRMS continued

CONSTRUCTION • Midlands

1 Wragge & Co Birmingham
2 Hammond Suddards Edge Birmingham
3 Gateley Wareing Birmingham
4 Freethcartwright Nottingham
5 DLA Birmingham
  Eversheds Birmingham, Derby, Nottingham
  Lee Crowder Birmingham
  Merricks Birmingham
  Pinsent Curtis Biddle Birmingham
6 Browne Jacobson Nottingham
  Garretts Birmingham
  Shoosmiths Northampton

CONSTRUCTION • East Anglia

1 Mills & Reeve Cambridge
2 Eversheds Ipswich, Norwich
  Hewitson Becke + Shaw Cambridge
3 Greenwoods Peterborough

Within each band, firms are listed alphabetically.
Source: Chambers and Partners Guide to the Legal Profession 2001-2002

CONSTRUCTION • North West

1 Masons Manchester
2 Hammond Suddards Edge Manchester
3 Kirk Jackson Manchester
4 Addleshaw Booth & Co Manchester
  DLA Liverpool, Manchester
  Halliwell Landau Manchester
  Hill Dickinson Liverpool
5 Elliotts Manchester
  Pannone & Partners Manchester

CONSTRUCTION • Yorkshire

1 Addleshaw Booth & Co Leeds
  Hammond Suddards Edge Leeds
2 Masons Leeds
3 Walker Morris Leeds
4 DLA Leeds, Sheffield
  Nabarro Nathanson Sheffield
  Pinsent Curtis Biddle Leeds
5 Eversheds Leeds
  Irwin Mitchell Leeds

CONSTRUCTION • North East

1 Dickinson Dees Newcastle upon Tyne
  Eversheds Newcastle upon Tyne
2 Watson Burton Newcastle upon Tyne

LEADING FIRMS continued

ENERGY & NATURAL RESOURCES • London

1 Denton Wilde Sapte
Herbert Smith
2 CMS Cameron McKenna
3 Allen & Overy
Clifford Chance
Freshfields Bruckhaus Deringer
Linklaters
Norton Rose
4 Ashurst Morris Crisp
Lovells
Slaughter and May
Vinson & Elkins LLP
5 Lawrence Graham
Nabarro Nathanson
Simmons & Simmons
6 Baker & McKenzie
Baker Botts
Beachcroft Wansbroughs
Clyde & Co
Coudert Brothers
Field Fisher Waterhouse
Ince & Co
Masons
Morgan Cole
Shearman & Sterling
Watson, Farley & Williams

ENERGY & NATURAL RESOURCES • The South

1 Bond Pearce Plymouth
Veale Wasbrough Bristol

ENERGY & NATURAL RESOURCES • Midlands

1 Martineau Johnson Birmingham
Wragge & Co Birmingham
2 Eversheds Birmingham
Kent Jones and Done Stoke-on-Trent
Knight & Sons Newcastle-under-Lyme
3 Edwards Geldard Derby
Hammond Suddards Edge Birmingham

ENERGY & NATURAL RESOURCES • The North

1 Nabarro Nathanson Sheffield
2 Dickinson Dees Newcastle upon Tyne
Wake Dyne Lawton Chester
Wrigleys Leeds
3 Addleshaw Booth & Co Leeds
Pinsent Curtis Biddle Leeds

Within each band, firms are listed alphabetically.
Source: Chambers and Partners Guide to the Legal Profession 2001-2002

LEADING FIRMS *continued*

PROJECT FINANCE • London

1. Allen & Overy
2. Linklaters
3. Clifford Chance
   Norton Rose
4. Denton Wilde Sapte
   Freshfields Bruckhaus Deringer
   Milbank, Tweed, Hadley & McCloy
   Shearman & Sterling
5. Baker & McKenzie
   CMS Cameron McKenna
   Slaughter and May
   White & Case
6. Ashurst Morris Crisp
   Herbert Smith
   Lovells
   Masons
   Simmons & Simmons

PROJECTS/PFI • The South & Wales

1. Bevan Ashford Bristol
2. Burges Salmon Bristol
   Eversheds Cardiff
3. Morgan Cole Cardiff
4. Masons Bristol

PROJECTS/PFI • Midlands & East Anglia

1. Eversheds Nottingham
   Pinsent Curtis Biddle Birmingham
2. DLA Birmingham
   Mills & Reeve Cambridge
   Wragge & Co Birmingham

PROJECTS/PFI • London

1. Allen & Overy
   Clifford Chance
   Linklaters
2. Freshfields Bruckhaus Deringer
3. Ashurst Morris Crisp
   CMS Cameron McKenna
   Denton Wilde Sapte
   Herbert Smith
4. Lovells
   Masons
   Norton Rose
5. DLA
   Simmons & Simmons
   Slaughter and May
   Theodore Goddard
6. Berwin Leighton Paisner
   Bird & Bird
   Rowe & Maw
   Trowers & Hamlins

PROJECTS/PFI • The North

1. Addleshaw Booth & Co Leeds, Manchester
   Pinsent Curtis Biddle Leeds
2. Eversheds Leeds, Manchester
3. Dickinson Dees Newcastle upon Tyne
   DLA Leeds, Manchester
   Nabarro Nathanson Sheffield
4. Masons Leeds, Manchester

Within each band, firms are listed alphabetically.
Source: Chambers and Partners Guide to the Legal Profession 2001-2002

property

A property lawyer's tools are land law and contract law. Most work involves a blend of the two. The acquisition and disposal of land and the creation and termination of relationships between investors, land owners and land users are, in the main, contractual issues. Add to this a body of common law and a swathe of statutes and you have the nuts and bolts of property law. Overlaying all of this is the property market, the most significant ingredient of all.

Clients vary widely in terms of their level of involvement with the property market. At one end of the scale is the residential conveyancing client who may only be involved in one property transaction in his whole life. At the other is the large institution whose representative is a property professional himself. In between are the users and owners of property. Each client requires a different style of service. The one-off user may need plenty of hand-holding, whilst the professional may simply need action without detailed explanation.

The firm you choose will determine what type of client base you'll be working with and increasingly the type of transaction you'll encounter.

In very recent years commercial property work has undergone a sea change. There has been a divergence of work, with the largest firms moving away from routine lease drafting and more conventional property work in favour of complex property deals that are more like corporate transactions. Increasingly, clients look to smaller London firms and the regions for traditional property services. While the bigger City firms handle the larger and more complicated deals. These newer corporate-style deals involve investment in property through joint ventures, limited partnerships and investment trusts. Additionally, there are large scale outsourcing deals and the property aspects of projects and PFI transactions. The City firms also specialise in complex property finance. The property lawyers in these firms are becoming more like corporate lawyers whose deals just happen to have a property asset base. There's a tendency for property lawyers to call themselves Real Estate lawyers these days. Don't be confused, it's just a name change.

The work of even the humblest property solicitor leans against other disciplines - company law, finance, revenue law and trusts to name but four. You may encounter areas such as liquor licensing, health and safety, telecommunications, environmental law, agricultural law, insolvency, project finance and planning. You will come to learn about the role of surveyors and property agents. You will interact with the Inland Revenue, local authorities, the Land Registry, Companies House, property agents, building surveyors, architects, banks and mortgage lenders, brokers, designers...and the list goes on. Think about how much real estate there is in this country and how many different relationships there are between owners, users, investors, sellers and buyers. You will see how much property work there is and how varied it is.

type of work

Property work is fundamentally transaction driven and requires a huge amount of documentation to be considered and amended. In an average day you'll spend a considerable amount of time in negotiations either on the phone or in meetings with clients, other lawyers and property professionals in related areas.

An example of a standard piece of old-style commercial property work would be the business lease. Typically you might receive instructions for a new lease from a client who has negotiated the basics with the help of a commercial agent. The main structure of the deal will be established but many points require further negotiation. A fifteen-year lease of one floor in an office block, for example, could involve a provision for one party to bring the lease to an end after a certain number of years. It could involve the right for the tenant to sub-let or transfer the lease to a third party. It could involve a major refit of the premises or a period, which is rent-free. During the lease period major issues between the parties include the review of rent at set times and the level of annual service charge payments to cover the costs of maintenance and services to the building. All of these issues must be dealt with before the lease is signed and the parties commit to the long-term relationship.

Clients always want certainty from you; it's your job to give them the nearest possible thing to that. They expect you, the experienced professional, to anticipate what might go wrong and to protect them ahead of time. Whilst a property lawyer generally works on a deal in which both sides have the same goal, the trick is to get the very best deal for your client and to get it done within the time scale that the client sets for you.

Victoria Sutcliffe is an assistant solicitor at Lovells. Property took her by surprise - as it does for a good majority of those who end up making a career of it. She liked the fact that from her first day as a trainee, she felt she was productive, in control and running her own files. "From day one the phone was ringing. As I walked in the door a client rang to say they were ready to complete and from then on the telephone didn't stop ringing. The clients don't stop asking lots of questions so you build up a very good relationship with them. More than in almost any other department you are responsible for your own destiny at a very junior level. There is an end product, which you can see. You can drive through any city centre and say I bought that, I sold that, I leased that."

skills needed

.....verbal and written negotiating skills.....attention to detail.....ability to think through a potential problem and give clear advice to clients.....pro-active time and case management.....ability to communicate well and forge professional relationships.....knowledge of wide scope of client businesses.

career options

Just as the fortunes of the property market have been cyclical, the fortunes of property lawyers rise and fall accordingly. A decade ago, the market dealt a serious blow to this part of the legal profession and it is only in more recent years that there has been a strong demand for property lawyers. For those qualifying into and gaining experience in commercial property work during the leaner years, the present up turn in the market has put them in a strong position and the salaries commanded have begun to match those in other core commercial areas. Those watching the legal profession have noticed that in the last couple of years, property lawyers have become a sought after commodity and all sorts of firms who may previously have paid little attention to their property departments have placed renewed emphasis on them. No longer just a support department to more glamorous and bigger-billing departments, property lawyers can hold their heads up high.

After a while in private practice, or perhaps as a result of other commitments, some lawyers look for change. In-house jobs in industry and commerce are popular. Such positions offer the chance to work for a single 'client' on essentially the same types of transactions as contemporaries in private practice.

The Land Registry or the Law Commission provide career options for those with a more academic bent and, increasingly, know-how lawyers play a prominent role in the education and on-going training of property lawyers in larger practices. In addition to keeping their teams up to speed on developments in the law the know-how specialist would be responsible for periodically updating the firm's standard documentation and producing news updates for clients.

LEADING FIRMS

PROPERTY (COMMERCIAL): FEWER THAN 25 SOLICITORS • London

1
- Boodle Hatfield
- Maxwell Batley

2
- Manches
- Speechly Bircham
- Travers Smith Braithwaite

3
- Finers Stephens Innocent
- Julian Holy
- Mishcon de Reya
- Nicholson Graham & Jones
- Stepien Lake Gilbert & Paling
- Trowers & Hamlins

4
- Coudert Brothers
- Fladgate Fielder
- Hamlins
- Osborne Clarke
- Park Nelson

PROPERTY (COMMERCIAL): 25-49 SOLICITORS • London

1
- SJ Berwin

2
- Dechert
- Denton Wilde Sapte

3
- DJ Freeman
- Macfarlanes
- Norton Rose

4
- Forsters
- Olswang
- Slaughter and May

5
- Field Fisher Waterhouse
- Gouldens

6
- Eversheds
- Richards Butler
- Rowe & Maw
- Simmons & Simmons

PROPERTY (COMMERCIAL): 50+ SOLICITORS • London

1
- Linklaters

2
- Clifford Chance

3
- Berwin Leighton Paisner
- Herbert Smith
- Lovells

4
- Freshfields Bruckhaus Deringer
- Nabarro Nathanson

5
- Ashurst Morris Crisp
- CMS Cameron McKenna

6
- Allen & Overy
- Lawrence Graham

PROPERTY (COMMERCIAL) • Wales

1
- Eversheds Cardiff

2
- Berry Smith Cardiff

3
- Edwards Geldard Cardiff
- Morgan Cole Cardiff, Swansea
- Palser Grossman Cardiff Bay, Swansea
- Robertsons Cardiff

4
- Hugh James Ford Simey Cardiff

Within each band, firms are listed alphabetically.
Source: Chambers and Partners Guide to the Legal Profession 2001-2002

SPECIALIST PRACTICE AREAS PROPERTY

LEADING FIRMS continued

PROPERTY (COMMERCIAL) • The South

1 **Blake Lapthorn** Fareham, Portsmouth, Southampton

2 **Bond Pearce** Southampton
Paris Smith & Randall Southampton
Stevens & Bolton Guildford

3 **Clyde & Co** Guildford
Cripps Harries Hall Tunbridge Wells
Thomson Snell & Passmore Tunbridge Wells

4 **DMH** Brighton, Crawley
Laytons Guildford
Lester Aldridge Bournemouth
Penningtons Basingstoke, Godalming, Newbury
Steele Raymond Bournemouth
Thomas Eggar Church Adams Chichester, Horsham, Reigate, Worthing

5 **Brachers** Maidstone
Coffin Mew & Clover Portsmouth
GCL Solicitors Guildford
Moore & Blatch Southampton
Rawlison Butler Crawley
Sherwin Oliver Solicitors Portsmouth
Shoosmiths Fareham

PROPERTY (COMMERCIAL) • Thames Valley

1 **Denton Wilde Sapte** Milton Keynes
Pitmans Reading

2 **BrookStreet Des Roches** Witney
Morgan Cole Oxford, Reading

3 **Clarks** Reading
Harold Benjamin Littlejohn Harrow
Linnells Oxford

4 **Iliffes Booth Bennett** Uxbridge
Matthew Arnold & Baldwin Watford

5 **BP Collins** Beaconsfield, Gerrards Cross
Boyes Turner Reading
Fennemores Milton Keynes
Manches Oxford
Nabarro Nathanson Reading
Pictons St Albans

Within each band, firms are listed alphabetically.
Source: Chambers and Partners Guide to the Legal Profession 2001-2002

LEADING FIRMS continued

PROPERTY (COMMERCIAL) • South West

1 Burges Salmon Bristol
Osborne Clarke Bristol
2 Beachcroft Wansbroughs Bristol
Bevan Ashford Bristol, Exeter, Plymouth, Taunton
Bond Pearce Bristol, Exeter, Plymouth
Michelmores Exeter
3 Clarke Willmott & Clarke Bristol, Taunton
TLT Solicitors Bristol
Veale Wasbrough Bristol
4 Davies and Partners Gloucester
Foot Anstey Sargent Plymouth
Lyons Davidson Bristol
Rickerby Watterson Cheltenham
Stephens & Scown Exeter, Liskeard, St Austell, Truro
5 Bretherton Price Elgoods Cheltenham
Davitt Jones Bould Taunton
Thring Townsend Swindon

Within each band, firms are listed alphabetically.
Source: Chambers and Partners Guide to the Legal Profession 2001-2002

PROPERTY (COMMERCIAL) • Midlands

1 Eversheds Birmingham, Nottingham
Wragge & Co Birmingham
2 Hammond Suddards Edge Birmingham
Pinsent Curtis Biddle Birmingham
3 DLA Birmingham
Freethcartwright Leicester, Nottingham
Lee Crowder Birmingham
4 Knight & Sons Newcastle-under-Lyme
Martineau Johnson Birmingham
Shoosmiths Northampton, Nottingham
5 Browne Jacobson Nottingham
Harvey Ingram Owston Leicester
Wright Hassall Leamington Spa
6 Edwards Geldard Nottingham
Higgs & Sons Brierley Hill

PROPERTY (COMMERCIAL) • East Anglia

1 Eversheds Cambridge, Ipswich, Norwich
Hewitson Becke + Shaw Cambridge
Mills & Reeve Cambridge, Norwich
2 Ashton Graham Bury St Edmunds, Ipswich
Birketts Ipswich
Prettys Ipswich
Taylor Vinters Cambridge
Wollastons Chelmsford
3 Ellison & Co Colchester
Few & Kester Cambridge
Greene & Greene Bury St Edmunds
Greenwoods Peterborough

SPECIALIST PRACTICE AREAS
PROPERTY

LEADING FIRMS *continued*

PROPERTY (COMMERCIAL) • North West

1 **Addleshaw Booth & Co** Manchester
Bullivant Jones Liverpool
Cobbetts Manchester
DLA Liverpool, Manchester
Eversheds Manchester
Halliwell Landau Manchester

2 **Field Cunningham & Co** Manchester
Hammond Suddards Edge Manchester

3 **Beachcroft Wansbroughs** Manchester
Davies Wallis Foyster Liverpool
Mace & Jones Liverpool, Manchester
Pannone & Partners Manchester

4 **Brabners** Liverpool, Preston
Jones Maidment Wilson Altrincham, Manchester

5 **Chaffe Street** Manchester
Cuff Roberts Liverpool
Gorna & Co Manchester
Kuit Steinart Levy Manchester
Wacks Caller Manchester

6 **Aaron & Partners** Chester
Hill Dickinson Chester, Liverpool
Walker Smith & Way Chester
Weightmans Liverpool, Manchester

PROPERTY (COMMERCIAL) • Yorkshire

1 **Addleshaw Booth & Co** Leeds
2 **Walker Morris** Leeds
3 **DLA** Leeds, Sheffield
Eversheds Leeds
Hammond Suddards Edge Leeds
Pinsent Curtis Biddle Leeds
Read Hind Stewart Leeds

4 **Andrew M Jackson & Co** Hull
Gordons Cranswick Solicitors Bradford, Leeds
Irwin Mitchell Sheffield
Nabarro Nathanson Sheffield

5 **Denison Till** York
Gosschalks Hull
The Frith Partnership Leeds

6 **Keeble Hawson** Sheffield
Rollits Hull
Wake Smith Sheffield

Within each band, firms are listed alphabetically.
Source: Chambers and Partners Guide to the Legal Profession 2001-2002

public interest law

Public interest law concerns the relationship between state and citizen. Whilst each area of law grouped under this heading is a separate subject in its own right, requiring particular skills and personal qualities, all areas concern the activities of public bodies, and in particular whether their actions are lawful. Challenging their decisions by way of judicial review is an important thread in civil liberties, immigration and education work. Lawyers involved in local government law see the other side of the coin. They advise public authorities on their powers and how to defend their decisions.

Each of these areas has been heavily affected by the implementation of the Human Rights Act, which enshrines the European Convention on Human Rights in British law. This came into effect in October 2000. All legislation and court judgments will have to be read in the light of provisions of the Act. It means interesting and busy times ahead for lawyers in these fields.

type of work

human rights/civil liberties: Civil liberties is a broad concept covering suspected miscarriages of justice, actions against the police, prisoners' rights, public order, discrimination and free speech issues. Redress will often be sought by judicial review, and there is considerable cross-over between civil liberties and areas such as crime and immigration.

As all these areas are covered under provisions of the Human Rights Act, the volume of judicial review is likely to increase at an alarming pace over the next few years. Lawyers and campaign groups practising in this field have attempted to train fellow lawyers and professionals in the implications of the Act for other areas of law, including commercial disciplines.

At **Bindman & Partners**, Stephen Grosz's work is characterised by its variety. A morning's work might include studying a European directive on freedom of access to information on the environment, advising a client on a school closure, meeting a student who failed exams because of insufficient provision for dyslexia, and considering new instructions from a homosexual naval officer.

An imaginative legal mind, an ability to adapt to different areas of law and an interest in using the law creatively and strategically are all important qualities in a civil liberties lawyer, according to Stephen Grosz. *"You need to try and push back the boundaries, and if you're working with campaigning organisations, as you frequently are, you have to understand their needs and priorities."* Grosz also looks for a sympathetic and understanding nature and a broad world view, as opposed to a narrow legalistic outlook.

career options

Places at the few firms which do civil liberties work and offer training are incredibly competitive. Such firms often prefer older trainees who have worked in relevant fields to students fresh from university. It is vital, then, to get involved in voluntary or campaign work at an early stage if you wish to train in this area.

There are a number of organisations which are particularly known for their campaigning work in civil liberties and human rights, such as Amnesty International and Justice. All can be joined, for a fee and amongst other benefits will send you newsletters with up to date information about their campaigns and recent changes in the law. For hands-on experience, it is best to contact your local law centre or relevant voluntary organisations.

A career as a civil liberties lawyer may be interesting but is unlikely to be lucrative. Law Centres, campaigning groups and voluntary organisations offer alternatives to private practice.

type of work

immigration: There are two types of immigration work: personal and business. Personal immigration clients are private individuals seeking advice. Work includes political asylum cases, nationality issues, marriage applications and family reunion cases. Much of this is public funded and is carried out by small firms. In business immigration, clients are often employers seeking advice on behalf of employees or, more usually, future employees. Work includes advising national and multinational corporations on work permits and investor applications and advising employers on avoiding breaches of the immigration acts. Large and medium-sized commercial firms undertake this work.

a day in the life....

A typical day, says Peter Alfandary, head of Corporate Immigration at **Reed Smith Warner Cranston**, might involve advising the English arm of a foreign company wanting to bring staff from New York to work in the UK, drafting an application for a work permit on behalf of a multi national client, advising a foreign investor on setting up a business in the UK, advising a human resources department on whether a potential employee has a legal right to work in the UK and telephoning the British Embassy in Beijing to sort out entry clearance for the wife of a Chinese executive.

A typical day for personal immigration expert Wesley Gryk could involve encounters with a whole range of clients. He may spend the morning with a lesbian couple advising them on same sex immigration issues, followed by an emergency meeting with a foreign wife abandoned by her husband. The afternoon could involve simple work permit advice, then more complicated advice to someone who has virtually no legal right to be in the country and has been 'underground' for twenty years. A junior lawyer's day may be just as varied – they may start the morning filing, but then be sent off on their own for a five hour interview at Gatwick airport or the Home Office, in sole charge of looking after the interests of an asylum seeker.

skills needed

....communication...tact, diplomacy and patience...good drafting and advocacy skills...an interest in current affairs and politics...liberalism (for personal immigration)...scepticism...presentation skills...a team player....

career options

Personal immigration does not offer the financial rewards enjoyed by those in more commercial disciplines, or those specialising in business immigration. But would-be personal immigration specialists are unlikely to be motivated by financial gain. Alternatives to private practice include working for a Law Centre or bodies such as the UN or Joint Council for the Welfare of Immigrants (JCWI). Leading immigration lawyer Alison Stanley, for example, was articled to **Winstanley-Burgess**, then spent several years as the solicitor to the JWCI before returning to private practice with **Bindman & Partners**. It is also possible to come to this type of work from a more commercial background. Wesley Gryk began his career as a corporate lawyer with large US firm Shearman & Sterling.

type of work

local government: Most firms with a dedicated public sector or local authority department will act on behalf of the authorities in a defensive or preemptive capacity attempting to stave off potential judicial review or advising on the liabilities of proposed new methods of service delivery. Other firms will represent the claimant(s) actively seeking to challenge the decisions of the local authority.

Although local authorities have their own in-house legal teams, they will frequently outsource work to private practice on a whole range of matters from development and urban regeneration projects, planning appeals, local government finance and vires (powers) to housing stock transfers and the implementation of "best value" techniques.

Niche specialists **Leonie Cowen & Associates**, for example, have been advising The London Borough of Tower Hamlets on the legal structuring of a charitable trust regarding the £20m-£30m multi-purpose Mile End Park millennium project. **Rowe & Maw**, acted for the Westminster City Council Auditor in the 'homes for votes' case. They also act for local authorities concerning PFI, social services and human rights advice. **Sharpe Pritchard** act for a whole raft of councils defending them against judicial challenges to their policies on childcare, education, and health.

a day in the life of ....

A typical day for Tony Curnow, head of the Public Sector Group at **Ashurst Morris Crisp**, might include drafting heads of terms for a local authority regeneration project, meeting with clients to discuss a housing transfer agreement, reviewing a compulsory purchase order case and chasing the Department of Transport, Local Government and Regions for the issue of a draft road closure order.

skills needed

....ability to get on with people at all levels...flexibility...political awareness...understanding of the relationship between central and local government...head for statutory interpretation...ability to master a complex regulatory regime...self-motivation...common sense approach....

career options

The obvious starting point for someone wishing to specialise in local government law is to apply for a training contract with a local authority legal department. You then have the option to stay at the authority or move into private practice. *"Somebody who'd done their training in a local authority, stayed on for a year or so, and then applied to us would be an attractive package."* Says Tony Curnow *"they might be more attractive than someone who'd been solely in the private sector, but it depends on the individual."*

On the other hand, firms like **Nabarro Nathanson**, **Eversheds** or **Ashurst Morris Crisp** may be able to offer broader commercial experience during training, as well as good quality local government work. A wider range of options may then remain open on qualification. You could continue in commercial private practice, transfer into more general public law work or move into a local authority.

Salaries are generally higher in private practice, but hours are often longer to match. The good news about local authorities is that pay and conditions are perceived to be improving.

type of work

education: There are two kinds of client in education work: institutions and individuals. Commercial firms tend to act for institutions including universities, schools, colleges and funding organisations. Smaller, niche firms act for individuals, including pupils and their parents, university students and children with special needs.

Advice to institutional clients covers more than just education law. **Eversheds**, for example, advises universities and colleges on employment law, industrial relations, constitutional issues, funding matters, student relations and discipline. At **Beachcroft Wansbroughs**, Julian Gizzi was involved in the Dearing Committee inquiry into the running of Higher Education and is also involved in funding and franchising issues.

David Ruebain, meanwhile, at **David Levene & Co**, might spend his morning with the parents of a disabled child trying to sort out funding for transport to school. His afternoon could be spent on the telephone arguing against an examining board on behalf of a 'special needs' pupil. Jack Rabinowicz at **Teacher Stern Selby** may have to deal with the parents of a child bully one day and the parents of a child who has been bullied the next.

SPECIALIST PRACTICE AREAS PUBLIC INTEREST LAW

skills needed

institutions:...commercial outlook...aptitude for statutory interpretation...the self-confidence to stick your neck out and take a view....

individuals:...a rights-based perspective..."you've got to decide that earning as much money as possible is not your priority"...a head for statute and case law...a feel for the way public policy is developing....

career options

There are a number of opportunities to practice education law outside private practice. Joining a local authority legal department is one obvious option – a significant part of local authority legal work involves educational institutions. There are also posts within the Department for Education, and some universities now have their own legal units.

LEADING FIRMS

HUMAN RIGHTS • London

1. Bindman & Partners
2. Bhatt Murphy
3. Christian Fisher
   Deighton Guedalla
4. Birnberg Peirce & Partners
   Hickman & Rose
5. Simons Muirhead & Burton
   Winstanley-Burgess
6. Irwin Mitchell
   Taylor Nichol
   Thanki Novy Taube

HUMAN RIGHTS • Midlands

1. Tyndallwoods Birmingham
2. McGrath & Co Birmingham

Within each band, firms are listed alphabetically.
Source: Chambers and Partners Guide to the Legal Profession 2001-2002

HUMAN RIGHTS • The North

1. AS Law Liverpool
   Harrison Bundey & Co Leeds
   Howells Sheffield
2. David Gray Solicitors Newcastle upon Tyne
   Irwin Mitchell Sheffield
   Robert Lizar Manchester

EDUCATION• London

1. Eversheds
2. Beachcroft Wansbroughs
3. Lee Bolton & Lee
   Winckworth Sherwood
4. Lawfords
   Reynolds Porter Chamberlain
5. Farrer & Co

EDUCATION • The South

1. Bond Pearce Southampton
   DMH Brighton
   Steele Raymond Bournemouth
   Thomas Eggar Church Adams Chichester

LEADING FIRMS continued

EDUCATION • Thames Valley

1. **Manches** Oxford
   Morgan Cole Oxford
   Winckworth Sherwood Oxford

EDUCATION • South West

1. **Veale Wasbrough** Bristol
2. **Stone King** Bath
3. **Michelmores** Exeter
   Rickerby Watterson Cheltenham
4. **Tozers** Exeter
5. **Bevan Ashford** Bristol
   Bond Pearce Plymouth
   Osborne Clarke

EDUCATION • Wales

1. **Eversheds** Cardiff
2. **Morgan Cole** Cardiff

EDUCATION • Midlands

1. **Martineau Johnson** Birmingham
2. **Eversheds** Derby, Nottingham
3. **Shakespeares** Birmingham
   Wragge & Co Birmingham

EDUCATION • East Anglia

1. **Mills & Reeve** Cambridge, Norwich
2. **Eversheds** Ipswich, Norwich
3. **Birkett Long** Colchester
   Wollastons Chelmsford

EDUCATION • The North

1. **Eversheds** Leeds, Manchester, Newcastle upon Tyne
2. **Addleshaw Booth & Co** Manchester
   Pinsent Curtis Biddle Leeds

IMMIGRATION:
• The South, Thames Valley & South West

1. **Bobbetts Mackan** Bristol
   Darbys Oxford
   Eric Robinson & Co Southampton

IMMIGRATION • Midlands

1. **Tyndallwoods** Birmingham
2. **Nelsons** Nottingham

IMMIGRATION • East Anglia

1. **Gross & Co.** Bury St Edmunds
   Leathes Prior Norwich
   Wollastons Chelmsford

Within each band, firms are listed alphabetically.
Source: Chambers and Partners Guide to the Legal Profession 2001-2002

SPECIALIST PRACTICE AREAS — PUBLIC INTEREST LAW

SPECIALIST PRACTICE AREAS — PUBLIC INTEREST LAW

LEADING FIRMS continued

IMMIGRATION • The North

1 David Gray Solicitors Newcastle upon Tyne
Howells Sheffield
2 AS Law Liverpool
Harrison Bundey & Co Leeds
Jackson & Canter Liverpool
James & Co Bradford
3 Davis Blank Furniss Manchester
Samuel Phillips & Co Newcastle upon Tyne
Thornhill Ince Manchester

IMMIGRATION: BUSINESS • London

1 CMS Cameron McKenna
Kingsley Napley
2 Bates, Wells & Braithwaite
Magrath & Co
Reed Smith Warner Cranston
3 Baker & McKenzie
Eversheds
Sturtivant & Co
4 Gherson & Co
Mishcon de Reya
Norton Rose
5 DJ Webb & Co
Fox Williams
Gulbenkian Harris Andonian
Harbottle & Lewis
Pullig & Co
6 Campbell Hooper
Penningtons

IMMIGRATION: PERSONAL • London

1 Bindman & Partners
Birnberg Peirce & Partners
Deighton Guedalla
Wesley Gryk
Winstanley-Burgess
2 Coker Vis Partnership
3 Bartram & Co
Gill & Co
Glazer Delmar
Luqmani Thompson
4 Powell & Co
Wilson & Co

LOCAL GOVERNMENT • London

1 Nabarro Nathanson
2 Rowe & Maw
Sharpe Pritchard
3 Ashurst Morris Crisp
Lawrence Graham
Léonie Cowen & Associates
Trowers & Hamlins
4 Berwin Leighton Paisner
Denton Wilde Sapte
5 Clifford Chance
Herbert Smith
6 DJ Freeman
Dechert
Jenkins & Hand
Winckworth Sherwood

Within each band, firms are listed alphabetically.
Source: Chambers and Partners Guide to the Legal Profession 2001-2002

LEADING FIRMS continued

LOCAL GOVERNMENT • South West

1. **Bevan Ashford** Bristol, Exeter, Plymouth
2. **Bond Pearce** Bristol, Exeter

LOCAL GOVERNMENT • Wales

1. **Eversheds** Cardiff
2. **Edwards Geldard** Cardiff
3. **Morgan Cole** Cardiff, Swansea

LOCAL GOVERNMENT • Midlands

1. **Wragge & Co** Birmingham
2. **Pinsent Curtis Biddle** Birmingham
3. **DLA** Birmingham
   Eversheds Birmingham, Nottingham
4. **Anthony Collins Solicitors** Birmingham
   Mills & Reeve Birmingham

LOCAL GOVERNMENT • East Anglia

1. **Steele & Co** Norwich

LOCAL GOVERNMENT • The North

1. **Eversheds** Leeds
2. **Pinsent Curtis Biddle** Leeds
3. **Walker Morris** Leeds
4. **Masons** Leeds
   Pannone & Partners Manchester

Within each band, firms are listed alphabetically.
Source: Chambers and Partners Guide to the Legal Profession 2001-2002

SPECIALIST PRACTICE AREAS

PUBLIC INTEREST LAW

shipping

definition of terms

P&I Club: 'Protection and indemnity' Club: a marine insurance club run mutually by and for ship-owners.

Charter party: Commercial instrument, essentially a contract for the hire of an entire ship for the purpose of import or export of goods.

Bill of Lading: a certificate of undertaking by the master of a ship to deliver goods on payment of the named sum to a named party.

Salvage: reward payable by owners of ships and goods saved at sea by 'salvors.'

Underwriter: an individual who agrees to indemnify an assured person against losses under a policy of insurance.

MOA: Memorandum of Agreement.

Suggest shipping law as a practice area to the majority of law students and you may well be met by a glazed look and a swift exit. At best you will call to mind images of Greek shipping magnates chewing on vast Havanas and news coverage of dramatic collisions at sea. In fact shipping law is an exciting, complex and unpredictable area of practice, involving many cutting edge principles of law.

Shipping law can be defined as "the law relating to all aspects of carriage by sea and international trade." It involves both contentious and non-contentious work.

Contentious work is divided into 'Wet' and 'Dry'. The difference, in essence, is that 'Wet' (traditionally known as Admiralty) work concerns disputes arising from mishaps at sea, ie. collision, salvage, total loss etc. whilst 'Dry' (traditionally known as Marine) arises from disputes over contracts made on dry land; charterparties, bills of lading, cargo and sale of goods contracts. Non-contentious includes registration of ships and re-flagging yet mainly relates to ship finance advice, which is essentially corporate in nature.

Other niche practice areas include yachting and fishing (often regulatory advice).

type of work

Shipping lawyers have a choice of non-contentious and contentious work available to them on qualification. On the non-contentious side advice is given on shipbuilding contracts, sale and purchase agreements, ship finance, contracts of employment for crew members and contracts of affreightment etc. Contentious work includes ad hoc 'consultancy' advice on day to day matters for regular clients, arrest of ships, together with conduct of High Court and arbitration cases from the time of the initial dispute through issuing of pleadings and interlocutory proceedings to final hearing and enforcement. Clients range from owners, operators, traders and charterers to P&I Clubs, other insurers and hull underwriters.

Very few lawyers will advise on both sides and those that do are generally located in smaller overseas offices where they are often required to turn their hands to most shipping related matters. Moreover, the type of firm you train with will normally pre-determine your eventual specialism.

There are a number of specialist firms in London such as **Ince & Co**, **Holman Fenwick & Willan** and **Clyde & Co.** where you will concentrate to a large degree on contentious shipping work for the duration of your training contract. Other corporate firms such as **Norton Rose** and **Watson Farley Williams** are known predominantly for their non-contentious work (namely ship finance) yet will also offer seats in other practice areas. Gina Power, four years qualified shipping lawyer at **Lawrence Graham**, started her career at medium sized City firm Penningtons precisely because she was not entirely sure which area of law she intended to specialise in. She was immediately attracted to commercial litigation and had a chance to do a six month seat in shipping. A broad choice of seats may prove vital if a trainee decides after six months that shipping is not for them.

Clare Matthews, shipping lawyer at Sydney Based P&I Club AUS, urges prospective trainees to obtain vacation work placements prior to deciding which firms to apply to. She decided to commence her training at **Ince & Co** after taking a placement there one summer. If you are unable to obtain work experience then try to talk to lawyers at the firms. They will invariably be happy to discuss any queries you may have and will largely welcome your interest and initiative.

Trainees at the bigger London firms are occasionally offered the chance to take a seat abroad and this is definitely something you should consider. Don't despair if this is not the policy of your chosen firm or if they do not actually have any overseas offices. Gina Power, for example, speaks fluent Greek, and pestered her partners at Penningtons to be allowed to do a 3 month stint with a Greek shipping firm. It was up to her to arrange this, yet she managed to gain valuable international experience with a top firm in the port of Piraeus.

Many cultures are still male oriented when it comes to business and prefer to deal 'man to man.' Indeed, within shipping law there is still quite a high drop-out rate amongst women and most of the top shipping partners are male. Nonetheless, all lawyers interviewed agreed that this should not dissuade female applicants. Many top female shipping lawyers are now coming through the ranks and achieving partnership staus at a relatively young age. According to Gina Power, *"although some shipping clients can be difficult at first, they all show enormous respect once they realise you are as effective, hard working and persistent as your male counterparts."*

a day in the life of....

All shipping lawyers interviewed baulked at the idea of describing a typical day; nothing about this area of law is typical - 'expect the unexpected' is the catch-phrase. Due to the global nature of your client base you are acutely aware of all the different time zones that you are working to on any one day. *"Organisation is the key,"* says Gina, who admits it is sometimes difficult for shipping lawyers to juggle their day. A shipping specialist from leading firm **Ince & Co**. describes how on one occasion he received a call from a client to say that a barge had capsized in the South China Sea leaving many casualties. By 10pm that night he was on a flight to Singapore (with a team including trainees) to take statements from all surviving crew members. This may not be a run of the mill occurrence for trainees but it is not unusual for shipping lawyers at a senior level.

Many cases are high profile, attracting media interest for both their factual and legal content. Consider the shipping casualties which have hit the headlines over the last 10 years; The Marchioness, Herald of Free Enterprise, the Braer oil spillage and the Sea Empress - all have involved lawyers in various capacities. Consider too, the cases you learn in contract law - many of the leading cases are complex shipping matters.

skills needed

dry/wet: ...no place for shrinking violets ....abreast of legal developments and industry trends...extremely familiar with contract, tort and court procedure....extremely flexible in terms of hours and availability to travel...good communicators...good humour, common sense, team spirit and self motivation....

wet: ...previous knowledge of sea life.....(many wet lawyers are ex-mariners or naval officers)

career options

Those interested in shipping law should be aware that jobs outside London are relatively few and far between. Shipping work is limited to towns with ports. After London, Plymouth, Liverpool and Newcastle are most important. In the larger firms with overseas offices there are opportunities for assistants to gain experience working abroad for a few years or even permanently. All interviewees considered this to be a good career move, particularly with regard to future partnership prospects back home. According to Gina Power, you are likely to undertake greater responsibility in a smaller overseas office where you are working in the same time zone and culture as your clients. This immediacy of contact is great for personal PR and you could end up returning to London with a host of new clients which you would not have otherwise obtained. Oliver Weiss is now based in the Greek port of Piraeus after lengthy stints in his firm's London and Hong Kong offices.

If, after qualification, you decide that shipping is not for you then your skills and solid grounding as a commercial litigator should allow you to qualify into another contentious department within or outside your present firm.

If private practice does not appeal, there is of course the possibility of going in-house. Ship owners, P&I clubs, operators and marine insurers all have openings for specialist lawyers. Claire Matthews feels that her knowledge of the day to day running of the shipping industry has increased substantially since working in-house. *"The advice is more immediate and quite exciting,"* she says, *"although in the long term you are not likely to make as much money as a top London partner."* The hours and working conditions are widely perceived to be much more attractive than life in private practice. The predominance of English law in international shipping matters also makes it relatively easy for in-house shipping lawyers to return to private practice in the future.

Some shipping lawyers choose to go it alone as sole practitioners or are setting up niche firms. One such lawyer is Nicola Ellis (Plymouth) who set up on her own in 1994. Her background was in general litigation, but she 'fell into' marine work on qualification after a spell at **Clyde & Co.** in Guildford, during which she handled some cargo claims. Having gained that experience she found herself handling similar work in subsequent jobs and being encouraged to specialise by one particular yacht-building client. She now deals with mainly yachting work, representing the insured rather than the insurer in the majority of cases.

LEADING FIRMS

SHIPPING • London

1. **Holman Fenwick & Willan**
   Ince & Co
2. **Clyde & Co**
3. **Hill Taylor Dickinson**
   Richards Butler
4. **Bentleys, Stokes & Lowless**
   Clifford Chance
   Holmes Hardingham
   Jackson Parton
   More Fisher Brown
   Norton Rose
   Shaw and Croft
   Sinclair Roche & Temperley
   Stephenson Harwood
   Waltons & Morse
5. **Hill Dickinson**
   Lawrence Graham
   Watson, Farley & Williams
6. **Barlow Lyde & Gilbert**
   Curtis Davis Garrard
   Fishers
   Middleton Potts
   Thomas Cooper & Stibbard

SHIPPING • The South & South West

1. **Davies, Johnson & Co** Plymouth
   Foot Anstey Sargent Exeter, Plymouth
   Lester Aldridge Southampton
2. **Bond Pearce** Plymouth, Southampton
   DMH Brighton

SHIPPING • East Anglia

1. **Dale & Co** Felixstowe
   Eversheds Ipswich
   John Weston & Co Felixstowe
2. **Birketts** Ipswich
   Prettys Ipswich

SHIPPING • The North

1. **Andrew M Jackson & Co** Hull
   Eversheds Newcastle upon Tyne
   Mills & Co Newcastle upon Tyne
   Rayfield Mills Newcastle upon Tyne
2. **Hill Dickinson** Liverpool, Manchester
3. **DLA** Liverpool, Manchester

SHIPPING: FINANCE • London

1. **Norton Rose**
2. **Watson, Farley & Williams**
3. **Allen & Overy**
   Stephenson Harwood
4. **Clifford Chance**
   Sinclair Roche & Temperley
5. **Linklaters**

Within each band, firms are listed alphabetically.
Source: Chambers and Partners Guide to the Legal Profession 2001-2002

SPECIALIST PRACTICE AREAS — SHIPPING

sports law

The term 'sports law' used to be a convenient umbrella denoting an amalgam of separate legal disciplines, both contentious and non-contentious, for sporting clients. The lawyer had to apply these general legal principles within a sporting context. But all lawyers interviewed agreed that a separate body of law relating to specific sports-related issues is now developing at an ever-increasing pace.

According to Andy Korman, Head of Sponsorship at sports specialists **Townleys** (which has just merged with Hammond Suddards Edge), this is best illustrated when national law and particular sports regulations collide. He gives the example of the well known Bosman Case, in which football regulations governing the transfer of players were at odds with European employment legislation. Regulatory bodies are increasingly being taken to court for imposing rules which are at odds with the prevailing laws of the land. Parul Patel, assistant solicitor at **Clarke Willmott & Clarke**, agrees and comments that increased professionalism and the globalisation of sporting concerns will inevitably lead to increased legislation nationally and across Europe. She points to the fact that sport is now such a major global industry, as an indication of the inevitability of further specific industry regulation.

The areas of law which retain particular importance in sports-related work remain intellectual property (the protection and exploitation of rights); EU and competition law (looking at the sports industry to see whether it is restrictive of competition); media and entertainment law (covering broadcasting, sponsorship, advertising); commercial/corporate law; crime & personal injury.

type of work

The area we call 'sports law' can be divided into three main aspects:

1. The regulatory, disciplinary, criminal and personal injury advice given to individuals, teams and ruling bodies.
2. Media/sponsorship and advertising.
3. Corporate and commercial advice, e.g. the stock market listing of a football club.

In addition, students should also determine whether they envisage a career in litigation or as a non-contentious lawyer. There is increasingly a greater willingness to litigate among sporting clients.

However one defines sports law it is obvious that prospective trainees should think carefully before deciding which firms to approach. Firms fall broadly into one category or another although most handle a cross-section of sports-related work as required by their clients.

Townleys advise exclusively on sports law matters and offer trainees four sports-related seats to be chosen from the areas of broadcasting, commercial, New Media, dispute resolution, governance, IP and sponsorship. The team works on sports as varied as triathlon, squash, football, rugby and bob-sleigh and has worked on the sponsorship of the Rugby World Cup legal programme; Fulham FC's commercial and player matters; Six Nations merchandising and Formula One brand protection work.

Denton Wilde Sapte, meanwhile, has a strong media bias to their sports work, advising individuals on their intellectual property rights and sponsorship. They advised Tracy Edwards (skipper of the first all-woman crew attempting to sail round the world) on various trademark registrations, on a publishing deal and on setting up her own website. The team is also involved in regulatory and disciplinary issues and recently defended Restrictive Practices court proceedings brought by the Director General of Fair Trading regarding Premier League Rules and broadcast agreements.

Another firm known for regulatory and disciplinary work is **Farrer & Co.** Karena Vleck advised the British Athletics Federation in the long running Diane Modahl case and is a non-executive director of UK Athletics. As well as dealing with constitutional issues she has been negotiating TV rights and sponsorship, agency and event agreements.

Nicholson Graham & Jones was probably the first City firm to establish a sports department and to approach the sector from a corporate angle. Many sporting disciplines are covered by their client base, including football, rugby and cricket as well as minor sports such as greyhound racing and snow boarding. Their involvement in acquisitions of businesses, competition law, property, insolvency, sponsorship agreements, players' contracts and constitutional advice shows the breadth of the team's work.

a day in the life...

'Sporadic' is the description most used by practitioners to describe the nature of the job. A typical day for rugby specialist Parul Patel might involve a lengthy contract negotiation for a player, advising a major international name on personal injury litigation and attempting to find clubs for out-of-contract clients. All agreed that, although their chosen field was considered by most to be a 'sexy' area to work in, sports law is by no means a soft option. The day to day legal work is as exhausting (and at times mundane) as any other specialism. Nonetheless, the high profile nature of the job was viewed favourably by all sport lawyers interviewed. Andy Korman, for example, gets a "*kick*" when watching a football team whose shirt sponsorship he has negotiated. Moreover, if commenting on your cases for television, fending off reporters and watching major events from the comfort of the directors' box interests you then you are likely to enjoy the discipline.

skills needed

"It is not enough to be passionate about sport" claims Andy Korman. "You need to be able to grasp many aspects of law quickly, and to understand how they impact on each other." Particularly important is a good commercial grounding, a knowledge of contract, media and intellectual property law and an awareness of EU and competition law. He cites the example of a trainee at **Townleys** whose Masters in intellectual property law and IT law made him particularly suited to the firm's New Media department.

However it is vital to show a proven track record of interest in the area. If students are offered the chance to do a dissertation at university then they should pick a topic relevant to sport. Trainees who can relate to the sporting issues of the day and understand the inherent legal implications are precisely what Townleys are looking for.

Parul Patel, meanwhile, considered language skills important, and pointed to the increasing globalisation of sport in this respect. Her ability to speak French and Italian is proving invaluable in her negotiations with European clubs on behalf of her rugby playing clients.

Unfortunately, for the majority of people, this is an area where good contacts can easily sway job interviews. A sports department will be much more likely to look at you if you have played rugby for your country or if your father is a premiership football manager. Jonny Searle, lawyer with **Ashurst Morris Crisp** and Olympic oarsman, also suggests that clients tend to treat you with less suspicion when they know you can empathise with them as a sports player. Despite increased professionalism many sportsmen and women are still cynical about lawyers and the business of making money out of sport.

Students should not despair if they fail to get a training contract offering a sports law seat. Andy Korman, for example, trained at a well known corporate firm in the City before joining **Townleys** on qualification. Likewise, Parul Patel joined **Clarke Willmott & Clarke** as a sports lawyer after qualification from leading regional firm Eversheds.

Although Eversheds was not known for its sporting client base she harassed the partners for anything sports-related that came in, managing to build up her own portfolio of experience. *"You will only get work if you ask for it"* she says. *"Be persistent, use your initiative and be up front about your interest in sport from day one."*

skills needed

...strong personal skills...not for prima donnas...people skills as well as paper skills... vibrant team players...energy...determination to succeed ...knowledge of the business of sport...technical appreciation of key sports...

career options

In private practice, sports specialists move into this area both by accident and design. Sports lovers often try to steer their careers in this direction, while corporate, litigation, intellectual property or personal injury lawyers who have acquired a sporting clientele may suddenly find themselves referred to as sports lawyers.

There are various in-house opportunities in the the sports world. Brian Clarke (ex-**Nabarro Nathanson**) is the European head of sports management agency IMG. You could work for a governing body such as the FA or the the RFU; for a sports broadcaster negotiating rights, or as an agent for individual sports personalities or teams. Lawyer Mel Stein has made a name for himself in this respect with his work for Paul Gascoigne.

LEADING FIRMS

SPORT: COMMERCIAL/MEDIA • London

1. Denton Wilde Sapte
2. Bird & Bird
   Nicholson Graham & Jones
3. Olswang
   SJ Berwin
   Townleys
4. Freshfields Bruckhaus Deringer
   Theodore Goddard
5. Ashurst Morris Crisp
   Clintons
   Collyer-Bristow
   Field Fisher Waterhouse
   Harbottle & Lewis
   Herbert Smith
   Memery Crystal
   The Simkins Partnership

SPORT: REGULATORY • London

1. Denton Wilde Sapte
   Townleys
2. Farrer & Co
   Max Bitel, Greene
3. Charles Russell
   Grower Freeman & Goldberg
4. Mishcon de Reya
   Simmons & Simmons

SPORT • South West

1. Clarke Willmott & Clarke Bristol
2. Osborne Clarke Bristol

SPORT • Wales

1. Hugh James Ford Simey Cardiff

SPORT • Midlands

1. Hammond Suddards Edge Birmingham

SPORT • The North

1. James Chapman & Co Manchester
   McCormicks Leeds
2. George Davies Manchester
   Walker Morris Leeds
3. Addleshaw Booth & Co Manchester
   Gorna & Co Manchester
4. Zermansky & Partners Leeds

Within each band, firms are listed alphabetically.
Source: Chambers and Partners Guide to the Legal Profession 2001-2002

tax

A significant percentage of a company's income is paid out in tax, so it's not hard to see why tax lawyers are so valuable to their clients. Good advice can result in a tax saving that can reap enormous financial benefits for the client. Even the most costly lawyers' fees are money well spent. In a nutshell, it's the tax adviser's job to tell the client exactly how to structure its business activities so as to be most tax effective.

type of work

Corporate tax lawyers are widely seen as 'anoraks.' In fact they need to be extremely commercial animals. Tax law is not a refuge for those who want to screen themselves from client involvement behind towers of statute books. There's no room for those who want to theorise about technicalities of 'black letter law' in isolation from the real world for which it was written. That said, if it is the thrill of the chase you are after, and the adrenalin of the all-night meeting, you may be unfulfilled.

Steve Edge, partner at **Slaughter and May** and probably the World's most well-known tax lawyer comments: "*Sometimes I'm the first lawyer to be involved on a big deal. But as the job is done, I'll see people who have been up all night on negotiations and have the tremendous satisfaction that they've moved mountains. More often than not the tax people will have been more remote in the latter stages of the deal unless a problem arises. When a problem does arise you have to react like the fire brigade and sort things out quickly!*" One thing in tax law is certain – no one has any patience with tax advisers who make a meal of things.

There is tremendous satisfaction in being able to come in and provide a positive solution under pressure in such circumstances and that obviously produces its own form of adrenalin. You certainly have to regard yourself as an ideas person and a problem solver, but you are unlikely to get the champagne and the glory for driving the deal to completion.

A good lawyer absorbs him or herself in the world of the clients. Be they corporate finance, banking or property-based, a good tax lawyer needs to understand these areas of law and the culture, constraints and regulations affecting the sector. So, as in all commercial areas of law, you need to be a business adviser, with a particular expertise in tax.

skills needed

….be more than just an 'anorak'…detailed knowledge of tax laws…ability to communicate extremely complex ideas in layman's language…a keen eye for detail…a forensic mind…laser-like precision…absolute confidence in your own judgment…common sense….

career options

Specialist tax lawyers are not two-a-penny so after just a few years of bedding down into the practice area you will become a very marketable commodity. In the last few years there has been a degree of movement of senior figures between tax departments in banks, accountancy firms, law firms and also to the Bar and to and from the Inland Revenue or Customs and Excise.

Some of the most respected tax barristers have only been called to the Bar for a couple of years but had previously been successful solicitors. The knowledge and skills developed in practice are so transferable that you then become free to select the context in which you deliver a service to clients or advise those who make policy decisions concerning tax legislation.

LEADING FIRMS

TAX • London

1
- Freshfields Bruckhaus Deringer
- Linklaters
- Slaughter and May

2
- Allen & Overy
- Clifford Chance

3
- Ashurst Morris Crisp
- Herbert Smith
- Norton Rose
- SJ Berwin

4
- Berwin Leighton Paisner
- Denton Wilde Sapte
- Lovells
- Macfarlanes
- Nabarro Nathanson
- Olswang
- Simmons & Simmons
- Travers Smith Braithwaite

5
- Clyde & Co
- CMS Cameron McKenna
- Field Fisher Waterhouse
- McDermott, Will & Emery

6
- Hammond Suddards Edge
- Theodore Goddard
- Watson, Farley & Williams

TAX • The South & South West

1
- Burges Salmon Bristol
- Osborne Clarke Bristol

2
- Blake Lapthorn Fareham
- Wiggin & Co Cheltenham

TAX • Midlands & East Anglia

1
- Pinsent Curtis Biddle Birmingham
- Wragge & Co Birmingham

2
- DLA Birmingham
- Eversheds Norwich, Nottingham

3
- Mills & Reeve Cambridge

TAX • The North

1
- Addleshaw Booth & Co Leeds, Manchester
- Pinsent Curtis Biddle Leeds

2
- Eversheds Leeds, Manchester
- Hammond Suddards Edge Leeds, Manchester

3
- Dickinson Dees Newcastle upon Tyne
- Walker Morris Leeds

Within each band, firms are listed alphabetically.
Source: Chambers and Partners Guide to the Legal Profession 2001-2002

qualifying in other jurisdictions

In an increasingly competitive international legal and business world, many lawyers view dual or foreign qualification as a desirable addition to their professional skill-set. Such qualifications enable them to offer a broader and more comprehensive service.

the US bar

Qualification at one of the US Bars permits solicitors to practise freely in New York as attorneys or to represent American clients in the UK. Some feel this makes them more marketable to the growing number of US firms based in London and beyond. City of London law firms based in New York may also look favourably upon this additional qualification.

There are only a small number of course providers authorised in the UK to prepare for and administer the examination. Central Law Training is a Birmingham-based legal education and training organisation. The New York Bar lecture programme and examinations are conducted from its London facilities. To be eligible for the NY Bar exam you must hold a three year full-time or four year part-time LLB degree qualification. There is the option of a five-month lecture programme or home study course. The former is the more popular option as it allows close contact and communication with the lecturer and other course students.

A California Bar programme is also offered, although less interest has been shown in this, as it additionally requires 12 months experience in practice as a solicitor and is only available via the home study method.

NY Bar exams are conducted twice yearly. The lecture programme commencing in February prepares for a bar exam in July and a September lecture programme leads to final examination the following February. All lectures take place on Friday evenings and Saturdays (drinkers and socialites beware!) at the Café Royal on Regent Street.

Pass rates on the lecture programme run at around 70-80%. Bar-Bri legal texts are used, the preparatory papers used by most US students.

Contact: Central Law Training, Wrens Court, 52-54 Victoria Road, Sutton Coldfield, B72 1SX. **Tel:** 0121 362 7703. **Website:** www.centlaw.com

The University of Holborn also offers two courses in preparation for the New York Bar Exam. Students must have completed the equivalent of a three year degree course, based on English common law, at a recognised law school or university. Students can opt for the eight week review course or part-time fifteen week course, both of which take place at the college in London on Friday evenings and at weekends, preparing them for the twice-yearly examinations in New York.

The review course covers an eight week period starting in October for the February examinations or in March for the July examinations. The courses are held on weekends. Students are taught by qualified American attorneys, many of whom were initially British barristers and several of whom practise in New York.

Any eligibility queries should be addressed to the New York State Board of Examiners, 7 Executive Centre Drive, Albany, New York 12203, USA.

qualifying as an australian solicitor

Increasingly, the sun-drenched climate and laid-back charm of Australia offers an attractive alternative to over-stressed northern hemisphere professionals seeking a lifestyle-driven career change. Australia's federal system supports several states with different legal jurisdictions and varying rules governing admission requirements to the professional bodies of solicitors and barristers.

Below, we provide brief information for one popular choice – the state of New South Wales incorporating the principal city of Sydney. Contact details for solicitors' professional associations in Victoria and Queensland are also listed.

"Australia offers an attractive alternative to over-stressed northern hemisphere professionals."

picture courtesy of the Australian Tourist Commission

new south wales

In New South Wales, a person is admitted as a Legal Practitioner to the Supreme Court of New South Wales. Once they have obtained a practising certificate from the state's Law Society, they are free to practise as a solicitor or barrister.

The Legal Practitioners Admission Board is the appropriate admitting authority in New South Wales and is responsible for administering the application process. English solicitors are required to apply for admission under Rule 100 of the Legal Practitioners Transitional Admission Rules 1994 which advises as to the requirements for transfer.

These requirements may necessitate further academic and practical legal training. But certain academic exemption clauses and practical exemptions exist dependent upon prior qualifications and relevant work experience. These courses can be studied at either the Legal Practitioners Admission Board itself or various educational establishments in New South Wales. A series of fees for registration, processing, admission etc. are payable to the board.

Contact: The Legal Practitioners Admission Board, Level 4 ADC Elizabeth Building, Corner King and Elizabeth Streets, Sydney, NSW 2000, Australia. **Tel:** 02 9392 0300. **Fax:** 02 9392 0315.

Contact: The Law Society of New South Wales, 170 Philip Street, Sydney, NSW 2000, Australia. **Tel:** 61 2 9926 0333. **Fax:** 61 2 9231 5809.
Website: www.lawsocnsw.asn.au
Email: lawsociety@lawsocnsw.asn.au

Contact: Law Institute Of Victoria, 470 Bourke St, Melbourne, Victoria 3000, Australia. **Tel:** 61 3 9607 9311. **Fax:** 61 3 9602 5270. **Website:** www.liv.asn.au

Contact: Queensland Law Society Inc. Law Society House, 179 Ann St, Brisbane, Queensland 4000, Australia. **Tel:** 61 7 3842 5888. **Fax:** 61 7 3842 5999. **Website:** www.qls.com.au

law society of scotland

Qualified solicitors from England and Wales seeking to practise in Scotland firstly need to be fully admitted to the roll in England and Wales. A certificate of good standing is required from the Law Society to The Law Society of Scotland.

There are no structured preparatory lectures or organised tuition programmes for the inter-UK transfer test held in Edinburgh, an examination consisting of 3x2 hour papers. The Law Society Of Scotland and Strathclyde University administer and oversee a home study programme, providing learning texts and communication support.

On successful completion of the transfer test, solicitors will be eligible to be admitted to the roll of Scottish solicitors, and thereby can practise freely. A £250 administration fee is required, payable to The Law Society Of Scotland. Additionally, examination fees are charged at £50 each.

Contact: The Law Society Of Scotland, 26 Drumsheugh Gardens, Edinburgh EH3 7YR. **Tel:** 0131 226 7411. **Fax:** 0131 225 2934.

overseas lawyers

becoming an english lawyer

Lawyers from Europe, Africa, the Caribbean and Australasia are among the main groups of overseas professionals who annually seek to add their name to the Roll of Solicitors of England and Wales.

The QLTT (Qualified Lawyers Transfer Test) is a Law Society accredited conversion test that permits lawyers qualified in selected countries outside the UK, as well as UK barristers to retrain and requalify as solicitors. The test covers four heads: Property, Litigation, Principles of Common Law and finally Professional Conduct and Accounts.

The Law Society determines which heads candidates must pass, dependent on their primary professional qualification. Candidates need to apply for a certificate of eligibility from the Law Society before applying to sit the test. Foreign qualified lawyers will usually have to pass sections of the test in conjunction with a two year experience requirement. This may be reduced if they have already completed an 'articles-style' training scheme overseas.

A full list of jurisdictions that fall under the umbrella of the Qualified Lawyers Transfer Regulations (QLTR) and the appropriate subjects and experience requirements can be obtained from the Law Society or via their website.

The Law Society confirms those types of previous experience which may be taken into account during the application process. Evidence of dates, written confirmation from employers, head of chambers etc. need to be submitted with any application, such as:

- Up to 12 months pupillage certified as satisfactory by the pupil master.
- Any period spent in practice at the Bar (i.e. – tenancy or squatting).
- A period spent in legal employment in the office of a solicitor or lawyer in private practice.
- Any period spent in legal employment with the Crown Prosecution Service or with the Magistrates/Court Service.
- Any period spent in legal employment in the Civil Service, Local Government, a public authority, commerce or industry provided that the employment is in a legal department which is headed by a solicitor, barrister or lawyer of at least five years standing.

For barristers, the experience must have been gained in England, Wales or Northern Ireland. Experience gained overseas may count if it occurred in a common law jurisdiction and in all cases, should be within the last five years.

Any unusual requests which do not fit into the above category requirements are usually considered by the Transfer Casework Committee.

test and study providers

There are two official test 'providers' – recognised educational establishments who offer the examination service and preparatory training and tuition courses. The Law Society refer potential participants to both.

The College of Law administers and runs the test but also offers a range of preliminary tuition options to prepare candidates for examination. These fall under three different categories; Distance Learning Courses, Evening Lectures/Weekend Courses, Revision Sessions.

BPP Law School runs the test twice yearly after focused study courses and sessions on key areas. Face to face methods or distance learning are available.

THE TRUE PICTURE

introduction	186
top 100 firms table	188
the true picture	191
international firms	396
prospects for newly qualifieds	399

a guide to training with 100 of the top firms

our methodology
This year we interviewed trainees at 100 of the top law firms in England and Wales (but not Scotland and Northern Ireland), asking about everything from seat allocation to social life. The 'True Picture 100' were selected by size of firm, size of trainee population and rankings in the *Chambers Guide to the Legal Profession 2001-2002*. The firms provided us with complete lists of their trainees and NQs and we selected our sample randomly from those lists. Our interviews averaged 30 minutes with each trainee or NQ and our sources were guaranteed anonymity. None of the True Picture has been vetted by any of the firms covered. What follows is uncut.

our findings
Responsibility varies between departments. In property you might handle a number of small files. Litigation experience depends entirely on the type of cases your firm handles; you may take small cases all the way through to settlement or you may be stuck for months on documentation on a big case. Corporate means long hours, which climax in dreaded all-nighters around closure. Big firms mean big hours. Outside London deals tend to be smaller and the pace calmer, however, hours are intense at the largest regional firms.

Most firms offer four six-month seats, some a six by four-month rotation. Trainees move between departments, either sharing a room and working for a partner or senior assistant or working for a number of lawyers, perhaps in an open plan environment.

Your choice of firm will be based partly on location, partly on size and partly on the practice areas available. Then it's a matter of chemistry. It's down to you to attend law fairs, open days and vacation schemes. Beg to visit law firms, shadow someone, meet a trainee. Go into reception and try to get a feel for things. Phone graduate recruitment and get chatting to them. This is a decision that will affect you for a long time. Make it an educated one.

During our interviews we noticed that different issues affect trainees at different types of firms.

what's new at magic circle firms?
- Salary rises. Although unlikely to continue, NQ salaries have soared again – and trainees are benefiting too.
- Armies of paralegals mean less dross work for trainees. But on big-ticket work you wont be in the front line.
- Hours can be grim. There's been masses of work in the past few years, but the numbers of M&A deals are falling.
- The chances of getting an overseas seat are high. Campaign for the most popular ones asap.
- Many trainees do not intend to remain in their magic circle firm for more than a couple of years post-qualification. They may predict that their quality of life after qualification will be abysmal.

what's new at mid-size firms?
- A surge in corporate/private equity work has meant higher salaries, longer hours.
- A wide spread of types of work on offer. If finance doesn't get you excited, find a commercial firm, which allows you to side step the whole 'City' thing.
- You are less likely to get an overseas placement.
- Partners know who you are and you're likely to know most people at the firm. At some firms, trainees can fit around one table in the pub.
- Technology and media firms are consolidating their position after catapulting up the leader board in the last couple of years. The technology sector is not as healthy as it was though.

- On qualification, some trainees find their firm can't offer jobs in the most popular areas of work. e.g. IP, employment and tax.

what's new at national firms?
- Some firms require trainees to move around the country, some offer the opportunity to do so, at others movement is almost impossible.
- Although salaries have improved, differentials between the offices may cause trainee pouting.
- You don't always get the same menu at each office. Make sure the one you choose does the work you think it does as well as other branch offices.
- The firm may be as big as the magic circle firms, but deals and clients are not usually blue chip.
- You get the advantages of a more intimate atmosphere in a smaller office, with the benefits of a larger network of lawyers across the country. You'll always be able to find someone who can answer your question – even if they are 150 miles away.

what's new at regional firms?
- At the top regionals you'll find great quality work. They compete with the finest in the City.
- Most prefer to recruit trainees with local connections. They've suffered from the pull of London on qualification, but this is beginning to change.
- Older trainees often appeal to the regional players. Not only do they have deeper roots locally, but they often bring first career skills and contacts.
- Pay is good in some cities. You'll earn less money than in London, but the cost of living is lower.
- There's a strong general trend towards commercial/corporate work. Many firms have shed private clients/crime/family/PI or are in the process of doing so.

what's new in niche firms?
- If you join a niche practice, experience in other areas of work may be minimal. You may not be able to qualify into another practice area. Be sure this is what you want to do.
- Niche practices are subject to fluctuations in the market. e.g. the consolidation of the insurance market has left some firms feeling the cold as they fall off the companies' panels of solicitors. Some firms have shrunk in size, others merged.
- A reorganisation of the NHS Litigation Authority panel has closed off defendant clinical negligence work to many firms
- Niche firms are attracted to applicants who can bring something with them – industry experience or good contacts.
- Competition for trainee places can be the fiercest in this part of the profession. For example, Wiggin & Co (media and technology), Bindman & Partners (civil liberties and human rights) and Sheridans (music and entertainment).

and finally…
As an applicant you are motivated by two concerns. Finding a firm you want to work for and finding a firm that wants you. We hope the True Picture will help on both counts. You may be wasting your time applying to firms, which are very unlikely to accept you. Look at the statistics in our selection table on page 38. There are some eyebrow-raising revelations there. Wiggin & Co is a niche media/IT firm acting for leading TV and telecoms companies. It's in Cheltenham, pays London salaries and is anything but traditional, with a full-time dress-down policy. A job in a million? Well, almost – it's actually a job in several hundreds. At the other end of the scale, on statistics alone, the easiest place to get a training contract is the biggest magic circle firm, Clifford Chance. The odds are just over one in 15. Applicants are often self-selecting, shying away from the magic circle and focusing instead on smaller firms. But, look at the statistics – on paper, with only four positions available, the odds of getting into small Thames Valley firm Boyes Turner are 1:550, compared to just over 1:15 for Clifford Chance.

THE TRUE PICTURE TOP 100 FIRMS

TRUE PIC RANK	FIRM NAME	CITY	TOTAL TRAINEES	PAGE NUMBER TRUE PICTURE	A-Z
1	Clifford Chance	London	225	227	444
2	Eversheds	London*	250	254	466
3	DLA	London*	138	250	462
4	Linklaters	London	286	305	500
5	Allen & Overy	London	220	193	420
6	Freshfields Bruckhaus Deringer	London	176	265	474
7	Herbert Smith	London	171	277	481
8	Hammond Suddards Edge	London*	100	273	478
9	Lovells	London	109	308	501
10	CMS Cameron McKenna	London*	110	232	446
11	Denton Wilde Sapte	London*	114	244	458
12	Norton Rose	London	120	329	516
13	Slaughter and May	London	150	359	541
14	Wragge & Co	Birmingham*	50	393	564
15	Ashurst Morris Crisp	London	106	196	423
16	Pinsent Curtis Biddle	Birmingham*	62	339	522
17	Beachcroft Wansbroughs	London*	55	202	n/a
18	Simmons & Simmons	London	154	353	539
19	Addleshaw Booth	Leeds*	63	191	419
20	Nabarro Nathanson	London*	56	325	514
21	Berwin Leighton Paisner	London	67	204	426
22	Garretts (Andersen Legal)	London*	52	268	422
23	Osborne Clarke	Bristol*	54	333	518
24	Masons	London*	60	317	506
25	SJ Berwin	London	78	356	427
26	Baker & McKenzie	London	51	198	424
27	Morgan Cole	Cardiff*	38	323	513
28	Taylor Joynson Garrett	London	47	364	546
29	Rowe & Maw	London	41	347	530
30	Irwin Mitchell	Sheffield*	27	293	489
31	Bevan Ashford	Bristol*	46	207	428
32	Barlow Lyde & Gilbert	London*	35	200	n/a
33	Bird & Bird	London	27	209	429
34	Shoosmiths	Northampton*	24	249	537

* Indicates branches elsewhere in England and Wales. Only head office location listed.

THE TRUE PICTURE TOP 100 FIRMS

TRUE PIC RANK	FIRM NAME	CITY	TOTAL TRAINEES	PAGE NUMBER	
				TRUE PICTURE	A-Z
35	Bond Pearce	Plymouth*	41	213	431
36	Lawrence Graham	London	30	297	493
37	Mills & Reeve	Cambridge*	32	319	511
38	Clyde & Co	London*	43	230	445
9	Olswang	London	58	331	517
40	Field Fisher Waterhouse	London	20	259	469
41	Burges Salmon	Bristol	38	219	437
42	Macfarlanes	London	34	311	503
43	Charles Russell	London*	28	223	441
44	Stephenson Harwood	London	44	363	544
45	Richards Butler	London	43	345	528
46	Theodore Goddard	London	33	368	550
47	Halliwell Landau	Manchester	19	271	477
48	Travers Smith Braithwaite	London	36	372	553
49	Dickinson Dees	Newcastle*	22	246	459
50	Dechert	London	26	242	456
51	Hill Dickinson	Liverpool*	20	282	483
52	Reynolds Porter Chamberlain	London	18	343	527
53	Browne Jacobson	Nottingham*	18	217	436
54	Penningtons	London*	20	337	521
55	Sidley Austin Brown & Wood	London	11	351	538
56	Walker Morris	Leeds	25	378	555
57	Weightmans	Liverpool*	20	386	559
58	Pannone & Partners	Manchester	19	335	519
59	Hugh James Ford Simey	Cardiff*	13	290	487
60	Davies Wallis Foyster	Liverpool*	15	240	455
61	Davies Arnold Cooper	London*	16	238	454
62	D J Freeman	London	28	248	461
63	Trowers & Hamlins	London*	29	374	554
64	Blake Lapthorn	Portsmouth*	15	211	430
65	Weil, Gotshal & Manges	London	16	387	560
66	Withers	London	21	391	563
67	Manches	London*	18	313	504

* Indicates branches elsewhere in England and Wales. Only head office location listed.

THE TRUE PICTURE TOP 100 FIRMS

TRUE PIC RANK	FIRM NAME	CITY	TOTAL TRAINEES	PAGE NUMBER	
				TRUE PICTURE	A-Z
68	Martineau Johnson	Birmingham*	25	315	505
69	Edwards Geldard	Cardiff*	24	252	465
70	Holman Fenwick & Willan	London	16	286	485
71	Cobbetts	Manchester	18	234	448
72	Freethcartwright	Nottingham*	15	263	n/a
73	Nicholson Graham & Jones	London	20	328	515
74	Gouldens	London	30	270	476
75	White & Case	London	16	389	561
76	Clarke Willmott & Clarke	Bristol*	17	225	n/a
77	Hewitson Becke + Shaw	Cambridge*	20	280	482
78	Watson, Farley & Williams	London	25	382	557
79	Ince & Co	London	19	292	488
80	Farrer & Co	London	18	257	467
81	Speechly Bircham	London	10	361	542
82	Ward Hadaway	Newcastle	16	380	556
83	KLegal	London	22	295	491
84	Bristows	London	14	215	435
85	Finers Stephens Innocent	London	8	261	470
86	TLT Solicitors	Bristol	14	370	552
87	Lewis Silkin	London	12	303	499
88	Mishcon de Reya	London	16	321	512
89	Laytons	London*	18	299	494
90	Cripps Harries Hall	Tunbridge Wells*	13	236	451
91	Taylor Vinters	Cambridge	10	366	547
92	Harbottle & Lewis	London	7	275	479
93	Veale Wasbrough	Bristol	12	376	n/a
94	Sinclair Roche & Temperley	London	16	354	540
95	Radcliffes	London	13	341	525
96	Lester Aldridge	Bournemouth*	11	301	498
97	Wedlake Bell	London	10	384	558
98	Howes Percival	Northampton*	10	288	486
99	Hodge Jones & Allen	London	12	284	484
100	Capsticks	London	11	221	440

* Indicates branches elsewhere in England and Wales. Only head office location listed.

the true picture 100

Addleshaw Booth

the facts
Location: Leeds, London, Manchester
UK ranking by size: 19
Total number of trainees: 63
Seats: 4x6 months
Alternative Seats: Secondments

Addleshaw Booth was once a northern firm with a small satellite branch in London. But that satellite has doubled in size and is set to double again. The firm has serious designs on the capital, but will have to go a long way to match its reputation and success up north.

the triad
Leeds, London, Manchester. Three offices and three distinct personalities. The firm was created out of a 1997 marriage between Addleshaw Sons & Latham of Manchester and Booth & Co. of Leeds. The London office followed as a result of the nuptials. *"They are definitely trying to develop a unified culture,"* one trainee told us. *"All activities are synchronised between the offices and you will work with colleagues from other offices."* But there is a *"bit of a north-south split because of geography."*

> "Decorum was thrown to the wind as team tribalism took over."

Training contracts are available in each location, and while trainees are encouraged to move, there is no obligation to do so. The option to move between offices appealed to most of those we spoke to, particularly as financial support is on offer to help with relocation costs. But seat allocation can be *"stressful,"* and some trainees told us that not everyone gets their preferred seats. *"There is the usual fight for seats,"* one source complained. *"It is not always clear where you are going to end up."*

we don't talk anymore
One enthusiastic trainee said *"If you want to work in the north, Addeshaws is the only place to go. A corporate firm, plus private client – a breadth of experience and excellent training."* Addleshaws does indeed provide an excellent level of choice for trainees. It proves that quality 'City work' is available in the north and yet offers the option of a stint working for private clients. It would be wrong to regard this as a mixed commercial/private training though. Addleshaw's practice is most definitely oriented towards large commercial clients. In corporate finance these clients include 3i, Airtours, Barclays Bank and Adidas.

The firm does not *"pull any punches with work"* and *"you're given responsibility, if you have shown that you are capable of it."* Northern trainees talked of feeling useful from early on. One said, *"after the first seat I felt like I was a junior fee earner."* Mid-seat reviews now supplement the usual end-of-seat discussion, but niggles remain. While some supervisors *"tend not to say anything for three months then fill in the form, and not say anything for another three,"* others get full marks. Most trainees have *"no problems seeing partners about work."*

on the bus
The firm *"is run more like a business than a stuffy law firm."* The Leeds office is *"open and friendly." "You just can't over-emphasise the atmosphere."* Many trainees live in the Roundhay area of the city, and often sit next to each other *"on the 'school bus' into work."* Amongst the Yorkshire terriers – the bigger law firms that scrap for work in Leeds – Addleshaws is perceived as

slightly more gentlemanly. *"It hasn't got the aggression of other Leeds firms,"* one source said. According to another, Addleshaws trainees are *"not overly ambitious."* We asked what Addleshaws wanted in a new recruit and were told the firm is not a place for *"highly academic geeky graduates."* *"Most trainees have gone to northern universities. There are a few Oxbridge, but a lot more are red brick."* *"They look for commerciality."*

The Manchester office has a different personality. *"It's very established. It still has quite a traditional feel to it."* One Leeds trainee observed: *"Manchester is perceived as more serious; they work longer hours and come across as a bit more unapproachable. It is perceived to have a bit of a chip on its shoulder as Leeds is the better office and gets the better work."* Miaow! Local rivalries aside, a Manchester trainee did confirm *"it is a bit more hierarchical. It does take itself more seriously,"* even though *"dinosaur partners are few on the ground."* Manchester trainees need not be jealous. The office is distinguished by the secondments on offer. Top clients Airtours and AstraZeneca regularly take trainees – *"there is always somebody off on secondment."*

The *"healthy competition"* between the two northern offices does not prevent co-operation and a bus service runs between the two branches three times a day. The next time you see a bus full of eager young lawyers tearing along the M62 on a Tuesday morning, it may just be the bunch from Addleshaws.

tornado!

The London branch will shortly be moving to prestigious offices in Cannon Street, opposite St. Paul's Cathedral. Rather like a tornado, it is pulling in qualified lawyers from the northern offices and other firms, and with *"the amount of work exceeding expectations,"* (it has trebled its fee income since it opened) all its September 2001 qualifiers were retained. *"London seats are sought after"* by trainees in each of the three offices. As a smaller office, *"you get more responsibility, because there are only eight trainees,"* but with such intense competition for seats, *"there are always people disappointed by what they get."*

here to stay?

Hmmm... Retention... 2001 was not a vintage year for Addleshaws. The firm retained only 12 of the 22 qualifying trainees, many of them in London. Sources spoke of having received nods and winks for jobs and then having them withdrawn. *"It has not been handled at all well and has been bad for morale."* We contacted the graduate recruitment office and were told that a greater number of jobs were offered, but not all of them had been in departments that were of interest to trainees. It's only fair to point out that both trainees and graduate recruitment believe this has been a rogue year and the pattern will not necessarily be repeated in the future.

mug shots

"Everybody works hard but there is a lot of office banter," one source said, building up to a tale from the London branch. A lawyer sent an email around the whole office demanding the return of his missing Tottenham Hotspur mug. A senior (Arsenal supporting) partner responded with team loyalty very much to the fore. In the ensuing email mayhem, everyone in the office got in on the act. Decorum was thrown to the wind as team tribalism took over.

There's plenty of socialising in each office. *"Trainees go out all the time,"* and spoke (nauseatingly) of *"friends as well as colleagues."* The usual range of sports teams is on offer in all locations and for entertainment in those quieter moments, *"we all have our photos on the firm's intranet and, when there's nothing to do, you can log on and have a laugh."*

and finally...

Addleshaws has *"no European ambitions"* and unlike certain other big regionals, is *"focused on just three offices."* This must be a good strategy as turnover increased by a healthy 22% to £75.3m last year. With a high profile role in the Manchester 2002 Commonwealth Games as 'Official Partner to the Games', it would seem the London office won't be overshadowing the northern homesteads just yet.

Allen & Overy

the facts
Location: London
UK ranking by size: 5
Total number of trainees: 220
Seats: 4x6 months*
Alternative seats: Overseas offices, secondments
Extras: Pro bono: Battersea Legal Centre, Privy Council death row appeals, language training.

It's one of the five firms that form the magic circle and is thought by some to be the quiet one of the five. Certainly, it's not cut throat, but it does handle some of the highest value work in the City. It's civilised but not snobby and trainees speak warmly of the firm year after year. Naturally, we were keen to find out about life at this softly spoken gentle giant, so we strolled down to One New Change for a look see…

moving stories
Blimey! You'd never know it was the 21st century when you step into A&O's sh-wish client reception. You'll think you've messed up your directions, taken a wrong turn at St Paul's Cathedral and landed in a rather old-fashioned but terribly expensive hotel. As you struggle to maintain friction on the smooth leather armchairs and thumb through a copy of Country Life, you'll notice the framed endorsement from HRH QE2 and you'll surely wonder if A&O is what you're really looking for. Plush it is, progressive looking it ain't. But trainees told us that *"the reception doesn't bear any resemblance to the rest of the firm or the rest of the building, it's so dated."* Their message is that you shouldn't judge this particular book by its leather-bound cover.

By 2004, the firm will have moved from the shadows of St Paul's, no doubt enabling it to update its public image and the reading material in its reception. Traditional *"classic"* could become anything, anywhere. There's even been talk of moving to the London Borough of Hackney. If you need evidence that life at A&O is not as it may seem from its reception, then just consider this; classicism and royal endorsement didn't hold A&O back from being the first City law firm to run a full time dress down (err… sorry, business casual) policy. Nor does it cause the firm to come across as upper crusty. Indeed, A&O is felt to be at the less élitist end of the magic circle. If circles have ends…

financial times
If it's not blue-blooded and stuffy, then what is it? What motivates trainees to sign up here? Trainees truly believe that *"it's the friendly face of the big City firms."* And who are we to say whether or not A&O is friendlier than other big firms? We will simply tell you that trainees have been saying it year after year and, even at other top firms, the idea perpetuates. Reputations arise and survive somehow and so it could very well be true. There's no evidence to the contrary, so maybe it's just like believing in God.

Aside from the reputation for friendliness, the main reasons for training with the firm are that it has a superb reputation, oozes respectability and pays shed loads. *"I had a desire to work for the best,"* said one trainee who saw the training as a golden ticket to a bright future. And he's not wrong. As an A&O lawyer no one will ever doubt your credentials and you'll never be short of job offers, should you choose to leave the fold. Then there's all those overseas placements and don't forget all that top-notch banking and finance work. Ah yes, don't forget the work. Forget at your peril that which will occupy your waking and working hours. Listen carefully while we say three words to you. Finance. Finance. Finance.

mind-blowing concepts
Many trainees are clearly delighted to be at the epicentre of all things City and financial. *"You will be involved in some of the biggest transactions in the City here and that's exciting,"* said one, adding *"you'll be working with some of the best people in their fields – creative guys and women."* Unfortunately, a few trainees

do realise that much of the firm's core business leaves them cold. *"It can be tough for those who find that they don't enjoy it that much and discover that it's not what they want. If they realise 'My God that's not for me – banking and corporate law,' then possibly they could become quite isolated here."* One or two, we are told, drop by the wayside. They do elsewhere too.

It's not a difficult concept. If you are uninterested in blue chip deals and international money markets then think carefully about this firm or any other in the magic circle. Trainees spoke to us of the frankness of the firm's recruitment material. *"They are very honest about it being a finance firm in their literature. You are not tricked into it."* Certainly not, trickery seems very unA&O.

> "The firm has its very own bar in the office."

seven days

"Did she decline? No. Didn't she mind? I don't think so. Was it for real? Damn sure. What was the deal?" Fact: Craig David wrote that song 'Seven Days' about a trainee's experiences in the ICM (International Capital Markets) seat. We're told it's a toughie and that *"hours are quite demanding."* We're told that many trainees steer well clear of it but some first-seaters apparently have no choice. We also hear that those who put on a brave face and enter the world of ICM come out of the experience pretty stoked. It's an interesting seat and by doing it you'll earn a fair bit of kudos amongst your peers. *"You've got to do a year in finance, which covers corporate, banking and ICM"* as *"banking and capital markets are the lead activities, along with corporate since Guy Beringer* [senior partner] *came along."* Working for the best in their fields also means that *"Godforsaken hours"* are likely to be a part of your work experience.

Are the hours relentless and unbearable? We asked. The answers varied in the detail, but each of the trainees stressed that corporate and finance seats are no picnic. *"It varies with the trainer,"* one said. *"I never worked an all-nighter, but that's pretty lucky. Certain trainers border on slave drivers; others accept that you should work hard, but to a point."* Another talked of being asked to work weekends at short notice and having *"three all-nighters in a row."*

human sacrifice

We perceived the rumblings of a *"backlash"* against hours amongst lawyers. *"People are reluctant to sacrifice their personal lives. With a 9.30am start you can't realistically expect to leave before 7pm. That's a quiet day. In a finance seat you can expect to work consistently, as a way of life, until 9-9.30pm and then you have the nutty periods coming up to completion. Those are necessary, rare and bearable because of all the adrenaline flying around."* We got the impression that it was the regularity of evenings in the office that hurt more than the odd early morning departure. *"Caution the students reading this that as a student you don't appreciate the bind of it."*

But, after the pressure's been on, and to quote Craig David again, are newly qualifieds "walking away to find a better day?" Do they all rush off to mid-tier or provincial firms or are they prepared to live with the long hours? *"In the future I will make that trade"* one trainee spoke categorically. Many uttered versions of the magic circle trainee mantra: "It's easier to trade down from the magic circle than it is to trade up to it." But for the medium term, they stay put – in their droves. If it interests you, here's the September 2001 NQ retention stats: Banking 11, Corporate 11, ICM 7, Litigation 7, Private Client 3, Employment/Pensions 2, Property 2, Tax 2, Hong Kong office 1, Departees 4. Total score 92%!

growth spurts

Despite the inevitable magic circle moans about hours, A&O trainees are very happy with their choice of firm. Our interview notes were filled with comments about *"camaraderie," "community,"* and *"making very good friends."* One trainee spoke of a "level playing field in the office," saying "Arrogance gets knocked out of people early on here… it no longer helps if you've been to, say, Oxbridge. We can all do well." The fact that the firm has its very own bar in the office is an indicator of the A&O 'we' not 'me' culture. After hours it's a good place for a quiet drink before going home or can be used just as a meeting point before hitting one of the bars nearby.

It would be wrong to assume that your training will all be corporate and financial. The firm has a department or unit for everything, including a few things that direct competitors won't touch, such as private client work. You can't flit from one niche to another, but these niche seats are a real attraction for some trainees. Certain, hitherto underplayed departments are putting on a growth spurt, for example IP litigation, property and employment. There's still a sense that some of these departments are "*on the periphery*" and merely orbiting the main action, but they are an important reality for those trainees who love corporate and finance less than they love the firm.

playing cards

There's a Law Society requirement for all trainees to do three months of contentious work and many A&O trainees have a "*don't give a damn*" attitude to litigation seats, almost treating them as a three-month holiday. The "*shunting through*" of the disinterested annoys those who are passionate about litigation. This is where the canny trainee will bring into play their secret weapon – the wildcard or "*priority seat request*". This is a one-off opportunity to stamp feet and demand a particular seat. "*Unless you state that it is your priority seat, your litigation seat will only be three months*" a source explained.

The combination of the "*priority seat*" and the ability to leave an unappealing seat after just three months* makes for happy trainees. "*People are sometimes reluctant to leave a seat after three months in case they offend a trainer who takes it personally, but sometimes it is personal.*" That said, everyone in the firm understands that it's silly to slog away at something when you could be more fulfilled and more useful elsewhere. Sadly, some of the most popular departments, eg IP litigation, only offer a three-month slot. Swings. Roundabouts.

pick me kate

Generally taken in the fourth, but sometimes the third seat, overseas placements are real application pullers. "*The demand never outweighs supply though*" our sources confirmed. So how do you get the one you want from an almost inexhaustible list? (Amsterdam, Bangkok, Bratislava, Brussels, Budapest, Germany, Hong Kong, Madrid, Milan, Moscow, New York, Paris, Prague, Rome, Singapore, Tokyo, Turin and Warsaw… Phew!) The selection process seems to be scrupulously fair, requiring an application form stating "*what type of law you want to do abroad and then your three preferred locations listed in alphabetical order. You can indicate in a bit of narrative which is your favourite.*"

The lucky trainees are identified by a process which, although not quite as rigorous as Nasty Nigel Lythgoe's Popstars auditions, is close to it. "*They look at your previous assessments and speak to previous trainers.*" At the end of all that, a trainee surely feels fit for the job. Star picker, Kate Friend, is nothing like Nasty Nigel, nor does she have a mullet haircut.

love hate relationships

A&O isn't standing still. Any suggestion that it's a conservative firm that's resistant to change comes from outside the firm and not within. Some of those we spoke to genuinely felt that A&O has started to tackle difficult issues with a forward-thinking attitude. "*They seem to be open to embracing new ways of working*" one said, discussing a recent firm-wide campaign called 'Values into Action', which touches on the insoluble problem of the life-work imbalance in large City practices.

As one trainee said, "*It's a brave partner that turns around and says no to a client's demands*" and yet that's at the heart of the problem in this service industry. A&O doesn't have the answer to these problems but it's nice to see it surveying staff on them. It's a frank and official acceptance that lawyers quite often have a *"love hate relationship with what they do"* and yearn for more of themselves and less of the job in their busy and well-paid lives. Oh, on the subject of pay, relax. It's irrelevant that headline rates for trainees and NQ's are a sliver below the headline rates for other magic circle firms. There was a 17% firm-wide bonus in 2001. You're bright, do the maths…

and finally…

The respectability of the magic circle clings to A&O and a training here is a golden ticket to a great career. But understand this – finance and corporate work will feature heavily. Be very clear that at times you will work much longer hours than you ever imagined. Be consoled that your salary will be huge and that in some way A&O retains a softness to its character that isn't evident at all other magic circle firms. We can't prove it, but we believe it.

Ashurst Morris Crisp

the facts

Location: London
UK ranking by size: 15
Total number of trainees: 106
Seats: 4x6 months
Alternative Seats: Overseas seats, secondments
Extras: Pro bono: Privy council death row appeals, Toynbee Hall & Islington Law Centres, language classes

Ashurst Morris Crisp continues to punch above its weight in the market. The firm enjoys an excellent reputation amongst the movers and shakers of corporate Britain, despite comparatively low numbers of fee earners when measured against its peers. The last two years saw the firm dealing with the heartache of two near miss mergers – first with Clifford Chance and then with US firm Latham & Watkins. Some speculated that these failed romances were evidence of discontent at Ashursts; that they would affect profits and this was the beginning of the end of the firm's rather rapid rise. The cynics have been proved wrong.

best of both worlds?

Ashursts is a firm with ambition. Profits, deal sizes and market share have increased rapidly over the last five years. Has this significantly changed the culture of the firm? One trainee thought not. *"I chose Ashursts because it had a reputation for combining a good atmosphere with high quality work. We are still on the outskirts of top firms but we get the same quality of work."* Sounds perfect. Not all trainees were convinced that they would continue to enjoy the best of both worlds though. *"We have grown so much since I joined the firm, we have even taken over another building to support the increased level of work."* Will this impact upon trainees? *"Partners are conscious that there is a certain atmosphere here and we want to keep it, they do try but I think it is going to get harder for trainees in the future."* Whatever the future might hold, the trainees we spoke to this year were certainly managing to enjoy their social lives, both within the office and outside.

taxing times

As a trainee you will experience four six-month seats. Three of these seats must be spent in one of the core departments of the firm (company/commercial, commercial property, litigation and international finance). Trainees can choose their last seat, subject to availability. Those we spoke to found the firm to be *"reasonably good about matching choices to actual places."* The most popular destinations include employment and tax. For a couple of years now the tax seat has proved to be of particular interest to trainees; they describe the department as *"really young, exciting and very sociable."* So next time you're having a party, make sure you invite a tax lawyer or two.

Trainees are sent to a number of Ashursts' overseas offices at every seat rotation. This provides the opportunity to travel to Brussels, Paris, Frankfurt, Milan, Singapore and Tokyo. Competition for these overseas seats varies from year to year but obviously some destinations, especially Paris, are very popular. We heard the firm occasionally creates an additional Paris seat if there is particularly high demand. Without a huge network of overseas offices, the opportunities for travel are slightly lower than at some magic circle firms, but still, you can choose from a reasonable crop. If the firm pushes forward with its latest round of merger talks (with US firm Fried Frank Harris Shriver & Jacobson), who knows what might become available. But then again, after two displays of pre-wedding nerves, Ashursts is developing a bit of a reputation as a 'bolter'... Aside from the opportunity to travel, secondments are available to household name clients.

Progress is monitored by formal six-monthly appraisals, but the level of informal feedback will vary between supervisors. *"Depending upon who you sit with, evaluation could be given daily, weekly or monthly."* Over the last four years, the number of trainees taken on by the firm has more than doubled year on year. This rapid growth has required many more lawyers to step into the supervisor role. One trainee told us *"If you have a problem then with most supervisors you need to be quite pro-active and bring it to their attention, you can't expect them to come to you."* Sounds obvious but it can be difficult, especially if you have only just started your training.

in the driving seat

Whilst talking to trainees, we try to get a feel for what it is that makes each firm different and who would enjoy working there. The first thing to get clear in your mind about Ashursts is that corporate work is really important. It does well in its other areas of practice, but corporate work is what it is best known for and its banking and company departments pull in over half of the firm's income. One source stressed this point *"If you don't want to do corporate work then you don't want to apply here."* To be even more specific, in addition to the regular diet of classy M&A deals that grace the desks of Ashurst's corporate bods, it is private equity (or venture capital) that is of prime importance. This aspect of the firm's work (most often acting for the equity houses) is also a key driver in its international strategy.

take the plunge

Trainees told us that on average their hours were fairly solid. Typical hours for one of our sources were *"a 9:30am start or earlier through to about 6:30pm or 7pm. This could be later in the corporate seats."* Occasional late nights and the odd weekend are all to be expected in City practice; it comes with the terrain. Opinion was divided on how easy it had been making the transition from study to practice. *"Everyone was telling me how hard commercial work was and how I would hate the hours... I have certainly survived. In my last seat I worked through the night twice and came in on a couple of weekends."* Another trainee found the sudden plunge into City practice more of a shock *"When I first started out the hours and the work seemed like the end of the world at times, but you get used to it. It isn't that bad."* You will be worked hard, but not to excess. Hours were certainly not a huge issue for our interviewees.

The quality of work you can expect to see is dependent upon the deal, department and supervisor. *"On smaller deals, I have been responsible for drafting quite big documents, on bigger deals there is less responsibility."* And some good news from another trainee: *"I only had one day's photocopying over a year; there is loads of paralegal support and the secretaries and document production staff are excellent."*

the usual suspects

Speaking to trainees and glancing at the trainee profiles on the Ashursts website, it's pretty clear that the firm knows its own tastes when recruiting. Oxbridge and all the usual red brick suspects are there in abundance. Bristol, Durham, Edinburgh etc. There exists only a tiny minority of students from the new universities so clearly a degree from a traditional and well-respected university will give you a head start when applying. One trainee went further. *"By and large it is what you would expect from a City law firm. I think that it has only been comparatively recently that recruitment focused away from solely Oxbridge."* We were also told the firm values independent minded applicants; those with a bit of character and confidence about them. Basically, *"someone you would want to share an office with."*

> "Next time you're having a party, make sure you invite a tax lawyer."

The divide between partners, assistants and trainees isn't really evident when it comes to socialising. *"In most departments the partners take trainees out for drinks on Friday evenings."* The firm organises a variety of events, including the intriguingly titled *"interactive cocktails,"* which presumably entails more than chit chat over a G&T (but we'd hate to allow our overactive imaginations loose on this one). There are three popular bars *"very, very close."* The *"full and noisy"* Lime Bar, the *"hip and trendy"* Light on Broadgate (*"it's really popular"*) and on Broadgate Circle a *"normal pub"* called The Exchange.

and finally…
Ashursts has been sloughing off the skin it traditionally wore. The blue-blooded reputation of old is little more than whispered about these days and is increasingly anachronistic. Its corporate punch defines it much more strongly. Retention rates for 2001 are pretty impressive; 47 out of the 50 who qualified in September 2001 elected to stay. It must be the pull of those party animals from the tax department.

Baker & McKenzie

the facts
Location: London
UK ranking by size: 26
Total number of trainees: 51
Seats: 4x6 months
Alternative Seats: Overseas offices, secondments
Extras: Pro bono: Waterloo and Royal Courts of Justice Advice Centres

Baker & McKenzie is a global firm in a big way. Since the original Chicago practice was set up in 1949, rapid international pollination has brought the magic of B&M to some 61 offices in 35 different countries, all staffed by local lawyers specialising in local law. The London branch is a prize bloomer on the Baker's shelf. General corporate and commercial work is the bread and butter of its practice, but it offers a thick spread of specialist work. The firm has a superb reputation in employment, pensions, IP, IT and e-commerce.

where everybody knows your name
Whilst B&M might not have the kudos of the magic circle firms, if you are looking to train in a truly global firm B&M should be on your list. All our interviewees enthused about the international work that crosses their desks and the contact they have with lawyers from other jurisdictions. One trainee summed this up by telling us *"the kind of work I am involved in is high profile, international and exciting, but at the same time I know everyone's name."* The intimacy offered by B&M derives from its smaller office.

what about my needs?
The trainees we spoke to told us they had received quality work from day one and felt valued in the execution of that work. *"You are not just told to get on with it and hand it in. Partners and associates are interested in your opinion as a colleague."* In some seats, but notably not project finance or corporate, trainees were given their own files and cases to handle, some of them

involving advocacy (an opportunity which is not always on offer at the very largest firms). *"I am doing my own advocacy at a tribunal. The sum is comparatively small and the client was given a 'trainee health warning,' but it has gone really well. My supervisor is really keen and thinks that more trainees should take on this kind of work."* You need to be proactive to ensure that these opportunities come your way. One trainee commented *"You do need to make people aware of your needs. To begin with I would find myself with no work all day and then at 6.15pm a huge workload would be dropped onto my desk. You need to make yourself heard."*

Hours are entirely dependant on the department you're in and the type of work it does. They range from *"a pretty regular eight hour day"* in pensions, through to *"9am to 9pm in corporate and finance – sometimes later."* The firm wants its trainees to get stuck into work as quickly as possible and the first few weeks can be *"rather daunting."* Trainees aren't hidden away from clients and in some seats around one third of the work is client facing. The dispute resolution department was singled out as offering the best opportunities to get client-handling experience.

the ego has departed

Whilst not exactly a workers collective, trainees felt Baker & McKenzie had a refreshingly weak hierarchy. *"People don't care about titles here; there is no ego barrier between trainee, partner and associate."* There seems to be less of a defined social stratum between lawyers and support staff too. The trainees also highlighted a real mix of backgrounds amongst the staff. It's something most trainees say about their firms, but at B&M it would seem to be especially true. Those we spoke to (even the Oxbridge graduates) commented on the lack of Oxbridge culture or dominance, the number of second career trainees and the high numbers of staff of different nationalities. Obviously the latter owes a great deal to B&M's international presence.

Training consists of four six-month seats, one of which must be commercial and one of which must be contentious. The contentious seat can be undertaken in a variety of different departments including IP, employment and EU. The IP seat gives trainees the chance to work with some of the firm's more glamorous clients in the world of fashion and cosmetics. One trainee was won over by the firm during the vac scheme when she was whisked off in a flash BMW to meet an Italian designer who had instructed the firm over a counterfeit clothing dispute. Trainees viewed these more specialist areas as being by far the most popular departments. These seats do *"tend to get a bit crowded"* and your choice is subject to availability. If your heart is set on one of the popular seats, state your case and be prepared to be flexible.

fears before corporate

Some trainees who had yet to sample the delights of the corporate seat expressed reservations about their social life going down the pan under an avalanche of paper work and due diligence. One first seat trainee whispered *"I've heard bad things happen there."* Speaking to those who have emerged on the other side, there is some comfort to be drawn. *"You can expect to do the occasional weekend and a couple of all-nighters, but we don't work really silly hours."* The corporate department, it was noted, does not expect you to miss Eastenders just for the sake of it. *"If there is no work to be done, nobody raises an eyebrow if you go home at 6pm."* Trainees also commented on how *"nice"* the people in corporate were. After researching the True Picture for several months, we almost began to believe that all the 'nice' people in the UK must be working in City law firms. Almost.

Across the UK employment work seems to be among the most popular area of practice. The good news is that Baker & McKenzie has one of the best employment departments in the country. It acts only for employers but is right at the epicentre of this ever-changing area of law and at any one time there are five seats on offer. Another sexy area of work is IP/IT/e-commerce with six trainee seats available at every rotation.

the matrix

In a firm with a matrix of overseas offices, you'd be disappointed if there were no opportunities for travel. B&M does not disappoint and offers a selection of overseas seats, though there's a slight bias towards travel coinciding with the corporate seat. The decision as to who goes where is made on merit, with languages and experience taken alongside personal preferences. Trainees tell us it isn't at all difficult to get away from the City for a few months. *"It just seems that you put in a request, explain your reasons and they will see what they can do. Most people who do want to go abroad will get the opportunity."* B&M trainees have so far found themselves in a variety of overseas offices including Sydney, Canada, Hong Kong, San Francisco and Frankfurt.

Of the 2001 qualifiers 72% stayed at the firm. Interestingly, four NQs joined the employment department and three qualified into IP. Most departments recruited NQs and, just to prove there are some trainees interested in mainstream corporate and finance, five qualified into those areas.

> "One trainee was whisked off in a flash BMW to meet an Italian designer."

meat markets

The firm organises a large number of social and sporting events for staff and specifically for trainees. They regularly socialise together, especially at the beginning of the training contract before the intake is scattered to the winds. There was some debate over the favourite B&M watering hole. Some opted for Brodies Wine Bar, whilst the hardier B&M socialites choose to dance the night away in Shoeless Joe's, an infamous bar in Temple. One trainee remarked *"It's tacky but loads of fun. Sometimes a big group of us go down together. It has even been known that the odd partner will turn up."* Others were not quite so convinced *"It's just a meat market. I think people should be banned from going there!"*

and finally

All in all Baker & McKenzie trainees seem pleased with their lot in life. If you are looking for a friendly atmosphere with an expanding international firm or are interested in the firm's specialist areas, you should certainly give them a try. The dough at Bakers isn't bad either – lets hope it keeps rising.

Barlow Lyde & Gilbert

the facts

Location: London, Oxford
UK ranking by size: 32
Total number of trainees: 35
Seats: 4x6 months
Alternative Seats: Hong Kong, secondments
Extras: Pro bono: St Botolph's Project

Barlow Lyde & Gilbert is best known for its truly impressive litigation and insurance work. It is top ranked for its financial, insurance industry and legal professional negligence practices and stands out for its excellent defendant personal injury department.

tripping

Since insurance and litigation comprise so much of the work, the BLG trainee will *"definitely do a seat in PI,"* and mostly likely one of the *"raft of divisions"* within insurance litigation. These include shipping, aviation, reinsurance and general insurance. There's an abundance of seats available in these divisions, but the firm does have other areas of work to offer its youngsters. On the non-contentious side these include company/commercial, corporate finance, banking and property, and trainees are tripping over themselves to get into the *"young and rigorous IT team."* Our sources thought it appropriate for us to emphasise that the majority of the typical training contract will be spent in contentious areas of work. While you don't have to be dead set on a career as a litigator, they thought it unlikely anyone would *"come here if they wanted to be a commercial property lawyer!"*

serious business

Each department or division has its own character. Reinsurance is *"very studious, almost academic,"* while company/commercial clocked in as *"the most laddish."* Second years report longer hours than first years and, as in all firms, the hours in deal-led departments are less predictable and often longer. Trainees talked of heading home at 5.30pm in general insurance, slightly later in other litigation departments, and in company/commercial things can go well into the evening, *"with the occasional all-nighter."*

Responsibility follows once trainees have proved themselves. They are then given their own cases with *"lots of hands on work."* As for supervision, *"most partners are willing to take trainees very seriously, and consider it in their interests to do so,"* although *"it all depends on what they have on."* Partners in personal injury can be *"very rushed and they don't always have the time."* Appraisals come round once every six months, but some wished there was more feedback. *"The problem is that you are not told if something is good."*

gurus

There's evidence that BLG is directing plenty of energy towards its corporate practice. The corporate department is steadily expanding, with partners poached from other firms. Our sources thought BLG was *"no longer a pure insurance firm."* *"It knows that litigation will not get it into the top ten,"* and wants to *"branch out"* into non-contentious areas. *"It's becoming more broad based"* and *"getting a more corporate 'magic circle' style."* Trainees talked of *"rumours that chargeable hours will go up."* A new Oxford office *"should pick up industries in the M4 corridor,"* and at least one commercial/IT seat is currently available in the branch.

But let's not overstate the shift in emphasis; it seems unlikely the firm will be slacking off on litigation and insurance. BLG is proud to have been kept on the panel of the NHS Litigation Authority – a vote of confidence in the quality of service it offers. *"If you want to learn about the law, there is a lot of expertise here in dispute resolution and a wealth of experience in arbitration."* Not content to simply praise partners, our sources referred to them as *"insurance gurus."*

happy families

The firm looks to recruit trainees with commercial awareness and, if possible, some experience in the insurance industry. Trainees come from a full range of university backgrounds and some have had previous careers. *"Many trainees are recruited from vacation schemes,"* as these schemes prove to be an ideal opportunity to test a candidate's ability to work and to see if they fit into the BLG culture.

And what of that culture? One trait, which is typical of insurance-oriented firms, is teamwork. Big insurance companies send a lot of repeat business to their lawyers and consequently the ability to get on with clients is paramount. Lawyers build up ongoing relationships with those who instruct them and contact will often be weekly or even daily. Hopefully relationships last and last. The concept of working as a team with others is hugely important. *"Barlows likes to think of itself as a big happy family of a firm."* And what family would be complete without some petty moans from the kids. *"Stationery can be more difficult to get hold of than it should be."* Oh really!

naughty and not nice

BLG has a Hong Kong office, and one trainee will usually head east for six months. Other shorter business trips arise during a few of the London seats, like aviation and shipping.

The firm continues to struggle to attain high NQ retention rates. In September 2000 only 10 of the 16 qualifiers stayed with the firm. Things improved only slightly in September 2001 with 12 of the 16 qualifiers staying on, despite all being offered jobs. As in last year's True Picture interviews, trainees thought the job offers were handled badly. *"They were slightly naughty. A couple of trainees were told they had jobs in certain departments, then told they didn't have room after all."* Most departees left for City rivals and one followed the BLG construction team, which defected to Berwin Leighton Paisner in 2000.

denver carrington

The *"excellent"* social life centres around pubs with a lyrical bent. Traditionally The Water Poet has been favoured but during its refurbishment trainees, displaying incredible imagination and taste for variety, adopted The Purple Poet. While there *"seems to be a distinction between lawyers and support staff,"* there are no *"hooray henries"* and trainees *"are reasonably close. Everyone gets along very well."* Client entertainment is pushed along by the fact that *"insurers don't mind a beer,"* and the firm is *"very good at laying on free drinks."* On the sporting front, there are teams for football, netball, cricket, and rugby sevens.

Emulating Dynasty-like excesses, BLG's offices are described as *"a white 'shoulder pads and red braces' scenario." "There are excessive amounts of marble; wherever it could be laid, it was – the lifts, toilets, the entrance hall."* Matters aren't helped by the *"pink and green paint around the windows"* and the fountain in reception. It's *"definitely a product of the late 80s."* Alexis Carrington eat ya heart out!

and finally…

"If you want to be a litigator, it's one of **the** *places to be."* But at the end of the day, not all those that remain with the firm after training will end up as litigators. Minor moans on specific issues aside, trainees are really happy at BLG. The depth of knowledge on offer in specialist areas of work should prove attractive to many students.

Beachcroft Wansbroughs

the facts
Location: London, Bristol, Winchester, Birmingham, Leeds, Manchester
UK ranking by size: 17
Total number of trainees: 55
Seats: 4x6 months
Alternative Seats: Secondments

The product of a tripartite merger three years ago, Beachcroft Wansbroughs is a large national firm with areas of particular strength in the health sector and insurance. It's by no means all that the firm does, but these sectors make up a good proportion of its business. Although the firm is spread across England, it currently recruits trainees into just three of its offices – London, Bristol and Manchester.

london: a mind altering experience

The London office presently offers trainees a range of seats unmatched by many of the other offices. The London trainees fall into two camps; those attracted to the corporate areas of the firm and those attracted to the contentious work. Actually once they have experienced some of the seat choices on offer some trainees change their mind about what they want to do after qualification. *"I wanted to be a litigator when I came here,"* one told us *"but now I find that I want to be something entirely different."* We learned that *"in the year above at least half wanted to qualify into health litigation"* but now trainees are attracted to *"burgeoning departments across the board."*

Arguably health litigation may have had its heyday in London. Certain other offices of the firm survived the cull of the National Health Service Litigation Authority (NHSLA) panel, but not London. As the corporate and commercial strengths of the London office grow, so the relative importance of clinical negligence diminishes. If you're after a career in clinical negligence, London may not be the best choice of office.

flounder and chips please

Generally London trainees seemed satisfied with their seat choices. They concluded that a six-seat rotation (which may be abandoned in favour of the more traditional four-seat rotation) had helped them in this respect. The most popular seats are corporate, employment and IT, plus a secondment to Unilever. Education, PI, commercial litigation, private client, projects/PFI and property are also on offer. We're told *"they stress the importance of you doing property."* The firm has a Brussels office but, thus far, it's not been possible for trainees to nip over on the Eurostar for six months of moules and frites.

> "Trainees are long distance runners, not sprinters."

With a fairly regular 9.30am-6.30pm day and more than adequate assistance from supervisors and young assistant solicitors, trainees reported an absence of stress. *"On one matter I worked on I saw the poor guy on the other side floundering. Throughout my training I have seen people who are really busy stop as they are walking along the corridor and take time to explain something to a trainee."*

bristol: in the bag

Home to the firm's administrative centre and the national head of training, Bristol's position as a trainee base was always in the bag. Its position on the NHSLA panel is also in the bag, so expect a slice of the clin neg action here. This office has always operated a four-seat training model and our sources confirmed that, while *"some people will get two of their preferred seat choices, you can guarantee one of them."*

Although there's no corporate seat as *"the department disintegrated about a year ago but it's just starting up again,"* plenty of other areas of work appeal to trainees. *"Employment is popular now, as is professional indemnity and most people want personal injury too. Commercial litigation is getting more popular."* Also on offer is *"the new clin neg seat and construction. Property litigation has trainees on and off."* The emphasis is on contentious work in Bristol.

on patrol

Bristol attracts some applicants who studied at one or other of the local universities, but not everyone has a strong connection with the area. Almost everyone raves about life in Bristol, in spite of a feeling that the firm is paying below the market rate for newly qualifieds. One trainee compared life in Bristol with that experienced by friends in big London firms. *"Sometimes they're working long hours for no reason… it's difficult to get hold of them and they're stressed out."* Our source told us that the average trainee day in the Bristol office is 8.45am-6pm. *"They don't like to see you working too late. The training principal is a visible presence. She walks around and has a word with you if you're still here at 6.30pm!"*

"The atmosphere is pretty relaxed… partners are not put on a pedestal" and once a month they pay for drinks in a local bar. The trainees socialise amongst themselves only sporadically – maybe this is why they can't decide which pub to make their local. *"It's in flux at the moment, it used to be the Cornubia but now it's usually O'Neill's."*

manchester: chop chop

In contrast, the Manchester trainees knew exactly which local bars were hot favourites. *"Mr Thomas' Chop House has real character – it's not a bleeding chain pub! It's where partners entertain their clients and on Friday nights you'll get partners and all sorts in there."* Its *"sister pub* [er, don't you mean brother?] *is Sam's Chop House and it's also popular."* So fond are they of their locals, Beachcrofts lawyers have named the staff room 'Harry's Bar' and enjoy a spot of TV or table football at lunchtime. Well this is Manchester after all…

We noted no regional bias in the recruitment of trainees. There's a mix of locals and those from the

North East, Wales and Northern Ireland. *"The firm has a big enough name nationally to attract people from all over"* we were told. We picked up on a preference for contentious work. Pre-merger, the Manchester firm – Vaudreys – was oriented towards personal injury and this is still a popular seat. *"We have a lot of PI but there's a growing field in professional indemnity,"* defending a mix of all sorts of professional negligence actions.

Litigation seats are popular because trainees like *"the cut and thrust of court life."* Take a second litigation seat and you can expect *"to have your own fast track files and do interim hearings in court."* Reflecting the fact that hours in contentious seats are generally regular and not excessive, it would be common to start before 9am and finish by 6pm.

extinction

Although a dying breed, we spoke to trainees in Leeds, Birmingham and Winchester and again the litigation bias came through. The firm's Sheffield office closed down mid way through 2001. As training contracts will no longer be offered in Birmingham and Winchester and may or may not be offered in Leeds, we don't propose to recount the training experiences of our sources in any detail. Suffice to say that there were no horror stories and trainees were generally very happy with their lot.

One message came across very clearly from each of the firm's offices – trainees perceive a north-south divide in the firm. It starts with the Professional Skills Course that they complete during the early part of the training contract. *"The PSC is regionalised,"* one trainee told us *"and so Bristol, Winchester and London trainees meet and the northern and Birmingham trainees meet separately."* Ask a Bristol trainee if they know their peers in Leeds and it's highly unlikely that the answer will be 'yes'.

The management does occasionally try to organise national events. In November 1999 the whole firm congregated near Reading and had motivation talks from Roger Black and Kris Akabussi. We have absolutely no idea how quickly the Beachcrofts trainees can cover 400 metres, but if September 2001 retention figures are anything to go by, they are long distance runners, not sprinters. The majority stay the distance post-qualification; in 2001 70% did.

and finally…

We'll admit that we approached True Picture interviews at this firm with some trepidation this year. Ever since merger the trainees have been off limits to our researchers. Despite one or two comments about post-merger, partner-level competition for top dog status, there was nothing to explain why our nosiness had been unwelcome. The firm hardly needs us to award its training a clean bill of health… but it has earned one anyway.

Berwin Leighton Paisner

the facts

Location: London
UK ranking by size: 21
Total number of trainees: 67
Seats: 4x6 months
Alternative seats: Overseas seats, secondments
Extras: Language training

It's been hard to give Berwin Leighton Paisner a good True Picturing this year, as the recently merged firm is so fresh and new that analysis of its training system is nigh impossible. But here goes…

"it's a good cultural fit"

So there's this firm called Berwin Leighton and this firm called Paisner & Co. Berwin Leighton sits in a grand building on the north side of London Bridge. Expansive, calm, sensible, established. Not too whacky, not particularly trendy. Good, solid, content, but it wants more… It spies plucky little Paisner & Co on Fleet Street, and "it looks like a good cultural fit." The whirlwind courtship resulted in merger on 1st May 2001. Though impossible to assess how the merger was fairing, everyone we spoke to reminded us of what a *"good cultural fit"* the two firms had.

Training at each firm had previously operated under a four by six-month seat rotation. Each firm had an impeccable record of retention on qualification. Trainees at each firm had a strong bond with their firm. But will the BLP training become a facsimile of the Berwin Leighton training, with its compulsories in property, corporate and contentious work? And will Paisners' trainees' *"guarantee"* of a seat in TechMedia for all those who want it vanish once the Berwin Leighton army have an equal chance of bagging that particular favourite?

berwins: the dominant partner

Berwin Leighton offered trainees fulfilling experiences in each of its large departments, although it was a rare and beautiful moment when we stumbled on trainees who had worked in niche seats, eg.employment or IP, or had been on a client secondment or worked overseas. To date, the two years were most likely to be rooted in property, corporate, banking, property finance, litigation or property litigation. Berwin Leighton's property-heavy client base provides the explanation for this.

Although they'd have preferred greater choice, trainees could indicate one 'preference seat' and would be reasonably assured of getting it. *"Corporate and commercial seats are popular and finance has become more so."* Indeed, if you look at the destination departments of those qualifying in September 2001, this 'mainstream' approach is reflected. The scores on the doors are: mainstream Corporate 7, mainstream Property 5, Banking 2, Property Finance 1, General Commercial 2, TechMedia 4, and then one each into insolvency, employment, litigation and tax. What, only one litigator? *"No one in our year is desperately keen to go into it… Litigation is just not that popular."*

healthy ambition

Berwin Leighton trainees saw themselves as *"not stuffy or arrogant, down to earth, those who enjoy challenges."* They freely admit to wanting to remain as lawyers; no one blushed at the idea of one day making partnership. *"Here, a majority of trainees might want partnership someday; perhaps about 60%."* Believe it or not that's quite high for a top firm and in real contrast to the answer typically received from magic circle trainees. Are these trainees an especially faithful lot? *"We seem to be a pretty loyal group of people,"* one thought. These are not the tarts of the legal profession, just out to get a few gold stars on their CVs before waltzing off into the sunset.

The firm's going to hate us saying it – again – but your average Berwin Leighton trainee isn't that unpredictable mate of yours that makes you edgy after he's had more than four pints. We heard – again – how a number of the trainees were already settled down with husbands, wives or established partners, yet the topic rarely comes up with trainees at other firms. These are the settlers of this world. Diligent, focused and self-assured but not cocky; hard working but not maniacal. They bear the hallmarks of well-rounded individuals who have a desire to make a real effort at work. One trainee confirmed that *"being keen really helps,"* but stressed *"it is not a keenness competition though."* The eager beavers we spoke to were all delighted with the quality of work and levels of responsibility they had been given.

le grand prix

There's scant opportunity to go abroad during the training contract, so make sure this doesn't matter to you. *"Not everyone wants to go. For Monaco, last time there was only two serious candidates so it's not a bun fight between 20 people saying 'I'm the best I want to go.' Quite a few are engaged or married."* (See, there it is again.) If Monaco doesn't suit, there's also a Brussels seat and, even closer to home, one trainee will pop out to Tesco three days a week (to work in the legal department, not on the tills). Other secondments include a stint with insurance giant Aon.

Berwin Leighton has a *"realistic approach"* to hours. *"Property and property finance are early starters,* usually 8.30am-6.30pm. The rest are 9-9.30am starts with a 6.30-7pm finish." In corporate, hours seem particularly dependent on the deal flow. One trainee remarked "*I did three or four weekends and five or six all-nighters. I worked after 9pm maybe once every two weeks. It wasn't a killer, but it did have its moments.*" "*You're not slogged to bits here… there's no whinge about hours – it's not an onslaught.*"

Manageable hours make for a healthy atmosphere and there's any number of sports that a trainee can enjoy with work mates. There are regular Friday night drinks on the partners' tab at local bar FOB and a brilliant 'concierge' facility that made our researcher green with envy. Just imagine being able to get someone else to book your flights, organise your dry cleaning and wait at home for the electrician! We also like the idea of clicking onto the web Qcam in the firm's basement restaurant 'Alibi'. The full time dress down policy allows for some sartorial flexibility, although many of the trainees we talked to wore suits anyhow.

paisner's story

Last year we covered Paisner & Co in the True Picture for the first time. The trainees made us laugh; they refreshed the parts that most trainees don't reach. We'll be honest, when we heard the two firms were merging, we thought that from a trainee's perspective, it was a bit of a shame.

Merger always seems easier for the larger partner in the equation and, whilst none of Paisner's trainees sounded overly concerned, it is obvious that things will change for them. Typically, trainees seem to have purposefully chosen a smaller firm. Last year it was ranked 66th (by size) in the UK. Berwin Leighton Paisner is now ranked 21st. Identifying the positives, one trainee told us that merger meant "*more money, more bodies and playing on all fronts… They are strong in areas that we're not. We didn't do property financing or planning like they do and we'll have more exposure to finance seats. I think the first years are after that. Lots of the first years want to do corporate work too.*"

Paisner's trainees will now have access to big mainstream departments at Berwins' Adelaide House – property, finance etc. and Berwins' trainees will now get their hands on more TechMedia work and private client seats. Thus far, "*graduate recruitment are receptive to your views,*" said one trainee.

routemaster

According to our sources, hours have been positively liberating at Paisner & Co. Trainees seem reassured that merger won't mean that they're suddenly working like dogs. "*It's a good cultural fit… they have a similar attitude to working and don't overburden you in the earlier years*" one trainee said. Every effort has been made to allow trainees to get to know each other and the rest of the firm at the other end of the 15-minute walk between offices. At the end of June 2001, property and corporate lawyers at Paisners were packing up and heading for Adelaide House and the litigators, construction and planning folk from Berwins were wending their way up to Paisner's old office – a rabbit warren called Bouverie House. Rumour has it that by August some of them had even remembered the route from the front door to their own desks.

The 'double decker' graduate recruitment brochure, hurried together following the decision to merge, displays the new BLP branding. You'll find more on the website and note a preoccupation with anagrams. The only sulky comment we heard on the branding was that Paisners had been subjected to memos and file labels bearing the old Berwin Leighton logo. Ouch! Rub the salt in.

There was initial anxiety over the shape of things to come. One trainee told us, "*When I first heard, I thought I was going to end up doing property due diligence for the rest of the two years.*" The general enthusiasm for merger from the top down seems to have rubbed off though, despite the fact that "*no one really knows what's happening.*" We learned that, as on Big Brother, the answer to many of the trainees' questions was: "*We'll get back to you on that.*"

and finally…

BLP will have had plenty of time to get to know itself by September 2003. Hopefully all staff will be housed under just one roof and doubtless there will be a whole new set of plans on the agenda. Something European maybe? It is a shame that Paisners will no longer exist as a punchy little alternative to the big firms, but we're sure that its influence will be felt within BLP. Could be an interesting place to be in the coming years…

Bevan Ashford

the facts
Location: Tiverton, Taunton, Plymouth, Exeter, Bristol, London, Birmingham
UK ranking by size: 31
Total number of trainees: 46
Seats: 4x6 months
Alternative seats: Secondments

Health-wise, this firm is really in the pink. It's a fast growing West of England firm that put down roots in the London market three years ago and has just opened a Birmingham office. It is well known for its public sector work, particularly in health, but also has a growing private sector client base.

safe seats
An accredited Investor in People, this isn't one of those desperately stuck-in-their-ways firms. Firms that see rapid growth (Bevan Ashford has doubled in size in the last five years) more often than not also experience a shift of power to younger, more go-ahead partners, and certainly Bevan Ashford has its fair share of ambitious partners. The latest outlet for ambition is the new office in Birmingham. None of our sources had any experience of this office, but we understand it has been set up to focus on health and PFI work. One or two trainees work out of Birmingham on NHS claims work or employment and healthcare advice. The London office also takes one or two Bristol trainees at a time for a six-month seat.

Bevan Ashford lost its Cardiff office earlier in 2001, when four partners bought out the Welsh business of the firm. After the *"initial shock,"* Cardiff trainees have come to terms with the loss and been welcomed into the Bristol fold. *"It was disappointing,"* said one ex-Cardiff trainee, *"but we knew our position was safe and the same seats are available in Bristol."*

west country life
Plymouth, Taunton and Tiverton are home to a cluster of the firm's trainees and, although not all of them are local girls and boys, they all have a love of the West Country. Even the most die-hard urbanite can be converted by the *"stunning drives to work."* If you want to work as a commercial lawyer but still smell the surf and the pasties, Bevan Ashford in the West Country has to be considered. The Tiverton office is located in a delightful 18th century house at the end of the small-town high street. It seems to be *"an exceptionally nice place to work"* where the town has *"a community feel"* and the partners are described as *"gentlemen."* Taunton is a tad bigger and the office slightly younger. Again, it's a real winner with the trainees who work there.

> "Plymouth are making a giant cactus and Taunton are building a huge wigwam."

Most of our West Country sources had spent time in more than one office, usually switching for a particular seat that was on offer elsewhere. Actually there's enough variety in each of the offices to allow a trainee to stay put for the whole two years, if necessary. The West Country offices' activities are primarily commercial (indeed Plymouth is wholly commercial), but seats can be taken in personal injury, matrimonial, crime, agriculture and private client. Throw in the specialist seats in Exeter, such as pensions and planning, and you soon note that practically every main area of law is covered. However, if you're after international capital markets work, you should be looking under 'A' for Allen & Overy.

the southernhay strip

The Exeter office was criticised in last year's True Picture for having a somewhat authoritarian feel to it. Trainee opinion was split this year as to whether that criticism had been fair, although all admitted that things feel more chilled now than a year ago. Trainees are now *"well over"* a couple of sticky incidents, so it's not surprising they are happier and that any negative atmosphere has *"dissipated."*

Early to bed, early to rise and all that; trainees often start their day in the office at eight-something but that means an exit as early as 5.20pm in some cases. *"Without a killer commute,"* you can be home in time to catch Neighbours on TV. There's the occasional evening when you'll be lucky to make the 8pm soaps, but *"there's no 'beds in the basement' mentality."* With an open plan layout, *"you feel as if you are a member of a large team and you get to know everyone."* Office drinks, held every Friday, are well attended and afterwards there's *"a bit of a scene on the strip"* (Southernhay – where a number of Exeter's law firms are located). There are plenty of organised events and the TSG is strong in the city. Best of all though was the genuine enthusiasm with which trainees talked about the firm's annual West Country Ball. *"It's going to be in Dawlish,"* one trainee explained, *"and it has a Wild West theme. Plymouth are making a giant cactus and Taunton are building a huge wigwam."* Hmm… we think trainees smoke too much pipe of peace…

bristol: health of the nation

With the 'golden triangle' of Cardiff-Bristol-London being re-drafted into a 'golden straight line' following the loss of the Welsh office, the Bristol trainee population just got a bit bigger. Unlike other firms' attempts to open up in the city (Eversheds recently closed its office there), Bevan Ashford has met with real success and it holds its head high with the other top-rung firms. *"We have an NHS client focus at the moment, but we will expand the client base and build off the back of the NHS." "The main types of work that we do here are healthcare and claims, projects and commercial work for NHS clients."* As in past years, trainees remind us that NHS clients' requirements are not all that different from private sector clients.

Most Bristol trainees will do a medical negligence seat and it is possible that some will end up doing two if they ask; *"it's the biggest department here."* The most popular seats are employment, commercial litigation and projects. Bevan Ashford has some super private sector clients – Allied Domecq, HSBC, Bank of Ireland and some other really sexy plcs that we could tell you about… but Bevan Ashford would probably have to shoot us if we did… did we mention the secondment to Orange? Bang!

b.y.o. skills

OK, it's not essential to bring your own skills as Bevan Ashford takes its training very seriously. Second careerers, especially medical professionals, can really come into their own as trainee lawyers and, in recognition of this, the firm recruits a number of those with first career experience. Even if you're not medically qualified *"you should have an interest in healthcare"* one trainee said. Social skills are also of importance as *"you must be a team player to work here."*

It's important to understand that the Exeter-Tiverton-Taunton-Plymouth experience is one half of the picture and the London-Bristol-(and now) Birmingham experience is another. The former is less oriented to healthcare than the latter. Trainees almost never move between the two groupings and few know any trainees from the other group. If you want to orient your work towards healthcare, or if you want to avoid it, then choose the correct grouping.

and finally...

Whether you're a West Country bumpkin and can envisage yourself saying something like *"Exeter is everything I need"* or you crave the bright lights of Bristol, Bevan Ashford has an office that is likely to suit you. The firm's health sector reputation and work will act as a real draw to some applicants, but fear not if you're inclined to the private sector rather than the public as blue chips instruct the firm too.

Bird & Bird

the facts
Location: London
UK ranking by size: 33
Total number of trainees: 27
Seats: 4x6 months
Alternative seats: Secondments

With a clear focus on technology, the firm's main strengths lie in communications, e-commerce, IT, IP, media and sport. With this focus comes a group of well known and hip clients, such as MP3, the FA, Vivendi and AOL... as well as some less hip government departments.

nest hopping
Bird & Bird takes on a relatively low number of trainees for its size and our sources thought this went some way to explaining the general satisfaction with seat allocation. *"I thought I'd be told what to do and have to grit my teeth, but it's not been like that at all – I've had input."* A number of trainees had spent three months in-house with a client during certain of their six-month seats. They were also pleased with the variety of work that had come their way in the office. *"It makes a real difference when you have a say in your training; you can adapt it to what you want it to be."* *"They consult with you, they're flexible and you're not just dumped into seats."* This suggests that, if you know what kind of experience you want to get, you'll be listened to. It also suggests that the firm expects its trainees to be proactive.

The most popular seats are employment, IP and 'Company C' (*"where the IT e-commerce-type stuff gets done."*) Although you'll usually get your first choice, some practice areas can get over-subscribed. Apparently last year well over half of one intake wanted to do an employment seat and there wasn't enough room, but *"they'll try to fit you in at some stage."*

> "There's no cranky type in a cloud of B&H smoke...no one has that much respect here."

catching worms
Trainees are allocated a supervisor, but work can come from many sources. *"You're not hamstrung by a single supervisor. You can wander around and grab work off anyone and you're encouraged to go and get it."* So do these trainee hunter-gatherers return to their desks with rich pickings or slim pickings? *"You're given as much as you can handle... I was doing work for the chairman in my first seat."* It can mean that *"you're sometimes thrown in at the deep end, but we don't have any nightmare supervisors. I've always been able to talk to other people and have my work checked."* Trainees are enthusiastic about the help and feedback they receive. *"Supervisors are always welcoming, even when they're quite busy. You can ask them silly questions – I do a lot!"*

freebirds
The words *"trust"* and *"responsibility"* cropped up a lot during our interviews for the True Picture. *"I was impressed by the level of involvement I had from day one,"* one of our sources told us. *"I've had quite a few moments where it's been a bit panicky, but they don't let you do anything that's going to expose you."* The trust placed in the trainees by the partners is sometimes evident in the trainees' relationships with clients.

"For some clients trainees are the first point of contact," although "client instructions won't get processed and sent out without someone seeing it." The firm pushes its trainees to perform but provides plenty of on the job training. "They're very pro-education – we get lectures every lunchtime, which are good for keeping up to speed." "They're also good at putting you on external courses," not all of them confined to black letter law.

And the picture is just as bright where hours are concerned. Trainees told us they usually left the office by 7pm at the latest, although most had experienced two or three all-nighters. On the whole "I'm a bit in control of my own hours, I don't feel any pressure to stay late." A bit in control… well that's better than nothing!

migration

What type of applicant does Bird & Bird want to attract to the flock? The website indicates that it's interested in graduates with science, engineering or mathematics degrees and those with language skills. However, the current trainee population doesn't seem to reflect this. "In my intake, half were law, half weren't, and only one had a scientific background." And just in case you make the mistake, "you shouldn't think of Bird & Bird as just an IP and communications firm. The firm is trying to broaden; I think one trainee even wants to qualify into property." Fancy that!

However, there's not much point in ignoring the fact that Bird & Bird has grown as a technology firm. One trainee said, "I'd encourage students to apply if they've got prior experience in IT, IP sciences or even just experience of living abroad." You certainly don't need a PhD in rocket science but "it's helpful to have some IT/IP/e-commerce knowledge because those are the firm's core strengths. It's not a technical aptitude you need, just a desire to learn." Language skills come in handy because of the international nature of the firm's work. It has a twinning scheme with its Stockholm and Paris offices. Periodically, London solicitors go out to one of the other offices for two weeks and foreign lawyers visit the UK. From time to time a trainee might get the chance to participate in an exchange.

A full six-month seat is available in the firm's Brussels office and there will soon be one in Paris.

larkin' about

The firm's style is an open one. "There's none of the hierarchy thing and I've never hesitated to knock on a door. Good news for non-smokers: "There's no cranky type in a cloud of B&H smoke who is so revered that everyone jumps to attention when he's around. No one has that much respect here!" But "we still wear suits" and it's a very commercial atmosphere. Lawyers are getting on with the serious business of case handling. "The bottom line very definitely matters, it's probably the watchword here."

It's not all work though. When we called to speak to them, some trainees were rushed off their feet. It wasn't that they had masses of work, it was the looming deadlines imposed by their busy social calendar. "We've got softball tonight; tomorrow there's our summer party with Jools Holland and on Wednesday cricket and rounders against a key client." A busy week then!

A quiet week might mean just the one social engagement – a Friday night meeting in Walkers, the pub just below the office. Trainees sometimes find themselves with a bundle of cash from the partners and the simple instruction to "go off for lunch!" Although they are "quite a tight group," trainees do mix with associates and partners. Every three months the partners throw a drinks party for the whole firm. Would you ever find the partners in Walkers on a Friday night? "Definitely, they tend to drag you out and they put their cards behind the bar!" Excellent.

are you experienced?

The trainees offered some tips for applicants. "If you've got some knowledge or some particular interest, really highlight it. They are looking for something that's a bit different. In your application be positive about what makes you different – if you've been fossil hunting in Kathmandu for six years, don't hide it." Experience of one sort or another is valued. Bird & Bird does take on more than its fair share of mature trainees and often it is the mature trainee that knows what he or she wants. Our True Picture interviewees seemed to have clear ideas about what drew them to the firm. *"In my covering letter I mentioned my background... I tried to get across that fact that I wasn't applying to fifty firms – that I'd tailored my application."*

"Bird & Bird's not for people who'd be happy to be working on menial stuff from 7am to 12pm... it's for people who want to contribute something rather than be time-servers." Trainees differ in style, *"some are quite studious and academic, some are more outgoing,"* but all are *"quite strong, in that they speak their mind."* They didn't study law because they couldn't think of anything else, nor did they apply to Bird & Bird and a hundred other firms. And once there, they want to stay. *"Most of us are ambitious. We're aware that it's going well at the firm and there aren't many places we'd want to go on to from here."* One said, *"I can't imagine anyone not wanting to be partner."* Six of the seven qualifiers stayed with the firm in September 2001.

and finally...

If you're confident, secure, brainy, optimistic, ambitious and into all that internet jazz, then this bird's for you. Even if you end up as a property lawyer...

Blake Lapthorn

the facts
Location: Fareham, Portsmouth, Southampton, London
UK ranking by size: 70
Total number of trainees: 15
Seats: 4x6 months
Alternative seats: Brussels, secondments

If you're set on living and working on the south coast and you want to try your hand at a truly broad spread of work, then maybe you can do no better than Blake Lapthorn. From the little guy in the street to the multinational plc, this firm's got a really diverse client base. Whether you know which end of the scale you're going for or whether you just want to keep your options open, it's is a good choice.

in the house
Training contracts are being hacked from a one-time high of ten per year to just five per year. It's a smart response to the frustrations experienced by many regional practices that see trainees jumping on the first train to London after qualification. By taking just five trainees a year, Blake Lapthorn can concentrate on recruiting the most committed five. If you have local connections, great. If you don't, apply anyway. The firm won't hold it against you. And don't read the reduction in training places as any indication of a shrinking profile. You'd be very wrong. Blake Lapthorn is actually strengthening its position as 'best of breed' in this part of the country.

Last year trainees moaned about having to repay the money loaned to them by the firm for law school fees. Hooray!! The repayable loan is gone! In its place is a bursary. Well done Blakes, we knew you had the cash. Gone too are the 'trainee houses' in Portsmouth; homes to the Billy No-mates new recruits until they found their feet, their own social scene and a four-week deposit. One source told us that it just seemed like the right time for the firm to sell those houses. *"By the end they weren't in great condition"* (sounds like student housing doesn't it?) and sometimes the trainees might get into a bit of a squabble, although it was *"nothing too hectic."* While some were happy about no longer having a *"knickers on the radiator"* relationship with work colleagues, others have found breaking up hard to do. Three *"chums"* still live together in the same house. Bless!

in the hot seat
In addition to the staples of corporate, property and commercial litigation, the firm undertakes a remarkable range of specialist work across its four offices, including aviation, pensions, banking, and professional and clinical negligence. Whilst there's no choice over your first seat and the firm likes you to

"*get a good all round training,*" there are some seats which are definitely more popular than others. "*Commercial and employment are the hot seats*" at the moment and we learned that a few trainees are also very keen on personal injury.

Certain seats, like the Brussels' secondment and some less popular slots such as the "*dreaded*" residential conveyancing ("*a bulk operation run by legal execs*" which "*some are prepared to put up with*") are only three months long, with the rest at six months. A couple of industry secondments offer a look at life from the client's perspective. And then there's the only really alarming seat option – six months in the probate department dealing with "*old grannies' wills.*"

big brother

We were intrigued by the firm's recent attempt to show how difficult it was to allocate seats. In an exercise akin to "*mud wrestling,*" the trainees were taken out for a meal and a few beers and asked to enter into a group discussion and thrash out the next seat allocation. There and then. "*It was bloody awkward to sit in the pub and argue for what you wanted… it smacked a bit of Big Brother!*" But "*everyone said their piece…*" and they learnt why they don't all get their first choice. The exercise was a one off. Seat requests are now written.

Regular group consultations with HR are a new and popular initiative and often wrap up with an evening out together. Trainee mentors join in, as does the training partner who is an approachable chap with whom our sources felt they could connect. It seems easy enough to raise issues with him, the best approach being to "*mug him on the way to the pub.*"

stay or go – you decide

We noted an increase in morale during this year's True Picture research. It's not that morale was desperately low before, but suddenly a number of things have changed for trainees – and they like it. For example, "*the firm used to leave job offers* [on qualification] *till late and the process was messy… They are now more open,*" said one trainee. In 1999 only three of the ten qualifiers stayed on, in 2000 it had sunk to an all time low of just one out of ten. In September 2001 the figure rose to five out of ten (although the popular jobs are still oversubscribed).

> "Some were happy about no longer having a 'knickers on the radiator' relationship with work collegues."

The NQ salary is much bigger this year. At £28K it's felt to be a realistic alternative to those big London bucks and way better than previous "*skimpy*" salaries. There's more of a feeling of "*openness*" and realism at the moment with the firm behaving towards its trainees "*more like a London practice.*" As far as trainees are concerned, this is exactly as it should be as "*they operate their business like a London firm and expect the same standards of trainees.*"

staying under the limit

There's a good emphasis on sports and social events and "*marketing are always organising something.*" In most of the offices there are Friday night drinks on a regular basis, but "*in reality only the fee earners go.*" The regularity of after hours visits to local pubs depends on office location. Southampton ("*very laid back… smaller headcount… partner involvement in creating a cosier atmosphere*") and London (which takes one trainee at a time) are inner city, and the scene is healthy. The Southampton staff have The Alexandra and The Varsity. London staff, although "*not out on the pop the whole time,*" enjoy a drink in The Hercules. The poor old Segensworth trainees, operating out of an office on the side of the M27, need to go for a short drive or walk 15 minutes to The Talisman… and then get back home somehow.

The upside to working in a side of motorway business park? Loads of parking. One converted traffic watcher enthused about her journey to work; "It's brilliant – you can get to work in the blink of an eye. At worst it takes 25 minutes... although at lunchtimes you do have to get in your car to go anywhere." Obviously this is a firm for the motorist. "It's not especially picturesque on the industrial estate" one said, (no, we thought it wouldn't be) "but you can soon drive to a nice river bank and just sit there and chat to your mates if you're having a bad day. And there's quite good cut price designer clothes at a nearby factory outlet."

the mr men

Some of our sources thought that Segensworth was "the most sociable. It's got the biggest gang of trainees." They also pointed out that although Harbour Court in Portsmouth has fewer trainees, it is home to many of the support staff, which makes for "a nice mix of people." But then we heard something really odd… We struggled with the concept that in 2001 there are some partners in the firm (a minority it's true) who still prefer trainees and staff to call them Mr so and so. Remarkable! If trainees at other firms would like to report this phenomenon, we'd be happy to start a nationwide campaign for first names.

We have no idea on the preferred forms of address of the 12 partners at Portsmouth firm Sherwin Oliver, with whom Blakes hopes to merge in October 2001.

and finally…

The Mr Men issue seems to be a vestige from a past in which trainees could list a number of things that they'd change. This traditionalism is at odds with Blake Lapthorn's reputation in the marketplace as a firm that keeps pace with developments in the profession and its clients' business. Trainees feel their position has changed in the last year and indicated that they knew they were being listened to. "When I applied to them I saw them as an innovative firm with a younger outlook and not set in their ways." From the trainees' perspective, Blake Lapthorn is becoming that firm.

Bond Pearce

the facts

Location: Bristol, Exeter, Leeds, London, Plymouth, Southampton
UK ranking by size: 36
Total number of trainees: 41
Seats: 4x6 months
Alternative Seats: Secondments

Bond Pearce is a serious commercial player, which has gained a fantastic reputation across the south and west of England. The London and Leeds satellite offices do not take trainees, so our True Picture report concentrates on its four larger offices.

plymouth: banter and piss-take

"Plymouth is where the firm started, and the administrative hub still resides there." It is housed in "all brand new" offices and our sources indicated that it attracts trainees who are "generally older and from round here… and will stay." Understandably, applicants are more likely to be attracted to Plymouth if they already have some ties in the region and the firm needs to award training contracts to those who are genuinely committed to a career in the area. Hence the preponderance of "West Country folk." If you train here, expect to defend your decision to "mates in London" who'll assume that "Plymouth is not great." Well, we expect they'd change their minds after a night out in the firm's local, Sippers. We learned that some "amusing characters" staff the Plymouth office and there's "a lot of banter and piss-take."

On a serious note, expect a commercial training (generally handling regional business) and some personal injury work. We're not surprised to hear that "commercial seats are more popular… PI is not considered that great a seat." In the first seat, one of our sources was "spoon fed quite nicely, which was a relief" but the pace picked up and the training became very hands on. Commercial litigation offers very

THE TRUE PICTURE OUR TOP 100 FIRMS

213

good experience, with attendance at plenty of court hearings. Seat allocation involves some *"jostling around"* and *"some won't get what they want or may have to be put in another office to get what they want."* One source indicated that previous attempts by trainees to sort out the seat allocation amongst themselves didn't go well and resulted in *"a lot of back-stabbing."* NQ job offers proceeded more smoothly and in September 2001. Three qualifiers stayed in Plymouth post-qualification.

exeter: sleeping on the beach

"Exeter is sleepy" and there are *"no night clubs… but we go to the beach instead."* However, the TSG is active in the city and there's no killer commute on the tube at the end of the day. Indeed, with contracted hours of 9am till 5.15pm, and an hour and a quarter for lunch, you'll be fully aware that you've bypassed the London experience. The seats on offer are geared towards the firm's commercial work and the trainees are themselves *"commercially minded."* As a result, *"some people don't want to do a personal injury seat."* Property can be a bit of a yawn as it involves a lot of compulsory purchase work for the Highways Agency.

Seat allocations are made after a *"15 minute chat with the head of training and then a bit of negotiation among the trainees."* Exeter trainees get on well with each other and one source emphasised that *"you receive a lot of support from other trainees."* It helps if junior colleagues can answer your queries because, while *"some partners are approachable, with others you feel nervous about asking questions."* In September 2001 none of the trainees qualified in to the Exeter office.

southampton: popping out to B&Q

The Southampton branch is *"split into three different offices, though they should be moving together."* Although not ideal, with *"good computer links it's not a problem."* The Southampton lawyers' long term links with big retail clients (Woolworths, B&Q and others) has resulted in *"quite a few secondments.*

There's definitely an opportunity to do one if you want to. They can be taken as a commercial or an employment seat." The secondments offer trainees the chance to take on a higher level of responsibility than they might otherwise experience and certainly far more than in their first seats where responsibility was *"limited… but I didn't want any more at that stage."* One trainee told us the high point of the training contract was *"finally feeling like I was getting somewhere in my second year rather than just proof reading."* Unsurprisingly, the low times are *"when it is quiet and you feel under used."*

Bond Pearce attracts high calibre trainees who are clearly just as capable as their friends and peers in the City; it's just that they have chosen to side step the big smoke in favour of provincial life. The office social committee ensures that things don't get too quiet: *"For £1 a month we've had subsidised trips to the theatre, beer and curry, a trip to the Dome and a shopping trip to London."* Bargain! *"I am perfectly happy here,"* one said, *"even though my mates are in London."* Southampton has done very well to retain so many of its young lawyers. In September 2001, five of the six qualifiers stayed with the firm and another has relocated from a different branch.

bristol: magnetism

The developing Bristol office put on a growth spurt in 2001 through a merger with local firm Cartwrights. Each of the trainees we spoke to across the Bond Pearce empire knew that the Bristol office *"is liable to increase in size dramatically."* If you desire a metropolitan life in the West Country, Bristol can provide it. If the truth be known, a number of our sources wanted to switch offices after qualification and move to the Bristol branch. It has good quality clients and competes easily with the leading firms in the city for good quality work. Bond Pearce's short history in the city has meant that *"there have only been five departments in Bristol, but this should grow."*

In September 2001, none of the Bond Pearce qualifiers were retained in the Bristol office, but two of the five Cartwrights NQs stayed on.

A Bristol trainee explained that the office was *"more high-powered because of a greater percentage of partners here... Therefore, trainees and others tend to feel it can be more pressurised, and that more fun is had at the other Bond Pearce offices."* *"Maybe one night a week, an email will go round about drinks after work,"* usually in the local Quay Bar. But even if it's Bristol you want, be prepared to take your turn elsewhere – *"you have to be willing to move around the offices."*

all together now

What becomes clear is that to train with Bond Pearce outside of Bristol, you have to appreciate a less cosmopolitan existence, but all the trainees we spoke to emphasised a good quality of work and a high standard of living. Salaries in each office are good for the area. Maybe it's just because we interviewed them on a lovely June day, but the trainees at Bond Pearce were positive and optimistic. *"Good work without being in London, really good clients, good quality of life and you can go to the beach."* *"Everybody mucks in,"* and people are *"enthusiastic and bright... casual, informal and friendly."* We also learned that *"there are some eccentrics at Bond Pearce. They don't repress people, or boot you out for being different."*

However, one trainee bemoaned the practice of *"opening the post each morning."* Fear not! *Chambers Student Guide* to the rescue. Two years ago we took up the challenge to free Bevan Ashford trainees from this loathsome task. So let the Bond Pearce anti-post campaign begin!

and finally…

Take note: all applicants for a training contract must now apply for and undertake a vacation scheme in order to be considered. The rise of the Bristol office looks set to continue and training opportunities in that office are likely to increase. It may have just been a two office Devon practice five years ago but just look at it now!

Bristows

the facts

Location: London
UK ranking by size: 93
Total number of trainees: 14
Seats: 4x6 months*
Alternative Seats: Secondments

It's top ranked in the UK for intellectual property law, so did we really need to ask why trainees applied to the firm? The answer held no surprises for our trusty researcher: *"I want to be an IP lawyer!"* Just as we thought then…

what's a test tube?

This niche firm exudes a confidence that comes from knowing it is a leader in the field. And that doesn't just mean simple trademark cases. Bristows regularly deals with scientific patents involving precise technical knowledge. World-class scientists are often called in to help with cases, and we heard of one trainee who interviewed his old chemistry professor as a witness. You don't have to have a science degree to work here, but it helps. Some of the current crop of trainees went a bit far; three actually have PhDs. *"At some stages, I have done more science than law,"* one told us. In reality, about half of each year's intake have experience in science and often orient towards the more technical work on offer.

> "Flying out to California to witness experiments."

The training contract is *"fluid,"* in the sense that trainees might do three months here and six months there.* *"The idea is that everyone does four seats of six months in IP, IT, property and commercial litigation."* But *"it's a lop-sided firm, IP is huge, so the training is lop-sided as well."* Invariably, with contentious and non-contentious IP seats available, trainees can expect about nine months of IP training *"at the sacrifice of a seat determined by firm."* A trainee's choice is limited in respect of *"which order and for how long in each one."* Just one minor gripe results from this unregimented approach: formal appraisals can suffer. *"It's supposed to be as soon as you finish a seat. But they have not been as regular as they should be,"* one trainee said. Another confirmed, *"they have been inconsistent in getting them organised."*

intellectual hot property

Clients range from FTSE 100 to small start-up companies, so you'll not be acting for *"just one type of client."* They come from pharmaceuticals, electronics, IT, media and e-business – you get the picture. In IP litigation, *"it can be excellent. You have great responsibility, but if the department is quiet, you may find yourself with bog-standard trainee work to do."* Working as a part of a team, trainees find that a lot of their work is *"more research based,"* although we did hear of one trainee flying out to California to witness some experiments. Cool!

big deal

But what of the other departments? Do they become sidelined? After all, IP amounts to over half of the firm's workload. *"Sometimes other departments don't feel as if they get a look in, but that is the nature of a niche firm,"* one trainee said. The non-IP departments are *"relaxed and small, so probably don't care that they are in the shadow of IP."* There's *"good work"* in commercial litigation and you're *"really thrown in the deep end in property."* In company, *"a big deal can be great, but if it's quiet it can mean company secretarial work."*

Partners supervise well and delegate appropriately. *"I'm never worried about making an horrendous mistake."* *"As soon as you prove yourself, you get more and more work."* Secondments are available to *"large blue chip companies,"* usually for three months, though *"if you have been doing a particular case, some have been called back for the odd week."*

no winging it

This firm knows it must continue to perform at the highest level to keep hold of its leading reputation. *"It is very established and people here really do know what they are talking about."* *"The thing that hits you is how intelligent people are."* What comes with this is a particular matter-of-factness: *"You can't coast. There's no winging it. You have to have substance."* Flashiness gets you nowhere in this *"friendly, quite conservative place, which is not ostentatious or showy at all, just very proud of what it does, with the knowledge that it does it well."*

The firm is actively expanding non-IP departments, but *"knows that it is very good at IP, and is going to keep building on those strengths."* A number of partners have been appointed in the last couple of years, so the firm is looking to take on *"more junior- and medium- experience assistants,"* which must bode well for future trainees.

ice cream and grass

Listening to the Bristows trainees describe their lives together, it's difficult not to imagine a 70s TV show with a name like 'The Smiley Gang'. We decided the show would have opening credits with the lead characters gambolling across the lawns of Lincoln's Inn Fields, high-fiving and chorusing 'hey, let's clerk!' Indeed, without an outdoor clerk, one of the features of a Bristows training contract is the rota that requires trainees to take turns issuing writs and collecting papers from court. *"On a sunny day, you can have an ice-cream and walk across the grass."* Sweet!

reaching the parts others don't reach

Come Friday, the Smiley Gang will enter into a *"long and involved debate"* as to where to go that night. *"But usually it doesn't work"* and, as in any good sitcom, they end up in their regular haunt (in this case *"The George"*) accompanied by a *"sprinkling of assistants."* Often teams will go out together and, particularly when a case has completed, *"there have been some pretty raucous nights out with clients, counsel, and* experts." 6pm is a typical end to the working day. One source said, "*I have only had to cancel social arrangements twice.*"

An annual dinner dance (*"talked about at length before and after"*) took place this year in Claridges. *"They thought 'everyone has Christmas parties – what's the dullest time of year? March!'"* In a move to encourage interaction, other-halves were told to stay home. This may have been an overly-cautious step, as the firm seems to be perfectly well integrated. *"There are no barriers between trainees and partners,"* one of our sources said, while another talked of Bristows being *"an incredibly friendly firm, from post room boys to top partners."*

> "There's no winging it. You have to have substance."

Retention rates are high. In a repeat of the previous year, all the 2001 qualifiers were offered jobs and only one is leaving to explore life outside of law. Trainees stick with Bristows on qualification even though, with such a thorough grounding in IP law, they could *"walk into jobs at big firms with headline salaries."* There's something about Bristows that makes them stay; it's more than just good hours and the firm being *"small, cosy and good at IP."* Staff are very approachable at all levels, and *"are keen to see that you are interested."* *"My friend said I was the only person she knew who was enjoying their job,"* declared one trainee with such enthusiasm that she admitted getting *"carried away talking about work."* Now that's refreshing.

and finally…

The depth of knowledge and expertise in this firm is something to be reckoned with and it has carved itself an enviable place in the profession. In short, *"it's a pretty happy ship."*

Browne Jacobson

the facts

Location: Nottingham, Birmingham, London
UK ranking by size: 56
Total number of trainees: 18
Seats: 4x6 months
Alternative Seats: None

The majority of Browne Jacobson's practice is corporate/commercial and insurance litigation, including personal injury. The firm also undertakes private client work, albeit for *"wealthy clients."* As one trainee put it, *"it's small claims up to big industrial disputes."* There really is more to this firm than just insurance, as it has sometimes been characterised, but it's true that insurance groups handle nearly half the firm's work.

pigs might fly

Most of Browne Jacobson's business is carried out in its Nottingham office and trainees tell us the firm prefers its recruits to have some roots in the area. If you've studied in Nottingham you're halfway there and any kind of Midlands connection will do. The firm has offered training contracts to some of its paralegals and we noted more than one ex-accountant in the current batch.

In addition to the main Nottingham office, Browne Jacobson has outposts in London and Birmingham. The relationship between offices is department-driven; *"Birmingham has more of an insurance market and if you're not involved with that type of work, you won't really have anything to do with that office."* One seat is available for a trainee in London in the professional indemnity group or PIG as it's affectionately known.

map reading

Trainees talk of being *"aware that you are with a firm of a substantial size."* Its name has grown in areas such as commercial property, banking, construction, trusts and healthcare, and the corporate/commercial seats have become the most popular amongst trainees. BJs has maintained its strong reputation in litigation and continues to be a regional leader in professional negligence and defendant personal injury. The firm has come out smelling of roses following the shake-up of the NHS Litigation Authority panel (which issues instructions to defend clinical negligence claims). Of late the clinical negligence practice in the Birmingham office has been recruiting heavily and will shortly make a seat available for one trainee.

Steady expansion in Nottingham has resulted in the firm taking over neighbouring office buildings, many of which are listed. The resulting offices are *"like a rabbit warren."* Some sources spoke of trainees disappearing for months on end and others wandering around in a confused state. Fear not, *"new trainees are handed a map when they first arrive."* In Nottingham, *"they are stepping up targets for the firm." "Having grown quickly, it is having to adjust."* But trainees see the firm's approach to growth as organic. Don't expect any big mergers. The firm is *"quite proud of the tradition of never merging."*

it's good to talk

Trainees are *"always subject to close supervision"* from *"very approachable people right up to partner level,"* although we did hear of *"a couple of people who have been reluctant to give feedback because they are too busy."* Trainees tell us that they *"do get involved in some of the bigger cases – but you also get mundane work."*

The official way to secure your seat of choice is to go and talk to the training partner although, apparently, it *"helps to speak to departments beforehand." "The big departments do have the space to give trainees what they want,"* so you can always guarantee a seat in commercial litigation and company commercial. However, not all trainees are offered jobs on qualification and some do leave simply because the firm has had a problem finding a role for them in their preferred departments. In 2001, five of the nine qualifiers were offered jobs and four of those accepted, each with the company commercial department as their destination.

it's a knockout

"It's a Knockout, for the whole firm, was lovely. The partners brought their families. I thought 'this is why I'm at this firm'." Browne Jacobson is very sociable. *"The Kids"* is the nickname attached to a pub called the Royal Children, which is the *"second office"* just over the road from the firm's Nottingham HQ. It's *"quite grotty"* apparently, but staff tend to prefer its laid back surroundings to the swanky bars in the centre of Nottingham. Proceedings are helped along by the fact that *"there are a number of young partners"* and the trainees are *"friends as well as colleagues."*

Each year the firm engages in a treasure hunt around the pubs of Nottingham. As the night wears on, staff find it increasingly difficult to search for clues and eventually have to be directed straight to the food and drink prize marking the end of the hunt. This poor navigation occurs even though (or perhaps because) there's *"not a single person in the firm you wouldn't feel happy to talk to."*

scream if you wanna go faster

What a website! Watch the fuses flash at you as you move your mouse over the circuit-board on the home page. We spent far too long playing with the site… OK, it was a slow day. Website aside, is Browne Jacobson a wired firm? No. It's *"relaxed"* but *"some of the partners are a scream."*

Once you've calmed down from all that web excitement, remind yourself of the fact that Browne Jacobson is a serious regional player. Its *"personality based atmosphere"* is *"coupled with the fact that we know we do some very good work."* The firm is *"small enough for everyone to know you, but big enough to be able to provide a scope and diversity of training – ideal for people that want to do well, but don't want to be one of 100 trainees."* One trainee said, *"I couldn't really ask for a nicer place to work."* It *"doesn't pay lip service to the work/life balance"* and hours are typically 8.30am to 6pm.

and finally…

If you fancy yourself as one of the merry men (or women) of Nottingham, you should consider Browne Jacobson. It offers an excellent range of work in the commercial sphere and can give private client experience to those that want it. What's more, it won't rob you of your social life or your sense of fun.

Burges Salmon

the facts
Location: Bristol
UK ranking by size: 42
Total number of trainees: 38
Seats: 6x4 months
Alternative Seats: Secondments
Extras: Pro bono: Bristol University Law Centre, language training

Burges Salmon is the cream of the crop in Bristol and the largest firm in the South West by a whisker. It offers a wide commercial practice and has a strong reputation in agriculture and private client work, which in the past has given the firm a slightly stuffier image than its top regional rival Osborne Clarke. If you want to practise law in Bristol, this firm will undoubtedly be on your list… so long as you can handle the corporate colour – salmon pink.

spinning around

The seat system involves six rotations of four months over two years. Four of the six are in compulsory areas, namely one seat in company/commercial and one in property. There is then a choice between tax and trusts or employment and pensions. The fifth seat is an option seat and the final one will be taken in your qualification department. This system gives trainees a chance to see a wide variety of work before deciding on an area for qualification. The gripe that four months is not long enough to get the real flavour of a department is remedied by the fact that preferred seats can be repeated before qualification.

Like most regional firms, Burges Salmon appreciates applicants who have some kind of connection with the area. *"If you have family here or studied here then that can be a plus. It is not a prerequisite, they just want to know why you are applying to the firm and if you will stay on after qualification."* It's also got *"a reputation for being a firm with a positive attitude to mature applicants."* This certainly doesn't mean fresh-faced graduates shouldn't apply, just that the firm is especially interested in those who have special skills or experience. *"In my intake almost 50% of trainees had a career before or had taken a couple of years out, but it isn't always like that. They are looking for the best regardless of age."* Perhaps it's this aspect of the firm's recruitment strategy, which results in the absence of a Burges Salmon 'type'. Trainees find a range of personalities and backgrounds amongst their peers.

blue chip blues

Generally trainees were happy with the levels of responsibility available. Interviewees all cited examples of handling their own files and running small cases with support from their supervisor. They also talked of plenty of paralegal and support staff to keep photocopying levels to a minimum. As with any big firm, you can't expect client contact and responsibility in every seat or during every deal and some found this disheartening, especially early on. *"In my first seat the department was completing on a huge deal. There was next to nothing that I could practically contribute and I really didn't feel like I was part of the team. They assured me that it would get better though."* Remember, this is all part of life in a firm that handles big deals for blue chip clients.

In 2000/2001 the number of mega-deals handled by the corporate team was impressive. Amongst them the £234 million disposal of Bristol Airport for FirstGroup, public takeovers of ARAM Resources, Oneview.net (valued at £135 million) and Pegasus Group. It also handled Motion Media's £141 million official listing, the £95 million acquisition of Annova for Orange and the US$50 million cross-border acquisition of the worldwide business of CODA for Science Systems. If we started listing all the high profile work the firm covered in its other areas of practice we'd be here forever. You get the picture.

beside the quayside

Burges Salmon is based on Bristol's quayside, with many lawyers enjoying a view of the river. It's an increasingly cosmopolitan area, surrounded by bars, restaurants and cinemas. Most trainees live within walking distance of the office, sparing them the interminable grind into work each morning that their London peers must endure. The firm organises a pretty extensive range of social events from balls and lunches to parties and charity events. When we called to interview trainees, they had recently been involved in a sponsored rowing competition for Comic Relief on Red Nose day.

There is an understanding that life does not begin and end with the firm and you won't be worked to the point of burn out. In the main part, hours are predictable. Trainees told us that a normal working day would last from 9am to 6pm with staff staying late only when it was essential. *"Hours are reasonably steady here but they can vary… when you do work late though, supervisors make sure that you know it is appreciated. It really helps give the impression that we are valued when hard work is noted and appreciated."*

the future's bright

Burges Salmon is pretty much a one-office outfit, so don't expect to be working in London or jetting off to practise abroad during your time as a trainee. Burges Salmon is expanding in Bristol though. The property department has recently knocked through a wall, spilling out into the building next door. We heard that it's eyeing up another floor in the building too.

If you don't want to be in Bristol, you don't want to be at Burges Salmon. But that said, the firm is increasing the number of client secondments available to trainees. Schemes currently exist with companies such as Orange, FirstGroup and British Aerospace. We spoke to a trainee who had completed a secondment. He described it as the highlight of his training contract.

in the pink

When it comes to qualification, what are the prospects for those who want to stay in the pink? *"When we qualified it really felt like we were in a buyers market,"* one newly qualified told us. *"It was the firm selling itself to us. We got the feeling that they wanted us to choose them rather than the other way round."* The fact that 95% of Burges Salmon's qualifiers decided to stay with the shoal in 2000 is an excellent endorsement of the training programme and in September 2001 the retention rates were similarly high – all trainees were offered jobs and only one did not accept.

> "There is an understanding that life does not begin and end with the firm."

One factor which may assist in retention is the idea that in this part of the country, you really can't do better in terms of high calibre deals and lawyers. Burges Salmon may decry its reputation for being serious and formal, but no one questions its status as the Rolls Royce of Bristol law firms.

and finally…

Having conquered Bristol, Burges Salmon is now taking on London business. Anyone who wants the quality of work and training found in London, but can live without pollution, a high cost of living and daily tube misery might have found a perfect match with this firm.

Capsticks

the facts
Location: London
UK ranking by size: 153
Total number of trainees: 11
Seats: 6x4 months
Alternative Seats: Secondments

Capsticks is the pre-eminent defendant clinical negligence firm in London and a number of its partners are ranked as the best in the field. But there's more to Capsticks than NHS litigation. Trainees were so keen to stress the work of other departments that we felt compelled to undiscover the secrets hidden within its grey office block in Putney.

a healthy start
The NHS, with all its associated institutions and divisions, is Capsticks' principal client. While the clinical negligence practice dominates the firm and represents over half of its workload, its four other practice groups – employment, commercial, property and dispute resolution – all undertake work for the NHS. There's some interesting commercial issues doing the rounds here; *"high-profile stuff, with PPPs, consent issues - you name it!"* The *"very profitable property department"* has *"a lot of massive multi-million pound deals"* for various Private Finance Initiatives. The commercial practice deals with nursing homes and advice on the contractual aspects of PFI. As Europe's largest employer, the NHS keeps the employment department pretty busy. These departments, while possessing nothing of the reputation associated with the clinical negligence department, are nevertheless sufficiently well regarded to enable departees to take up positions with City firms. Training with Capsticks does not cut off your options; you will not be limited to the health sector for the rest of your career.

top dog
But if clinical law is what you want to do, you're reading the right page of this book. Capsticks was founded in the 1970s specifically to act on behalf of the NHS. The firm handles small clinical negligence cases and high value catastrophic claims. It is at the cutting edge of work in the area and has developed 'NHS Online', a database of *"law and practice related to healthcare, clinical negligence, primary care, quality assurance, risk management and other matters related to the NHS."*

Capsticks sits on the NHS Litigation Authority (NHSLA), a position reviewed every three years. *"Obviously clinical law is a big part of the firm and if we weren't on the panel at the next review that would be bad."* So long as the firm remains so highly rated, it seems unlikely that its position will be under threat, especially when *"the last few years have shown a marked increase in clinical negligence actions."* The NHSLA shrunk its panel size this year and the government has further plans to concentrate clinical defence work in the hands of a smaller group of firms. This bodes well for Capsticks and there's no reason to doubt that previous growth rates of over 20% per year will continue.

second opinion
Capsticks places great store by its vacation schemes, and *"rarely recruits"* without trainees previously having participated in a vacation scheme. It acts as an opportunity to demonstrate *"a commitment to healthcare issues."* *"They give you three or four mini seats of four days doing similar things as a trainee. It revealed the culture and attitude of the firm."* Trainees are eased into working life by several weeks of training courses, including an all-important introduction to the NHS. *"They are conscious of the fact that you do not know what you are doing."* However, by the end of the first seat, *"some people did have their own files."* The level of supervision *"is quite amazing."* Trainees *"never felt afraid to go and knock on anyone's door."*

With six seats of four months, trainees normally take a seat in each department and then repeat a seat during the final four months as preparation for qualification. Trainees can avoid one seat *"if they are desperate – as long as it isn't clinical law!"* Appraisals take place at the end of each seat and, at meetings with training principals, trainees are asked to give feedback on where the firm can improve. *"They ask for our opinions,"* one trainee told us, clearly pleased to feel involved in the development of the training environment.

ooh matron

While there are no overseas seats, limited secondments will come up on an ad hoc basis – usually one or two days a week to various hospitals and health authority clients. Salaries are good, but reflect shorter hours. 9am till 6pm is normal and the offices are empty by 7.30pm. It's *"a really good benefit of the firm."* This is a young firm. It is also a firm with a high proportion of women to men, from trainee level right up to the partners. There are five doctors on staff, four of whom are also qualified as solicitors.

Perhaps trying to empathise with some of the crumbling and neglected buildings of the NHS, the firm occupies a 1960s tower block. *"It could be more aesthetically pleasing,"* said one trainee diplomatically. The office started as one storey but has grown over the years to seven. Putney is *"cost effective as a location,"* and trainees prefer being out of the City environment. Providing assistance to the directionally challenged, the Capsticks offices are *"ten metres from Putney tube station."*

public body and soul

One issue may have you puzzled. If an interest in clinical negligence is a pre-requisite to joining the firm – you must do a seat there – how does the firm find trainees happy to qualify into the other departments? In 2001, three of the seven NQs went into clinical law, with the remainder passing into other departments – take note, full retention. So what happens? Is a proportion of each intake forced to renounce their devotion to clinical negligence and swear un-dying allegiance to the property department? Trainees were reflective.

The NHS will feature in your work wherever you end up. Experience, an association with, or some enthusiasm for the NHS will garner the approval of the firm's recruitment partners. We noted some trainees with previous careers, family members or work experience in the health sector. A number of Capsticks lawyers contribute articles to various journals and take on committee roles, and trainees have contributed to a research project on obstetrics. It is closely connected to the development and evolution of the NHS and the legal implications of changes in its organisation and activities. Displaying an interest in public health is more important than a specific interest in clinical negligence work. One source spoke of *"a warm feeling"* that comes from working for a public body.

off to edith's

In the parochial language of these Putney lawyers, *"Friday lunchtimes will generally mean Nando's,"* and Friday evenings will find most of the firm in Le Piaf – *"the Capsticks wine bar."* A social committee organises comedy nights and go-karting, and the firm likes its sports. A cricket team is well established, but a netball team *"just didn't seem to happen this summer."* It's in a mixed five-a-side football league and the young lawyers have been known to take it all quite seriously. *"There's lots of competitiveness among the boys."* Trying to impress those female trainees? Sports aside *"we do all get on very well. There is no sense of competition."* As if to prove the point, three trainees went on holiday to Greece and several others took a long weekend in Nice with some post-qualifieds. *"There's always something going on socially."*

We couldn't write a piece on Capsticks without including a little gem we unearthed quite by accident. One of the firm's partners (a leading figure in clinical law), apparently left university and spent five years making model soldiers. It is unclear whether such activities would prove to be a help or a hindrance in obtaining a training contract with the firm today.

and finally…

This is firm with a very distinct focus. If the health sector is something that motivates you, or if your previous experience has led to a desire to combine clinical issues with law, then look no further.

Charles Russell

the facts
Location: London, Cheltenham, Guildford
UK ranking by size: 44
Total number of trainees: 28
Seats: 4x6 months
Alternative Seats: None

Old and traditional. Excellent for private client. Two centuries of experience. But Charles Russell has moved on. *"Don't expect an old fashioned firm. It's not wood panelling or old school anymore."* How does a law firm bring itself out of the 19th century and into the information age? It gets into media and telecoms law, of course. And it expands.

temptation
Although the firm offers training contracts in three offices, the trainees remain pretty static. They don't move between branches and *"if you're training in Guildford, you're training in Guildford."* The offices are *"not massively close. They are quite individual,"* although the two provincial offices do tap into the know-how of the London HQ.

The Cheltenham office was lauded for offering *"the resources of a London firm and work which is akin to a London firm."* It's probably as commercial a firm as one can get in Gloucestershire, however, it's a small office and *"there are only four seats, so you have no choice at all."* Maybe the provincial location does hinder a bit in terms of work but, set in the picturesque Cotswolds, it's a lively town ideally suited to shopaholics and those who love horse racing.

The Guildford office provides *"London work, but with Guildford salaries,"* and was felt to be more personable than the London HQ. *"The whole office knows each other."* The City does represent temptation; one Guildford trainee felt *"a bit more flexibility would be nice. It would be good to be able to go to London for one seat."* But with only three trainees, the choice of seats in Guildford is good.

getting cosy
The majority of Charles Russell's trainees are based in London. They're enthusiastic about the benefits associated with training at a medium-sized City firm. *"I wanted a City firm and a high quality of work, but something cosier than a big firm."* The one trainee working in the insurance seat in the satellite office in the Lloyd's building will surely know the meaning of the word cosy. Our sources confirmed the high levels of responsibility offered in most seats and pointed out that there can be *"really long hours in some."* The firm puts the pressure on trainees from time to time. *"In corporate finance, I had an assistant role, rather than a trainee role,"* one trainee reported.

There's no stay-late culture at Charles Russell. *"You work as hard as the people you are with,"* and *"they are very apologetic if you have to stay late."* Partners are accessible, *"you can ask about anything"* and they *"will take the time to explain something to you."* Echoing the comments of trainees in previous years, one said *"you do get thrown in a bit, but there's usually someone you can ask for help."*

brand warrior
Charles Russell has always been renowned for its private client work. It bucked the trend of City firms by not just retaining its private client department, but expanding it. Entire teams of family lawyers were poached from rival firms, further strengthening its reputation in this area. This side of the firm grew because of the work others ignored. However, the firm's commercial practice has also grown and now far exceeds the private client work. All this expansion has had practical consequences. Charles

Russell's home, a *"really tedious looking office block"* seemed to be a source of some amusement for our interviewees. Following the race to expand, space is now at a premium and *"they have had to shove things round a lot."*

The firm has made big efforts to establish itself as a key player in media and telecoms law. Clients include Cable & Wireless, ntl, Ericsson, and Scoot.com; evidence of the reputation the firm has developed with dot.coms and techy clients. Once the commercial business has been done, entrepreneurs push their individual business in the firm's direction. The strategy must be working. Last year the firm reported a 23% rise in profits.

al pacino in devil's advocate

"Which film role would you most like to have played and why?" A serious question posed on the training contract application filled in by some of our sources. Despite this question (which seemingly encourages wild flights of fancy) the trainees are a fairly normal bunch. *"They look for a diverse mix of people and they like mature students,"* one trainee said. *"The firm tends to be going for niche areas and the trainees reflect this"* another thought. Indeed, if you want a flourishing media department, why not recruit a freelance photographer and someone from the music industry. Charles Russell has. *"Media is a niche market we think we can do well in."* It provides some *"good fun media clients."* As you might expect, it's a trainee hot seat.

If you're unsure whether you want to work for corporates or individuals then training at Charles Russell provides both. *"People who don't know what they want to do apply here for its diversity."* Some decide after a while that, no matter how interesting the clients are, private client is still private client. *"You can think, 'here's me drafting another will for someone'. You will get some poor work"* and *"general proof-reading can get you down."* It's perhaps as a direct result of the diversity that one trainee felt that the training experience lacked uniformity, with some supervisors much more adept at delegating decent work than others. We heard just one more gripe – salaries. Trainees are *"not paid as much as others in the City."* And more worryingly, *"if they want to expand, they will have to increase the salary, or else they will lose trainees."* Salaries for 2001's NQs are actually £43,500 – not quite magic circle, but not a million miles off – so in this instance we beg to differ with our source.

hello!

Unlike the glitz and glamour of the celeb-packed parties the firm's exciting media clients might enjoy, Charles Russell's social life does not set the trainees alight. *"It's not very exciting and it's occasionally all a bit 6th form disco. Often the social events are for clients, so they are not for you to enjoy."* At one (now famous) shindig for client Cable & Wireless, a partner grabbed a flute off the salsa band and proceeded to flaunt his dexterity to the attendant lawyers and executives. It seems unlikely that a Charles Russell party would grace the pages of its magazine client, HELLO! We're told the mag is not prescribed reading in the office – yeah right!

Sports are important and the London office fields hockey and cricket teams. In the other offices the smaller numbers of staff inhibit anything too spectacular, although things are improving in Cheltenham because *"the office seems to be getting younger."*

and finally…

If you join Charles Russell, expect to stay put. This *"forward-looking firm"* recruits to retain and there are no secondments, overseas seats or moves between offices by trainees. But should you decide to move on, you will have received a training that will equip you for the magic circle or a high street family practice. There is no vacation placement scheme with this firm, so if you are thinking about applying you will have to go simply on what you manage to research for yourself (or as one of our researchers did many years ago, talk your way into a summer job with the firm).

Clarke Willmott & Clarke

the facts
Location: Taunton, Bristol
UK ranking by size: 84
Total number of trainees: 17
Seats: 4x6 months
Alternative Seats: None

Less than two years ago the legal press ran a botched story about Clarke Willmott & Clarke's decision to stop taking trainees. They got it wrong. One look at the firm's website will show you just how keen the firm is to recruit its stars of the future. But take note: it's looking for trainees that will stay post-qualification and beyond.

changing times
In rather less than a Taunton minute, this firm has morphed from a 14-office organisation spread across the West Country to a two-centre firm in Bristol and Blackbrook (Taunton). The firm's business plan for its Somerset offices has resulted in staff either disappearing into the sunset or consolidating in the Blackbrook office. Blackbrook, on the side of the M5 just outside Taunton, will double in size and absorb the two remaining Somerset branch offices by the end of 2001. Bristol and Blackbrook are both modern and open plan and a far cry from some of *"ye olde"* CWC branch offices. No more will local townsfolk wander in off the street and present trainees with almost any type of legal problem imaginable. *"Sometimes a humbling experience,"* in the old days trainees would find themselves *"part solicitor, part office bod and part secretary."*

CWC has spent the past couple of years upping the stakes and raising its game. The firm is now building its hand from the region's commercial clients. *"We're looking for a higher calibre of client"* explained one trainee. Another confirmed *"I perceive the client base as medium-sized businesses – regionals with the odd nationals. Limited companies not blue chips.*

But if you want a high street firm, don't come here. Our clinical negligence work is legal aid, as is some of the family, but there's no criminal legal aid work." And how well have staff at CWC ridden the wave of change? *"The younger partners have been more adaptable. The firm has lost a lot of older partners and admin staff."*

what am i doing here?
The firm has a clear leaning towards contentious work and property. There are no compulsory seats, but it's *"more probable than not that you'll do a commercial property seat and it's fairly probable that you'll do a personal injury seat."* We got hold of a handy list of the seats currently available to trainees. This is how they stack up: four in personal injury, three each in property and litigation, two in employment and one each in crime, family and corporate. You'll note that only a few trainees get the chance to work on M&A or other types of corporate transactions.

> "No one is going to be saying 'hit the deck' and give me 1,000 chargeable hours now."

The lesser emphasis on corporate deals and a regular 9am-6pm day mean that life is fairly chilled at CWC. There's plenty of time for surfing or sailing or whatever else healthy West Country folk get up to after work. No one is going to be saying *"hit the deck and give me 1,000 chargeable hours now!"* Good for you… go breathe some fresh air or something.

getting to know the M5
What's the practical reality of working for a firm split between two locations? Is this really one firm or is there 'competition' between the two offices? Which one is top dog? Trainees had clear opinions on these

questions. One trainee told us "*Historically this was a Somerset firm, but it is changing. Taunton takes clients from Somerset, Dorset, Devon and wherever. Bristol attracts a large client base from the Bristol area itself. It would be wrong to say that the main focus was on either office.*" But another confirmed there's an element of "*Somerset viewing Bristol as the big lights.*"

The only real trainee bugbear is the uncertainty as to where they will be from one seat to the next. When requesting a seat, trainees are asked to state their preferences for work type and location. "*There seems to be no rhyme or reason to seat allocations*" one trainee thought. "*You look at the results and just ask 'But why?' Before the results you're all on tenterhooks.*" Taunton is about a 45 minute drive from Bristol. Some trainees who live in Bristol but work in Blackbrook commute daily and vice versa for those living in Somerset but working in Bristol. Others relocate. For six months. Until they switch back again.

You'll have no problem if you want to spend all four seats in Blackbrook. Chances are you'll pull that off. It's not unheard of for a trainee to secure a Bristol-only training, but to rely on it would be inadvisable. Bristol is seen as having young partners and a more go-ahead attitude. It has just developed a new niche in sports law, having hired in experts from various firms. If and when a trainee seat becomes available in that department, we expect competition to be stiffer than a McDonald's shake.

ever been to a harvester before?

Over in Blackwood on the Hankridge Farm business park, the animals have made way for the lawyers, Sainsbury's and wait for it... a Harvester restaurant. After we'd sniggered a little (sorry, us London types get terribly snobby about where we eat) we allowed the trainees to tell us about their environment. "*Our Harvester is pretty good! There's nice trees and a pond and a huge beer garden where at lunchtimes you can sit in the sun and do a lizard impression.*"

As in Bristol, Blackwood trainees perceive that the open plan layout of the office promotes "*a lot of interaction between people, an exchange of ideas and a free flow of thought processes.*" It almost sounds telepathic, this "*open atmosphere with no airs and graces.*" Indeed, thought one trainee, "*You won't get on here if you have airs and graces.*" After all, "*this is a firm that doesn't have people pulling rank.*" Expect lawyers to be "*jumping ideas off each other regularly,*" and plenty of "*focus*" on the "*facts and figures.*" CWC is intent on revamping its old image and taking on the region's commercial players. In 2003 the Bristol office is moving to super-cool new premises. If you want a preview, go check out the hole in the ground in St George's Square.

who's in and who's out?

Out this year – "*The dead wood.*" In this year – "*Independent minded people,*" maybe even "*those willing to disagree*" rather than be just yes-trainees. Also in are those with a regional connection. "*Coming from UWE is a common theme. A local connection certainly helps; they are keen to retain trainees.*" The good news – "*If you have an ounce of personality you will get on well here.*" More good news – the recruitment policy is an enlightened one. Part-time training contracts will be considered for those wishing to combine on-the-job training with part-time LPC study. Paralegals get a fair crack of the whip in the quest for a training contract and the firm has declared its interest in those who can show they have pursued academic study "*in the face of adversity.*" It likes mature applicants who can bring something interesting to the party. NB – please don't bring a bottle to interview.

So you're in the door. Will you want to stay post-qualification? We assumed the answer would be a resounding 'Yes!' But in recent years it's turned out to be a qualified 'yes'. "*Historically most haven't really wanted to stay here,*" we heard. After qualification, numbers tended to dwindle. Why? "*The pay structure. We were always billed as being at the top of the firms in the South West, but that never filtered through to salary.*" We understand that the 2001 NQ salary is a whopping £30K Bristol and £27K in Taunton. Once regional costs of living are factored in, this compares favourably with many regional firms.

and finally…
All but one of the ten 2001 qualifiers stayed with the firm. Reflecting the balance of the firm's activities, most are going into contentious and property jobs. None are going into corporate. What has kept them is a low-stress life in an area of the country that they really love. Some people would miss the London legal scene and its *"bright lights and ego trips."* If that's what you're really after then look elsewhere.

Clifford Chance

the facts
Location: London
UK ranking by size: 1
Total number of trainees: 225
Seats: 4x6 months
Alternative seats: Overseas seats, secondments
Extras: Pro bono: Hackney and Tooting Advice Centres, language training

The biggest law firm in the world. The best known name in the legal profession. Almost blanket coverage of anything commercial and dominance in the financial sphere. Phew! It's big and brash. Do you need to be equally so in order to secure a place in the mega-est of all the mega firms? Or is it really true that this is one of the easiest firms in the country to get into? Magic circle it is, élitist it ain't. Whilst we're sure it has its fair share of bright sparks from the ivory tower unis, there's such a wide spread of graduates and, so long as you have ability and a good academic record, the firm is not snobbish about which uni you went to.

world domination
It's been ahead of most in the race for globalisation for some years and in many jurisdictions it blows other Anglo-Saxon firms out of the water. The big men put their heads together in 1997 and came up with the plan to take over the world. This signalled a rush on overseas law firms and before long any City of London practice worth its salt was wooing potential merger partners. At the start of the new millennium Clifford Chance tied the knot with New York's Rogers & Wells and Germany's Punder. It now has over 650 partners worldwide.

Trainees tell us the global nature of the firm is a day to day reality for them. This is a multi-national, multi-ethnic, multi-lingual firm and you don't need to step out of its gargantuan and imposing Aldersgate Street offices (aka Gotham City) to evidence this. As one trainee put it, *"the international nature of the firm and the opportunities are a very definite lure for a lot of people. It's noted for its international outlook and staff."* That trainees felt things were now at the stage where *"to be a trainee here and not go abroad is frowned on. Increasingly, assistants and partners would think it was odd."* Only around a quarter of the trainees elect to stay in London for the whole of their training and they usually offer some sort of explanation, for example wives and husbands.

chutzpah and balls
We noted a highly developed understanding amongst trainees as to what Clifford Chance was all about. We sometimes feel like bashing our heads against the wall when trainees can't identify any distinguishing characteristics of their firms. There's no danger of headaches following trainee interviews at CC. They describe the firm as *"innovative and brave"* and having *"chutzpah and balls."* They talk of *"a definite idea that we're all in it together and for the firm."* Strength in numbers, achievement through playing the game as a team, together. As they said: *"The needs of the firm come first."*

"It is a sort of mantra and it kicks off straight away when you join. It's not subtle at all. The firm has a mission statement put together by management consultants. [McKinsey, we understand] *We even had the managing partner down to speak to us on the first morning about how*

he wants the firm to be one big unit… it's very laudable and very corporate speak." But it seems to work. Trainees frequently uttered various edits and remixes of the mantra during interviews, often unwittingly.

lonely planet

It is a well-known fact that a person could, if they wanted to, live their whole life inside Gotham City, although long-standing rumours of beds in the building are still unsubstantiated. The London office is so huge it spreads round a road junction. Entering the building, ascending the escalators and stumbling into reception on your first day you'll surely feel its enormity and your diminutive stature quite acutely. *"At first I was over-awed and kept getting lost. The lifts were very confusing."*

So then, presumably, you have to come to terms with the size of the workforce (around 1,000 lawyers alone). Well, no, it seems you don't. One trainee concluded that all of the large London firms would feel the same. *"I think when you hit a certain number, say 600, you don't notice the difference."* And as for it being a sea of unfamiliar faces, *"when I joined I seemed to keep meeting the same people over and over again…"* Another agreed: *"The size didn't bother me in the slightest. Each department or group is like its own separate practice, a microcosm of the firm."* Bit by bit you learn about different groups and what they do.

Thankfully there's a bible for trainees, detailing the activities of the different groups in the firm. Written by trainees, the handbook is aimed at clearing the mists of bewilderment and enabling trainees to make seat choices. *"It's outrageously difficult to work out what you want to do and the handbook gives trainee contact names and tells you what goes on in those departments. You read it fairly cynically and there's coded hints which give stuff away and you hear stuff on the grapevine."* Stuff? What stuff?

i am not a number…

Picking a seat is akin to picking a flavour on a trip to a Baskin-Robbins ice cream parlour. *"People like dif-* *ferent things – some absolutely love corporate and finance work."* And a good job too because there's an endless supply of that type of work. *"There's no denying it, the finance practice is the powerhouse of the firm and corporate is catching it up… emphasise to the students that it's a large part of what this firm is all about."* Emphasising the vastness of the finance and corporate practices, each group has a code number. Trainees talk of having worked in 30J (financial services) or 50H (derivatives and regulatory) or 50T (Eurobonds and securities) or 50Z (banking finance). One or two, such as 50S (securities) are a *"badge of honour,"* as they're deemed to be punishing seats with complex work and *"horrendous"* hours.

Opinion is split as to whether it's better to start your training contract with a clear idea of what you want to achieve or to stay open minded. *"Some come with set ideas and get disappointed."* Generally, the level of satisfaction with seat allocation impressed us. Most trainees got what they wanted, although most had adopted a necessary policy of flexibility.

fancy a quickie?

Retention rates on qualification are good and it's no surprise that the majority go into the two biggies –finance and corporate. One trainee let us in on a secret about the run up to qualification: *"It's difficult to say whether people get their first choice of job because people don't like to talk about it. They don't like to be seen not to be getting it."* Before applications are made for NQ jobs, *"fourth seaters have a chat with certain partners about the likelihood of getting an offer."* So that way nobody gets to feel like a loser when they attempt to get a job that won't be offered to them? *"Exactly, but this year, for example, no one's going into employment as they don't need any NQs, so everyone's a loser there."*

The niche departments are tiny in comparison to the mainstream practice areas. Even real estate and litigation appear somewhat on the sidelines in terms of the trainee experience. Most will only do three-months in litigation. These 'split seats' are not universally popular. *"Three months is such a short time*

– *it's a wasted seat. If you make it clear that you are very keen on litigation you can get six months, but if you are not sure you'll only get three.*" There's little prospect of moving from one niche seat to another to another… and given that litigation and real estate are practically niches in the training experience, you can almost predict where your time will be spent.

> "World domination has provided a strong theme."

The niches offer the best hours by far and time spent in them is in contrast to the experience in corporate and finance seats where *"you don't really know from day to day when you'll leave work. Your social life has to be kept at the behest of work and you can only be certain of making dates with people at the weekend."* On the subject of dating, our researcher wondered if there was much inter-trainee… 'stuff'. Sadly, we have nothing interesting to report. *"There's not much inter-trainee dating as even though most of the male trainees don't have girlfriends, most of the females have boyfriends."* Ah… sorry lads!

dumb and dumber

If you want to go abroad to one of the 29 countries in the CC Empire then you certainly will. It is not unheard of for trainees (usually those originating from key Asian locations like Singapore or Hong Kong) to do two six-month seats abroad. But who gets to go where?

Many trainees speak second, third or even fourth languages to varying degrees of competence. Early on, independent assessors formally test language skills and your overseas prospects will be determined in no small part by your performance in the language testing. Ironically, *"people are sometimes handcuffed by their language skills."* If you speak fluent German for example, this might act against you in your bid to go to New York or Hong Kong, where language skills are unnecessary. We heard a story of one trainee who was adamant that she would go anywhere except Frankfurt. She ended up in Frankfurt. Trainees offer a tip: if you want to avoid a location for which your languages make you ideal, dumb them down in the assessment. As one trainee told us, *"It's easy enough to throw the tests."*

Even those who confess that dumbing down was widespread, or that they'd done it themselves, subscribe to the notion that trainees owe it to the firm to go where their talents are of most use. *"Look at it from the point of view of the firm,"* they said, *"Why would they want to waste an important aspect of your talent."* Remember the mantra: 'The needs of the firm come first'. One trainee said *"the firm provides a lot for you so it will demand a lot in return."* Quid pro quo. Mutual scratching.

feng shui classes

Some outside the firm say that Clifford Chance is too big to have character. They joke about a grey-suited army of clones. Whilst *"the firm's too big and diverse to bottle its atmosphere,"* there have been attempts to make the working day feel less formal. A full-time business casual dress code is interpreted liberally in some departments. *"Obviously it's no jeans, but I have just one suit and I can't imagine owning more than one."* In other departments things are very different. *"Corporate is still smart suits. If you are in client meetings all the time, there's no point in dressing down."*

The amenities are spectacular. The fitness centre and restaurant in the basement are well used and there's an endless list of courses you can sign up for, from scuba diving in the firm's pool (looking for emotional and physical wrecks?) to feng shui. It's a fact that the recent £50K NQ salaries were the result of strategic placement of flutes, mirrors and pot plants on trainee desks throughout 2000/2001.

An army of paralegals and proof readers help to reduce the monotony of certain trainee tasks. *"The trick is using the support staff,"* said one sussed female trainee. *"If you know how the system works and you're a bit smart you can delegate and supervise."* You go girl!

dead at the weekend

What about those legendary magic circle hours that you'll have heard about? *"If you get a group of trainees together"* we were told *"all they can do is whinge about the hours. They are a pain and I have cancelled plans. But when you haven't had long hours for a while you forget about them. Once you have caught up on your sleep it washes out of your mind."* Summarising the regular hours of a trainee is difficult. In the non-corporate and finance seats trainees talk of commonly leaving at 6.30pm and meeting up in local pubs like the Hogshead and the Lord Raglan. As for the *"powerhouse"* seats, *"it's pretty standard that you do 9am to at least 7ish in corporate and then every few weeks something will build up a head of steam."* In finance seats *"standard days are 9am-7pm with the expectation of a late night or two every week."* In these seats *"your social life is not brilliant… people don't tend to be party animals."*

We wondered if the firm's move to Canary Wharf in 2003 will impact further on the time trainees get home at night and whether isolation from the rest of the legal community will cause lawyers to question their commitment to the firm. We noted the 'magic circle training is my passport to a glittering future' mentality, so there are sufficient trainees who already question their long-term commitment to the firm. Adding geographic isolation is an eyebrow-raiser. *"The firm is doing a good job of trying to make the move seem more palatable,"* one trainee told us. *"They are organising trips down there on a boat with cocktails and giving talks on the facilities."* Most of our sources had been too busy to take the booze cruise. *"A fair few people have already moved house to Docklands and love it"* a trainee remarked, *"but I just think it's dead at the weekends."*

and finally…

Big could mean bland, but trainees at Clifford Chance don't subscribe to that theory. World domination has provided a strong theme and the opportunities for trainees seem greater than ever. A word to the wise: keep reminding yourself of the focus of this firm's work. Finance rules. Finance and corporate transactions mop up the bulk of lawyer-hours at Gotham City. Hours in those practice areas are rigorous and the 'kinder hours' departments are thinner on the ground. If you have little interest in international blue chip deals and finance, are you really going to be happy working in this firm?

Clyde & Co

the facts

Location: London, Guildford, Cardiff
UK ranking by size: 39
Total number of trainees: 43
Seats: 4x6 months
Alternative Seats: Overseas seats
Extras: Language training

Clyde & Co has a strong reputation in shipping, insurance and international trade. It is the nautical nature of the work, combined with a strong international perspective that makes the firm stand out from the pack. It operates out of offices in London, Guildford and Cardiff, with trainees based in London and Guildford only. Like most firms with a maritime bent, this is an environment in which you should expect to be stimulated, pushed and challenged. Be prepared for bracing sea air.

ship to shore

Clyde & Co boasts on its website that it's a big hitter in all areas of commercial law. Certainly, whatever the firm does it does it well; profits were up 32% last year. There's a mere nod in the recruitment part of the website towards the work upon which much of the firm's reputation rests – insurance and shipping. Understandably, the firm doesn't want to be mistaken for a two trick pony and there's no doubt that it has other areas of excellence, but bear in mind that as a trainee you will see plenty of work from its core areas. The hard facts speak louder than the marketing. The firm's own figures show that over 50% of its work is in shipping and insurance. Just as sand from a day at the seaside manages to spread its way through all your belongings, Clyde & Co's focus on shipping and the insurance market will seep into the training experience. *"There are no compulsory seats here, you don't have to do a shipping or insurance seat but, wherever you are working, you can't avoid that kind of business. At the end of the day it is what we do."*

town or country?

Before trainees plunge into work, they need to decide which office floats their boat. The quality of work is the same in Guildford and London, so it is very much a lifestyle choice. Around two thirds choose to train in London, with the remainder preferring a suburban lifestyle in sunny Surrey. To this end, one of our sources felt that the staff in the Guildford office tended to be *"a bit older and more likely to be married with kids."* London is only 30 minutes away on the train if you fancy some overpriced drinks.

speaking in tongues

There is no identikit Clydes trainee. Recruits hail from different continents, different age groups and often bring experience from previous careers. This year we heard that a former policeman and an ex music journalist had been taken on. The firm looks favourably on applicants with language skills and if you do have languages, it's likely they'll be called upon. *"The fact that I speak Italian seemed to help when I applied, but I didn't think that I would get a chance to use it. I was so wrong! I have had plenty of contact with Italian clients in all my seats so far."*

welcome to the family

When researching for the True Picture, we often hear the same tired patter about how friendly everyone is, how open and welcoming the fee earners are, how different that makes them from all the other firms. Zzzzzz. We normally take these claims with a pinch of sea salt. There did, however, seem to be a particularly strong feeling of community amongst Clydes trainees. *"There's only fifteen of us coming in each year so you don't get lost in the crowd."* *"It really is a warm atmosphere and people get to know you as soon as possible."* The HR department adds a few little touches to make your first weeks easier. One initiative is to ensure that you have contact with one of the lawyers from your interview panel during the first seat. *"It means that there is a familiar face as soon as you start."*

The hours aren't too gruelling, with the typical day running from 9am to 6:30pm. One source explained *"because we are running our own files and our own cases much of the time, many deadlines, evenings and weekends are self imposed. There is certainly no culture of imposing deadlines just for the hell of it."* You can expect a handful of late nights in most seats *"the latest I have stayed has been around 10pm; that has happened once or twice in both seats, but it can get a bit later than that in corporate."* True enough! But even in the corporate department you won't be put through the kind of endurance tests to which trainees at the mega-firms are subjected.

king of the castle

Clyde & Co makes a real effort to ensure trainees feel like real grown up lawyers from the start. At most firms, trainees share an office with their supervisor or are grouped together in trainee rooms, but each Clydes trainee has their own office. Our sources valued the feeling of independence afforded by being king of their own small castle. *"I didn't want to be shadowing someone for a year thinking 'I could do that'. Here I am called a case handler from day one, running my own files from my own office."* But does this independence mean trainees are cast adrift too early? According to those we spoke to, not really. *"It is great to have privacy and the status your own office gives, but it only works because we know help is there whenever we ask for it."*

You can expect to be responsible for your own small cases and clients immediately after the induction. *"Obviously there is supervision and the cases which trainees get cracking on are small fry, but it is better than spending your time photocopying and filing."* Trainees in the Guildford office seemed to get even less of the boring admin work as the tedious stuff and photocopying is usually covered by support staff. The flip side is that you must expect to be pushed. *"This is not a firm where you have your hand held as you tread water for a couple of years."* Retention is reasonably high; of the 17 trainees who qualified in September 2001, 14 were offered jobs and 13 accepted.

london 4: guildford 1

For a firm with such an international reach (offices in Caracas, Dubai, Hong Kong, Paris, Piraeus and Singapore) there are only two overseas locations on offer. Three trainees are sent out to Dubai every six months and they tend to have a pretty fantastic time. Two of the seats are in commercial and a third is in litigation. The firm has just added a seat in Hong Kong and the lucky trainee will spend most of their time in litigation, with the opportunity to gain some IP experience.

Back in Old Blighty there is plenty of organised socialising. The London office enjoys a free bar every Thursday evening and with regular social events and staff meals. Spare a thought for the Guildford office, however, which has a free bar only once a month. Our hearts bleed! Many of the hardier Guildford drinkers manage to make it up to London to crash the weekly City bash so it isn't that bad. The favourite pub for London trainees is The Ship, whilst Guildford trainees picked RSVP from the large selection of chain bars on offer in the town centre.

and finally...

With its welcoming atmosphere, diverse mix of people and excellent responsibility afforded to all trainees from a very early stage, Clydes will suit the motivated applicant who's eager to get going on real work. In terms of the work, the firm does have a wide breadth of departments, but do remember where its core strengths lie. Definitely an option if you have a taste for shipping, trade and insurance and are interested in joining a truly international practice.

CMS Cameron McKenna

the facts

Location: London, Bristol, Aberdeen
UK ranking by size: 10
Total number of trainees: 110
Seats: 4x6 months
Alternative Seats: Overseas seats, secondments
Extras: Pro bono: Islington Law Centre, language training

The firm was born out of a merger between Cameron Markby Hewitt and McKenna and Co in 1997. Sometimes when two reasonably laid back, medium-sized firms collide and start to compete with the Premier League, the atmosphere can sour as lawyers have to become a little more cut throat to prove themselves. This isn't the case at CMS Cameron McKenna; the charm and calm evident in the workplace of each firm before merger still shows through at the merged firm.

unholy alliance

Camerons still seems to have a slight sense of unease following the merger and feels that it has yet to achieve the status it deserves. But this can manifest itself in positive ways. *"We don't think we have made it yet and it is an exciting place to be. We are not sitting back, we are trying to push forwards."* Some of our sources thought the firm was *"still searching for its identity post merger."* Certainly, the firm is searching for a stronger identity internationally.

Camerons sit at the hub of the CMS Alliance, a collection of European firms working together to provide a pan-European legal service. The Alliance has not had an easy time of things since its creation in April 1999. First it was suggested that some of the members were of an inferior quality and merely there to make up the numbers, then the Dutch member of the Alliance got cold feet and took up observer status. An 11-month delay in appointing a managing director of the Alliance added further complications. It is now thought that the planned merger between the firms will take twice as long as originally anticipated. It is too early to say if the Alliance will fare any better in the future but there's no doubting Cameron McKenna's determination to be a significant European player.

At the end of the 1980s, Cameron Markby Hewitt was the first western firm to open up offices in Eastern Europe. Others followed suit, but Camerons is still closely associated with its eastern European practice and also with its pan-European energy work. The firm won the 2001 *Chambers Global* 'Energy Law Firm of the Year (Power)' Award for Western Europe.

broaden your horizons

For adventurous souls, overseas seats are available. As ever, some are more popular than others, so don't expect to be guaranteed six months in the Hong Kong office. Prague is a top destination, as is the less conventional hot spot of Warsaw. We heard about the trainee who spent six months in Kazakhstan and *"had the time of his life."* Sadly this seat is no longer available since the Kazakh office was taken over by rival Denton Wilde Sapte in November 2000. A new seat in Vienna looks set to become popular. If you want to go to one of the sexier of the 37 locations in which Camerons has either its own office or an Alliance partner, then you will face an interview and should start making your case to move out there as early as possible.

For those who don't want to go overseas, the firm has offices in Bristol (originally set up to serve the needs of Lloyds TSB and now focusing on banking and insurance work) and Aberdeen (which serves clients in the oil industry). *"Normally the Bristol seat is quite unpopular, but this year three out of the four trainees who went there had asked to go."* And if you don't want to go? *"I don't know anyone who has refused as such!"* Those who go to Bristol seem to enjoy the experience; the quality of work and attention from more senior fee earners is excellent. *"The offices are very flash and are located right on the wharf. The firm gives you a great flat too; it really isn't that bad."* The Aberdeen slot is less popular. We couldn't track down anyone who had been there recently, but were assured that *"they did come back!"* That's something anyway.

nothing toulouse

The Camerons approach allows trainees to take on as much responsibility as they feel they can handle. This means that you need the confidence to point out if things aren't going to plan. *"There was a time when I was running 30 files and I needed to ease the workload a bit. I just pointed it out and it was sorted. Then in a different seat I felt like I was kicking my heels a bit so I asked for more responsibility. Again, it was fine."* You need to use your initiative to get on here. As one trainee put it *"We are here to learn, but it is appreciated if you suggest a solution rather than ask a question."* There is no doubt that support is there but, reading between the lines, if you expect to be spoon fed, you are going to struggle.

> "If you expect to be spoon fed, you are going to struggle."

For those wanting to stretch their wings fully, Camerons offers a range of client secondments, many of them to household name clients including a major high street bank. *"Being on secondment was the high point of my training contract,"* one trainee told us. *"I was treated like I was already a qualified solicitor."* There are also opportunities for those with language skills to undertake client secondments overseas. We heard about a placement with Airbus in Toulouse.

Our colleagues on the *Chambers Guide* pointed out to us that the firm rules the roost in product liability work where it acts for large pharmaceutical manufacturers, offering regulatory advice and defending claims about products such as the MMR vaccine and breast implants. This department is ideally suited to those from a medical or pharmacological background or those who know the pharmaceuticals industry well. The highly ranked construction and engineering practice group works for major players in the industry on contentious matters and issues pertaining to PFI and health and safety. Again, it's ideally suited to those with relevant industry experience.

shear joy

One of the first things that strikes the new recruit is the atmosphere. We were frequently told how "*human*" and good-natured staff were. "*You walk around the office and you will hear conversation, but more importantly you will hear laughter.*" The firm seems to have a more laid back approach to practice than some of its rivals and they won't expect you to give up your life outside work. "*I have only worked late a couple of times and I have done a weekend, but every time it was my choice,*" one trainee said. Obviously it varies from seat to seat; litigation and property were singled out as providing the steadiest hours.

> Winner of the 2001 *Chambers Global* 'Energy Law Firm of the Year (Power) Award'

Socially the historic (if somewhat cramped) Hand & Shears is under significant pressure from the advance of the chain pub, specifically the Hogshead (which lies between Camerons and Clifford Chance next door) and a string of trendy bars in Smithfield. Wherever trainees regularly meet for drinks, there's no bar room pecking order. "*The managing partner comes down to the pub every now and again and if you are standing by the bar you normally talk to him, especially if you have had a few drinks!*"

and finally…

With a relaxed atmosphere, high quality work, some exceptional opportunities and an ambitious vision of the future, Cameron McKenna is undoubtedly an interesting place to be.

Cobbetts

the facts

Location: Manchester
UK ranking by size: 79
Total number of trainees: 18
Seats: 4x6 months
Alternative Seats: Brussels, secondments

On its website, Manchester firm Cobbetts speaks with pride of its status as a "premier independent commercial law firm." Around half of its work is in the property sphere, but trainees quickly confirm that there's plenty more on offer. So read on if you fancy a career in footie-mad Madchester, the gun capital of Britain, home to the Stone Roses, Oasis, Beckham, Affleck's Palace, canals, rain… oh and Mick Hucknall!

every move you make

With the volume of property work at this firm, it comes as no surprise that one of your first two seats will be in the property division. The other will fulfil the Law Society's requirement that you cover something contentious. "*We are a big property firm and a lot of trainees come here to do that.*" Oliver Twist-like though, unless you ask for more, there will be no second helpings of property. It will sweep you away into high productivity and early responsibility. "*Property's a bit of a blur. You have good support but a big caseload. You get stuck in*" one trainee told us. Another agreed "*It's high volume, lower value work. Trainees can get early responsibility.*"

Second years get the pick of the other seats, most popular of which are employment and commercial (no big surprises there then). Also on offer, corporate (dealing with owner managed businesses through to some blue chips), banking, various breeds of litigation, private client and insolvency. Corporate was felt to be the seat for least responsibility, with "*times when you are frustrated by your fair share of leg work.*" Once a year, one lucky so and so will get to spend three months in an affiliated Belgian firm. This Brussels seat is not massively oversubscribed, so if you show the enthusiasm and the aptitude for it, it could be yours. Generally the message is that you should be *"really pushy about what you want to get."* There's no programme of regular client secondments; any that do take place are on an as-and-when basis. When we interviewed for the True Picture, one trainee was working at the Royal Bank of Scotland.

We were impressed by the emphasis placed on monitoring trainees' progress. Many firms now offer three-monthly appraisals – Cobbetts trainees meet the training manager every month to discuss the work they have covered and what else they need to do. Every third month the discussion involves the training partner and a written report from the trainee's supervisor.

independence

We asked trainees how working at an independent firm might differ from working at the Manchester branch of one of the national firms. *"Although we have had a couple of mergers,* [notably with Slater Heelis in 1998] *this is not an amalgamation of firms, which inevitably changes the culture. Any changes here have evolved."* One trainee also thought that any single office of a national firm would constantly have to show that its performance and profitability was competitive with other branches in other regions. They felt the absence of this factor meant the main driving force didn't have to be chargeable hours. *"Fees don't have to become the only indicator of someone's worth."* Trainees also liked the idea that the managing partner and management team are based in their office and devise strategy from Manchester and not London or Leeds.

The North West theme is strong, with almost all trainees having their roots or their education in the region. *"A local connection is not essential,"* one trainee explained, but for an applicant it would be *"a selling point. They want to be confident that people who do come here will stay."*

in the club

"Trainees are well looked after here," we were told. *"From day one you are encouraged to socialise and build up a close network of friends. Hours don't seem to be the main focus; it's not as ruthless as some firms in Manchester."* What about those hours then? *"8.30am-5.30pm or 9am-6pm and people do take lunch."* Sounds jolly reasonable to us. It led us to wonder if this is a consequence of the firm's property focus rather than, say, a corporate focus – the latter typically producing deal dependent swings in hours.

All those we interviewed emphasised the importance of the Cobbetts social club. At £2 a month, with the pot of cash matched by the partners, membership brings staff all sorts of goodies in the form of nights out and trips to various events. *"The social club is great. We just had a subsidised trip to London, including travel and a night in a four star hotel for just £15. We've been to The Clothes Show, The Comedy Store on Deansgate and once a month we eat around the world."* We should point out that this involves local restaurants rather than long haul flights. Once a month, the day after pay day, a different team will host drinks after work in the office. The most uninspired aspect of the social life is the All Bar One just opposite the office. Another firm in the chain gang…

staying power

With toptastic retention rates for NQs (usually total, 90% in September 2001), Cobbetts is a firm that hangs on to its lawyers. Of the nine staying in 2001, *"Five of us are going into the property division and four into the corporate one. Within that split people are going into different types of work. No litigation job was offered this year."* And why do they stay? *"Hours are good, the management seems to be in tune with people's needs… people respect your wishes."* Getting the job they wanted in an environment they enjoyed working in was of paramount importance to the trainees at this firm. Money was a secondary consideration, although trainees did talk about salaries.

"We are striving to be one of the biggest practices in the North West, so we are really growing… On the one hand we are driving forward, but on the other hand the firm is not paying as much as some others. We are caught between two stools. We are not the old Cobbetts but we are not yet up there with the big boys." It has to be said though, the difference in salary between Cobbetts and the highest payers in Manchester is not vast.

> "It's not as ruthless as some of the firms in Manchester."

'not one but two armani outlets'
In trying to sum up the culture at Cobbetts, trainees came up with the following ideas. *"It's quite a traditional northern practice, it's not flamboyant. It's quite straight and that's OK for me."* Another suggested that *"by and large the Cobbetts person is down to earth and personable. When recruiting they are definitely looking for the Cobbetts person; someone fairly outgoing, but they don't tend to recruit mavericks."* It's not felt to be an overly ambitious or cut-throat place to work. But perhaps the firm has high ideals in terms of image. After all, the website does point out that it is "positioned right in the middle of the city's most exclusive shopping area (we are flanked by not one, but two Armani outlets!)"

and finally…
If you're looking for a commercial firm in Manchester, but one that's not too gargantuan, then look seriously at Cobbetts. If it's an independent you're after, you'll certainly want to apply. While trainees stressed the property focus of the firm, there was no sense that their training is dominated by property work. If international corporate finance and overseas trips to New York and Asia are what you really want, forget it. But if you want a good solid commercial training in the North West then what are you waiting for?

Cripps Harries Hall

the facts
Location: Tunbridge Wells, London
UK ranking by size: 102
Total number of trainees: 13
Seats: 6 or more of varying length
Alternative Seats: None

On the Cripps Harries Hall website you'll find a phenomenally detailed history of the firm, starting with the birth of William Cripps Snr in 1832. Frankly this might be off putting to some students, raising questions as to how progressive this firm could possibly be. Forget about the starched collars and earnest expressions worn by the firm's forefathers and learn the real history lesson – this is a firm deeply rooted in its local area.

jack of all trades
Commonly, trainees told us that they had been attracted to the firm because of the range of clients and work on offer. Most had no idea as to what sort of lawyer they wanted to become. *"I wanted my training to be as broad as possible,"* said one. Another agreed *"Cripps is a good mix of corporate and private client work."* There's a notion that *"when you qualify into one area, you have had a real breadth of training. That makes you a better lawyer."* Early months are typically spent in departments like residential conveyancing and private client. *"The firm's location between London and the South East means that there's lots of people with money from the City living here; so there's lots of private client work."*

After a couple of short stints with private clients, *"nearly everyone does commercial property, as it's a big area for the firm,"* and more meaty commercial seats. *"The firm is 150 years old and historically it's had a large private client base, but in the last 10 years what has ballooned is the commercial practice."* That commercial practice is described by trainees as *"good clients and smaller size deals." "You're not talking about big household names – well one or two – if you want to act for an ICI* or a Virgin then this is not the place… There are clients attracted from London because of the value offered. It is medium-sized businesses and start-ups."

life in the cul de sac

The number of seats you'll do is impressive. All those we spoke to had done, or were on course to do, at least six or seven different seats in a panoply of practice areas. A plan is laid out at the beginning of the training and may involve some seats of just two months or others of five or six. There's an acknowledged degree of flexibility to take account of an individual's preferences, but business needs have a strong influence on the seat planning. As a trainee *"You have to be adaptable; it's sometimes frustrating"* as *"seats can be too short to get an idea of what's going on. You've hardly got there and worked out where to make coffee and it's time to pack your bags."* For HR it's assumed to be a complex *"juggling act."* The general view is that frequent moves allow trainees to *"get to know lots of people in the firm."*

As Cripps has grown in size and become more and more the commercial player in Kent, it has expanded its offices but remained in Tunbridge Wells. None of the trainees knew of anyone who'd done a stint in the firm's London office. Located in a small street near the Victoria Centre in Tunbridge Wells, the firm occupies six Georgian buildings, two on one side and a terrace of four on the other. *"It's like a small cul-de-sac where you know all the neighbours. Some buildings are more up to date than others."* Trainees are impressed by recent updates to IT and library facilities. When we researched, the firm had just taken on a new IT guru to add momentum to the pace of change.

There has been a marked transition from a sleepy *"traditional"* firm, with a core of local private and small business clients, to teams of younger, more commercially driven partners bringing the business forward. This is the same strategy that successful regional practices are following all over the country. And it's one that appeals to trainees. *"If I were to change anything about the training here,"* one said to us, *"I'd make the business clients bigger."* Undoubtedly that's just what the firm is trying to do. The firm had always been linked to the Solicitors Indemnity Fund (SIF) which provided it with defendant professional negligence work. Now that the SIF has closed down, the firm is seeking out new business from insurance companies and beginning to take on claimant work in this field.

It's *"not funky"* and maybe it's slightly more *"conservative"* than the *"progressive"* image the firm wants to portray, but trainees are seeing changes *"working through the system."*

or is it ramsay street?

If we gave an award for the firm offering trainees the best hours, then Cripps would definitely win it. *"The hours are 9am-5.15pm on the dot!"* with *"an hour and a quarter for lunch, which everyone takes."* One trainee remarked that *"City friends are working a hell of a lot longer and they are stressed. Here you are not generally stressed but we're given talks on how to handle it."* It's official, at Cripps you can get home in time to watch Neighbours. We even heard about one or two people who went home to watch it at lunchtime. Sad. Sad. Sad.

Any hint of stress can be worked off in either the local gym – LA Fitness – or the local pub – Sankeys. For some reason the trainees' voices all took on the same tone when we asked about the local pub. *"Every time I have been there it's just full of Cripps people. It's an old man's pub."* Old-man it may be, but Cripps lawyers just can't stay away. It has been suggested that if the firm stopped using it, the pub would go out of business. *"Sankeys is up for sale at the moment… and yes it's already been suggested that the firm buys it!"* Relationships with partners are easy and convivial. *"You know there's a hierarchy, but it's not imprinted onto everyone's foreheads. There's a good culture of referring things to others and seeking help."*

So, just like any good soap opera, there's a pub the characters love to hate. But what else does Tunbridge Wells have to offer and would an outsider move into the neighbourhood to train at the firm? Being so close to London has its advantages. It's just 45 minutes by train to the capital and the same to Brighton, so when you get fed up with Tunbridge Wells, the bright lights are at hand. *"This town's not very exciting"* one trainee warned us, *"there's not a great deal going on at night."* But it is pretty and the shopping's good.

hi mum

On the down side, proximity to London has a financial impact. Trainee and NQ salaries can hardly be described as bumper. In fact, it was the one consistent moan we had in our research interviews with Cripps' youngsters. *"Accommodation is expensive and the salary is quite tight. I would have expected to have had more cash to spare than I do,"* said one. Another spoke of trainees having to live at home with family, if local, and yet another of trainees having to spend more of their holiday allocation with parents than they would like. Those trainees that receive a bursary to cover law school fees must pay half of it back to the firm out of their salaries.

It's unrealistic to expect a regional firm to match a magic circle salary, but the cost of living in Tunbridge Wells certainly makes the cost of living in Newcastle upon Tyne look positively third world. Yet, we noted that the geordie firm that we researched at the same time as Cripps was paying an equivalent salary. These issues do have an effect on the minds of young lawyers, especially when they constantly have to read about sky high salaries in the City.

In September 2001, four of the eight qualifiers stayed with Cripps; two went into corporate, one into employment and the other into commercial litigation. The departees scattered to London or back home where they originally came from. We were surprised that the firm did not have a stronger 'you're not from around here are you?' attitude towards recruitment. But maybe, with the firm being so close to London, that's an unrealistic goal.

and finally…

Unquestionably, there is a good training on offer at Cripps Harries Hall in both the commercial and the private client spheres. But *"it's not City money or deals."* Trainees caution against using the firm as a safety net application: *"It's not for those who simply see the firm as a second choice to London. They wouldn't be happy as they'd always be comparing it to London."* What you will get is an inclusive and relaxed working environment and (bank balance aside!) a good quality of life.

Davies Arnold Cooper

the facts
Location: London, Manchester, Newcastle-upon-Tyne
UK ranking by size: 64
Total number of trainees: 16
Seats: 4x6 months
Alternative seats: Secondments

Davies Arnold Cooper's recent history has been a tortured one and parts of its trainee population have been left disgruntled. The firm has banked its future on the insurance and property markets, which has led some pundits to question whether the DAC strategy is inspired or pure, unadulterated madness. But it's not all doom and gloom and we've taken the opportunity to find out what it is that DAC has to offer.

in or out of focus?

But lets get all the difficult topics out of the way first. We asked trainees why they chose to train at the firm. One told us *"I signed up four years ago and then it was a top employer, really profitable, sexy and Olswangy. That was then."* Some of our sources started work at DAC just after it had gone through a night of the long knives exercise. In early 1999 staff numbers were slashed in Manchester and London. Some trainees who were due to start their contracts in Manchester found themselves moving to London.

So what on earth happened? Sometimes the truth gets blurred over time but, the way we understand it, late in 1998 the firm decided to abandon the idea of 'full-service' in favour of selected 'pillars of strength'. It eventually identified just two of them; the insurance industry, and property and banking. The Manchester office, for example, lost its entire corporate department. Some of our sources reported dismay and anger that their training had turned out so radically different to what they'd expected. Others felt that the change in focus had not affected them. Those trainees whose aspirations matched the firm's new focus were completely positive about their experiences.

good at what it does

Most trainees work in London and just a few are in Manchester as it has fewer departments. All of our sources praised the quality of training at DAC, telling us that tasks were far removed from photocopying and administrative chores. *"DAC offers a good training, just in fewer areas"* we were told. *"The media department is not here any more, the motor team upped and left to Barlow Lyde & Gilbert last year, half the banking team have gone. Some property people went to Nabarros… it has been a source of angst amongst trainees… it's worrying when senior people leave."* It must have been.

But there are those who look at the dramatic changes much more bullishly. *"Yes, I was concerned, but the restructuring was quite positive. If it's necessary, it's necessary. Any restructuring is in the past. The firm has moved forward from that. It's not even thought about now, it's in the past."*

one man's meat…

The golden rule in determining whether DAC is your kinda place is finding out whether they do your kinda work. During interviews for the True Picture, those interested in corporate work emphasised that, with hindsight, DAC was not somewhere they would apply to again. On the other hand, if litigation is your thing then you're laughing. Roll up your sleeves and get stuck in. *"In personal injury, you can run your own files. If you are going to be a litigator, it's good experience and good responsibility."* PI tends to be a first seat for many trainees, along with ELPL – employers and public liability. What's on the menu at DAC these days? *"Slippers and Trippers and RTA personal injury, reinsurance, construction, corporate (which is general commercial stuff), property (which is a good team), banking (which is really property finance), insolvency and product liability."*

The message is that applicants should judge DAC on what it now offers rather than harking back to the firm that it once was. The firm is very clear that it is primarily a litigation practice, so no one's going to take you that seriously if you start moaning about not getting enough corporate work.

DAC easily attracts second careerers, particularly those who have spent time in the medical profession, engineering or insurance. The firm's reputation in personal injury, product liability (defending group actions against clients in the pharmaceutical and healthcare sectors), construction and various types of insurance litigation acts as the bait. Arguably, it is these highly focused trainees who will be happiest at the firm. Property is an important department and has taken on one of this year's qualifiers.

cutting out the middle man

We quizzed our sources as to why they got so much responsibility. *"Whilst there's a lot of partners and junior NQs, the lawyers are missing in the middle… maybe they became edgy about all the axing, maybe it was the pay."* We heard a variety of responses to our questions about the atmosphere at the firm. Satisfied trainees applauded DAC for embracing the idea of flexible working. Senior solicitors attempting the fine balance between career and family were felt to be on a winning ticket. Then there were comments from the flip side: *"Morale is very poor,"* we heard from some. *"It's a sea of confusion as to what the firm is doing. Trainees sit in the pub and have a whinge every day."*

The DAC training has stood September 2001's NQ qualifiers in good stead; seven of the 11 stayed with the firm and, of those who left, some headed to firms like Macfarlanes and Lawrence Graham. As a general rule, those that left wanted more of a non-contentious 'City' experience than DAC could offer them.

you decide

The hours at DAC are totally manageable. *"No one is stressed over hours here. There's no macho-ism."* Curiously, one or two trainees thought that a few more lawyers doing a few longer hours might be good for the firm. *"The firm is not very driven; it's lacking a bit of effective management – they are trying, but it is drifting."* On the other hand (and with interviews at this firm there always seemed to be a real polarisation of views…) other trainees disagreed, saying *"this is a practice that is going somewhere in terms of international commercial contentious and non-contentious work. Trainees with ambition will receive all the support they could possibly require. If some want to sit on their laurels and purr about their first class degrees from Cambridge and moan then that's what they'll do…"* The firm's head honcho, the lovely Danny Gowan, is felt to be making an impact in terms of intra-firm communication. And we heard from one source that *"the person at the bottom of the food chain now knows what those at the top are designing for the future."*

So who do you believe? The trainees who are resentful, having spent two years doing a more limited range of work than they had signed up for, or those who see their future at the firm. Both the disgruntled and the satisfied have valid points. This firm is right for some applicants and it ought to be the case that in future years there will be no *"influx of trainees wanting seats that are no longer there."* We expect this to be the last year that we hear so many moans from trainees.

and finally…

When applying, be clear about what you want from your training contract. The work on offer here is, in the main, contentious (some of it the best in the field). Remember also that this is a firm with many of its eggs in the insurance basket and that sector has led a number of law firms down a rocky road in recent years.

Davies Wallis Foyster

the facts

Location: Liverpool, Manchester, Warrington
UK ranking by size: 63
Total number of trainees: 15
Seats: 6x4 months
Alternative seats: Secondments
Extras: Language training

Davies Wallis Foyster is a moderate-sized practice in the North West of England, offering a range of services to its commercial and insurance clients. Sounds straight forward… but don't be fooled!

stardate: 3 09 01 . 9

Before you do anything else, open up the DWF website. The home page, with its revolving planets and inter-galactic background, comes straight out of Star Trek. This aroused our initial suspicions and then… a trainee told us about senior partner Jim Davies. *"Jim is probably the friendliest person you are likely to meet."* Aye Aye Captain!

So if Davies Wallis Foyster is the Star Ship Enterprise, and Mr Davies is none other than the legendary Capt. James T Kirk, who's brainy Vulcan Spock, the lovely Lieutenant Uhura, dotty Doc McCoy and Scotty? And will you live an exciting life on the bridge during your training or will it be warp speed to Planet Insurance Claim for two years of road traffic accidents and 'trippers and slippers' cases?

down in the engine room

Trainees in Manchester still undertake six seats of four months but a new rotation is on trial in Liverpool, where an initial six-month seat is followed by three seats of four months. At that stage the trainee and the training manager will sit down together and discuss how the final six months will be best spent. Many go into their intended qualification department.

But is it all insurance work? After all, this firm has aligned itself with the insurance industry, in particular with giants such as Admiral, Royal & Sun Alliance and DAS Legal Expenses. One trainee was clear that *"not all our eggs are in one basket."* Every trainee will do an insurance seat, covering non-contentious as well as contentious work. Some of our sources talked of handling their own small RTA and employers' liability cases in this seat and it's generally felt to be a hands on experience.

> "The Klingons may be from the planet Qo'noS, but usually DWF trainees are from the North West."

Commonly trainees will also spend time in property, commercial litigation and corporate departments but the range on offer is increasing and they are now seeing work in banking and finance, employment and IP. Aside from the insurance giants, the firm works for *"a wide range of corporate clients. Some plcs and local companies, large and small."* Corporate clients include Princes (the canned food people), Safeway, Bank of Scotland, Liverpool John Moores Uni and Manchester Airport. The private client work that's undertaken is described as *"wealth protection for the directors of corporate clients."*

the federation
The nature of the firm's business in Manchester is very similar to its business in Liverpool. One trainee thought that Liverpool was the *"lead office,"* but there seems little to support the idea that one office is of greater importance than the other. True, Manchester currently has fewer trainees than Liverpool, but everything else gives the impression of balance between the two offices.

Trainees don't usually move between Liverpool and Manchester and at this time, there are no trainees in the new Warrington office. There's *"no joint training and no shared work at trainee level,"* but the firm encourages social interaction between the different cities. One scouse trainee said, *"I do know the trainees in the other office as once a year we go over to Manchester for a get together and they come over here for a night out. The firm pays."* Sounds great.

the klingons
The crew of the Starship Enterprise just keeps getting bigger. The firm is growing at all levels. On the one hand, a mass of non-qualified staff are being taken on in the new Warrington office, handling matters such as bulk conveyancing and debt recovery. On the other hand, DWF has attracted some leading lights at partner level. In 2001 star corporate name (and one time head of Addleshaw Booth's Manchester corporate department) Andrew Needham came wibbling out of the transporter beam, heralding a push on the firm's corporate business.

We asked what was happening to the September 2001 qualifiers and learnt that *"all the trainees are staying and that's common. We have a tradition of 100% of trainees being offered jobs and people rarely moving on."* We also learned that three of the eight second-year trainees had started their training contracts at other firms, but had jumped ship and moved to DWF. Why is the firm so successful in recruiting and retaining staff? *"There is a tremendous amount of enthusiasm in the place from partners through to fee earners,"* one trainee explained. *"You don't wake up and say 'oh no, another day in the office' and when you get there it's not just heads down and work."*

what planet are you from?
The Klingons may be from the planet Qo'noS, but usually DWF trainees come from the North West.

"Most have a North West link or studied at northern universities, but at partner level there are some southerners." Trainees told us that the ideal recruit would be "someone who won't hide away when the phone rings. The sort who will go out and get things done – someone who can take the initiative." We noted a matter of factness to the trainees we interviewed; they were exactly of the type they thought best suited the firm – "candid" and clearly "intelligent" life forms.

The trainees we spoke to understood that to be a successful lawyer you need to learn more than the law. We heard how one trainee had supplemented his legal training with a dose of reality training. Instead of moving from one seat straight into the next, he was seconded to the marketing partner for a fortnight to learn a few client-winning tricks. Many trainees are seconded to one or other of the firm's insurance clients for a few weeks of life on the other side.

it's a social life jim…
Trainees are energised by the social scene. "On a night out you'll have support staff and partners all out chatting to each other. You don't have to stand on ceremony here." It doesn't take long to beam yourself from the "tatty round the edges" Manchester office into one of "nine or ten bars between us and the traffic lights at the end of the road." Most popular with younger crewmembers at the moment is Bar 38 and a new venue called The Living Room. Over in Liverpool, the Mersey beat can be heard regularly in vodka bar, Revolution (a client), and another Living Room.

The working day is rarely longer than 9am–6pm "or not even that sometimes," so there's simply no excuse not to mix with colleagues. This might be over a Chinese meal and a few drinks or (more in keeping with our view of the firm) weapons poised at the local Laser Quest.

and finally…
One trainee told us that he thought the firm was "in touch with the future." We were mightily impressed and wondered if contact was made through a Romulan Warbird or some other inter-galactic vehicle. Jokes aside though, one does get a sense that this firm has a clear idea of where it wants to be, how fast it wants to grow (warp speed). The new bulk operation in Warrington and the plumped up corporate practice illustrate that DWF is not resting in dry dock tinkering with its established insurance work. The boosters are on and it's boldly going out to find business.

Dechert

the facts
Location: London
UK ranking by size: 52
Total number of trainees: 26
Seats: 6x4 months
Alternative Seats: Overseas offices, secondments
Extras: Pro bono with various law centres

After going steady for over six years, the relationship between Dechert in London and Dechert Price & Rhoads in the USA has been consummated. The two firms are now fully merged and are no longer just good Black & Dechert workmates (sorry!).

keeping an eye on things
The full effect of the union on the character and practice areas of the London office will become apparent in time. Dechert trainees have certainly been keeping a keen eye on developments and most of our sources were positive about the future. As one trainee put it, "the consensus seems to be that there will be exciting changes in some departments and others won't really be affected." Some wondered about aggressive US working practices infiltrating Dechert's more laid back atmosphere. "Everyone's a little concerned about the US office bringing higher billing targets over to London. It hasn't happened yet but we'll have to wait and see."

high street clients

Some of our sources were attracted by the nature of the work. One trainee said, *"I chose Dechert because it is not too obsessed with corporate, corporate, corporate. It's an important area, but not the be all and end all."* Another source confirmed *"If you are a die-hard machismo corporate law wannabe then Dechert probably isn't the firm for you."* Actually it's property which is Dechert's largest department and the firm boasts an impressive list of household name clients: Currys, Dixons, Tesco and WH Smith to name but a few. Understandably, the firm *"is very keen to ensure that all trainees spend some time in property."*

You will spend four months in each of six seats at Dechert, but if you're concerned that four months may not be long enough to gain sufficient experience, you need not worry. Trainees can spend up to three of their seats in the same department, providing extensive experience in one area of practice before qualification. One trainee told us *"The six rotations provide a more informed choice upon qualification. I am looking to qualify into a seat which I would never have considered until I gave it a go."*

> "Friends and family will recognise you after qualification."

The range of seats is impressive. The largest departments are property, corporate, litigation and financial services but the employment team is really on the up and the Customs & Excise and Fraud teams have a superb reputation.

familiar faces

Despite the trainee diet being something other than corporate three times a day, that department is described as *"growing and ambitious."* It's where the biggest hours are to be found so, when the pressure mounts on deals, don't expect to be out of the door at 6pm on the dot every night. You should expect *"a handful of late nights over your two years of training, especially in corporate, but weekends are rare."* Across most departments the hours are pretty steady, with a standard day running from around 9am to 6-7pm. Your friends and family will still recognise you on qualification!

There was no consensus amongst trainees as to which were the most popular seats. There has been some fighting over the IP and investigations seats in the past, but the popularity of seats fluctuates between years. This season's trendsetters are to be seen in property litigation. Described as *"the place to go,"* trainees can expect to run their own files and it offers the opportunity to undertake advocacy, making interim applications before masters in the court. Corporate inevitably involves less responsibility and the work can *"drag on if we are under pressure."* Whatever the new black is next season, *"the options tend to shake themselves out."*

st bernard

Dechert was one of the first UK firms to appoint a dedicated head of training and all our sources applauded the efforts of Bernard George, director of training at Dechert and former head of the College of Law. He is approachable and helpful, both during the day and when cornered in the pub after hours. We could print a more extensive account of the superlatives heaped upon him, but we've been warned that too much exaltation will go to his head.

Over the years, Dechert has earned a reputation at the *Chambers Student Guide* as one of the cosier of London's mid-tier firms. Judging by this year's interviews, little has changed. *"It is supportive and comfortable here. Starting at a City firm is quite a daunting experience, but the firm does everything it can to ease you into the work."* The level of feedback and supervision from senior assistants was commended. *"Sometimes I feel guilty about the amount of fee earners' time I take up,"* one conscientious interviewee told us, but another trainee added *"I would be lying if I said the same about **all** the partners."* Trainees are given the opportunity to put their views across to the bigwigs at quarterly meetings, where *"the top brass do genuinely turn up and our concerns are taken seriously."*

renovation required

Trainees are not all fresh out of university; the mature trainees we spoke to felt that Dechert valued the experience they brought with them. *"About one quarter of us have worked in other areas or had previous careers."* With a relatively small intake each year, trainees at Dechert get to know each other fairly well. One interviewee commented *"we manage to go out for lunch together almost every day."*

Trainees seem resigned to the fact that much of their post-work socialising will take place in The Clachan. The main (and some say only) attraction of this regular haunt is its proximity to the office. *"It's quite convenient given that it is effectively built into the side of the building!"* Perhaps it should be incorporated as *"it is the cliché of the second office. There is almost always someone there in the evenings."* The location of the office is appealing. *"It couldn't be better. We are so close to Covent Garden and Leicester Square."* Sadly, the office space itself provides no reason to get out of bed in the morning. We heard complaints that it was *"a bit tired looking"* and *"in need of renovation."*

Overseas travel is possible, with a seat available in Brussels. The long-anticipated US seat has been confirmed and in 2002 a couple of trainees will be able to spend a few months in Philadelphia.

and finally…

Dehert has a pretty good record of retaining newly qualifieds; in 2001 all the trainees were offered jobs and only one did not accept as he had decided to emigrate. *"The orders have come from on high that we need to do all we can to keep NQs"* and this has resulted in a pretty good deal for those qualifying into the firm. If you are looking to train at an upwardly mobile medium-sized firm, which won't throw corporate work at you for the duration of your training, Dechert is one to consider.

Denton Wilde Sapte

the facts
Location: London, Milton Keynes
UK ranking by size: 11
Total number of trainees: 114
Seats: 4x6 months
Alternative seats: Overseas seats, secondments
Extras: Pro bono: Princes Trust Business Centre

The product of a union between Denton Hall and Wilde Sapte, Denton Wilde Sapte is now coming to terms with life post-merger and is making its presence felt as one of London's ten largest law firms.

haunted house

Our sources felt it was impossible to identify a typical Denton Wilde Sapte trainee or indeed for there to yet be a character to ascribe to the recently unified firm. One said, *"I don't see how there could be – two quite different firms have been thrown together."* This is true. Part of the rationale for the merger was to bring Wilde Sapte's banking and finance portfolio together with Denton Hall's expertise in energy, property and media/sports. The merger is generally regarded by the market to have been a resounding success, with the two complementary practices slotting together like pieces of a jigsaw.

The two firms have kept their separate premises with the banking, corporate and energy departments based in the former Wilde Sapte homestead in Fleet Place, and property, litigation and media occupying Denton Hall's old Chancery Lane offices. Something of the feel of the pre-merged firms would still seem to haunt these offices. *"Things are much more chilled in the Chancery Lane building… there is a bit of an intense feel to the Fleet Place office."* This comes as no surprise, given the nature of work being undertaken in each office. Aside from this, Fleet Place came up trumps for being smarter and more spacious, and it has a staff restaurant.

happy families?

Aside from those with split personalities, who else would fit in here? We heard that "*Most people would get on, as long as they are unpretentious and can use their initiative.*" Trainees alluded to a good atmosphere, saying "*I really hope we don't lose the family feel, but it is inevitable we are going to start attracting the kind of trainees who apply to the magic circle because now we are in the top ten* [in London]."

Even with the 'family atmosphere', we did hear of a couple of trainees who hadn't found life at the firm quite as easy as others. As with any of the big firms, trainees are pushed and the key to keeping your head above the water is maintaining a decent relationship with your supervisor. "*I've been really lucky,*" one source said, "*but a friend in his first seat didn't get on with his supervisor at all and had a bit of a nightmare.*" To be fair, this situation will be comparatively rare as the firm has a policy of only placing trainees with supervisors who show enthusiasm for the role. Another trainee whose chum hadn't hit it off with their supervisor told us "*If supervisors do treat trainees as a perk then they are not given trainees the next year. At the end of seat appraisal you get fifteen minutes on your own with an independent partner where you can talk about your supervisor's performance.*"

musical chairs

Trainees will experience a contentious seat and a transactional seat. The firm prefers the contentious seat to be spent in the litigation department, although there is also the opportunity for trainees to discharge this requirement in employment or IP, where there is a fair amount of dispute resolution work available. The transactional seat can be spent in a variety of departments; in the main part trainees will do a stint in banking, property or corporate. There are plenty of smaller departments for trainees to chose from ranging from aviation and shipping to competition and media. The perennially popular media department is an attraction for many budding solicitors. Before you get too carried away with visions of an ab fab lifestyle, it's worth noting that whilst the client base might be exotic, the work itself is not wildly different to that undertaken in other departments. "*It can involve celebs and the world of entertainment, but you are just dealing with contracts.*" The media group, which occupies the fifth floor of the Chancery Lane office, does have more of a glitzy feel to it though. The walls are lined with movie posters and lawyers don't go short on freebie tickets to sports fixtures and premières.

There is no guarantee you'll get the seat you want, so if you fancy a pop at any of the oversubscribed departments the advice, as ever, is to get your request in early and be consistent in what you ask for. It is worth pointing out that Denton Wilde Sapte has recently changed its policy on dishing out the plum placements and preference is now given to those who wish to qualify into the niche departments, rather than simply to third and fourth seaters.

playtime

We were told that the social life at the firm was quite lively with a very active social committee "*Midweek we go to the Old Monk, the Knights Templar, the Cheshire Cheese or the Old Bank of England. We like to mix it up a bit.*" There is also occasional socialising at the weekend, when trainees tend to meet up in the West End. Retention rates for 2001 are healthy. 100% of trainees were offered jobs and five declined to take the firm up on its offer.

risk

DWS offers an international experience for trainees, both in the diverse range of lawyers in the London offices and by way of overseas seats. "*Some of our meetings are like the UN,*" one trainee said. "*I just came out of a conference where we had a German lawyer, a Portuguese lawyer and an Australian lawyer working on an international deal.*" Those winning an overseas seat go to one of the offices in "*Dubai, Gibraltar, Hong Kong, Paris, Cairo – the list just goes on.*" Competition for the foreign experience is fierce and not everyone gets the location they want. The firm has adopted a strategy of taking interest in countries that rivals have by-passed. It has associations with local firms in Zambia and Tanzania for example, and has offices in places like Uzbekistan and Kazakhstan (which it acquired from CMS Cameron McKenna a year or so ago). Much of its work in these jurisdictions is energy based.

The firm also has an office in Milton Keynes. It is unlikely to follow Wimbledon FC's example and attempt to relocate the whole operation there, however, as there are only around twenty fee earners in the office (largely handling commercial property work) no trainees are sent to the city of concrete cows.

and finally…
With a liquorice allsorts selection of diverse seats and a smorgasbord of overseas offices, trainees at this firm are in danger of being spoilt for choice. Last year when we interviewed DWS trainees there was just a hint of sectarianism between the Denton Hall and Wilde Sapte camps. This has eased as the merged firm begins to look for its own unique identity. The next generation of trainees will probably only ever have known the firm as Denton Wilde Sapte. Whether the ghosts of firms past will continue to haunt the hallways is another matter though.

Dickinson Dees

the facts
Location: Newcastle-upon-Tyne, Stockton on Tees
UK ranking by size: 51
Total number of trainees: 22
Seats: 4x6 months
Alternative Seats: Brussels, secondments

Right up there with Alan Shearer, Gazza and Jimmy Nail, Dickinson Dees is one of Newcastle's proudest home grown talents. In Dickie Dees' promotional material, it claims to be the biggest and best firm in the North, to provide a better service than most major City of London law firms and to be much cheaper. We wholeheartedly agree with two out of three of these comments!

northern connection
Let's cut to the chase. Who would apply to Dickie Dees and is it mainly the province of those from the North East? Trainee opinion was mixed on this. *"There is a wide range of people here, geographically and socially, with trainees from Nottingham and Warwick as well as the North East."* Other trainees felt that *"if you have a connection with the area it's a plus. The firm will want you to stay and become a part of its future."* The fundamental question is do you want to live and work in this beautiful part of the country? If the answer is yes then maybe you can do no better than work for Dickie Dees. The firm aims for 100% retention on qualification and certainly makes its trainees feel valued in an attempt to meet this target.

bending over backwards
When you load up the Dickie Dees website it flashes the proud declaration: 'if it's legal we'll do it.' The firm does indeed offer a huge range of practice areas, which will guarantee interesting and varied work for those who qualify into the firm. Of the four seats you will undertake, three are in compulsory practice areas. You must spend six months in each of the property, litigation and banking departments. Trainees are consulted over the final seat, but there is no guarantee that you will get your first choice. If this sounds as though you won't have much say over which areas you train in, don't be too concerned. There's plenty of variety in the work you'll see. *"Insolvency is quite a popular area and I wanted to get some experience there… I pointed this out and they ensured that I saw lots of insolvency work during my litigation seat."* Interviewees lavished praise on the structure of the training programme and the quality of their induction. *"They are very flexible with training and it is up to you what you make of it. Nobody tries to push you too hard and if you have a problem everyone bends over backwards to help solve it."*

Trainees had no complaints over responsibility. Not only are they in control of their own files in property, they get to try their hand at advocacy in litigation. *"We do have to do photocopying when things are rushed, but that is part of the team atmosphere and everyone gets on with it… there are opportunities to do advocacy, the standard repossession hearings and more complex litigation. We are fully briefed and there is support."*

Additional opportunities include an overseas seat in Brussels, where there are two vacancies every year. We were told that *"trainees don't fight to go to Brussels,"* but there is never any difficulty in filling the places. Bear in mind, however, that the work is largely research based. There are also opportunities to go on six-month client secondments.

wobble on the tyne is all mine

There were no complaints about the atmosphere in the office. *"It really wasn't what I expected from a law firm. Everybody seemed to know my name almost as soon as I walked in the door on my first day."* This is very important to the firm and something they are anxious to keep up. *"I think we are looking for people with a human touch, who are good lawyers, but have social skills too. We don't want to lose the atmosphere we have built up here."* The Newcastle HQ has recently moved to new offices on the Quayside. Given the comparative cost of property in the North East, Dickie Dees can afford more spacious and impressive premises than many London firms. One trainee told us she was looking out at the Millennium Bridge from her office during our interview and, unlike London's offering, *"it won't wobble when you walk on it!"* The firm recently opened a branch office in Stockton on Tees, which operates across all the firm's practice areas. One trainee is based at this office and there are no plans to extend this number.

out on the toon

The mainstay of the trainee social life seemed to be the local Trainee Solicitor's Group. *"The TSG is really active in the North East and we socialise lots with people from other firms."* Informal socialising with colleagues certainly takes place with regular post-work drinks in local bars such as the Pitcher & Piano.

> "Right up there with Alan Shearer, Dickinson Dees is one of Newcastle's proudest home grown talents."

There is no doubt that Dickie Dees is the jewel in the crown of Northern Eastern law firms. None of the trainees or newly qualified solicitors we spoke to could fault the quality of the training or the progressive and friendly feel of the firm. Dickie Dees is instructed by national clients and you will be given interesting areas of work and client contact early on. Against this you should consider that you will be paid less than your London counterparts, but this is offset, of course, by the lower cost of living in the North East. The £30K salary on qualification in September 2001 was at the top of the scale for the region though.

You won't be dealing with blue chip clients all the time, and you may end up feeling frustrated that you don't have the opportunities presented to the super-ambitious in London, but Dickinson Dees has some killer names on its client roster: Go Ahead, Arriva, Northern Electric & Gas, Northern Rock, the Environment Agency and various NHS trusts, just to mention a few. It gets the best of business from the region and some good instructions from beyond.

and finally…

Few trainees feel happier or more valued than those at Dickie Dees, something you would expect from a firm that has taken the still rare step of achieving Investors in People accreditation. If any of our words of caution just sound like Southern snobbery to you, then you've probably made up your mind to apply already.

DJ Freeman

the facts
Location: London
UK ranking by size: 66
Total number of trainees: 28
Seats: 4x6 months
Alternative seats: Secondments.

Having just put its 'old quill pen' logo into retirement, the firm's brand imagery now comes in the form of four snooker balls. Each one represents a 'chosen area of business', namely property, insurance, media and communications, and commercial litigation. This is what the firm focuses on. It doesn't pretend to be something it is not.

the four snooker balls
We asked trainees to help us understand the snooker ball approach and learned that the demarcation between the four departments is not as simple as it seems. For example, *"In the media department you've got litigation and company and commercial in the same department, which is good because you don't have to go to a different department to see the different types of work."* Another illustration of the point comes in property; *"It includes commercial conveyancing, construction litigation and property litigation and a company and commercial team who are instructed by property companies."* And so it becomes clear: each of those snooker balls is a client sector not a practice area... except commercial litigation!

A word of caution, if you want a continuous stream of big-ticket blue chip M&A deals then perhaps you should look elsewhere. *"Big corporate deals do happen,"* said one trainee, *"but not 24-7."* Chances are you'll be applying to magic circle firms if that's your bag. One very exciting highlight is the public international law seat, which may involve some interesting international border dispute cases and, for the lucky trainee, the chance to drop into the zone in dispute. Please, please, please understand just how rare an opportunity this is in the UK legal profession. Cherish it.

when 3 become 1
The different departments are spread between three offices and, as they spend six months in each department, trainees move offices a fair few times. All three buildings are on Fetter Lane (very handy for nearby Fleet Street newspaper clients, the High Court and barristers chambers) and a short walk to the West End. *"It's definite that they are looking for a single office,"* one trainee reassured us. Mind you, we heard that a year ago...

> "Girl power is in evidence at partner level."

The trainees at DJ Freeman know that their edge of the City choice has paid off in terms of hours and lifestyle. *"My regular day has averaged 9.30am-6.30pm... I've only very rarely worked after 9.30pm... It's a big plus to be able to hang onto your own life."* Trainees get on well together and are often to be found in nearby pubs of an evening. The current hangouts are The Hogshead on Fetter Lane, Simpson's on Breams Buildings and in the summer, The Cartoonist. We noticed an alarming penchant for fancy dress at DJ Freeman. *"We usually have a fancy dress Christmas party and the partners really go for it!"* At the Millennium party there was a Louis XIV theme and we understand that, amongst the partners, big wigs were *de rigueur*.

the rellies
The 'Aunt and Uncle' scheme ensures that in addition to your formal mentor, there's someone fairly close to your own age to whom you can go for advice on minor niggles. *"It's someone to talk to, maybe over a drink in the evening – everyone knows the odd difficult supervisor."* Indeed, dear reader, everyone, everywhere does.

One thing you might chat over with your aunt or uncle is the amount of responsibility being handed down to you. Frankly, it seems to depend on the individual supervisor. *"Some don't like to give responsibility, others do – sometimes too much. Thinking about it though, in hindsight it was great. My supervisor might have been more canny than I gave credit for. I really had to use my initiative."* Most seem really happy with the work they get. *"Very rarely do people say they feel undervalued. In insurance for example, there's a whole paralegal department dealing with document handling. There are paralegals in property and litigation too."*

meeja darlings

The firm's reputation in areas like defamation and broadcasting give it appeal for many students. Happily, the trainees don't all seem hell bent on becoming libel lawyers and so they're not all plotting and conspiring against each other for the sexiest seats. The other point to note is that just because you did your corporate experience in, say, the property department, you wouldn't be prevented from qualifying into media corporate. The business focus of the departments gives a holistic view of client needs. Experience translates between departments, just like learning to play a good game of snooker probably sets you up to do quite well at pool.

> "We noticed an alarming penchant for fancy dress at DJ Freeman."

The firm's highly regarded property department has taken a bashing in the last year. After a number of partner-level departures from the department, the legal press is now questioning the efficacy of the snooker ball approach. What's really behind the troubles is still a bit of a mystery, but you could always try asking in interview… (er, maybe not then!)

A reasonably *"relaxed"* firm, DJ Freeman trainees are able to accept the demands placed on them without feeling over-burdened. One trainee indicated that the absence of a pressure cooker environment made her feel more ambitious and none of those we spoke to foresaw burn out.

zig-a-zig-ah!

At trainee level, girls make up nearly 75% of the population. These days that's not particularly unusual. But girl power is truly in evidence at partner level as well and that's almost unheard of in a City practice. We learned that the 40-odd% proportion of female partners doesn't drastically alter the atmosphere of the firm on a day by day basis. OK, a number of partners work from home some of the time so that they can more sanely handle the family/work balance, but there are other female partners, we're told, who exhibit the same tough guy traits more typically ascribed to men.

We struggled against the urge to assign Spice Girl names to all the partners… Libel Spice… Restrictive Covenant Spice… Coco Spice… and then we reminded ourselves that that this is not a female-dominated practice; it is merely a practice which has an appropriate gender balance. So, the bottom line – don't assume this is a matriarchy, but do take heart that as a young female (or male) lawyer you need not contend with an abysmal 10-15% female partner ratio, as you will at most other firms. You Go Girl!

and finally…

DJ Freeman is a firm that has dared to be different. If you subscribe to the snooker ball philosophy and think that your own aims can be achieved within the firm, then go on – fill in that form. DJ Freeman looks like a very pleasant place to be. On qualification, retention is pretty good. Nine of the 12 September 2001 qualifiers stayed with the firm. Most trainees feel at home at DJ Freeman, anticipating that it will provide the life/work balance that they will want in future years.

DLA

the facts
Location: London, Birmingham, Liverpool, Manchester, Leeds, Bradford, Sheffield, Glasgow, Edinburgh
UK ranking by size: 3
Total number of trainees: 138
Seats: 4x6 months
Alternative seats: Brussels, secondments
Extras: Pro bono: Princes Trust

A national firm uninhibited in its aspirations. Back in 1999 it announced that within three years it would become a top ten firm in London and the dominant practice nationally. Its 2001 mission statement is even grander: within five years it will be a top five pan-European full-service firm. DLA certainly has the boldness to dream and to dream big. (By the way, in this particular dream sequence we've not discussed the training experience in Scotland.)

bond villains
Let's build you up to the European crescendo. Only 15 years ago, DLA was five separate firms – Alsop Stevens, Wilkinson Kimbers, Dibb Lupton, Broomhead and Needham & James. Those five firms combined through successive mergers into Dibb Lupton Broomhead and Alsop Wilkinson. Dibbs had the guts, balls and aspirations that the more subtle Alsops did not. After those two entities merged in 1996 there was some fall out. Until and through 1999 partners left the firm on a periodic basis.

The merged firm, Dibb Lupton Alsop, somehow acquired a reputation as an aggressive upstart. And like something sticky on the sole of your shoe, some reputations are hard to shake, whether or not they're justified. *"We have a past reputation for aggression,"* said one trainee, *"and I asked various partners where the reputation came from but they didn't really know. I've never noticed it from within."* That sentiment was repeated right up and down the country during our interviews. None of the trainees felt that DLA was a harsh training ground.

Track the legal press back to 1999, and you'll find statements from the firm's chief executive, Nigel Knowles, pointing out the benefits of a big firm in terms of full-service, critical mass and geographical spread. Bond villain, Blofeld kept popping into our heads… (Please note, we're just musing about the firm's plans for taking on the world, not destroying it. Nor are we suggesting that Mr Knowles sits in his swivel chair, petting a fluffy white cat.)

olympian ideals
DLA's European alliance of firms, collectively called D&P, is a relatively fresh arrangement. Press reports indicate that DLA would like to achieve full mergers with the allied firms. *"The overseas alliance is exciting,"* one trainee said. *"It makes DLA one of the most dynamic and exciting firms to work for."* Visits from the D&P lawyers have become commonplace in the various UK offices of DLA. Trainees in a number of offices spoke of European and Singaporean attorneys working with them for months at a time and in February 2001 Manchester hosted the D&P Olympics (which we understand was only marginally less extravagant than the Sydney Olympics).

They also talked about pan-European departmental training weekends held in Brussels, Madrid and…wait for it … Birmingham. Trainees were really up to speed with the firm's plans. *"It seems to have a very good business structure and in a way it's run more like a company. Business decisions are made by committees at different levels and they're steering the firm in a conscious way, not haphazardly. We understand the big thinking."*

up for it
Aside from those who want to jump on board for the ride through Europe, what type of trainee is DLA looking to recruit? *"Most are down to earth,"* we are told. *"There's a genuine culture of co-operation; not looking out for number one."* *"It helps to be enthusiastic,"* another suggested, *"we are all pretty up about the firm."*

Indeed, they pretty much all are. The Leeds office must have been particularly pleased with itself when in November 2000 it swallowed up almost the whole of Garretts' struggling Leeds outpost.

The different offices exhibit a high level of local bias in their recruitment, with those offering family or educational ties in the relevant region making up the bulk of the trainee population. The London office is the exception in this respect. Does this make for stereotyped office environments? We amused ourselves with the idea of a Liverpool office (*"generally a good laff"*) staffed by Harry Enfield's Scousers…eh? eh? eh? Broadly speaking, across the country the trainees saw themselves as *"strong, outgoing"* and *"confident."*

Once recruited by a particular office, a trainee is very likely to work in that office for the whole two years of the training contract and beyond. *"There's a brilliant retention rate on qualification."* In almost all offices it's 100%, with Leeds being the exception this year and the London office drawing a few NQs from Birmingham and further north. The NQ salary of £32K in the regions (£33K in Birmingham) and a hefty £47K in London has helped with retention. *"We weren't expecting that much,"* trainees confessed, confirming their satisfaction with the figures. The disparity between the regional and London offices doesn't cause dissent. *"Up here it gets you a nice car and a house…it can't harm!"* Jolly good.

rampant hormones

The firm's profits for 2000/2001 were blooming with health. Turnover increased by 25%, and partner profits by 36%. This, and the expansionist attitudes flying around like rampant hormones, must be encouraging to young lawyers. One of our sources in the London office told us *"it would be a nice firm to be a partner in… many of the partners are quite young and others are young at heart, if not actually young."* He felt that the partners' willingness to socialise with younger fee earners and trainees (which seems to involve them *"putting their cards behind the bar"*) *"definitely makes me feel more a part of the firm."* Trainees in other offices agreed. A northern trainee remarked that a partner had emphasised that she had a future with DLA, saying to her *"This is your business."* Others talked of feeling valued and being *"a resource to be utilised."*

So if you stick with just one DLA office, will you know any trainees in other offices? The Liverpool-Manchester tie is a tight one and you only need to look at a map of Britain to see that Leeds and Sheffield aren't a million miles apart. We're not aware of any trainee places in the Bradford office. Trainees in the regions feel a lot closer to each other than they do with the London trainees. *"London is perceived – by them – as the most important office in the firm. That's London lawyers for you! That office has the largest turnover and is growing quickly."* With regard to other regional offices, a regional trainee would consult with lawyers in other offices *"on a relatively regular basis… I'm not pretending that it's every day but a couple of times a week."* Once a year, trainees meet formally on the annual trainee residential course, which is *"a bit like a school trip but with alcohol."*

chain gang

The national trainee Saturday night out is a recent institution. Last summer there was a 'big one' in Manchester, attended by trainees from all offices except… London. A London source confessed, shame-faced, that none of them had bothered attending. *"I do feel more remote from the other offices… they are a lot closer to each other."* Perhaps the truth behind the London crew's absence lies in the DLA regions' proclivity for drinking in chain bars… All Bar Ones, Henry's, Hogsheads etc. etc. etc. We're not sure about the dress code for the big nights out, but in the office we learned that the dress code was rather uneven and a bit too formal for most trainees.

There are enough hours in the working day to include some winding down after work. At one end of the scale, London trainees in corporate might do *"two or three all-nighters in six months and work regularly until 9-10pm. In banking I did eight all-nighters and* was in regularly until 10-11pm. I never went home before 7pm in that seat." At the other end of the scale, insurance litigation in Liverpool would be a regular 9am to 5.30-6.30pm. In each office the hours in corporate were seen as the rough end of the stick and consequently we did hear that it was an unpopular seat for many. But not all. Take a cross-section of the DLA trainee population and you'll hear a wide range of ideas about what they want to do.

vive la différence
Generally the same seats are on offer in each of the offices and certainly the three-month Brussels secondment (supplemented by three months spent in London on EU competition work) is open to all. But, you shouldn't assume that the firm does everything everywhere. Marine work is only available in Liverpool, aviation, tax and competition in London only and when we conducted our research interviews, the Birmingham office had no IP seat. So find out up front if your desired seat is on offer in your desired location.

We detected no hint of compulsion in seat allocation. *"There's no edicts as to what you have to do,"* consequently *"there's never enough people for corporate seats."* While *"it's common that you get what you want"* in almost all offices, we heard dissent in only one – Leeds – where not everyone was totally over the moon about the seats they'd done. Retention is particularly high on qualification and in September 2001 only three of the 65 qualifiers chose to move on. Two of them were from the Leeds office.

and finally…
If you want the cachet of a national firm training on your CV, then do look at DLA. Although the firm's hunger for European presence is being sated by its current forays onto the continent, be aware that at this time there's a limited number of opportunities to actually go and work the other side of the Channel. Trainees have been geed up by the firm's ambitions and a healthy number of them see themselves as reaping the rewards in years to come.

Edwards Geldard

the facts
Location: Cardiff, Derby, Nottingham
UK ranking by size: 76
Total number of trainees: 24
Seats: 4x6 months
Alternative Seats: Secondments

Edwards Geldard is a firm of two halves. The East Midlands pairing of offices in Derby and Nottingham has little contact with the Cardiff office so far as trainees are concerned. Besides an annual training meeting, trainees keep themselves fairly separate.

big fish
Primarily a commercial firm, Edwards Geldard does have a private client practice and trainees will occasionally take up seats in this highly regarded department. For the most part, however, it's commercial work all the way. Sources were keen to point out that this is not a small or parochial firm. The quality of work is *"exceptional, given that it is a regional firm."* Edwards Geldard has some very large clients, including three of the 12 UK rail companies and two of the 10 power companies. The construction department has worked on projects worth around £100 million. A lesson in the effectiveness of take-overs, Edwards Geldard picked up prestigious and coveted work for the Welsh Rugby Union's Millennium stadium project through the firm it acquired in 1997, Gaskell Rhys & Otto-Jones. The Welsh Development Agency is one of its biggest clients in commercial property and will occasionally take trainees on secondment or send its own to the firm.

The Cardiff office attracts those who seek a commercial training and sure enough, the firm will *"try and push you towards anything commercial."* This means 'compulsory' seats in commercial litigation (top-ranked by the *Chambers Guide*), corporate, and commercial property, which is *"a very big area."* Further more, Edwards Geldard has outstanding practices in competition, IT/IP, employment, planning and environment. Its clinical negligence and personal injury work attract many trainees.

cardiff roots

Traditionally the firm's HQ, the Cardiff office's fee income is equal to the combined income of the East Midlands offices. Typical of local commercial firms, *"many trainees have a Welsh background."* In September 2001, five of the seven Welsh qualifiers stayed with the firm. Interestingly, two took jobs in the employment group, two went into IP and one went into litigation. Across Edwards Geldard, trainees are given no choice of seats in their first year. In the second year, the situation is reversed and allocations are decided on collectively by trainees in each office, before reporting back to the HR manager.

close to home

The close relations between the Derby and Nottingham are described as *"fluid."* Property and litigation practices are run as single teams between the two offices and the odd trainee will transfer between the two locations, depending on where the work and seats are available. Commuting is unproblematic. Seats are normally undertaken in corporate, commercial, litigation and commercial property, *"but if you really want to do another seat, they will let you do it."* The most desired of these 'other seats' are usually employment or insolvency, although several more specialist seats are available.

till death do us part

In Derby the firm is keen to build on the amount of corporate work it wins in the region and trainees tout it as the *"most productive corporate department in the East Midlands."* *"There are a lot of big businesses in Derby,"* they told us. Hours are *"never horrendous,"* and *"nobody expects you to be at your desk for the sake of it."* This is a young, honest and plain-speaking office. Three-monthly appraisals are *"always quite candid."* You can *"sit and have a chat with partners,"* but there's also a feeling *"of needing to get work done."*

Winning a training contract in the Derby office requires applicants to pass the Pub Test. The *"senior partners test is whether they could sit in a pub with you."* Simple! *"They are genuinely friendly."* Supervisors tend to be quite young and there is a *"good social rapport"* with them. Bizarrely, *"everybody seems to be married to everyone else,"* and *"everybody seems to be called Williams."* Just like finding a spouse, the Derby office is looking for those who will stay till death do us part. *"If you join, you join for the long term."* Trainees are viewed as *"future partners"* and on qualification *"if you are good enough, the firm will find a place for you."* Salaries at trainee level are nothing to write home about, *"but when you qualify, you do very well here. That is why retention is good."*

discovering gravity

The major recent event for Edwards Geldard in the East Midlands was the merger with Nottingham firm Eking Manning. Despite being the larger firm overall, it was actually the Edwards Geldard posse that moved into the Eking Manning office. *"It's lovely and old, but a bit of a rabbit warren,"* one trainee told us. *"Everybody seemed to gel quite well. The two firms were very similar anyway."* Each was focused on corporate and commercial work. Four trainees were brought into the fold as a result of merger and, of the combined population of seven who qualified in September 2001, all but one stayed with the firm. In Nottingham they told us *"As a trainee, you're a valued member of the team,"* but everything you do is *"checked by a supervisor before being sent out."* The appraisal system is described (very simply) as *"nice."*

There's more than a hint of competition between the two sides of the firm since the merger. Traditionally Cardiff has been the head office, but East Midlands trainees are now talking of a 'gravitational pull' towards the Derby and Nottingham branches. Both sides of the firm *"have very strong client bases of their own"* and are *"self-sufficient,"* but work is referred between the two sides of the firm, particularly "*because they do have additional specialisms in Cardiff.*" While there is "*plenty of work in Derby*" following the merger, there is "*a definite move towards Nottingham.*"

pancake surprise

That move towards Nottingham may not be too difficult to explain. Three of the eight Derby trainees live in Nottingham and the Nottingham office is thought to have the better social life. "*Every Friday all the trainees are in the bar with partners, assistants, and secretaries.*" The bar in question is The Limelight – part of the Nottingham Playhouse. The choice of watering hole has nothing to do with picking up luvvies and everything to do with its proximity to the office.

The Derby branch does have a free bar in the office once a month but, with most people driving to work, Derby trainees are more inclined to play golf and squash together than settle down in the bar on a Friday night. The two Midlands offices do field combined cricket and football teams and play in a league with clients. The firm's social life reached an all time high in 2001 as a consequence of "*a fabulous pancake eating competition for Comic Relief in the boardroom of the Derby office.*" We would have loved to witness the spectacle: "*As many as you can eat in five minutes.*" Hmm, nice….

> "In the Derby office everybody seems to be called Williams."

Doing their best to stay in with the in-crowd, Cardiff trainees will join their peers from other local law firms at Bar Essential and there's involvement with the local TSG. A special list of the Top 10 most hilarious internal emails is maintained and updated throughout the year for the entertainment of those at the Christmas party.

and finally…

Like any firm with different branches, it is worth considering the specialities of individual offices before applying. To date it has been viewed as a more serious player in Cardiff than England, so it will be interesting to see how the firm fares in the East Midlands post-merger. The trainees are certainly confident of success and the atmosphere is at least more intimate than at the giant Midlands firms. As one said, "*not many other firms give you this quality of work combined with this kind of environment.*"

Eversheds

the facts

Location: Birmingham, Cambridge, Cardiff, Derby, Ipswich, Leeds, London, Manchester, Newcastle, Norwich, Nottingham
UK ranking by size: 2
Total number of trainees: 250
Seats: 4x6 months
Alternative Seats: Overseas seats, secondments
Extras: Pro bono; Battersea Law Centre, Mary Ward Legal Centre, Manchester Uni Advice Centre

Eversheds easily compares to the City giants in terms of turnover and number of fee-earners, but it is not a City firm in the purest sense of the term. From the late 80s, it grew by taking over regional firms and then re-branding them as Eversheds. The 'franchise' phase has come to an end now that the firm has finally become truly profit-sharing. Eversheds has branches everywhere. Its London office may be medium-sized by City standards but, viewed on a national level, Eversheds is huge. In addition to corporate/commercial, litigation and property, each office provides a range of specialist areas of work, but it's difficult to generalise about the Eversheds experience.

eat me… drink me

In the provinces, Eversheds offices tend to fall into regional groupings – Derby and Nottingham are classed as one profit centre for example, and Norwich, Ipswich and Cambridge are grouped together.

The firm *"still holds a smaller firm atmosphere, but in a larger firm."* Trainees were enthusiastic about this intersection of the national and local. Several sources cited the mix of the *"specialisms and trappings of a big firm, but with a less formal atmosphere"* as an important attraction. Being a large national firm, *"it gives you the opportunity to move between offices if you need to."* We checked this with Grad Recruitment and actually it is relatively rare for trainees to move.

Eversheds has plentiful resources; *"precedents are available via the Eversheds intranet"* and, out there somewhere, you'll always always find someone with the answer to your question. However, this does not mean a steady supply of City work in the provinces. Some trainees were very much aware that they were doing *"regional work."* One source confirmed, *"if you do want City work, you will not get exposure unless you are in London or Birmingham."* Conversely, the London office can claim to offer *"a provincial experience in a City firm,"* as one trainee put it. The quality of the work is *"slightly limited compared to major City firms, but probably better than other regionals."* One trainee with experience of work in the magic circle described Eversheds London as *"a lot friendlier."* It is *"generally fairly easy-going"* and *"not full of sloane ranger types or highly aggressive domineering types."* We won't tell you where he used to work!

not afraid to shout

None of the trainees we spoke to had any complaints about the quality of training on offer. Appraisals take place every three months with *"ongoing informal feedback"* and seats *"start off with a general induction explaining the type of work you will be doing."* As in most firms, an *"open door policy"* abounds. Trainees *"would not have a problem going directly to the head of department"* and are *"not afraid to shout."* Expectations are realistic – *"you are learning, so won't be expected to get everything right. You can talk to your supervisor and partners will explain things." "There is no them and us. Most partners are down to earth – they don't want to be elusive."* Trainees help each other and *"there are always five people you can email about a problem."*

Sometimes trainees have had to speak up. One regional trainee felt that *"collectively, we do seem to have to fight for things. We had to go out and research salaries ourselves to offer proof that other local trainees were being paid more."* The branch in question immediately increased salaries, but the feeling lingered that *"the disadvantage of it being a national firm is that they will sometimes say they can't do something we request because Eversheds don't do it, even though there are national variations between offices."*

doing deals

As for getting the seat you want, *"you approach the training partner and put in your preferences, but it is down to them and priority is given to second years."* One source spoke frankly about the situation. *"At the end of the day, it does come down to personality – whether you are known or not known. If you really want something badly and you know that it is a popular seat, then you will approach the partner. Behind the door deals do go on, but they are the exception not the rule."*

Eversheds brands itself as 'Business lawyers in Europe' and, with two seats in Paris and one each in Monaco and Brussels, those with a taste for the continent might be drawn to apply. But one source was sceptical about the opportunities for trainees in regional offices to take overseas seats. *"If they were really keen on spending time overseas, that might be an unrealistic expectation."* One trainee thought *"the number of overseas seats will expand,"* and another told us *"ad hoc secondments to clients are regular."* The scope for movement between regional offices is less than might be expected at trainee level but after qualification this can be a real boon.

behind the brand

Beware. Eversheds has many offices and though it has plenty to shout about, the hype is not always justified in all locations. Offices vary in their performance in different fields. The 'top of the tree' reputation the firm has earned in employment law in

London, Cardiff, Manchester and Birmingham for example, does not necessarily carry over to Leeds. An outstanding IP department in Leeds is removed from lower profile teams in Manchester and the Midlands. And how certain can you be of securing a seat in the IP department in Cardiff, with just one assistant and one partner? If you desire a particular location and you know what you want to do, check that the Eversheds office is your best bet over other local rivals. As often as not it will be, but the Eversheds name does not mean the same thing in all practice areas in all locations.

no cross words

The firm's website makes much of the *"Eversheds way of thinking."* We were keen to identify the Eversheds trainees' way of thinking. Our sources found that most had some *"experience beyond just university... even if it is just working abroad for three months."* If you don't click with those *"appalling little puzzles"* on their website, then don't worry. *"Outgoing and sociable"* are the characteristics our sources emphasised, in a firm that has adopted business casual as its full time dress code. *"We are all quite laid back – we don't take ourselves too seriously and we are not that competitive with each other. Partners don't like you it if you are aggressive."* One trainee thought this was why being a trainee solicitor was *"not as stressful as I might have expected."*

Many trainees cite the regional atmosphere as the real attraction of Eversheds, but it will differ between offices. For example, you'll be one of just six trainees in Derby, while in Leeds there are 30+ lawyers training at any one time. City trainees can typically expect to be away by 7pm. Back in the regions, a 7pm finish would be considered quite unusual. But, everywhere we interviewed, we learned *"there is no pressure to stay late – it won't impress anyone."*

local pickings

The social life varies from office to office, but generally reflects the outgoing nature of the firm and was described by all sources as *"good."* One trainee told us of a social outing to the Tweenies pantomime, but hastily added that this was *"primarily for those with families."* Hmmm…

The social scene in each of the offices caters well for grown-ups and each has its own regular pubs. Nottingham trainees talked about wild nights out at the local dog track, but since the *"burnt tangerine"* coloured meeting rooms in Nottingham are described as *"bright and bad for hangovers,"* we suspect there's a high price to pay for student-like excesses. Certainly, the firm has been known to advise clients on how to resolve disputes resulting from raucous Christmas parties!

having it all

On the surface, Eversheds seems to offer it all – a wide range of specialisms, friendly local atmosphere, the resources of a national firm and a *"London experience in the regions."* Eversheds trainees are *"dashingly good looking - no, that's probably not true."* They come from the dreaming spires of Oxbridge, and the new local universities – De Montfort, Nottingham Trent and Liverpool John Moores were all mentioned. *"They always advertise for Oxbridge students, when in fact they take people from a wide range of universities."* Of the 110 trainees who qualified in 2001, 105 were offered jobs on qualification and 85 accepted.

Comparisons to the magic circle aren't really appropriate. Eversheds is not a City firm, but a very very large collection of regional offices with their sights, like Manchester United, set firmly on Europe. Call them the JD Wetherspoons of the legal profession if you want, but strength in numbers has its benefits. Until Clifford Chance takes over your local butchers and turns it into a corporate practice, Eversheds will continue to offer one of the best quality training contracts in the regions.

and finally…

Trainee experiences will vary as much as the firm's workload. In addition to Eversheds' staple practice areas, you might get the chance to see specialist work in areas like education, clinical negligence, environment, healthcare, licensing and shipping. It all depends on which office you apply to. Amusingly, the firm's internal newsletter is called *"The Shed."* Sheds forever then!

Farrer & Co

the facts
Location: London
UK ranking by size: 88
Total number of trainees: 18
Seats: 6x4 months
Alternative Seats: Secondments
Extras: Pro bono: Battersea Law Centre

Farrer & Co is assumed to be one of the most traditional firms in London. With its royal connections, long history of private client work and aristocratic reputation, many students will ignore the firm. But instead of just turning the page, read on…

rich list
Almost every seat on offer at Farrers is out of the ordinary. Trainees cover five areas of law over the course of six seats. *"They wanted me to see around the firm,"* one explained, taking us through the 'compulsories'. You'll certainly do something in private client (domestic or international) or charities. *"You're only dealing with those who have money and the landed gentry. In international it's oil-rich Arabs and other European and Asian super-rich."* The charities department works for trusts, national charities, museums and schools. Secondments are available to the London Business School and the Science Museum.

The litigation seat can be taken in family, media or general litigation. *"Media is popular as it sounds trendy."* Celebs aren't in regularly, but one trainee said, *"I have seen some famous people."* Media clients also include internet start-ups. In family, you'll be instructed by *"sloaney types and people who are rich."* The well-respected property department offers commercial, private, and estates (agricultural) options. Its clients include the Duchies of Lancaster and Cornwall. The fourth 'compulsory' is a commercial seat chosen from IP (*"very in"*), general commercial (including banking) and employment (which is growing). *"The companies are usually those set up by entrepreneurs, venture capital outfits and partnerships."* Deal sizes are not the biggest available and *"you're not going to be one of 24 people working on a deal."*

A fifth seat is chosen from the pack by playing a 'wildcard' and, in the sixth seat, trainees warm up to qualification by returning to their intended practice area. *"The warm up is a jolly good idea,"* one trainee said. In September 2001, all eight of those who qualified stayed with the firm.

twitching
"I didn't want to go into major corporate areas or be one of a number on a treadmill." This is what trainees say when asked why they chose the firm over big City players. Sure, *"the money wasn't as good, but it had a good name – it wasn't a tough decision."* Farrers is a firm where relationships between people are important and *"one strikes the right balance between work and extra-curricular activities."* One trainee summed it up by saying *"I like the fact that you can sit with a partner who is as likely to talk to you about bird-spotting, wine and gambling on the horses as the ins and outs of agricultural property law. My day is not solely concentrated on the business of learning the law. People are not automatons here."* The relaxed approach doesn't mean the law isn't treated as *"an academic subject,"* but it does mean that Farrers is *"not a cut throat firm."*

a toffs firm?
We asked trainees if Farrers was stuffy and aristocratic. *"It's slightly annoying,"* one of our sources retorted *"it's not a toffs' firm and to hear it labelled as such is slightly grating. No one here is particularly toffish, although some of the partners are from a wealthy back-*

ground." There's probably a fair degree of self-selection amongst applicants; not everyone wants to act for the super-rich and landed gentry. Undoubtedly applicants with an understanding of the wealthier elements of society see this firm as a potential home more quickly than those brought up on the wrong side of the tracks.

> "The cricket team even plays against the royal household ...they usually win."

Yes, the accents are (in the main, but not exclusively) a bit posher than at your average law firm, but there's no evidence whatsoever that Farrers wishes to keep recruiting the more privileged of society. *"Looking at the next few years, there's only one or two Oxbridge grads coming in – that was not the case five years ago."* We learned that *"Farrers goes for quite a lot of CPE/ year out people."* Among the current batch of trainees there's a former teacher, an ex stockbroker, an ex soldier and a football mad northerner. The hallmark of a Farrers trainee is *"self-confident, but not over-confident… someone who's at ease in different social situations."*

proper pubs
Lincoln's Inn Fields has been the firm's home since 1790. *"The old building is the public face of Farrers and contains the family and some private client teams, the meeting rooms and library."* It backs onto Imperial Buildings; a modern building that houses the rest of the staff. But you won't spend all your waking hours at work. The average trainee quits around 6pm-6.30pm, often slipping into one of the local hostelries afterwards. *"There's a couple of bars below Imperial Buildings – Jamie's on Kingsway, All Bar One and the Pitcher & Piano."* *"Estates and private property prefer the White Horse,"* *"a real dive which sells excellently kept beer."*

"Friday nights in Jamie's are always good fun. You'll get a cross-section of the younger half of the firm. But if the boys can convince the girls, we go to a proper pub!" Well done boys! We asked if there were dress down Fridays. One trainee set us straight. *"Ha! ha! – that's when we don't wear collar stiffeners – no we don't have dress down and I don't think we ever will."*

college ties
The training experience is *"like being in tutorials back in college – one to one."* And like any good college, Farrers has a dining room with a complex set of rules for troughing. Before 1pm non-partner staff can chow down, except on Wednesdays when they can eat at any time. Meals are free. One trainee took the college theme one step further when talking about appraisals. *"The half term assessment is otiose. I know how well I am doing by just talking to the person I sit with."*

Indeed, there's plenty of talking; it's the Farrers style. *"There's a good team feeling. The partner I sit with will ask my opinion on things."* More talk at group level too: *"Once a quarter we have a breakfast meeting with the management board. They tell us how the firm is doing financially. It's quite detailed. We put an agenda of our own forward too. In terms of information about the firm, they are fairly forthcoming."* Anything the trainees don't manage to say in these meetings comes out in the Christmas review. *"The trainee panto takes the piss out of partners!"*

loyalty and royalty
In the same way that one develops allegiance to a college, trainees grow fond of Farrers. *"I have immense loyalty to the firm, which is shared by the other trainees."* Certainly this spirit is needed in the firm's sporting endeavours. There's a cricket tour every summer and the team even plays *"against the royal household… they usually win. We play at Windsor, it's quite cool."* On learning of the annual partners v rest of the firm football match, we asked if the more senior partners could squeeze their bellies into the football strip. We were told *"It's more the younger ones that play in the match, although the cricket brings out some of the stuffies."*

"There's definitely a pride here – at Rugby Sevens we do well – the partners like to see us winning against a City firm. It is like a college thing." At the risk of labouring the point, we suspect that you can't underestimate Farrers' *"good sporting tradition."* It bonds the lawyers together. *"There's a sense of duty to the job here. Mucking in."* The firm values commitment and boy, do they get it! *"I love the firm – I can't imagine working anywhere else. I feel surrounded by like-minded interesting people."*

where's the but?

Having been bowled over by the praise, we looked to find some negative comments from trainees. *"It sounds sucky, but there's nothing I'd change."* Anything students should bear in mind that might put some off? *"You get important clients, but in commercial you don't have the massive deals."* And what of salary? *"Honestly, it is not as high as the big firms, but our lives are a lot nicer. It's an understanding place. People who leave here tend to go in-house."*

Don't come here looking for international secondments, the furthest you're likely to get is a short visit to an offshore tax haven like the Channel Islands. Don't expect Farrers to suddenly start changing its business either. Yes, areas like banking are growing and the firm has scooped up teams of lawyers from other firms (eg Nabarro Nathanson and Crockers Oswald Hickson) but in the main these add-ons have been in the private client/charities/media aspects of the firm's activities.

and finally…

There's a perception that Farrer & Co is stuffy because it is the Queen's solicitors, but trainees tell us that this is not borne out. There are some well-spoken staff at the firm and, yes, clients are of a certain breed, but Farrers doesn't appear to hold élitist views. If the question of how the other half lives fascinates rather than fazes you then take a second look at this firm. If you are the other half, your application may be in the post already.

Field Fisher Waterhouse

the facts

Location: London
UK ranking by size: 41
Total number of trainees: 20
Seats: 2x6 and 3x4 months
Alternative seats: Secondments

Field Fisher Waterhouse is a pleasant and growing mid-tier commercial practice. In the City but not just handling City work, it offers personal injury, IP, e-commerce and media seats alongside the more conventional property, banking and corporate departments. Its increased profile hasn't had an adverse effect on its reputation for being a pretty nice place to work.

fashionable lawyers

No longer a no-name, FFW is a label you'd be able to wear with pride at law school. If law firms were clothes, it would have once been the equivalent of a C&A brand and now it's probably closer to Stüssy or Kangol. With the new image, FFW has a new energy and pride and this hasn't escaped the attention of trainees. *"People didn't know our name before but they do now. We're definitely not stagnant as a firm. Things are changing."* Indeed they are.

> "You'll need to change your clothes on a regular basis."

Over the last couple of years, trainees told us that the firm's corporatisation was moving at a faster pace than their keenness to become corporate and banking lawyers. This year, the qualification stats and comments from trainees indicate a harmonisation of aspirations. Today's trainees do seem to be after what the firm is now offering. In September

2001 eight out of ten stayed post-qualification, some going into corporate. *"The corporate groups have grown in the last couple of years and younger people coming in have a slight change of focus,"* one trainee concluded.

as if by magic

But it's not the banking and corporate work that's made FFW a trendy place to be. To understand what's led to the firm's inclusion in the in crowd, you need to look at its IT/IP and media work. As well as having lawyers who sport goatee beards, the IT/IP/media departments have managed to court press attention, win great clients and earn a reputation for spearheading the new image of the firm. But rather like kids' TV hero Mr Benn, as a trainee at FFW you'll need to change your clothes on a regular basis. The firm is positively schizophrenic in its appearance. *"Commercial and corporate want to hang onto the uniform, IP and employment want total dress down."* Ding ding. Round one – goatees v pinstripes. We got the impression that IP/IT was by far the coolest place to be. *"The head, Mark Abel, has strong views on how a department should be run. It's very egalitarian, with lots of team meetings where we give input."*

Property is a sociable department and the partners there recently took their team out on the London Eye. The two teams – travel and tourism and Professional Regulatory Group (PRG) – that moved into a second office building *"just two minutes away"* have issued a standing invitation to the rest of the firm for Friday evening drinks. What's clear is that despite differences in style, the lawyers all want to get on with each other. *"Partners like to like the people they work with,"* said one trainee who also stressed that it was this *"similar wavelength"* test that she'd applied when choosing a firm for her training contract.

your money or your life

So what's the firm offering trainees? *"A broad range of work and a decent salary"* is the common answer, closely followed by comments pertaining *to "reasonable working hours,"* and *"this is a lifestyle firm."*

There's an acknowledgement that a FFW training offers *"a trade off"* between being the best paid at one of the biggest firms and as happy as Larry at one of the lower stress, lower profile firms. The range of work on offer is wide. On the one hand you can take your place in the *"burgeoning corporate or IP groups,"* on the other you can get involved with work in the PRG (especially for the General Medical Council). The personal injury department shuns 'trippers and slippers' for more serious claims.

While the different types of work on offer are varied, the general theme is commercial. *"People accept that they will be doing broadly commercial work, otherwise they wouldn't be applying here."* This might be a great firm to choose if you're still uncertain about what type of commercial lawyer you want to be. *"I joined because I wasn't 100% sure what I wanted to do. I didn't want to be swamped in a huge firm but I wanted a City firm with a good range of work."* The hours do vary from one department to another, so don't expect it all to be plain sailing and to be out of the door at 6pm every night of your training contract. One trainee recounted his busiest time *"I worked extreme hours for the guts of a year. As one big deal went quiet, another kicked off."* For the most part you'll find it easy enough to slip away between 6pm and 7pm. Unsurprisingly, corporate and banking will demand more of your time.

a fine line

The social life is pretty good. We have to say that, as the trainees we interviewed this year thought we'd been a bit down on their partying in last year's True Picture. So, for the record, *"the social scene has not run out of steam."* If you like the idea of trooping off to the Comedy Store or the dog track or a quiz night with 20 of your closest work buddies, then look no further; this is the firm for you. Staff also get their kicks from team sports.

There's no single pub that could be termed 'the second office', but one of the most frequented is The Fine Line, just across the road. The trainees are a close knit bunch. *"Because of the numbers you get to know each other well."* As for getting to know partners well, opinion was divided. *"You wouldn't regularly see any of the partners in the pub,"* one trainee said. But another thought differently: *"You do see partners in the pub on Friday. A group of the fee earners will go and the partners will join in. You get to know them on a personal level, learn about their families etc".* Maybe it depends on which department you're in.

on a flight to self discovery

The Vine Street offices are *"quite dull."* You'll share a room with your supervisor who'll be either a partner or an assistant. *"The good thing is that everybody gets the same aerodynamic* [er, don't you mean ergonomic?] *desk. So you're not hidden away in a dank, dark corner."* We should hope not! Whilst in charge of the controls on your own personal flight deck, you'll probably be pleasantly surprised at the *"one to one contact you'll have with your supervisor and their work."* Client contact is good and *"if you do the research, you'll write the letter."*

Secondments to clients like the BBC, Colt Telecom and Mitsubishi Bank are really popular. Aside from needing to *"jump up and down a lot"* because *"you should display keenness,"* the selection process is felt to be scrupulously fair and open.

Excellent news – it's *"a good training"* and *"they don't try and kill you!"* On the negative side, there is a sense that *"the firm is still finding itself and developing from an old-fashioned firm."* The *"ructions"* between old and new don't seem to turn trainee hairs and the transition that they perceive the firm is experiencing is now *"more than halfway through."*

and finally…

FFW is pitched as a lifestyle firm. The quality of work and clients means it's no soft option but it still feels pretty darned comfortable. If you're after a corporate/banking future, you could happily put this on your shortlist. If e-commerce or IT/IP gets your vote, it is also a firm to try for. And at law school you'll no longer have to explain who and what the firm is because your contemporaries will already know.

Finers Stephens Innocent

the facts

Location: London
UK ranking by size: 95
Total number of trainees: 8
Seats: 4x6 months
Alternative Seats: None

Finers Stephens Innocent is a chimera, created in 1999 out of the merger of general commercial firm Finers with media practice Stephens Innocent, followed by an influx of refugees from disbanded firm Edward Lewis. It offers commercial work, a media practice and a private client department all packaged up West End stylee.

be flexible

Trainees undertake a six-month seat in each of the corporate/commercial, property and litigation departments or 'brands'. (Note the media influence coming through already.) The remaining three practice areas of IP/media, employment and private client present attractive options for a fourth seat. Within media there's a sports law practice and a family seat can be taken in the private client department. Employment is very popular, especially since it recently formed its own department.

There's an element of trainee choice in the allocation of seats. According to one trainee, you must be persistent. *"They accommodated me, but you have to keep chipping away at them."* Nothing's set in stone though, and we learned of one trainee who extended a seat to a year and another who sandwiched a six-month seat between two lots of three months in another. But trainees must fit in with the business needs of the different departments. As with most firms, where you ultimately sit and when will require you to *"fit around the firm's logistics."*

if you don't ask…

Whichever department they were in, all those we

spoke to had found themselves handling *"such varied work,"* even if the subject matter was not that hot (property for instance?). We heard about one department that had never previously taken on a trainee. At first the lawyers were wary of delegating work, but our source *"nagged so I got work and they realised I could do it. I ended up doing the work of a qualified solicitor."* Responsibility is there for the taking, we're told.

Feedback flows readily; *"they are pretty good at praise or constructive criticism because they realise that they have to train us... we won't just turn out like they want."* There are no fancy seats abroad, but one trainee managed to work for a month in the US with the friend of a partner – *"if you don't ask, you don't get."* The firm is also *"very pro-education,"* so find a course, ask a partner, and you just might get to do it.

making your mark

Having acquired a new identity, FSI is moving forward and promoting itself. The words *"innovative,"* *"modern"* and *"forward thinking"* cropped up in our interviews and trainees pointed out that *"it's really trying to do something with itself at the moment; there's a strategy."* One familiar face from the old days is Mark Stephens, Head of Media. If there is a TV or radio show that needs a legal eagle to give an opinion then he's the man for the job. (Don't scare yourself by checking out his CV on the website.) *"He's a larger than life character. Everyone knows Mark and he does raise the firm's profile."* *"Mark always drags you down"* one trainee said, adding that she meant *"to his office to get involved in work,"* not that he depressed everyone.

Not only is the firm new to the True Picture, but effectively it's new full stop. There's the general bit (used to be Finers), the media bit (used to be Stephens Innocent) and the Edward Lewis *"good guys"* (see the Legal Week archives at www.lwk.co.uk for saucy scandal involving the EL 'bad guys') Now here comes the science bit – no, not really! But has there been happy covalent bonding or nuclear meltdown in this new firm? By all accounts, the atmosphere is just fine. Most of the trainees we spoke to found themselves in the odd position of working for a firm they didn't actually apply to. That is to say, they began their training at one or other of the firms before merger. There were inevitable teething problems at first. *"It was difficult to make a firm in the beginning,"* but things are well on the way now.

"There's a media atmosphere – but it's not solely media. Some trainees joined Finers and have no interest in media. Finers used to be property-orientated." On the other hand, *"Stephens Innocent was very media based. FSI is not as relaxed as Stephens Innocent was – but it's a fairly relaxed environment."* The consensus is that the merger increased the amount of media work, which in itself benefits the profile of the nascent firm. But trainees wanted us to emphasise that this is not solely a media firm; *"It's too big to be just that. It has every other facility too."* The September 2001 retention statistics illustrate the opportunities available. Seven of the eight qualifiers stayed with three of them going into corporate jobs and the rest spread across the rest of the practice.

westenders

Since the merger, the firm has out-grown its Great Portland Street building and the family and private client departments are in a separate building round the corner on Clipstone Street. It's not just the location; the style here is *"very West End."* It is *"more relaxed than other places. You don't have to be seen to stay late and there's no one-upmanship,"* but don't assume this means you won't have to work hard. Average hours seem to be around 8.45am to 6.30pm. According to one source, *"the latest I stayed was 7.45ish."*

So, it's a game of happy families. *"The firm is friendly and approachable, we're not in awe of the partners, you can just walk in to chat to them."* Most of our interviewees gained this impression right from the start. *"I've fitted in really easily – after a week it felt as if I had been here for ages."* *"If you have gripes, it's made plain who you go to. You don't suffer it on your own so it's never recurring."* Forget 'media darlings', think *"ambitious, dynamic... personality and quirks are allowed."* A few words of advice from one trainee though; *"for quieter people it would be more difficult, but it's all right for me."* Importantly, *"there's no one staid and up themselves, there are no hooray henries."* Glad to hear it!

paper cups 'n' nibbles

One trainee reckoned *"everyone knows who I am."* Is this a Mini-Mark snapping at the heels of his illustrious media idol? Idol or not, there's no overt sense of hierarchy and *"younger partners will come out to the pub sometimes."* Local haunts include Villandry, Mash, the ubiquitous Firkin and Ha!Ha!'s (*"great name"*). Another Starbucks is opening up round the corner (just what we need) and *"there's usually someone from the firm"* in the Clipstone Café. Or you could try the firm's effort; *"Wind Down – once a month…meeting room… paper cup…nibbles"* – OK, you've really sold that one to us.

> "Forget 'media darlings' think ambitious, dynamic... personality and quirks are allowed."

Another of the firm's new traditions is 'Dress-Down August', *"influenced by the Stephens Innocent side of things."* Fridays are dress down, irrespective of the month. There are also staff lunches once a month. But the firm's efforts aren't as lame as we may have led you to believe. There is a social committee, which has organised *"four functions in as many months."* The driver of the social life seems to be informal e-mails inviting everyone for a drink, lunch or whatever. You can take it or leave it; people are *"laid back."*

and finally…

If you want to specialise in media, go for it, if not, that's OK too. The client list is impressive, including celebrities, sports personalities, American press and broadcast organisations, hotels and on-line ventures.

Apparently, *"the only people who don't fit in well are those who don't like working late or staying for functions when we're all supposed to meet clients."* We suspect these are people who'd be better off not being lawyers at all.

Freethcartwright

the facts

Location: Derby, Leicester, Nottingham,
UK ranking by size: 80
Total number of trainees: 15
Seats: 4x6 months
Alternative Seats: None

This firm came into existence following the 1994 merger of Freeth Cartwright with Hunt Dickins. Overnight it became one of the biggest law firms in the East Midlands. There's no training in the Derby office and only one seat in Leicester, but the firm has four offices in Nottingham (although they may soon be brought together under one roof). Freeth's work is split fairly evenly between commercial property, private client, corporate and commercial services and dispute resolution (which includes the firm's outstanding clinical negligence and product liability departments).

are we nearly there yet?

Since the merger, there has been a bit of chopping and changing and a new chief executive from the Bank of Scotland was appointed in 2000. *"Crime and housing went a couple of years ago, but there are no plans to get rid of anything else."* The process of putting the firm together is ongoing. *"They are still struggling a bit to put the systems in place that a firm of this size needs."* For example, *"the library resources are poor."* There is talk of moving to a single office in Nottingham, but the firm's branches in the three different cities, departmental collaboration aside, tend be fairly distinct. For example, as one source explained, *"the Leicester office gets on with being the Leicester office."*

In response to our question about the firm's ambitions, one source said, *"They are not quite focused on what they should be delivering. The firm does not quite know where it is going."* Still unsure of itself, it has *"not quite reached the point of having the resources and outlook of a big firm."* But it's still a really nice place to work, and is at least happy with its regional status. It's *"a very good East Midlands firm, but not a national firm, and with no ambitions to be."* Profits increased by a whopping 33% in 2000/2001 so the firm must be doing something right.

wish fulfilment

"Before starting, they have an induction day for new trainees, with presentations about the different departments." Unusually, trainees at Freeths are able to select the location of their first seat. New trainees are not used to mop up unpopular seats, as happens at many firms, and getting the seat you desire is generally not a problem. *"There are enough seats for people to go where they want."*

Freeths is still feeling its way in the organisation of the training contract. Although mid and end of seat appraisals are now in place, *"some people don't give it as much time as they should."* One trainee admitted, *"I had one really bad seat, and there was no system to monitor that or pick it up in advance."* Although the firm has put in place a *"mentoring system, it is not particularly well followed through."* Still, *"if you work, hard it is appreciated,"* and there is absolutely no stay-late culture. 8.30am to 5pm are the prescribed hours.

hard or soft boiled

The quality of work varies with the breadth of practice areas. There are *"good clients, with good work, but it is not there all the time, so there can be some real crap. Certain departments are very good, but you cannot say that across the board."* Perhaps this reflects the nature of a firm of this type. *"It's not like a hard boiled City firm or a tough regional firm."* However, this does not stop the occasional trainee finding a job in the magic circle post qualification, if they are that way inclined.

Retention rates have been a bit wobbly in the last few years, despite a healthy number of job offers. In 2001 five jobs were offered to seven trainees but only three accepted. In several cases, departures merely reflected personal circumstances – Nottingham isn't necessarily going to remain the centre of every young lawyer's universe forever.

A trainee observed *"the corporate side needs to be built up."* Trainees tell us *"Freeths is not a big corporate firm. They can't offer consistently high quality work. You will get dross in between good stuff."* But maybe Nottingham is not the best place to go for a corporate training. *"It tends to fall in between Birmingham and Leeds, which is where a lot of work goes. But you do pick up the local work."*

dodgy gear

"The variety of training on offer," attracts some trainees, because they *"don't know what they want to do."* On the one hand they can work for corporate clients, on the other *"they can try out private client work."* Most trainees have local roots and many will study for the LPC in Nottingham.

Freethcartwright has an astoundingly good reputation for certain areas of its work. *"It is one of the best places in the country to do product liability."* Indeed it is. Freeths handles high profile claimant work such as the soya breast implant actions and the Measles Mumps and Rubella Vaccine litigation. Its work of this type, as well as a clinical negligence practice that is top rated in the Midlands, prompts some trainees to apply to the firm. In 2001 the clinical negligence team was just pipped at the post for *The Lawyer's* award for 'Litigation Team of the Year'. These strengths are felt to be down to the presence of some *"very talented individuals."* Naturally there's stiff competition amongst trainees for the chance to work with these high fliers.

let me entertain you

"Freeths looks for trainees to get involved" in the life of the firm, so expect team-building exercises, such as quad biking. There's a good informal trainee social

life and *"a good trainee scene in Nottingham."* The warm atmosphere extends up and down Freeths. Partners are *"very approachable, mix at all levels, and are not stuffy at all."* One trainee, possibly slightly confused, confessed, *"there's never been pressure to stop talking in class."*

In some bizarre East Midlands ritual, trainees at the annual Christmas party are 'obliged' to perform a comedy sketch or routine for the amusement of partners and assistants. Trainees dress up and mercilessly lampoon the partners, who just lap it all up. Inflatable sheep have previously been featured. *"Most partners do not consider themselves to be on a special level."* Clearly not!

and finally…

After all the changes, this firm is passing through its adolescent existentialist phase, touting its trendy name around, but still questioning why is it here and what is it doing. One trainee summed up two years spent at the firm: *"You will not do better in finding a balance between experience, work, and the social side. It is very rounded, but maybe diluted in terms of big work."*

Freshfields Bruckhaus Deringer

the facts

Location: London
UK ranking by size: 6
Total number of trainees: 176
Seats: 4x6 months*
Alternative Seats: Overseas seats, secondments
Extras: Pro bono: RCJ CAB, Tower Hamlets Law Centre, death row appeals, language training

A member of the magic circle and a leading international law firm, Freshfields is always at or around the top of the tree in every area in which it works. As the sixth largest firm in the UK, Freshfields handles nothing but top quality, big-ticket work. A Freshfields training will most likely turn you into an excellent lawyer and give you a Willy Wonka Golden Ticket to the best jobs in the legal profession… and to infinity and beyond.

bricking it

The firm has a reputation for recruiting not only extremely bright graduates, but a particular strand of 'blues and blondes' from the dreaming spires universities. The stereotype has been around for some time now and trainees are used to hearing it. When we innocently asked whether there was a typical trainee at Freshfields, they immediately responded *"I suppose you want us to tell you about the blues and blondes and how we are all from Oxbridge."* So, for the record, Freshfields is casting its net wider than Oxford and Cambridge. Several of the red brick university graduate trainees we spoke to decided to apply to Freshfields because they perceived it to have been more pro-active in marketing to non-Oxbridge students. One trainee told us *"they sponsored an event at my university and, to be honest, they were the only one of the top firms to take an interest in the lower red bricks."*

Most of our interviewees thought the Freshfields trainee profile was changing, although the old identifying features die hard. *"There are quite a few public school types, but I attended a state school and that isn't rare."* Some kicked harder against the stereotype. To be fair to the firm, whilst it has more than its fair share of Oxbridge recruits (probably more than half), it is not an Oxbridge closed shop. The defining characteristics of a Freshfields trainee are confidence and self-belief. They know they are amongst the élite of the legal profession and they know their Golden Ticket will get them through virtually any door in the future. Of the 75 trainees who graduated in 2001, 74 were offered a job and only three declined.

tales of the unexpected

What kind of a person would you expect to meet at Freshfields and is it the right place for you? First off, Freshfields trainees usually have a track record of academic excellence. But the firm is interested in more than this: *"They take it for granted that anyone at interview has all the basics. Freshfields are also looking for people with personality who can get on with other employees and clients."* Anything specific, we asked? *"There is no secret way in, no boxes to tick off. Sport, travel, anything that shows teamwork would be good. You don't get many here whose only stories from university are about property and trusts!"* Our sources stressed that the firm was far more interested in people's innate abilities than in just churning out legal clones. *"At interview there are no psychometric tests; they are trying to get to know you as an individual, not just a commodity."*

We noted a high proportion of trainees with language skills and travel experience. You can certainly expect to join the ranks of young, dynamic and interesting people when you start your training at Freshfields. This is rather fortunate because, to be frank, you are going to be seeing rather a lot of them. We checked whether Freshfields intends on remaining (with Slaughters) the last bastion of formal dress in the magic circle. It most certainly does, so you'd better start shopping for a few smart suits.

c u (much) l8r

Many graduates are put off the magic circle by the hours they are expected to put in. It's sometimes hard to get to the truth about trainee hours, but our sources at Freshfields left us in little doubt that they are full on. Hours certainly vary between seats; in corporate finance (which all trainees experience) they can be especially gruelling. *"I had to work quite a few all-nighters. Once I went all the way to morning and then on past 10pm the next day."* Everyone had spent quite a few nights working through until 3am or 4am, although this was described as *"not a real all-nighter!"*

None of this should necessarily scare you off applying to Freshfields in particular; it's just the way it is in the very largest firms in the City. If these hours are not for you then practice in the City may not be up your street either. It's simple: the bigger the deal, the bigger the firm, the longer the hours. Any top firm's reputation is built on total commitment to its clients. Your social life/sleep is very much a secondary consideration. Still, the work you will see can be interesting and the firm pays for dinner and taxis home after 9pm. Best of all, it will even issue an M&S gift voucher for you to buy a clean shirt in the morning. The girls apparently prefer a trip to the lingerie department. Whilst many trainees find adjusting to the long hours culture difficult, few find it impossible. Please, make sure you go in with your eyes open.

show me the money

Killer hours at times, but the financial rewards are there for the taking. Newly qualified solicitors at Freshfields are reaping the rewards of a latterly buoyant market and now take home £50K a year. We expected to hear of a champagne and bunting response to the latest rises in salary. But some trainees were reflective. One source expressed concern that higher salaries for trainees and NQs would lead to the further erosion of their social lives. *"There is a feeling that if we are expected to push ourselves harder then the extra money may not be worth it. I would rather earn a bit less and be able to have a bit more of a life outside of work."* Don't be surprised at this; it's a commonly held idea amongst junior lawyers once they reach three or four years PQE.

Most of the trainees we spoke to were absolutely delighted with their new found wealth and saw remuneration as quite separate from the number of hours they end up working. *"If you work for Freshfields then you accept that if the deal needs to be done then you do it. That commitment is there regardless of the money."* And more bluntly *"If someone were to tell me that I needed to pull my socks up and put more hours in, I would be interested to learn where in the day the hours would come from. We are already right on the button and the partners know it!"*

brief flings

There is a fair deal of flexibility in terms of seat rotation. You can normally choose to move on after three months* if a seat isn't your cup of tea. *"Some people use the three-month rotations to get a wider perspective of practice areas before qualification, but the real advantage is that you can escape a department which is not going well for you." Your first seat you will normally be a compulsory six months in corporate or finance and the pressure is heaped on from the first day you reach your desk. "It can be a baptism of fire, but that is where they need the bodies."

> "I ran a deal myself... pretty small... only about six million."

Bear in mind you are going to spend at least nine months in corporate and finance seats; there is no avoiding the hard core commitment the firm has to these areas of work. Big-ticket deals for international blue chips are the fuel on which Freshfields runs. Non-corporate and finance seats are seen to offer an easier ride. When choosing optional seats, the cool kids prefer employment, pensions and benefits (EPB), IP and tax. If you fancy having a go in these areas, you'll meet with stiff competition and there's only room to indulge a few trainees at a time.

erfolg!

Following mergers with two German firms (hence the Bruckhaus Deringer bit of the name) and success on the ground in… well, pretty much everywhere in the world… Freshfields enjoys a massive reputation internationally. On a global scale, when it comes to quality it is unsurpassable. The resulting opportunities for travel are considerable. At trainee level this extends to an impressive list of overseas seats. Hong Kong remains the most popular choice and there are perennial hot spots in Paris, Madrid and New York.

We'd never be able to list all the locations here, so just assume that your desired location is on offer. Whether or not you get there is another question though. "*As a general rule, if you want to do an overseas secondment then you will be able to go, providing you aren't too picky about where exactly you end up. The firm certainly won't guarantee you six months in Hong Kong or Paris.*" Language skills, your experiences in earlier seats and your performance so far will all determine your prospects of reaching your desired destination. Secondments are also available to clients such as IBM, Marconi and Morgan Stanley.

six million dollar man

After a few weeks of induction courses, you can expect to be right in the thick of things. It's not uncommon to be plunged straight into the middle of a major deal as soon as you start. Generally the level of paralegal and admin support is excellent. "*There is really good paralegal support… quite often on deals we are able to delegate proofreading to paralegals and then just check it afterwards. The buck still stops with us, but it allows trainees to focus on more interesting stuff.*" Despite this, you should expect to undertake some of the dross yourself from time to time. "*You can find yourself stuck doing pretty low quality work. It can be frustrating, but you are at the bottom of the food chain in the team and just have to get on with it.*"

Trainees are left to run their own 'small' files from time to time and this kind of responsibility was picked out as a high point for many interviewees. "*I pretty much ran a deal myself,*" one trainee told us. "*It was very small… only about six million.*" Oh, is that all? How dull… With a smaller trainee population than nearest rival Linklaters, this work, whilst still thin on the ground, tends to come round a bit more often.

outta here

Freshfields does not have a booming social life, largely because the demand doesn't seem to be there. Beyond the normal range of sports, Freshfields funds the occasional social event for trainees. "*If we do decide to get together, the firm is generally happy to sponsor a dinner or a night out.*" The hours do change your perspective a bit and not all our sources were sure they wanted to socialise with colleagues given that they saw so much of them at work. "*We don't go out together a lot. We might meet up for a quick drink on a Friday before we go our separate ways. You need to spend the time off with your friends from outside work.*"

In any event, the bars on the firm's doorstep are not that flash – the Cheshire Cheese, the Old Bank of England; they're hardly the trendiest hangouts. The office sits on Fleet Street in the vicinity of the Royal Courts of Justice, rather than in the heart of the Square Mile.

and finally…

So is Freshfields really that different from the other magic circle firms? Trainees were generally cynical about there being any real differences in lifestyle or culture between any of the magic circle firms. The corporate (as opposed to finance) emphasis of the work will have an influence, as will the emphasis on international expansion. Beyond that you'll have to test the waters for yourself… only you will know whether you gel with the Freshfields folk you meet at a law fair or interview day.

Garretts (Andersen Legal)

the facts
Location: London, Reading, Birmingham, Manchester, Cambridge
UK ranking by size: 22
Total number of trainees: 52
Seats: 4x6 months
Alternative Seats: Overseas seats

Garretts is the legal arm of Arthur Andersen. It seeks to provide a full range of commercial legal services to an international client base, but admittedly a large part of its business comes from Arthur Andersen. The firm has 'enjoyed' a series of friendly jousts with the Law Society in recent years. In a perfect world they would like to merge the law firm operation with the accountancy and consultancy businesses, but this presently represents a clear breach of Law Society regulations. The restrictions look unlikely to be relaxed until 2003, when, finally, increased crossover between Andersens and Garretts will be allowed. Other jurisdictions allow multidisciplinary practices (MDPs) and it seems unlikely that the Law Society will be able to hold out forever.

new religion

The trainees we spoke to emphasised the Andersen link as being a key factor in their decision to join the firm. "*I wanted to join a big international organisation that was not just all about law… you get a much better grounding in business here.*" Trainees emphasised the importance of the MDP principle and were eager to be fully integrated into an organisation that provides clients with expertise in tax, management, financial and accounting services and law.

They believe the approach will enable them to learn to view things from the clients' perspective. "*We work so closely with Andersens that we do get a better sense of commercial awareness and a greater understanding of what clients really want.*" Other trainees said they had already made contacts within Andersens, which they could use whenever they had a question about tax or accountancy. To get on at Garretts you have to buy into the Andersens way of doing things. As one trainee put it, "*you need to believe in the Andersen project more than you need to buy into the soul of a law firm.*"

running out of leeds

If you have done your research on Garretts, you'll have seen that, up North, last year was a tough one for the firm. The Leeds office, having been bombarded with questions over profitability and rocked by a stream of high level defections, was taken over by rival law firm DLA in November 2000. What effect did this have on trainees and newly qualifieds in other Garretts offices? "*We were all a bit concerned at the time, but it is much better now. Certainly nobody is expecting this office* [Manchester] *to close.*" We were assured that Leeds was just 'one of those things'; the firm couldn't tap into the tough market in Yorkshire and Garretts wanted to focus elsewhere.

london weighting

With Leeds now gone, Garretts is spread out across Birmingham, London, Manchester, Cambridge and Reading. Trainees are taken on at all offices. Having interviewed in all branches, we found, as last year, a perception that the London trainees do better than their colleagues outside the capital. *"There is definitely a feeling that the London office is the first among equals. I never wanted to work in London anyway though, so I suppose it is the price I pay."* Much to the chagrin of provincial trainees, overseas secondments are only available to trainees in the London office. We couldn't work out if this preferential treatment derives from the fact that London trainees are based at Andersen's global HQ on the Strand, or because, according to one London trainee, *"London is slightly harder to get into."*

prov plus

For applicants who are unsure about where to apply, the best advice is to think hard about where you want to train and why. The quality of work is broadly the same at all offices, but you may need to accept that the price of working outside of London is a feeling of being left a little out of the loop at times. On a more positive note, the provincial offices integrate trainees more closely with AA staff from day one. In London the lawyers are separated from Andersens staff with their own two floors at the top of the Strand HQ. In the provincial offices the layout is open plan and you are constantly exposed to the full complement of Andersens' business advisers. You will be surrounded by and working with them on a daily basis.

In all offices trainees do four seats of six months, one of which must be corporate and one of which must be contentious. Predictably, the corporate seat involves longer hours, but trainees were on the whole very positive about the department. *"Corpo-rate is where we are really driving at the moment. There is a real buzz about the place and it's exciting being there."* When choosing their optional seats, trainees indicated a pretty clear preference for tax and IT/IP and told us that in property they had the chance to run their own small files. Lawyers at Garretts work pretty regular hours, so it should be safe to make plans for dinner more than two days in advance. In London *"Trainees get in at around 9:30am and then leave at 6.15pm. All-night sessions don't tend to happen here."*

i was just passing

The Andersens connection has positive effect on Garretts social life. Whilst there are comparatively few trainees, there are plenty of like-minded Andersens employees floating around. *"I know quite a few Andersens people from university"* one trainee told us, *"and you develop contacts and hit it off with people you meet when you get here… it means we are not just socialising with other lawyers at after work drinks."* Astute trainees will double the number of work related freebies, gatecrashing AA events as well as their own. The Andersens youngsters reciprocate. But hey! This is what it's all about, right? The only fly in the ointment is that it can be daunting to have your clients strutting around the office, having dropped by to see an Andersens advisor. *"It can be a bit disconcerting. You don't always want clients popping up in front of your desk without warning!"*

and finally…

Once they've bought into the concept of MDP and invested two years of their lives with the firm, newly qualifieds are reluctant to leave Garretts. Out of the 22 trainees coming up to qualification in 2002, 21 were offered jobs and 20 accepted. Garretts trainees are really upbeat about the AA link and have high hopes for the future of the MDP. There seemed to be a real perception that the defections and the closing of the Leeds office have been left behind now. Garretts are certainly improving their profitability all the time, yet hours remain reasonable even in the London office. One newly qualified summed up the reason why he trained at Garretts by telling us *"I am doing work of the same quality as friends of mine who are newly qualified in the magic circle, earning nearly the same money but not working the silly hours."*

Gouldens

the facts
Location: London
UK ranking by size: 82
Total number of trainees: 30
Seats: Non-rotational
Alternative seats: None
Extras: Pro bono: Waterloo Legal Advice Centre

The hallmark of the training at this impressive mid-sized firm is that there is no rotation between different practice areas. You get your own office from day one and receive good quality work simultaneously from the three core departments; corporate, property and litigation. If one of the specialist areas, such as employment or IP, takes your fancy then it's up to you to speak up and show your interest.

tailor-made
In theory, trainees tailor-make their training contract to fit their own requirements. So, subject to Law Society stipulations, if you realise that, say, litigation really doesn't turn you on then you need not do any more of it than is absolutely necessary. Conversely, if a particular area interests you, then this can become the focus of your work.

It's easy to see the benefits of not having to spend six months in a department in which you have little interest. One trainee we spoke to could not over emphasise the value of this. He mentioned a friend at another firm whose experience in a seat he detested *"was enough to put him off the law for good."* However, is there is a danger of specialising too early on? Could the result be a less well-rounded training? Do Gouldens' trainees have sufficient experience to know what's good for them and to exercise the control over their training appropriately? We set out to find the answers to these questions.

being watched
It seems that trainees aren't left to fend for themselves and someone will always be there to monitor progress, ensuring they cover a wide enough range of work and no gaping holes appear in their knowledge base. A mentor will check up on each week's activities and there are further, more detailed and strategic reviews periodically throughout the two years. Another issue to think about is the scenario in which a trainee takes on work which turns out to be a complete chore or involves working with a partner with whom they don't gel. There's an obligation to see it through to a conclusion; they can't just escape after six months as one might in a rotational system.

One trainee told our researcher that training at Gouldens was *"like learning to swim."* It figures. You can't learn to swim unless you jump in and practise your strokes. Watching from the side of the pool doesn't work, nor does stacking and re-stacking the polystyrene floats. Trainees must learn to swim very early on. *"I did feel as though I was thrown in at the deep end"* said one, adding that on his third day at the firm he had to introduce himself by just walking into people's offices. Sounds like the mentors watch closely from the side of the pool like lifeguards, rather than holding trainees hands.

self starters
It's hard to say whether it's a product of the training or whether these are prerequisite skills for aspiring Gouldens' lawyers, but the trainees we speak to each year display levels of confidence and self-belief rarely seen outside the magic circle.

Trainees must be clear about what they want and have a *"go-getting"* attitude. The type of person who needs to be shown over and over again how to do something would *"sink pretty quickly"* here. If you want to know what type of applicant is attractive to the firm, look at the web profiles of current trainees. High achievers all.

Trainees told us that the *"massive learning curve"* was initially uncomfortable but the end result was a *"seamless transition"* into a qualified solicitor. Indeed the benefits of the non-rotational system perhaps become more apparent in the months leading up to qualification. Towards the end of the training contract the department in which you are to qualify into is where most of your work will come from.

just say no

The ability to prioritise is imperative; you have to juggle several types of work at once. *"It can be difficult to balance competing demands as work comes from the different departments simultaneously."* Sometimes the different departments don't liase with each other when allocating work and so *"trainees can start to drown."* You need to know how and when to say no. You need to *"be confident enough to make your views known to senior partners."*

The flip side of this is that increased exposure to work that interests you brings with it greater responsibility and a lot of satisfaction. A young Gouldens trainee will often face a more senior lawyer on the other side of a deal and they take pride in their progress. One told us how good it felt *"finding out that you can cope and stretch yourself."* Trainees here are seen, and see themselves, as fee earners from day one.

that'll do nicely

Gouldens' trainees are certainly not strapped for cash. But be under no illusion; market-leading salaries mean lawyers here work hard, but probably no harder than those at any top-tier City practice. Continuing the tradition of high retention rates on qualification, 13 of the 15 qualifiers stayed in September 2001.

One recurring comment is that there is *"a very loose hierarchy."* On Friday evenings plenty of the partners wind down with their employees at Seamus O'Donnells (affectionately known as 'The Smokey Irish'), which is handily located a short step across the road from the office. The 'Gouldens card' is accepted at a few of the local bars and, every now and then, enthusiastic trainees can be found making use of the firm's excellent credit rating. And what a credit rating! Although it's only ranked 82nd by size in the UK, Gouldens turnover is around about the 40th largest. Average profits per partner compare well with the magic circle and beat many of the top ten firms. No wonder they can afford those high salaries.

and finally...

You've got to be prepared to have a bash at things and be able to cope without molly-coddling. It is quite apparent that Gouldens' trainees have more self-confidence than many of their counterparts at other firms. They do need it to cope with the often-competing demands from partners and the impressive levels of responsibility that they take on.

Halliwell Landau

the facts

Location: Manchester, London
UK ranking by size: 49
Total number of trainees: 19
Seats: 4x6 months
Alternative seats: Secondments

It's been another successful year for Mancunians Halliwell Landau. Fee income increased by 20% in 2000/2001 and the firm now boasts a turnover of more than £26 million. If you want an idea of the drive behind this firm, just look at its nitro-fuelled growth – five years ago turnover was just £6.3m. Often described as confident and ambitious, Halliwells has a reputation amongst lawyers in the region for being aggressive and ruthless. Fiercely independent, Halliwells has spurned the lecherous advances of City firms eyeing up its Manchester base and it has recently opened its own small London office. There's no question of Halliwells being taken over, but a merger with a like-minded London firm is not out of the question.

independents' day
Following this rapid growth, the firm recently appointed a new senior partner, Alec Craig, to help propel the team further forward. What is it about Manchester and managers called Alec? Star spotters take note, three of Manchester's biggest celebrities now live just round the corner from one another as Alec has moved just down the road from Beckingham Palace. Expect to see Posh, Becks, Brooklyn and Alec jogging together in the near future.

> "There's no chance of just blending into the background for two years."

Independence is an important part of Halliwell's identity. This is not the Manchester branch of a national firm; the new London office is likely to remain a small outpost. Halliwells is not interested in following the example of firms like DLA and Addleshaws and changing focus from a regional firm with a London office to a City firm with regional offices. Like the music scene in 1989 – Manchester is where it's at.

Everyone is expected to play a part in driving the firm forwards. *"As an independent firm competing with the big boy's regional offices, we really have to push ourselves."* One thing our sources were keen to impress on us was that Halliwells do not only handle regional work. *"We are the largest* [independent] *firm in the region and of course local work is crucial, but we have big national clients and we are going to continue pushing for more and better work."* Do trainees recognise the aggressive approach that some outside the firm speak of? *"The firm has grown exponentially, so it has a very ambitious feel,"* one trainee said, *"but I have never seen the aggressive side which outsiders perceive it to have."*

gonna get myself connected
As with all regional firms, Halliwells looks favourably on applicants with a connection to the area. Predictably, a significant proportion (about 60% according to one source) of trainees hail from the North West or studied there. We assume this makes for an awful lot of Man Utd supporters on the staff. A number of the current trainees have had additional experience beyond academia or pursued first careers before deciding to delve into the law. All six September 2001 qualifiers stayed with the firm.

Trainees undertake four six-month seats and there's a set menu of one seat in each of commercial litigation, corporate and property. The fourth seat is picked off the *à la carte* menu and the firm tries hard to deliver the chosen seat. Employment and IP were the most popular this year. Unfortunately, with only one place available at a time in each of those departments, you may have to use your elbows a bit to secure the seat. *"Normally, you will specify your top three choices in order of preference. It tends to work out that second year trainees get priority over first years."*

work those contacts
Halliwell Landau gets top marks for the level of client exposure trainees experience. *"We are always introduced to clients and this extends to marketing initiatives as well. The firm wants all of its fee earners to always be on duty and ready to sell the firm to any potential new clients."* Our sources did feel that this could be daunting, especially when required of you from the very outset, but it certainly makes the training experience a very real and valuable two years. We'd put money on this firm's NQs being able to handle themselves without any difficulty at all.

The firm has an impressive reputation in banking and acts for a number of the retail banks, including Bank of Scotland, RBS, Co-operative Bank, Lloyds TSB, Anglo Irish Bank and Barclays. In corporate work it recently had a fine old time acquiring the Pontins holiday business and its IP lawyers advised Umbro on its sponsorship of Chelsea Football Club.

going for it

Perhaps because of the firm's ambitious outlook, hours are longer than you might normally expect for a regional practice. *"Typical hours here are about 9am-6.30pm in property and litigation and longer in corporate, say 8.30am-7.30pm. It is rare for trainees to work very late, but when it happens it is really appreciated by supervisors."* Getting your nose down and cracking on with the work is important at Halliwell Landau. *"There is a hard work culture here. Isn't it the same at every firm?"* Well… it's rare to find a commercial law firm with a slack approach to work! Some trainees felt there was a culture of needing to be seen to work hard, even when there isn't that much to get on with. *"You couldn't really sail out of the office at 4pm claiming that you had nothing on. I don't think that would go down very well."* This firm didn't get where it is today by…

But it isn't all work, work, work. Halliwells is a sociable firm. Trainees regularly troop off to one of the local bars for post-work drinks and the social committee organises monthly events to jolly everyone along. Particular praise is due to the social committee for its performance in organising trainee functions, but there's scant effort and zero imagination in the selection of the midweek drinking venue. *"We normally just go round the corner to the All Bar One."* We learned that at the cricket and rounders matches *"all the boys start taking it far too seriously."*

and finally…

The working environment can be quite pressurised and supervisors expect trainees to be a productive part of the team. This is a firm with a reputation for being a gutsy, 'go get 'em' swashbuckling outfit and would probably best suit someone with a real determination to succeed as a lawyer. It sounds like an environment where half-heartedness won't get you very far at all and there's no chance of just blending into the background for two years. If the expansion continues, you will have a good chance of quick promotion within the firm. Perhaps you should ask yourself first whether you are as ambitious about your career as Halliwells is about its practice.

Hammond Suddards Edge

the facts

Location: Birmingham, Leeds, London, Manchester
UK ranking by size: 8
Total number of trainees: 100
Seats: 6x4 months
Alternative Seats: Overseas seats
Extras: Language training

Just imagine it… trainees at Edge Ellison, a reputable Birmingham law firm, woke up one day last year to find they were trainees at Hammond Suddards… Edge. The joining of Edges with northerners Hammond Suddards was billed as a merger, but viewed by many as a shotgun wedding for the under-performing Midlands firm. The resulting training experience is one of the most distinctive of the 'big regionals'.

living together

The relaxed Edge has been taken up a gear by the bullish northern firm. You have to pity the Edge trainees who have been jumped into an entirely different training scheme. Even though, as one source put it, *"all the bluster and aggression you put out is not going to make you a better firm,"* the Hammonds approach was probably needed by Edge. Fortunately, *"the strain of the merger has gone. It is going forward now."* Several senior lawyers were lost after the merger but, for the trainees we spoke to, it is no longer an issue.

HSE requires its trainees to take up seats in at least three different offices around the country. The firm makes no secret of this and warns potential applicants from the outset. Still reading? Well, there are benefits. The firm provides trainees with gorgeous subsidised accommodation in city centre locations. It might be a long time before you can afford a flat of the same quality again. The Barbican in London and Manchester's Salford Quays are probably way beyond the means of contemporaries at other firms. But are desirable flats enough to make up for the disturbance of moving around? Some trainees love it. For them it is an opportunity. *"You go out a lot more with people from work." "Trainees become a lot closer because you live together." "Moving makes you feel part of the firm."*

breaking up

Not all were enthusiastic. *"It is frightening the number of relationships that have broken up because of moving around."* Trainees are effectively *"living at the firm for four months at a time."* Getting the seat in the location you want can be a *"total lottery." "You are so insecure about where you will move to. You're living in a strange city with someone you didn't choose."* No wonder some trainees will apparently *"sit around and moan how they don't want to be there."* Moving is difficult if you already have a mortgage. However, the firm will not increase the salary for those not taking subsidised accommodation. As a policy it seems more geared to recent graduates, despite the fact that the firm is happy to take trainees with previous careers.

iron fist

It is easy to see what the firm gains by its insistence on this tour of Britain. Moving offices creates greater synergy and ensures trainees make contacts in each office. It encourages the *"same standard of service from different offices. They are keen to prevent competition between offices and the firm becoming a franchise operation."* Certainly trainees *"don't build any huge loyalty to any particular office."* The approach applies at all levels, and assistants and partners are also known to move around. It would seem to work. *"You do feel part of the whole firm." "It is a national firm, but you happen to be in one office,"* was a sentiment expressed by many.

The HSE training is further distinguished by its organisation around six seats of four months. *"If you don't know what you want to do, it's great,"* but *"you can get more settled in six months."* Breadth rather than depth is the Hammonds way. *"You have to prove yourself in a shorter time to get the responsibility."* If you do like a particular seat, you can choose to repeat it. But ultimately, *"graduate recruitment has an iron fist."*

wrong purple sweetie

Seats begin with an informal appraisal and conclude with a formal review. But this is a *"robust firm – not touchy-feely,"* (unlike the old Edge Ellison). If you are doing something wrong you will find out. The firm seems keen to remain *"rough and ready northern." "You know exactly where you stand, which is great, as long as you have a thick skin."* One trainee cited the lack of pretension as the best thing about the firm, although this didn't stop it taking *"a month choosing the right shade of company purple."* Partners are down to earth and *"you will not be too scared to ask anyone a question."* However one source felt the firm lacks *"a person responsible for trainees in each office."* Furthermore *"there are still inconsistencies among the supervisors"* in their approach to training.

Reports on the quality of training were generally positive. *"Responsibility is appropriate. I have some of my own files and the supervising partner will check now and again."* They *"tend to treat you like just another fee earner." "You assist on some very interesting stuff,"* although *"when a big deal comes along, there is exciting work being done by someone, but it's not the trainees. At these times, they will get the horsework, like photocopying."*

r-e-s-p-e-c-t

There is *"mutual respect between offices. The quality of work and lawyers is on a par."* One of the main effects of the merger was a bolstered City presence. There are no "bad departments" and "IP is glamorous." The Enterprise and Technology Unit has caught the eye of many trainees – "commercial but with a technology/enterprise twist." One trainee told us "there are some high profile media jobs in London," though we're still not sure if he was remarking on the firm or the capital in general.

> "Trainees become a lot closer because they live together."

Overseas seats have now become available in Paris, Brussels, Munich and Turin. Winning them means further applications and interviews, and speaking the language helps. There's only one seat available in each office, so don't apply here because you never got round to going inter-railing in your gap year, and would like to catch up now!

philosophy

"If you're very ambitious and money driven, you will fit in with the firm's philosophy." You should expect a "commercial firm and the pressures that go with it." With the usual exceptions (yes, corporate), trainee hours are reasonable and "not too stretching." As for social life, "great, and lots of it." The "very young partners" are known to put their card behind the bar and, if you click with your flatmates in the HSE flats, you can expect to be hitting the town rather often. "There's always something going on, whether it's football tournaments or internal quizzes." (The latter, presumably, a hangover from the old Edge Ellison group 'mind-mapping' exercises.) The bottom line is that on qualification retention rates are high. Of 41 qualifiers in 2001, 38 were offered jobs and only one of those chose to go elsewhere.

After all the speculation, we think we know the real reason behind Hammonds' desire to merge with Edge. (No, it wasn't just the potential for naming the new entity 'Ham 'n' Egg'.) The Edge Ellison offices were situated opposite a major Birmingham hotel, popular with celebrities and celebrity-spotters. "Yesterday we were all crowded at the window to see Ronan Keating." Those northern softies.

and finally...

A great firm if "you don't know what you want to do, or where you want to do it." This is a "young, dynamic firm." Demonstrating its tireless ambition, it recently swallowed up two niche practices – sports law firm Townleys and banking and insolvency specialists Wilde & Partners. It wants to "expand," "play with the big boys," "get into Europe," and have its own particular shade of Hammonds purple. It has the drive and energy to achieve all this.

Harbottle & Lewis

the facts
Location: London
UK ranking by size: 109
Total number of trainees: 7
Seats: 4x6 months
Alternative Seats: Secondments

Harbottle & Lewis has a particularly easy selection procedure. Just like Slaughter and May, it is limited to a CV, a letter and a casual chat with the partners. "The interviews were unlike other firms. It wasn't the usual grilling," one trainee told us. But training at this well known media and entertainment firm will not be like two years of S&M.

popstars

Harbottle & Lewis was set up by theatre supremo Lawrence Harbottle about 40 years ago. His name became synonymous with legal needs of the UK entertainment industry. So presumably it's one long round of fashionable parties, film premieres and backstage passes? Mmm, nice image, but no. "*It is not that glamorous on the inside,*" a source said.

Admittedly you are more likely to encounter a celebrity in this firm's offices than at your average London law firm. Harbottles has individual and corporate clients from all aspects of media and entertainment. Film, television, publishing, music, theatre, sport, new media, IP – it's all there. You'll recognise all the names too: Robbie Williams, Hear'Say, Kate Moss, Comic Relief, the Ginger Media Group, the Arts Council and all manner of broadcast and digital media organizations. Unsurprisingly, "*there's a real buzz about the place.*" No kidding.

breezing through

But let's get things in perspective. "*In reality, you have not got celebrities wandering around the office all the time.*" "*Breezing through reception, you might look over occasionally to see a famous face,*" but "*we are not here to party with famous people.*" Put it this way, "*there are five floors and only one is devoted to entertainment. The rest of it is normal commercial work – entertainment clients do have boring stuff too.*" The firm undertakes corporate, property and litigation work for regular clients and not just those in media and entertainment. When applying for a training contract, it is worth considering Harbottle & Lewis as a normal commercial firm first and foremost.

"*Company and commercial is the largest group in the firm,*" one trainee confirmed, "*so you do get a general commercial training.*" Virgin Atlantic and various other companies in Richard Branson's empire are important clients. However, as several trainees admitted, "*our clients have intrigue, and people do apply here for that element.*" Tellingly, "*everyone wants to do the entertainment seats,*" and one trainee confessed that their reason for applying to the firm was because they "*wanted to work in the music industry and thought I may as well try it as a lawyer.*"

the laying on of hands

"*The training contract is hands on from day one,*" our sources emphasised. "*You do get thrown in at the deep end, but in a good way. They would never let you struggle,*" but "*there is a lot of responsibility.*" Another said, "*I inherited about 50 files in property, but when I needed the support it was there.*" Trainees understand that working in a firm of this size (just 18 partners are assisted by 73 other fee earners) means that they are stretched from early on. "*They do rely on you*" and "*you definitely get to work on a range of stuff.*" Such is the variety of work, you could easily be advising on aircraft acquisition one month and pop merchandising rights the next.

> "Breezing through reception, you might look over occasionally to see a famous face."

Compulsory seats in litigation, property and company/commercial generally leave just one six-month slot left for an optional seat. "*They actually tell you what seats you are going to do, then ask you what you want to do. But they will try and accommodate your wishes.*" As in every firm, the specialist IP group "*attracts a lot of people.*" The firm has kept pace with the internet revolution and has a number of dot.com clients. For those in the know, the IP group won the 'Trademark Team of the Year' at the 2000 awards of the industry journal '*Managing Intellectual Property*'.

frequent fliers

Our sources thanked their lucky stars that they hadn't ended up training in a City firm. "*I said at interview that I would rather earn less and have a life than earn mega-bucks.*" It must have worked. "*Hours are nowhere near as bad as the City,*" one trainee said, and "*there is no mentality of lurking around looking for work to do.*" "*You work hard during the day because you know that you want to be away in the evening.*"

Officially, appraisals take place every month. In reality, they occur every two months. But opinion was divided as to whether appraisals were "*too relaxed*" or "*taken seriously.*" The two client secondments available to trainees are unanimously popular. One is six months spent entirely in-house with a commercial client. The other is for two days per week, also for a client of the firm's commercial department. In 2001, three of the four qualifying trainees were retained, going into corporate/commercial, film/tv and property. It's interesting to note that some of those that leave the firm upon qualification take up in-house legal positions. This is mirrored at the top end too, with partners also going in-house. One recently became the head of Sony's legal department.

west end boys and girls
If you're an incurable shopaholic or a die-hard movie-buff, you'll be delighted with Harbottle & Lewis' location in the heart of the West End. The building is "*big and old, with the entrance on Hanover Square and one side on Oxford Street.*" Trainees spoke of a welcoming atmosphere; "*almost without exception, I get on with everyone here, including the support staff. It is a very, very friendly place to work.*"

We weren't overwhelmed by reports of non-stop socialising, although on the last Friday of the month "*the whole firm meets for drinks.*" And sometimes the lawyers outdo even the most eccentric of their clients – "*There are some very mad people here – big characters.*" Harbottles has mustered up cricket and football teams and there are "*rumours of a netball team.*"

and finally…
Apply for "*a great working environment*," but don't expect to be hanging out with celebs the whole time. "*We are too busy to think about the famous people. Nobody gets carried away with it.*" Obviously the firm's entertainment industry connections mean that it attracts plenty of starstruck applicants. As one experienced entertainment lawyer once said to us, make sure you really want to be the lawyer and not the client.

Herbert Smith

the facts
Location: London
UK ranking by size: 7
Total number of trainees: 171
Seats: 4x6 months
Alternative seats: Overseas seats, secondments
Extras: Pro bono: Privy Council death row appeals, language training

Herbert Smith is one of those household name law firms. If you didn't know which firms made up the magic circle, you would be forgiven for assuming that Herbert Smith was one of them. It is a part of the Gang of Eight firms that prompted the creation of the City LPC and competes with the leaders in practically all areas of its work. The firm has a long held reputation as **the** litigation firm, a reputation that is more than justly deserved, but to ignore the firm because you have no desire to be a litigator would be madness.

a balanced diet
One thing you can't say about Herbert Smith is that your training will be slanted towards any particular area of the firm's business. We examined the claim that at Herbert Smith you'll get the broadest possible commercial training and it seems to ring true. As for compulsory seats, "*you have to do a litigation seat and general corporate. You don't have to do property unless you want to.*" Or unless it is chosen for you as a first seat.

What commonly happens is second seaters get to choose from the seats left vacant by second years and first seaters get the leftover leftovers. Second years prefer specialist areas of work such as IP, employment, EU, tax and corporate recovery. They also tend to gobble up the client secondments and overseas seats. Certain corporate groups have become regarded in the same light as the last turkeys in the shop on Christmas Eve, and these are often left for first seaters. Some trainees thought it wasn't such a bad thing to get the corporate stint out of the way first though. At least it then leaves you with three bites at the juiciest seats later.

true or false

So what's the problem with corporate? Is the firm attracting too many budding litigators? Is there some deep dark secret locked away in the growing corporate practice? It's a bit of both, according to our sources, who provided unusually consistent and strong opinions on this topic.

True or false time: All trainees apply to the firm because they want to become litigators. Well that one's false(ish). Plenty do, and with the firm's stellar reputation why wouldn't they? *"I was interested in litigation and drawn to Herbert Smith by it."* But trainees also want to experience a range of commercial work; they just realise that their best chance of getting oodles of world class contentious experience is at Herbert Smith. We never once heard a trainee say that they joined because they wanted to be a corporate or finance lawyer.

As to the statement that trainees feel intimidated by the corporate groups. Oh dear – true(ish). In every firm there's a sense that a corporate seat will be a full on experience. At Herbert Smith it was rather depressing to hear that the experience can be an unpleasant one. Bottom line: *"Some of the supervisors are not friendly or nice."* *"In certain groups there are difficult characters. Others are deemed more friendly. It's just easier to work hard with nicer people. Because of the reputation, most trainees would never apply to certain groups."*

the big trip: part I

We discussed with our sources the extent to which we ought to write about the difficult nature or *"big egos"* of some supervisors. They thought we should raise the issue, but wanted us to stress that the vast majority of supervising solicitors and partners were fab. *"Some of the people here are not great supervisors. Some of them are working towards partnership so they have no time and don't want to supervise. It's a problem that the firm*

could do something about." Trainees want *"someone who actually cares about what you are doing. Someone you admire and want to be like. If you're trained by somebody you don't want to be like, you don't have the incentive to try and impress or follow them. The good supervisor will display a real interest in your ability and how well your work is matching it."* Those good supervisors certainly do exist and the trainees love 'em. One source illustrated this by saying, *"in my second seat most of the trainees in the department came to see my supervisor."* That's the difficult stuff said. Let's move on.

the big trip: part II

In recent times Herbert Smith has invested pots and pots in overseas offices, reflecting its desire and ability to keep pace with the globalisation of legal services. Admittedly there are more overseas opportunities on offer at some competitors, but Herbert Smith trainees tend to apply to the firm for reasons other than a six-month stint in the sun. It's a definite plus though. For one trainee it was important that the firm *"had anchor points outside of the UK,"* for another the overseas offices added *"kudos,"* but the chance to go abroad is not the be all and end all. There are exotic locations like Hong Kong, Tokyo and Singapore on offer as well as a number closer to home in Europe. And how do you secure one? The same way that you gun for a popular specialist seat; *"a bit of lobbying, but not too much. A well drafted memo setting out your reasons is better than pestering."* Client secondments on offer include: BAA, BskyB, Cable & Wireless, Coca-Cola, IBM and Warner Brothers.

essay crisis

What of the hours? Litigators tend to have *"an earlier start but an earlier finish. Corporate starts later in the day but often works later. There's a bit of an 'essay crisis' mentality going on there. You see the corporate lawyers as the same type of people at university who had essay crises. That category still exists in the workplace!"* To be fair though, it is in the nature of corporate work that hours will *"vary wildly"* from one month to the next, depending on the flow of deals. One trainee said, *"I worked hard for three weeks solid until midnight every night and then had four months of leaving at about 6pm."* Commonly, trainees talked of having left the office by 7pm.

There was a bit of a moan about the fact that a certain amount of the trainees' work was *"mundane and dull."* Examples being *"a lot of bill narratives – really dull when you have not worked on the case"* and *"putting bundles together and paginating."* Trainees certainly gave us plenty of examples of work they were really pleased to do, including handling small applications in court themselves. But as with all of the mega firms, deals and cases are extremely valuable and of the size that involves a number of lawyers of varying levels of experience. Guess where the trainee is in the food chain. Actually, on some matters you won't be at the bottom of the food chain as there will be a paralegal. A few trainees indicated that one or two more paras would improve their lot. Want, want, want.

trolleyed

Strange but true... drinks trolleys are a regular feature of life at Herbert Smith. Many groups (but not all) have an in-the-office wind down session from time to time over a few drinks. We giggled as we envisaged a be-suited partner trundling a squeaky-wheeled trolley down the corridor, pouring sherry for his colleagues. *"Actually one corporate group has champagne on theirs,"* we were told. Another trainee, aware of the different trolley habits of the different departments he'd been in, preferred the idea of some groups – *"giving you a bar tab."*

Everyone we spoke to had participated in the healthy trainee social scene. Thursday and Friday nights see trainees gathering in Futures (below the office) or one of the trendier bars, such as The Pool Bar or The Light. With a *"generous budget"* for entertaining, the vacation scheme season is *"nine weeks of partying."*

with friends like these

Friendships are made easily at Herbert Smith. Maybe it's the bizarre initiation ritual they all go through in week one. Under the pretext of it being a treasure hunt, packs of trainees are sent around the building and into the City wearing Herbert Smith Baseball caps and clutching a Polaroid camera. *"It helps us get to know each other and bond."*

No one can accuse the firm of élitism in its recruitment. Calls to randomly selected trainees (or their voicemails) reveal accents of all types. There's a natural desire to recruit plenty of Oxbridge grads and trainees told us that the vac schemes seem full of them, but there's not the overwhelming Oxbridge dominance that one would find at Freshfields or Linklaters.

It used to be said that Herbert Smith lawyers were aggressive sharks, but the trainees and NQs we spoke to were all sweethearts. Do you have to be tough to survive? *"You do have to be fairly confident and you have to be quite assertive,"* one trainee told us, whilst another thought that some trainees were a touch over-confident. *"In certain seats if you are not super-confident and cocky you'll be shot down, in others you'll be shot down if you are!"* Clear as mud then.

dealing with the overflow

The majority of trainees stay with the firm on qualification. 2001 proved no exception. Of the 57 qualifiers, 54 were offered jobs and 50 accepted. But choosing your NQ job can be harder than finding a needle in a haystack with the lights out. The difficulty seems to be that the specialist and sexy departments and litigation groups are massively oversubscribed and everyone knows it. *"You can make two choices. But if you put a group down as second choice, they know that and may judge you as not being committed. So some people only make one choice. The firm wants you to stay and if you don't get your choice they will tell you what's available."* This year there was a fair division across the core departments, with 19 heading for corporate and finance and 14 choosing litigation.

Apparently a number of wannabe 'specialist' lawyers *"chicken out at the last minute"* and apply for a department or group that they feel sure is not oversubscribed. The main message is that there are plenty of litigation jobs on offer, but too many people want them. If you want to work as a corporate lawyer you can guarantee it. We presume that with the keener interest the firm has taken in its corporate groups in the last couple of years, it will also have borne this in mind when recruiting students.

and finally…

The best thing about this firm is definitely the pick 'n' mix counter near the canteen. It's representative of the breadth of training on offer really. You won't have to spend nine or 12 months in the corporate/finance departments with just three months of litigation as at some firms. Nor will you have to fight for more than a few months of non-contentious experience.

Herbert Smith is aspirational and it becomes ever more so, as evidenced by its international strategy. It has a need to compete at the highest level in areas of work previously overshadowed by its super-strength in litigation. But this has never been a firm where the boat gets rocked. Solid, successful, secure and plain old sensible it certainly is, but wild and wacky… er nope.

Hewitson Becke + Shaw

the facts

Location: Cambridge, Northampton
UK ranking by size: 85
Total number of trainees: 20
Seats: 4x6 months
Alternative Seats: None

With one foot in the shoe-making capital of England and the other in the heart of Silicon Fen, Hewitson Becke + Shaw has been a name in the eastern half of the country for years. But times they are a changing for HB+S. It has caught the updraft of hi- and biotech work in Silicon Fen and is vigorously pursuing its corporate and technology practices. It spent much of 2001 in (ultimately fruitless) merger talks with Oxford firm Linnels.

on the plus side

Profits rose by 35% in 2000/2001, no doubt in part a result of the burgeoning technology sector. The work for this type of client (many of them spin-outs from the University of Cambridge) is not limited to IP/IT advice. The corporate team handles venture capital work for early stage technology companies, M&A and MBOs. There's a substantial international element to the work, many clients coming from the US. One trainee talked of the impressive work he'd assisted on. *"Clients are national and international, and although they are not blue chip, I worked on a few MBOs, one worth £20 million, another £14million."* Obviously in corporate you won't get to lead a deal but one trainee confirmed he felt *"part of the team, even though my work did not make or break the deal!"*

subtract two

Rumours of the closure of the small branch office in Saffron Walden circulate. Its closure would be indicative of a firm in the process of change. One trainee thought, *"In the two years I've been here it's become more progressive and aware of changes in legal market. There's a noticeable demarcation between old school partners and newer recruits. Although there's slightly more home-grown partners, people have come from London."* The main body of the firm's work is in corporate and property, with substantial amounts of technology and private client work. We wondered how many firms of the size of HB+S had a separate bioscience team. The view in Cambridge is that *"it's an upwardly mobile firm and it is prospering and taking on more people all the time. It has definitely got a good future, although some work depends on whether there's a recession in the technology sector."* The loss in 2001 of two of the country's top IP partners seems a cruel blow, but we presume the offer they received from US firm Dorsey & Whitney was one they simply couldn't refuse.

But, especially in Northampton, it's still a touch traditional. A source said, *"The firm is not particularly unconventional and it's progressing only slowly."* Some supervisors are better than others at taking you to meetings, but overall there's ample opportunity for *"getting involved in good deals, drafting and talking to clients."* Private client work was not unanimously popular. *"It's both landed gentry and old grannies' wills – sometimes this sort of client doesn't like dealing with trainees' and partners can be quite protective."* In litigation seats you will find yourself going to court (*"mainly County Court stuff"*) and trainees talked of having their own files.

you're not from round here, are you?

We wondered if HB+S had a preponderance of Cambridge University graduates amongst its ranks of trainees. One source said *"there are a few trainees from both Oxford and Cambridge, but there's a mix from a fair range of good universities like Leeds, Cardiff and Durham."* What's apparent is that the firm is not just recruiting those with a regional connection. Indeed, one Northampton trainee said, *"we don't seem to have anyone from the region."* The firm, particularly in Cambridge, has recruits who have taken an alternative route to becoming a lawyer – the army and a chemistry PhD were both mentioned, and some trainees have worked as paralegals in one of the offices.

> "It has caught the updraft of hi- and biotech work in Silicon Fen."

The Northampton branch is divided into *"three buildings within 50 yards of each other."* The main office, housing over half the staff including the property and debt recovery departments, *"looks quite grand."* But the three-way split does hinder the interaction between departments to an extent and IT resources just about manage to keep pace. *"We only recently started doing time recording on PCs,"* one trainee confided.

Maybe it's a result of the distance from the graduate recruitment department in Northampton, but Cambridge trainees told us that the seat allocation system in their office was erratic. The firm has no particular preference as to which departments trainees visit, but commercial seats are generally more popular than private client ones (which are often used as a 'soft' introduction to the training contract). In an environment where *"some partners maybe still cling onto their own little empires,"* it seems that going to see department heads may secure a seat in a particular practice area. *"Stronger personalities get the seats they want."*

your starter for £100

The Cambridge office has its own events committee and when it has managed to drag people a bit further than the local pub, visits to the Newmarket races and West End theatres have followed. Closer to home, in The Bird in the Hand, *"the partners put £100 behind the bar every Friday night,"* and *"everyone from reception to equity partners are there bantering."* Not to be outdone, the Northampton office also has a £100 bar tab in its local, Yates'. *"We also get everyone in the pub,"* they said. Hangovers aside, a five-a-side football team plays against other young professionals at the weekends. The two offices take it in turns to host the firm's Christmas party and, traditionally, it falls on the staff of the host office to provide the entertainment. A particularly memorable sketch was entitled *"Who Wants to be the Managing Partner?"* We understand Chris Tarrant continues to sleep soundly…

leader of the pack

There's a hint of competition between the two offices. Trainees in the Cambridge office told us *"we are the leader of the two offices. Northampton is more private client work, whereas Cambridge is more commercially driven and brings in bigger name clients and fees."* Whether or not Cambridge does actually lead, the bottom line is that *"in truth, they can feel like separate firms."* Staying loyal, it is rare for trainees to move between the offices while still training. Seats are duplicated between the offices, so there is no need to travel in order to access certain departments. In a recent round of qualification, six of seven trainees took up NQ positions with the firm.

Typical hours for trainees are 9am-6pm and the latest we heard of was 11pm on a deal in corporate. Salaries are typical of medium-sized firms in the regions, though perhaps not enough to live the good life in the property hot-spot of Cambridge. *"The Cambridge property market is evil – you couldn't even contemplate buying a one bed flat as a trainee."*

light and dark blues

We found it very difficult to get trainees to talk about the proposed merger with Linnells, either because they'd been told to keep schtum, or they were as in the dark over matters as were. The most we got was *"people are waiting for it to happen."* It was a union clearly designed to pick up university spin-out work in the hi- and biotech sectors and to capitalise on the Linnells client relationship with Oxford University (HB+S acts for Cambridge Uni). The merger would have created the only firm to have offices in both cities. Exciting stuff, but HB+S needs to find a new Oxford mate.

and finally...

With its direct access to the exciting work of the Silicon Fen, it wouldn't be surprising if the Cambridge office was the envy of Northampton trainees. The firm has achieved more than most would have expected way back in 1989 when it crawled out of its chrysalis. But will the *"slow evolution"* of the firm, refocusing on certain key areas around the *"Cambridge phenomenon,"* continue to be slow in the light of recent slumps in the hi-tech sector? It's very much a case of watch this space.

Hill Dickinson

the facts

Location: Liverpool, Manchester, London, Chester
UK ranking by size: 53
Total number of trainees: 20
Seats: 4x6 months
Alternative Seats: Secondments

This deceptively large firm first set sail in 1810 as a specialist shipping practice. It now has four offices, but is ostensibly a Liverpool operation and 53 of the 77 partners are Mersey-based. The firm has built its name and reputation on more than shipping though. Insurance and litigation now amount to nearly half of its work.

no weighty dicks

An insurance giant would have been created had the much-publicised merger with local rival, Weightmans, proceeded. Here at the *Chambers Student Guide*, we were gutted to learn that talks had broken down – we'd been desperate to write a True Picture about the merged firm as we'd convinced ourselves it would have been called Weighty Dicks. But some things are just not meant to be. After the abortive merger talks, Hill Dickinson concentrated on surviving the upheavals and consolidation in the insurance market. It has earned a certain amount of kudos by retaining its place on the NHS Litigation Authority panel. In case you don't know, the NHSLA oversees the conduct of clinical negligence claims brought against the NHS.

The firm is instructed by an enormous number of insurance companies and, whether or not trainees express any enthusiasm for one, *"everyone does a defendant insurance seat, often personal injury... there is no escaping it. Everyone does at least one, maybe two."* Good news – the insurance work is far wider than PI, and also covers transport claims, public sector services, specialist disease claims, employers' liability and professional negligence. More good news – the firm offers many other areas of practice, including company/commercial, property, construction, private client and IP. The latter group has worked for Liverpool FC and Hear'Say. The firm is certainly far less oriented towards company/commercial than contentious work and consequently this has a bearing on the seats that you'll be likely to cover. But trainees emphasise that *"it is a big firm, it does almost every type of law there is and it has the facilities to let you do whatever you want."*

trainees in transit

"I wanted to stay in the North West" was the most common reason why our sources applied to Hill Dickinson. Like most other regional firms, it tends to recruit those with a commitment to the area. The firm's three northern offices are not too far apart from each other and the majority of trainees will choose to take a seat in an office other than the 'home' office. *"Most do a stint in Chester or Manchester. If you are living in Liverpool, it is not that much of a hassle."* Some thought Chester and Manchester offered a better experience because of their smaller size.

The firm is putting extra effort into its Manchester office, which is home to less than ten partners. A contingent of IP lawyers from the firm's old satellite office in Stockport headed up the A626 to join them and recently the combined force of lawyers moved into bigger premises on Fountain Street. The Manchester office is heavily focused on personal injury litigation for some of the countless insurance companies on the firm's books. It also handles mercantile and goods in transit work. Trainees told us that the office *"does have a different atmosphere to other Manchester firms. You are not expected to work ridiculous hours and there is more of a social side to it."* Life in the small Chester office manages to be both *"commercially orientated"* and *"a bit more laid back."*

The London office offers something of a regional experience in the City. Its work mirrors that of the Manchester office – insurance litigation, mercantile, goods in transit – and it too has a smaller number of lawyers. The office takes two trainees, and while it is not a regular feature of the training contract, trainees from Liverpool will occasionally undertake a seat down south. Rather than take work from Liverpool, the London branch tends to be self-supporting.

hill training

Our sources observed that *"you don't have much choice over seats in the first year,"* but things improve in the second. Trainees feel in control of their work, saying, *"you get as much responsibility as you want."* Many enjoy the experience of managing their own files in some seats, but in others there will be the odd bit of photocopying, especially *"on a big deal, after the office juniors have gone and you're the most junior person left in the room."* Some things are universal!

Assistance is available from partners and assistants. *"In any seat there are two or three post-qualifieds who will be a good first port of call for help."* Hours are reasonable, and as one trainee said, *"I have never felt any pressure to stay late."* Even at partner level there's a tendency to *"come in early and finish on time."* Retention rates are comfortably high, out of 10 trainees qualifying in 2001 all were offered jobs and 8 accepted the offer. Cheerily enough, one trainee also told us *"most qualifying trainees get jobs in the departments they want. It is very rare for people not to be taken on."* A few trainees are seconded to Manweb or insurance clients.

trial experience

Come Friday night, you'll find half the firm in Trials, the pub opposite the main Liverpool office. The Trial experience begins straight after work and then, around 8pm, a group of trainees will relocate to another bar. Our sources described Hill Dickinson as particularly sociable. *"You have to have good banter to survive here,"* said one trainee. *"Almost everybody in the office has a nickname… You do actually come to work and enjoy yourself."*

Once a month, trainees meet with five of the partners to discuss relevant issues, air any grievances and generally promote communication. But there was some stark advice from one trainee. *"You will not get on in this firm if you are a Man United fan."* We think he was joking… Naturally, the firm fields a football team of its own.

and finally…
Expect a lively and down-to-earth firm, partners that will impersonate each other and plenty of good humour and insurance litigation. But make no mistake, the number and calibre of plc clients on the firm's books will ensure that you won't feel consigned to insurance work for your two years of training.

Hodge Jones & Allen

the facts
Location: London
UK ranking by size: 151
Total number of trainees: 12
Seats: 4x6 months
Alternative seats: None

Hodge Jones & Allen is a very different kettle of fish to the other firms profiled in the True Picture. It carries out the full range of high street work from its location in the inner city neighbourhood of Camden Town. Yet, it is a cut above your average high street firm, handling such high profile work as the MMR vaccine group action and acting for Gulf War veterans. Oh yeah, and there's also a thriving commercial property department.

doing a stretch
The work you'll handle here includes crime, family, employment, housing for tenants (*"we won't act for landlords"*) and top-notch clinical negligence and personal injury. And, lest we forget, commercial property. All the trainees we spoke to agreed that the training here was *"first class."* We got the impression that at a run-of-the-mill high street firm, trainees are left to muddle through on their own for two years. However, at Hodge Jones you'll certainly not be regarded as just another pair of hands. Trainees enjoy an *"individual, quality training,"* sitting in with a partner and generally doing four six-month seats. We say 'generally' as not one of our four interviewees had actually done this! Many extend seats beyond six months. We learned of one trainee who spent six months on an important case and then stayed on in the department for another six so she could get a broader overview of the area. Another trainee obtained exemption from a year of the training contract from the Law Society, having carried out police station work before training.

on call
Trainees are invited to indicate seat preferences but ultimately what the firm says goes. It attempts to accommodate everyone and a second year trainee's wishes are likely to prevail over those of someone who can wait their turn. Employment is flavour of the month, partly because *"it's trendy everywhere at the moment."* Expect to spend time in the family and criminal departments. The firm has a 24-hour call-out rota to police stations and trainees often enrol on the Police Accreditation Scheme, which means they can represent people in police stations before they're qualified. *"You become useful to the firm out of hours, so I felt important from the start."* One trainee told us how they made strong friendships with the firm's qualified solicitors through handing over details of Friday night call-outs at 8.30am on a Saturday morning.

red tape
This firm's staple is legal aid (now known as Public Funding). It is vital that you understand how this system will impact on your working day if you really want to go into this area, so we asked some trainees to tell us about it. The view is that Public Funding is both *"a help and a hindrance."* Not only do you have to adjust to your new job when you start, but *"legal aid is a whole other thing to get to grips with."* You have to think *"am I

sending the right form?" and *"which rules apply and when?"* There is no escaping the fact that funding arrangements and bureaucracy form a big part of the work load; *"half of it"* according to one source.

On the bright side, after the *"endless forms,"* once you have Public Funding, you're in control of the case, not the client. You have a budget you can work to without having to ask the client to proceed at every step. Another positive aspect is that only firms awarded franchises by the Legal Services Commission can do work under Public Funding. QED only those firms with good procedures, offering top-quality service, are awarded a franchise. Trainees gushed about the franchise-winning case management system in place at Hodge Jones & Allen. All the files are computerised so that *"you hardly ever refer to the hard files"* and the system produces standard documents, taking some of the dross out of the working day. Thirdly, there's always the risk that a private client won't pay, but you're onto a sure thing with government funding! Or… you could always work in commercial property, the firm's new money-spinner, which has *"completely taken off!"*

cheese…

OK, it's a legal aid firm, but don't expect a group of 'right-on' tree hugging/protesting hippies! If you do you'll be *"absolutely shocked."* There's a slightly cheesy quote on the firm's website about its aims: *"…to give help to the disadvantaged in society who have suffered injustice."* One trainee assures us there *"really is an atmosphere of being ethical and helping the under privileged… but we have to be a viable business."* It seems you can't be 'right on' and make money in the legal profession these days. The odd trainee has found it too business-like and moved to a smaller firm on qualification, but most trainees are impressed by the efficiency. You mustn't get the impression that Hodge Jones operates like a law factory; the ethos and the business sense *"complement each other well"* and the firm is *"still catering to clients' needs."* One trainee went as far as to say *"this is how a firm should be."* In September 2000 all four trainees stayed on qualification. In September 2001, two out of four have left, but only because there were no jobs in the departments they wanted.

Does the drive for efficiency make for long hours? From what we can gather, hours seem to be a personal thing. Some trainees worked from 9.30am-5.30pm, regardless of which department they were in, and one reckoned *"partners kick you out at 6pm."* Then there were others who found themselves staying until 7.30-8pm, especially in family and crime. The majority of solicitors, including partners, don't stay late but there's no stigma attached to those trainees who linger behind to finish off work.

…parma ham

It's not one big party at Hodge Jones & Allen, but they seem to be a sociable bunch; *"everyone knows everyone."* Trainees *"get to know everyone by moving seats."* One trainee confirmed *"you could ask questions of anyone on the team, not just your supervisor. There's a real team spirit."* In crime particularly, the doors are always open so that *"anyone can walk into anyone's office."* Each trainee is assigned a qualified solicitor mentor, who's meant to take him or her out to lunch once a month and generally give advice. Each department also has some sort of informal lunch or drinks arrangement whereby they go out together; in family it's lunch every Wednesday.

In true Ally McBeal style, the Mac bar is *"our second office – it's just across the road."* Thankfully there's no Barry White soundtrack accompanying these trainees' lives. The Eagle is another popular haunt, especially for things like leaving parties and *"if you want to find someone – go in the Parma Café!"* It's where you'll find the criminal department (chasing the hamburglar no doubt). More healthy pursuits include netball and rounders in Regents Park during the summer and an annual summer outing. According to one source, the social life is *"not as good as I would have thought, considering there are 11 trainees. But it's left to us and none of us can be* bothered organising anything!" What?? This is Camden Town! Oh well, there's always the last Friday of the month to look forward to, *"that's the best night – we get paid!"*

the real ideal

It's clear that these trainees have principles, which they don't want to compromise. The firm's website indicates it values voluntary experience as much as good academics. Many trainees have done a year or two at a refugee or law centre prior to their training contract. Our sources thought that the firm's real emphasis in recruiting was on interpersonal skills and an applicant's ability to handle clients. Voluntary work is simply taken as evidence of this.

The nature of Hodge Jones & Allen's work means that trainees are given a lot of responsibility and client contact from the word go. This kind of work attracts *"strong, confident, focused, together"* people; *"you wouldn't like it otherwise."* If you do like it, *"you can take as much responsibility as you want." "You need to be able to deal with clients."* The website suggests that the firm is keen to recruit trainees from among its own paralegals. A couple of our trainees had indeed started like this, but another reckoned that many paralegals had been encouraged to apply for a training contract, yet weren't offered one in the final analysis.

and finally…

If you have never even thought about doing wussy commercial law, it is likely you've known for a while that you want to do legal aid work. You've probably done voluntary work at a homeless shelter, for a charity or at your local Citizens Advice Bureau… hell, you might even have had a first career already. It'll help if you enjoy contact with the public, a quick pace and a bit of stress… and you won't mind working hard for less money than your contemporaries in the City. If you won't need mollycoddling through your training contract, Hodge Jones & Allen might be for you.

Holman Fenwick & Willan

the facts

Location: London
UK ranking by size: 77
Total number of trainees: 16
Seats: 4x6 months
Alternative Seats: Overseas seats, secondments

One of the top-ranking shipping practices, Holman Fenwick & Willan was founded in 1883. It is old. Whilst it would be nice to think that three crusty sailors had climbed ashore and decided that after years dodging pirates and weevils on the high seas, what they actually wanted to do was found a prestigious and respected City law firm, we suspect this was not the case. We're told that Holman Fenwick & Willan is not simply a shipping firm and anyone who implied it was would be heading for choppy waters… Look at our strength in commercial arbitration and dispute resolution they said…

many sails on this mast

OK, let's be clear. Holman Fenwick & Willan is one of the leading specialists in shipping and all its tributaries. As it states on the firm's website, it was one of the first "to recognise that transportation, insurance, trade, and finance were inextricably linked." The firm has experience in charter parties, bills of landing, carriage contracts, and the *"bumps and scrapes"* that occupy the Admiralty department. The firm has *"casualty and response teams"* of *"lawyers and mariners"* who *"operate 24-hours a day on a world-wide basis."*

But, there's more. The firm is actively developing other areas of work. Recent partner recruitment has been into banking, insolvency and fraud. One trainee explained the logic of the expansion; "as *clients' problems grow, it follows that practice areas are going to grow."* This is not to say that shipping will not be a significant part of your training contract, it just means that seats are not limited to matters maritime. But your clients might be…

contentious issues

Above everything else, trainees wanted us to understand that it is litigation and not shipping which will shape your training. Three out of the four seats will be in contentious departments. *"It's a great place for commercial litigation... as complex and varied as you can get."* Indeed, *"non-contentious is small. You have got to want to do commercial litigation. If you want predominantly company/commercial, you should head elsewhere."* Whilst *"a training contract in shipping won't hold you back in the City"* and the firm can still provide excellent experience in a range of seats, our message still seems to be; if you don't think shipping will float your boat, think carefully.

getting wet

For a firm of its size, HFW recruits remarkably few trainees. Our sources were positive that it's a bonus to be just *"one of only a few trainees."* The firm is small enough to know everyone and to be *"immediately known as a personality,"* rather than just a number. We often hear how small trainee populations allow for interesting work and early responsibility. One trainee said, *"I never felt out of my depth,"* indicating that the increase in responsibility grew *"organically."* The quality of work is generally good, and while there may be *"some photocopying, I would always feel happy that I could complain."* Despite the occasional *"difficult personality,"* all the partners *"have been easy to work for."*

> "The Admiralty department goes sailing in Docklands every Tuesday."

Getting the seat you want is not generally a problem as there just aren't that many trainees to compete with. Preferences are usually met, though *"it may help if you get to know people through working with them in a previous seat."* HFW can be hierarchical, but let's not go overboard here, *"all law firms are hierarchical,"* and this firm is certainly *"not oppressively so."* Even Lord Byron (who is a partner at the firm) is called 'Robin' by trainees because, well, that's his name! Maybe a better description of the HFW atmosphere would be *"collegiate."* It's *"both hierarchical and friendly, if that makes sense."* Er, we think we understand! One trainee emphasised that HFW is not as pretentious as he thought other firms might be. *"People have a joke, but it is professional at the same time. We know that we do have to get back to work, and work hard."*

round the world

We spied trainees with previous careers, including former insurance brokers and underwriters (was that at Lloyd's of London possibly??) and quite a diverse range of nationalities from various parts of Asia, Europe and Africa. This probably explains why one department goes by the name of the 'Kruger National Park.' Increasingly however, trainees are coming straight from university.

Client and overseas secondments are available *"if you ask"* and, with offices in Paris, Hong Kong, Greece, and Singapore, the option for travel is there. One or two trainees will be sent out to an overseas office every six months. Languages will stand you in good stead when you are making your case to travel. We were told that a trainee with fluent French who wanted to travel would have a one in three chance.

winding down

Acting for international businesses in maritime and trade, the typical client is thought to be entrepreneurial, meaning that they like their lawyers *"down to earth."* Trainees get City salaries but don't seem to work the hours of magic circle trainees. Late nights are only occasional and, as always, *"it varies with the department."* As fitting for a well-aged firm, it is located in a *"beautiful old building, but the dry shipping litigation department is down the road."*

The social life is *"department driven."* Indeed, the Admiralty department *"goes sailing around the Dock-*

lands every Tuesday." There's also a strong sporting element, but don't worry, *"the sports are relaxed – it doesn't matter if you don't know how to hold a bat."* There is more to socialising here than sport. The same interviewee also told us that HFW trainees certainly know how to hold *"a big glass of wine."*

and finally...
The firm has traditionally been successful in retaining its trainees on qualification. Out of the 2001 qualifiers all were offered jobs and all decided to accept. Smashing. Holman Fenwick & Willan may be just right for the trainee who's hungry for litigation. The firm *"no longer has the smell of a North Sea firm about it,"* but make no mistake, shipping still dominates. Big ships don't change course that quickly.

Howes Percival

the facts
Location: Leicester, Milton Keynes, Northampton, Norwich
UK ranking by size: 145
Total number of trainees: 10
Seats: 4x6 months
Alternative Seats: Secondments

Compared to most of the firms profiled in the True Picture, Howes Percival is a stocky little firm. Its workload divides into three hefty chunks of corporate, commercial property and litigation, with smaller portions of employment, insolvency and private client served up on the side. This makes for a meat and two veg training, with a compulsory rotation through each of the three core areas, and a second helping of the seat into which the trainee wants to qualify.

driven by pizza
Welcome to the East Midlands and Howes Percival's Northampton HQ. Trainees tell us that the town's not a backward place as such, but *"it has only just got its first Pizza Express!"* Many, but not all, of the trainees give Northampton a break after a while and move around between the other two Midlands offices in Leicester and Milton Keynes. It definitely helps if you have a car and you can drive it. Even if you're not regularly commuting between offices, *"you still need a car just to attend meetings."* If you've got the burden of student loans to pay off, this can be tough, so Howes is buying a Northampton flat for trainees and is considering similar investments elsewhere. It's only Norwich that doesn't shuffle its trainees around in this manner, recruiting independently, then keeping trainees firmly within East Anglian borders.

home alone
The trainees we interviewed were impressed with the firm's approach to training. One said *"I'm really pleased with it. I've had lots of work and no way are you just shadowing or watching people all day."* It has been a *"hands on training. You actually get proper work to do."* Client secondments are not regular but *"one person did just go to DaimlerChrysler,"* which, along with Scania and Start-Rite, is amongst the firm's more high profile clients. But, while the *"quality of work is good, supervision has occasionally been lacking."* Although *"nothing goes out without a partner seeing it,"* trainees spoke of partners away, assistants off sick, and being left alone in the office. This experience *"can be good or bad,"* but no doubt ensures trainees grow up quickly. Hours are *"not horrendous."* One source confirmed that to handle its burgeoning business, the firm *"needs more fee earners."* This must surely give comfort to those coming up to qualification.

the new sheriff
We learned of some teething troubles during seat changeovers – think principals on holiday and previous trainees handing work over without much explanation. One source said, *"it wasn't very well planned. It does need more structure."* Some gripes were put down to a now-departed training manager *"who*

had no background in HR," was absent for extended periods and did not like to tell the partnership things they did not want to hear. A fab replacement has been appointed. We decided to call him John Wayne as he's *"more assertive,"* a *"very impressive chap"* and has a *"deputy."* Trainees are convinced that *"things will improve."*

gunfight

We wanted to find out if there was a stand-off relationship between the Midlands and East Anglian offices or whether the firm worked together as one posse. *"It does feel like one firm, with lots of interaction between the offices."* The *"partners are very tightly knit – they talk to each other on a daily basis."* The trainees themselves meet every three months to talk about the firm and its future, creating their own agenda with a couple of suggestions from partners. *"We discuss where law is going and what we can do to market the firm."* It comes across as a progressive step by Howes Percival, which implies that it sees the trainees as a valuable part of the firm.

> *"No one actually lives in Milton Keynes."*

Yet retention rates have been shaky. While it is great to see that a Howes Percival training has previously prepared newly qualifieds for *"DLA, Burges Salmon, Cameron McKenna – certainly major City firms,"* it must be a bit gutting for the firm to see the kids leaving home and moving in with these other firms. No trainees have been retained in Norwich for two years and there are variable rates in other offices. So what's up? *"Part of the problem is location"* and the firm offering *"jobs where they feel like it,"* but not necessarily where newly qualifieds want to be. Some of our sources were perplexed by it all and in September 2001, only one of the three qualifiers stayed with the firm.

Howes Percival is waking up to the problem. *"Partners are beginning to recognise that we do have to be more proactive about retaining staff."* The movement of trainees around branches is regularly discussed. *"There are arguments about the geography but that will not go away."*

children of the revolution

Inevitably, it all comes out in the bar. Of the firm's different branches, it's Leicester that has the biggest social scene. One trainee told us *"Leicester's parties are fantastic. They know how to enjoy themselves. Watching the partners let their hair down is entertaining."* Located on a leafy pedestrian street on the outskirts of Leicester's city centre, at the end of the week the office trots off to local bar, Revolution. The Leicester office, and to a lesser extent Milton Keynes, have *"younger partners that are very forward thinking,"* although Friday nights just aren't the same when *"no one actually lives in Milton Keynes."* Elsewhere socialising *"tends to be more departmentalised."* Individually, partners are friendly and chatty but, come Friday, *"they will not be in the pub."* *"Northampton has the older crowd."* Still, *"people in the firm are particularly nice."*

Howes Percival has *"quite a strong male culture."* Of 27 partners, two are female. *"They are not coming in at partner level,"* even though at assistant and trainee level there are *"many more women."* *"Amost all the trainees are girls"* – a remedy for gender imbalance at the top in the future maybe, but one frustrated by low retention rates on qualification. The firm is *"slightly old school. A lot of young partners act middle aged"* one trainee indicated. Generally our sources thought Howes Percival was slow to change. While the younger Leicester office is *"work hard and play hard, it's the only office that you can describe in that way."*

and finally…

For *"high quality work in the regions,"* and the chance to square up to *"big regional firms like Wragge and Co,"* Howes Percival has a *"good training, you can't knock it."* Meat and two veg with a dash of HP sauce.

Hugh James Ford Simey

the facts
Location: Cardiff, Merthyr, Bargoed, Blackwood and nine others in Wales and the South East
UK ranking by size: 62
Total number of trainees: 13
Seats: 4x6 months
Alternative Seats: None

Hugh James Ford Simey came into being following the 1999 merger of Cardiff's Hugh James and West Country firm Ford Simey Daw Roberts. Retreating from the opportunity to have the longest name of any UK law firm, the merged practice became a firm of real diversity. It has a large network of thirteen branches. While its trainees come in three varieties: Welsh, Welsh and Welsh, its business ranges widely from crime to e-business. And what contrasts – from the large commercial practice in Cardiff city centre, to the small high street practices in the mining valley towns.

> "From a trainee's perspective it's a defiantly Welsh firm."

miners and rugby
Although it has a broad ranging practice, the firm's business is dominated to an extent by claimant personal injury and commercial/insurance litigation. High profile cases include 16,000 miners' Vibration White Finger claims, and about 6,000 miners' industrial deafness claims, so we're talking more than just pavement slippers and trippers cases. The rest of the work is evenly spread between commercial property, commercial services, construction and private client. The high number of non-solicitor fee earners suggests a volume of lower value work but you'll see the firm's name associated with big deals and sexy clients too. Roots to the fore, the firm is proud of its commercial contract work, securing the construction of the Millennium Stadium and the services of the Welsh Rugby Union coach.

satellite communications
No seats are available in the English offices, so trainees spend their two years rotating around the Cardiff and Merthyr offices, with one or two going up to Bargoed and Blackwood. Each of the year 2000 in-take completed their LPC in Cardiff. Like any regional firm, there's a desire to recruit those who are committed to a career locally. *"They do want trainees with a connection to the area,"* and each of the trainees we spoke to applied to the firm because they wanted to stay in Wales.

Despite its English offices, from a trainee's perspective it's a defiantly Welsh firm. With eight offices in Wales and five in England, does Hugh James Ford Simey hang together as a single entity? The Welsh trainees have little to do with the offices across the Severn and trainee opinion was divided as to whether even the Welsh offices were close. Some observed *"a one firm feeling,"* while others argued *"it is disparate. There are satellite offices that feel like individual firms, with Cardiff as the epicentre."* The number of offices at least provides *"more resources, horizons and experience."*

For once we didn't roll our eyes when we heard a trainee describe their firm as *"a big firm, but a small firm… It has a name, but not anonymity."* That trainee summed up life at Hugh James very neatly. It has around 60 partners and 450 other fee earners, but sitting in the wills department of a small valley office, you wouldn't know it.

in the valleys
Trainee moves between the Welsh branches are highly likely. Indeed, they're sometimes necessary to accommodate trainees' seat choices, as not all seats are available in all of the offices. Only apply if you are willing to get out of Cardiff and spend six months in a valley town. One source in a valley office said *"some trainees are reluctant to leave Cardiff but pleasantly surprised when they actually come here."* The firm does

try to be flexible – it created an employment seat for one trainee – but realistically, choice is a luxury item rationed to second years only. While there is no *"set pattern,"* seats are commonly taken in defendant insurance litigation, commercial property and *"some form of conveyancing, wills or family seat in a valley office."* And for the first time this year, trainees will be able to take a seat in the firm's sports department, top ranked by our colleagues on the *Chambers Guide*.

> "Such a fiery baptism should be an advantage at a later stage."

Life in the branch offices is *"relaxed. It's smaller so you get to know people better."* In the commercial world of Cardiff the atmosphere *"is slightly different – more formal. Not a problem, just a bigger office."* But with its *"roots in the valleys, it's a friendly firm with approachable staff."* Lower salaries were said to reflect *"really good hours."* Although the Merthyr branch is empty by 5.30pm, it wants to move away from the high street and expand its commercial work.

m for mirther

The social scene varies between offices. With trainees *"spread about different places, we don't go out much as a group."* Hugh James *"does not throw money at trainees."* Some observed that, as a group, *"trainees at other big firms in Cardiff are closer and the firm organises stuff for them."* In Cardiff, trainees go out for lunch together most days and *"will tend to go for a drink after work, with occasional bigger nights out."* However, some thought *"Cardiff has changed. It was very sociable, but every department has enclosed upon itself a bit."*

Things are better at a branch level. Step forward the legendary Merthyr partners. This is where we ask you to imagine a drum roll and the mass gasping of breath. *"They are bonkers! Just bonkers!"* Their reputation continues to grow, and not just among the Hugh James trainees. For those not in the know, their 1999 Christmas party rendition of Village People's YMCA was described as nothing less than *"the funniest thing I have ever seen."* A repeat performance in 2000 was put down to the fact that *"they haven't bothered to get different costumes." "Their parties are legendary,"* despite most partners *"having no rhythm."*

unwrapped

Returning to more serious matters, Hugh James does not go easy on its trainees. *"The level of responsibility was higher than I expected."* It arrives on your desk from day one and overwhelmed some of our sources. *"You are not wrapped in cotton wool."* The firm is *"not very big on supervision. You get an awful lot of responsibility for a trainee solicitor."* On the plus side, *"it is character building and gives you a lot more confidence."* But is it too much? A trainee described a low point as *"when you are up to your eyeballs in work and, no matter what you say to anybody, it is not taken off you."* Still, trainees thought it a *"a good training contract,"* there are *"no nightmare photocopying stories"* and such a fiery baptism should be an advantage at a later stage. *"We are more confident than trainees at other firms."*

With an almost unparalleled variety of seats on offer, *"you can get a wide range of experience."* It's high street and commercial experience all rolled into one. Every single one of Hugh James' September 2001 NQs were retained by the firm, and *"none had to take jobs where they didn't want to go."* Bravo!

and finally…

Although it is a large firm, you can get small firm experience. *"The best of both worlds."* We freely admit that this has become one of our favourite firms on the *Chambers Student Guide*. Hugh James has a huge amount to offer to those planning to stay in Wales, provided they have the willingness to embrace responsibility and try their hand at anything. And of course there's the *"Valleys humour on a daily basis."*

Ince & Co

the facts
Location: London
UK ranking by size: 87
Total number of trainees: 19
Seats: 4x6 seats
Alternative Seats: None

Ince & Co's work is around 40% shipping and aviation and 25% insurance related. If these areas of work wet your whistle then you can't do much better than set course for Ince & Co. There's a few other areas on offer too.

calling incernational rescue
The firm's website includes a rather dramatic red 'emergency response' button. When we first saw it last year, it got us thinking. Gerry Anderson must have got his inspiration for Thunderbirds from somewhere and we reckon it was Inces. Clearly nowadays when disaster strikes, it is crucial that the lawyers land before Thunderbird One. After all, what does Virgil Tracy understand about contributory negligence and damages? Plane crashes, piracy, oil spills and fires – these form the bread and butter of Ince & Co's work and it must surely be one of the few organisations proud to boast of its involvement in almost every major disaster over the last ten years. It's not just the nature of the work that sets Ince & Co apart from other mid-tier firms; the structure of its training is different too.

brains (and balls)
Training at Ince & Co is not for the faint hearted! *"You have to be really tough if you want to train here,"* one source told us. For starters, you won't get an easy introduction to the work by simply sitting with and shadowing a partner for your first seat before you get your hands dirty. *"You are handling your own (small) cases from day one."* Trainees do sit with four successive partners, but accept work from different partners throughout the two years, building a reputation with and learning from all of them as time progresses. *"You sink or swim based on your standing,"* one trainee explained. *"Once you establish a reputation with partners, you start getting more and better work."* Sound daunting?

Assertiveness, confidence and the ability to say no when under pressure are essential if you are to survive. *"You can find yourself being given work by several different partners… nobody will run your life for you. If you are having problems you need to make it clear."* We should point out before going any further that there is much to be gained from this extra pressure. Trainees highlighted the challenging nature of the training environment as both the best and worst aspects of their time at the firm. *"The pressure does get to you every now and again. There was a time when I was working for fifteen partners at the same time,"* one said. Another added, *"It means you learn very, very quickly. I am a better lawyer and a better person for having been thrown in and made to find my feet."*

the ince way
Training 'the Ince way' will have positive and negative impact on case handling. As trainees are not moving from department to department every six months, they don't have to abandon interesting cases half way through. *"The satisfaction I received from finally finishing a complex case that ran for almost a year was brilliant,"* one source told us. And those less interesting cases? *"You can end up with that nightmare case, which just chases you around and won't go away… you might be desperate to pass it on to someone else but it isn't an option."*

In spite of the somewhat scruffy feel of the office building and artwork that is less than inspiring (pictures of ships and oil rigs), trainees are essentially pretty fond of the firm. They get together with colleagues in All Bar One and Foxtrot Oscar. The Ince way clearly appeals. Of the 2001 qualifiers, the firm offered jobs to 100% of trainees, only one trainee did not accept.

lonesome tonight

Trainees occasionally reported feeling isolated and unappreciated when working late. A bit like John Tracy floating around outer space in Thunderbird Five, nobody seems to notice you plugging away late in the evening. *"At some firms if you work late there's a 'lets go for it' team atmosphere. Here nobody really knows if you do pull a late one. It can be frustrating."* But the flip side is *"if there is nothing going on then you can just go home at 4pm and nobody bats an eyelid."* The vast majority of Ince & Co's work is contentious; this tends to mean that hours will not be wildly unpredictable (unless, we assume, you're on the super-cool emergency response team).

In such a challenging environment, it's obviously important that there's support and guidance available when you need it. We found this year's trainees more comfortable about asking for assistance or reporting problems than in earlier years. This is largely because the firm has become cosier under the influence of Ince & Co's own Jeff Tracy – senior partner, Peter Rogan. *"He is much more of a people person… more interested in making sure trainees feel looked after."* If problems do arise, there is now somewhere employees can turn to. *"The new Senior Partner has introduced a committee composed of the 'nice partners'. Anyone can turn to this committee for help… it does work."*

There have been more changes on Tracy Island. The firm now has a monthly drinks get together, which predictably enough has proved popular with trainees. The senior partner delivers news of important changes to small groups of staff himself, and we're told that the big guy is *"one of the few people in the firm who actually means it when he says that his door is always open."* Anyway, enough… we are sure his ego is big enough already!

brighton rocks

There are opportunities for trainees and newly qualifieds to travel as and when the work requires. Despite the fact that there are no formal overseas secondments available, trainees have found themselves heading for Bahrain, the Yemen and Newfoundland in past years. Half the trainee population had the opportunity to go out to Singapore this year, the other half were despatched to Brighton (the lucky things). Trainees go where the work takes them and, with a bit of luck, it will lead you further afield than Brighton Pier.

and finally…

Ince and Co will not suit everyone, only those who'll be happy with the pressure and the challenging nature of the work. Against this, you will certainly not be bored. Perhaps the best endorsement of the firm's training came from a trainee who had a great deal to say about how tough the work had been, how much pressure he had been under and how hard he had been pushed. We asked him whether, if he had his time again, he would have picked a different firm. *"Absolutely not. No way. Coming here has been one of the best decisions I have made."* F.A.B.

Irwin Mitchell

the facts

Location: Sheffield, Leeds, Birmingham, London
UK ranking by size: 30
Total number of trainees: 27
Seats: 4x6 months
Alternative Seats: None

Irwin Mitchell has been an established name up north for over 80 years. It has a fantastic reputation in personal injury and clinical negligence, but has broadened its work and now covers corporate services, insurance litigation and private client.

it's a disaster

For a firm previously tagged as northern personal injury specialists, the last few years have seen big efforts to rebrand and expand. From an historical base in Sheffield, the folk at Irwin Mitchell sacrificed their delicate regional sensibilities and you'll now also find them in Leeds, Birmingham and London. It wants to *"create an image as a streamlined national firm."* Trainees tell us *"now, the hype is true – they are a national firm."*

Happy to deal with the little things in life, the firm works for a range of clients from private individuals to large plcs. It also specialises in the extraordinary. Indeed, Irwin Mitchell has niche expertise in disaster law and has worked on high profile cases like the King's Cross Fire, the Marchioness, Piper Alpha, CJD and miners' disease claims.

IM offers its trainees a particularly diverse range of seats and it is this diversity that appeals to the many applicants who are not sure where they would like to specialise. Some of the trainees we interviewed at the firm had discovered unexpected affinities for employment and even commercial property. 80% of trainees were offered jobs this year, and all of those lucky recruits chose to stay on. And what an eclectic range of departments they are going into: aside from mainstream commercial seats, criminal, IP, wills, employment, insolvency and clinical negligence all took on NQs.

wealth in experience

The firm happily recruits mature trainees, those with families and those of its own paralegals looking to upgrade to a training contract. There seems to be no need to scoop up impressionable youngsters fit to be moulded into identi-solicitor. IM trainees are not the *"over-confident"* types, but nor are they the *"quiet ones"* and certainly, *"Oxbridge is not important."* Strangely, with such a wealth of experience on offer at IM, *"PI is not so popular now with trainees, but it does vary from intake to intake."* At the moment, employment is the buzz department, especially in Birmingham.

The three main offices – Sheffield, Leeds and Birmingham – have a similar spread of work. Seats can be taken in company/commercial, property, litigation, PI, employment, IP, crime and family. The popular business crime seat is only available in Sheffield though. Hours will of course vary with the department and the case, but for those we spoke to 8:30am to 6pm was the norm. Salaries are good as a trainee but were regarded as *"crap"* upon qualification. Ouch!

angelic apparitions

This is a firm that won't deluge you with work, but will put it in your way if you want it. *"They don't throw you in at the deep end,"* but *"effort is noted."* If things get too hairy, it'll probably get picked up. There's *"good communication"* and your progress will be well monitored. Trainees experience a *"steady increase in responsibility."* The firm recognises that, at the end of the day, you are just a trainee. Six month seats are punctuated by visits from the *"Angel of the North,"* Auntie Sue Lenkowski – the graduate recruitment manager who glides between offices and *"keeps an eye on you."*

Competition for seats is diluted by the fact that trainees tend to both *"huddle"* and *"natter,"* in an attempt to co-ordinate between themselves. Friends made during early seats may scatter to the winds during your second year as they move offices. *"You don't see trainees from your early seats too often, but there is always good banter on email."* When everyone groups together for national training meetings, *"it's like we've never been apart."* Sweet.

you... leeds... now!

But this is not a perfect world. None of the trainees get to choose their first seat and the big big bugbear is that you won't always get your first choice, even in later seats. *"Some have just had to take what they've been given,"* and even worse, *"some were forced to move to Leeds!"* And while we wouldn't recommend it as a quick fix solution, *"you won't have to move if you have a family."* Overall, a willingness to relocate is recommended and, as one trainee noted, *"it can actually be a positive thing."*

The social life varies between departments and between offices. With two trainees in London and four in Birmingham, you will have to wait for the monthly trainee meetings to hook up with all your buddies. PI in Sheffield and employment in Birmingham are both known to be very sociable departments, with the Sheffield PI and Catastrophic Injuries mob in the bar *"three or four times a week."* But if you want to square up against the DLA trainees down at Babylon (swanky and suited in Leeds), then don't expect to be there with a posse from commercial property, where there is *"no socialising at all."*

fishy tales

This is a *"genuinely friendly firm."* Partners will almost invariably say, *"well done,"* and the firm is *"not stuffy at all in any of the offices."* You need a gsoh when you receive an instruction from a client who 'accidentally' boiled the tropical fish in his employers' office tank (true!). Maybe this is why IM trainees are *"slightly more off the wall than other trainees."* Can only be a good thing we think.

and finally...

Apply for the relaxed atmosphere, the *"breadth of experience and quality of work"* and, of course, some of the most unusual cases you could wish to come across. Fundamentally, like Grant and Phil, you can be proud to be a Mitchell.

KLegal

the facts

Location: London
UK ranking by size: 92
Total number of trainees: 22
Seats: 4x6 months
Alternative Seats: Brussels

This is one of two accountancy-tied legal practices included in the True Picture. The other profiled firm is Garretts (Arthur Andersen). The other tied firms in the UK are Landwell (PricewaterhouseCoopers) and Tite & Lewis (Ernst & Young). Arthur Andersen's Garretts may have started the move towards MDP in the UK, but KLegal (KPMG's brainchild), has made noticeable strides in the two plus years since its conception in July 1999.

what's an mdp?

You may well ask and if you're about to fill in the KLegal application form you really ought to know. MDP stands for multi-disciplinary practice. Simply put, it is the concept of accountants and lawyers and other professionals working together in the same partnership. At present UK regulations prohibit solicitors from being in partnership with non-solicitors to offer legal services. This is unlikely to change until 2003. Currently the Law Society is inching its way forward on the subject. MDPs are already a reality in a number of other countries.

What's the point of an MDP? Again, this is another question on which we suggest you form a view. We asked KLegal's trainees for some ideas and, more particularly, why the nine of them employed by the firm in 2000/2001 had decided to take the plunge and become the firm's trainee guinea pigs. *"I knew KLegal wouldn't be a typical firm as it has just started"* one trainee voiced the feelings of all those we spoke to. Another said, *"I liked the idea of a law firm that went beyond law."* From a third we heard, *"I was keen on getting a good legal training but I didn't just want to work with lawyers. We work in client service teams here with people from KPMG."*

To what extent the MDP ideal of improved client service and focus is a reality or the Holy Grail, we can't judge. This is where you try to form your own view. Trainees tell us that *"KLegal is looking for those who believe in MDP. If students don't understand it, then that can be overcome, but if they don't believe in it then that's another matter."*

older brother or big brother?

Just how close is the relationship with KPMG? Trainees conclude that around 70% of the law firm's business comes from KPMG, either by way of the accountants' clients instructing the lawyers directly or KPMG having a retainer and instructing the law firm on aspects of the retainer. The remaining 30% comes from contacts of the KLegal lawyers.

The lawyers occupy two and a half floors of the KPMG building, *"but we are completely separate."* In addition to Chinese walls, *"all the files have to be locked away. We can go into KPMG areas but all our doors are locked off."* There's definitely a sense that KLegal feeds off KPMG and not vice versa. Of great amusement to us, but of real interest to trainees was the KPMG knowledge management database. *"Kworld! It's the world I live in,"* one of them told us. *"I can get anything off it – information about client service teams, fee generation figures. It has so many research tools it's a joke. It takes time to get used to it but when you do… brokers' reports, analysts' reports – it's all there."* Uh oh… why are we suddenly thinking about Wayne and Garth?

evangelism
In the last year alone the firm has doubled in size, pulling in lawyers from across the City. *"It is intending to take on a hundred lawyers a year for the next three years,"* one of our sources told us. Thus far, lawyers have arrived at a firm that hasn't yet been around long enough to have its own traditions and each of them brings a different approach or style of working. Terminology has been borrowed from KPMG (trainees talk about their supervisors as their 'managers' and there's a whole additional 'director' layer between senior solicitor and partner) and a set of ethics – the 'Values Charter' has also leapt the Chinese wall.

Trainee opinion on the importance of the KPMG Values Charter is divided. Some are positively evangelical about it. *"It's an idea about how people should behave at work. That you should try and obtain the facts before making a judgement, that you should have respect for the balance between work and home life. Appraisals are tied into the values, so if you treat people appallingly you wouldn't get the same reward. I think it has teeth."* Others are less impressed; *"It's KPMG's charter, I don't have any attachment to it."* What all agree on is a *"keenness to maintain openness"* and that the hierarchy is not oppressive. The absence of long-held traditions leaves trainees feeling like they are a part of something *"pioneering,"* that *"nothing is set in stone"* and their opinions count for something.

getting to know you
With a constant stream of lawyers joining the firm and a whole accountancy practice to get to know, we wondered if life at KLegal was one long round of introductions and hand shaking. *"We do work on the same projects as the KPMG people, they organise a lot of evening seminars to let us know what they can offer us and then there are drinks afterwards. We have started to do similar things for them."* But the numbers can be bewildering. *"Knowing that we have access to the resources of KPMG feels overwhelming. Sometimes after the event you realise they have a whole dedicated team in something and, if you'd known, it would have helped. It will take a little time to realise what we have actually got!"*

> *"KWorld! It's the world I live in."*

As well as lots of terribly useful people to assist them, the lawyers have the KPMG amenities and social scene to tap into. From womens' footie to the scuba diving club, masses of things are on offer to the KLegal trainees. Sadly with only one man and eight women in the first ever trainee intake, KLegal wouldn't really have boosted the prospects of the KPMG men's football team.

Many trainees reported starting work around 8.30am and finishing around 6.30pm and so most have the energy for a full social life at the firm. It's the trainees who organise monthly drinks events for the whole firm in different local bars. *"Recently we had a pub quiz to bring out those who would not normally come. We've had salsa classes and softball after work... birthday drinks and leaving drinks."* Leaving drinks? Already?

for those who still believe the world is flat...

What sort of person leaves a career in one law firm to come to a brand new firm? *"Someone who is comfortable with change,"* is the easy answer. Trainees find the idea of being a part of KLegal's development exciting. *"I want to grow with it and help it develop,"* one of our sources said. *"It's unique being here at the beginning."* Another talked about the future, saying, *"In terms of career aspirations, I am thinking about my position in five or ten years time. I'll have a lot more choice than at a traditional law firm. Not only can you progress as a lawyer but you can move around KPMG as well. There are opportunities* [for qualified lawyers] *to second to KPMG. One of the directors in property has gone over to transactional services, for example. And there will be international assignments in the future."*

Which brings us to the topic of international work. At present there is only one three-month Brussels secondment for trainees, but in most seats some of your work will have an international angle to it. Our sources spoke of working with KLegal lawyers in other countries on cross-border work and on UK work referred by their foreign counterparts.

No one's suggesting Klegal has already perfected the training experience and we heard one or two suggestions as to how matters could be improved. For example, the first intake would have preferred group training for the Professional Skills Course rather than the individual study that they undertook. But, for a Year One assessment, it's fairly impressive. The trainee population will leap from nine to 22 in September 2001; a clear indication that new graduate recruits are seen as key to continued growth. It's unclear whether the range of seats on offer will increase or whether there will just be more seats in the areas of work currently available to trainees. For the record, these currently include corporate and commercial, banking and finance, IP and TEC (technology), property, employment and tax litigation.

and finally...

The accountancy-tied law firms are a new breed in the UK legal profession and, before you try to leap on board one of them, you ought to collect your thoughts on the question of MDP. There's no point in getting all the way to interview and having no opinion...

Lawrence Graham

the facts
Location: London
UK ranking by size: 37
Total number of trainees: 30
Seats: 4x6 months
Alternative Seats: None

Mid-town... mid-size...middle of the road? No! Wait! That was just to get your attention. Lawrence Graham is so skilled at hiding its light under a bush that we decided to shout a bit on its behalf. Lawrence Graham – excellent firm for property and environmental work, pretty nifty on smaller corporate deals and very commendable in private client. Go check 'em out.

the bigger breakfast

Having always been blessed with a reputation as a good place to work, it has recruited an HR adviser from a US bank. Overhauling its graduate recruitment operations, Lawrence Graham has ditched the usual glossy brochure, refocused on where it aims to recruit and reduced the number of students interviewed. Partners have attended workshops on giving feedback, performance-related bonus schemes have been introduced and a culture apparently too accepting of under-performance has been attacked. Does this mean the end of the old Larry G charm?

Well no. The firm hasn't turned into Brutal, Nasty & Co – *"no one would raise an eyebrow if you left at 5.30pm."* But it is definitely trying to *"revamp its image"* and become more performance oriented. *"It knows it is going to have to increase the workload."* However, the firm has been concentrating on broadening the client base, rather than billing existing clients more. Despite considering plans to raise the annual target for billable hours from 1,300 to 1,400, trainees have found *"there are no strict billing targets or the strict attitude there is at some firms."* The firm's makeover has not resulted in any major shift in culture, although one trainee did admit to having *"breakfast lectures in the corporate department."* (To learn how many eggs per day are good for young lawyers?)

the comfort zone

Our sources were generally very complimentary about their training. The work is of a distinctively high quality. *"From the start, it was more like being an assistant than a trainee."* Interestingly, Lawrence Graham actively considers where its trainees would be best suited. *"The firm thinks forward and advises what seats they think you should do"* and recommends accordingly. *"It was suggested that I do this seat and now I'm qualifying into it."* Retention rates are high. In September 2001, eight qualifiers were offered jobs and six accepted. In line with recent changes, the firm has been recruiting more into corporate.

So would you fit in? *"Lawrence Graham trainees are a bit less scary than other trainees. There is a bigger spread of characters than is usually found in the legal profession."* We did wonder why the trainees thought the rest of the legal profession such a scary place. Trainees are open amongst themselves about seat preferences and *"rumours about partners' personalities do affect seat choices."* Trainee numbers are relatively small, so rather than just being an accessory for partners, they are actually productive creatures. Nevertheless, some felt *"the seats are slightly less organised than they should be."*

don't be fooled

With the renewed focus on performance, Lawrence Graham has achieved some good results. In the last financial year, profits increased by 35%. The firm's business consists primarily of commercial property, company/commercial, litigation, and… tax and financial management, which is one of those euphemistic names used by City firms to make their private client departments sound more interesting. One of the most profitable departments in the firm, this is no ordinary private client practice. The firm serves a small number of very wealthy families. V-e-r-y wealthy. Think huge. One partner's entire practice is built around just one family. Most of these particular clients reside abroad and, with the amount of work available, Lawrence Graham is desperate to expand this aspect of its practice. A seat is available in the department for those interested in taking on the role of the trusted advisor.

able seamen

Lawrence Graham has an office in the Ukraine. Part of an international association of law firms called ABLE, the work of the Ukrainian office is primarily shipping. However, trainees are unable to spend time abroad and there are no secondments to clients either – something several trainees felt was a shame. Boo! The furthest trainees will go is to one of the four seats at a second, smaller London office. Like its Ukrainian cousin, it too is focused on shipping and is nestled just down the road from Lloyd's of London.

Thankfully, our sources were over the moon about the location of the firm's HQ on the Strand. *"It's perfect! You're not stuck in the City, you're close to Covent Garden and, if you want to do court work, the RCJ is just opposite."* And just think about all those retail opportunities!

alligators and champagne

It may be true, but then again it may be just a legal urban myth (like the alligator kept in the basement swimming pool of a prominent magic circle firm).

Lawrence Graham's partners – allegedly – once looked into buying Dalys, the bar around the corner from the Strand office. Why? Simple. It is so frequented by the firm's employees. As one trainee put it, *"they should just put my salary straight in there."* Trainees *"go out together all the time."* *"There are plenty of characters at the firm. Everybody goes to Dalys, and you can talk to anyone."* So are the ensuing antics quiet and restrained? *"It's lucky the legal press aren't in there."*

> "One partner's entire practice is built around just one family."

Organised events include *"summer soirees on the roof of the Strand office, with Pimms and champagne."* There are *"lots of client dos,"* and the firm's annual summer party took place this year at London Zoo (though we don't think the animals themselves are clients). Not even the gators. There are a number of sports teams too. *"It's the kind of place where you can just start something up."* What, like urban myths about reptiles?

And it has a gym. But it's very small. *"It has everything there; lots of blokes in the firm use it. It's just… very small."* Perhaps lacking the space to exercise their testosterone is the reason why *"there is no macho culture in Lawrence Graham."*

and finally…

The recent review of working practices hasn't created a magic circle environment although, if the increase in chargeable hours continues, some changes may be noticed. *"If you didn't like it here, you would struggle to work anywhere."* So what would improve Lawrence Graham? On the sweltering July day when we interviewed trainees, one of them had the answer. *"If we could just get the air conditioning sorted out, that would be great."*

Laytons

the facts

Location: Bristol, Guildford, London, Manchester
UK ranking by size: 100
Total number of trainees: 18
Seats: See individual offices
Alternative Seats: None

Laytons has four offices in four very different locations. Commercial work is its common thread. Each office may *"have its own particular strengths"* and its own recruitment procedures, but how else do you tell one Laytons office from another?

the geography lesson

"Each office is equal; Laytons is not London-centric," and the branches attract work in their own right. *"The offices are independent yet inter-dependent.* [ooh! almost sounds like psychobabble] *It depends on what matter you are dealing with, who the client is and where the expertise is."* We became confused at this point, so a trainee helped us out with an illustration of Laytons' working practices. *"Within dispute resolution there is an employment team. That team liases with the national employment team. Within each office different departments rely on each other for various aspects of their work."*

Perhaps the best example of working together comes in relation to High Court hearings. The proximity of the London office to the High Court means that the capital's litigators provide support to all the other offices. But in spite of this co-operation on work, the national intranet system and *"national teams,"* geography has a powerful effect. One trainee admitted, *"I haven't even been to the other offices. We do seem to work independently."*

the maths lesson

Let's talk about the training contract. Manchester and London adopt a standard four by six-month seat rotation. With a limited number of practice groups in Manchester, trainees have no choice over seats, but move between company/commercial, dispute resolution, property and family. However, trainees pointed out that *"departments are not made too distinct. You will do different things in just one seat."* London trainees feel that matters are slightly more flexible in their office, with the possibility of repeating certain seats if strongly desired.

Guildford and Bristol are more unusual. Two seats of nine months are accompanied by one seat of six months. While it might be nice to think that this is the result of enlightenment, following the advice of a Feng Shui expert who specialises in legal training, the reality is that there's a more limited number of practice groups in these offices. Indeed, the firm is close to switching to a to a humdrum four by six-month rotation in these offices.

manchester: distinguished family

Manchester looks to recruit trainees with local roots. The family department (a niche practice within the firm) succeeds in attracting some *"high-profile clients,"* and trainees find work here *"exciting."* The Manchester office has clung to its old home (*"with a conservatory"*) in a converted building in St. John Street, at the heart of Manchester's legal community. It's a short step to the chambers of the city's leading barristers. But make no mistake; it's not all private client work. One Manchester trainee was keen to stress the wealth of regional corporate clients that instruct the office and the interesting work in corporate finance and venture capital being undertaken by the firm's lawyers. Although it has a pleasant atmosphere, trainees felt that the office would benefit from *"more social events"* and that they themselves would like *"more appraisals."*

london: gravy boats

The trainees in the London office indicated that supervisors were *"good at nurturing you"* and praised the level of feedback from *"partners who are fairly amenable to going down to the pub for a chat."* The London office sits right on the Thames on Victoria Embankment, opposite the OXO Tower so *"the meeting rooms have wonderful views."* In London the emphasis is on company/commercial work and for such a modestly sized office, it packs a pretty big punch. We sneaked a look at its corporate client and deals lists and spotted plenty of international work and some sexy clients. Po Na Na and Red Bull both instruct Laytons' London office for their corporate deals and there's been plenty going on in the hi-tech start-up market.

bristol: keen as mustard

The Bristol office may lack any distinctive architectural features, (which is a shame, given its strong construction practice) but fear not, it's certainly not lacking in ambition. Trainees told us that the partners were *"very, very keen on marketing and bringing in more clients."* The partners also seem as keen as mustard in their approach to training. One source said, *"you are a fee earner from the very beginning,"* working alongside *"partners that are keen to let you know your strengths and weaknesses."* This isn't foreboding at all, with trainees reporting the firm's desire to keep the branch *"like a family network."* Well that's nice.

guildford: va va voom

Having outgrown them, the Guildford branch grudgingly moved out of its old Edwardian buildings in Hampton Court and now occupies two floors in a new modern office block. One trainee told us, *"it's a big leap to tinted windows and air-conditioning!"* Still, the new route to work must be a refreshing change for the partners of this office, where there is *"definitely a cult of motorbikes."* The office relocation apparently generated a lot of *"Surrey media interest."* Great news for a branch whose *"aim is to be number one"* in the county. Trainees told us that the work of the Guildford office is *"very much focused on the big house-builders. Commercial property buys the land and then, after development, it handles the sale of individual plots."* Top marks for supervising partners. They let you *"see a job through to the end"* and provide *"instant feedback all the time."*

ahoy there!

The firm builds by *"employing the same kind of people." "You have to fit in with the culture of Laytons"* and this years qualifiers would seem to have done so; the firm retained them all. With such a small trainee population, this means an absence of competitiveness and usually more than enough attention from partners to go round. Trainees will occasionally move between offices, but this is not a regular feature of the training contract. The only universal experience seems to be the promotional *"bright green umbrellas! Really embarrassing to walk around with!"* Pretty useful in the rain though, we bet…

> "In the Guildford office there is definitely a cult of motorbikes."

For the sporty types the European football tour was a real winner. Indeed, each office offers various sports teams, but we were unable to find out which office performed best on the field. Also on the sporting front, Laytons hosts an annual sailing regatta for staff and clients. *"We splash around in the Solent for a bit"* and (if the post-match activities on the football tour are anything to go by) presumably then find a suitable watering hole. Trainees recommend even the driest of landlubbers set course for the regatta as it's a good mixer. One said, *"I met some of the other trainees for the first time at the sailing."* It may be a rare occasion that the firm gets together *en masse* but it does happen at the annual ball. Vodka and Red Bulls all round!

and finally…

Around half of the firm's work is corporate and commercial, with property coming in as the second of the biggest practice areas. Litigation, employment, insolvency and a smattering of private client work (including family) complete the picture. Laytons may not be the first name you'll come across in your search for a training contract, but its reputation is not to be sniffed at.

Lester Aldridge

the facts
Location: Bournemouth, Southampton
UK ranking by size: 120
Total number of trainees: 11
Seats: 4x6 months
Alternative Seats: Occasional secondments

First Bournemouth and now Southampton, commercial player Lester Aldridge is raising its profile on the south coast. If you're thinking of applying, you'll be pleased to hear the firm's name carries further than Dorset and Hampshire.

driving the merc

Trainees tell us that there's more going on at Lester Aldridge than you'd think. *"We are seeking to be a regional player on the commercial side,"* one source declared. Rather than just local businesses, *"we have some very big clients… BP and Mercedes, for example."* Another trainee explained, *"we want to expand. It is very much a driven firm."* This is not parochial south-coast work then? Oh no. *"There are London firms on the other side of transactions."*

Developing this theme, trainees were keen to point out that they feel they *"get more responsibility than trainees at London firms."* But the limitations of training with a smaller practice do sometimes hit home. *"The seats on offer will always be a product of the business needs of the firm."* A trainee observed, *"we all understand that it is a business and they have to decide where they need people, but it does sometimes mean we don't get experience where we might want it."* However, it isn't unheard of for the firm to *"create a seat if necessary."*

The majority of the firm's work is in litigation, corporate and banking. There's also a significant private client department, (top-ranked by *Chambers Guide* in the South) which amounts to a fifth of the firm's workload. Are you surprised? This is practically the retirement capital of England – there must be a few folk wanting to set their financial affairs in order before settling down in a deckchair on the pier for the next 15 years. There's a unit that focuses entirely on immigration and a specialist debt recovery service known as 'LA Fast Track'.

baywatch

Sun, sea, sand and if you're sick of the grind of study or London, then come to LA and hit the beach! Listen to this, "*You can eat your sandwiches on the beach and some staff go for a swim during lunch.*" Sounds more California cool than Sterident and bifocals. Ah ha… we finally get to the heart of the matter. Bournemouth has an unjustly earned reputation for being a retirement town. Trainees tell us "*it is not actually full of old people. It's a fairly decent part of England to be in.*" "*A pleasant atmosphere, sunshine and a fair buzz.*"

Our sources indicated that the firm wants to attract redbrick university graduates and knows that it needs to recruit "*people who will stay after training and who will be quite happy to be in Bournemouth and take it for what it has to offer.*" There's been a real problem in past years with trainees high-tailing it off to the City after qualification. It's a problem that all regional firms have faced, but particularly those in the south. Understandably Lester Aldridge is not looking for those who'll do a two-year stretch in the south and then follow the scent of City salaries. They are succeeding. The 2001 batch of qualifiers were all offered jobs and four of the five stayed put.

rising up the firm

The relatively new Southampton office takes just one trainee at a time. Informal client secondments out of the 'Fast Track' debt recovery department are available to "*large clients in Canary Wharf.*" Hours are reasonable. One trainee confirmed that the usual day was "*9am-5.30pm. I have never felt pressed to stay late.*" Commenting on extremes, one source observed "*I might be in the office until 6pm-6.30pm sometimes.*" But there's no idling; "*we all have billing targets. They want to see us out there, being commercial and drawing in clients. You are given a fair degree of instruction in terms of marketing. The firm sees a lawyer as a practitioner and a marketer.*"

There is a clear incentive to rise up in this firm. The seven-floor building has lovely sea views from the fifth floor upwards. Secure an office on one of these floors and you can do your work looking out onto the ocean (OK, the Channel). Since the appointment of a new managing partner, Lester Aldridge has been on a mission to become more sociable. Dress-down Fridays were introduced and once a month (after work) staff ascend to the seventh floor boardroom for 'Happy Hour' drinks. The firm's regular watering hole is Downes Wine Bar. A trainee observed: "*We are all there, from the senior partner right down to the most junior admin assistant.*"

barking mad

Lester Aldridge pulled a rather novel promotion tool out of its box recently. The 'Shockingly Normal' campaign featured photographs of partners emblazoned on large postcards, adopting a variety of bizarre positions. Although unlikely to become collectors' series, you may wish to keep an eye open for 'Suited partner on beach on one leg clutching surfboard' or even 'Partner ironing'. It's one way of getting noticed. Whatever next?

More eccentricity maybe… One partner brings his dog into work each day. "*Sparkle*" is described as "*part of the furniture.*" Said canine "*wanders around the floors. It will come and pester you for your sandwich and even grab the food off your desk.*" Fortunately, Sparkle remains popular and we couldn't uncover any plans to balance some sandwiches on the window ledge of that seventh floor boardroom.

and finally…
"An approachable firm, with a good solid training that you can enjoy." This firm certainly has ambitions, as proved by its bold move into the Southampton market. Some might argue that this is the most likely south coast arena for high quality commercial work and that it's the only way that Lester Aldridge can grow. By the time students reading this start their training contracts, the firm will have had two years to establish itself in the city and matters will be clearer.

Lewis Silkin

the facts
Location: London
UK ranking by size: 98
Total number of trainees: 12
Seats: 4x6 months
Alternative Seats: None

Lewis Silkin is a firm with an irreverent character, so it says. There's a notion amongst employees that this firm has something special – they call it 'silkiness'. We were keen to find out whether the declarations of difference were a reality or just super-slick marketing hype from a firm that has learnt a thing or two from its advertising agency clients over the years.

goldilocks and the free beers
In spite of the firm's reputation in certain areas of work, notably employment, advertising and social housing, most trainees told us that it was the profile of the firm as a whole that attracted them. *"I wanted a firm in London that was not too large and not too small,"* one trainee said. *"I looked at the brochure and it looked more like a left wing firm; it has its roots in Peckham… Somewhere like Clifford Chance is not my thing. Those places are like an extension of the tube – everyone avoids eye contact until they get to their own area."* So be prepared to get to know everyone at Lewis Silkin pretty quickly. *"As long as you're not shy that's fine. And those with high opinions of themselves or who are arrogant won't enjoy it here. There's a certain sort at law school who are not going to fit in."* So, this is a not too small, but not too big firm for the not too quiet, but not too over-confident type. Right…

Earlier in 2001 the firm moved from its old home in Victoria Street, SW1 (*"civil servant land"*) to the offices formerly occupied by Withers, just north of Fleet Street. It moved its trendy designer furniture into the reception and started referring to itself as a City firm. OK, so technically it's not actually the City, but what's half a mile between professionals. *"There was a groundswell of concern amongst assistants before we moved,"* one source told us. The assistants put forward a list of their concerns about going 'City'. *"There were concerns that the firm would become a billing machine when we moved, we'd be paying higher rent and our charge out rates would go up. Everything seemed to be being done in a rather Machiavellian, cloak and dagger way and partners couldn't talk like before."* But the move has been well received. *"It's a hell of a nicer office to work in"* and *"near to barristers chambers, the High Court and other lawyers."* Down in the basement the firm has its own canteen, a good location for the end of month drinks parties.

the ivy or the canteen?
Staff canteens often act like a barometer for the atmosphere within a firm. *"On any given day you'll get a pretty good mix of lawyers in there. You'll stroll down and just see a table of people and go and sit with them. Roger* [senior partner] *and Trevor* [managing partner] *will be in there and Roger will say 'come and sit over here.'"* Now we happen to know that Roger Alexander quite often lunches at The Ivy and, given the meeja orientation of the diners there, it's probably where he learned the art of pulling aside a chair for those strolling past his table.

In some senses the firm is a bit of a duality. Slick and media-savvy on the one hand and brown rice and social conscience on the other. *"It does give a damn about the bloke next door and it wants to work for RSLs*

[Housing Associations]," one trainee said. Another told us how he had enjoyed *"dealing with ordinary people's problems, but at a non-high street level."* Applicants who see themselves as *"a little more ethical than most"* or as wanting to work for a firm that is *"not after the mega bucks, but getting it right for clients"* should look at this firm.

this season's fashions
Unless you work in either social housing or construction, you might not come across the 'right on' clients. Those you'll encounter will have a style of their own though. Be prepared for your client to be way cooler than you are and to be wearing a much trendier suit… if he wears one at all. The firm has a full time dress down policy, which ranges from *"suit no tie"* in litigation, through the *"chino man"* look in property and corporate to the odd Hawaiian shirt in IP/media areas, where *"the combats come out."* The general rules are that lawyers dress to suit their clients and that sitting at your desk in a suit and tie is *"silly."*

> "IP/media and employment are hot seats… you can effectively guarantee one or the other."

"IP and media have become hot seats." There's two available at each rotation and they are almost always seen as second year seats. Employment falls into the same category and, again, there are two seats available at any one time. With only six trainees recruited each year, this means that you can effectively guarantee one or the other, *"although you can't necessarily do both."* First years invariably do a property seat and either a general litigation or a general corporate seat.

pavlov's dog
Aspiring employment lawyers will note that the firm is a leading name in this area of work. Indeed, the employment team (which ten years ago was barely more than one man and a dog) has expanded like a science experiment gone wrong and was described by one of our sources as *"an amorphous blob on the third floor."* It also gets a good deal of the publicity afforded to the firm by the media. So are the non-employment lawyers just a teeny weeny bit jealous of their terribly popular colleagues? *"The employment team has a distinct position. They organise nights out together and are close as a team. It is pretty self-contained, but it doesn't feel like it's dominating the firm."* There's a rule of thumb – if a face doesn't ring a bell *"they must be an employment lawyer."*

Recognising everyone seems to be important at Lewis Silkin and *"largely, people get on well. It's rare to find tensions… if there's a firm event there will be a high turn out across the board."* One trainee told us that partners *"have hearts"* and we assumed from this that they also have pulses. *"Some are more serious than others, some are busier than others. The partners with a social conscience and those with a commercial side all get on fine with each other."* If a partner barks at you, it's likely you'll get an apology or an explanation afterwards.

the billion pound vision
We started looking for the 'but'. Our sources told us it was the pay. If you are happy earning less than many of your contemporaries at large City firms and can see yourself saying something like: *"You're generally pretty well paid as a lawyer – sure I could get paid more elsewhere, but I don't mind. Maybe I'm just foolish,"* then apply. Traditionally, Lewis Silkin has paid less than City outfits, but the office move seems to have had an uplifting effect on salaries; having checked them out, they ain't that bad. The other 'but' is the volume and size of transactions. One trainee said, *"don't come here for the biggest transactions in the world or to see your firm's name on the financial pages." "If you have a billion pound vision of being super-corporate boy, it's a waste of time applying."* But these trainees are disparaging of *"the biggest corporate deals for companies that make ball bearings."* They

want their deals to be for sexy, stimulating and interesting clients. Ball bearings? No. Ad agencies, restaurants or community housing co-operatives? That's fine.

Lewis Silkin presents itself as a lifestyle firm, where the balance between working hours and play and the family can be met. It's not stupid, it knows that this is what will attract new talent to the firm. Having a life does seem to be a genuine tenet of the firm's ideology. It is part of the silkiness that trainees have learned to speak of.

disappearing act

9am-6.30pm is a regular day. Some may go earlier, say, in property where commonly they have less interest. Others may stay longer, if their enthusiasm and eagerness to impress overrides their desire to pop down to the Cheshire Cheese for a couple of pints. If you want to work until the early hours in the corporate department, you'll have that opportunity, but don't expect to block off too many pages in your diary for 'midnight champagne completions' or 'proofing till dawn'.

If life's so great, then why doesn't everyone stay when they qualify? Three out of 2000's qualifiers are still at the firm and in September 2001, a massive two out of six remained post-qualification even though *"there were seven jobs on paper."* Hmmm: *"If it reflects badly on the firm, it's a shame that it does."* A couple of the departees are leaving the law already. One's gone into publishing and the other into teaching. A third was looking for a job as a sports lawyer and the fourth just wanted to leave the country.

and finally…

Lewis Silkin is just a little bit cooler than many firms in a non-moneyed, unglamorous way. It's doing deals for interesting clients and taking a leading role in employment, advertising and social housing. If you simply can't see yourself at a blue-blooded firm or working as a tiny component in a big machine on a mega-deal then you'll probably fit in.

Linklaters

the facts
Location: London
UK ranking by size: 4
Total number of trainees: 286
Seats: 4x6 months
Alternative Seats: Overseas seats, secondments
Extras: Pro Bono: Newham Rights Law Centre, Free Representation Unit, language training

"Well done! You've got what it takes to make a legal hot-shot. Now all you have to do is apply, get an offer, pass your degree, qualify and you'll be all set for a glittering career at Linklaters." Following our abysmal performance on the Linklaters website legal skills test last year (when we were advised to join a circus) the 2002 team were delighted to receive this ringing endorsement of our lawyering skills. Either Linklaters' standards are slipping or we're getting better at fudging tests. Before we take it up on its kind offer though, we thought we would find out a bit more about the firm.

it's magic!

Linklaters is one of the five mega-firms with a membership card for the *très* exclusive magic circle. For its lawyers this means blue chip clients, big billing, whopping salaries and long hours. The firm has an outstanding reputation in almost every single commercial practice area. Applicants need to be super-bright with an impressive CV. Language skills are described as "advantageous," as so much of the work is cross-border. Linklaters is the linchpin of Linklaters & Alliance, a huge collection of top quality European law firms. Linklaters' London office is the nerve centre of this operation.

The question we really wanted an answer to was 'what is the difference between Linklaters and its magic circle peers?' In short, why would you choose this magic circle firm over the four others? One of the problems magic circle applicants have is that, on paper, the five firms look similar. One way of distinguishing between the magnificent five is to base your decision upon the trainee stereotypes. Slaughters are allegedly arrogant and ruthless, Freshfields are floppy-haired, blond Oxbridge types (think Hugh Grant if he joined a gym and got highlights), Clifford Chance are that little bit more egalitarian and diverse, Allen & Overy folk are friendlier. Legend has it that Linklaters trainees are very career minded and ambitious. Whilst making a decision based upon these stereotypes might be a little more accurate than tossing a coin, we hope to provide our readers with something a bit more constructive. As one trainee told us *"it is great to be told how much brighter we are than everyone else but, with my hand on my heart, I am not sure it is 100% true!"* So modest!

separated at birth?

Within the magic circle, it is often hardest to distinguish between Linklaters and Freshfields. In some ways (reputation, practice areas, size and profitability) the two might have been separated at birth. One significant difference is in the number of trainees at each firm. Linklaters boasts an impressive 257 trainees to Freshfields 155. This has implications for the trainees' working environment. First, the good news: *"I haven't ever worked a weekend. In corporate, if there was a load of work to get through, a partner would give it to us to share out amongst the trainees. I would take evenings and someone else would work through the weekend according to our preferences."* Next, the bad news: *"It isn't always the way, but often on the big deals you can just get stuck doing really low grade work. It is very disheartening, but there are not always enough of the smaller deals to go round such a huge trainee population."*

culture shock

Quality of work is part of the conundrum trainees at the mega-firms face. The benefits of cutting your teeth on huge deals with blue chip clients are clear; you'll see nothing but the highest calibre of lawyering going on around you. The problem is, no matter how bright you are, the firm isn't going to give you the opportunity to lose its clients' money. The bigger the firm, the bigger the deal, the smaller the trainee's input into the final product. On a big-ticket deal there can be an awful lot of low responsibility work.

One trainee told us *"In my first seat there was something of a culture shock. I hadn't been prepared for quite how grinding the work could prove to be. When we were under pressure, the hours almost made me weep, especially having been a student for the last five years!"* The firm is aware of this problem and does try to ensure trainees are not stuck with such work all the time. *"The situation is better than it used to be, we have more organised teams of paralegals who do most of the admin work. At the end of the day, why should the client be paying for a trainee solicitor to do basic paperwork?"*

man on the moon

Returning to the stereotypes, one Linklaters myth (which seems to hold true), is just how 'keen' the trainees are. One source told us *"Whatever you do on a deal, it is a brilliant feeling when you read about it on the front cover of The Wall Street Journal the next day. You might just have done admin, but you get a feel for the impact of the firm's work."* Speaking to trainees, we were reminded of the story of a cleaner at Cape Canaveral who, when asked by the President what he did for NASA, put down his broom and said "I'm helping put a man on the moon." In a similar show of team spirit, commitment to the good ship Linklaters emerged when some interviewees enthused about the (often) mundane nature of the work. *"We are always kept briefed on the significance of what we are doing. Even if I am just photocopying files, I can read them and follow what is going on. I am always a part, if only a small part, of a much greater whole."*

Whether trainees are just proofreading or running smaller deals themselves, enthusiasm is essential to getting on at Linklaters. *"You need to buy into the spirit and appreciate that, whatever you are doing, you are playing your role within the team."* This is not to say Linklaters' trainees dream of leaving the firm in a golden coffin after 40 years service. The prospects of a calmer life outside the magic circle commonly entice Linklaters' assistants. They are like gold dust in the recruitment market – and they know it! As one trainee put it *"most people are keeping an open mind on qualification. It's one thing to believe in the firm, the work and what you are doing, but another to decide that this is all you want to do with your life."* Or as another trainee said, rather cockily, *"There isn't a single-mindedness to stay within Linklaters. Most of us think we might be partners, but equally we might leave a few years after qualifying. It's great to have that choice."* Well, if you do some very basic maths, you'll see only a tiny proportion of each trainee intake ever make partnership. The rest… well, the world's their oyster. It's a tough life.

health warning

We couldn't write about training in the magic circle without mentioning the hours. There's no escaping it; the hours can be hardcore. Those huge salaries are there for a reason. *"Corporate is certainly the hardest seat. Average hours in some teams can be from 9am through to 10pm or later."* As we've already mentioned, supervisors can be flexible about how tasks are divvied up, but whether you put the hours in at the weekend or in the evening, if the work needs doing, you will be office bound. *"This is a crucial issue now, particularly in the corporate and finance departments. We are a service industry; one that's on call 24 hours a day."* Corporate is very big at Linklaters, it is a compulsory seat but die-hards can take the option to repeat and spend a year in the department.

Most trainees, whilst not happy about the hours, are resigned to the inevitable. *"It is in the gift of the client now. Whenever they ask for something to be turned around in double-quick time it is expected that we will work through the night to do it."* But there was some criticism of the double-quick culture. *"Sometimes a deadline will be set and we do wonder if it is quite necessary. Perhaps people are a little too willing to see us put in 90 hour weeks."* Whichever way you look at it, if you want to work at Linklaters, you will have to accept that it carries a social life health warning. Departments other than corporate and finance carry slightly lower hours.

pu-lease

A key part of the Linklaters' experience is its burgeoning international practice. Some trainees cited the international nature of the work and the expansionist perspective of the firm as one of the reasons they applied in the first place. *"Linklaters has big plans for global expansion,"* one trainee explained. *"It underlines the ambition that drives the firm forwards. I wanted to be part of a firm that is going places."* Overseas offices mean overseas seats for trainees. And you won't have to knife anyone in the back to get the chance to travel. *"Pretty much everyone who wants to go overseas will get the opportunity, quite a few people go twice!"*

Trainees have a wide range of destinations to choose from. Offices offering secondments include the ever popular New York, Hong Kong, Tokyo and Singapore and the much less sought after Frankfurt and Munich. We heard it's become so hard to find volunteers for Germany that the firm has resorted to 'bribery.' *"If you really want to go to New York or another over-subscribed seat then you can volunteer to go to Germany first time round and they will repay the favour!"* The list of locations is almost endless and client secondments are also available.

the fresher approach

A few years ago Linklaters attempted to inject new life into its training with a radically redesigned programme – 'the Fresh Approach'. It included frequent contact with trainees whilst still at law school and an accelerated process by which trainees chose the department they would qualify into. The choice was so accelerated that trainees found themselves plumping for a qualification job during the first few weeks of the training contract. Hastily made decisions could be reversed, but many trainees were uneasy about making such an important decision without sufficient experience to enable informed choice. To be fair, the HR department was quick to react to this unease. The situation now is one whereby the best parts of the Fresh Approach have been retained, most notably integration into the beating heart of the firm through contact with students at law school. Trainees are now consulted about where they want to qualify during their third seat.

looking after their own
Socially, the scene mirrors that at Freshfields, with many trainees taking the view that they see quite enough of their colleagues during the working day (and night). *"The firm organises quite a few activities – annual balls, sports and nights out… as a general rule I prefer to spend my spare time with people who have nothing to do with work!"* For those interested in burning the candle at both ends, there are certainly opportunities; *"You tend to socialise quite a bit with your intake. Some of us got on quite well together at law school. Others had gone to university together."* Ah yes… university chums. We note that a large proportion (and quite possibly the majority) of trainees graduated from Oxford and Cambridge.

When you find yourself stuck on difficult and boring deals, the Linklaters *esprit de corps* comes to the rescue. *"I am currently on a terrible deal – to be honest the work has been pretty miserable – but the partners looked after us socially, which helps make up a bit for being shafted work-wise."* Trainees tended to congregate either in local pubs such as The King's Tavern for quick post work affairs, with the Barbican and Smithfield areas popular for more concerted late night drinking.

and finally…
Linklaters would offer any bright, articulate and hard working law (or non-law) student a sensational opportunity to learn the legal and practical skills required to work on high value corporate deals. Corporate work is the currency of this firm and as a trainee you'll see plenty of it. The best advice we can give to any aspiring Linklaters trainee is make sure you are prepared not just to give it a go, but to give it your all.

Lovells

the facts
Location: London
UK ranking by size: 9
Total number of trainees: 109
Seats: 4x6 months
Alternative seats: Overseas seats, secondments
Extras: Pro Bono: Privy Council death row appeals, language training

The last couple of years has seen Lovells "careering through Europe like a runaway train" (*The Lawyer* 20.11.00). For Lovells' current crop of trainees this is no ordinary English train – it's a big, swift, safe, clean and luxurious one. Passenger satisfaction is almost 100% and they'll travel with the company again. Other trainee operators beware!

your friendly eurostar
Lovells' reputation as the City's Mr Nice Guy survived yet another year of True Picture interviews with trainees. They spoke of a friendly and forgiving environment with an almost luvvy-duvvy atmosphere. But the firm packs a strong corporate punch. It is one of the largest in the City and is expanding in Europe. It has no particular specialist profile, preferring to remain a good all-rounder.

getting on board
Why apply? *"I wanted a top ten firm for the experience, the chance of a foreign secondment and I needed to find a way to pay for law school."* This response is a fairly standard one, but why Lovells? *"The top ten firms are much of a muchness and in the end it comes down to personal taste and this was mine."* *"It had a good reputation among students and a friend here seemed to be enjoying it more than friends at other firms."* There's no magic formula. It seems that most were not thinking Lovells-or-nothing, but when it came round to the interview stage, the firm charmed them with its *"genuinely friendly approach."*

finding your seat

Trainees are generally happy with the seat allocation, telling us that *"you'll get your first choice at some stage."* The most sought after is IP (*"popular because it's wide-ranging"*) and there's been an increase in applications for banking and corporate seats. The property seat is known to be one where *"you have your own files and issues like a real solicitor."* Litigation is also valued for giving *"more responsibility and client contact than others."* Naturally, trainees have mixed experiences, but most speak on the phone to clients and other solicitors. Most have had more responsibility than they had anticipated. One trainee told us of *"holding my own meeting and finalising an agreement after six months at Lovells,"* another of being *"thrown in at the deep end, but the seniors really helped me out. It's not a question of sink or swim."*

> "It's a relaxed, but not laid back environment, which can get hectic."

Industry secondments and foreign placements are popular. Secondments are available to clients like Barclays, BAT, Esso, 3i, John Lewis, Prudential and Merck. The firm offers eight overseas placements to Brussels, Frankfurt, Hong Kong, Moscow, New York, Paris, Prague and Tokyo. There are no language requirements except for Germany and, to a lesser extent, France. Seats abroad not only offer the excitement of living in another country, but because the offices tend to be smaller, *"you get more responsibility and there's a wide span of work."*

getting up to speed

At first the learning curve is steep and *"it can get quite stressful when you're in the middle of something and you can't speak to anyone,"* but *"you don't feel too out of your depth; the partners don't push you too much."* Although *"sometimes you don't understand things as the deal's going on, you can ask afterwards."* Each new seat comes with training sessions to get you up to speed. Hours can be long, especially in banking and corporate. *"At first some hours are a shock. In one department I was there till midnight on my first day and all night on my second day."* But trainees rarely work weekends and the hours do level themselves out. It's usually a *"relaxed, but not laid back"* environment, which *"can get hectic, so you need a pragmatic approach and you need to remember that the rewards outweigh the bad times."* *"Sometimes it's not so nice doing due diligence at four in the morning, but you get out of it what you put in and your hard work is appreciated."*

During the training contract you'll have an opportunity to do pro bono work, an area in which Lovells has always been active. Trainees have worked for charities, environmental groups and the Big Issue (not selling it though) amongst others, although it seems they do less and less as their training contract moves on – *"I did a lot of pro bono work in my first seat, but I don't do so much now."* Away from work, the social scene is an active one. Those we spoke to were looking forward to go-karting, Dragon Boat racing and ensuring the softball team remained *"the best in London."* Some had been involved in corporate days out, taking clients to rugby internationals and playing golf.

customer satisfaction

As in all firms, you will receive feedback on your performance. *"After each six-month seat you write 2-3 pages of what you thought about the seat. The department responds and then you discuss. You've always got the opportunity to disagree and they encourage you to have your own opinion. It's very constructive."* Half of our interviewees had taken up the offer of a three-month appraisal, saying *"you need to know how you're performing whilst you're on the job."* (Gosh!) Some trainees stressed the importance of appraisals; they *"play a big part in getting what you want on qualification."*

do you really like it?

Generally, trainees found it easy to raise issues. One said, *"I was sceptical of the open door policy, but they really do listen."* In addition to a seat supervisor, trainees have a mentor/contact partner to whom they *"chat to about seats or tactics or problems."* Depending on the partner, this system can work very well as *"they're mostly very responsive."* The graduate recruitment staff came in for particular praise in our interviews. *"They follow everything up and make an effort for you."* A Trainee Committee meets to discuss (mainly) social events, but also provides a forum to raise training issues.

we're lovin' it, lovin' it, lovin' it

The variety of work on offer at Lovells appeals to many – *"I wanted a wide training contract and they've given me the opportunity to do what I wanted to do. Friends at other City firms have really had to fight to get the seats they wanted."* The firm's recent European drive has not gone unnoticed. *"It's forward looking and there's ambition,"* said one trainee, whilst another enthused, *"you definitely feel it's international and you deal a lot with overseas clients."* There's almost a sense of deep gratitude to the firm and the practical effect is a good rate of retention on qualification. 95% of September 2001s NQs stayed.

passenger profile

Trainees are keen, hard working and ambitious. They seem to have perfected the art of enthusing. *"It's exciting when you get a big deal done or when you see what you've been working on in the papers."* They also value straight-talking; *"I like the way the firm lives up to what it promised in the brochure."* When asked what kind of people they thought the firm recruited, our sources mentioned *"dedication, a willingness to take part in the culture of the group, people who are friendly, relaxed and who have the ability to get on with others."*

There is certainly an element of the group being more important than the individuals – *"they want people who fit into the environment."* *"The culture fits me,* it's a happy place and it's easy to talk to people."* The open door, *"no lines drawn"* policy extends down to the Bottle Scrue, the firm's local, where partners and trainees buy each other drinks. *"Partners treat you well."* One can't help but think the firm should be called 'Luvvies' with all this mutual admiration.

automated ticket sales

Trainees believed they were part of a group where *"there's no average characteristic."* *"There's a mixture of law and non-law, some who have worked, and the ages of my intake ranged from about 22 to 29."* You also need a little extra on your CV – *"There are people who are sporty, well-travelled and into music. At the interview they seemed very interested in my extra-curricular activities."* You've got to have a team-ethic and you've got to be well balanced; this is no place for eccentrics. Indeed, we did wonder if it's really a place for the exceptional. The trainees' responses to some of our questions were generally fairly bland and things they thought exceptional are, in reality, the rule rather than the exception.

Having more than good grades on your CV is not an exceptional requirement; recruiting non-law grads is perfectly normal and having an interest in travel, sport or music is not daringly different. One trainee thought it important that we stress Lovell's willingness to recruit from state as well as public schools, yet it would be incredible if any large law firm did otherwise. There's no room here for rocking the boat and individuality is not the first characteristic that springs to mind. These comments may sound harsh, but it's one possible explanation why different trainees' answers to some of our questions were word for word the same!

In the end most trainees are the gap year, top-drawer British university stock. We sometimes adopt a 'school days' classification of trainees. These aren't the head boys and girls, the sports captains, those with that *je ne sais quoi*, but the nice, harmless, uncomplaining and clever ones – the goody-goodies.

and finally…

So where's the catch? Well there isn't one if you know you want to be a City lawyer. The firm may not be considered part of the magic circle, but it's a top London firm and the work won't differ from the work done by magic circle trainees. There's no doubt that these are some of the friendliest and happiest of all the ambitious people you'll meet in the Square Mile. Don't cock a snook at Lovells for being so lovely as, more often than not, the difference between a miserable training contract and a great one lies with your work colleagues.

Macfarlanes

the facts

Location: London
UK ranking by size: 43
Total number of trainees: 34
Seats: 4x6 months
Alternative Seats: Secondments
Extras: Pro bono: Privy Council death row appeals, Tower Hamlets Law Centre

A smallish City practice which punches high above its weight and is sometimes thought of as a mini-Slaughter and May. The hallmark is quality and the long held reputation is for small 'c' conservatism. The former is about as likely to change as we are to join the Bolshoi Ballet, but the latter is coming under threat. Leading the charge is 'Beanie man', who makes an appearance on the firm's website and on the bookmark in this guide.

ready to work?

What can you expect if you decide to train at Macfarlanes? For starters, the trainees are generally regarded as being an exceptionally bright lot, which perhaps fits the firm's *"sometimes rather academic atmosphere."* Macfarlanes' trainees tell us that the firm has a *"chilled"* atmosphere (although we'd like to stress that they don't mean Ibiza chilled – more like cool, calm and collected chilled). No matter how it's defined, chilled doesn't equate to lazy days. Training is structured in such a way that recruits take on considerable responsibility at an early stage and maybe more so than at other City firms. *"There is an emphasis on hitting the ground running. You are paid from day one and are expected to get on with it from day one. It is quite a challenge."*

Most interviewees felt that this baptism of fire, whilst a daunting induction, was the best way to pick up the skills they would need on qualification. In some firms, when trainees are expected to make a flying start, they become snowed under with work in their attempts to impress with their multi-tasking skills. Sometimes trainees find it hard to say no to the demands of partners. A relatively simple device is employed at Macfarlanes to prevent this from happening. *"Every week we fill in a form which details how much work we have on – it ranges from 'Ready To Work'* [bored] *to 'Help'* [help]." In some departments, only trainees fill in these sheets, in others they are used by all fee earners. *"It is much easier to fill in the form with everyone else than to go and complain to a partner that you are overworked."* Macfarlanes has an outstanding reputation in corporate work and is instructed on headline grabbing deals on a regular basis. Recent highlights included acting for Saatchi & Saatchi on a £4 billion acquisition and advising Virgin over the sale of a 49% stake in Virgin Atlantic.

forces of conservatism?

Macfarlanes seems to have its own distinctive way of doing things. This is often put down to what has been described as the firm's 'conservative' approach, perhaps implying a conventional and unadventurous style. The trainees we spoke to felt Macfarlanes' style was typified by a quiet professional confidence. *"We really aren't a conservative firm. That rumour is just perpetuated by legal guides."* Miaow! But surely this perception must have come from somewhere? *"It is more about professionalism. I can't believe that we are that* different from other firms… if conservative means not wearing jeans and a baggy T shirt to meet a banking client, who isn't conservative?" On this theme, Macfarlanes has yet to succumb to the current trend to introduce a full time dress down policy. Friday is a business casual day, but we were told that a fair few trainees feel more comfortable wearing a suit.

Macfarlanes is also going its own way by retaining a diversity of work. Many firms primarily identified with their commercial work bade farewell to departments such as private client and agriculture, focusing upon smaller amounts of higher value work. Macfarlanes, however, is still proud of these practices and continues to perform superbly in both. Much of the agriculture work is investment focused rather than landed gentry, suggesting a good sense of commercial awareness mixed in with ye olde legal charm.

flexible friends

The seat rotation allows for a fair amount of flexibility. Most trainees will spend six months within one of the three core departments – company/commercial and banking, litigation, and property. There's is good news for those who want to spend more time in one or two departments. One trainee told us *"There are no really hard and fast rules. A friend of mine asked if he could stay in commercial for another seat, rather than doing property, and that was fine."* The vogue seats vary year on year, perhaps reinforcing the idea that there isn't really a particular Macfarlanes type.

The latest batch of qualifiers seemed to have had something in common though as most of those who recently received their spurs chose to move into the corporate department. In terms of the smaller departments, we received a pretty broad endorsement for employment and tax and financial planning seats. Hours are not short, so be prepared to really put your back into it when the workload is high, especially in the corporate and commercial seats. This does not seem to put trainees off, however. In 2001 all 15 trainees were offered a job and all bar one accepted.

stiff little fingers

There are no mixers, attractive parasols or other frills with a Macfarlanes training contract. The two years are served straight up in a stiff three fingers of London based practice. The firm has recently introduced two external seat options, however. There is a client secondment available at venture capitalists 3i, and there are two opportunities to spend six months researching in the Court of Appeal. At a time when many firms are ploughing considerable energy and resources into beefing up their overseas presence, Macfarlanes remains aloof to potential suitors attempting to woo them with offers of overseas mergers. Instead the firm flirts with the idea of international expansion by remaining close friends with a variety of legal pals in various jurisdictions. For those desperate to read about overseas travel, we did hear about an interesting perk. *"When we finished a deal, the whole team were give the choice of getting a free return ticket to either New Delhi or Las Vegas as a thank you."* Ooh… tough call.

nobody leaves

Macfarlanes runs a friendly office with good levels of social interaction between trainees, assistants and partners. One trainee said, *"I feel I can walk into anyone's office to discuss things… well perhaps not the senior partner's!"* We'll let him off on that one. Speaking of partners, there is an unusually strong loyalty amongst the brethren (around 50% Oxbridge) at Macfarlanes. According to a gentleman's agreement (which, unusually for gentleman's agreements, has actually been honoured), no partners have defected to join other firms since the early 1980s. Perhaps one explanation for the loyal partnership lies in the firm's profits. Macfarlanes does not publicise its profits, not out of shame – hovering around 40th in the UK by size, profits per partner are estimated to lie around the top ten nationwide. Go figure!

and finally…

Why did our interviewees choose Macfarlanes? *"Their reputation for training is second to none. I asked a *few people where they would train if they had their time over again and lots of people said Macfarlanes."* Yes, we hear that a lot too. Need we say more?

Manches

the facts
Location: London, Oxford
UK ranking by size: 74
Total number of trainees: 18
Seats: 4x6 months
Alternative Seats: None

Split between London and Oxford, Manches offers general commercial work and a large family department. At a time when most commercial practices have long since shed family work to focus higher value commercial work, Manches has opted to keep its highly regarded family specialism and it attracts many applicants.

town and gown
We interviewed trainees in London and Oxford and the atmosphere seemed to be broadly similar at both offices. London trainees benefit from a higher salary, more practice areas to choose from and a slightly more active social life. The London office has spurned the financial district and is tucked away in the more sedate West End surroundings of the Aldwych, a short walk from Covent Garden and Trafalgar Square. Those who head for the dreaming spires of Oxford enjoy more regular hours, a competitive salary for the region and, perhaps, a slightly more laid back atmosphere. *"The work certainly gets done but we have a calmer pace here than London. I don't know why, maybe its something in the water in the City."* Er, no!

In spite of the reputation for family work, it's important to keep sight of its largely commercial perspective. The vast majority of the firm's work is focused around corporate clients and it is in commercial areas that most of your time will be spent as a trainee. Take a look at the clients listed in the firm's promotional material and you'll see names such as Nestlé UK, Pearl Assurance, the Internet Society of England, Oxford University and Oxford University Press. Much of this work comes from the firm's strong reputation in IP and publishing.

extra time
Hours vary between the two offices and different departments, but typically trainees have their noses down from 9am-6.30pm. While neither office seems to expect trainees to work silly hours, London trainees reported working until 1am on a couple of occasions. Weekends are encroached upon only *"in exceptional circumstances and almost always by choice."* Whenever trainees stayed late, there was a sense that this was noted by supervisors. *"If you do put in the extra time it is certainly recognised and appreciated; it does make you feel valued… it is never just expected of us."*

retail therapy
The firm has an impressive commercial property department and boasts several well known retailers on its books, from high street names like WHSmith and Jigsaw to the more up market Liberty. Presumably trainees feel a rush of pride for the firm's work when they pop out for a spot of retail therapy. One of Manches' big growth areas at the moment is IP, where it has *"a real determination to push and expand the department at the moment."* It is the smaller and more niche departments (especially employment) which prove to be most popular with trainees and, with fewer seats available in these departments, there is some jostling for the places.

As a rule, the firm will attempt to allot all trainees at least one place in the niche departments over the duration of their training contract. If you are especially keen to see a particular department, make it clear where you want to go as soon as possible. Less popular were the commercial property and corporate finance seats, although we heard that *"everyone* who goes has a really good time." Whilst many trainees were initially attracted to the firm for its family reputation, those who were prepared to throw themselves into commercial areas were very glad to have had the experience. As a trainee, you will share an office with your supervisor. Often this will be a partner, but around one third of trainees share with senior assistants.

family issues

With highly rated departments in both London and Oxford, Manches family work remains a popular choice for trainees and, with plenty of bodies needed in the department, you won't need to muscle in to try your hand. *"It is pretty much accepted that almost everyone will have a go in family, so there isn't competition for the places."* We got a very good impression of 'family life' in the Oxford office, where trainees had a unanimously positive view of the experience. One told us *"The work progressed steadily in terms of difficulty and the knowledge required. I felt fortunate I was working with such patient people."*

> "Almost everyone will have a go in family, so there isn't competition."

However, some trainees in the London office felt slightly uneasy during their six months in the family seat. One told us *"I never really felt like I was trusted to get involved in the work and there was lots of photocopying."* Another trainee commented *"there wasn't really an inclusive culture in family. If you made a mistake then that was it, no second chances, you were 'demoted'."* And it gets worse *"The supervision I received was just demoralising, I didn't enjoy the seat at all."* But we spoke to another trainee who had undertaken the family seat later on in his training contract and seemed to find it both easier and more rewarding, probably because he was more experienced and felt confident enough to be more pro-active in asking for support. The trainees who had difficulties in family had much better experiences in other seats and are now happily settled at the firm.

lara croft

Last year, a couple of trainees mentioned that there was a bit of laddish culture in some departments. This year, none of the interviewees perceived this and many pointed out that the vast majority of current trainees are actually female. Whilst the majority of partners are male, there is a groundswell of strong and influential female partners who ensure Manches' claim to be a progressive law firm is more than just lip service. We put it down to the 'Lara effect'. The lovely Ms Croft is one of the firm's best known clients.

Opinion was divided on the extent of the social life at Manches. Whilst everyone found the firm to be generally friendly, trainees clearly don't live in each other's pockets. A trainee at the Oxford office told us *"Some trainees might feel the social life at work is not so good, but I prefer to keep work and social life separate. The social life is inevitably better in the London office."* One of our London sources told us that *"trainees do go out together occasionally, but any regular socialising is done on an individual basis. Partners and trainees socialise at specific events such as the Christmas party."* One trainee mentioned that the most active social bonds seemed to be those built around sport.

NQ retention was good in 2001, with the vast majority of trainees staying on post-qualification. All bar one were offered a job and two more trainees elected to leave, one to return to the north and another to see if he could hack life with the big boys at a large City firm.

and finally…

You will get the opportunity to experience a wide diversity of practice areas from corporate and IT to employment, family and private client. Manches will appeal to anyone looking to qualify as a family lawyer, or perhaps an applicant with a broad interest, who doesn't want to be tied down to one specialism before they have even begun work. Certainly, for those looking for a training contract in Oxford, it's got to be on the shortlist.

Martineau Johnson

the facts
Location: Birmingham, London
UK ranking by size: 75
Total number of trainees: 25
Seats: 6x4 months
Alternative seats: None

Martineau Johnson is an impressive firm. It not only manages to achieve great things in the commercial sphere, but leads the way in other specialised areas of work, such as education and charities/private client. Many of the strong bets in Birmingham are national firms with a number of offices throughout the UK. Like its larger and similarly independent rival, Wragge & Co, Martineaus keeps most of its lawyers in Birmingham, with just a few flying the flag in London.

six of the best
One of the first things we discovered about the Martineaus training was the popular six-seat system. Martineaus likes its trainees to cover four main areas: education or private client (large Midlands charities and landed estates, rather than old grannies' wills), litigation, property and corporate. The other two seats are usually return visits to the trainees' preferred areas of work, with a view to getting further and better pre-qualification experience. Trainees have no choice in their first seat – it's odds-on that new recruits will end up in private client, education or property. *"One of the main reasons is that these are seen as easier introduction seats and there's not an amazing amount of pressure in them."*

As one trainee pointed out, in a seat of only four months there's no point in dragging your feet. *"I've always been thrown in to work and had my supervisor saying 'You can do this can't you?' – and you do."* Indeed, one of the things that struck our researcher was how involved and in control of their work the trainees were. When we telephoned to arrange interviews, they knew their diaries inside out several days in advance – which meetings were liable to be long ones and which were liable to be cancelled. Some talked about fitting interviews in around the completion of transactions. More than most, this firm gave off the smell of busy and usefully employed trainees. OK, so it was just an impression and who are we (with hundreds of trainee interviews under our belts) to judge!

growing your own
Responsibility is felt to be appropriate, although *"property feels like a mass production seat."* That's not all bad, one trainee explained. *"In some seats you're stretched by the intellectual nature of the subject, but not the volume. In property and private client you're stretched by the volume."* So how many hours a day does it take to deal with the volume or the head scratching? Commonly, hours might be 8.30am-6.30pm. *"Officially, it's 9am-5.18pm! You need to do a minimum of 73 six-minute units per day."* Ah yes, time recording – the bane of any lawyer's day. *"If you don't record 73 units your time sheet comes back to you."* Some of the office procedures were described as *"a bit prehistoric,"* but the firm is just switching over to on-screen time recording, which might lead trainees into *"a wilderness of creativeness."* More than once we heard that Martineaus was *"fairly conservative"* and a little *"slow at responding to trends." "It will change, but slowly; certain old fashioned views are still held. It's traditional but the partnership is getting younger."* One trainee thought that the move away from *"conservative"* was well under way. *"Since I joined, about ten people have been made partners and a couple have left. The focus is changing."* We're told that Martineaus likes to *"grow its own"* partners and, consequently, *"people see good prospects here."*

anyone for tennis?

Good prospects. Maybe that's why trainees stay post-qualification. In September 2001, there was full retention, apart from one guy who moved back to Guernsey (but not, we understand, as a tax exile). Jobs were taken in corporate, IP, employment, litigation and private client. *"All of these were first choices and a property job was offered too."* Salaries are comparable to other big firms in Birmingham. The firm's got it sussed – when trainees choose their department for qualification and accept a job, their trainee salary immediately receives a boost of around 50%. Not bad and hardly indicative of a firm that's slow in responding to trends.

The London office offers one IP seat and *"it's fairly popular."* So is IP lawyer and senior partner, Bill Barker, who has a reputation regionally as *"a terribly nice chap"* and a trainee as his tennis doubles partner. If IP is at the popular end of the range of seats, then close to the other end is the trade and utilities seat. While trainees might not get a massive buzz off the work there, it does illustrate a very good point. This firm covers more than the usual standard practice areas and offers numerous niche opportunities in leading edge departments. Just as in education and charities, this firm is top-ranking in the Midlands for its energy work.

wwwalkies

The firm is housed in two buildings either side of Cathedral Square. Being in two buildings *"is not so ideal"* and *"the offices aren't terribly modern,"* but all the IT kit is bang up to date and splitting the firm in two has not affected the *"synergy between departments."* The two-minute trip between offices makes for a pleasant break in the day and the firm's resident guide dog isn't complaining. He belongs to one of the trainees. *"Winston is a legend,"* we're told. Check him out on the Martineau Johnson website – he's adorable. That website, by the way, www.graduates4law.co.uk gets our seal of approval. Factor out the inevitable 'loving it-loving it-loving it' quotes and you're left with a very informative resource.

Martineau Johnson is located slap-bang in the heart of Birmingham's professional community, so no chance of avoiding lawyers from other firms, accountants and clients on a Friday night out in the many many bars that exert a magnetic pull on Brum's yuppies. The Old Joint Stock is popular, as is *"The Mailbox, B3, Brindleyplace (via McDonald's), All Bar One, Pitcher & Piano…" "Some might go out for a meal, some might go to a club – Bobby Browns – where all the suits in Birmingham go. It's a bit of a meat market."* We bet it is! At least the girls are working off the excesses with a healthy programme of sporting fixtures. *"There's a group of about 15 girls who play netball, five-a-side football and hockey. It's a good way to meet other law firms."* We're not sure what the boys are doing.

regional news round up

Whilst the firm has most success in recruiting those with either a Midlands upbringing or a degree from one of the region's universities, clients seem to be located all over the country and *"solicitors on the other side are mainly in London."* If Martineau Johnson's London and Birmingham offices were reversed, we'd be very surprised if the firm wasn't a household name amongst law students. But the powerhouse is in Birmingham and, as a result, applicants need to be certain that Birmingham is where they want to be based. You don't need to know the city like the back of your hand though; one trainee told us that she had *"only ever been shopping in Birmingham before."* But do make sure you know why you're choosing a career in Birmingham. No sloppy seconds applications from wannabe Londoners please.

Martineau Johnson had been in merger talks with rival firm Mills & Reeve from East Anglia, but now it's back to competing against them for education and charities clients and Mills & Reeve is back to building up its Birmingham office. Currently, Martineaus is declaring its independence and merger seems to be off the menu. A 25% rise in turnover last year and a 50% boost in partners' profits followed a reshuffle in which a quarter of its equity partners gave up their equity status. Again, this hardly smacks of conservatism…

and finally…

Thoroughly respectable in all areas of commercial work and superb in its niche areas, there's an awful lot on offer at Martineau Johnson. The firm has an established position in Birmingham and, if you don't fancy a training contract at the local branch of one of the national firms, it could be just up your street.

Masons

the facts

Location: London, Bristol, Leeds, Manchester, Glasgow, Edinburgh
UK ranking by size: 24
Total number of trainees: 60
Seats: 4x6 months
Alternative Seats: Overseas seats, secondments

Masons' stated aim is to become the leading legal advisers in construction and engineering, information technology, energy and infrastructure. Happily much of this goal has been achieved and, both nationally and internationally, it has an impressive reputation in the construction and engineering industries. To the slight irritation of the firm, Masons has earned such a good name as a construction firm that it overshadows its success in the other areas of its business. But don't turn the page if you are not dead set on construction. You will find yourself acting for a variety of clients, from Bradford & Bingley and MCI Worldcom to the more traditional, top flight construction bods.

don't forget your hardhat

Anyone thinking of qualifying as a construction lawyer should make a beeline for Masons. It is firmly cemented at the top of the pile in construction work. For those who understand there's more to life than hard hats and JCBs, the firm also has a good general commercial practice and an excellent reputation in PFI and IT. One of our sources stressed *"we are more than just a construction firm and there most certainly are other options for those who want them."* Most trainees choose not to qualify into construction law. One told us *"Originally I was interested in construction, but I was exposed to other areas of work and discovered my real skills lie elsewhere."* Even so, if you are applying, remember where this firm's real strengths lie. With so much of Masons' reputation and income coming from the construction industry, it will colour your training to a greater or lesser extent. Believe it or not, over the last few years we have come across the odd trainee who admitted to not appreciating the firm's leanings until after they started their training contract.

Masons takes on trainees in its London, Bristol, Glasgow, Manchester and Leeds offices. Of this year's intake, 29 young bloods herded to the London office and between five and six trickled into each of the regions. Interaction between the offices is encouraged; all trainees attend a two week induction and, subsequently, they will meet at national training sessions and social events, such as the Summer Ball in London.

outsourcing and outlaws

On the whole, trainees in London have the greatest choice in terms of the seats they undertake. This is simply because their office has more departments than the other branches. There isn't a rush for any seat in particular, although we did get a sense that many trainees were keen to try their hand at IT. Having pulled off some pretty impressive outsourcing deals this year (it was instructed on a £2.5 billion deal for Rolls Royce and a £1.8 billion deal for BAE), it is understandable that there is something of a buzz in this department at the moment. The firm has also recently launched the excitingly named 'outlaw.com', an e-commerce and new media information service, which has gone down very well, winning awards along the way. One thing is clear, IT is an area which the firm is pushing hard.

In London, trainees must complete two stints in the CEPA group, in either the construction, energy or infrastructure departments. Aside from this, you will be free to choose, subject to the Law Society's requirements. As with most firms, there is no guarantee that you will get the seats you want, although many interviewees emphasised how flexible the HR department was when matching trainees to their chosen seats. *"If you make it clear what you want then they will do all that is humanly possible to place you."* Other popular seats include employment, environmental and property. You see, there really is more than just construction here!

Hours vary from seat to seat, but were not a concern for Masons' trainees. Most of our interviewees knocked off on average between 6pm and 7pm. You should expect to work the occasional late night and to come in at the weekend when there is a rush on. Extra effort is recognised though and supervisors don't expect you to put your life on hold for the firm as a matter of course. *"We get on with the work here and put in the hours when it is needed. I haven't lost my identity outside of work – I have friends at other firms who seem to have lost themselves a bit."*

exploration

It's a well known fact (amongst construction lawyers) that English law is the preferred choice of those entering into major projects in construction and engineering around the world. Masons has been quick to capitalise on this fact and has built up a presence in international work. It operates out of offices in Dublin, Brussels, Guangzhou (China), Hong Kong and Singapore. It's a bit disappointing therefore, that, so far, overseas seats have been thin on the ground. There is a regular slot available in Brussels, though this is normally oversubscribed. Just before going to press we learned that Hong Kong will now offer a place to one trainee. Occasionally, as and when the work requires, trainees may jet off on a short business trip to one of the Asian offices. The Masons website mentions that new opportunities for overseas seats are constantly being explored, so you never know.

naming faces

Masons recruitment material proudly boasts that it gives trainees as much responsibility as they can handle. The trainees we interviewed echoed this view. *"The level of responsibility I have been given has been a real high point of my time here. Everyone is genuinely involved in the work and there is a minimum of photocopying and tedious admin."*

Masons is also keen that trainees get to meet clients as early as possible, enabling them to deal more effectively with enquiries at a later date. *"We have lots of client contact in meetings and over the phone… supervisors certainly don't try to keep the trainees hidden and we are brought out at marketing initiatives and seminars whenever possible."* Trainees also attend construction conferences, where there's an opportunity to put faces to client names and vice versa. It's all about absorbing trainees into the firm's core industry sector. Out of 24 trainees who finished their training contract in 2001, 18 were offered jobs with the firm.

hot desks and cold feet

Masons offices were praised to the rafters by the trainees we interviewed. Last year, we were told that the hi-tech London office bore a certain resemblance to that on Ally McBeal (presumably without the unisex toilets). We were told this year that the Manchester office was used as a film set for the ITV drama 'Cold Feet'. The offices in Glasgow and Manchester operate a hot-desking system. Even though it's just these two smaller offices which work the system, trainees felt that hot-desking epitomised the open and unregimented feel of the firm. The larger offices see trainees sharing a room with their supervisor. All trainees told us that there was an active social life in their office. The firm organises regular events, such as the annual ball and individual offices organise trips. We heard that the London office trooped off to Amsterdam recently. Individual teams and departments regularly meet in bars or go out for subsidised meals.

and finally

Whilst Masons does a lot more than just construction, there's a good deal of pride in the firm's top of the tree reputation. Don't expect two years of construction disputes, but do expect to act for clients in this industry across different departments.

Mills & Reeve

the facts

Location: Cambridge, Norwich, Birmingham, London
UK ranking by size: 38
Total number of trainees: 32
Seats: 4x5 and 1x4 months
Alternative seats: None

A cracking, but no longer little firm that commands considerable respect in the profession and has latterly been seducing leading lawyers from big City firms. The small London office is at present *"irrelevant"* to the trainee experience; it has a pure insurance focus and no trainees have yet taken a seat there. So concentrate on the other three locations and pick the one that appeals, in the knowledge that moves between them are possible.

norwich: bootiful

So what do you know about Norwich? Bernard Matthews turkeys, the Norfolk Broads and Norwich City FC. (The Canaries currently sit in the middle of Division 1 by the way.) The fair cathedral city is the original birthplace of the spreading Mills & Reeve Empire. Its roots lie with the landed and moneyed folk of the region and to some extent the Norwich office still exists to serve them. *"Private client work is how the Norwich office grew up,"* one trainee explained. *"It still has a particular specialisation in the agricultural sector, but in the present climate these areas are not growing."* Adding that the Norwich office has long viewed itself as a commercial practice, the trainee stressed that *"private client, trusts and agricultural planning are specialist niches,"* not the mainstay of the operation. The mainstay is the region's business activity and consequently you can fulfil your corporate desires from this one office, should you so choose.

> "If you love the law, you can get involved in making it."

The location of the office is *"fantastic – right in the centre of the city and within 50 metres of all the good bars like Ha!Ha!, and the Slug and Lettuce."* The local is The Hogshead. (Hmmm, yet another chain gang then). Presently in an older building, we're told that new premises are to be built for the firm.

cambridge: a city with momentum

Just one good reason to consider a training contract in the Cambridge office is the city itself. If the attractions of the university buildings, punting and oodles of history doesn't inspire you to fill out the application form then maybe the office's client base will. Welcome to Silicon Fen. Welcome to top hi- and biotech R&D and spin-outs. Say hello to a hugely successful IP practice and corporate deals coming off the back of the brains and boffins of Cambridge University. Become a matchmaker to those with money and those with ideas. Help 'seed' new businesses. It's exciting stuff. *"The deal flow is very good here,"* one trainee told us. *"I deal with venture capitalists and AIM listings."* The trainee added, *"It tends to be relatively small fry compared to the City,"* but remember, small also equals hands on.

319

"There's no long hours culture at Mills & Reeve," with most trainees citing 8.30am-6pm as common hours. In corporate it varies as you ride the ups and downs of the deals and we learned that IP can also involve longer hours. The Cambridge local is the Flying Pig and once you get beyond the early clinging-to-other-trainees stage, you'll probably find yourself sharing a few drinks with more senior colleagues. As in Norwich, trainees felt that the office had *"a welcoming nature."* A first year in one of the offices recalled *"Everyone was looking forward to our arrival at the firm."*

birmingham: going public

"Birmingham is predominantly public law – NHS trusts, local government etc." Bolted on two years ago when Mills & Reeve looked westwards to the Midlands, this office initially set its sights on insurance litigation and then shortly merged with a struggling medical negligence partnership. That aspect of the work has suffered lately with the firm being dropped from the NHS Litigation Authority panel and a fair few lawyers were lost from the practice as a result. Good job then that NHSLA work wasn't the only reason for being in Birmingham. Trainees were not overly concerned at the loss, saying *"it was only one seat and we still do med neg work."* Forever looking for the silver lining in the clouds, some thought that the broader clinical governance issues handled for NHS trusts were actually far more interesting than the NHSLA cases had been.

The Birmingham office is smaller than the East Anglian ones, but is by no means a tiddler. *"We're about to move up the road into improved accommodation. Just about central Birmingham but not hard down town."* It sounds as if the M&R training experience is slightly different to that at one of the corporate big-fish firms that dominate the legal landscape in central Brum.

Does the distance from the firm's East Anglian heartland put the office out on a limb? We're told that Brum is *"a distant third"* in terms of intra-office social activity but, in terms of work, its public sector focus is strong and as a result there are very positive reasons for choosing to spend some or even all of your time there. It seems that moves are also afoot to increase the proportion of private sector work.

making up the law

Our discussions with trainees across each of the three offices left a particular impression. Mills & Reeve, we conclude, is a firm for those who are really interested in the law. Much of its business is in particular specialist areas, such as higher education, IP, employment, agriculture, corporate governance, charities and more. Yes, it's possible to mainstream in company/commercial or commercial litigation or commercial property, but the niche departments offer up the opportunity to get to the leading edge of things. *"If you love the law, you can really get involved in making it"* and feel like you are *"in the thick of things."* It's not beyond the realms of possibility that in a niche seat you could be involved in the preparation of a big House of Lords case. East Anglia may be famous for poultry, but there's no way you'll sit in front of your keyboard pecking at the same letter for two years.

"Different niches look for different things in their trainees, that's why there's no Mills & Reeve clone," a source said. Becoming quite specialised at trainee level brings with it inherent complications though. A specialist department might attract more wannabe qualifiers than there is room for and, once your appetite for an area of law has been whetted, it then means that you'd be looking around for an appropriate new home post-qualification. Thankfully, most do get a job in their desired department and in September 2001 nine of the 12 stayed. One commented that happy matches in small departments require not only that the area of law fits you, but that your face fits the department. Clearly they usually do.

and finally…

A thoroughbred firm in East Anglia (and now the Midlands and London), where you'll find the going rewardingly challenging. The local racecourses at Newmarket and Yarmouth may be for flat racing, but at this firm the jumps are there for you to attempt. Trainees with a good academic pedigree and a keen interest in the law should apply. But make sure that these are parts of the country in which you want to live and work.

Mishcon de Reya

the facts
Location: London
UK ranking by size: 99
Total number of trainees: 16
Seats: 4x6 months
Alternative seats: None
Extras: Pro bono: Mary Ward Legal Centre

One of the most well-known of London's smaller commercial practices, Mishcon de Reya has a whopping profile derived from involvement with famous clients and headline-grabbing cases. Princess Diana instructed the firm and Geoffrey Archer, Fat Boy Slim and Craig David are among its clients. It hit the headlines on the Irving/Penguin/Lipstadt libel shocker and athlete Diane Modahl's doping litigation. Mishcon de Reya never seems to stay out of the limelight for long. If you like what you do to be in the public eye and exciting, then this firm might just do the trick for you.

the far side
Even before we interviewed trainees at Mishcons, we knew we'd be in for a treat. With hundreds of applications for just a few trainee places per year, there's no way this firm could be recruiting dullards. Although we couldn't quite put our fingers on it (and we're not totally sure we can even now), there's something just a little bit different about this firm. If ever there was a Gary Larson cartoon masquerading as a law firm, then this is surely it.

So this is The Far Side then? *"Well most of the trainees do come from somewhere else."* (Yes, just as we thought.) *"One is ex Israeli army, one is ex secret service, one is an ex builder, one an ex secretary. You get all sorts; it's a bizarre mix."* Blimey, it's the X Files too then…

Not only are the Mishcons' recruiters picking trainees who are out of the mould, but we had it on good authority that their own behaviour was… slightly unorthodox. *"When I applied, they had an odd interviewing technique. Some of them got you to sing a song, others to tell a joke. One asked how you'd explain a credit card to a seven year old."* We spoke to three people who all knew their jokes had been awful, but got through anyway.

big personalities or tricky characters?
Corporate has become a very popular department with trainees and family is a perennially popular seat. Consequently, these are the preserves of third and fourth seaters. The property department has good work, but it is litigation for which the firm is perhaps best known and trainees told us, again and again, that this was viewed as the heart of the training experience. *"Often people find that they will do two seats in litigation,"* *"it's such a big department here."*

Most partners and supervisors are seen to be approachable, but *"one or two in litigation are a bit weird."* *"Nobody is pompous, although there are a couple of egotists."* Try as we might, we couldn't get anyone to name names. But what does that matter? Find us a firm that doesn't have its big egos. A grey and pin-striped training, acting for widget makers – no. The press camped outside the office from time to time – yes. You'll never have to watch someone's eyes glaze over when at a dinner party you're asked where you work.

who let the dogs out?
Late in 2000, Mishcons entered into a merger with a top music law firm called Eatons. As well as bringing clients like Craig David, Gabrielle, Fatboy Slim and

the Bee Gees with it, Eatons also brought a dog, Lottie the Lurcher. Given that one of the existing Mishcons consultants was already in the habit of bringing Murphy the Labrador into the office, we wondered how the two dogs got on with each other. *"You see them coming and going, but I've never seen both of them together."*

It's not just the dogs that are on show. The relatively small number of trainees makes each one a figure in the firm from the moment they join. *"Trainees are treated as members of the firm"* and *"you can't hide... although we do try sometimes!"* Some supervisors are acknowledged to be better than others at involving trainees in everything they do, but most trainees were happy with the tasks they were asked to perform. One said, *"I have not been kept in the background, but I am slightly jealous of some of my intake as they have had more experience than other trainees. Most of the time responsibility and client contact has been there though."* Disparities follow from the nature of the supervisor not the nature of the clients or the work.

wish you were here

Trainees painted a picture of a very image conscious firm and talked of postcards produced by the marketing department for clients. These seem to include quirky slogans such as *"Everything you ever wanted to know about sex discrimination but were too afraid to ask"* and *"something about us being interested in ideals not just deals."* Ah yes, ideals. If you study the firm's website there's a hint that this is a firm with a certain set of ideals. *"It's a left of centre firm and that's reflected in its client base and the pro bono work it does. Most people here read the Guardian, I would say. There are certainly more Guardian readers than Telegraph readers."*

Trainees regard the firm as an unusual but interesting place to work and see this as its unique selling point. If working on rewardingly responsible tasks, but rarely beyond 9am-6pm, is important to you then this is somewhere that will suit. If you're looking for a firm that defines its Dress Down Friday such that *"combats, T-shirts and trainers"* are acceptable, you have found the right place. If you are the sort that expects the unexpected, you'll thrive. Those we spoke to were thriving, although only five of the nine September 2001 qualifiers stayed with the firm. This was primarily the result of a deficit in corporate and employment job offers.

unforgettable

"The impression I got before I started was that you really had to stand out, but actually I think that their biggest priority is that you will get on with the people here. Big personalities exist in the firm and they don't want to recruit people who will antagonise them." We asked if there were any common traits amongst trainees. The following points became clear. *"It attracts individuals – the stereotypical lawyer doesn't fit here."* The firm is *"not looking for sheep"* and the Mishcons type just wouldn't want to hack it in a large and faceless law firm. The money may be less than at the magic circle (at all levels), but money is not the main motivator. Cash came way down the list of priorities of those we spoke to.

High up on the list of priorities was that work was interesting and didn't steal away the opportunity to have a life outside the office. There was no evidence that trainees were of the sort that needed to ensconce themselves in an intense work-centred social scene. Once a month on 'First Thursdays', there are drinks in the boardroom, but opinion was divided as to which of the local bars was the firm's favourite. Given the imminent office move to Red Lion Square, north of Fleet Street, this lack of attachment seems no bad thing. Trainees look forward to the new offices and more space and maybe something more *"funky designer"* than the present *"80's look."*

and finally…

Mishcon de Reya is easy to understand. It's a quirky place for smart people who enjoy variety. We have no doubt that it receives hundreds of high quality applications, but it genuinely seems to have its own definition of what makes a good potential Mishcons lawyer. They'll know you when they see you.

Morgan Cole

the facts
Location: Cardiff, Swansea, Oxford, Reading, London, Croydon
UK ranking by size: 27
Total number of trainees: 38
Seats: 4x6 months
Alternative seats: Secondments.

Once upon a time in 1998, a Welsh firm, Morgan Bruce, with offices in Cardiff, Swansea and London, merged with a Thames Valley practice, Cole & Cole. Before a year was out, the firm had added a niche Lloyd's insurance firm, Fishburn Boxer. It was set to be the dominant force in the Thames Valley and a leading regional player.

the master plan
The rest of the legal profession assumed the Morgan Cole master plan revolved around insurance work. In early 2000 the firm added a new branch in Croydon devoted to personal injury work for insurance companies. Then it acquired a whole team of defendant professional indemnity lawyers from Lawrence Graham. More than a third of its revenue now comes from insurance clients. The theory seemed proven.

Any recently merged firm comes under intense scrutiny from legal pundits and Morgan Cole has taken a lot of flak in the legal press. Stories emerged of defections at partner and assistant level. It's true that several partners have left – around 10% – most of them from the Oxford office. The big story of 2000 was the departure of a crack trio of corporate partners to set up a new branch office of a US firm. The big story of 2001 was the decimation of the employment department, when the region's best known employment lawyer and some of her team flew the nest to Nabarro Nathanson in London. Just before finishing this book, we learned of the defection of four property partners from the Swansea office.

So is the tale of Morgan Cole one of woe or does it have a happy ending?

what's with the long face?
Cardiff is the prime location for Welsh trainees (although not all of them are actually Welsh); 12 out of the 16 work in that office. *"There are more opportunities to specialise to a greater extent in Cardiff,"* although Swansea also offers the three main departments – property, litigation and business services. In Cardiff, seats are also available in areas such as insurance, employment, banking and property litigation. Trainees told us that they were pretty happy with seat allocation and had *"a certain degree of input"* into the hand they were dealt. Seat three is where you are most likely to get your first choice, *"even if it's at the expense of first years."* Every year there's been an opportunity for a 'Welsh' trainee to go on secondment to ICI in Slough. That slot is now shared with Thames Valley and London trainees.

> "They are very keen to throw substantial work at you early on."

Responsibility comes with the territory, *"depending on how capable you are and how much your partner is prepared to delegate."* In litigation, for example, you will handle cases yourself, instructing counsel and even conducting the advocacy in small hearings, *"mostly mortgage repossessions"* and the like. *"They are very keen to throw substantial work at you early on,"* but, *"they don't flog you completely to the bone. Senior people are quite enthusiastic about you enjoying your work and don't like faces down to the floor."* Hours average out at 9am-6pm, with days in some departments a little longer.

knowing me knowing you... ah ha
The Welsh offices are open plan in some departments. This is *"aimed at getting everyone closer together*

and working as a team." It's easy to get to know teammates through the various sports that keep staff in tip-top shape. A popular sporting pastime is the dash to the pub after hours. *"On a Friday, a lot of the younger people go out for a drink. There are a few good new bars in Cardiff that we go to. Ha!Ha!, the Med Bar and some other pubs round the corner."* The TSG is also strong in south Wales and provides an alternative social scene.

"The Morgan Bruce culture has survived the merger," we were told. *"Not a lot has changed, it was always fairly progressive and that still holds true. There are partners who are quite traditional – the older ones – but the firm as a whole is not overly traditional and the regional directors seem to be young and progressive."* We were told that post-merger, Morgan Cole's Welsh bits feel *"stable"* and a *"comfortable"* place to be. We got the impression that looking eastwards from Wales was like looking beyond the comfort zone, but we also wondered what Welsh trainees might have said had we interviewed them after the Swansea property partners shocker in August 2001.

quakes in the valley
No one we spoke to in either Oxford or Reading was in the least bit Welsh and nor had they worked there. It's almost as if the bridges over the Severn are down in this respect. It's not like the trainees don't interact between the regions though, *"they are on the other end of the phone."* The firm has expended considerable energy and resources on the integration of the three regions and, following initial *"computer hassles,"* there are now good communication links; *"the library services and IT are going really well."*

"But," the trainees said, *"it's still effectively three separate firms."* Geography has a lot to answer for. It would be wrong to over play the issue though, as *"the firm feels more knitted together than before."* Alas, the Oxford office has a habit of dropping a few stitches. Trainees talked about the partner losses, saying *"the major feeling has been instability."* Last year there was a feeling of *"who's next? Everyone was looking over their shoulders."* Rumour has it that staff were running a sweepstake as to which partners would be next to go.

bull fighting
Whilst *"still not feeling as secure as we could,"* things do appear to have settled down and this may be because the powers that be have *"grabbed the bull by the horns and said where the firm is going."* And where is that? *"The firm-wide strategy has been rolled out and accepted. We're focusing on hi-tech stuff. Here in Oxford that also means biotech clients and university spin-out work. It's also realised that it does have a lot of clients in the energy sector and, of course, there's the insurance focus which has historically been a big one."*

The firm is aiming for strong, technology based clients. The variety of seats on offer in Oxford and Reading is *"fantastic"* and, for the corporate-minded trainee, things are definitely moving their way. One trainee commented on how his application to the firm had been based on notions of high street work and legal aid. *"This is a commercial practice now. We simply don't do crime any more."* So make sure you know what's on offer. As ever, the website is a great starting point.

There are slight differences between Reading and Oxford. *"Oxford is more formal,"* one trainee said. Reading is more dressed-down in look and possibly attitudes too. We heard an interesting observation from a London trainee: *"Cole & Cole trainees were chosen for their intellectual abilities, Morgan Bruce trainees for their personalities. Oxford is a bit more stiff upper lip. In London, we're closer to the Welsh but I think that Morgan Cole is all about taking the best bits out of both firms."* In September 2001, 18 of the 23 qualifiers stayed with the firm.

london: the city and the borough of croydon
Morgan Cole has been on the pull in London. Its Fleet Street office is just one of two in the City, with the other being a specialist Lloyd's of London prac-

tice called Fishburn Morgan Cole. So strong was the Fishburn brand, it kept it following merger with Morgan Cole. In 2000 another dimension was added in Croydon (and many would argue that Croydon is indeed in another dimension). While Fishburn is handling top level insurance work, Croydon is devoted to higher volume, lower value insurance work, much of it personal injury. One or two trainees sit in each of these offices and movement between the London offices is common.

> "A popular sporting pastime is the dash to the pub after work."

Fleet Street offers the usual litigation, property and business services. *"There's not a lot of choice,"* one trainee admitted. But you can supplement your London experiences with six months in one of the Thames Valley offices. This will happen if a TV trainee wants some time in London. Time seconded to client NFU has bred more of a sense of variety. The 9am-6pm hours are standard in London too, so no one's complaining about being overworked. And its shadows-of-the-High Court location ensures that you'll be in and out of that building and getting great experience more often than a cuckoo in a clock.

and finally…

There's a quote from the firm's own website, which seems to say it all. "Commercial people are always moving and organisations forever changing." Indeed they are. Good clients, good lawyers and a strategy – what more ought a firm need? Whatever turbulence it may have experienced in Oxford, bear in mind that this is just one part of the firm and the air has been considerably calmer elsewhere.

Nabarro Nathanson

the facts

Location: London, Reading, Sheffield
UK ranking by size: 20
Total number of trainees: 56
Seats: 6x4 months
Alternative seats: Overseas seats, secondments
Extras: Language training

A broad and very sound commercial practice and a sure-fire winner for property, property litigation, pensions, planning, public sector and private equity work. The firm covers a complete range of work, not just areas that start with the letter 'p'. This is a nice, nice firm; we've yet to speak to a trainee or newly qualified lawyer who doesn't regard it as a kind and fulfilling environment in which to work.

p-p-p-property

A key question to ask is whether or not this is first and foremost a property firm. A quick look at the graduate recruitment website left us wondering why the firm was reluctant to mention that particular p-word. Is it trying too hard to look like something it's not, or has it achieved a sufficiently broad focus to have lost the property label? The facts: around a third of its revenue comes from property and certainly the property industry regards it as one its key firms. But only a part of your training will revolve around land law, leases and all the stuff that drove you nuts in uni. This is not going to be two years of hell in a Re Vandervell's Trusts-themed Groundhog Day. If property is not your thing, then just do your one compulsory seat in the department and move right on along to something that does interest.

The new six seat regime, which started in September 2001, means that the minimum requirement for any of the three compulsories (property, litigation, corporate) is reduced to a mere four months of each. With compulsories completed early on, the final seat is intended to be the period in which trainees try on their qualification department for size. A few lucky trainees are seconded to clients – recently Ofgen and IMG sports management. Six seats look set to be popular, increasing the *"breadth of experience"* and allowing trainees the option of *"toying with specialisms."* The firm hopes it will make the transition to qualification even smoother.

how much love is there in this room?

Earlier in 2001, the partnership elected a new senior partner, the then 39-year old Australian Simon Johnston (more pin up than pinstripe). Managing partner Nicole Paradise is of the same generation. What does this say about a law firm? Factor in a once-a-week dress-down policy at *"the fairly casual end of smart casual – as long as your not taking the mick"* and an almost soft-focus view on the lines of command and you can imagine that it's easy to feel good about the working environment. *"It is a relaxed place to work. You don't see too many stressed people, which you would expect to at a law firm of this size,"* one trainee commented. That trainee was not a lone voice.

It's too big to be Central Perk, but at the right time on a dressed-down day, sat in the café (or *"break out area"* as they call it), you could be forgiven for thinking you were on the set of 'Friends'. These lawyers are, in the main, so chummy with each other that it verges on heart-warming. But it can get confusing. One trainee told us that it can be a problem deciding on a qualification department because it's hard to work out why you want something. *"You get distracted because you got on so well socially in the department and you really need to ask yourself 'did I enjoy the people or the work?'"* Tough choice, you poor things.

So is Nabarros a bunch of air-kissing, luvved-up, cappuccino-drinking non-City types or can they kick ass with the big corporate boys in EC1? *"Yes, our corporate boys are very corporate,"* one trainee responded to the challenge. *"If you want City work you can do it here and you don't have to go to the magic circle."* We agree – to a point. And as for them being the air-kissy types? Naah.

blizzard conditions

"No one's snowed under the whole time," one trainee said, commenting on the rigours of trainee hours. 9am-6.30pm or thereabouts, we're told, which sounds jolly reasonable. It doesn't take a rocket scientist to figure out that big hours come off the back of big-ticket deals and corporate hard play, so surely there ought to be a few blizzards leaving you office bound. *"Not often"* said one. Yet, another told us that in his first week in one department he was in until 11pm most nights. With 15 AIM flotations in 2000, venture capital clients such as Alchemy Partners and companies such as Investec Henderson Crosthwaite on the books, if you want to buy yourself some red braces and pretend you're Gordon Gecko then go ahead and indulge yourself. Of the 25 trainees who qualified in September 2001, 20 stayed. 12 went into corporate areas of work and five went into property. The firm looks for anything up to a third of its NQs to go into property-related work.

the baby sitter

Nabarro Nathanson has no fear of delegation. Trainees sit with their supervisor, but that supervisor may not be a partner. Indeed, most are not and some may not even be senior solicitors. It is not unheard of for a trainee to sit with a two-year qualified lawyer and, whilst this is a very calming experience, one or two trainees did wonder whether it was the best system. *"I don't like it. Younger supervisors are not doing such juicy work, so they can't pass any down."* Others found the idea of sitting with partners daunting. *"They choose people according to whether they make suitable supervisors. I wouldn't like to sit with partners. I enjoy the fact that I can socialise with my supervisor."* Sounds rather too comfortable. Wherever we interview, trainees do look back with pride at their performance on some of the darker days of their training contracts; they understand that under pressure they grew fastest. Sometimes it really is only good if it hurts.

on the fringe

There are so many specialist areas to choose from (although the firm has just lost the whole of its private client department to Farrer & Co) that, collectively, niche departments could hardly be described as being on the periphery of the firm's business. IP/IT is a really popular choice, with two seats available in the firm's Reading office. The other Reading seats are in property and corporate, but the firm's looking to add a charities/litigation seat soon. Reading recruits two of its own trainees and borrows two from London at every seat rotation. The IP/IT work exerts a strong pull on the London office and trainees are usually pleasantly surprised at the smaller, more intimate feel of the Reading outpost.

it's a steal

Nabarro Nathanson prides itself on its links with industry. Real industry that is, not just services, call centres and coffee shop franchises. Where better then to have a branch office than Sheffield? The origin of the Sheffield office is the legal department of British Coal, which Nabarros picked up in the early 90's. This is still a premier energy (especially coal) practice. Don't go searching for a pick axe just yet though; seats can be taken in company/commercial, property, employment and pensions, defendant personal injury, environmental and litigation. It's been known for one of the six Sheffield trainees to swoop in and make off with the one Brussels seat on offer at any one time. So much for the overseas seats being the preserve of London trainees. A Reading trainee went to Paris recently and we learned that German seats are now on offer.

If you're set on training in the north of England, you shouldn't forget to look at Nabarro's Sheffield office. The spirit of the London office is evident there too and trainees told us of frequent interaction between the three offices, including plenty of email and video conferencing links. Proof positive that the information superhighway is faster than the M1 every time.

close contact

Nabarro Nathanson is still deliriously happy with its relatively new north Holborn home. We took the tour, cooed at the atrium ("*so light, so spacious*"), marvelled at the lighting effects on the 'bridges' between different departments and got positively jittery on caffeine in 'break out.' The trainees (and probably their seniors) see their new home as a statement of who they now are, collectively. "*It oozes a corporate image*," one said, "*smart and professional and corporate.*"

Showing its caring side, there's been a renewed emphasis on pro bono activities since the firm's move to Holborn. Ex senior partner, David Branson, runs the programme, which includes community projects and financial and training support for the trainee solicitor employed by the Mary Ward Legal Centre. We also couldn't report on Nabarros without mentioning ContactNN (and its Reading incarnation TVC). It's a programme of events put on by the young lawyers at the firm for other young professionals. It's a great example of trainees being taken seriously as future work winners. Full marks NN.

Top tip: The firm takes around 80% of its trainees off the back of the vacation scheme. Need we say more.

and finally…

Magic circle trainees may consider themselves snappier, slicker and better paid than those at a firm like Nabarro Nathanson; their firms have a certain kudos as the blue chip élite. It's hard to find Nabarro's trainees who'd trade in their lot for a job in the magic circle though. Their salaries are not far off and their hours are certainly shorter. That warm fuzzy feeling that washes over you at Nabarros, how much is that worth? The firm wants the legal world to know it strides with greater confidence these days. And, yes, it hates being labelled as 'just a property firm'.

Nicholson Graham & Jones

the facts
Location: London
UK ranking by size: 81
Total number of trainees: 20
Seats: 4x6 months
Alternative Seats: secondments
Extras: Pro bono: Battersea Law Centre, language training

A medium-sized firm based in the heart of the City, Nicholson Graham & Jones underwent something of a rebranding a couple of years ago. Perhaps in an attempt to give itself a stronger identity in the market, the firm acquired the snazzy slogan: "A Better Partnership." So we thought we'd find out if it was…

painting by numbers
After speaking to trainees, it still seems as if the younger generation of lawyers at NGJ do not have a very firm handle on exactly what makes the firm different. We even had difficulty drawing out what it was about the firm, which had initially attracted our interviewees. This is certainly not to say that trainees accepted the NGJ contract as a last resort. "*I had lots of offers, but changed my mind about the kind of firm I was interested in going to. I knew I didn't want to go to a large firm and the atmosphere just seemed right for me here.*" The typical trainee seemed to be looking for a successful medium-sized firm with a comfortable atmosphere. NGJ passes with flying colours on all these counts, but is not quite so hot on standing out from the crowd (despite the recent lick of conceptual paint).

modest ambitions
The firm has a broad commercial practice with a few niche areas of work, including IP/IT and employment. There are some large clients on the firm's books and the quality of work for trainees is as high as at any of the leading mid-tier practices. Unlike some of NGJ's contemporaries, trainees did not feel that the firm was straining to compete with the mega firms. "*We are ambitious, but we know what we are good at and we don't need to try and take on the huge firms.*" The firm has a successful property department, indeed, most of NGJ's highest profile work is in this field. Property is one of the areas of business the firm has chosen in order to stamp its mark. It also has small but perfectly formed litigation and sports departments.

weekends away
The structure and quality of internal training events were praised. "*We fast track the Professional Skills Course at the beginning of the training contract.* [Many firms do.] *We all get to know each other and trainees tend to form a tight knit community as a result.*" Once a year, all the fee earners are whisked off to a hotel for a training weekend and a spot of group bonding. These activities are seen to be of equal importance. The serious stuff is tackled on the Saturday, with a 'do' in the evening and there's an optional sports day on the Sunday. Trainees felt that this interweaving of training and socialising was indicative of the relaxed attitude which pervades the firm. "*The training weekend is always enjoyable and has been instrumental in pooling ideas to increase the firm's profile and identity. You feel comfortable enough to make a contribution in the open sessions.*"

The absence of a rigorous hierarchy promotes a feeling that NGJ is a calm and welcoming place to work. This doesn't mean you'll be slacking for two years. As one trainee put it, "*we work hard (sometimes very hard), especially in corporate, but it is not like some firms where you are on call 24-hours a day.*" Corporate aside, typical daily hours are from around 9am to 6-7pm. One trainee told us that in his first year he had stayed beyond 8pm on no more than ten occasions.

weekends together
Trainees must undertake compulsory seats in corporate/commercial, litigation and either

commercial property or construction. They then choose their final seat. Popular destinations include IP and employment but, with only one seat available in each of these areas, it's important to make it known early on that you are interested in gaining experience in either of these departments. The firm also has a specialist sports law group. Before all you sports fans dash off the blocks to apply, bear in mind this is a small niche and certainly not one of the main practice areas. Simply put, if you are coming to NGJ intent on qualifying into this area, there is a very good chance you'll be disappointed. There are few guarantees in this world and this isn't one of them.

> "We are ambitious, but we know what we are good at."

With a manageable workload and the time to hold on to your life outside work, NGJ trainees get to know each other after hours. *"We don't just meet up during the week, we socialise at weekends too. Other people I went to law school with are quite surprised that we meet up on Saturdays as often as we do."* Many trainees choose to live near one another. Clearly, NGJ is the kind of place where you can expect to make friends. Friends that will be there for some time too. All 2001 qualifiers were offered jobs and only one did not accept.

made for sharing

NGJ's international goals are not realised by mergers or a string of overseas offices, but through membership of Globalex, a coalition of international firms. NGJ is a founding member of the group and the sole UK representative. Through this alliance, clients can consult lawyers from Singapore to New York and Sweden. The firm has use of a Brussels office, funded jointly by all Globalex members. With this modest strategy, it should not come as too much of a surprise that there are no overseas seats available. But there are a few client secondments, which crop up on an ad hoc basis.

and finally…

If you don't want to go to a mega-firm, have no strong opinions on specific practice areas and don't aspire to world domination, but are drawn to a cosy firm that doesn't need to dress itself up in glitz and glamour, then there is every reason to apply to NGJ. Perhaps next year interviewees will be a bit clearer about their reasons for choosing the firm. Like waking up with a hangover on the sofa the morning after, you'll be very glad you got there, even if you can't for the life of you remember how.

Norton Rose

the facts
Location: London
UK ranking by size: 12
Total number of trainees: 120
Seats: 6x4 months
Alternative Seats: Overseas seats, secondments
Extras: Pro bono: Tower Hamlets Law Centre, language training

Norton Rose's domestic presence and profits have risen again, as the firm continues to challenge the top ten for work and clients. Outside the UK, a programme of overseas expansion has given the firm a high profile international presence, with an impressive European operation. The large number of overseas offices means that there are plenty of opportunities for trainees to travel over the course of their training contract. One other introductory point of interest is that Norton Rose is one of the three firms to have snuggled up with the magic circle to set up the City LPC.

don't mention the email

You'll have heard the now famous story of the smutty email sent to a Norton Rose lawyer, which travelled around the world via millions of computer screens. Bear two things in mind. First, this could have happened at any firm and does not suggest disproportionately high hormone levels at Norton Rose. Second, the powers that be have yet to see the funny side, so best not to mention Ms Swires if you are invited to interview.

so norton rose

What kind of person would fit in at Norton Rose? When asked this question, trainees strongly insisted that there is no Norton Rose type. *"That is just the point, the only type here is an individual."* Hmmm… they all say that dear. We're told that there's no culture of Oxbridge domination at Norton Rose and a handful of non-UK nationals will join the firm in each intake. You won't be joining a team of legal clones, but bear in mind that a lack of Oxbridge 'dominance' still means that between 30-40 % will hail from the dreaming spires.

The firm has a rather unconventional (and slightly complex) seat rotation system. First off, you will pay three compulsory visits to banking, commercial litigation and corporate finance seats. After this, trainees pick an optional seat. There are a variety of options for the final seat. There's a full explanation of the rather convoluted system in the Norton Rose A-Z profile at the back of this book – read about it there. We are writing this on a Friday afternoon and life is too short. It can be difficult getting into some of the smaller, more popular seats. IT/IP and tax are each very popular, but with only about ten seats available, you may have to wait your turn before you get a chance.

We're told that the banking and corporate finance departments *"house the real meat of our work."* Trainees should expect to do their share of administrative work (something you must accept at any of the big firms) and the working day can easily run late into the night, if your team is up against a deadline. Certain teams, and specifically teams in banking and corporate, have a reputation for long hours. *"The team I am in at the moment has lots of work on. It is not at all rare for us to still be at it at 10pm."* On the plus side, you shouldn't find yourself working too many weekends or staying late every seat. Hours aside, responsibility and client contact are there in abundance, especially for those who use their initiative and request more 'hands on' work. *"I have had as much responsibility as I could possibly want. Supervisors will ensure, whenever they can, that you get all the responsibility you can handle – you just have to ask for it."*

eastern promises

Our interviewees identified the multitude of overseas seats as a real crowd-puller. *"By and large, everyone who wants to go abroad will get the opportunity,"* they said. You'll be able to choose from a wide range of destinations throughout Asia and Europe. Decisions as to who goes where are made on merit, although, in some instances, language skills are required. Take Paris for example; we're told *"a very high level of proficiency is required for the corporate seat, but a basic grasp will get you through banking."* Language training is available if you need to brush up on your skills. Two of the seats (Greece and Singapore) will focus on the firm's shipping specialism. Norton Rose had to close down its Hong Kong office for three years due to a restrictive covenant imposed by a former business partner. The office will reopen next year and the firm intends to waste no time in restarting the popular Hong Kong seat. An additional seat was recently added in Singapore, allowing another trainee to travel to the Far East.

smells like team spirit

The concept of team working within departments is crucial to Norton Rose's identity. More so than most, Norton Rose trainees spoke of 'the team' as opposed to 'the department' or even 'the firm' itself. *"Much of* the socialising is focused around teams. We go out for welcome drinks, goodbye drinks and welcome back drinks!" The team you join will determine the hours you find yourself working and there are differentials between teams. One source said, "*it is unusual for the department, but we have a mountain of work on at the moment, so we're often still here at 10pm*" Team spirit and loyalty seems to help trainees cope with the hours, which can be gruelling at times.

As you flick through the pages of the True Picture and read about other top firms, you may notice that not all of them have as full a social scene as Norton Rose. "*We work hard but socialise together too. Unless you're the sort who can't enjoy yourself unless you're in the pub by 7pm, then you'll have a good social life here.*" Our sources also told us of a good deal of interaction between trainees and assistants, with "*high levels of banter within teams*" and "*a total lack of egos or barriers.*"

The firm organises a free bar (complete with savoury snacks) on Monday evenings. This varies in popularity, with some perceiving that regular attendance "*might make you look a bit tight and a bit sad.*" Demand picks up, however, during the summer (vac scheme season) and before Christmas (need you ask?). Several trainees thought the bar would be better held on a Thursday or Friday evening. If you want to go further than The Old Monk (the local pub), the offices (by Liverpool Street Station) are "*conveniently located for City bars and Brick Lane restaurants.*" Pappadums all round then?

and finally…

The seat rotation system will ensure that you complete a tour of duty in several different departments and you will find a plethora of practice areas in which NR has a stonking reputation. Shipping, IP, energy and EU are all big areas, but the focus is on corporate and banking. This is where the money is made to fuel the growth. It is where the bodies are required on qualification and where, at times, the long hours are required.

Olswang

the facts
Location: London
UK ranking by size: 40
Total number of trainees: 58
Seats: 4x6 months
Alternative Seats: None

Olswang has attracted a huge amount of attention over the last few years. It aligned itself with IT and media work and developed a truly impressive practice in these areas, as well as more traditional work. It's one of the few law firms frequently described as trendy. Perhaps all of this explains why Olswang receives more applications per year than Clifford Chance, despite offering only a fraction of the number of training places. Olswang is proud of its exceptional growth and has boasted of being the fastest growing law firm in London.

masters of cool

It's a fashionable outfit with a distinctively different feel. Walking into the reception area, you can tell this isn't a.n. other stuffy law firm. From the laid back atmosphere, to the much discussed "*funky sofas*" and Sky TV playing in the background, there's "*not a hint of Dickensian gloom*" about the place. Trainees are proud of the firm and love the quirkiness that makes Olswang what it is. When you meet Olswang trainees at university law fairs – and we hope you will – you'll see from who they are (cool meeja) and the way they dress (also cool meeja), that life at the firm will be far from oppressive and overly formal.

But we ought not to hype it up too much. Whilst much of the work focuses on glamorous industries (we heard about trainees who saw their names on film credits), in the main part you are just the boring lawyer the client has to go and see. The majority of the work is no different to what you will see at other commercial firms; contracts, finance, regulations. Olswang has a strong corporate/commercial practice and excellent commercial property work, as well as its leading work in telecoms and all aspects of media and technology. If you want a firm that only does media, you are in the wrong place.

ease and whizz

The training entails four six-month seats and trainees divide their time between company/commercial, entertainment, litigation and property. There's some flexibility within this arrangement and, in the past, it's been easy for trainees to substitute the ents seat for a second bite of the corporate cherry. But there are problems with overcrowding in some departments. A rapidly expanded trainee population has caused a few logistical problems in the last year. One trainee told us, *"The last intake was 23 compared to ten the year before and nine the year before that, so it is getting quite difficult to accommodate everyone's needs."*

We also heard that these large numbers have resulted in a less than rigorous approach to time management and feedback from supervisors. Trainees told us that when conducting appraisals, some supervisors would whizz through the form giving top marks for any area where a trainee's work had been satisfactory, whilst others took the process more seriously. This has led to inconsistencies and problems evaluating performance across the firm. As one source put it, *"appraisals and specific training issues are not always perfect. Part of the problem is that we have poached so many partners from other firms, there is no uniform structure for dealing with such things."* This is currently being addressed by a restructuring of the HR department and should be further eased by smaller trainee intakes in 2003 and beyond.

on the piste

The learning curve is steep at Olswang and trainees can't expect to stay on the nursery slopes for long. The firm has certainly been very busy in the last few years. *"The work can be erratic, with a huge package landing on your desk without much prior warning. You have to use your initiative, but that is what training at Olswang is all about."* When a department is busy, everyone needs to pull their weight and this can extend to late nights and weekends, *"especially in corporate."* One trainee told us that *"the average across departments on a normal day would be about 9am to 6.30pm. In all my time at the firm, I have done two weekends and about ten late nights."*

But the rewards are there. One trainee told us, *"the entire corporate department trooped off on a skiing trip together, as a thank you to the staff for all the work we had done on a deal. How many firms do you know who do that?"* Not many. Another source said, *"working at Olswang has provided me with opportunities, which are hardly typical. I have given lectures at universities and written an article for one of the partners that was published in Music Week."* No matter how trendy the firm is, we still find it hard to imagine David Gray reading the article over his cornflakes.

don't forget your pj's

Socially, the firm has had an enviable commitment to junkets, jollies, and jamborees. Aside from the skiing trip, one source gave details of a departmental beano in Paris and another told us of the time the litigation department was whisked off for a hotel break together. *"It was quite rowdy. I'm not sure that we are going to be asked back!"* This is definitely a firm where you'll experience a very sociable life and can let your hair down with colleagues. *"We go out lots, both on firm sponsored events and on evenings we organise ourselves… normally about twice a week. In fact someone recently organised a sleepover."* OK, that's more information than we needed to know…

tears before qualification

Very recently, as the cynics had predicted, the firm's rapid growth shuddered to a halt. In September 2001 50% of Olswang trainees weren't offered a job on qualification. Olswang denied that this had anything to do with the pace of the firm's growth outstripping the demand for legal services, but without any credible explanation, we have difficulty concluding otherwise. Our theory? Olswang is just behaving as it always has – boldly. In times of plenty it grabbed as much of the action as it could and now that corporate belts are being tightened (particularly in the new technology sector) it is responding quickly. It's still svelte enough to do so. It is slashing training places from 23 in 2000 to a projected 15 in 2003. Hopefully there will be fewer tears in subsequent years, when NQ job offers are announced.

going through a rough patch

So how does this leave the trainees steaming on towards qualification next year? We were surprised that, after some *"initial panic,"* the majority of first years were quite philosophical about their predicament. *"The whole industry* [new technology] *is going through a rough patch at the moment, but if you are up to scratch, then they will keep you on. I want to qualify into corporate anyway so I am not that bothered."* When first year trainees heard rumours that only two of the trainees coming up to qualification in September 2001 were to be offered jobs, HR sat down and reassured them that, a year from now, decisions would not be made arbitrarily. Trainees had worried that the *"sometimes random appraisal evaluations"* might count against them. They are under the impression that, if they prove their worth, the firm will do its best to offer them a job. Time will tell. Clearly Olswang trainees are made of stronger stuff than us weak-willed, namby pamby *Student Guide* hacks; this all sounds like quite a stressful experience to us.

and finally…

Olswang has an outstanding reputation in some of the freshest and sexiest areas of work. It won the *Chambers and Partners* 'Law Firm of the Year Award' in 2000. But times are getting leaner in the technology sector and an over inflated market has been forced to right itself. Investors have realised that 'zero risk' ventures fronted by spotty-faced thirteen-year-olds aren't going to treble fortunes over night after all. Olswang looks like a resilient firm and it has a fair few eggs in other baskets. It will no doubt cope with these challenges and bounce back. Bear in mind the problems the firm has had over the last year, but put them in perspective. The surge in recruitment between 1998 and 2000 was unsustainable and the firm is now looking to find the right balance between the work available and the numbers it recruits.

Osborne Clarke

the facts

Location: Bristol, London, Reading
UK ranking by size: 23
Total number of trainees: 54
Seats: 4x6months
Alternative Seats: Overseas seats, secondments

If you want to practice in Bristol, Reading or London and want a top quality commercial training you should consider short-listing Osborne Clarke. From its roots in Bristol, OC has successfully spread east to Reading and London.

make your mind up time

A bit like choosing one of the three contestants on Blind Date, trainees get to pick from each of the firm's locations. The original and largest office is the Bristol nerve centre with 28 trainees stationed in the South West. In second place comes London, weighing in at 20 trainees and, finally, Reading with a tally of just six. The majority of seats are on offer in all three locations, but Reading misses out on some. Unsurprisingly, the main focus of the Thames Valley office is IT and e-commerce. The office also handles banking, employment, pensions and incentives and general corporate/commercial, so it isn't quite silicon chips with everything. Both the London and Bristol offices offer a broad spectrum of, well… pretty much everything.

OC has a brilliant reputation in corporate finance in the South West and pulls off significant deals. It's looking way beyond the Bristol region for its work and clients, just like rival top dog Burges Salmon. In London, Osborne Clarke continues to stake its claim as a serious City player, rather than just a branch office of a Bristol firm. The IT-flavoured corporate deals continue to flow in, in particular from clients like the NatWest IT Fund and other technologically-minded venture capitalists. Trainees are encouraged to move around offices, with graduate recruitment ensuring temporary relocations are as painless as possible. Relocation is not compulsory for those who have family or mortgage commitments.

getting fresh

The four six-month seats are assigned one by one as you progress through your training. *"There used to be a requirement that you did a litigation seat, a property seat and a corporate seat, but now, as long as you fulfil the Law Society's requirements, most combinations are fine."* IT seemed to be an especially popular choice. *"It covers loads of different areas, including video games. Lots of the IT specialists are young and have come in from outside the firm, so there is a really fresh feel to the department."*

In terms of evaluating your performance, the firm is *"big on feedback"* by way of *"three-month reviews, which are fairly informal and conducted by your supervisor and someone from HR... every six months there's an end of seat appraisal, which is much more formal."*

silicon implants

Resisting the trend to merge with European partners, the firm has helped create an alliance to realise its aims of international practice and furnish clients with access to *"over 550 lawyers in 15 cities."* This provides trainees with the opportunity to undertake overseas seats. *"There is a chance to go to pretty much every office we have dealings with. This has included Cologne, Frankfurt, Paris, Helsinki and California."* When matching trainees to destinations, *"languages are very important... for most seats you will need a high level of proficiency, but for others languages are not a prequisite."* The firm recently opened up an office in California's Silicon Valley, providing exciting opportunities. *"If you do a seat in IT, you also get the opportunity to go to California."*

you're not at school anymore

On the subject of adjusting from study to work, one trainee said, *"it wasn't so much that I was cast adrift, but the firm expect you to get down to the work pretty quickly. It is an intense working environment – you're not at school anymore. If you find you have too much work on then you need to point this out."* The work can, at times, be uninteresting as well as abundant. Our sources talked of *"a fair bit of copying and proofing from time to time."* This is especially true in the first couple of months. *"As with any firm where you see big deals involving large sums of money, the firm isn't going to let you learn by your mistakes, if you're losing several million quid for a client."* However, a fairly steep learning curve means it shouldn't be too long before you get your teeth into some decent work. *"Responsibility comes with experience... this is a firm where you will get plenty of both."*

> "The managing partner drops in regularly to find out any gossip."

Hours at Osborne Clarke should not be too much of a concern. Typically trainees work from 9am-6pm, however, late nights are not unheard of. In London, *"a rough night at Osborne Clarke means being in the office until around 9pm."* Late? You could be home in time for The Sopranos. *"You should expect to be held back in the office about a couple of time's a month."* In Bristol and Reading, *"we get lots of City work, so the hours are about the same."* Perhaps partly because of the resonable hours, trainees are, in the main part, happy to stay with the firm on qualification. Out of the 19 trainees who qualified in 2001, 16 accepted NQ jobs.

catching up on the gossip

The atmosphere within the firm is more relaxed than you might think, although the hours are *"closer to City than provincial practice."* The firm is low on formality; *"there is a complete dress-down policy here all week long, all communication is on first name terms and much of it is done informally over the intranet."* The trainees told us that the firm sought their opinions: *"The managing partner drops in regularly to find out how we are all getting on, to get our feedback on important developments and to find out any gossip."* The managing partner, Leslie Perrin, is a dynamic character and well known in the legal profession. We suspect he loves the gossip.

instruments of torture

Partners regularly socialise with trainees, buy drinks in the local pub and participate in firm-wide social events with what sounds like disproportionate gusto. Organised events ranged from the frankly embarrassing – *"A group of partners are getting together to form an Osborne Clarke band, but I am not entirely sure what type,"* to the cringe-worthy – *"the managing partner is always the first to dress up for costume parties."* In addition to the firm-wide balls, the post-AGM summer party and other formal events, individual teams are *"always organising drinks."* Reading trainees will sometimes travel to Bristol for bigger events, but the day to day social life in the smaller Reading office seemed rather more sedate than the other two.

and finally…

OC offers an excellent commercial training within a regime that allows you a life outside of the office. In spite of what we found out about the hours and the steep incline into the work, you will not need to work to the same intensity as at some firms in the City. As one trainee put it *"I never wanted to practice in the City, but I wanted high quality work. I have a training contract and a CV, which will be respected by the market."*

Pannone & Partners

the facts

Location: Manchester
UK ranking by size: 61
Total number of trainees: 19
Seats: 4x6 months
Alternative Seats: None
Extras: Language training

You could go back to 1851 to dig up a bit of history about Pannone & Partners – if you really wanted to. The firm is not only a leading name on the Manchester legal scene, it has a national profile for some of its cases and clients (Asil Nadir, Saudi nurse Deborah Parry, conjoined twins Mary and Jodie) and its senior partner Roger Pannone. Mr P is a very busy man. He's a past president of the Law Society, the current chairman of the Law Society's Working Party on International Human Rights and now chairman of the 2002 Commonwealth Games to be held in Manchester.

piranhas need not apply

If Mr P wasn't a cool enough figurehead for the firm, get this – Pannones has one of the UK's few female managing partners and about one third of all partners are women. This is a firm with ethics and a pretty 'right on' attitude to gender balance. Forget funny handshakes and backslapping business bunk-ups on the golf course. The trainees we interviewed believe that having a female managing partner adds something to the way the firm operates. *"It makes a difference,"* one source said, *"maybe in the working practices. It's accepted and encouraged that you have a life outside of work. It's not a bums on seats all hours mentality."*

Other trainees referred to the relative ease with which top-flight lawyers could reach the dizzy heights of partnership. *"Partners here tend to be born and bred Pannones. It's an encouraging prospect that, if you are hot and good, you can get there quickly. You can* expect to get to salaried partner, if you are good, at about three years PQE." This doesn't mean that the young lawyers at the firm are snapping at promotion like a pool of frenzied piranha. "It's enthusiasm rather than ambition," one trainee thought. Another told us that "if you're competitive, bordering on aggressive, then this is not the right firm for you." "People who jump on others to get to the top are not tolerated."

the doctor will see you now

The firm has acted on matters that receive considerable media attention, such as the work for the victims of Thalidomide and the Manchester air crash. Its personal injury and clinical negligence practices have an excellent reputation nationally and are a real draw to applicants for training contracts. Those with a previous qualification in the medical profession will fare well here. One of the current trainees is a doctor and in the clinical negligence team there are five former nurses and a midwife. Most of the trainees do a seat in PI, indeed, "you need to do PI before you do clinical negligence." Unfortunately, three of September 2001's qualifiers wanted to stay in clinical negligence but only one job was available. This seems to have been the primary reason why only four of the seven NQs stayed with the firm.

northern exposure

Although some "tasks can get monotonous, like preparing costs for Legal Aid claims," most of the time trainees feel they are being stretched and getting their teeth into real work. "It's very hands on. I was allowed to get into the heart of things rather than tinkering around the edges." Our sources spoke of working for a number of lawyers and, as a result, "being exposed to lots of methods of working." This necessitates learning how to prioritise and "shout up if you have too much work."

As more and more firms bulge at the seams and switch to open plan working, growth at Pannones still hasn't led to a shift away from trainees having their own offices. "Having your own space is wonderful," said one. "You can get your head down and get on with it. I love it. It also shows that you're expected to have a certain capability."

amazing slim cats

Maybe it's the tranquillity of having their own space, maybe it's part of the firm ethic, maybe they're just plain lucky, but the Pannones trainees know that their work hours are a dream. "9am-6pm and no weekends" was the standard response to our question on hours. "There's no reason why I should have to put my life on hold," one said. Trainee and NQ salaries may not be the fattest, but the hours, prospects of promotion and quality of work are "sufficient to keep us here." It helps that the cost of living in Manchester is not so high that, even as a trainee, you can get yourself a mortgage on a tidy little property.

On the Manchester Airport corporate deal that some trainees got involved in, they met their peers at City firm Ashurst Morris Crisp. Our sources compared experiences. "They get paid wads of money, but we felt that they didn't seem to have the same responsibility as us or the variety. They were amazed at what we did."

detective stories

Is there a Pannones type? "People here are quite down to earth. They want to do a good job in a supportive atmosphere... the firm tends to attract people who are not brash, not arrogant." But you do need to be "game on." We heard an anecdote about a trainee who went knocking on doors to find witnesses for the client's case. It's not unusual for a trainee to "go off to investigate the scene of an accident to take road measurements and test the voracity of a client's story." Sounds fun. Certainly when combined with the opportunity to slant your training towards commercial work, should you so wish, it makes for real variety.

You can tell straight away from their accents that typically trainees have a connection with the North West. But even if you don't already have your own social scene in Manchester, you will "walk into a complete social life" at the firm when you start. Apparently, "you can't go anywhere in Manchester without bumping into other lawyers. Trainees at the firms all tend to know each other. There's a real network."

There's no chance of going undetected on a Friday night at either of the Pannones regular haunts – the nearby Hogshead or (heaven help them) Aussie-styled pick up joint, Walkabout.

and finally…

If you're interested in clinical negligence you'd be a fool to not apply to this firm. But, there's also plenty on offer for those whose goals lie in the commercial sphere. This is a firm that retains an air of difference; rather than being neither fish nor fowl, it's actually both fish and fowl. If you join the firm with private clients in mind, but then want to "*jump ship halfway through*" and end up working for corporate clients, there seems to be nothing to stop you.

Penningtons

the facts

Location: London, Godalming, Basingstoke, Newbury
UK ranking by size: 57
Total number of trainees: 20
Seats: 4x6 months
Alternative seats: None

A long established four-office partnership spanning commercial work as well as private client, family and clinical negligence/personal injury. Those students interested in taking a peek at both sides of the fence, rather than concentrating on either commercial or private clients, should get their bifocals on and see what Penningtons has to offer.

london: first mondays

The London office has been turning out lawyers for 200 years and is the key location for the firm. The trainee population totals ten and this is where the regular "First Monday" trainee convention takes place on (unsurprisingly) the first Monday of each month. Late in the afternoon, the branch office trainees converge for an hour-long lecture and afterwards there's a 'meet and greet the country cousins' session in the various bars local to the Cannon Street office. We're told that the bar below the office, Mithras, is closing and maybe that's because it doesn't appeal to the new school sensibilities of the trainees. The Slug and Lettuce has more of a buzz.

buckle up

If Mithras is a bit too old school and its presence won't be missed, will trainees miss the old image of Penningtons? The firm has undergone a rebranding exercise within the last year. The old 'buckle' logo has gone in favour of a more modern presentation. "*There's a new marketing manager,*" we're told. "*People realised that we needed the sweep of a new broom, although some people had grown attached to the old buckle.*" Others confirmed the firm's aspirations to be seen as a dynamic outfit. "*It's traditional but becoming a more forward-looking organisation, starting with the launch of the corporate ID.*"

Unlike some firms known for private client work, the trainees didn't view Penningtons as "*stuffy and aristocratic.*" They did view it as a place which suits those who are "*affable, conscientious and… subtle,*" saying "*you can't overstep the mark here. The lawyers here are not brash characters.*" So, is this new corporate image all spin and no substance? Apparently not. Trainees observe a partnership that is determined to move forward and feels "*younger and more entrepreneurial,*" but still "*reputable.*"

the element of choice

In London two compulsory seats are taken in litigation and property and then, "*subject to availability,*" trainees choose from corporate, commercial, matrimonial and private client. Tastes differ and, while some opt for the latter two seats, others find corporate and commercial more stimulating. We noted a few regrets that the commercial seat was oversubscribed. "*Everyone wants to do it,*" one trainee said, explaining that the work was particularly varied there. *"You get to do a little IP, for example."* One of our sources suggested that the choicest work could be shared out more evenly amongst the trainees. We got the impression that the training best suits those who are happy to be flexible about the type of work that they do.

The benefits of a smaller firm are obvious to Penningtons trainees. *"It's easy to feel appreciated,"* especially when the female senior partner (still a very rare breed in the City) asks you how your weekend was, as you pass her in the corridor. But small also has its drawbacks. Last year across the firm there was a pretty low retention rate. It was especially low in London where only one of the five qualifiers stayed. Perhaps this will improve as the firm continues its metamorphosis into an even more commercial practice.

godalming: that special feeling

In the heart of the home counties, quite posh with a quaint antiquity. Cute cobbled streets, where the wives of wealthy commuters shop in upmarket boutiques. This is Godalming. So does the firm's Surrey outpost mirror our description of the town, or is there more to it? *"It's busy, but very personal,"* our source pointed out, adding, *"Penningtons is not purporting to be a Clifford Chance or a Denton Wilde Sapte."* There's a distinctly local flavour to the staff at the office and to many of the clients (*"private limited companies and local landowners"*), but the umbilical cord to the London office isn't a long one. In just 45 minutes you're in Waterloo and then it's on to meetings and court appearances.

On offer are seats in private client, property (commercial/residential mix), litigation (particularly personal injury and clinical negligence) and corporate/commercial. It is likely that you'll do all four in Godalming. *"No one I've known has worked elsewhere."* With two trainees hired per year, the only sticky issue is whether or not the job on offer at the end of the day matches the type of work you want to do. Being one of four has its plus points: *"From day one you're made to feel a bit special."* This brings with it *"responsibility and expectations. There's no one to hide behind; you need to be reasonably confident."* No big trainee gang to hang with, but no bar on socialising with more senior lawyers – perhaps down the road in The Wharf or The Sun. *"I've ended up being invited out to lunch with two or three partners for no apparent reason."* Good for you.

basingstoke: a safe environment

Pretty much the same four seat options on offer here as there are in Godalming, so it's a decision of geography. If Hampshire is your scene then be prepared for an even smaller trainee crowd. At any one time there'll be just the two of you. Cosy. Naturally the life of the office as a whole will be important to you, but chances are you'll already have friends in the area. *"It doesn't feel isolating,"* we were told, and *"it feels like I am getting good quality work."* Certainly trainees receive sufficient attention and supervision and refer to *"being protected on workloads... and a bit sheltered,"* with responsibility being *"somewhere between enough and nearly enough."* The overall impression is that the office is *"well established with good local clients"* and *"a pleasant place to work."*

Basingstoke is described as having an *"ad hoc"* social life, with events like skittles and darts. *"The youngsters might meet up for a meal and a pint"* from time to time, but chances are you'll have your own social scene locally anyway and the 9am-5.30pm working day certainly allows you to pursue that.

newbury: well connected cousins

Newbury – infamous for its bypass and its eco-warriors. But will you feel like you're going out of your tree in Berkshire? The seat menu reads the same as those at Godalming and Basingstoke, putting it in the position of commercial leader in the town. Again, trainees benefit from the type of intimate and personalised training only truly possible in smaller firms. Like their counterparts in Godalming and Basingstoke, they have access to the resources (both in terms of facilities and lawyers) in the London office. So are these regional trainees seen as country cousins? *"I only sense it a little; nothing overt is said about it."*

and finally…
Two hundred years of stability, work of polar extremes and a very healthy work/life balance. This will be of interest to a certain breed of applicant. Chucking the buckle has appealed to the younger element of the firm, those that will push ahead with the transition to a more commercial practice.

Pinsent Curtis Biddle

the facts
Location: Birmingham, Leeds, London
UK ranking by size: 16
Total number of trainees: 62
Seats: 4x6 months
Alternative Seats: Overseas seats, secondments
Extras: Language training

Pinsent Curtis is one of the big regionals, up there with Eversheds, DLA, and Hammonds. It traditionally marked itself out by not making an issue of European expansion and not having the aggression or bluster of some of its rivals. One of the Yorkshire terriers in Leeds, it didn't posture, or blow as much hot air. Then in February 2001 the firm took the bold step of joining forces with City firm Biddle.

such a lovely couple
Pinsent Curtis looked at merging after its London office struggled to make an impression in the City. Several partners had flown the nest to make homes elsewhere, and a managing partner had moved in with a large bank. There was something missing. Biddle had been a bride in search of a groom for some time, having previously held talks with Field Fisher Waterhouse. The scene was set, and romance was to blossom. The coming together brought strengths in private equity and pensions, and more importantly, a larger base from which to grow in the City. What do such dramatic events do to your training contract? Not much, apparently. Outside the capital the trainees were blasé *"It hasn't really affected us here."* No major changes then? *"Maybe more in London, I suppose."*

it's like i've always known you
As mergers go, this one has been pretty exemplary. For those training in the regions, the merger has barely registered and the London trainees spoke of no longer being able to distinguish or remember who was originally associated with each firm. One of Biddle's perceived strengths had been media work with clients such as ITN. The honeymoon was brief for the media lawyers though – within days of the merger, several of them were packing their cases and taking their little black books with them. But isn't there always adjustment in any new relationship? There was a certain amount of desk-shifting as lawyers joined their new counterparts – *"everyone changed building."* The newlyweds still have their original pads, but it can only be a matter of time before the firm finds a somewhere bigger for its London base. *"There's been a much bigger emphasis on London since the merger. They were keen for all of us to work together."* The City office has been reported as spiriting work away from the provincial branches. Trainees deny this.

> "Someone coming here would not have any sense that it was a firm that had come through a merger."

Biddle adopted the Pinsents training contract, but *"it has not disrupted training. You tend to work for several people in a single department, so its not made* much practical difference," although *"where you are working with Biddle partners, there is still the atmosphere of a small firm."* It required *"a change of mentality, but not too much of a dramatic change." "Someone coming here would not have any sense that it was a firm that had come through a merger. I have been impressed with how quickly it has been sorted."* The merger has meant *"more departments and work opportunities."*

So do the regional offices begrudge London its new found attention? *"It does feel very much like one firm. I have been to meetings and events in different offices."* Trainees described the level of contact. *"We're all linked together. There is a firm intranet and you can see what people look like before you speak to them."*

brains required

So, how could the trainees at Pinsent Curtis Biddle be described? Gushing, we decided! Maybe some people are just easy to please, but our sources were unable to find anything bad to say about their training. *"I would recommend it to anybody,"* declared a Leeds source. *"It is really well organised. There's an in-house Professional Skills Course and loads of training and development seminars." "I've not been making tea or photocopying. I've only done things requiring a brain."* Funny, our photocopier requires a BSc in engineering…

the chosen

Each trainee is allocated a mentor. *"I was pleasantly surprised at the level of support,"* said one source. *"Because you are sitting with a partner, you can always ask a question."* Three-monthly appraisals provide a *"more formal setting"* for feedback. *"I've never been completely overwhelmed, nor overly bored." "There's a real mix of work."* Seat allocation was usually to the satisfaction of all; *"you don't hear much grumbling about not getting seats."* They're on offer in a *"real variety of areas."* Trainees can take seats in *"any department that there is,"* and this includes some top-rated practices such as Administrative and Public Law, Employee Share Schemes, Environment, and Financial Services. Trainees told us *"we are getting more and more interesting clients across the board,"* although some are still *"run of the mill."*

There is no *"coat on chair syndrome,"* [pretending to be at your desk after you've buggered off home] and 6.30pm seemed a typical time to head out the door. Corporate is a key area for the firm, and it is *"very keen"* for you to do a seat there. Future trainees should also take note of the firm's *"carefully selected 'Chosen Markets',"* in which it is *"striving towards"* being a market leader. These include Financial Institutions and Foreign Controlled Companies. The chosen markets represent the medium-term ambitions of the firm.

is that you or the pigeons?

The atmosphere in Pinsents Leeds *"made me choose the firm,"* one northern trainee said. *"It's an enjoyable place to work and it has a good reputation in Leeds."* Like the other big local firms, students apply to Pinsents for *"high quality work outside of London."* Again, they retain the option of going to London. The calibre of lawyer in the office is high, in part due to the migration of partners and assistants from the capital. *"Open plan and open door,"* the *"nice and airy"* Leeds office is centrally located in premises variously described as *"very glam"* and *"impressive."*

Many trainees actively sought a commercial training outside of the Big Smoke, with the option of a seat in the City. Although Birmingham's not exactly the Left Bank, trainees thought Pinsents was less *"pretentious"* than other Brum firms. It's *"laid back without being unprofessional. Not slack, but quite relaxed."* We noted a tendency towards graduates of Birmingham University but that may be the result of self-selection. Birmingham is not everyone's cup of tea, but *"it's good if you don't want to work in London, but do want good work and to have a life."* True to stereotype, the office is in the middle of a roundabout and accessible through an underpass that *"smells of pigeons."*

moving on

As long as it can be accommodated, trainees are free to move around between branches. The firm does not press people to switch, but generous relocation packages are provided. *"It's not uncommon to move. Everybody that has asked has been able to."* Trainee numbers are fairly balanced between the three branches, with around 20-25 trainees in each location. One trainee told us that on qualification, it is *"unusual for the firm to lose any trainees."* However, we checked with grad recruitment and this year it lost 20% of its qualifiers.

Client secondments are regularly available. One trainee said, *"I really enjoyed it. You still have support from Pinsents. I was working with a legal director and liaising with people from all over the country."* A seat is available for one trainee in the firm's Brussels office and, as a result of an alliance with Swedish firm Magnusson Wahlin, *"people have started going to Scandinavia on secondment."*

living it large

While all our interviewees were happy with the social life of Pinsents, none seemed overwhelmed. Departmental and firm-wide events do go on, but trainee groups will not be found living it large on a Saturday night. But then, that wouldn't really be the Pinsents way. We weren't entirely surprised to hear one trainee say *"no-one begrudges you for leaving early to play cricket."* London seems to have the best perks, with a drinks trolley brought around the office on a Friday and an annual treasure hunt across London.

and finally…

There's definitely a good training contract on offer here and the chance to work in some excellent departments. Without the aggressive approach and European ambitions of its competitors, the long-term future of the firm will depend on its success in building a strong City practice. If you are thinking of applying, look carefully at the firms' list of 'Chosen Markets'.

Radcliffes

the facts

Location: London
UK ranking by size: 117
Total number of trainees: 13
Seats: 4x6 months
Alternative seats: None

Nestled in the warren of streets next to the Houses of Parliament and Westminster Abbey, Radcliffes has been a fixture in SW1 for what seems like forever. It has the air of a traditional old firm, and one that has been a name in private client and charities work since the dawn of time. But trainees tell us that sleepy little Radcliffes is not quite so sleepy any more.

all change

We heard the winds of change sweeping through the firm's Great College Street office. If you've kept your eyes on the legal press over the last couple of years (yes, of course you have) you'll have noted the loss and acquisition of lawyers on a reasonably regular basis. The end result is that, following cabinet reshuffles and the departures of certain lead lawyers to other firms, a couple of departments are now headed by young 30-somethings. The firm has a new non-solicitor chief executive (the former head honcho of a very successful Birmingham barristers' chambers) and at the end of 2000 it merged with a seven-partner commercial firm called J Benning & Peltz. A firm of this size (and we're talking about less than 40 partners) will often find that its areas of expertise are dependent on the skills, experience and connections of its partners. Hence Radcliffes finds itself with mini-focus areas in Italian and South African work and an interest in the Far East. But, as a trainee, you should be clear that there's little prospect of a six-month secondment to Cape Town or Singapore. This is not a big City outfit.

plucky pigeons without holes

It's precisely because it's not a big City outfit that trainees choose Radcliffes in the first place. These youngsters don't want to sacrifice themselves on the altar of billable hours and they don't want to over-specialise during their training. It's not just that they can select from tax and private client work, family and charities on the one hand and company/commercial on the other, it's also that there's a generalist nature to the seats on offer to them. "*If I was at Clifford Chance, I might be doing an IT seat, a banking seat and an asset finance seat. Here, all of that work is covered in just one seat. It's good if you want a broad exposure.*" Another agreed; "*within CoCo you don't get 25 different specialist seats, but you touch on a lot of different work. You are not over specialised so you get the larger picture.*"

With variety comes responsibility. If you're not prepared for it then think again about an application to Radcliffes. "*You have to have pluckiness. Trainees here are expected to work like assistants from the beginning. You just find yourself with files and things to do. Partners like you to just get on with it and not come back every two or three minutes with questions – some would be irritated by that. So you have to be resourceful and have the ability to just get on and have confidence in what you do.*"

calmer chameleon

The quality of tasks to be performed by trainees may be high and the range may make one feel "*like a chameleon,*" but trainees are quick to point out two things. First, the value of deals is low compared to many in the City. They talk of working on £5-10 million deals, but point out that a deal's a deal irrespective of how many noughts are on the end of the price tag. Smaller deals and smaller teams means trainees get closer to the front line.

Another issue trainees discussed with us was the low pressure hours that they work. "*Unless you are particularly busy and involved in a corporate deal then you won't be here beyond 7pm and most trainees leave around 6-6.30pm.*" This enables you to get home well in time for the evening news – just to check whether or not one of the several camera crews you passed on the way to the sandwich shop caught your best side (as you accidentally stood behind the reporter).

pimms and croquet

TV crews and politicians are two a penny in this location so no one back in the office will be that impressed when you tell them that you spotted Michael Portillo having lunch in the nearby Atrium restaurant. But the bad news is that "*you have to battle with the tourists to get to the tube.*"

The decent hours at Radcliffes have allowed for some charming social events to take off in the last year, since trainees initiated a social committee to put on firm-wide jollies. One of the favourites has been Pimms and Croquet in the adjacent Victoria Tower Gardens. Spiffing! So is this a terribly civilised and upper crust firm? "*Trainees are half private school and half state school*" we're told "*...it's not really rah!*" The crowd that makes up the numbers for Pimms and Croquet is the same one that also enjoys a night out at the dogs and participates in the "*Curry Club events*"

softball or hardball?

With just a dozen trainees, "*it's a firm where you're very evident.*" There'll be no hiding in the background trying to blend in with the furniture or the photocopying machine. Trainees say that it's important to be outgoing "*but not ruthlessly so*" and that "*cut throat back-stabbing*" is about as unRadcliffes as you could possibly get. It comes across as a very gentlemanly place where fair play goes down better than hard play.

Then again, we did sense that there are some among the trainees who think that a ballsier approach is both necessary and on the way. "*I would make it more commercial in its overall view and there's a vein running through the firm that agrees with me. Those on that side are fighting a battle… there's more to this firm than wills and estates for landed gentry. I think we have proved that to our clients but one needs to press on.*"

mirror mirror

Returning to the topic of change, trainees know that the new *"trouble shooter"* chief executive was brought in with the intention that he'd kick ass (if you'll excuse a rather unRadcliffes phrase). The reception may look like *"a cosy antique shop or a living room,"* but trainees tell us that having a *"traditional feel"* doesn't make the firm *"stagnant and old school."* Moreover, we heard that it is *"trying hard to reinvent itself. It looks in the mirror and doesn't like what it sees."*

"The really grumpy miserable partners are the exception not the rule" and whilst *"at the top it is an old boys club,"* this is not how the trainees see the firm as a whole. The firm engenders a sense of participation and belonging, and trainees perceive that the firm has been jolted awake and now knows where it is going. More than one of our sources talked of this being a *"good time to be on board"* at Radcliffes as it changed *"for the best."*

a deeper understanding

We got the impression that trainees really understood why they are at Radcliffes – they certainly have to. The nearer they get to qualification the more their commitment is questioned. The fact that all three of September 2001's qualifiers turned down *"scary offers"* from law firms in the City says a lot. But they fully appreciate their worth, and if the trade off between pay and personal lives diminishes they could be tempted to question the decision to stay. From time to time assistants do head east for the big money in the City and they go well qualified and with a good name on their CVs. The fact that there's not an exodus of assistants confirms the point that trainees made during our interviews; *"if you're motivated by big money, you'd have made a different choice in the first place."*

and finally...

Radcliffes is a blend of all things truly traditional with an emerging commercial appetite. If you want to bounce from mental health and clinical negligence work to big money divorces to general commercial work and corporate transactions then you can at this firm. *"It's different from the rest"* the trainees told us. Indeed it seems to be, but that doesn't mean that it hasn't recognised what the competition is doing and isn't keeping pace.

Reynolds Porter Chamberlain

the facts

Location: London
UK ranking by size: 55
Total number of trainees: 18
Seats: 4x6 months
Alternative Seats: None

RPC has traditionally been known as an insurance firm. And for good reason. Half of its workload is in insurance, it is highly rated by the *Chambers Guide* in insurance and professional negligence and it has a second office near Lloyd's of London, just to be closer to the action.

getting in the door

Several trainees at RPC have insurance as a background and one applied because he had heard *"good feedback on the firm having worked in the insurance industry."* There is no doubt that experience or an understanding of the insurance industry will go down well at interview. However, you don't need to have already had a successful first career just to get in the door.

Besides insurance, practices in commercial litigation, corporate, property and construction each account for around 10% of the firm's work and then there are token amounts of private client and media and technology. Trainees were keen to stress that the training contract does provide a breadth of experience. Just insurance *"would be a narrow way to think about it. Although there is an insurance slant to a lot of the work, there is more to it than that."* The diversity of work was enough to make one trainee declare *"we're getting the same training as everyone else!"*

mucking in

When asked about the high points of the training contract, one trainee said *"high points? It's a job in law!"* Despite this, all those that we spoke to had complimentary things to say about the training. They told us that *"the amount of work and responsibility you take on is very much up to you, which is probably a good thing."* The focus is on *"them training you. They want to give you responsibility when you can handle it. You are working with good people who are willing to take time out to help you."* It therefore comes as no surprise that *"most partners are very approachable."* You are *"not expected to ask questions about everything, but you can talk to partners if you have a problem." "Generally speaking, people muck in as a team."*

breaking ground

Trainees recognised that a good training means some hard work. *"In the first seat you weren't sat twiddling your thumbs, but in the second seat it has got a lot harder, with a lot more responsibility. You are given files on which you are asked to make decisions."* But this brings with it the opportunity to excel. One trainee said, *"on certain cases I was aware that we were breaking new ground in law."*

The trainee population at RPC is fairly small and this breeds intimacy. No… not that sort!! *"In large firms you are vying for attention. At RPC, with such a small number of trainees, you are not in competition with friends."* Sure enough, the trainees *"all get on with each other."* Once a month, on the 'First Thursday' in fact, lawyers in the Holborn office will meet up in the Three Cups bar. There are various sports teams – hockey, cricket etc.

taking off

A variety of seats are available at RPC. *"I don't think it's a good idea to specialise too early and at this firm there are a lot of departments that you can sit in."* Unusually, the firm still has a family practice, although the clients and cases taken on are not those to be found in your run of the mill high street practice. Some of the high profile divorces handled by RPC have ended up splashed over the pages of national newspapers. National newspapers also cause the firm's defamation lawyers to be kept busy. Since the media team arrived from Davies Arnold Cooper, RPC's reputation in this field has gone from strength to strength.

> "The trainee population at RPC is fairly small and this breeds intimacy."

We can't avoid talking about the i-word, so we'll let you know that RPC has one of the largest insurance and reinsurance practices in the country covering contentious and non-contentious matters. Within the firm, *"City insurance is really taking off – that is where trainees are looking to qualify."* The firm receives instructions from the London market's reinsurance of foreign insurers and represented the London insurers over losses caused by the Indonesian riots. In 2001, and no doubt amid the popping of corks, RPC became a full member of the NHS Litigation Authority panel and should benefit from changes in the way that medical negligence claims are handled and the further concentration of NHS litigation work among a small number of firms. The firm also sits on seven insurer's legal negligence panels including Zurich, Hiscox, and Bar Mutual.

this is my minder

RPC takes care of its trainees. Each is assigned a partner from a different department who is their mentor or *"minder"* as they put it. While these partners do not actually shadow the trainees around the office, looking surly and wearing dark glasses (or so we're told), they do meet with trainees every three months to review the training, provide feedback and help in the selection of the next seat. 'Help' from the 'minders' would seem to work: "*if you do want to do a seat, you will generally get to do it.*"

The firm wants to develop through natural growth. "*It is not the type of firm that wants to merge and expand ridiculously. It wants to grow through its own trainees.*" Six of the seven qualifiers stayed with the firm in September 2001, three of them going into insurance groups. Still, salaries are felt to be "*not quite in line with other firms.*"

evil baddies

RPC is the British member of a worldwide network of law firms called 'Terralex'. Despite sounding suspiciously like a member of the Decepticons, evil baddies in the Transformers, Terralex helps member firms serve their clients', through the exchange of professional information among members, and the provision of jurisdictional expertise and service in locations around the world. Or so the website tells us…

Do you see yourself as an RPC trainee? If you're not sure, you can look on the firm's website and see the current trainees' profiles. The firm "*likes you to be interesting,*" and "*tends not to get overly ambitious people.*" "*No one expects the job to be your life.*" Judging from the trainee profiles, sports are popular – one trainee was a member of the British ski team. "*People are expected to have a life outside of work.*" For one trainee, this means DJing in his spare time. Trainees were also keen to point out there is "*no Oxbridge bias.*"

and finally…

With only about ten new recruits a year, the trainee population is small enough for you to make an impression from the outset. The work is dominated by insurance and if you specifically want international finance and wall to wall M&A, it might be wise to look elsewhere. But if litigation's on your mind… get applying!

Richards Butler

the facts

Location: London
UK ranking by size: 46
Total number of trainees: 43
Seats: 4x5 and 1x4 months
Alternative seats: Overseas seats, secondments
Extras: Pro bono: St Botolph's Project, language training

Richards Butler is a mid-tier firm whose core reputation is in shipping and media. Outside those departments are a whole raft of other practice areas, such as banking, employment, planning and insolvency. Its strong international base (begun around 50 years ago) is more important than it may at first seem. A large proportion of the firm's revenue is generated overseas.

beefing up corporate

One of the main events of 2001 was the installation of a new managing partner. True to form he gave interviews to the press and expounded on the firm's strategy for the coming years. It seems the firm is in the process of restating its commitment to corporate finance. It's an area in which Richards Butler is a leading name in Hong Kong, but which hasn't been noted as a key strength in London for some time. The trainees we spoke to confirmed that corporate and finance seats were becoming a much more popular way to spend time during the training contract. Some trainees spoke of being surprised how much they'd enjoyed the 'City' work on offer at the firm. "*I never thought I'd like banking, but I really liked getting involved in deals.*"

what's the deal?

Trainees view the wide range of departments on offer to them as one of the firm's best selling points. "*If you don't know what you want to specialise in, this is a good firm to come to,*" "*it's not like the firms where, for instance,*" there's no let-off from finance work." Let's illustrate the range of work by referring to two relatively recent deals – the redevelopment of Battersea Power Station (into offices, bars, hotels and flats) and the liquidation of the Romanian state shipping fleet. Some trainees intimated that the firm's reputation in shipping has led to distance developing between that department and the rest of firm. *"Shipping is very separate from the rest of us… I don't know anyone there."* One source indicated that, if you are interested in shipping, this is the right time to apply to Richards Butler as *"it's a big firm for shipping and you've almost got the job in the bag if you say you're interested in shipping."*

Those unsure of what interests them should be aware of the stiff competition for seats in some of the smaller and sexier departments. Consequently, some trainees *"don't bother applying to media, IP or employment,"* perceiving it to be *"a waste of time."* For those that are lucky enough to grab a seat in the highly rated media department or in IP, there are secondments to clients like the BBC, MTV and Rank. Getting through the competition is well worth it. As for those secondments – *"they're fun! It's a very different environment, more hands on and you get more responsibility, plus there are no timesheets to fill in."* On the MTV seat you get *"proper dress-down and the TV is on all day."* The secondment to Rank is an employment seat with a difference. *"You handle your own cases… I was drafting my own tribunal pleadings."*

the wrong trainers

The size of the firm is something many applicants factor into their decision to approach the firm. *"It's not a hamburger factory,"* said one trainee. *"The firm still has personality, so as well as having great work and some high profile clients, the firm has character."* Excellent… but what sort of character? A common thread is that most people are chatty and cheerful (*"down to earth and not snobby"*), which is an advantage for trainees as *"you never feel on edge or unable to approach people."*

We like to amuse ourselves here on the Chambers Student Guide. Sometimes we come up with a 'school days' classification for the trainees we interview. So we've decided – Richards Butler trainees are like those of your old classmates who couldn't be bothered to wear the right trainers. You remember them – the clever and friendly ones who were interested in absolutely everything, except how others perceived them.

the smooth and the hairy

Richards Butler trainees seemed to posses a shade more realism than many of the others we interviewed for the True Picture. Fully aware that the rough comes with the smooth, and nonplussed by it, they told us that *"sometimes you're not ecstatic about being here, but it's not horrible… the training works for me."* Client contact varies between different seats, with some trainees *"looking forward to working with clients, as I haven't had much client contact,"* while others were more than happy with the level of contact and responsibility they'd been given. It may sound obvious but an *"excellent supervisor makes for a good seat"* and *"some supervisors are control freaks, others are more relaxed."* Even those who hadn't built up the best of relationships with certain supervisors told us that *"there are always people you can speak to when things are getting hairy."*

reality check

The firm's website indicates that it's looking to *"recruit for future partners,"* and although most of those we spoke to *"don't know anyone in my intake who's dying to be a partner,"* they are generally keen to stay at the firm after qualification. That said, Richards Butler has historically retained only a portion of its qualifiers. *"They try to accommodate you, but they can't if everyone wants to do the same thing."* Some think that getting the job you want on qualification boils down to luck, most are philosophical – *"I'm doing the training, I'll get the experience, and then I'll think about what to do."*

Richards Butler recruits from *"a good mix of universities"* and *"there's a breadth of ages."* There is no set

Richards Butler type, but the trainees we spoke to were relaxed and cheerful and possessed a healthy dose of realism. There are no wide-eyed romantics and no power-hungry despots-in-waiting. In 2001, 15 of the 20 qualifiers stayed with the firm.

pure poetry

If a colleague says to you 'See you in the Poet after work', you'll have to ask him to be more specific. There are the three Poet pubs in the area (The Water Poet, The Poet and The New Poet) and trainees also frequent a few bars further afield. The firm has a basement restaurant called 'Writs' that doubles as a venue for the '531 club' (no we don't know why it's called that) which serves up free drinks once a month and is mainly attended by trainees and the support staff. Otherwise the canteen is good for catching up on news, and is *"quite a good gossip machine."* Those not on the hunt for juice and scandal relax on the roof terrace.

The trainees are a *"tightly-knit"* bunch, but they told us *"there's not much interaction between the different groups except at trainee level."* We find it impossible to characterise the relationship between trainees and the partners and senior assistants simply because opinion varied so widely on that topic. One source said, *"we don't really have much to do with senior assistants and partners."* Another told us that *" partners from some areas socialise more than from others, anyway, I wouldn't want the partners to come along all the time,"* whilst a third described the partners as *"young, friendly and approachable."* It's perfectly possible that all three are correct.

and finally…

Internationally Richards Butler has a great reputation in corporate and finance, yet at home these are seen as areas for improvement. No home improvements are required in the superb media practice and it is strong in shipping across all its offices. The key watchword for applicants is 'variety' but remember these other words – Paris, Hong Kong and Abu Dhabi. Get your bags packed!

Rowe & Maw

the facts
Location: London
UK ranking by size: 29
Total number of trainees: 41
Seats: 4x6 months
Alternative Seats: Brussels, secondments
Extras: Pro bono: Royal Courts of Justice CAB

In many ways Rowe & Maw comes across as a pretty run of the mill, medium-sized commercial practice. Corprorate transactions provide the bulk of the work and the firm has a substantial litigation department. As an outsider, it's difficult to ascertain what makes the firm stand out from the crowd… so we spoke to a few insiders and got sleuthing.

dope filled conference rooms

There is no question that the firm has performed well over the past couple of years in terms of growth and profits; one might almost say that it's having a bit of a renaissance. Indeed, turnover rose from £46 million to £56 million in the last financial year. Emphasising the firm's broad church commercial practice, the *Chambers Guide* shows Rowe & Maw performing strongly in medium deal corporate finance work, pensions and pension litigation, partnership, construction and construction based professional negligence work, and administrative and public law.

We noted a succession of quirky, headline-grabbing cases and events. Rowe & Maw were instructed on the construction of the world's largest Buddha statue in India and could once boast Mr Blobby as a client. Currently it's acting for GW, the company licensed by the government to produce large quantities of cannabis to be used in the production of non-smokable medicines. Rowe & Maw also scored something of a marketing coup earlier in 2001 when it became the first law firm to advertise on British television with some rather garish hoardings in England's World Cup qualifier against Greece. We got the impression that maybe, just maybe R&M's boring image was beginning to change.

dinner party pokémon

In last year's True Picture we commented on Rowe & Maw's staid image and its particularly bland website. And we exposed the scandal of the business card-less trainees. We could not possibly comment on whether or not it's the result of our exposé but we're delighted to report improvement in all these areas. Trainees can now play twenty-something pokémon at dinner parties, the website opens with a snazzy Flash animation and our sources report a little more dynamism within the firm.

The firm has broken with a long-standing bias towards Oxbridge recruits and recognises that good trainees hail from a variety of universities. The effects of this shift are working their way through the system. One source said, *"out of 25 trainees in my year, I think about three have come from Oxford or Cambridge."* Those we interviewed came from a wide range of institutions themselves. So what now constitutes a typical Rowe & Maw trainee? Well, basically, they are bright graduates who've shied away from the mega-firms in an attempt to live a more balanced lifestyle. One trainee told us *"coming here was, in many ways, a quality of life decision."* And another said, *"when I came for my interview a trainee told us that no one she knows at the big firms ever has the chance to see their friends. I just didn't want that."*

Whilst you will not be expected to give up your life outside work, hours can vary so don't expect to be out the door promptly every evening. Typical hours run from 9am to 6pm-7pm. Most of the trainees we spoke to had worked a weekend and a couple of late nights.

don't bank on lloyd's

Trainees must complete two compulsory seats – corporate and litigation. Beyond this, most trainees seem to end up with the seats they angled for. We heard that *"in the large departments it's almost as if there aren't enough trainees to go round,"* but the smaller departments are often oversubscribed. Two areas of work in particular – the Lloyd's seat and the IP seat – drew a lot of favourable comment. However, with only a couple of places in each, there's no guarantee you'll see one or the other. *"There aren't many openings in the small departments, so there is a bit of strategising about the optional seats – working out how many people are applying* [for each seat] *and how to maximise chances and not waste a choice."* At each seat rotation, two trainees get to go out to Brussels and there's also an array of client secondments on offer.

We heard a few moans about insufficient (though not inadequate) paralegal support. Insolvency litigation was cited as the only department with enough of it. In general, litigation often turns out not to be the hive of challenging activity trainees had hoped for. *"It can be good because you are in a department with loads of other young people, but it sometimes means you are treated like a paralegal as well… the trainees can just blend into the support staff."*

don't underestimate the power of the grey side

Perhaps smarting from the cruel nickname, 'Slow & Bore', trainees told us about two divergent forces battling within the partnership. *"One group is in favour of the old school, gentlemanly practice and the other is keen to see a new, more dynamic firm start to compete on a larger stage."* So which side is winning the war of the Roweses? *"Definitely the more 'modern' side… we are really pushing to expand and move up the rankings."* Sounds like interesting times ahead. The firm recently shed its private client department in an attempt to focus on more profitable areas of business. The boring, safe image may soon be gone forever.

mad for it

Die-hard clubbers beware. Rowe & Maw is a perfectly friendly firm, but the social life is not massive. *"Before I came here I had hoped there would be a big social life but now, whilst we do go out sometimes, we all value our space and tend to do our own thing. That isn't a bad* thing; it means we keep in touch with non-work friends." We did track down an R&M trainee pub though – The Booksellers. Trainees mingle over post-work drinks, particularly on special occasions. *"Birthday parties are quite a big thing here."* Great, who's for the bumps then? Perhaps there have been some nasty accidents as, according to the figures graduate recruitment gave us, out of the 13 2001 trainees, between 8.03 and 9.49 went on to qualify into the firm.

and finally…

Rowe & Maw has struggled a bit with its identity problem in the past. Our interviewees understood that this was changing, but we were left with a sense that the evolving firm currently suffers from a mild dose of schizophrenia. There are signs that the traditional and sluggish elements of the firm are making way for the ambitions of younger and more go ahead partners. Whether the Rowe & Maw charm, quirky cases and gentlemanly attitudes will survive in the future we don't know, but it'll be more exciting times for the trainees.

Shoosmiths

the facts

Location: Northampton, Nottingham, Reading, Banbury, Fareham
UK ranking by size: 34
Total number of trainees: 24
Seats: 4x6 months
Alternative Seats: Secondments

Shoosmiths aims to give trainees the best of both worlds – an excellent training without long hours, six figure property prices and Ken Livingstone. To this end, Shoosmiths has based itself in six regional offices spreading north from the south coast right up to Nottingham. Admittedly, it's not chosen the sexiest of locations, but not everyone is hell-bent on working in EC1.

sh sh sh shoopeople

When asked why they chose Shoosmiths, every trainee we spoke to was clear about not wanting to be based in London. From one we heard *"I cut the country off at Oxford and only looked at places further north."* Trainees were also keen to ensure they received a high quality training within a smaller office environment. They didn't want to feel *"part of a monstrously huge legal machine."* As one put it, *"it's not that Shoosmiths is a small firm, but the division between offices means that you will be one of a small group of trainees."*

Shoosmiths' practice is divided into three divisions: claims compensation, commercial services, and financial institutions. Claims Compensation and Property Direct handle the bulk of Shoosmiths work. These two divisions specialise in high volume, low cost, low value conveyancing and personal injury work. Don't worry though, trainees rarely get involved in the nitty gritty of this area of the firm's business. The low value work is handled by large teams of staff, many of whom have no formal legal qualifications. Trainee solicitors spend their time in the higher value finance and commercial practices. Whilst 'secondments' to the conveyor belt divisions do happen *"when there is a rush on,"* trainees speak positively about it. One told us of his time in Property Direct: *"I was effectively managing a group of junior staff and dealing with more complex issues as they arose… I really enjoyed it."* From time to time trainees also get the opportunity to spend time on secondment to clients, including Barclaycard and the Open University.

To give a flavour of life around the country we infiltrated the different offices which take on trainees. Basingstoke handles 100% personal injury work and no trainees are based there full time.

northampton court

The biggest office taking the most trainees, Shoosmiths' Northampton HQ is based at 'The Lakes' just off the M1. With a population of twelve trainees, it has a dirty half-dozen young guns joining the office each year. Despite the firm's out-of-town side-of-motorway location, we were told The Lakes is as pleasant an office environment as one could wish for. *"The offices are new and very smart… surrounded by lakes with swans on the water, it is a great area to work in."*

> "If we do stay till around 2am, it's so rare that we tend to have champagne."

Flora and fauna aside, there are two compulsory seats – litigation and commercial property – and an opportunity to spend some time in corporate, which is *"quite a popular destination."* As in all offices, trainees have the chance to conduct small pieces of advocacy themselves. *"One of the high points for me was making an application in the Royal Courts of Justice* [in London]. *Walking through those arches gave me a huge sense of pride."* But you'll not be expected to work anywhere near London hours; *"by 6:30pm the office is almost deserted… no secretaries, no partners and no trainees."* When working late is necessary, the extra effort is appreciated. *"If we do stay till around 2am, it is so rare that we tend to have champagne afterwards."* (Presumably the closure of a deal is the trigger for both the work and the champagne.)

It seems that in last year's True Picture we were guilty of a grave injustice. We reported that there were no pubs nearby. This year trainees were pretty darned quick to point out there's *"not only one, but two!"* Sincere and grovelling apologies to the Shoefolk. With the largest choice of seats on offer, it is possible for trainees to request to be transferred from one of the other offices over to Northampton to broaden their horizons. Or maybe the real attraction is the swans. In Northampton, 2001 retention statistics are fighting fit; six out of the seven trainees accepted the firm's offer on qualification.

nottingham forest

The smaller Nottingham office has a different feel to the Northampton nerve centre, not least of all because the office is completely open plan. *"It helps to break down barriers; all the fee earners sit together with the secretaries in the middle."* The Nottingham office takes five trainees at a time and we learnt that this has an impact on the interaction between staff. One trainee said, *"as there are so few of us, we tend to socialise as a group with all the staff under the age of 30 – assistants and support staff too."* You won't be spoiled for seat choice in Nottingham on account of the fact that there are only four available. Trainees rotate around commercial property, litigation, corporate/commercial and employment. *"Whilst there aren't many seats, personnel are flexible about the kind of work you see in each seat so there is some choice."* Hours seemed to be more regular than in Northampton, with late night sessions a rarity. In 2001, both trainees were offered a job on qualification, one accepted and one decided to leave for personal reasons.

banbury cross

The Banbury office is another intimate affair, with only two trainees currently based in the Oxfordshire outpost. Banbury is the only one of the offices to offer a family seat, which means every now and again a trainee from another office will spend six months getting some experience in that department. Banbury is about to go open plan in swanky new premises. As to be expected in a training population of two, the opportunities for socialising as a group are limited and, again, this leads to more interaction with staff as a whole and less of a *"trainee mentality."* In September 2001, the one qualifying trainee was retained. 100% retention!

reading lists

The Reading office is another *"smart modern building just off the main road"* and another location where it is almost essential that you can drive to get to and from work. With so much IT business floating around the

Thames Valley, it is not surprising that much of the Reading office's work is focused in this area. Like all the smaller offices, barriers between trainees and other staff are broken down by the absence of *"trainees flocking in like students during Freshers' Week!"* Three out of four Reading trainees took jobs on qualification.

ships in the nightlife

Fareham traditionally undertook personal injury work, but that operation has now been farmed out to the Basingstoke office. It is now a general commercial boutique with a specialism in shipping. In the past, only one trainee was anchored at the Fareham office, but in 2002 a flotilla of three young tugs will make their way over. The office was described as young and sociable and regularly meets in the two local bars, The Waterside and The Parson's Collar. In 2001 the lone trainee in this office was offered a job, but chose to set sail for new waters.

waving the flag

Despite their separate locations, staff from all offices come together for social events from the Summer Ball to quiz nights. Training courses are conducted on a firm wide basis, with staff descending upon Northampton for most inter-office events. Trainees praised the quality of these training sessions and the time invested in their personal development by the HR department and partners. The firm takes great pride in its Investors in People award. One trainee told us, *"It really wasn't just about getting the flag."*

Shoosmiths is a firm with separate offices united by a common endeavour. *"There is no rivalry or competition, though I have heard it wasn't always that way, we have a very strong team identity."* Trainees get to know one another at the beginning of their training and most manage to stay in touch throughout the two years, regardless of the geographical division. *"We all email each other and keep up with what is going on around the country. I think regardless of where we are, we all know what each other are up to."* Bless!

and finally...

The firm has a very specific identity with a unique approach to practice. It takes pride in lower value as well as higher value work, although trainees will focus primarily on the latter type. Shoosmiths is clearly not trying to compete with the top City firms and neither is it demanding to be called **the** best provincial firm. But it's well up there nationally.

Sidley Austin Brown & Wood

the facts

Location: London
UK ranking by size: 58
Total number of trainees: 11
Seats: 4x6 months
Alternative Seats: None

Sidley Austin Brown & Wood is a new firm created from the merger of two big US practices, both of whom had London branches within a stone's throw of the Bank of England. And for good reason.

mind boggling

The coming together on May 1st 2001 of Sidley & Austin with Brown & Wood resulted in one of America's largest law firms, with over 1300 Ally McBeals of various ages and genders. This merger was completely driven from the US, so the two London branches suddenly found themselves joined at the hip. The firm still has both of its original homes in the City, but plans are afoot for full *"physical integration."* Social events have promoted other forms of integration and *"partners make the effort to attend." "It takes time, but we are getting there."*

In terms of clients and new work, the benefits of the merger were *"visible from day one."* It brought together the broad structured finance prowess of Sidley & Austin, and the US-backed repackaging practice of Brown & Wood. Its big name finance clients include Morgan Stanley and JP Morgan. The firm undertook a recent high profile deal involving a ground-breaking collateralised debt obligation transaction for Deutsche Bank and has niche strengths in the interlinking areas of commercial mortgage backed deals, conduits and synthetic transactions. For securitisation, it is ranked alongside the biggest guns of the magic circle. So, did that make sense to you? If not, is your interest piqued? If it's yes to either question, then apply straight away.

silly questions

So you're still reading. Excellent! *"A large part of the practice is banking related." "Property and tax departments act as support to corporate and banking."* Sidley & Austin previously had a broader based corporate/commercial practice, but was knocked by the loss of its telecoms lawyers, resulting in a conscious decision to specialise more on capital markets. Trainees, therefore, rotate around just four seats: tax, property, banking, and corporate. Work in banking *"can be very complicated." "You are working on transactions in quite small teams"* and, with the nature of the deals, *"client contact is limited."*

There is no litigation seat. Sidleys trainees previously had three months seconded to top City litigators Barlow Lyde & Gilbert to gain experience. To meet the requirements of the Law Society, trainees now undertake an in-house course of seminars, *"which is just not the same."* Some feel they are not getting as broad an experience they would like. However, future trainees are warned at the outset of the highly specialised nature of the work, and hence the training. As for the quality of training, most partners are *"decent"* at sitting down with trainees and explaining things. A source confirmed, *"I have been able to ask the silliest questions."* Everyone is *"really approachable,"* but the training is *"very much on the job." "If you approach people doing interesting work, you can get involved."* But trainees must be *"proactive,"* because work *"will not always be given to you."* Still, with *"not as many trainees to share the work with, you are recognised for what you do."*

limey blimey!

Despite a network of twelve overseas offices around the US and the Far East, trainees do not go abroad. Our sources reported that the firm values those with previous careers. Several of the current crop have postgraduate qualifications in aspects of international law and finance. Trainees are paid *"less than magic circle,"* but upon qualification, *"very well – Mid Atlantic plus."* Now if we were to give a prize for the understatement of the book, it's got to be this description of NQ salaries. Theses lucky so and so's get a colossal £75, 520 per year. Blimey!

Almost everyone is offered a job, *"around half stay and half leave."* Positions tend to come up in banking and corporate, but trainees should not expect to qualify into property. *"The chances are low. It is very specialised, and they only take on 2-3 year PQEs."* Positions in fashionable areas like IP and employment would also be very hard to come by at Sidleys.

born in the usa?

While trainees insisted the firm is *"not like the myth of US firms,"* if the work is there, it will be done, including during evenings and weekends. Property and tax were thought slightly better for hours – 9am-6.30pm were common. But if a run of transactions hit you in banking, it will be tough, with very long hours and weekends. One trainee described her low point as these hours, especially if they entailed *"monotonous work and proof reading."* Otherwise, there is no pressure to be seen in the office late. Working in a US firm in London does not mean a *"marked difference"* from UK firms though; the number of US-qualified lawyers in the office is not huge. *"Day to day, it's similar to any other magic circle type environment."* Except in terms of size, we suspect. Typical of US firms, Sidleys has a full time dress-down policy.

Although one source admitted, *"we will always be part of the US mothership,"* it is clear that as an overseas branch of a US firm, the London office does have a level of autonomy. Work does *"come through connections with the US, but at the same time, we do have a lot independent clients." "The policy is for us to stand on our own two feet." Sources reported "concentrating more on Europe," and the firm has had talks with a German firm regarding another possible merger.

going round in circles
What is on offer at Sidleys seems to be the quality of deals available in the magic circle, coupled with "*a smaller environment.*" Trainees talked of a lack of pretension, bravado or arrogance. "*Even the managing partner stops you in the corridor and asks you how you are.*" The firm has social events, but no regular get togethers in the pub. On a Friday night there's not a huge amount of "*socialising among trainees.*"

> "Working in a US firm in London does not mean a marked difference from UK firms."

The old Sidley & Austin offices in Threadneedle Street, are "*very much dark wood – what the Americans would want the UK office to look like!*" We laughed at a trainee's description of the large circular boardroom. "*When all the doors are closed, you can't actually find your way out and you end up in the kitchen or a cupboard.*" Sounds like a French farce!

and finally…
It could never be described as a broad training, but if you are interested in banking and financial markets, this "*very very specific firm*" is an "*exciting*" place to consider. Fairly small, it actually has a surprisingly down to earth atmosphere, given the magic circle quality of work being undertaken. But you have been warned: "*trainees should have an interest in international finance.*"

Simmons & Simmons

the facts
Location: London
UK ranking by size: 18
Total number of trainees: 154
Seats: 4x6 months
Alternative Seats: Overseas seats, secondments

Last year we were happy to report on an optimistic atmosphere and broadly happy trainees at this top 20 City practice. This was in spite of a jittery time for Simmons in recent years as the firm was rocked by a series of high profile partner defections. The exodus seems to have been halted, profits have risen dramatically and the firm has moved into swanky new offices. All in all, there really is no reason why we shouldn't be able to report on an excellent training environment at Simmons.

you're only cheating yourselves
But we can't. Despite repeated requests, the Graduate Recruitment department refused to give us free access to their trainees to conduct confidential interviews. Instead, a handful of trainees were very kindly picked for us. We are unable to confirm that the trainees to whom we spoke had not been handpicked for a reason and we certainly could not guarantee them the anonymity that trainees enjoyed at other firms. Simmons' appearance in the True Picture is, consequently, an abbreviated one. The True Picture is not designed to be a marketing opportunity, but law firms with nothing to hide have nothing to fear from us. Far from having skeletons in the closet, Simons recently finished 24th in a DTI sponsored survey to find Britain's best employers. Only two other law firms in the True Picture 100 appeared in the survey results. OK, by now you can tell we've got the hump with Simmons.

happy, happy, joy, joy
Anyway, what is not in doubt is that Simmons is a large international practice. "*I chose the firm because of*

their size and the international perspective of the practice." Good answer, but why choose this firm over international rivals like Norton Rose or CMS Cameron McKenna? *"It was the people, the environment and the atmosphere. This is a really friendly firm."* This is a comment we hear about the majority of firms where we interview. Maybe it really is true of Simmons but, without being able to conduct confidential interviews, we can't confirm one way or another.

> "Everyone who wants to travel should get to go."

beans on toast for all

We were told that there is no typical trainee, with a broad cross-section of backgrounds, ages and universities represented. *"There is as much Oxbridge as anywhere else, but certainly not a public school or collegiate culture."* We heard several times that Simmons trainees were *"well rounded and down to earth."* And there was a distinct absence of *"the trainee partner"* (meaning an over aggressive, ambitious trainee who eats, breathes and dreams about law and the greater glory of the firm). Interviewees reported a good level of interaction between all levels of fee earners and support staff. This has been assisted by the move to the new offices, where *"the partners' dining room has been abolished. We all eat together now."* Great. Pass the ketchup.

playground hair tug no.1

Seats are served in the standard four by six-month rotation, with no compulsory visits apart from the Law Society's contentious/non-contentious requirements. Simmons is well known for its successful niche practices in IP and employment and these always tend to be attractive stop offs for trainee solicitors. Trainees told us they normally received the seats they asked for, if not in the order requested then eventually and, if not your first choice then your second. *"Graduate Recruitment and HR bend over backwards to helps us."* Just fancy that!

playground hair tug no.2

With a global network of overseas offices, trainees are offered a large number of secondments outside of the UK. Opportunities are available in Shanghai, Hong Kong, Abu Dhabi, Lisbon, Milan, Brussels and Paris amongst others. Languages are especially important for the Brussels and Paris seats. How easy is it to get overseas? With so many seats available there's no reason why everyone who wants to travel shouldn't get the opportunity. Guess who is really supportive and helpful when the seats are being allocated.

and finally

So that's about it, responsibility (super), feedback (smashing) and office atmosphere (great). Maybe we are a bit too cynical. Maybe everything is just fine and dandy. Before you write us off as jaded old hacks however, imagine that you have just started as a trainee and we ask you to spill the beans on what life at your firm is really like. You have no guarantee that your anonymity will be protected. Would you be entirely candid? You may very well say no. We couldn't possibly comment.

Sinclair Roche & Temperley

the facts

Location: London
UK ranking by size: 113
Total number of trainees: 16
Seats: 4x6 months
Alternative Seats: Secondments
Extras: Pro bono: Hoxton Law Centre, language training

Sinclair Roche & Temperley is a medium-sized City of London outfit with an international practice. The firm is best known for its shipping work, but is also well respected in aviation, trade and energy.

love at first sight
Like many medium-sized firms, it can be difficult getting a handle on that particular *je ne sais quoi*, which we always hope will make a firm stand out from the crowd. When we asked trainees why they joined the firm we got the usual – *"I really liked the atmosphere when I came for interview."* A touch of love at first sight – *"They came over to my university to do a presentation and it was all go from there."* And the slightly more helpful – *"I wanted lots of international work, but in a more intimate atmosphere. That was exactly what SRT offered."* One trainee told us *"I was a known face from day one. You don't have to work for someone here for them to know you."*

It's an international firm in every sense. 65-75 % of SRT's client base hail from outside the UK, so you will certainly not be joining a bunch of Little Englanders. The trainee population also reflects the firm's international perspective, with trainees flocking from the four corners of the globe… even the Midlands. *"Trainees come from all over. In my intake, four are from the UK and the rest from Zimbabwe, China, Korea and Romania."*

weigh anchor
Training is structured into four six-month seats and, with its heavy emphasis on the firm's core shipping practice, trainees are keen to take a break from the open seas whenever the opportunity arises. *"Corporate and property are normally rather popular as they are separate from the firm's core shipping practice. It is nice to see a bit of variety later on during the training."* Whilst there can be no doubt that SRT has firmly laid anchor in its nautical niche, there is more to the firm than just shipping, so you should get the chance to see other work. However, trainees report that across the departments there seemed to be something of a disjointed approach, with the firm lacking a cohesive inter-departmental ethos. Perhaps this is because of the sharp differences between the shipping and non-shipping work. Trainees further noted that this could at times adversely affect the quality and diversity of work available to them. *"If the firm took a slightly more holistic approach to practice then we might see more work being shared around from different departments. This could give us a broader and more interesting training."*

A sea change may lie ahead. The firm is undertaking a softly softly review of the way it approaches practice, intending to place a renewed emphasis on teamwork and training. One source said, *"We have a new head of HR starting soon – a qualified lawyer. The firm is taking a bit of a step back and reviewing training procedures."* Another confirmed, *"we have started grouping fee earners more logically; for instance, commercial litigators now sit on the commercial floor… there are also trade groups set up, which focus upon specific practice areas. It is part of an evolutionary process of change within the firm."*

the financial times
You will not have to work the unsociable hours that plague some of the larger international practices. *"My hours are normally about 9.30am to 6pm,"* one trainee said. *"There are very few late nights or weekends."* In fact, rather than complaining about being worked too hard, when we asked whether there had been any low points of their training contract, we were told that trainees occasionally end up kicking their heels when there's not enough work to be getting on with. Once again, we heard about differences in attitudes between departments when it came to finishing a quiet day. *"In most departments, if you have finished your work at 5:45pm then you go and nobody comments on it. In others you might be better shuffling papers for three quarters of an hour."* Which departments? A different source leaked the info: *"I have heard this can happen in Finance."*

contact details
The trainees we interviewed welcomed the idea of a general overhaul of training. *"In the past, feedback and supervision have been quite poor,"* one said. *"We were

supposed to have an appraisal for every seat which we completed, but increasingly these became too informal and might not even take place until a month after we had left the seat." Admittedly, we hear this is a problem at some other firms too. So is everything fine now? *"The new system is a lot better – there is a formal hand over process after we change seats, but we still do find appraisals taking place after a seat has been left well behind."* This year all bar one of the eight qualifiers were offered jobs. Of these, five accepted.

> "I've attended client lunches and have run my own client meetings."

Trainees seemed happy with levels of client contact in most departments. *"I handle client contact when my partner is away… I have attended many client meetings, client lunches and have even run my own client meetings."* Slightly less contact was afforded in others. *"Client contact is normally regarded as a reward here. If you prove yourself, then you get it."*

trapped or trappist?
Whilst there will be some opportunities to travel if you join this firm, these opportunities are slightly limited given the firm's international reach. *"Whenever trainees do get sent aboard, it tends to be because they have language skills."* With overseas offices in Bucharest, Shanghai and Hong Kong, you are going to need more than just GCSE French. Client secondments are also thin on the ground, though again, not entirely unheard of. *"They do happen occasionally, but generally only if you have experience in a specific area which could be of merit."* The advice to those who want to vary their location whilst training is to make it clear that you want these opportunities early on and have a very good case as to why you have something to contribute.

And what of the social scene? In addition to the usual sporting fixtures, there's a drinks reception in the building at the end of each week. It is well attended. *"We don't tend to all go out en masse every night, but there is usually a group who will push on after the drinks on Friday."* The main SRT haunt after hours is The Old Monk, just around the corner from the office, where *"you can normally find someone you know."*

and finally…
Trainees were optimistic about the changes afoot within HR and valued the level of client contact in most departments. Whilst there are few opportunities to travel as a trainee, bear in mind just how much of the firm's work is international. If you want to travel, these opportunities will certainly arise regularly after qualification.

SJ Berwin

the facts
Location: London
UK ranking by size: 25
Total number of trainees: 78
Seats: 4x6 months
Alternative seats: Overseas seats

Can you handle it? It's a fair enough question. This is one firm which you ought to be certain suits you before you end up there by accident. A young and very corporate-oriented practice with a full on feel and energy levels to leave you spinning. SJ Berwin may not be as slick and sophisticated as the magic circle, and possibly to the establishment City practices it is just a bit on the wide side, but if you want to be judged on who you are and what you can do rather than where you've come from, then this is a firm to consider.

naked ambition
The website states that trainees at the firm are "bright, commercially aware and ambitious." Our

years of research lead us to agree. One trainee put it less subtly: *"On the PSC course that we share with other firms we're always the mouthy ones at the back asking questions. We attract strong personalities."* Indeed you do. Another confirmed *"this firm is not for the fainthearted. We have a brash new boy image and we are happy with it."* The bottom line is that, if you're intelligent and very hard working, you'll make it here. Whether you're quieter or plain mad, bad and dangerous, ideally you'll justifiably confident in your abilities and driven to do well. You should be able to handle the heat when the kitchen gets hot. Some feel that, if there were less of the driven and ambitious and more of the calmer and quieter types, *"it would be healthier for the firm."*

One of the urban myths that used to circulate about SJ Berwin was that it was a sweatshop. We can't find any real evidence of slavery or drudgery. Yes, lawyers here work very, very hard and probably harder than at the vast majority of law firms in the UK but, time and time again, trainees tell us that they have no problem with this. Clearly not a firm for slackers, *"it attracts a certain type; the very competitive type, but healthily so."*

Maybe not always so healthy though. Take the issue of seat allocation. *"There's big brash characters here and you have to be willing to be arsey, when needed, to fight for the good seats."* There are good seats and bad seats? Not exactly – there are mainstream seats and over subscribed niche seats. The compulsories are two corporate seats (although these include areas like financial services and tax) and a contentious seat. This is important to remember. Corporate, and in particular private equity, is *"the driver of the firm."* It has a great reputation for property and a large property department, but a property seat is not strictly compulsory, although it is likely.

european competition

"People need to know that this is a corporate firm and that you need to fight from the start and be a little political." The EU and media seats are good examples of areas of practice for which the firm has a superb reputation, but more people wanting these experiences than there are places available. *"Lots of trainees miss out on seats that they want. You've got to be a strong character as nothing just falls into place here."*

> "It's a high octane firm stacked with big big characters."

More seats are available overseas than ever before but, although there's a healthy degree of interest from those without the ball and chain of *"mortgages or relationships"* (Hmmm – not sure we quite understand why either are a problem), competition is not overly fierce. At the time of our interviews, a new Paris office was opening up to join the Brussels, Madrid and German offices. SJ Berwin is intent on developing as a European firm and trainees spoke of the daily reality of the European presence. Even from London, their work involved dealings with the continental outposts. Much of the impetus for the firm's growth in Europe has been the private equity market and, consequently, much of the work overseas will be in this area.

just love those hours

Typically, a trainee would work *"at least a good 9am to 7pm"* but then, when things get busy (remember the corporate focus), you might have a month of *"from 8am till well past midnight."* Some just relish those hours, apparently subscribing to the 'it's only good if it hurts' school of thought. *"They enjoy the atmosphere of 'we're corporate and we're doing the deals'. A lot of trainees thrive on it… they like to feel important and partners are actually quite happy to see people busting a gut."*

There will be the odd compensatory quiet day to wind down from the big days and nights, but a couple of our interviewees thought it important to mention there weren't really any wind down departments. *"So many people want to do the non-corporate jobs in the firm that, when you get a seat in one of those depart-*

ments, you have to really perform to stand out." But "*if you want to qualify into corporate then you're laughing.*"

glittering prizes

It would be wrong to suggest that the firm didn't value effort, commitment and hard work. SJB pays right at the top end of the scale, it knows how to make appropriate gestures of thanks (yummy hampers and palm pilots for Christmas) and super-hard work has led to a few lawyers getting a super weekend break for two. Sound like a game show? Perhaps, but it's more Millionaire than Weakest Link. You can achieve what you aspire to here without worrying about fellow players stabbing you in the back.

Just like on Millionaire, going to the next level of responsibility and being challenged seems to be a decision you make for yourself. "*You make your own responsibility to a large extent here and there's plenty of opportunities.*" The best way to get responsibility is to "*go in and take it when people are busy*" and to prove your worth. There's a clear sense of being "*an asset now, not just for future.*" We're told that "*the size of clients means that deals are not always enormous… your bread and butter is reasonable-sized deals*" which suits because "*on the biggest deals it can get boring for a trainee.*" Little chance then that you'll spend two years "*twiddling your thumbs or photocopying.*"

no place to hide

Walk into the bar opposite the office and you'll see a whole range of lawyers and staff from the firm. One can almost imagine a stranger entering the bar hearing 'You're not from round these parts are you?' Not the best place to hide then. "*If you'd had a stressful week you wouldn't go to Centros,*" one trainee told us. As so many of our interviewees mentioned the bar as a regular hang out, we concluded that they couldn't be feeling that bad about their lot in life. Other trainee haunts are The Blue Lion and The Union. The trainees have a social budget, which is "*generally quite flexible and high*" and, for the sporty, there are a number of team opportunities.

It would be fair to say that the area in which the firm has chosen to locate is not the flashiest London has to offer. It's at least a ten-minute walk to the nearest tube stations and has a bit of an armpit-of-King's Cross feel to it. Maybe, on a wet February morning, you'll question the wisdom of the decision to locate there. But hey – there's plenty of parking for the partners.

> "The best way to get responsibility is to go in and take it when people are busy."

The firm's dining room is used by anyone who wants a free lunch. (If, of course, there is such a thing as a free lunch…) Some might use the facility to hang out with buddies; others might see an opportunity for strategically placing themselves next to an important partner. Either is OK.

In past years, the turnover of junior lawyers has been high and it's not perfect now, but the firm has listened to the concerns of its staff and various initiatives have been put in place to smooth out some of the perceived difficulties. A mentoring scheme runs long after qualification and the firm accepts that trainees deserve confidential and independent advice in the run up to qualification. There's a certain frankness and honesty on the part of the firm in its admission that being a lawyer is a challenging job. Young lawyers need support when things get tough and sticky and, whilst you won't get acres of slack in which to nurture your own personal crisis, you'll probably not be ignored.

and finally…

S J Berwin is a high octane yet down to earth firm stacked with big, big characters. If you have ambition, you're smart and you're maybe just a bit sassy with it, you'll do just fine here. Think corporate, think private equity work, think quickly.

Slaughter and May

the facts
Location: London
UK ranking by size: 13
Total number of trainees: 150
Seats: 4x6 months
Alternative Seats: Overseas seats
Extras: Pro bono: Islington Law Centre

This firm plays by its own rules. Our usual research methodology involves us selecting trainees at random to ensure objective and confidential interviews. Slaughter and May provided only a short list of seven names. Bah humbug! It's not as if the firm has had a bad year or that trainees are likely to slate the quality of their training. Frankly it's no more or less than we anticipated. Slaughter and May probably couldn't care what we write; it's confident in the belief that year on year many of the brightest graduates in the country will apply to it. It is a part of the magic circle after all. What follows is a True Picture based on the experiences of 'identified' trainees. Their responses may not have been as candid as randomly selected trainees.

pure and simple
We've always been keen to get to the bottom of the myth that life at Slaughters is a bit like living in Siberia – harsh and somewhat wintry. That may only be possible from within, but we'll do our best. Slaughters has no marketing department – *"they don't feel the need."* Maybe this explains why the firm is the subject of so much speculation and hearsay. *"It manages fairly well without dispelling the old rumours,"* one trainee said. *"It's not at all flashy,"* but *"understated with the emphasis being on quality of work and subtlety."* It's half the size of some magic circle peers, yet it outperforms all on profitability. The average equity partner takes home a cool million every year.

In the years before we were allowed to speak to even 'screened' trainees we used to joke about whether they existed at all. We now know that's not the case. Two trainees-in-waiting even worked with us on the *Student Guide* team this year. We're pleased to report that they were both delightful, but it was no surprise to us that both were Oxford graduates. On the question of universities, one of our sources said, *"You will not only get the typical Oxbridge type, but all sorts really."* Another said, *"They talk about the old boy network, but young partners are from a variety of backgrounds."* Talk of a Slaughters type was dismissed, but words such as *"courtesy"* and *"gentility"* were used.

One trainee told us that the firm was *"hierarchical to an extent. It is always very clear who the partners are."* As for the aloofness perceived from outside the firm, *"you do feel part of a separate band because you get so much crap from people at other firms. There is a Slaughters camaraderie."* Probably it just comes from knowing that yours is the best performing firm around.

your last life-saving experience
Applicants have no extended forms to fill in or 'Describe a situation in which you saved the lives of dozens of small children from perilous danger on top of Mt. Everest' questions. Your CV, a covering letter and an hour's chat with a partner and that's it. Anything more would come too close to a three-ring circus to be in keeping with the firm's understated approach. Several trainees gave the selection procedure as their reason for choosing the firm. Reaching interview apparently means you're up to the job, the chat is just to gauge your personality.

corporate and may
This is a corporate firm – big blue chip deals amount to about two thirds of its workload and trainees must complete two of their seats in corporate departments. *"Don't apply unless you want corporate work."* Non-corporate departments are referred to as 'satellites'. *"They do their own work, but they are mainly there to support the corporate stuff."* You have probably heard of most of the clients – many are FTSE100 and they no doubt instruct the firm because its work is utterly reliable and its lawyers truly impressive.

Trainees are exposed to the highest quality clients, deals and lawyers (some of whom have god-like status). But don't assume quality clients and deals always means quality work for trainees. While good work is available, Slaughters trainees suffer from the same problems as their magic circle peers. *"If you are working on a major transaction with lots of people, as a trainee you will get the dregs – photocopying and proof reading."* When the deal is sizeable, *"there is not always that much left at the bottom."* If you want to be the partner's right hand man you may be looking at the wrong size of firm. And if you want to be the partner sooner rather than later – or even eventually – this is not the easiest place to achieve that. The demands placed on qualified assistants are especially high and a large number of them leave the firm before partnership is ever on the cards. The vast majority of trainees stay post-qualification though – in September 2001, 44 out of 48 stayed.

time gentlemen please

The hours *"come in bursts. You might have three weeks of ten o'clocks."* The experiences of those we spoke to ranged from *"10am to 5.30pm for six months"* to *"100 hours per week"* for the length of one overseas seat. (Clearly physically impossible, but we get the drift.) If the work is there, you are expected to stay. The firm has a reputation *"for turning a job round quickly."* *"It is totally client driven. If the client demands something in a short space of time, you do it… It does mean some very hardcore hours."* Trainees reassured us that there is no staying late for the sake of it and there are no billing targets so you're not competing with your peers. If there's no work, you go home, but *"there is no denying that you have to work really hard. That is what makes the firm what it is."* A million a year for the big guys – you do the maths.

friends forever

Bucking the trend, Slaughters has only a small number of overseas offices. It has no plan to acquire or merge with foreign law firms, opting instead for 'best friend' co-operative alliances. It has persistently refused to build any kind of capacity in the US. Trainees insist this does not remove the opportunity for overseas seats, confirming their availability with the best friends. The numbers of overseas placements do not compare favourably with some others in the magic circle, though anything up to half will go overseas. Currently there are openings in Brussels, Paris, New York, Singapore, Hong Kong and a string of other European locations.

> "The average equity partner takes home a cool million every year."

Slaughters doesn't go in for a lot of organised socialising. *"It's not big on trainee entertainment. We don't get wined and dined."* You'll probably note a more business-like approach on the vacation scheme, if you do one. Trainees find their social lives tend to remain independent of the firm or limited to their trainee peer group. While good friends are made, large groups of young lawyers do not regularly decamp to a bar on a Friday night. Don't expect to be shouted a pint by a partner come 5pm.

fill that form

Trainees are asked to select all four seats during their LPC year. But, these selections are not then set in stone. Remember, the satellite nature of non-corporate departments will mean that there will not always be enough seats in niche areas.

An end of seat appraisal system is in place, but trainees felt *"some partners are not great at filling out the form"* and *"feedback is definitely lower than in other firms."* In a similar vein, one source complained that there is no mechanism for trainees and NQs to convey to their seniors what they would like to change. *"A more flexible system would be better."* The trainees do not fair as well as magic circle peers on the trinkets and benefits scale. Accessories such as laptops and mobiles for junior fee earners have been hard to come by. In-house amenities are not great. And then there's the offices…

a hill of buns

If you are reading this as a student or prospective applicant, by the time you might begin working at the firm, it will have abandoned its present home and lodged itself in the sunny towers of Bunhill Row, EC1. And what a relief it will be to all those presently shackled in the firm's *"disgraceful"* and *"windowless"* offices. Wherever all those profits were going, it wasn't on accommodation.

And in case you have been wondering, no, the firm does not regularly make 'S&M' jokes. It is permitted, once a year, at the annual firm dinner and is made by the senior partner – the reward for all those years of hard graft, no doubt.

and finally…

There is more misinformation about this firm than any other. What emerged from our limited investigation is a serious no-frills firm that has never felt the need to run with the pack. *"Things are slightly quirky here"* – well, that's one way of putting it. It'll be interesting to see how its long-term position is affected by the decision against overseas expansion. Only apply if you want to make corporate work your life.

Speechly Bircham

the facts

Location: London
UK ranking by size: 90
Total number of trainees: 10
Seats: 4x6 months
Alternative Seats: under review

Its size means that Speechly Bircham falls close to the bottom of our True Picture 100, but there's no reason to regard the training on offer as bottom of the league. This is a medium-sized commercial firm on the edge of the City, with clients stretching from plcs to individuals.

school dinners

The firm has a high partner-assistant ratio and, with just five trainees taken on per year, it's not too hard to understand why trainees felt that they were given a satisfying level of responsibility. *"Friends at other firms say 'Wow, you did that?'"* one trainee told us when we asked how the Speechlys experience compared with those of friends elsewhere. *"Partners here seem willing to discuss the tactics of a matter and you're not just sent off to paginate a bundle."*

A number of those we spoke to feel Speechlys is a firm where the law really matters and is respected as much as, say, the doing of a deal. *"It does feel very academic here. People don't just want to get the job done. People are really interested in the law. The senior partner, for example, has an encyclopaedic knowledge of tax."* Trainees alluded to the importance placed on research-based tasks and the concept of learning the law during their training. There are very regular departmental training sessions at lunchtimes, with *"good hot lunches and sandwiches."* We asked if the firm had a canteen. *"No, but there's a crisps and chocolate machine!"*

across the board

With the concept of schooling in mind, we were keen to find out what sort of a place this was – oak panelled hallowed halls or new state of the art technology institute? There's no straight answer. *"It has a mixture of partners,"* one source said. *"Some are very old school and some are not. As a result it is not consistent in its ethos."* Maybe matters were clearer before the firm's move out of its old *"awful, dingy and dark"* Fleet Street offices to *"a new purpose built office with lots of natural light."* With the new address came new branding: *"new logos, letterheads and brochures to keep up with the times. It's not been a radical decision to market, but there's been a noticeable change."* One trainee thought this was a firm that went at *"its own pace."* It struck us as one that is unlikely to be looking for dramatic change.

A quiet confidence exudes from Speechly Bircham. It has a great reputation in a number of its seven core areas of practice, earning *Chambers* rankings in investment funds, private client work, employment, property and property litigation. Each department takes trainees and each of the trainees we interviewed commented favourably on the likelihood of getting the seats they wanted. Most trainees *"came to the firm with an open mind,"* with just one or two having a leaning either to corporate or to private client work. Speechly Bircham is one of the few firms in the City that still *"deals with clients across the board from private individuals to huge organisations."*

waiting patiently

The 'variety is the spice of life' approach means that trainees end up covering several work types; an attractive proposition to those who don't know what they might want to practice after qualification. Ideally, the firm wants trainees to undertake one seat on each of its four floors/departments: corporate and tax, private client, litigation and property.

On learning that *"corporate is the most popular seat,"* we asked what type of work was done in the corporate department. *"It's the larger firms that tend to have big clients,"* one trainee explained. *"We do work such as MBOs and private equity, rather than big M&A."* They also pointed out that *"this is a domestic UK firm and going overseas is a no no."* The only down side identified by trainees was the absence of any opportunity to spend time in a foreign office. *"It's not going to happen in a little firm"* one told us, while another said, *"if you want to get lots of international work then you can't stay here."* The message from the graduate recruitment office differs slightly. On overseas seats they said *"Not yet."* On international work they said *"It's growing in construction and corporate."*

cheeky beers

Trainees come from *"a mix of private and state schools."* Curiously, of the ten trainees at the firm in 2001, two of them were German. We could find no explanation for this and had to settle for *"it's co-incidence."* The firm likes applicants with languages and, *"if they had two applicants at the same level, they would go for the one with languages."*

No one needs a translator for email sent on a Friday afternoon to those on the *"cheeky beers list."* Bars like Smiths, ten minutes away in trendy Smithfield, or the Hoop & Grapes, closer to the office, have become popular with the trainees, assistants and some of the younger partners. A social committee organises theatre nights, family days and recently a trip on the Eurostar to Lille. It was travel that enticed two of the five NQs away from the firm in September 2001. We learned that one may be returning to the fold after six months of globe-trotting.

making a name for yourself

For those applicants more inclined to be one of the herd (Baaa!), being just one of ten trainees would be a daunting prospect. No blending into the background, no anonymity. Speechly Bircham's trainees recognise that *"it's easy to make your name known"* and consequently there's a whiff of an idea that they sometimes behave *"quite cautiously and are keener than they need to be."* No one is cruising. The average day is 9.30am-6.30pm and, when a trainee worked until 4am one night, it was so unusual it was seen as a scandal. The next day the partner thanked the trainee.

and finally…

Speechly Bircham comes across as a stable firm that values quality and really respects the law as an intellectual discipline. We're not talking about pile it high sell it cheap legal work at this firm. It might be a shade too conventional for some, and it'll be too up-close-and-personal an environment for others, but there's undoubtedly many an applicant who will fit straight into the *"personalised"* atmosphere.

Stephenson Harwood

the facts
Location: London
UK ranking by size: 45
Total number of trainees: 44
Seats: 4x6 months
Alternative seats: Overseas seats
Extras: Language training

If you're not after one of the biggest firms but you want a broad commercial training, Stephenson Harwood may well be on your shortlist. It performs well in a number of areas, including litigation, corporate finance, shipping, banking and employment. But the last two years have seen a number of changes, which the aspiring trainee ought to understand.

grimly reaping the benefit
The firm has a clearly stated aim to become more profitable. It had felt that it was becoming flabby and inefficient and was slipping down the league tables. Following the implementation of a three-year plan in May 1999 a number of partners have exited stage left. Those that stayed already earn more from a leaner and reorganised partnership. There's a handy set of pie charts on the firm's website explaining the sources of its revenue and you'll do well to look at them. The plan was to beef up the finance-related work and to absorb various other specialisms into larger departments. For example, the once highly regarded IP department was the subject of partner losses and the remaining IP work is now covered by the Business Technology subdivision of the corporate group.

Trainees seem to understand that the firm's evolution (well, we could hardly call change from above a revolution) is for the health and well-being of those that stay. Survival of the fittest. Saying "Goodbye" to the weakest links. There's no mass exodus on qualification and all but one of the 14 September 2001 qualifiers remain with the firm. But, seeing so many partners go has been unnerving for some; the word "*panicky*" described the feelings of one of our sources when they realised what was happening.

The good news is that profits are up already. But the cull may continue yet.

wok's up at S.harwoods?
One thing that sets Stephenson Harwood apart from a number of similar-sized competitors is its proliferation of overseas offices; three in Europe – Brussels, Madrid and Piraeus and three more in Asia – Guangzhou (China), Hong Kong and Singapore. Only the Brussels and Chinese aspects of that menu are 'off today, sir.' The others are enormously popular and distinctly attainable. "*It was the best six months of my life. I only went home to sleep – I was always out,*" said one trainee of his time in one of the Asian offices. "*Although you're doing lots of behind the scenes work, there's also lots of responsibility*." At any one time, two trainees will work in Hong Kong, one in Singapore, another one in Madrid and, whenever anyone can be persuaded, the Greek seat is filled.

speak now or forever…
String up the bunting, start the parade. The trainees have a new voice. There is now an official forum (Working Development Committee) for trainee issues. As yet there's been nothing too major on the agenda (other than the budget for the footie team), but it's good to know that, should something arise, there is an outlet. One trainee was at pains to point out that, in his experience, senior partners take a keen interest in trainees and check their workloads are properly monitored. "*The head of department asked how I was and if I had too much work.*"

Trainees talked of billing targets and this is perhaps no surprise, given the firm's efforts to improve time recording and efficiency. For a first seater, the notional target is 72 hours a month and "*easily attainable.*" One confirmed "*I've never been pulled up if I didn't meet my targets.*" Newly qualifieds have a target of 129 hours a month. "*It's certainly not a doss – you won't be flogged to death, but you have to work hard like any other*

City trainee." Maybe not every other City trainee perhaps. One told us, over the two years of her training, she had averaged "*9am-6.30pm. I am over-keen. Certainly there are those that do 9.30-5.30pm.*" Really late nights can probably be counted on two hands over the course of the two-year contract and there's no weekend working (except for the really keen volunteer).

bloody nightmare

The first of your four seats will be allocated to you, but then follows an element of choice. We sneaked a look at the seats on offer. Eight in corporate areas, six in banking/finance, nine in litigation, six in property, four in shipping, three 'biztech', two employment, two in private capital and one in insurance. From this information, you can see the orientation of the firm's work and estimate your chances of a seat in each area.

We concluded that networking has an important role to play in seat allocation. The HR department is officially in control, but trainees indicated that, to get a particular seat or one of the client secondments, "*You go and see a partner and chat. It's all to do with personalities.*" Another confirmed that "*personalities are important. A partner must like you for you to get a seat. Relationships are important when you're working with someone.*"

The firm has a full time business casual dress code (except for client meetings) and this assists in keeping the atmosphere quite relaxed. "*It's a bloody nightmare for the blokes though, as they just adopt the (unflattering) chinos and blue shirt combo!*"

coolin' off

There are definitely a couple of bars that you can walk into on a Friday night and spot faces from the firm. Most popular are Coolin', Shaw's Booksellers and the "*great thai*" restaurant above the Rising Sun. Sometimes you might find a partner or two around in one of the bars, but it's usually the youngsters. Some departments have more of a fun reputation than others. "*Ship finance are more sociable than most,*" we understand.

Trainees get drawn into social events with clients. "*You get invited to dinners and drinks, sporting events too. When you get invited to a client do you feel the partners have confidence in you. You really get the impression that people regard you as assistants to be.*" Er… good! One trainee's first impression of Stephenson Harwood was that the lawyers were "*genuine, nice professionals*" and that there was "*no back-stabbing or bitchiness.*" When probing further, we heard comments such as "*confident but not egotistical,*" and "*egos are less on display here.*" So would this be a bad place for the applicant with a colossal ego? One trainee said that her friends at magic circle firms would simply never have considered the firm. "*You don't get a lot of kudos for being at Stephenson Harwood. You don't get huge deals that hit the front page of the FT all the time. You might not always see your deal in the press.*"

and finally…

This is a comfortable-sized firm with a view of the front of St Paul's Cathedral ("*A&O only get the back view*"), undergoing a major refit to ensure seaworthiness and success on its future voyages. With the prow facing directly at City work, the firm may not yet be yelling "I'm the king of the world!" like Leo in 'Titanic,' but despite partner losses, absolutely nobody is expecting this ship to go down.

Taylor Joynson Garett

the facts

Location: London
UK ranking by size: 28
Total number of trainees: 47
Seats: 4x6 months
Alternative Seats: Brussels, secondments

Another good year for Taylor Joynson Garrett, as the firm continues to impress and expand in its two core areas of IP and e-commerce and its general commercial practice. It is right at the top of the tree in IP work, both hard and soft, but clients also value its experience on corporate transactions.

and now for the science bit
Intellectual Property is what the firm's built its name on and, as is often the case with strong IP practices, TTG is keen to find applicants who have a science background, especially those who completed a science degree before moving into the law. Despite this mutually beneficial opportunity for science graduates, the firm still finds it hard to recruit as many as it might like. So, if you were looking for an excuse to burn your lab coat, this could be it.

> "If you were looking for as excuse to burn your lab coat, this could be it."

Those with a techy or scientific background will fare well in the firm's 'hard' IP groups, where complicated patents are protected for all sorts of clients, often in pharmaceuticals, agro-chemicals, oil and hi-tech. Those without such skills may feel more at home with the 'soft' IP work. This relates to trademarks, copyright and design rights for clients wishing to protect their brands or work from explotation by others.

popularity contest
Last year we reported unease amongst the trainees we interviewed about the assignment of seats. Either we just happened to interview a string of unlucky trainees or things have improved dramatically. This year's interviewees reported that there were no real concerns with seat assignment. Fantastic, everyone's happy then.

Trainees are asked to specify which supervisor they'd like to sit with, rather than simply nominating a department. We did wonder if this led to a popularity contest amongst partners, but assume that they're much more grown up than that. It sounds like a great system, but does it work? *"I got all my seats in the order I asked for them and with the partners I asked for,"* one trainee told us. Another said, *"generally you receive the seat which you ask for. I didn't get my first choice for my second seat but have been reassured I will be going there later."* Predictably enough, the most popular seats were based around the firm's core practice areas of IP and IT/e-commerce. There are always plenty of trainees needed in these departments so there's no fighting to get them. IT is an important area for the firm, which cleverly combines expertise in corporate finance and IP. IT/e-commerce clients on the TJG books include Arriba, ebay and Priceline.

As is the case at all firms, the employment department proves to be particularly sought after, but there is only room for a couple of trainees at a time. TJG also offers private client services. This seat is seen as a particularly varied one and trainees speak favourably of time spent there. *"Private client work brings in a wide range of interesting cases, it was excellent training."*

group bonding
Taylor Joynson Garrett has a distinctive atmosphere. All the trainees we spoke to were keen to emphasise *"just how close knit we are. Trainees just seem to bond really well every year. This is a place where you can make friends."* You will also have the opportunity get to know and socialise with partners. *"We have dealings with partners at all levels. Friends of mine at larger firms never get this kind of opportunity."* Science graduates aside, what kind of person are the firm looking for? *"You must have a good group mentality or you will not get on here,"* one trainee told us. According to another source, *"nobody here is strikingly ambitious, certainly not to the point of treading on peoples toes… there are a couple of stars here, but they are not precocious at all."*

i think therefore i bill
Whilst you won't put in the kind of hours expected at the largest City firms, trainees did mention that when there is a lot of work on, the pace does begin to get to

you. When there was no rush on trainees found themselves working fairly regular days. The latest we heard of anyone staying was 10-11pm. *"My team in corporate went through a period where we were still at it past 10pm. It continued for a couple of weeks, but then eased off."* Another trainee told us *"One of my main problems was time management. I value my free time, but quite often found myself working late on Fridays which is quite frustrating."* The firm offers a variety of training courses to help deal with this and other problems. *"I was encouraged to attend a time management course, which really helped me control my workload and my hours."*

For those seeking a deeper understanding of life, the firm offers a popular philosophy course. *"It was taught by PhD students from Kings College London and was a great opportunity to socialise with and get to know partners and other staff outside of work or a bar!"* We heard that in some departments there was a culture of having to be seen to be in the office. *"I did get a bit of a feeling in some departments that I should be around when other people are working late, even if I didn't have much work to be getting on with."* Before anyone jumps on us for saying anything at all critical about the firm, we must point out that this is not a concern in all departments.

There is an overseas seat available in Brussels, offering EU/competition and commercial work. In the past trainees have had the opportunity to spend time with an affiliated law firm in Hong Kong. There is no formal programme of secondments, but clients do arrange for trainees to spend time with them on an ad hoc basis. Over the last couple of years trainees have spent time with clients, including Alliance & Leicester and Visa.

and finally…

This is a place where you will have an active social life with your colleagues. There's also a great sense of loyalty and pride for the firm and maybe this is why the negative aspects to last year's True Picture piece were vehemently denied in this year's interviews. Loyalty and pride led to 17 of the 23 trainees accepting jobs on qualification in 2001.

Taylor Vinters

the facts

Location: Cambridge
UK ranking by size: 105
Total number of trainees: 10
Seats: 4x6 months
Alternative Seats: Brussels

Taylor Vinters is one of a select band of Cambridge based law firms, serving the dynamic and innovatory science economy that has developed around the University of Cambridge (a major client) and the Cambridge Science Park. High growth businesses abound and the area has the largest cluster of biotech ventures in Europe.

there at the birth

A location in Silicon Fen means *"you are exposed to all sorts of hi-tech work. It is very exciting. You get to be there at the start of new businesses and talk to people who are excited about what they do."* With knowledge-based industries on the doorstep, most trainees are *"fighting to do IP at some point."* One explained *"a lot of City firms don't realise how technology businesses start here from the ground up. We have a few plcs, but will also work with small companies started by a few graduates."* Work is cross-referred between departments. *"Commercial property finds new businesses places to house themselves. Private client serves the millionaires who appear."*

But the firm is not entirely geared towards science, technology and academia; it is highly regarded for personal injury work and has a noteworthy rural business department, specialising in bloodstock and equine law. *"We have everything under one roof."*

the f word

Surprisingly, trainees do not typically have a link with Cambridge (town or gown). *"Strong candidates will be considered from anywhere."* Taylor Vinters has a good record of recruiting those with first career experience. Although not essential, one of our sources indicated "it is good to have a general interest in science/technology or to have converted from a science to law."

Trainees described a firm that is "not hierarchical," but one adopting "more of an 'all hands on deck' approach." As an illustration, "the term 'fee earners' is never used. There are just 'lawyers' and 'support staff', which demonstrates something of the ethos, I think." This makes for a good atmosphere. "People like it here. Support staff don't come and go," and "you are just as likely to go out with secretaries as with supervisors." Staying late won't impress anyone, even though "they do work very hard in corporate."

motherly love

Trainees were pleased with induction week; it is "done amazingly well. The managing partner made herself very available. You are integrated into partners' lunches. There's loads of IT training." If you are nervous about the start of your legal career, those overseeing things "were all sweet and motherly."

Many first seaters are thrown into the firm's excellent personal injury department. "It's a funky young team and you will enjoy it." But it's not an easy start. "You are expected to produce billable work." The firm lays on the responsibility. "If you are competent, you won't be treated as a trainee and the quality of the work reflects this." "They gauge what they can get out of trainees well. For one client, I am almost their key contact. London trainees would not be allowed anywhere near them." One source told us "there were times when you felt you weren't getting enough support, but the firm realised this, and changed things." "Most partners are lovely and help you at a drop of the hat."

talking it over (and over)

Most trainees will almost certainly do a seat in company/commercial but, beyond that, nothing is prescribed and the firm is very flexible with second years. A secondment is available to the Brussels firm Renouf & Co, which has formed associations with a number of non-competing regional firms, including Taylor Vinters. As well as offering the firm a 'hotline' for advice on EU law, the Renouf link gives the lucky secondee an enjoyable three months in the Brussels trainee community.

Back on home turf, some noted that "the start to a particular seat can be sloppy," depending on who your supervisor is. "There is an attitude of only later working out what to do with the trainee." However, the firm is aware of this, and "realises you can't afford not to train people properly." "It has been discussed" and, where it occurs, it is being addressed. Appraisals with seat supervisors take place every three months and each appraisal is reviewed in turn by the overall training supervisor. That's effectively four appraisals per seat. According to one source, it works both ways. "You are appraising them, and they do welcome feedback." Trainees are not "left not knowing what is going on. They are direct about your strengths and weaknesses."

> "Most partners help you at the drop of a hat."

hms vinters

The firm has "a business plan; a vision of where it is going." The managing partner "won't accept staying still. She wants to mark the firm out." The firm is "modernising in terms of IT and the way it does business." With recent knocks to the hi-tech sector, some might argue that the firm's future will be less rosy than in previous years. However, Taylor Vinters is "concentrating on the corporate/commercial side and on clients who have IP as their base. Three NQs are going into the corporate team." One trainee said, "if you were really set on doing corporate, you would be in the wrong place training here." We hesitate to contradict any of our interviewees – after all this is their shout – but Taylor Vinters corporate department has a really great reputation and it handles some really interesting deals. OK, they're priced in millions rather than hundreds of millions, but this can actually work to a trainee's advantage in terms of responsibility.

The firm is *"keen on retaining its own trainees. If you have chosen an area, they are keen for you to get to know the clients and integrate."* Most trainees are offered jobs and retention is fairly high. In September 2001, three of the four qualifiers accepted jobs with the firm. *"The firm goes for people who are independent, charismatic and not robotic."* Recently, four trainees all lived together and harmony reigned. *"We all got along."* Cambridge is not a cheap place to live and while competitive for the region, salaries are considerably lower than those paid in London and not enough *"to pay rent and pay back student debts. Offering interest-free loans would help."* Taylors' office building in the Cambridge Science Park is not exactly aesthetically pleasing. *"It's big and grey and like a battleship."* The firm occupies only a part of the building at present but, with expansion on the horizon, *"we should be occupying all of it next year."*

i'll ride in the van

There's more to the social life than just *"heading to All Bar One after work."* From the Cambridge Science Park, visits to the Q-Ton bar take place on a Thursday. *"People drive to work, so won't necessarily go on the razz on a Friday." "Friday night tends to be Thursday night,"* (Just like Manhattan then!) There are plenty of firm-wide sports and events. *"We organised a netball team and the firm paid for everything. They throw money at you to do that sort of thing." "You can go and play cricket three times a week for the firm. And at the big match next week, everybody is leaving at 3pm to go and support the team."* For a recent trip to the nearby Newmarket races, staff hopped on a coach and a separate van was booked to transport the alcohol. Hmmm...

and finally…

Quality of life was emphasised by all our sources, so *"if you want to earn to live, you have to come here rather than London. Life is not taken up by work."* And the work and clients are both varied and innovative. What more could you ask for?

Theodore Goddard

the facts

Location: London
UK ranking by size: 47
Total number of trainees: 33
Seats: 4 x 6 months
Alternative seats: Overseas seats, secondments
Extras: Pro bono: Springfield Law Centre

Statistically, this is one of the most popular firms in the UK for training contract applicants. On last year's figures, you'd have had about a one in 150 chance of getting a place. The firm's popularity derives from its mid-tier size, a reputation for high quality work and a reputed feel good factor amongst employees. Oh! and one more thing… a leading 'meeja' and entertainment department. This is a City firm with a twist.

howdy neighbour

This is the first year that Theodore Goddard has come out to play with *Chambers Student Guide* researchers. We were delighted to find that our very near neighbours (at the back of trendy Smithfield and in the shadows of Clifford Chance's 'Gotham City' office building) were really jolly nice indeed. But how disappointing to hear that there's no great rivalry with the Chancers or with next door neighbours CMS Cameron McKenna. Not even the occasional water bomb lobbed at an open window.

There's no need to question whether or not Theodore Goddard is a friendly firm. Just accept that it is and that trainees do make a point of reminding us of the fact. But, hey, they do at most firms. They also point out, without hesitation, that their lives are better than those of their neighbours because *"our hours are not horrendous."* Typically the working day runs from 9.30am to no later than 7pm. Typically you'll work at the weekend only once or twice during your two years of training and you'll only work late into the night on a limited number of occasions.

hidden attractions

The hours suit those who have interests beyond the law. The firm's media and entertainment department attracts a few trainees who also continue to pursue the arts.

For those less cultural evenings, local bars provide the distraction. There's an ad hoc scene at Spirit, Extra Time or The Hogshead *"once or twice a week."* Every other Friday evening, the firm serves up drinks in its restaurant. Also a popular lunchtime venue, the restaurant is a large glass atrium affair that opens up onto a pleasant patio. You'd never guess that Theodore Goddard had such an attractive office space by looking at the front façade of the building or its rather drab – OK ugly – reception.

The dichotomy in interior design is almost symbolic of a dichotomy in the firm's activities and its persona. The popular media and entertainment practice sits side by side with corporate finance and banking. In many ways this is a traditional City practice, in others it has much in common with a more 'West End' firm.

a-list celebs and nobodies

Whilst a number of the trainees are clearly media types, the media and entertainment work would be *"wasted on others."* The position is that this specialist work does not in any way dominate the firm and so only those who have a real interest in it actually sit in the IP, film, music and e-com/theatre seats. It's clear to us that the firm has taken care to recruit the right proportion of media/showbiz-focused trainees (a number of whom have already worked in the industry) and the right proportion of more conventionally-motivated trainees. Given the fierce competition for training contract places, it sounds as if you should be certain about what you want from this firm. If you're attracted because you want to be a media lawyer then be prepared to compete with many others. If you're attracted because the firm is successful elsewhere in its work then don't be afraid of making that point clear.

Speaking up for yourself has been a way of life in the past. Trainees told us that the allocation of seats and the offer of jobs post-qualification have not always been subject to the most systematic of processes. Methods of getting seats included *"batting your eyelids at the right people,"* *"getting to know the partners in the relevant departments"* and reminding the powers that be that you were *"shafted"* on your previous seat allocation. Not altogether satisfactory. This 'if your face fits' approach often left a few trainees on the sidelines, feeling as if their names had been left off the guest list, while others got just what they wanted. *"Those who had not gone out and got themselves a seat found that the nasty seats were dumped on them."* The problem boiled down to a lack of understanding about how the seat allocation worked or, indeed, whether there even was a system.

fall of the iron curtain

For those of you who are not graduates of Eastern European politics, Glasnost refers to the enlargement of individual freedom of expression in the political and social aspects of life. Far be it from us to imply that life as a Theodore Goddard trainee was akin to communism in Russia because, for the record, we are not. However, there's a post-Glasnost feel to trainee life these days; a voice has been found and they think it may be audible.

A new graduate recruitment and training officer is already displaying a more trainee-friendly approach. When we interviewed for the True Picture, trainees had just had a series of *"pow wows"* with the powers that be and, as one told us, *"no one went in there thinking 'I had better not say that, in case I don't get a job.'"* It looks as if the firm is now receptive to the *"trainee action to have things become more transparent and open."*

Trainees know that there is *"still some way to go and that it's not going to be all sweet-smelling and rosy overnight,"* but they have already seen job offers on qualification come out earlier than ever before and a more formalised application process has been set up for those jobs. All in all it sounds far better than the old *"secrecy as to what was available on qualification and who would be invited to qualify into which areas."* In September 2001, all qualifying trainees were offered jobs and only two chose to leave.

come together

In the past there have been merger talks with various firms and when we interviewed there were talks with international firm, Salans Hertzfeld & Heilbronn HRK. Salans has offices in Paris, New York and Eastern Europe and a reputation in the financial sector. *"The merger would allow us to be seen as a firm with a global capacity, which we are not at the moment,"* one trainee said. But then the merger was shelved. It didn't surprise us to learn that overseas secondment opportunities were not at the top of the list of reasons why trainees chose the firm. A three- or six-month posting to the Brussels office is not massively oversubscribed, nor is the sometimes-available seat in the firm's associated Paris office. Of real interest to some are the client secondments, which include one to record company V2. We can't understand why…

Compulsory seats are limited to *"something contentious"* and *"something City."* Beyond that, personal preferences influence the remaining time, with some trainees' two years looking much more corporate than others. A hefty range of in-between areas such as property, construction and employment complete the package.

the missing link

The Professional Skills Course and on-going legal training seem to be well run and regular and it was good to hear that there's some vital non-legal training on offer, including a course on body language. As the session progressed, one trainee told us *"you could see people moving from a slouching into an upright position."* We wonder how many sessions it takes to evolve into the *"always smiling… gracious and charming"* senior partner, Paddy Grafton Green.

One or two trainees pointed out that, in spite of the firm's media work, *"it's not a trendy firm, it's a City firm."* *"Funky? No."* You won't see trainees in cargo pants and ponytails like you might at a West End media boutique, but you will see a preponderance of approachable seniors and a sea of friendly faces. *"If someone turns up in the canteen that I don't recognise then it's a real surprise,"* one source said.

and finally…

Theodore Goddard is a firm that's undeniably popular with its employees as well as applicants. Maybe not exclusively City but undeniably City-led in its work and hanging onto a reasonably *"staid"* image. If you want to come to this firm for entertainment work then be prepared to prove you deserve it. As for a merger? Who knows what the future holds?

TLT Solicitors

the facts

Location: Bristol
UK ranking by size: 96
Total number of trainees: 14
Seats: 4x6 months
Alternative Seats: None

May 1st 2000 was TLT's big day. Two Bristol firms, Trumps and Lawrence Tucketts, came together in a move perceived to be phase one of a strategy to create Bristol's number three commercial firm. The city's two traditional big players, Burges Salmon and Osborne Clarke are assumed to be looking beyond the Bristol area post codes for their business and TLT is thought to be working out and getting in shape to wear their cast off clothes. Third in Bristol? Why not?

one plus one

Getting in shape means that there's now plenty of emphasis on the corporate, financial and banking practices. If anyone needed further proof of this shift, they only need to look at the firm's abandonment of its personal injury practice. "*We are more commercially oriented and focused now*" one trainee stated, "*and we have a stronger corporate identity.*" A branch office in Kingswood has closed and the merged firm is perceived to be more "*gutsy and forward looking*" than either of its component parts. Not all work for individuals has gone though, with the firm having taken an 'if it ain't broke don't fix it' approach to its successful family and private client departments. But if you're looking for the high street experience of "*crime or lots of legal aid, don't come here.*"

Corporate and commercial seats are the most popular amongst TLT trainees, along with commercial litigation. Banking is a very busy department and has a "*loads of work*" reputation. The number of banks on the firm's books is impressive and it is known to handle recovery work for Lloyds TSB, Woolwich and Barclays. When you speak to trainees about the merged firm, it takes a little while to pick apart who brought what to the party. In our interviews Trumps and Lawrence Tucketts came across as a pretty good match. Neither set of trainees suddenly found the range of seats on offer to them post-merger had changed much. As with most firms, "*there's an unwritten rule that where there is competition for a seat, the more senior trainee has a better chance of getting it.*" No seat is compulsory and it looks as if the days of the unpopular seat in residential conveyancing are numbered.

two houses

The firm is not yet under one roof, but it is working on it. "*It's not ideal being in two buildings*" especially when there's a ten minute walk between them. Bush House was the old Lawrence Tucketts' home and now contains the commercial departments; Redcliffe Street was Trumps' old home and now contains the admin and private client parts of the firm. Although integration of lawyers from each firm has taken place to an extent, there's still some way to go. "*It's still a good culture, but it's twice the size now and more anonymous – I don't recognise everyone in both buildings.*"

Freakily the local pub for each office is called The Shakespeare, although one has more 'e's than the other. The Redcliffe Street version, down by the quayside, also fills up with Burges Salmon lawyers on a Friday night. We're not aware of any Montague and Capulet style rumbles with them though. "*Actually we have some ex Osbornes and Burges Salmon lawyers in the firm,*" one trainee told us, and another pointed out that Bristol has "*a really close legal community.*"

> "The Bristol legal scene is big and vibrant enough to attract applicants from all over the country."

TLT lays on a fair few social events by way of a social club. The social budget produces trips to the theatre, barbecues and recently a booze cruise to France, which was "*subsidised and very, very cheap. For £25 we had a night in hotel, a free bar and a meal.*" We were charmed by "*Tuesday Sandwiches,*" an old Trumps tradition that has survived merger and allows lawyers to munch and chat with colleagues from outside their own department.

team players in crumpled t-shirts

TLT is still viewed as the poorer cousin of Osborne Clarke and Burges Salmon, maybe because it is newer, maybe because it's not so slick and there's less to hype up in terms of big deals and clients. "*We see them at sports and social things,*" said one of our sources of the other two firms. A couple of trainees talked about feeling scruffy in comparison when challenging them at sports. "*Burges Salmon will turn out in fully matching kit*" and TLT players will just about muster up "*a few crumpled firm T-shirts.*"

Ask the trainees if the razzle-dazzle of one of the élite Bristol firms appeals and quite commonly you'll hear: "*I wouldn't want to work there – apart from the*

371

salary. *I like it here.*" There's a notion that TLT trainees take themselves less seriously. Whether it's true or not, we couldn't possibly say.

go west young man

"The pay is actually pretty good for the regions" one trainee admitted. Trainees certainly have enough to make a good life for themselves in Bristol. A number of them are doing the 'This Life' thing and sharing houses. *"Bristol is a large enough city to really enjoy. Accommodation is affordable, as it's a studenty town. And it's easy to get to the countryside."* Most trainees had either an upbringing in the South West or were at university in Bristol. *"Lawrence Tucketts always had a good relationship with Bristol University and they ran an essay competition there for years, so the firm's name was known."*

There's clearly self-selection by applicants, with most applications coming from the region, but TLT is open to considering those without connections. Trainees tell us that the Bristol legal scene is big and vibrant enough to be able to attract applicants from all over the country. It should appeal to those with no desire to live and work in London; those who like the idea of a 9am-6pm working day with the benefits of living in an interesting city in a beautiful part of the country. If you want *"champagne at 3am deals you will get them"* once in a while, but *"don't come here if you want that all the time."* All five of September 2001's remain with the firm, working across the board from family to corporate finance.

and finally…

So why TLT? *"They didn't make me build a bridge out of lego in my interview!"* Fair enough, what else? *"Variety."* A place you can remain yourself, where *"you are not required to conform."* *"The firm doesn't regulate what you do on the LPC"* and during the training contract, *"you're not over specialised."* There's a sense that you don't sell your soul by signing up to a TLT training, but *"if you want to make millions by the time you are 25, don't come here."*

Travers Smith Braithwaite

the facts
Location: London
UK ranking by size: 50
Total number of trainees: 36
Seats: 4x6 months
Alternative seats: Overseas seats
Extras: Language training

A corporate led practice handling decent-profile jobs, often larger than to be expected for a firm of its size. This firm is a favourite with many applicants because of its small size but big, yet non-flashy reputation. It's thoroughly respected and pleasant rather than breathtakingly sexy or brash.

flying ducks

If you look at the TSB website, you'll see that in a moment of twisted irony, the firm adopted three flying ducks as a symbol of its exclusivity. Geese? Oh… they're geese. Ah well… It proclaims: "we don't want many, just the best." It has, without doubt, chosen to focus on the élite. Almost half of the current trainees graduated from Oxford and Cambridge colleges. Add in King's College, London and you've got over 60% of trainees coming from just three universities. Smells like a plan to us. Among its buzzwords are "quality," "intelligent," "articulate" and "pleasant" and these are undoubtedly the hallmarks of those that have been recruited. Travers is the perfect example of a firm that is recruiting in its own image.

Two words jumped out during our interviews; *"camaraderie"* and *"loyalty."* Trainees rebuffed the idea that their firm had a public school/Oxbridge reputation. *"It's not like that!"* one trainee protested. May be not, but the figures don't lie. If we're honest, we know full well that plenty of other firms would be delighted to have the TSB proportion of Oxbridge graduates. It's simply the case that TSB can attract them.

club classics

How do we describe a typical TSB trainee? *"Lowish-key, but quietly confident"* one told us, adding that *"actually you could be either brash or bookish, it wouldn't matter."* *"Hard-working and good humoured,"* another offered. Most seem to have bought in to the slogan: *"We take our work, but not ourselves seriously."* *"It's twee and a cliché, but it's close to the truth,"* one admitted.

Trainees come across as calm, contented individuals with an appreciation that their lives are pretty good because they have been fortunate enough to train in a nurturing environment. *"To say it's like a family here is going too far,"* we were told, but *"yes, it is a bit like a club – but that doesn't mean it's exclusive. If it's a club it's because it's inclusive."* Outsiders in other City firms still sniff traditionalism about the firm, but maybe it's better described as classic rather than traditional.

just good friends

Trainees like each other – a lot – and many of them build up *"real friendships"* at work. In the True Picture last year we indicated that there was a lot of *"gossip and snogging"* and sure, the odd liaison crops up amongst the trainees, but apparently *"you're not going to see trainees draped all over each other in the Bishop's Finger. It's more discreet than that... maybe it goes on here because we are all such good friends."* We learned of eight trainees going off on a surf weekend together and another group taking a skiing holiday.

Regular Friday and midweek trainee nights out take place in the Bishop's Finger and a number of the other pubs and bars around trendy Smithfield and Clerkenwell. Having loosened the corporate belt and expanded into a neighbouring building backing onto Smithfield, the extended family is pretty comfortable in its swisher offices. *"It's nice working round here. Certainly better than Fenchurch Street or places like that."*

Every department has regular drinks evenings. *"You'll maybe go for a curry afterwards with some of the younger partners. There are plenty who are still quite young at heart. You'll never let your hair down completely but it's always nice to get to know them as people."* As one put it, *"I wouldn't phone up Chris Carroll* [the managing partner] *and say 'fancy a drink?' but maybe at a leaving drinks party or an event I might chat to a senior partner."*

and in the blue corner

There's no sense of being pitted against your fellow trainees, infact there's an absence of competition for seats, as your seat choices are all sewn up before the training contract begins. Before starting, trainees come to *"quite a raucous"* Easter drinks party, part of which is designed to help them select their seats. *"Each of the departments does a presentation to let them know what the work entails."* One of our sources recommended that you *"sign away your life on the dotted line before the champagne"* though.

Trainees suggest that new recruits with clear ideas about seat preferences should *"write in before starting so that a trainee or NQ can call you to chat about that area of work."* They also suggested that it is best to be very particular about which seats you indicate a preference for. The trainees who seemed happiest with the four seats allocated to them appeared to be those that had indicated the least flexibility on their selection forms. The good news is that, *"although you might feel you have limited choices right at the beginning, the departments are quite wide and you can make it known within the department what work interests you."* It's not such a big firm that departments have become over-specialised.

no fear and loathing

Compulsory seats are taken in property, corporate (including banking) and litigation. A fourth seat can be taken in a more specialised area such as tax, (*"I'd rather chew my own foot off than do tax but some love it"*), commercial (*"seat of the month at the moment"*) or employment (*"renowned for being really friendly"*). Private Equity is really growing at the firm and is seen as an energetic area of business. *"The most popular seats are those with the most dynamic partners or the top assistants. No seats are loathed or hated. Of course, there's always one or two difficult partners but, aside from that, all the seats are OK."*

You're not going to be flogged to death here, our sources tell us. Average hours are totally manageable and you'll almost always be able to fulfil evening social engagements. None of the trainees or NQs we spoke to had worked a weekend and had done only a modest number of late nights in corporate.

the trade off

If life at Travers is so good, then why does anyone apply to the magic circle? *"Travers isn't a household name for students like, say, Slaughter and May or Freshfields."* One trainee appreciated that *"some people really thrive in cut a throat world,"* but pointed out this means *"in your 20's, when you're in a really exciting city, you're stuck in the office."* Our TSB sources all valued their leisure time. Other contrasts with the mega-firms become apparent: *"The big firms get the sexiest deals. If you are working on them, great, but you are the trainee and not necessarily getting best experience. My best experience was working on a small million pound deal practically alone. Yet I worked on a multi-billion pound deal too."* Be aware of the trade off between the sexiness of a deal and the level of responsibility on offer to trainees.

Don't start planning a life as a jet-setting trainee. There's one Paris seat for a good French speaker and a new opportunity to go to the USA but, for most, international ambitions have to be fulfilled at their desk in London. On the subject of qualification, you'll almost certainly want to stay with the firm and it would be unusual if you weren't offered a job. In September 2001, 15 of the 17 qualifiers were offered positions and all accepted.

and finally…

New managing partner Chris Carroll is undertaking a strategy review. We'd put money on it not leading to radical change – this is Travers Smith Braithwaite after all. Trainees certainly expect *"more of the same."* European mergers don't seem to be a priority as the firm has a strong enough name to attract good European 'best friends'. As a trainee you'll figure out quickly that friendship is valued highly at this firm.

Trowers & Hamlins

the facts

Location: London
UK ranking by size: 69
Total number of trainees: 29
Seats: 4x6 seats
Alternative seats: Overseas seats
Extras: Pro bono: currently 'between law centres'

Trowers & Hamlins is leagues ahead of the rest in social housing, it is also well recognised for its construction work and won the 2001 *Chambers Global* Middle Eastern 'Law Firm of the Year Award'. The rest of the picture is built from the standard range of corporate and commercial work.

it's all in the blend

The most popular seats are construction and property, with most trainees doing a corporate seat (a mix of commercial and banking). As well as the compulsory litigation, other seats on offer include public sector, employment, projects, housing and private client. With its Middle Eastern offices, the firm offers seats in Muscat and Abu Dhabi. It also has offices in Exeter and Manchester for those who pine for their student days. Most people get their first choice of seat, and if not, *"no one got more than one seat they didn't want."* It's not just a firm for those interested in public sector housing or the Middle East, it should appeal to those looking for a broad range of experiences before making up their mind as to where they'd like to specialise *"They give you a good blend of training."*

As with most training contracts, the level of responsibility and the complexity of cases you'll handle will differ from supervisor to supervisor. Trainees reported not getting dogsbody work, but *"good work, where you learn a hell of a lot."* *"Because the firm is smaller, I'm dealing with assistants in other law firms."* *"In my last seat I've been treated as a qualified solicitor, I've sometimes held meetings on my own."* For those who want to act for big name clients, in the UK the firm's larger clients and the *"full on"* work is mainly on the property side. In the Middle East, Trowers has large multinational clients such as Credit Agricole, Enron and BP. There's quite a bit of competition for the Middle East seats, and the firm takes on the *"odd Arabist,"* so you have to *"make it clear that you want to go."*

Hours are fairly stable, *"I've had two to three nights in until 10pm, but the worst it has ever got is having to come in on a Bank Holiday to switch over seats." "Occasionally I've had panic days, but you can always say 'I've got a lot to do, can I give this to you tommorrow?'"*

trowlin' around

As with most small groups of trainees, the Trowers & Hamlins recruits are a cohesive bunch. However, when compared to other firms, they don't seem to go out together that much. It may be a reflection of the firm's desire to recruit people who have "independence, resourcefulness and initiative" (as it says on its web blurb). There's a trainee lunch every Monday, but otherwise there is no organised social scene. *"We just meet up and let off steam,"* usually in the local All Bar One. Those on the look out for a cheesy night-out popping down to The Mineries (*"it's a bit of a cattle market on Fridays"*). The sports scene is well developed, with a mixed hockey side and a womens' football team.

the bottom line

Although the firm usually retains a high percentage of trainees, there's no Trowers type. There *"really is a mixture of people in the firm,"* one trainee said. *"There are few red-braces types and there are a lot of eccentrics,"* and this eclectic mixture of people is a bonus, as *"you'll always find someone who understands your view."* The partners are appreciated, *"they never treat you as an inferior, they're friendly and there isn't a noticeable hierarchy."* This open style means that people are relaxed here and the firm manages to keep a reputation as a serious player without being too hard nosed. *"The bottom line (ie billable hours) is not the most important thing here, you're not on a conveyor belt."*

With regard to retention rates, they differ every year. Because of the firm's policy of not hiring in bulk (as stated in the website), most trainees stay at the firm, unless they want to specialise in an area where the firm does not have a heavy workload, for instance in capital markets. In September 2001, five out of the thirteen qualifiers left, though the year before, 12 out of 13 stayed. *"It's a question of what you want to do, and if it's something Trowers does, then you'll probably stay."*

what do you want from me?

What is the firm looking for? According to the trainees, *"you need a personality, they don't want completely wacky people, but they like sparky people who are a bit different."* This is not a hierarchical firm (*"you get to know everyone in office from the managing partner to the post room boys"*) and, as it is medium-sized, there's a lot of interaction with the partners. Consequently, *"you need confidence, as you're working with partners and you have to explain what you've done to them."*

You need to have a *"bit of oomph about your character; it's not for the quiet or shy,"* one source said. Another confirmed *"we're ambitious, but we don't take ourselves too seriously and we're not the kind who want pots of cash and to be on the front page of The Lawyer."* Having said this, we found it really hard to identify any common ground between the trainees we spoke to; they were all very different from each other. They ranged from the relaxed, open and friendly type, who saw both sides of the coin, to the excessively cautious type who recited marketing spiel and who didn't suffer non-lawyer fools gladly.

As for credentials, it helps to be interested in property and social housing. *"You're expected to know where the firm's strengths lie,"* but loving property work is not necessarily a prerequisite (*"I hated property at uni"*). The firm's huge reputation in social housing will not overshadow your training contract, although a lot will be linked to it. The banking seat, for instance, is primarily concerned with housing finance. If you're not interested in this area, but want to work on big deals, then this is probably not the firm for you, because this is the area with the *"serious clients, serious deals and serious work."*

and finally…

So this is a firm where you can be an individual and get a balanced training. You don't need to have wanted to work in property and construction since the time your friends wanted to be astronauts and vets. You need to be a go-getter, but not aggressively ambitious. It's not a place for those who like to go with the flow, because the trainee intake isn't large enough to hide in. You'll get a solid training, without the advantages a big firm might offer in terms of pampering, but with the advantage of a more homely atmosphere. And afterwards? Again, it's up to you. There's room for you to stay at the firm, but with its size and the range of departments, *"you can keep your options open, because you can go either way afterwards – to the high street or to the big City firms."*

Veale Wasbrough

the facts

Location: Bristol
UK ranking by size: 111
Total number of trainees: 12
Seats: 4x6 months
Alternative Seats: None

A Bristol firm providing services across the board to regional businesses and local individuals. It is pre-eminent in property and does well in litigation, commercial and a number of specialist areas like education, energy and claimant personal injury. It's felt to be well on the road to recovery after some high level departures in previous years.

survivor

A few years ago, Veale Wasbrough entered into talks with national behemoths Eversheds about a possible take-over (the preferred method of expanding the Eversheds empire). Unfortunately for Eversheds, Veale Wasbrough didn't snap up the bait and the national giant's Plan B (setting up a brand new office from scratch) failed miserably. And what of Veale Wasbrough? After countenancing the possible dissolution of the partnership, it might be assumed that that Veales would be left directionless. Trainees assured us that enough time has passed for the firm to be back on the ball again and vigorously pursuing its future as an independent.

After departures around the time of the failed merger, the firm is expanding again. *"It has grown to the point where they are having a big office reshuffle. Generally it's the strong teams in the firm that have grown and brought in good work."* With fewer lawyers on the ladder between the partners at the top and the junior assistants on the lower rungs, *"the firm is increasingly young, and you feel positive about a long-term career here – that there could be a space for you."*

room for manoeuvre

Occupying the middle ground of the Bristol legal market, trainees feel that Veale Wasbrough *"offers a very good training and does actually care about training, as opposed to just having trainees."* They have the firm's target clients *"bashed into"* them – *"medium size enterprises."* For those not wanting a pressured life in London or the macho boots-and-all training of some of the big regional firms, life at Veale Wasbrough will appeal. It's a *"nice size of firm,"* offering *"room for manoeuvre and responsibility."* An absence of posturing and pushiness is evident and this might in part be the result of it having a mixed public sector/private sector client base.

True to the doctrine of regional firms, *"they recruit quite a lot of non-law graduates and want to know you are not going to shoot off to London after qualifying."* Increasingly, this means a growing emphasis on vacation schemes and those who have participated in them. The smart applicant would do well to get on one.

Some thought the training would benefit from *"more consistency between the supervisors,"* even though *"when your supervisor is busy, there are other people around to ask."* Some felt the younger partners made better supervisors, others praised the *"network of supervision."* One trainee confirmed *"I was never made to feel silly by asking questions of anybody... My first supervisor accepted that I didn't know anything."* Levels of responsibility increase over the course of the training contract, but the biggest factor was acknowledged to be the flow of instructions from clients. *"When there is plenty of work, you will get the responsibility."*

you can run but you can't hide

Veales likes its trainees to gain experience in three core areas; litigation, commercial, and property. A variety of practices are on offer, however, including construction, employment, estate and tax planning and personal injury. There are four seats in the property department. Indeed, as one of the firm's core areas of business, *"you'd be lucky to get away without doing some sort of property seat."* Property is one of the firm's real success stories and it has attracted leading names to the department. It handles work for local and central government and was involved in the regeneration of Bristol Harbourside for the City Council.

Of the other departments, commercial litigation is popular and *"difficult to get into."* Although a rare trainee will gain experience in the estates and tax planning, trainees do not undertake a seat in the family practice. The claimant PI department offers good cases and lots of client contact. It gives trainees a chance to see the other side of the law – acting for individuals. The employment department offers a really popular seat, having rebuilt itself following the departure of some of its lawyers a couple of years ago.

school days

The firm has some noteworthy niche departments. Trainees can take up seats in the first-rate education practice, which looks after the interests of over 600 independent schools. Education and property share clients and work through PFI projects relating to schools. If the education niche wasn't enough to distinguish Veale Wasbrough from a multitude of mid-size regional practices, there's also the superb specialist work it does in medical partnerships for over 200 doctors' practices and the cables and pipelines advice it gives to clients such as Esso.

Despite a reasonable range of departments taking trainees, *"not getting the seat you ask for,"* is a problem. The reality of training with *"a smaller firm,"* is that *"they are limited by the resources they have."* Departments take only the trainees they need at any given time, and the firm will seek to place trainees in departments where they may later be recruited. Small niche practices may not always be seeking to expand.

> *"Partners are more into their wine than their spiritual enlightenment."*

While plenty of NQ jobs are offered (*"this year they wanted to keep all of us on"*) the offers are *"not always in departments where people wanted to go."* In a moment of magnanimity, the firm took one 2001 qualifier on for six months until a suitable vacancy came up elsewhere. The firm does want to retain all of its trainees and is *"actively recruiting from other firms,"* such is its desire to build up lawyer numbers. Some of those we spoke to thought that to get the really big clients, a move to London or bigger local rivals would be necessary.

spiritual enlightenment

Veale Wasbrough is part of the *"nice legal community"* in Bristol and operates out of offices *"just behind hippodrome in the centre of town."* One source admitted, *"some departments do tend to have a very independent life from the firm,"* but *"you get to know most people."* There is a culture of co-operation and it's something that the firm makes efforts to promote. One trainee told us *"everybody goes out of the way to help, from managing partner to support staff."*

The firm has *"quite a good social life"* and wander into local bar, Encore, on a Friday night and you'll bump into *"twenty people from the firm."* Whilst the usual Friday afternoon email will ensure good attendance figures in the pub, it's certainly not the only use that the recently upgraded IT is put to! Life is pretty sweet at Veale Wasbrough. *"When you have got the work, you stay and put the hours in,"* but no one seems to work long hours. Put it this way, the *"staying late culture"* in company/commercial means staying *"till six o'clock."*

Each year, a number of the firm's partners go on a weekend retreat to *"Cant Farm somewhere in Cornwall."* Images of saffron robes, meditation and yogic flying popped into our heads, but we understand the partners are *"more into their wine than their spiritual enlightenment."* Cant Farm may or may or not be the place where the new managing partner develops his *"very American approach to marketing. He has a pro-marketing viewpoint."* OK, maybe we're off beam with the notions of group chanting and hugging, but this is definitely not a crusty old school firm.

and finally…

An open medium-sized Bristol firm, offering a good training and the possibility of some niche experience, if you can push your way in. Just make sure you apply for a vacation scheme placement.

Walker Morris

the facts

Location: Leeds
UK ranking by size: 59
Total number of trainees: 25
Seats: 6x4 months
Alternative Seats: None

Leeds-based Walker Morris seems destined to forever fight a rearguard action defending its decision to remain a single-site firm. Barely a month seems to pass without the arguments for and against being peddled back and forth in the legal press. Regional loyalties are certainly important – *"the whole firm supports Leeds United."*

close attention

Walker Morris touts itself as one of the most profitable firms outside London. Company and commercial, commercial litigation and commercial property make up over three-quarters of its workload. Fee income has increased by 20%, and clients include Starbucks, Debenhams and Caterpillar. *"More and more quality work is coming into Leeds, and you get the opportunity to do it."*

Organised around six seats of four months, the firm has strong preferences as to what seats trainees do – *"corporate, litigation and property,"* but *"you can do one with a slant on it – like contentious IP."* Sources emphasised the *"quality of work you are given,"* and *"speed of introduction to partner work,"* something that can be put down to the size of the firm. *"They still do smaller stuff and you get involved. It can be you and an assistant on a small deal."* 'Partner work' may be complex to understand, but *"by working closely with assistants you really learn stuff."* *"Responsibility is thrust upon you, but if you need help, it is there."*

appraise me!

Seat appraisals can be *"difficult to arrange"* and some occur months after a seat ends. *"Partners are busy. There is not really a system."* Why not just go and see the partners? *"Some might say, just come and see me, but you wouldn't always feel comfortable."* As a result, *"it's up to the trainee to have a good relationship."* No wonder *"something more formal would create uniformity."*

rock paper scissors

Seat allocation is unusual, with the firm making the decision for the first three seats. *"You are randomly put somewhere. It's not like they think you'd be good in a certain department."* One optimistic trainee thought *"you learn about departments which you might not have opted for." However, most dislike the lack of choice. *"Without career planning, you could easily find yourself beginning the second year having not done a seat you want to qualify in."*

> "Responsibility is thrust upon you, but if you need help, it is there."

In the second year, trainees meet to take a collective decision as to the location of their final three seats. *"We thrash it out amongst ourselves."* If preferences don't clash and trainee relations are amicable, this method can be democratic. However, previous years have seen disagreement. Unconfirmed reports suggest entire days spent playing 'Rock, Paper, Scissors'. Those with stronger personalities may prevail over the more polite and ill feeling can follow. *"It works till the sixth seat, but then people start to hold their cards close to their chest."* Partners prefer not to get involved, but will take the final decision if there is no agreement. Some felt let down come qualification. *"If you've only had one seat where you want to qualify, you will not get that job."* With larger intakes of trainees, some thought this *"policy of least aggro to partners"* unlikely to work in the future.

talk to the hand...
Trainees grumbled about the amenities that make for comfort and ease of working. *"There's no air conditioning, just air management. It doesn't condition the air, it just blows it around!"* Others moaned a bit about IT, but we understand it's improving. With *"faxes and photocopying – there is a lack of support. It is quicker and easier to do it yourself."*

One or two trainees felt *"there's a feeling that you should be grateful to be here."* One year, a group of trainees went to see the training partner. The partner took the views on board and went to see the managing partner, *"but nothing happened."* *"There has sometimes been a feeling that, as a trainee, your voice isn't heard. Opinions may be asked, but nothing happens."*

As for NQ job offers, we heard there is *"no real procedure."* *"No one knew what was happening. People apply elsewhere because they are kept hanging on."* Confirming this view, the retention stats for 2001 were so so. Of the ten qualifiers, four left the firm, some for rivals in Leeds.

WM likes trainees with added variety. We heard of archaeologists, careers in marketing, and football trials for England. (Not all the same person, mind you.) Hours are good with *"no pressure to show your face late from partners,"* who are a *"pretty relaxed bunch. They will help you out."* Trainees do not undertake client secondments or overseas seats.

face painting
There is a great social life. Just outside the office, trainees flock to Wharf Street, while the partners tend to the posher Sous le Nez. One source described staying in Wharf Street until funds ran low, then moving to the up-market bar, where partners buy the drinks as you listen to their stories. And what stories! One partner was apparently a roadie for the Rolling Stones.

There are also activity days. *"Trainees just slaughter the partners in paintballing. Everyone is in masks, so you can shoot close up and they don't know who you are!"* There are regular restaurant visits and the 'Insolvency BBQ' is always good. (Presumably, you have to bring your own food, sauces, beer, coals, matches, deck chairs…)

staying a singleton
So, that dogged single-site policy… *"If it ain't broke don't fix it, is their attitude."* But, with expansion, several departments have now moved *"over the road."* Trainees are divided over the firm's evolution. *"There is no problem attracting international clients,"* contrasted with *"there will probably need to be a lot of change in the next five years."* For training purposes, *"its great.*

You are in one site, and there's no chance of being moved around." (Just tell that to the exhausted Hammond Suddards Edge trainees.)

and finally...
Walker Morris is an enviably profitable firm that provides access to some good work. But how long it can continue without employing a dedicated graduate recruitment manager remains to be seen. The trainees are calling for one: *"They need to come into the 21st century."*

Ward Hadaway

the facts
Location: Newcastle
UK ranking by size: 91
Total number of trainees: 16
Seats: 4x6 months
Alternative Seats: None

Ward Hadaway is growing and has recently undertaken a successful merger with another local firm, Keenlyside & Forster. It may not yet have the all round presence of some regional rivals, but its commercial litigation department is recognised as the best in the North East. For the last two years, all its trainees have been offered jobs on qualification and all have accepted. It must be doing something right to have achieved this 100% sucess rate... or maybe its just the Newcastle Brown and the fog on the Tyne...

where the heart is
Many trainees, eager to stay away from London, will head to Leeds and Birmingham. But there is an alternative. As the major city in the north – and by that we mean The Real North – Newcastle acts as the centre for legal activity. Trainee salaries tend to hover around the £17-18K mark, slightly lower than the young Ally McBeals in Leeds, and light-years away from London money. But fat wallets are obviously not the primary motivation for Newcastle's lawyers.

Among trainees, it is *"unusual not to have a connection with the area,"* and many have studied at one of the local universities. *"They think that people from the north and north east are likely to stay,"* and this is certainly a firm that recruits to retain. But don't worry, it will take trainees from any background and a stint on Byker Grove is not always necessary.

desires
Unsurprisingly, the firm's work has a strong regional bias. *"Most clients are from above Leeds."* But the firm is not content to limit its horizons. *"They have been really trying to improve the client base"* and the firm *"is now competing on a much wider basis."* Ward Hadaway has talked of breaking the dominance of the big firms in Leeds, which is seen by many as the biggest legal market outside of London. Trainees discussed the firm's desire to build a profile on a national level, but stressed that this didn't mean the firm is parochial in its existing achievements. *"Corporate finance tends to be national work"* and the firm already has some international clients, including a number from the US.

prize fighters
You learn independence quickly at Ward Hadaway. Trainees *"are not checked on. You are left to manage your own workload." "Partners do the big stuff and then pass work down to trainees to do the smaller stuff."* Yielding criticism from our sources about their training was tough. Feedback has been limited to six-monthly appraisals, but talks have been taking place over the introduction of three-monthly reviews. Colleagues were universally described as *"approachable"* and, in seeking to help us understand the firm's culture, one trainee pointed to the fact that all lawyers have the same model of desk, irrespective of their seniority. Whilst not a scientific test, they felt it was indicative of something!

A trainee described her feelings on starting with the firm. *"I was surprised at the level of responsibility. There is no photocopying."* With a relatively small intake of trainees each year, there are usually no problems with seat allocation. The range of experiences available to a trainee unsure of their interests at the outset is commendable. *"They like you to get a broad experience."* But the real body of the firm's workload is in litigation and it has some of the leading litigators in the region. The department generally has several multi-million pound disputes in progress at any given time. The firm also has a strong reputation in property but it's commercial work *"where trainees want to get experience."*

abracadabra

Several sources mentioned the firm creating seats to meet requests from trainees. *"They are open to ideas, and very flexible."* Although there is no regular seat in the private client department, if a trainee did want to take a seat there, they'd probably be accommodated. One year, a trainee asked for an IP/IT seat and, lo and behold, it was created and subsequently made available on a permanent basis. The firm touts itself as a leading e-business adviser in the North East, acting for start-ups and IT businesses moving into the area, rather than simply large companies with IT issues. And if, like most trainees, you are interested in employment law, the firm has a growing specialist team with half its work originating from outside the region.

how the other half live

Trainees enthused about the rapid expansion of the firm, which has been fuelled by mergers such as recent one with Gateshead-based property specialists Keenlyside & Forster. Turnover recently exceeded £10 million and trainees talked confidently of the firm becoming the biggest in Newcastle. Presumably local rivals, Dickinson Dees, might have something to say about that though. The firm has 40 partners and a total of 114 fee-earners. One trainee described how, upon joining, she was surprised at how big the firm actually was. To cope with growth, *"we've got a new building and half the firm is moving in."* Future trainees can expect to work in the new offices and some of our sources were eager to try out the new open-plan environment on offer there.

new faces

We were told *"there's a set of twenty-to-thirty-somethings who will be in the pub on a Friday night."* Each week they dash down to the nearby Pitcher & Piano after work to rub shoulders with other city professionals. Ward Hadaway is clearly a very sociable firm in a very sociable location. After all, *"it's Newcastle!"* Trainees and NQs will regularly meet up at weekends. *"You can't come in hung over all the time, but some of the time is OK,"* one source confessed. The firm will organise events of its own, such as summer BBQs and a 'new faces' drinks do whenever somebody new joins the firm. Trainees also highlighted a very good local TSG, with the firm paying for the tickets to the annual ball. It smacks of a firm that looks after its own.

> "Located near the Millennium Bridge, trainees are privy to the military manoeuvres that take place on the river."

Located near the Millennium Bridge in Newcastle, trainees are privy to the military manoeuvres that take place on the river, as well as the various TV crews that use the bridge as a backdrop. While day-to-day tasks may not always be as exciting as storming the Tyne Bridge or making a TV show, Ward Hadaway certainly has some very satisfied trainees. It encourages them to *"take the stuffiness out of law."*

and finally…

The firm is on a mission to expand, raise its profile and push its name as a brand. *"It's a young firm, there are people who want to bring it on and develop it."* It is anticipated that, in the future, recruitment will increase, so maybe its time to hop aboard this Geordie bandwagon?

Watson, Farley & Williams

the facts
Location: London
UK ranking by size: 86
Total number of trainees: 25
Seats: 6x4 months
Alternative seats: Overseas seats
Extras: Language training

Set up in 1982, Watson, Farley & Williams is a medium-sized London firm with international offices and international clients. It's a potent force in the specialist areas of shipping and ship finance and is also well known for the quality of its work in tax, corporate and banking. But if you train here will you survive on a diet of ship's biscuits and develop scurvy? Or will you feast on a variety of work and come out the other end of your contract in good shape?

unshippy shipmates
"OK, so which one of you is the son/daughter of a Greek shipping tycoon?" our researcher asked. "Which of you previously worked at Lloyd's of London? Which one is an ex-naval commander?" Silence from the ranks indicated that maybe this wasn't the shippiest of shipping firms after all. As one of the trainees told us, "*if there's a 'but' about working here it's people saying I work for a shipping firm. I've got minimal interest in ship finance and my training has been pretty non-shipping. The firm is trying to get that across in advertising campaigns.*" Is the firm protesting too much? After all, there are three compulsory seats: litigation ("*about 95% shipping litigation*"), corporate and finance (much of it ship finance).

It is likely that you will end up working on shipping matters of some sort, trainees confirmed. "The upside is that the shipping trade will never ever disappear. They will never find a substitute for shipping goods so there's huge job security. Also salary wise some of best paid lawyers are shipping lawyers and you are very very marketable. WF&W has such a good name that you'll never have a problem." You will be pleased to learn that trainee and NQ salaries keep pace with those of the magic circle.

don't panic
Having accepted that shipping, and more particularly ship finance, will feature in your training contract, what sort of experience will you have? "*Much of your time as a trainee is spent going along to the registries and registering or discharging mortgages of ships. When I was told I had to go to the Bahamas to do one I got really excited… but then they told me it was at the Bahamas Maritime Authority in Aldgate East.*" You'll also be involved helping with loan documentation, learning how to amend precedents, drafting corporate authorities and powers of attorney, creating transaction bibles (rather a yawn at times) and just generally "*learning the ropes.*" For some trainees shipping-related work is not the easiest to connect with, but "*some people do enjoy it. It depends what sort of person you are. The majority come to it with an open mind.*"

Aside from the compulsories, seats can be taken in banking, property, tax, IP, EU and employment. The last three are perennially popular so make your desire to do them known as early as possible. That said, "*lobbying is very low-key. Because we do six seats and there's not so many of us, you get less panicky.*" Similarly, when it comes to qualification, the smaller number of trainees means the process of finding out if you'll get your ideal job is less formal than at the largest firms. In 2000, four out of the 13 qualifiers chose to move to larger firms "*They went to Slaughters, Ashursts, Linklaters and Freshfields*" we were told. "*Maybe they didn't realise that their salary here would be the same. Maybe they wanted to go to a top ten firm with a higher profile.*" In September 2001, seven of the nine qualifiers stayed, going into various areas of practice.

fantastic voyage

No, the firm's not offering to shrink trainees to microscopic size and inject them into the senior partner for a trip down the alimentary canal. But the firm will guarantee you an overseas seat in your first year. That's right, you heard correctly: every first year trainee gets at least four months in Singapore, Paris or Greece. The chance to go abroad is a major reason why trainees choose this firm. It's one of a small group of medium-sized firms that can offer an overseas experience somewhere other than Brussels. If the mega-firm doesn't float your boat, but you are dead set on getting a stamp in your passport, Watson, Farley & Williams just might be your firm.

It came as no surprise to us that the Singapore slot is a dynamite experience. The firm bought the office from rival shipping firm Sinclair Roche & Temperley in 1998 and within a year or so one of the trainees had campaigned so hard to get out there that a regular posting was created. There are now two seats available in the Singapore office. Two more in Paris (usually filled by one of the many linguistically well-endowed trainees) and a seat in Piraeus in Greece make up the full set. The Piraeus seat is the least popular because some see it as *"solitary confinement."* But it's usually filled. As the junior member of staff in a small overseas office, the resident trainee finds that the administrative buck stops with them, but that they are challenged in ways that are unlikely in London. *"Everything comes to you. You get to test yourself."* At this time there are no seats in the firm's Moscow or New York offices.

speaking in tongues

If a desire to work abroad is a common denominator amongst trainees then so is a second language. Those of you who binned languages at GCSE level need not bin your applications to WF&W after reading this, but trainees left us in no doubt that languages are valued highly. Language lessons are on offer at lunchtimes.

For some reason, girls outnumber boys in the trainee population by some distance. It's a trend we've spotted at a huge number of firms. One trainee suggested that it was because *"educationally girls outperform boys and the firm wants to get the best."* Whatever the reason, the lads aren't too upset. The only problem seems to be that it's not helping the football team get promoted.

With just a dozen or so trainees taken on per year, you are going to get to know your intake well. Trainees do seem to bond together, even though characters range from the *"self-contained and conscientious"* to the *"loud and lively."* That range of personalities is reflected at all levels throughout the firm and when it comes to partners, *"some are reserved and some more outgoing. Some are more approachable than others. The more senior ones you are not so close to."*

young guns havin' some fun

Our sources had no nightmare tales to tell (other than the odd dodgy dish in the firm's canteen – oops sorry, 'Rooftop Restaurant') and confirmed there were no seats to avoid at all costs. Each shares a room with their supervisor – usually a partner but often a senior assistant. *"Sometimes it's nicer sitting with senior assistants. They are less manic and closer to your level. Most partners are receptive so long as you don't ask silly questions."*

The graduate recruitment website calls for those who can offer *"real enthusiasm, youth and dynamism as well as a good academic background."* Trainees confirmed that almost all of their number had come straight through academia and were in their early/mid twenties. We did not find the orientation towards older, nautically inclined trainees that crop up with regularity at some other shipping firms.

The social life is healthy, perhaps because the firm sits on top of an All Bar One. Very handy. *"We really ought to have a corporate card there,"* one insider told us. If you balk at chain bars, there's always Finches or The Paper Mill and every few Fridays the firm will bung a bit of cash behind a bar for a firm-wide social. Fee earners and support staff get to rub shoulders, occasionally with partners (although it's usually the younger ones who hang around for more than one drink).

to be or not to be

Here's something that's not on the firm's website. In 1999 and 2000 Watson, Farley & Williams spent quite a bit of time chatting up a US firm called Hunton & Williams. Despite the fact that neither firm would've had to change its surname, the marriage was not to be. One trainee said, *"we were a little apprehensive. It was the unknown and we wondered about the culture change if we merged with a US firm, but we were kept briefed."* Firms merge when they think it makes good business sense. So will WF&W try again?

And what's this culture the trainees spoke of so fondly? Well, nothing hit us with hurricane force, in fact a number of trainees disagreed with each other about WF&W's style. *"Far from radical"* thought one, whilst another felt that the firm was *"slightly maverick in approach."* They reached agreement over the idea that the partners were *"quite forward thinking"* and unafraid of accepting new ideas or a non-establishment approach. A trainee could come from either Eton or Essex, they told us.

fancy that

Fancy a magic circle salary without magic circle hours? Trainees here claim to have just that. One after another told us the average day was 9.30am-6.30pm with the very occasional late night and about one weekend per year. Few complained about the levels of responsibility. After a challenging seat overseas, proofreading and colour copying in the property department can feel a bit lame and tax can leave a trainee feeling rather remote from the client, but, overall, work is pitched about right. When a supervising partner is too busy, trainees find they can easily chat to another lawyer if they have a question about work and the solid bond they develop with each other acts as a good *"safety net."*

and finally...

So where's the catch? Maybe it's that the firm is so respected for its shipping and finance work that other departments have a hard time coming out from the shadows cast by those areas. No matter how hard the firm's marketing department works at plugging the corporate or IP or employment lawyers, trainees still find themselves explaining that there's more to the firm than just shipping.

Wedlake Bell

the facts

Location: London
UK ranking by size: 127
Total number of trainees: 10
Seats: 4x6 months
Alternative Seats: None

A smaller firm tucked away in Covent Garden, but with a satellite office in Guernsey. 33 partners and 51 other fee earners handle a workload made up mostly of corporate and banking, property and construction, and private client.

keeping it in the family

First year trainees complete property and litigation seats and then choose between a range of options, including corporate, banking, commercial, construction, private client, employment and media/IP. The private client department *"is no longer just old gentry,"* increasingly, clients are *"directors from blue chip companies looking for tax advice."* The Guernsey presence is indicatative of the importance of offshore work in this area of the firm's business. However, the firm is mainly concerned with *"a lot of SMEs and a lot of family businesses."* *"It doesn't do household name client work."* What this means is that, unlike larger firms where the client-lawyer relationship may never develop very far, at Wedlake Bell lawyers will really get to know their clients.

Applying to Wedlake Bell is a relaxed process, involving an interview that is *"just like meeting someone in a pub."* Trainees report the firm *"tends to go for people who've gone off and done something completely different"* before applying. This ensures the firm gets *"people who are well-rounded,"* and *"not staid pin-striped suit types."* Not many trainees have come straight through from university, and *"they do like to recruit people from vacation schemes."* You know what you've got to do then!

free agents

The firm has a reputation for providing a good quality experience. One source confirmed that he received *"assistant solicitor work."* Proud of its young protégés, the firm doesn't lock them in the photocopying room or *"hide from clients the fact that trainees are working for them."* Trainees sometimes act as the clients' first port of call and think the training provides them with *"an excellent level of responsibility, when compared to friends at other firms."* With only one or two trainees in a department and a fairly high partner to assistant ratio, *"if assistants aren't around, trainees will be given the work."* The responsibility is there from the outset: *"You are expected to get to grips with it and just get going,"* although, *"nothing goes out without it being checked."*

Rather than being tied to one supervisor, trainees are attached to departments and tend to be *"free agents"* who ask for work and receive it from *"lots of different sources."* Some found that certain partners shirk the responsibilities of supervision. *"If you are not interested in a partner's department, you will be given dogsbody work."* Some felt that supervisors *"don't delegate work properly because they have their own targets to meet and may not be interested in training you,"* unless you have *"expressed interest"* in qualifying into their department. Among trainees, this results in a *"quiet dissatisfaction."*

haven for refugees

Although trainees will grumble about salaries being *"not particularly high compared to other firms, it is put in perspective when you talk to people from elsewhere."* Indeed, the quality of life at Wedlake Bell actually attracts those who have gained a few years experience in bigger firms and want to ease down a notch. *"Two people in the banking department are from Freshfields,"* one of whom was quoted as saying, *"you can actually plan a social life!"*

Trainees disagreed whether a move in the opposite direction would be possible for NQs. *"Moving up to bigger firms has not been a problem in the past,"* while some thought *"the work you get is just not of enough quality to enable you to transfer across."* Either way, two of four qualifiers were offered jobs in 2001, with one accepting the position. In 2000, there was 100% retention. However, some trainees felt the long-term prospects of some departments may be undermined by the small size of the firm, and the lack of critical mass necessary to compete in certain areas.

There are *"a lot of old partners here."* Some sources felt the firm was *"a bit of an old-fashioned law firm, run as a gentleman's club, rather than a business."* Interestingly, of 32 partners, only 3 are female. Still, younger partners *"are moving up through the firm,"* and are *"desperate to get the name of the firm known"* and *"have a very clear vision of where they want to take it."* The last year has seen a 13% rise in revenue to £14.2m, particularly due to work in the corporate finance and IP/media departments.

always one nearby

Wedlake Bell has a reputation for being friendly and open. Sure enough, *"people do get on every well here"* and *"everyone is amazingly friendly."* Hours are more typical of a regional firm; one of our sources told us he'd *"stayed to 7pm only twice in two years."* It has a great location in Covent Garden, *"opposite All Bar One."* However, the firm's lawyers are drawn to the more down-to-earth Lamb and Flag nearby. *"We may move in the next couple of years,"* said one source, confirming it will be because of the *"end of the lease"* and not just to get away from All Bar One. Training at Wedlake Bell won't always mean a champagne-filled high life (it was recently reported in the legal press, that at a PR event for the corporate finance team, trainees were found taking coats and fetching ashtrays), but you'll definitely be closely involved with work you show an interest in.

and finally…
Wedlake Bell is thought to allow for a good *"quality of life, given the experience you are getting."* The training can be excellent and it will appeal those who want hands on experience on work for clients they will get to know well. The ideal applicant is probably the sort of person who knows their neighbours and everyone in their local pub. If the anonymity of a City mega-firm sounds preferable, you've just read about the wrong firm.

Weightmans

the facts
Location: Liverpool, Manchester, Birmingham, Leicester
UK ranking by size: 60
Total number of trainees: 20
Seats: 4x6 months
Alternative Seats: None

These are testing times for the Mersey-based Weightmans. Traditionally seen to epitomise law firms in the insurance sector, it has suffered some heavy blows of late. There's a depth of expertise in the firm however, and it continues to be top ranked by the *Chambers Guide* in defendant personal injury and professional negligence.

riding the waves
Insurance work and litigation have changed dramatically in recent times. The Woolf reforms cut the volume of claims brought to court and restructuring in the insurance market has shrunk the legal budgets of major insurance companies. So how has Weightmans faired? Following the breakdown of extended merger talks with Liverpool rivals Hill Dickinson, trainees spoke optimistically of the firm getting back on its feet. Unfortunately, the firm's brand new retail and leisure department defected to Manchester's Halliwell Landau after just a few months and it fell off legal panels of two major insurance clients – AXA and CGNU. Turnover has dipped by 4%, but it's not all bad. The firm has secured a place on the prestigious NHS Litigation Authority panel at a time when other firms were being chucked off.

Not all of Weightmans work is in insurance litigation. There's a reasonable amount of public sector (including 13 local police authorities) work and good practices in company/commercial, commercial property and employment. One of our sources spoke cheerily, saying *"Morale within the firm hasn't suffered. We know that there are exciting things going on."*

northern roots
Trainees can undertake seats in all four offices. The firm is keen for them to move, but relocation is not compulsory. However, with different opportunities available in each office, travel may be necessary to experience the full range of seats available. *"If you're not prepared to switch, you will be limited,"* one trainee confirmed. There is more movement between the northern offices among trainees and qualified lawyers, although one source may have exaggerated slightly to declare *"Manchester and Liverpool are interchangeable."* Typical seats for trainees are insurance litigation, company/commercial, professional indemnity and e-commerce. Commercial seats tend to be the most popular, with employment seen as the jewel in the crown.

Weightmans trainees do usually have roots in the North West. Maybe the firm looks for a regional commitment, or maybe the local law students just gravitate towards the firm. Their rewards are good. Salaries for Manchester are competitive and in Liverpool they are outstanding. *"The firm wants to grow organically."* No artificial pesticides or treatments are used on trainees and Weightmans aims to retain all its NQs. The September 2001 round of job offers enabled all the qualifying trainees to stay on. And why not? The firm views them as *"a long-term investment"* and trainees describe it as *"friendly," "friendly,"* and *"friendly."*

no need to scream
Feedback on trainee performance is organised around *"formal three-monthly reviews, where you say where you think you are."* (In Liverpool, stupid!) Not the most rigorous of assessments then. *"I was encouraged to handle files and do drafting, but it was all checked. There are no horror stories."* It is *"very much a caring company. There is open communication all levels."* Indeed, one source spoke of *"emotional support."*

> Stop press: The firm has just won a place on the new legal panel of Shell International

Trainees get a hands-on experience not always possible at bigger firms. *"My friends at larger firms won't get their hands on as much work." "You learn by being given responsibility."* Hours are very reasonable – 8.30am to 5.30pm. *"I have not been asked to work late. You would only do it out of choice."* Another source expanded, *"I have never never worked past 5.30pm. Or weekends! I've been told, 'You are a trainee, go home'!"*

football focus
Weightmans has invested heavily in IT. Its website states that this *"reduces the cost of service delivery."* In a move to put its business online, Weightmans ensures that clients receive email updates on new legislation within 24 hours of their announcement. In addition, and perhaps providing one of the slightly less exciting 'webcasts' on the WorldWideWeb, the firm will provide 'live' status reports for clients on existing cases. Unlikely to be rivalling Big Brother for the number of 'hits', we think.

There are no complaints about the social life, although if you are one of the single trainees in the Birmingham and Leicester offices, you'd better get used to socialising with partners and assistants. Presumably not a problem when *"working in one of the smaller offices, you know everyone."* The firm has the usual array of organised office and departmental parties, as well as a football team that plays matches against clients. With all those employees from insurance companies on the pitch, presumably it's not a time to tackle anyone from behind. This firm must surely be a conundrum for the avid football fan. How do you explain a major Liverpool player setting up shop in Manchester? *"There is no rivalry between the offices."* What? None at all? *"We meet up with the Manchester trainees fairly often,"* one trainee told us, and another explained *"I actually live in Liverpool, but commute up everyday."*

and finally…
The profession will have to wait and see how Weightmans picks itself up after a challenging year. With an atmosphere and ethos to envy, it seems the dent to morale has been minimal, although we did sense that those we interviewed were fully aware of how much hard work the firm has ahead of it. Any student looking at the firm would do well to consider the depth and experience on offer in insurance litigation.

Weil, Gotshal & Manges

the facts
Location: London
UK ranking by size: 71
Total number of trainees: 16
Seats: 4x6 months
Alternative Seats: New York

Weil, Gotshal & Manges is a major US firm with over 800 lawyers worldwide. Its growing operation in London recently hit turnover levels of £37.7m. 23 partners are assisted by 89 other fee-earners, the annual intake of trainees is steadily increasing and the firm has just taken over another floor in its London office building.

are your shoes clean?
Winning a training contract with Weil Gotshal means a *"very very informal and laid back interview"* that is *"more like a chat."* The firm aims to *"make sure you will be happy here. Everyone will know you and you have to fit in."* Reflecting the atmosphere of the firm, the training environment is one where *"you can go into a partners office and say 'help!'"* One source described the firm as the sort of place where you could *"put your feet on the table."* *"Laid back but professional"* sums things up nicely and the offices are *"totally dressed down to a very high degree."* But this should not be overstated. *"Everyone is also incredibly serious about how things are done."* Many partners have a magic circle pedigree. They have *"magic circle standards, but want a more informal atmosphere."*

Those offered a place are eased into firm life by a number of social events. Shortly after trainees join the firm, it flies off for its annual retreat in a European city – recent destinations included Edinburgh and Barcelona. Some of the current trainees have international backgrounds, but surprisingly few have foreign language skills.

lawyers that lunch
The firm has *"quite a lot of individual characters,"* who display *"different ways of dealing with trainees."* But there's consistency in the quality of tasks trainees are asked to perform. *"I have never ever had photocopying,"* one told us and the worst we could uncover from another was a feeble grumble about *"administrative stuff like proofreading."* Work oscillates between *"enormous M&A or banking transactions and small repeat securitisations."* With a smaller office by City standards, *"you are never that far from a partner."* Opportunities to shine are, therefore, *"never that far away."* Magic circle firms sit on the other side of transactions although, in contrast to those firms, as a Weil Gotshal trainee, *"you are more likely to be in small group and to get more exposure."* Two appraisals take place per seat: *"Every three months, we will go out for lunch with our supervisor,"* With increasing numbers of trainees, *"HR are taking it very seriously."*

all american?
As the largest department, trainees will almost certainly gain experience in corporate and it's also where many NQs are retained. Clients include household names like Estée Lauder and Telewest. Other seats can be taken in property, capital markets, tax, litigation, securitisation, project finance and e-commerce. The banking practice was undermined this year with the loss of its last English-qualified banking partner. No client secondments are available, although an overseas seat is up for grabs in the New York office. *"You get to see what an enormous machine it is. It's a completely full-service law firm over there."* Trainees thought other opportunities would become available. *"They are talking about Frankfurt and Silicon Valley."* But ultimately, the London branch *"needs to keep trainees back to do the work."*

In spite of *"massive backing in the US,"* *"you wouldn't walk in and say 'oh it's American'."* There are *"US voices around and people are flying off to New York all the time,"* but as well as *"US lawyers here, there are Kiwis, and Australians."* *"US-qualified lawyers do the US work."* Our sources felt the London office could exist on its own without the backing of the US and, with offices in Prague, Budapest and Brussels among others, Weil Gotshal London is seen *"more like the head of Europe."* Indeed, our sources thought the goal of the firm now was *"to expand and get much more into Europe."* To this end, *"they are recruiting"* The annual trainee intake increased this year from six to ten. In 2001 the firm retained all of its qualifiers.

We confronted our sources with the reputation that surrounds the working culture of US firms. *"The myth of slave labour in US firms is not borne out in reality."* With *"absolutely no stay-late culture,"* it is *"nothing more than is expected of you than at City firms."* Trainees pointed out that, with fewer trainees, *"if you work hard, it is noticed"* and when longer hours do hit, *"it is probably slightly better because it is more laid back."* Admittedly, there are *"very long hours in New York,"* but by working in the London branch, *"you get the US links without the punishment of working in the NY office."*

american vampire in london

The main feature of the Weil Gotshal offices? *"It is all glass."* Completing the look, *"it has these blinds which come down automatically and turn in the direction of the sun."* Hmmm, afraid of sunlight? A decorative pond (regular tap, not holy water) in reception was apparently removed because *"people kept falling in."* We have unconfirmed reports of the *"banking department playing golf down the corridor."*

and finally…

"You're not just one of 120 trainees. We feel special!" Weil, Gotshal & Manges provides high quality training in a smaller and fairly casual environment. The firm expects a lot of its trainees in terms of commitment and ability, but the rewards are huge.

White & Case LLP

the facts

Location: London
UK ranking by size: 83
Total number of trainees: 16
Seats: 4x6 months
Alternative Seats: Overseas seats
Extras: Language training

White & Case is an American giant with offices all over the globe. But the London office has the feeling of being its own small firm. True, the offices are located in the heart of the City and the clients are top-notch corporate and finance businesses, but by London standards this office is intimate and friendly.

so many offices, so few trainees

The trainees we spoke to believe they had found a winning combination. The small size of the London office makes for top quality training. *"Trainees are treated as junior lawyers and part of the team,"* gushed one enthusiastic interviewee. Another of the same ilk boasted *"compared to friends at magic circle firms we're exposed to more advanced work and have greater exposure to clients pretty much from the start because there are so few trainees."* It goes on – *"we hit the ground running but there's always the back up so we're never out of our depth."* On the other hand, the massive global face of the firm means plenty of international work and high profile clients. It also means that *"you will definitely go abroad."* And we're not just talking mini-breaks to the Bratislava office! Each trainee gets a six-month seat abroad because the firm *"likes to circulate its trainees."* No one's complaining: there are currently opportunities in Brussels, Hong Kong, Moscow, Paris and Singapore. Our trainees found the seat abroad the most challenging, *"I was given as much responsibility as I could take."* We were however reassured that it's *"not bad or evil not to go."* Phew!

london loves

Back in dreary old London (you love it really), a litigation seat is compulsory. This can be in the litigation department… beg your pardon, the Dispute Resolution department or in IP. The latter is much sought after as *"it's an en vogue area – internet and e-commerce are hot topics."* Summer students have picked up on this too; *"they all want IP."* Trainees also undertake a seat covering banking, asset finance and projects. For the really keen, asset finance has now become a seat in its own right. You are unlikely to choose your first seat but, after that, trainees' preferences are taken into account, which includes timing. One trainee chose the location of their seat abroad, the order of their second, third and fourth seats and when to fit in their litigation seat, in which they managed to do a reduced stint, having done some abroad.

The trainees believe that the style of training they receive is unique amongst corporate firms of this standing. *"It's not as large and institutional as other City firms. It's tailored to individuals so it's about doing the relevant thing at the relevant time. It's not just 'this is our training programme – you must fit in'."* Others found that *"the emphasis is on you."* We gathered that the environment is consistently supportive as, unsurprisingly, *"the learning curve went from zero to being able to do it, but people listened and helped me."* Following on from this, a newly qualified said that the firm is also *"very good at pushing when you've found your feet, and if you feel able to take on more, you can."*

pound of flesh myth exploded

Surely the culture of this place can't be perfect too? *"It's a bit sick – but I can't think of anyone who doesn't really like it! The only gripes are demanding clients and some long hours, but you get that anywhere in the City."* Ah, the hours – got them! We've all heard how these American firms expect their pound of flesh for the wads of cash they pay... *"We're not expected to work like New York lawyers. It depends what the work load is like, but 9.30am-6.30pm are average hours. If you work late, it's because you need to, not for show."* One trainee told us of working on a matter from 9.30am to midnight on two or three nights a week for two months. *"It's no worse than the magic circle though."* Fair point.

american all-stars?

We wondered if the fact that it was a US firm affected the atmosphere. One trainee said *"quite a few Americans work here, but I've nothing to compare it against, so I can't say how the American culture has impacted."* The firm has a complete dress-down policy. *"There's a very low freak factor!"* Perhaps the explanation of the *"pretty relaxed, personable and much less stuffy"* atmosphere is the size of the London office and nothing more. *"There's no bowing down to the senior partner, I just wander into his office without knocking."* Sounds fab.

The mother firm is also driving the expansion. *"The London office has been expanding quite a lot recently to break into big deals on our own."* The rate is phenomenal; two trainees thought that the number of lawyers had perhaps doubled in only six months while they had been away on their overseas seats. As for the work ethic, *"if you've got clients who say they want the documents on Monday, we're not going to tell them they have to wait because we don't work over the weekend in London!"* It seems that the chief influence exerted by the Americans is the feeling of a global network in which the different offices help each other. *"The global cultural differences are because people in different offices are of different nationalities, but it's not like a BakerMac franchise."* *"It's still one global firm. Picking up the phone to Tokyo is like dialling an extension within the building. I think that's the American influence."*

eyes wide open

On the one hand we were assured that *"recruiters have their eyes wide open – you don't have to be from Oxford."* But it seems our researchers just know how to pick 'em – the majority of our interviewees were! A huge degree of common sense (they don't necessarily hand that out at Oxford) and a willingness to travel also help. Trainees wanted us to stress that the firm has only recently started marketing itself and that the recent summer students have been from all sorts of backgrounds. It seems we should all apply just for a laugh; *"this was the only interview I positively enjoyed. I pissed myself laughing all the way through!"* Current trainees get on well with each other. They gave the impression of being warm, friendly and ever so slightly laid back; the type of people who are able to take everything in their stride. In 2001, all of the qualifying trainees were retained by the firm.

The social life here exerts *"no pressure either way."* It ranges from informal groups going for lunch or drinks on a Thursday night, where *"there's always a good turn out - the Corney & Barrow gets a lot of attention,"* to more organised affairs. These include five-a-side footy every Friday or the Social Club's various activities, such as wine tasting. The expansion calls for more organisation; *"there have been organised* events for us to get to know people because of the expansion – it was very enjoyable." There is even a 'retreat' every year for everyone at the firm to get away and *"consolidate."* Whatever that entails! It can be glamorous too; the European offices recently got together near Versailles. Alternatively, there are those who prefer to keep work and home separate, and that's no problem.

beige & case

White & Case is now spread tentacle-like through three buildings, but they're all about thirty seconds apart. *"It doesn't affect day to day work, but there's less bumping into people."* For those who care about their surroundings, the buildings *"have good spaces and are very light. The décor is good – modern, beige, no garish colours, clean and there are plants, I like plants!"*

and finally…

White & Case's selling points are that it's a huge firm worldwide with big clients, yet feels like a small firm in London. The implications for training are obvious; *"I didn't realise how much control I would have over what I would be doing."* Trainees want something more than *"the training contract treadmill."* As if all this weren't enough, if you've got the travel bug, we recommend you take a look at White & Case.

Withers

the facts

Location: London
UK ranking by size: 72
Total number of trainees: 21
Seats: 4 x 6 months
Alternative Seats: None

Withers has a reputation for being a bit of an establishment firm, a bit old world and a bit stuffy. Unusually for a City firm, Withers undertakes private client and family work. It's this private client connection that's behind the perception that Withers is more Aled Jones than Vinnie Jones. But there's signs that the old reputation is disappearing. With one of the most impressive websites going and some *"brand new spanking offices,"* can it cast it off forever?

leg room

The new offices by the Old Bailey are certainly popular with trainees and offer much more leg room than they were accustomed to in the old days in Gough Square. *"We all have huge wrap-around desks and plenty of cupboard space."* The offices have helped to makeover the firm's image. *"It is a bit of re-branding, taking the firm into the 21st century. Clients are really impressed when they see our offices."* With a dress-down policy recently introduced, does this mean that Withers are now the coolest kids on the block? Trainees told us that whilst the firm has a more modern feel, it certainly has not completely changed its atmosphere. *"The dress-down policy is quite confusing. It certainly isn't jeans and trainers and never will be - this is Withers!"* The poor trainees seem to spend quite a while agonising over their sartorial selections in the mornings – *"it's a bit confusing really, especially in private client. Sometimes it is just much easier to wear a suit."* Perhaps more importantly, we heard that there's a groundswell of young, talented lawyers pushing the firm forwards, especially in the corporate department.

rich list

40% of Withers revenue comes from private client and charity work. Private client is a compulsory seat, so be prepared to get involved in this type of work. Whilst trainees feel that private client is still quite traditional, the huge variety of work in the department ensures that it is rarely dull. Withers acts for 15% of The Sunday Times rich list and boasts a number of entrepreneurs and celebrities on its client roster. Traditional maybe, but mundane it ain't. Obviously there are strict rules on confidentiality (damn!) so we can't start naming names.

But do you have to have the same pedigree as

Withers' clients to stand a chance of winning a training contract? One trainee added at the end of the interview: "*Don't worry if you didn't come from Oxbridge, we do have this Eton/Oxbridge reputation, but HR are looking across a broad range of institutions.*"

keep it in the family

Family is one of the firm's main strengths. Indeed, along with Manches, the firm is recognised as having the best family department in the country. The department has a huge case load and is always very busy. "*It is a pretty daunting place to be, but the client exposure and potential for gaining extra responsibility are brilliant.*" This extends to advocacy as well; we head from trainees who had spoken before masters and made applications before district judges.

Sure, it's one of its proudest practice areas, but it would be a mistake to assume that private client and family law is all there is to the firm. "*Withers is not just looking for people who have an interest in family. They are looking for all-rounders.*" In fact, we were told that Withers sometimes finds it hard to attract enough trainees for its corporate department because of a perception that everything begins and ends with family and private client.

the italian job

Withers has a strong Italian connection, with around twenty fluent Italian speakers and a representative office in Milan. This dates back to a merger with McKenzie & Mills and offers some fantastic opportunities for those with relevant language skills. "*I wondered if I would get the opportunity to use my Italian, but I do, lots. I have been involved in PR and marketing with Italian clients.*"

The training bods at Withers have a few tricks up their sleeves to ensure their trainees are happy. External trainers come in and lead sessions with groups of trainees. "*It is an opportunity to bitch about any problems we might have in complete confidence. We know that, in the end, something constructive will be done about the issues we raise.*" All the trainees we spoke to felt these sessions were a very positive aspect to life at Withers. We even heard a couple of stories about struggling trainees having their problems solved by these group sessions.

clocking off and snuggling up

Working hours are a dream. Most seats will involve regular hours and some trainees described being in the office at around 8pm as a late night (a proposition that would bring tears of laughter and despair to the eyes of trainees at many of the other firms we cover in the True Picture). Working at the weekend is also a rarity for Withers trainees. "*Not only does it not happen regularly, it is really rather frowned upon,*" one trainee explained.

> "We get on really well and sleep over at each other's houses and stuff."

This is not to say that you won't work hard but you'll be able hold onto your social life. As one trainee put it, "*I wouldn't have it any other way!*" Socially, Withers trainees were one of the closer bunches we encountered. "*We get on really well and sleep over at each others houses and stuff!*" At this point our researcher made his excuses and left! We were relieved to hear that "*we don't live in each others pockets though.*" Following the firm's relocation to Old Bailey, the mainstay of Withers social life, The Cheshire Cheese, has gone forever. Trainees have found a new home in McGovern's on Fridays and The Old Monk on school nights.

and finally...

Of the 12 trainees qualifying in 2001, eight became fee earners with the firm. The remaining four were offered jobs, but decided to take up positions elsewhere, as their department of choice (litigation) was oversubscribed. With a comparatively low number of trainees, you will not feel neglected or just a face in the crowd. Trainees are happy with the quality and variety of work they receive but warned students: *"If you are not ready for the responsibility, you had better get ready PDQ. We're under plenty of scrutiny, as we are quite a small group."* None the less, with such a positive atmosphere and all the touchy feely group therapy, most trainees seem to get through in one piece.

Wragge & Co

the facts
Location: Birmingham, London
UK ranking by size: 14
Total number of trainees: 50
Seats: 4x6 months
Alternative seats: Brussels

In the last five years Birmingham-based Wragge & Co has gone from contender to champion in the Midlands and now, if you look at City deal tables, you'll see that Wragges can handle itself against the big London players. Many believe that this is **the** commercial practice outside London*. If you want a top commercial training but you don't want to live and work in London you need to put this firm on your list. But expect to meet with stiff competition. If you can win a place, it'll be worth it and maybe you'll understand why year after year Wragges wins the hearts and minds of its trainees.

big hug
Wragge & Co has almost doubled in size in the last three years. Growth seems to be fuelled by an increased flow of good quality work, rising profits and high retention rates. This is officially a big firm now, so no applications to Wragges on the basis that they are a cosy medium-sized player. Growth raises a key question; is the firm losing its famous embracing ethos?

Trainees and NQs tell us that the firm is as 'inclusive' as it ever was. *"Some people say that they don't feel as if they know so many people and that's not surprising with the sheer number of people and finding your way around, but the management team has made a point of saying that they want to keep the ethos."* That ethos is one of drawing in and bringing on staff of all types. By way of example, *"paralegals are all full-time permanent employees"* rather than just short-term temps. A number of them do get to take up training contracts and one trainee was formerly a secretary at the firm. Focus groups are formed to discuss certain issues and initiatives that affect the firm and these are drawn from all levels of the firm. Individuals do feel as if they have a voice, not only through these groups (of most relevance to trainees is the trainee committee), but also through open and relaxed relationships with partners.

room for one more?
Is a Wragges partner a different breed of boss? Possibly. Wragges trainees tell us that it is Birmingham's largest occupier of office space. They are bursting at the seams because until late 2001 its main office building is partly sublet to another company. Until that extra space becomes available, staff must all breathe in and squeeze together. The solution to the problem is, at present, open plan working. Partners and all. Indeed, trainees tell us this illustrates an important point, *"The majority of partners are open plan... I sit sandwiched between two partners and they are very keen to be seen to be accessible and human."* In one team everyone except the partners seems to have an office. *"It was a case of them leading by example"* a trainee confirmed. *"Pensions and employment do the same; the partners took the crappiest workstation positions to lead by example."*

Effectively turning a space shortage into a social spirit level is rather canny. *"There's a pretty crafty management team here, they really put their points across well"* a trainee explained. While open plan working may be very sociable, it's not always the calmest or quietest of environments and, if you're a particularly private person who hates being seen out in public, this may have some bearing on your choice of firm. If you desperately need peace and quiet there are *"breakout rooms"* available and apparently certain departments have devised rituals to avoid lawyers being disturbed at crucial times. *"You need to learn to read body language,"* one trainee told us, *"but to make it perfectly clear, wearing a baseball cap means 'No really, please do not disturb me'."*

where the heart is
Lawyers are working very hard at Wragge & Co. *"In corporate, 8.30am-6.30pm and then sometimes you'll get 36-48 hour days. That happened twice in six months for me"* a trainee told us, confirming that his experience was typical of that department. *"In litigation it would be 9am-6pm on average."* So what stops London lawyers all rushing to Wragges, if they really are doing the same type of work? Money perhaps and just the plain fact that for some the image of Birmingham is still *"that hole in the middle of the country."*

Trainees tell us that if you've never been to Birmingham before (and a number hadn't) you should take a visit and see for yourself. *"Birmingham is quite vibrant at the moment. It's just like London, but on a smaller scale. Travelling to work takes between ten minutes and half an hour."* Trainees warn, however, that Wragges is not to be viewed as a second choice to London firms. *"You must go in with the right attitude – make sure your heart is not in London."*

A nearby development at Brindleyplace provides plenty of popular drinking spots, including a Pitcher & Piano and a popular bar called The Mailbox. The Old Joint Stock is the favourite hang out but, wherever you go for a quickie, you're likely to bump into lawyers from Pinsents, Martineaus and Eversheds and plenty of folk from the accountancy firms. *"There's a real professional community… most trainees live in shared houses with other professionals,"* so there's no reason to think that just because all your friends are going to London that you'll be Billy No-mates. Now we're not sure exactly what the trainee who told us *"my intake are incredibly tight"* actually meant, but we're sure he was smiling when he said it.

stop smiling
Wragge & Co felt we weren't serious enough in our piece about them in last year's True Picture. We suggest that they recruit a few boring trainees for us to talk to or perhaps starve them a little or rough 'em up before they talk to us. Sorry, but these trainees are still high-high-high on the happy side. Maybe it's the funny red pills that look like M&M's that seem to make an appearance on Wragges' website.

> "Recognition, respect and thanks. That's what it's all about."

Undoubtedly a well developed sense of fun and an upbeat disposition is an advantage at Wragge & Co. We're not suggesting that you need to be a party animal or the most dynamic person you know, but if you like things to be done in a very established and traditional way, think carefully. If you need to be a part of a rigid hierarchy so that you know your place in it then Wragges may not provide that comfort. A flat hierarchy makes it hard to brown nose, one trainee told us. *"Sometimes you see people trying and it's so obvious. It's really amusing, but it doesn't last long."*

You'll do three compulsory seats, corporate and litigation and property. A fourth option can be chosen from areas of practice including employment, IP (*including an option of one seat in the smaller London satellite office), EU (including a Brussels slot), and Finance and Projects. These seats are all currently very 'in' seats. Some trainees prefer to take their optional seats in the third six months rather than the final six as it makes their choice of department on qualification a little easier. And the opportunities on qualification are many. Wragges is usually very proud of its 100% retention rate on qualification but just missed it in September 2001, when 15 of the 17 stayed.

because you're worth it
You are unlikely to go abroad for part of your training contract. You will certainly work for international clients, but as one of our trainee interviewees stressed this will be from your desk in the UK and not overseas. *"If you have strong international desires, go to the City to a firm with plenty of overseas offices. Wragges won't give you the same opportunity."*

The only fly in the ointment seems to be the issue of salaries. It's not something that affects trainees so much as those at about two or three years PQE. *"It hurts a bit when you see £50K on qualification in London, but rent here is just £200-300 per month and you spend much less money here. Trainees are already buying property."* Others echoed the sentiment. *"Initially Wragges resists the London pull but at 2-3 years qualified people start to wonder what they should do."* *"Some of us think 'maybe I'll go for two years, burn out and come back.' The salary pulls."* But, we ask, how many London firms have David Ginola on their website? And how many can boast the workplace awards that the firm has won in various national surveys?

and finally...
Trainees work hard, but have it pretty good in terms of the environment in which they spend their week. The rapid growth experienced over the last few years seems unlikely to be sustained forever but, given the limitations of office space right now, that might be seen as a good thing. When asked to sum up what's best about Wragge & Co, one trainee put it succinctly *"Recognition, respect and thanks. That's what it's all about."*

international firms...international locations

It's all gone global! The globalisation of the world economy has led to the creation of the global law firm. Several UK firms claim the title. Many were already international, with offices in several jurisdictions, mainly practising UK law and staffed by UK qualified lawyers. In the last couple of years international mergers have appeared on the menu. Clifford Chance was the first, with mergers in Germany and the US. Freshfields, Lovells and Linklaters soon followed suit, and now everyone's trying to be a player. Slaughter and May remains resolute. It has a few international offices and other firms with whom it has 'best friends' relationships.

So you want to be a global trainee. You can go to a UK firm, which is a top international player. Or you can go to a firm with foreign offices and apply for an overseas seat. Or you can choose to train at one of the US firms in London. There are so many options now available that, provided you select the right training contract, you can guarantee three, six or even twelve months overseas.

the top international players

We picked our Top 15 international firms from those featured in the True Picture, after consulting research from *Chambers Global 2001-2002*. We counted the number of rankings each firm received (including rankings for firms that have merged with the top 15 firms since the publication of *Chambers Global*. Each ranking represents recommendations from the market place in an individual practice area in a separate country or region. The number of rankings received is shown in brackets. All of these firms have multiple offices in other jurisdictions.

For more information refer to *Chambers Global* on www.chambersandpartners.com

trainees abroad

Favourite overseas locations for trainees are New York, Hong Kong, Singapore and Paris but, in these days of globalisation, the list of locations grows ever longer. In the Middle East, Dubai is a trainee hot spot. Seats in Eastern Europe are now more common and trainees from UK firms can work as far afield as China, Venezuela and Australia. Closer to home, secondments to Brussels offices are the most plentiful and, if a firm only offers one overseas seat, it will usually be Brussels.

Although the time abroad gives you experience of working in another jurisdiction, you are, with some exceptions, unlikely to practise foreign law. However, as international merger follows interna-

THE TRUE PICTURE GLOBAL TOP 15

1	Baker & McKenzie (89)
2	Clifford Chance (75)
3	Allen & Overy (73)
4	Freshfields Bruckhaus Deringer (68)
5	Linklaters (66)
6	White & Case LLP (51)
7	Herbert Smith (27)
8	Norton Rose (26)
9	Lovells (24)
10	Slaughter and May (24)
11	Weil, Gotshal & Manges (23)
12	Ashurst Morris Crisp (20)
13	Simmons & Simmons (20)
14	CMS Cameron McKenna (15)
15	Denton Wilde Sapte (15)

tional merger, offices are increasingly staffed by lawyers who are dual qualified. It's also very common for UK offices to have a complement of overseas lawyers.

Repeatedly, trainees tell us that overseas seats are hard work. Offices abroad are generally much smaller than main offices in London and this requires trainees to shoulder more responsibility. Almost all trainees welcome this; for most an overseas seat is the highlight of their training contract both in terms of work and personal experience.

How do you ensure that you get your preferred seat abroad? Generally, trainees feel that selection is based on merit and suitability for the job. Language ability is essential for some seats like Paris, Madrid or Milan, but unnecessary for most Asian or Middle Eastern seats. We're told of trainees 'dumbing down' their language skills in order to avoid being sent to an unpopular seat – Frankfurt, for example. The trick to securing certain of the most popular seats is still, to a degree, a case of waging an effective campaign of self promotion. At firms with less of an emphasis on overseas placements, at least half of the trainees usually decide against time abroad as a result of commitments in the UK, or simply a desire to spend all of their seats in the home office. Sometimes (although less commonly than in previous years) trainees have told us that they feared six months away from the action in London might mean that they were out of sight and out of mind. Invariably, the award of an overseas seat will be an endorsement of recognised ability.

Remember, an overseas seat is an opportunity for networking and will give you valuable work experience. In New York you'll get the opportunity to meet finance trainees as well as associates from the US firms. Brussels will give you proximity to the EU institutions and opportunities to meet stagiaires or other interns.

It may be hard work. It may be an eye-opener. It may even be lonely if you're in one of the less frequented locations. But the overwhelming feedback from those we spoke to is that working as a trainee abroad is an unmissable experience.

So what's on offer in the locations to which trainees are most likely to be sent? Here's what we found out.

brussels

Very much an EU/Competition seat and can be research-intensive. Many trainees had already spent some time in EU/Competition departments back in London. This improved their time in Brussels. Having said that, much of the work will be linked to *"big ticket"* corporate deals.

hong kong

Project finance, corporate and banking work are the most common practice areas. Some firms also offer litigation. Depending on the firm much, indeed possibly all, of your work will be based on Hong Kong law, *"which is different but familiar."* Hours can be long; 12 hour days are *"fairly regular."* Saturday mornings are a standard part of the working week (but are dress-down).

new york

Unsurprisingly, finance work (such as securities) and general corporate feature highly. Trainees thought that hours in New York were similar to those in the London. However, the day can be *"very fast-paced,"* partly because hours are governed by *"the fact that you are working with Europe and you have to deal with everything before they go home."* New York offices are very much smaller than London offices of UK firms, so there's more responsibility. You may be the only trainee.

paris

Lots of corporate, international finance and M&A work, with a French language element. Some firms do some domestic French work. Probably some translation work will be required of you. You'll only be sent out to Paris if your French is good. As for the hours, you shouldn't expect to get out of the office early. Nevertheless trainees admit that by 7.30/8pm *"everyone is heading out."* In some Paris offices the long continental lunchbreak dies hard and in August… *"everyone is on holiday."*

frankfurt

This is likely to offer finance-related work, so more of a business and transaction driven seat than six months with black letter law. Socially there is an expat scene and there is certainly a tendency to mix with other English speakers. But, German language skills will usually be required.

madrid

Mostly corporate work and you need to be a Spanish speaker as this is the language of business here. There's a sizeable contingent from the UK firms in Madrid. Spanish firms operate around the two hour siesta from 2pm to 4pm. This means that the official working day stretches for a whopping ten and a half hours from 9.30am–8pm. (But you do get a snooze.)

singapore

Desperately popular with UK trainees. The lure of Asia is intense. Shipping is a common area of work for those lucky enough to secure a secondment here. English is spoken in all offices as it is the official language in this polyglot society. The working week, like in Hong Kong, is Monday to Saturday lunchtime.

piraeus

"People don't want to go to Piraeus" – or so we kept hearing. It's Greek and it's shipping. We assume that it's the latter which is the main turn-off. It may also be the fact that you're unlikely to be in a big gang of trainees from your firm – usually you'll be the only one posted. A handful of firms have offices out there so it ought to be possible to hook up with other UK trainees.

prague

Way better in the summer. A beautiful City with stunning ballet and theatre but sometimes you miss the buzz of London and having your friends around. The architecture and culture are fabulous but the food is dire and it's virtually impossible to get a decent coffee. Lots of corporate work.

tokyo

Becoming ever more popular amongst City trainees. You must love noise, karaoke and pachinko. Space is at a real premium in Tokyo, so flats are never spacious. Be prepared for complete culture shock. A unique experience if you can get it.

moscow

If you're a Russian speaker and your firm has a Moscow office you are in the frame for a secondment there, whether you like it or not. It may be difficult to convince HR that you are best suited to New York or Singapore. Not a large number of trainees in the city but the chance to really get to know colleagues and the workings of a small office as well as your clients' business needs in eastern Europe. Take your long johns in winter and invest in a fur hat, whatever your feelings about it. Temperatures of -18º are quite usual in winter.

middle east

Depending on where your firm has offices, seats can be taken in Bahrain, Abu Dhabi, Dubai or Muscat. These secondments will not throw you into a totally unfamiliar environment as the expat scene is so very strong in these Gulf locations. Female secondees may notice more of a difference than their male counterparts, as Islamic tradition and laws do need to be respected and this will often require modification of dress and behaviour between men and women. If you're unhappy about the prospect of making these adjustments, don't go. Some firms have offices in Cairo.

prospects for newly qualifieds

The last six months of your training contract is a time when you need to make some big decisions about your career. A tiny minority will leave the law; the two years of training have taught them enough to realise they will be happier in another job. The time spent training will not be wasted as they'll have acquired plenty of useful skills and an impressive CV to help them on their way. Most trainees will need to decide whether they want to stay with the firm that trained them or move on to pastures new – either another firm or an in-house legal department.

Those who move on usually do so because their own firm is unable to offer them a job in the department they want. In our research for the True Picture, we spoke to a number of trainees looking elsewhere for employment law, sports law and other more specialist positions. But what of the market as a whole and the prospects for NQs generally? We asked our colleagues at Chambers and Partners Recruitment to give us the low down on the NQ jobs market in autumn 2001.

private practice

For newly qualified solicitors, the market this year is not as strong as the booming market of the past few years. *"There is good news, however: the majority of newly qualifieds are being offered suitable positions by their own firms,"* says Chambers' London consultant Jo Salt. She adds, *"we still have many vacancies in banking and finance, with UK and US firms paying between £50,000 and £80,000. And we are still placing a large number of newly qualified solicitors into corporate law positions, despite there being fewer M&A deals around."*

But the weaker state of the market is having some effect. *"It is more difficult to achieve the goal of many newly qualified solicitors – the move from a smaller firm to a larger firm, or regional firm to London firm, immediately upon qualification. Similarly, those trainee solicitors not offered a position in their first choice specialisation, are finding it harder to move elsewhere,"* says Chambers' consultant Paul Thomas. Some newly qualified solicitors, it seems, may have to make compromises.

> "The lowdown on the NQ jobs market in autumn 2001."

Are there any lessons in all this for students commencing training contracts over the next few years? It is impossible to predict what the market will be like when you come up to qualification. The best advice, therefore, is to play safe. *"Don't burn your bridges with the firm where you are doing your training contract – even if it isn't ideal,"* advises Paul Thomas. *"If the market turns out to be tight when you qualify, you may need their goodwill. There are always more jobs for solicitors with one to two years' PQE than for newly qualified solicitors. If the market is strong when you qualify, we can place you anywhere. If it's tight, we can still find you a good position, but we may advise that you'll need an extra year's PQE to land your dream job."*

So, will we see the recent meteoric rises in salary slow down with the tightening market? Quite possibly. There are already rumblings of client dissatisfaction with increased fees for work and there seems to be a growing reluctance on the part of firms to keep raising salaries. It is likely that they will remain fairly static until the next positive shift in the recruitment market. A continued slow down in business may result in an oversupply of lawyers and this will inevitably affect those with less experience. Four years ago law firms could almost get two NQs for the price of one today. The bottom line seems to be that NQ salaries at large commercial firms are high already, don't expect them to go higher.

industry and banking

It's not hard to see the allure of the in-house culture – more predictable working hours, more opportunities to become involved in business decisions, incentivised pay structures, which have the potential to translate into large bonus payments or share options. But, lack of infrastructure and hands on supervision may deter some NQs

> "Using a specialist consultancy like *Chambers and Partners* is the most likely way of securing one of these jobs."

Most in-house positions in commerce and industry are broad corporate/commercial roles, with an emphasis on negotiating commercial contracts, joint ventures and M&A activity. Sometimes a need arises for candidates with a specialist slant, for example IP, employment or, increasingly, IT. Those with an eye to moving in-house would benefit from qualifying into corporate or commercial departments and trying to ensure a broad commercial mix during their training contract. Opportunities for litigators and property specialists are far more limited.

Good in-house positions can be found in the large commercial centres in the UK, although many leading companies are still based in London and the home counties. This is also where the best salaries are to be found. Whilst it's true to say that the majority of positions are for those with 2-5 years' PQE, Chambers' consultant Nick Lee says *"More opportunities are opening up for newly qualifieds. In-house legal teams are expanding as companies want to reduce external legal costs following the recent hike in private practice rates"*.

Newly qualifieds can also consider positions within the banking sector, although as most are for those with experience in banking and/or capital markets, successful applicants tend to come from the magic circle or second-tier banking firms. These jobs generally come up throughout the year rather than in March and September, when training contracts end. Secondments to a bank during training or afterwards are very useful for making contacts and for giving an insight into the reality of the job.

More positions arise in international investment banks than in retail or commercial banks, simply because they have more lawyers (typically 50+). Other financial institutions, such as building societies or leasing companies, are more often based in the regions and the positions are, therefore, less well paid. However, they tend to be more generalist and might suit those who don't wish to specialise at an early stage in their career. *"In any one year there aren't many NQ banking and finance jobs,"* says Deborah Kirkman, of Chambers' banking division *"Legal departments are relatively small and traders relatively demanding, so there's not much time to train people up"*. Using a specialist consultancy like Chambers and Partners is the most likely way of securing one of these jobs.

Whether it's banking or industry, much of a candidate's success has to do with his or her attitude. *"Teams are small and employers are keen to find the right 'fit'. Personality will often take precedence over experience."* advises Stuart Morton of Chambers. Commercial awareness is also an important attribute, which can be cultivated by keeping abreast of developments in industry-related publications such as the *Financial Times*. Candidates must, of course, be able to demonstrate an interest in and an understanding of the in-house legal environment. But, ultimately, there's no substitute for enthusiasm.

A-Zs

universities and law schools A-Z 403

solicitors A-Z 419

barristers A-Z 566

Cardiff Law School

Centre For Professional Legal Studies, PO Box 294, Cardiff CF10 3UX
Tel: (029) 2087 4964 Fax: (029) 2087 4984
Email: Brookfield@Cardiff.ac.uk
Website: www.cf.ac.uk/claws/cpls

contact
Mr Ian C Brookfield
Tel: (029) 2087 4941

university profile

Cardiff Law School is long established, well-resourced and enjoys an international reputation for its teaching and research. In the most recent assessment of research quality conducted by the Higher Education Funding Council, Cardiff achieved a grade 5 rating, placing it in the top dozen law schools in the country. Cardiff offers opportunities for students to pursue postgraduate study by research leading to the degrees of M.Phil and Ph.D. In addition, taught Masters degrees in the areas of canon, commercial, marine affairs and medical law are offered in full and part-time mode.

legal practice course and bar vocational course

Within the Law School, the Centre for Professional Legal Studies is validated to offer both the Legal Practice Course and the Bar Vocational Course. Students are taught by experienced solicitors and barristers who have been specifically recruited for this purpose. All students pursuing the vocational courses are guaranteed placements with solicitors' firms or sets of chambers, while students studying the Bar Vocational Course additionally enjoy a one week placement with a Circuit or District Judge. Cardiff's Legal Practice Course has three times been rated 'Excellent' by the Law Society; one of only three out of the 31 providers of this course to hold the top ranking.

facilities

Recent developments within the Law School include extensive IT provision together with dedicated accommodation for the vocational courses which house a practitioner library, courtroom facilities, and fixed and movable audio visual equipment for recording interactive practitioner skills activities. In addition, the main law library contains one of the largest collections of primary and secondary material within the UK. The Law School is housed in its own building at the heart of the campus, itself located in one of the finest civic centres in Britain and only a short walk from the main shopping area. The University has its own postgraduate centre, together with a full range of sporting and social facilities.

University of Central England in Birmingham

Faculty of Law & Social Sciences, Franchise Street, Perry Barr, Birmingham B42 2SU
Tel: (0121) 331 6600 Fax: (0121) 331 6622
Email: lss@uce.ac.uk
Website: www.uce.ac.uk

contact

Please apply to:
Admissions Officer,
Faculty of Law & Social Sciences,
Perry Barr,
Birmingham B42 2SU

Tel: (0121) 331 6600
Fax: (0121) 331 6622
Email: lss@uce.ac.uk
Website: www.uce.ac.uk

college profile

Based in Birmingham, UCE's School of Law has been a major centre for legal education and training in the city for over 30 years. Its close links to the city's legal community ensure its courses reflect the modern needs of the profession. A wide range of law courses is taught by experienced and well-qualified staff, in a law school noted for its friendly and approachable atmosphere, in which students are treated as individuals. Its facilities include a legal practice resource centre, fully-equipped IT workrooms, and a court room and solicitor's office, both with audio-visual recording.

lpc/postgraduate diploma in legal practice (full or part-time)

The LPC course is designed to give you an advantageous start to your career in a competitive professional environment. It offers a wide range of commercial and private client options. Interactive teaching and learning methods replicate typical transactions which you will encounter in practice and are designed to develop the self-sufficiency and confidence necessary when embarking on your training contract.

cpe/postgraduate diploma in legal studies (full or part-time)

The CPE places emphasis on the development of legal skills by use of interactive teaching and learning methods and problem solving techniques. Part-time students may study in the day or evening, or a combination of both.

ma legal practice/legal studies (part-time)

These research based courses are for students who have completed the LPC or CPE respectively and who wish to acquire further specialised knowledge.

pgdip/llm european legal studies (full or part-time)

European law in its political or economic context.

pgdip/llm international human rights (full or part-time)

European or USA pathway. USA pathway includes a semester working in the USA.

pgdip/ma immigration policy, law and practice (part-time)

The implications of current law and practice in the UK.

City University, London

The Law Department, Northampton Square, London EC1V 0HB
Tel: (020) 7040 8301 Fax: (020) 7040 8578
Email: cpe@city.ac.uk or law@city.ac.uk
Website: www.city.ac.uk/law

college profile
City University, London, was granted a Royal Charter in 1966. The University is located within walking distance of the Law Society, the major City firms of solicitors, the Bar Council, Inns of Court, Royal Courts of Justice and Central Criminal Court. The Law Department has close ties with the professions and places special emphasis on careers advice. There is an active mooting programme including an Inns of Court sponsored competition. Guaranteed places are available for both the BVC and the LPC.

cpe/diploma in law (full-time or part-time)
The City CPE has a strong academic focus providing a solid foundation in law. It is the largest university CPE/Diploma course and benefits from specialist staff with unrivalled experience, including visiting academics from Oxford, Cambridge and other established universities. It can be converted into an LLB by completing additional course units on a part-time basis and may be converted into an MA by thesis.

graduate entry llb honours degree (full-time)
City's graduate entry LLB is a programme for non-law graduates who want a broader two year course leading to a qualifying law degree. The course is designed both to provide a general knowledge of the central areas of the law and to allow special interests to be developed. The academic work and examinations are of first degree standard and the course is taught jointly with the department's three year undergraduate LLB degree. Separate tutors and tutorials give this course its own special identity within the department.

llm programme (full-time or part-time)
Taught Masters degrees in International Law, Human Rights, Anglo-American Law and Environmental Law are available within a modular framework. Distinctive features of the programme include interdisciplinary content, with contributions to taught modules from non-law academics, and good contact with specialist staff, facilitated by the relatively small size of the courses.

---

contact
Contact the Law Department for full course brochures

cpe/diploma in law
Applications for the full-time course should be made to the Central Applications Board by February. Part-time (2 days per week) applications direct to City by 30 April

graduate entry llb
Applications should be made to City preferably by 30 April

llm programme
Applications should be made to City. No specific closing date

City University London

The College of Law

Braboeuf Manor, Portsmouth Road, Guildford GU3 1HA
Tel: (0800) 328 0153 Fax: (01383) 460 460
Email: info@lawcol.co.uk
Website: www.college-of-law.co.uk

contact
Freephone:
(0800) 328 0153
Email: info@lawcol.co.uk

college profile

The College of Law, the largest legal training establishment in Europe, has branches in Birmingham, Chester, Guildford, London and York. The College has an excellent reputation with law firms and chambers and its teaching staff are professionally qualified as solicitors or barristers. The College's Careers Advisory Service uses its specialist knowledge and extensive contacts to help students gain training contracts and pupillages. It offers the following courses:

postgraduate diploma in law (full-time, part-time or distance learning)

The PgDL is the law conversion course for graduates of disciplines other than law who wish to become solicitors or barristers. Students will receive in-depth tuition in seven foundation subjects from tutors with a proven track record in providing legal education. Successful students receive a Diploma in Law and are guaranteed a place on the College's Legal Practice Course.

legal practice course (full-time, part-time, or block learning)

The LPC is the vocational stage of training for prospective solicitors. The College's LPC has been developed in consultation with both City and provincial firms to address the real needs of today's legal profession, and ensure the course meets the demands of life in practice.

bar vocational course (full-time)

The BVC is the vocational stage of training for prospective barristers and is available at the College in London. It has been developed in conjunction with practising barristers to prepare students for life in their early years at the Bar. Practitioners from highly respected sets of chambers also contribute to the delivery of the course.

For further information about courses at any of the College's branches please contact Admissions.

The College of Law
of England and Wales

University of Derby

School of Education, Human Sciences and Law, Kedleston Road, Derby DE22 1GB
Email: edhumlaw@derby.ac.uk
Website: www.derby.ac.uk/schools

contact
School of Education
Human Sciences and Law
Tel: (01332) 591 122
Email: edhumlaw@derby.ac.uk
Website: www.derby.ac.uk/schools

college profile
At Derby, you will join a university dedicated to lifelong learning that encourages and welcomes students of all ages and backgrounds.

llm/ma in conflict studies and dispute resolution
The programme provides students with a critical understanding of the ways in which conflict studies can be interpreted with insights available from a variety of disciplines. It aims to balance a theoretical examination of conflict and dispute resolution with specific case studies and individual research. Students are encouraged to explore new areas of knowledge through the multidisciplinary approach employed by the course and to reinforce their areas of previous interest and experience.

llm/ma in international law and diplomacy
This degree offers a unique opportunity to learn a variety of disciplines relevant to understanding the legal, and more generally normative dimension of decision-making, with respect to the United Kingdom, the whole Atlantic area, Africa, the Balkans and the Middle East.

llm in commercial law
This challenging programme provides an opportunity for students to engage with key aspects of the law relating to commercial activity. A particular focus of the course is the study of the dynamic commercial environment linking key economic and business management concepts with legal regulations. The course aims to balance a theoretical examination of commercial law with specific case studies and individual research. Students will be encouraged to apply knowledge to issues in contemporary commercial activity and develop skills of critical analysis and research.

UNIVERSITY *of* DERBY

University of Exeter

Centre of Legal Practice, Amory Building, Rennes Drive, Exeter EX4 4RJ
Tel: (01392) 263 157 Fax: (01392) 263 400
Email: Jenny.L.Cook@exeter.ac.uk
Website: www.exeter.ac.uk/law/centprac.htm

contact
Jenny L Cook

college profile
The Centre for Legal Practice was established in 1992 to provide postgraduate programmes relevant to the practice of law. It offers the Diploma in Legal Practice, which is recognised by the Law Society for the purposes of vocational training for solicitors, and the Diploma in Law, which is recognised by the Law Society and the Council of Legal Education as covering the academic stage of training for non-law graduates. The Centre is validated by the Law Society and is presently rated 'Good', whilst being commended for 'an excellent rapport between staff and students', 'very good pastoral care of students ' and a 'committed and enthusiastic course team'. The Centre offers dedicated postgraduate facilities, small teaching classes, a consistently high pass rate and excellent links with local and national firms - all in a beautiful location.

legal practice course (full-time)
The programme is of 34 weeks duration beginning with a three week Core Foundation course. This provides instruction in the practical legal skills of client interviewing and advising, advocacy, writing and drafting and legal research and in the pervasive subjects of Professional Conduct, Financial Services, Accounts and Human Rights. The three compulsory subjects of Business Law, Conveyancing and Litigation are studied over a seventeen week teaching block. Students then choose three elective subjects from: Corporate Finance, Commercial Contracts, Commercial Leases, Housing and Welfare Law, Employment Law, Family Law, Insurance Law and Private Client. The emphasis of the programme is on participative learning and subjects are taught on a practical transactional basis.

diploma in law course (full-time)
Students follow a programme of study for 36 weeks, beginning with a structured introductory reading course for two weeks before coming into residence. A residential Foundation course runs for four weeks preceding the commencement of the Michelmas Term. Thereafter students observe the normal ten week University terms. Students study the following subjects from the LLB syllabus: Criminal Law, Contract Law, Law of Torts, Public Law of the EU and UK 11, Land Law, Constitutional Principles of the EU and UK, Trusts Law. Students also submit a 4,000 word dissertation on an area of legal study not covered within the seven foundation subjects.

Inns of Court School of Law

4 Gray's Inn Place, Gray's Inn, London WC1R 5DX
Tel: (020) 7404 5787 Fax: (020) 7831 4188
Email: icslcourses@icsl.ac.uk
Website: www.icsl.ac.uk

contact
Please apply to Admissions at the address above for further details or to request a prospectus

college profile

The Inns of Court School of Law is the leading provider of postgraduate legal training for both solicitors and barristers and has a well-established CPD programme including the PSC and Higher Rights. All students have remote access via a PC to course materials and online databases. The ICSL's Pro Bono partnership gives vocational course students the opportunity to work with live clients at the School's Advice Clinic or to work with a voluntary partner.

bar vocational course (full-time or part-time)

The ICSL seeks to train lawyers that will be well-equipped for the future, and the use of IT is regarded as fundamental to the teaching and learning process. It is the only institution to offer the BVC in part-time mode. The five core lawyer skills are taught: Advocacy, Opinion Writing, Drafting, Negotiation and Client Conference Skills, plus Legal Research and Case Management, as well as addressing issues of Professional Conduct and Professional Ethics.
Places offered: 650.

legal practice course (full-time)

The LPC has been highly tailored to meet students' future needs in practice, with a heavy emphasis on learning via the use of IT resources. The foundation course consists of: Ethics, Skills, The European Context and Taxation, followed by compulsory subjects of Business Law and Practice, Litigation and Advocacy, and Conveyancing, with a choice of electives.
Places offered: 100 full-time.

llm in criminal litigation (full-time or part-time)

Run in association with City University, this LLM is the only postgraduate degree course in the country to be devoted exclusively to Criminal Litigation. It allows students to examine critically the four key subjects that underpin the criminal justice system – criminal procedure, sentencing, criminal evidence and criminal advocacy.

INNS OF COURT SCHOOL OF LAW
PIONEERS IN PROFESSIONAL
LEGAL TRAINING

London Guildhall University

Department of Law, 84 Moorgate, London EC3M 6SQ
Tel: (020) 7320 1616 Fax: (020) 7320 1163
Email: enqs@lgu.ac.uk
Website: www.lgu.ac.uk

contact
Robert Hawker

college profile
London Guildhall University was one of the first providers to obtain accreditation to run professional law courses. The teaching style of these courses is considered to be one of the friendliest and most thorough available. The University prides itself on giving students personal and individual attention; it is committed to keeping class numbers low; and its IT facilities include MIMICS and other software programs that are found in practice. Students receive training that is relevant, professional and with the right level of assistance to ensure success on their course. Its location in the heart of the City of London means there is easy access to underground and mainline stations.

legal practice course (full-time or part-time day and evening)
Many of the teaching staff are either recently out of practice, or still in practice, and therefore the emphasis is on the provision of professional training. Welfare and commercial electives are offered, including some rare subjects such as Immigration and International Trade.

Class sizes are deliberately limited and skills training is provided in smaller groups to ensure personal and individual attention. Computers are utilised within the classrooms along with video cameras to ensure that all the latest training and practitioner tools are made available to students.

A unique (to London) part-time day course is offered to provide flexibility in training modes.

common professional examination (full-time or part-time day or evening)
Training is by both lectures and tutorials with an emphasis on the seven foundations of legal knowledge. The course prides itself on an intimate atmosphere with personal and individual attention offered to all students. A variety of teaching and assessment methods are utilised including research assignments, case and statute analysis, and oral presentations.

Fee assistance is provided to those students wishing to continue with the LPC at London Guildhall University. The University also offers a flexible mode of study that helps students commit when considering undertaking a professional course.

Manchester Metropolitan University

School of Law, Elizabeth Gaskell Campus, Hathersage Road, Manchester M13 0JA
Tel: (0161) 247 3050 Fax: (0161) 247 6309
Email: law@mmu.ac.uk

contact
Contact the Admissions Tutor for the relevant course

college profile
The School of Law is one of the largest providers of legal education in the UK, and enjoys an excellent reputation for the quality and range of its courses. The School's courses are well designed and taught, combining rigorous academic standards with practical application.

bar vocational course (full-time)
This course provides the vocational stage of training for intending practising barristers. Adopting a Syndicate Group approach, the BVC is activity based and interactive. Extensive IT and audio visual facilities combine with dedicated, well equipped premises to provide an enjoyable and stimulating experience. Excellent student support is provided including mentoring by practising barristers and an Additional Professional Programme which is designed to bridge the gap betweeen student and professional life.

legal practice course (full-time or part-time)
This course is for those wishing to qualify as a solicitor. Offering a full range of commercial and private client electives the Legal Practice Course, taught by professionally qualified staff, prepares you for every day practice. There is a dedicated Resource Centre and an excellent pastoral care programme for LPC students. Consistently recognised by the Law Society for its high quality.

postgraduate diploma in law/cpe (full-time or part-time)
An increasing number of graduates enter the legal profession this way, with employers attracted by the applicant's maturity and transferable skills. The course places emphasis on the acquisition of legal research and other relevant legal skills. Subject to successful completion of the PgDL, the school guarantees a place on the MMU LPC or BVC, provided that Law Society and Bar entry requirements are met.

Middlesex University

Middlesex University Business School, The Burroughs, Hendon, London NW4 4BT
Tel: (020) 8411 5090 Fax: (020) 8411 6069
Email: headmissions@mdx.ac.uk
Website: www.mubs.mdx.ac.uk

college profile
Middlesex University Business School (MUBS) is the largest business school in London and is located at the Hendon campus, within 30 minutes of Central London by underground rail. The law group has been offering both undergraduate and postgraduate programmes for over 26 years and hosts the Centre for Research in Industrial and Commercial Law, with current projects in Employment Law (Whistleblowing), Environmental Law and European Law.

undergraduate programmes
The University offers three qualifying law degrees which provide exemption from the first stage of professional legal education for those seeking a professional career in law. Those are: the LLB (Hons), BA (Hons) Business Law and BA (Hons) Law and Criminal Justice. A combined honours, non-qualifying degree is also offered in Legal Studies.

postgraduate programmes - llm in employment law
Designed for practising lawyers, human resource practitioners, trade union officials and advice workers. Applications from students with a non-law background are welcomed. Students who have not practised law previously will undertake a pre-course block on legal principles and methods.

pg diploma in law/cpe (full-time and distance learning)
Designed for non-law graduates who wish to pursue a career in law. The programmes are recognised by the Law Society and the General Bar Council, while the CPE board approves the CPE programmes. The Pg Diploma is studied one year full-time, whilst the CPE is offered as a two year distance learning course. The programmes provide the academic stage to your legal education that leads to qualification as a barrister or solicitor. Students who successfully pass the programme have a guaranteed place on the full-time LPC at the College of Law.

contact
Campus Admissions
Middlesex University
Business School,
The Burroughs,
London NW4 4BT

Tel: (020) 8411 5090
Fax: (020) 8411 6069
Email: headmissions@ mdx.ac.uk
Website: www.mubs.mdx.ac.uk

Northumbria University

School of Law, Northumbria University, Sutherland Building,
Newcastle-upon-Tyne NE1 8ST
Tel: (0191) 227 4494
Fax: (0191) 227 4557
Website: www.northumbria.ac.uk/law

contact
lpc: Dawn Hayes
(dawn.hayes@northumbria.ac.uk)

bvc: Margaret Bell
(margaret.bell@northumbria.ac.uk)

cpe: Stuart Hill
(stuart.hill@northumbria.ac.uk)

college profile

The School of Law at Northumbria University is known for its excellence in the provision of academic and professional legal education. Situated in central Newcastle, the School has over 60 full-time teaching staff and is one of the largest departments in the University. Full-time, part-time and distance learning modes of study are available. The School is validated to run the Bar Vocational Course, the Legal Practice Course and the Common Professional Examination/Diploma in Law Course. It also offers the Professional Skills Course and an extensive LLM programme, including courses in Mental Health Law, Medical Law, Commercial Law, European Law, International Trade Law and Commercial Property. The Law School has dedicated lecture and workshop accommodation together with its own Law Skills Centre which includes a large practitioner library, court room and offices with full CCTV facilities plus open access IT equipment.

lpc (full-time or part-time)

- the vocational training course for students who wish to qualify as solicitors
- a wide range of corporate and private client electives
- practical workshops

bvc (full-time)

- the vocational training course for students who wish to qualify as barristers
- practical skills training in dedicated accommodation
- strong practitioner participation

cpe (full-time or distance learning)

- the academic stage of training for non-law graduates who wish to qualify as solicitors or barristers
- structured study materials
- opportunity to obtain a law degree with an additional study programme
- guaranteed places for successful students either on their Legal Practice Course or, subject to the requirements of the General Council of the Bar, on their Bar Vocational Course

UNIVERSITY of NORTHUMBRIA at NEWCASTLE
Promoting Excellence in Higher Education

Nottingham Law School

Nottingham Law School, Belgrave Centre, Nottingham NG1 5LP
Tel: (0115) 848 6871 Fax: (0115) 848 6878

contact
Nottingham Law School,
Belgrave Centre,
Chaucer Street,
Nottingham NG1 5LP

bar vocational course

Nottingham Law School has designed its BVC to develop to a high standard a range of core practical skills, and to equip students to succeed in the fast-changing environment of practice at the Bar. Particular emphasis is placed on the skill of advocacy. Advocacy sessions are conducted in groups of six and the School uses the Guildhall courtrooms for most sessions. The BVC is taught entirely by recently practising barristers, and utilises the same integrated and interactive teaching methods as all of the School's other professional courses. Essentially, students learn by doing and Nottingham Law School provides a risk-free environment in which students are encouraged to realise, through practice and feedback, their full potential.

legal practice course

The LPC is offered by full-time and part-time block study. This course has been designed to be challenging and stimulating for students and responsive to the needs of firms, varying from large commercial to smaller high street practices.

Nottingham Law School's LPC features: integration of the transactions and skills, so that each advances the other, whilst ensuring the transferability of skills between different subject areas. Carefully structured interactive group work which develops an ability to handle skills and legal transactions effectively, and in an integrated way. A rigorous assessment process that nevertheless avoids 'assessment overload', to maintain a teaching and learning emphasis to the course. A professionally qualified team, retaining substantial links with practice. An excellent rating from The Law Society's Assessment Panel in every year of its operation.

the postgraduate diploma in law (full-time)

The Nottingham Law School PgDL is a one year conversion course designed for any non-law graduate who intends to become a solicitor or barrister in the UK. The intensive course effectively covers the seven core subjects of an undergraduate law degree in one go. It is the stepping stone to the LPC or the BVC at Nottingham Law School, and a legal career thereafter. It operates on a similar basis to the LPC (see above), though inevitably it has a more academic bias.

Semple Piggot Rochez

Website: www.spr-law.com, www.spr-consilo.com

college profile
SPR established the world's first online law school and is the foremost provider of internet based law training. SPR is committed to excellence in its provision of teaching and resources to a global community of law students and practitioners. SPR provides tuition and support for students enrolled on the University of London's External LLB and LLM programmes. These programmes include:

the graduate entry route a (fast track) and route b llb programmes (incorporating four extended study weekends (Friday-Sunday) and one four day revision seminar) at £1,150 p.a. and £1,050 p.a. respectively.

the graduate route a/undergraduate scheme a online llb programmes (incorporating one four day revision seminar) over two and three years respectively each at £950 p.a. with registration via Scottish Knowledge.

the graduate route b/undergraduate scheme b online llb programmes (incorporating one four day revision seminar) over three and four years respectively each at £850 p.a. with registration via Scottish Knowledge.

the online llm A taught masters degree over two years at £1,050 p.a. with registration via Scottish Knowledge. For students who qualify for the LLM scholarship fund the fee is £600 p.a.

SPR's Online LLB students can also attend the seminars which are automatically provided to SPR's Face to Face Graduate Entry students. The Online Student fee is £300 for the entire series of four three day seminars or £100 for one three day seminar.

facilities
SPR's students are given unlimited access to the SPR website which provides an extensive online law library (including access to Butterworths, Westlaw, Justis and Lawtel); excellent online course and revision materials; sound files of lectures and interviews with leading members of the judiciary, the profession and academics; tutor support of the highest calibre; virtual tutorials held in real time in each subject. SPR also provides:

consilio (www.spr-consilio.com) Consilio is SPR's free online interactive magazine for law students providing a wealth of fascinating items and useful materials.

cpd direct (www.cpd-direct.com) A new online service from Butterworths Lexis Direct and SPR providing online CPD in a wide range of practice areas.

legal web tv (www.legalwebtv.com) Internet broadcasting channel for the legal profession.

site readership Unlimited access to the SPR website for an annual subscription of £500.

saturday courses LLB and CPE students of any university can enrol on SPR's Saturday courses. In addition to six hours of lectures on one Saturday each month throughout the academic year, students have unlimited access to the SPR website, for a total of £600 p.a.

contact
Jane O'Hare
Director of Studies,
Semple Piggot Rochez,
173b Cowley Road,
Oxford OX4 1UT
Tel: (01865) 201 546
Fax: (01865) 726 378
Email:
janeohare@spr-law.com
Mike Semple Piggot
Semple Piggot Rochez

SEMPLE PIGGOT ROCHEZ

Staffordshire University

Staffordshire University Law School, Leek Road, Stoke on Trent ST4 2DF
Tel: (01782) 294 689/294 452 Fax: (01782) 294 335
Email: ph3@staffs.ac.uk Website: www.staffs.ac.uk/schools/law/welcome.html

contact
Pat Holdcroft
CPC Administrator
Tel: (01782) 294689
Fax: (01782) 294335
Email: ph3@staffs.ac.uk

Julie Gingell
LPC Administrator
Tel: (01782) 294452
Email: jg5@staffs.ac.uk

college profile

Staffordshire University Law School offers a comprehensive range of academic and professional postgraduate courses. An enthusiastic team of well qualified staff with a commitment to academic development, legal research and publication is able to offer a breadth and depth of specialist legal knowledge and experience. This is complemented by a £3 million purpose-built state-of-the-art Law School building which exemplifies the University's commitment and approach to legal education and support. The spacious building with its exciting design, set in an attractive setting, is based on a central law library surrounded by teaching and study rooms. It includes two mock courtrooms, staff rooms, study areas and extensive information technology provision. The combination of dedicated staff and a purpose-built building provide an unrivalled resource for law students, providing a focus for legal practitioners, and a centre of excellence for legal education and professional training. Its library and Legal Information Technology Centre provide access to wide ranging information sources, expertise and facilities.

legal practice course (full-time or part-time)

Rated 'Very Good' by the Law Society. The course offers:
- unique practitioner-student mentoring scheme
- comprehensive support in securing training contracts
- excellent, dedicated LPC facilities
- full range of Masters top-up awards
- dedicated teaching staff involved in professional practice

common professional examination/postgraduate diploma in legal studies (full-time or part-time)

The course offers:
- a postgraduate legal qualification ('upgrade' to Masters)
- completion of the academic stage of legal training (equivalent to LLB)
- Certificate in Social Welfare Law and Practice on completion of the CPE '8th Subject'
- 'credits' towards further degrees or vocational courses
- guaranteed Staffordshire University Legal Practice Course place (full or part-time routes)
- mentoring scheme and assistance with work experience

University of the West of England, Bristol

Faculty of Law, Frenchay Campus, Coldharbour Lane, Bristol BS16 1QY
Tel: (0117) 344 2604 Fax: (0117) 344 2268
Email: law@uwe.ac.uk
Website: www.uwe.ac.uk

contact
Gabriel Fallon
Tel: (0117) 344 3769
Fax: (0117) 976 3841
Email: gabriel.fallon@uwe.ac.uk

college profile

The Bristol Institute of Legal Practice, which is part of the Faculty of Law at the University of the West of England, Bristol, is one of the largest providers of professional legal education in the United Kingdom. The Law Society has recognised the quality of its Legal Practice Courses by awarding them an 'Excellent' rating. It is also proud to be one of only seven providers outside London to be validated by the Bar Council to run the Bar Vocational Course. Moreover, the Higher Education Funding Council for England and Wales rated teaching across the Faculty as a whole as 'Excellent'.

courses

The Bristol Institute of Legal Practice offers the following courses:

legal practice course - lpc (full-time and part-time): The Institute's Legal Practice Courses have a national reputation for quality, which has been recognised by the Law Society with its award of an 'Excellent' rating. Moreover, it currently offers more elective subjects (13) than any other provider in the country. The Faculty has very good links with both local and national firms of solicitors.

bar vocational course - bvc (full-time): In 1996 the UWE Faculty of Law was successfully validated by the Bar Council to run the Bar Vocational Course. When validating the course the Chairman of the Bar Council remarked among other factors taken into account was 'the standard of the facilities to be made available for the Course and the strength of support from the local Bar'.

common professional examination (full-time and part-time): The Faculty has run CPE courses for over 20 years. Both the full-time and part-time versions of the course are recognised nationally as being high quality. They are also very popular and highly respected by the Legal Profession. The courses have very high pass rates and, on the successful completion of the Bristol CPE, students also receive a Postgraduate Diploma in Law.

University of Wolverhampton

School of Law, Molineux Street, Wolverhampton WV1 1SB
Tel: (01902) 321000 Fax: (01902) 321570

contact
Lynn Leighton-Johnstone
Recruitment & Admissions
Tel: (01902) 321 999

college profile
Based in Wolverhampton and offers courses for students intending to become solicitors. The law school has been offering these courses for over 20 years. Its LPC programme has had consistently good ratings. The lecturers are drawn from ex-solicitors, barristers, academics and individuals from business and industry. There are excellent IT facilities, a well-stocked library and a sports centre.

legal practice course (full/part-time)
The vocational training course for those intending to practise as solicitors. The core subjects of Business, Litigation and Conveyancing are taught, together with a range of commercial and private client options. Professional skills courses, practical workshops and seminars are all part of the training. Close links with local practitioners, mentoring and CV distribution. Purpose built courtroom. Exclusive LPC resources room. Group social activities.

common professional examination (full/part-time)
The academic stage of training for non-law graduates wishing to become solicitors or barristers. A full programme of lectures and tutorials is offered on this demanding course. Students are taught by ex-solicitors and barristers. Places on the LPC are guaranteed for successful students. Flexible studying choices are under review.

Addleshaw Booth

Sovereign House, PO Box 8, Sovereign Street, Leeds LS1 1HQ
Tel: (0113) 209 2000 Fax: (0113) 209 2060
100 Barbirolli Square, Manchester M2 3AB
Tel: (0161) 934 6000 Fax: (0161) 934 6060
25 Cannon Street, London EC4M 5TB
Tel: (020) 7788 5000 Fax: (020) 7788 5060
Email: grad@addleshaw-booth.co.uk
Website: www.addleshaw-booth.co.uk

firm profile
Addleshaw Booth is more than just a leading UK law firm, it is a national player with an international capability. The firm has an impressive list of clients who have chosen it because of its high quality, bespoke service. The firm was awarded *The Daily Telegraph* / energis Customer Service Award 2000 in recognition of its innovative approach to customer service. Having developed its own client-focused approach, the firm is dedicated to building on its success by continually looking forward. To help it anticipate and embrace change and meet the challenges ahead, the firm looks to its graduate trainees as its future.

main areas of work
Banking and financial services; commercial property; corporate finance; commercial services; litigation and dispute resolution; enact (housing); private client.

trainee profile
Graduates who are capable of achieving a 2:1 and can demonstrate commercial awareness, motivation and enthusiasm. Applications from law and non-law graduates are welcomed, as are applications from mature students who may be considering a change of direction.

training environment
During each six month seat, there will be regular two-way performance reviews with the supervising partner or solicitor. Trainees have the opportunity to spend a seat in one of the other offices and there are also a number of secondments to the in-house legal departments of clients such as Astra Zeneca and Airtours plc. Trainees are seated with a qualified solicitor or partner and work as part of a team, enabling them to develop the professional skills necessary to deal with the demanding and challenging work the firm carries out for its clients. Practical training is complemented by a series of high quality training courses provided by the in-house team and by courses run by the College of Law, tailored specifically to the firm's needs.

sponsorship & benefits
CPE and LPC fees are paid, plus a maintenance grant of £4,000. Benefits include corporate gym membership, season ticket loan.

vacation placements
Places for 2001: 40; Duration: 2 weeks; Remuneration: £150 p.w. Apply by 23 February 2001.

Partners 128
Assistant Solicitors 470
Total Trainees 63

contact
Mrs Simran Foote
Graduate Manager

method of application
Employer's application form

selection procedure
Interview, assessment day

closing date for 2004
26 July 2002

application
Training contracts p.a. 40
Applications p.a. 2,000
% interviewed p.a. 10%
Required degree grade 2:1

training
Salary
1st year (2000)
£18,000-£18,500 (Manchester & Leeds)
£22,000-£22,500 (London)
2nd year (2000)
£19,000-£19,500 (Manchester & Leeds)
£23,500-£24,000 (London)
Holiday entitlement
25 days
% of trainees with a non-law degree p.a.
40%

post-qualification
Salary (2000)
£29,000 (Manchester & Leeds)
£40,000 (London)
% of trainees offered job on qualification (2000) 85%

other offices
Leeds, London, Manchester

Allen & Overy

One New Change, London EC4M 9QQ
Tel: (020) 7330 3000 Fax: (020) 7330 9999
Email: graduate.recruitment@allenovery.com
Website: www.allenovery.com

Partners	386*
Associates	1196*
Total Trainees	446*

denotes world-wide figures

firm profile
Allen & Overy is one of the world's premier international law firms, with major strengths in banking, international capital markets and corporate work. All departments work closely together to meet the needs of clients which include governments, financial institutions, businesses and private individuals.

main areas of work
Banking; international capital markets; corporate; litigation; property; private client; tax; employment and related areas.

trainee profile
Intellectual ability is a prerequisite but as Allen & Overy is a commercial firm it also looks for people with a good level of business understanding. The firm looks for creative, problem solving people who can quickly identify salient points without losing sight of detail. You will need to be highly motivated, demonstrate initiative and the ability to alternate between leading and being part of a team.

training environment
Within a highly pressurised environment, trainees obtain a balance of practical and formal tuition. You will experience at least four different areas of work, but will spend a significant amount of time in at least two of the following departments: banking, corporate and international capital markets. Your preferences will be balanced with the firm's needs. Seminars provide practical advice and an introduction to each area of law. Overseas placements are available. A positive, open and co-operative culture is encouraged both professionally and socially. A range of sporting activities are available.

benefits
Private healthcare scheme, private medical insurance, season ticket loans, subsidised restaurant, gym membership, 'cybercafe', six weeks unpaid leave on qualification.

vacation placements
Places for 2002: 90; Duration: 3 weeks; Remuneration: £250 p.w.; Closing Date: 31 January 2002. Places available in London, Brussels, Frankfurt and Paris.

sponsorship & awards
CPE and LPC fees and £5,000 maintenance p.a. (£4,500 outside London, Oxford and Guildford).

contact
Graduate Recruitment

method of application
Application form & online

selection procedure
Interview

closing date for 2004
CPE candidates
End Feb 02
Law students End Aug 02

application
Training contracts p.a. 120
Applications p.a. 4,000
% interviewed p.a. 10%
Required degree grade: 2:1

training
Salary
1st year (2001) £28,000
2nd year (2001) £32,000
Holiday entitlement
25 days
% of trainees with a
non-law degree p.a. 40%
No. of seats available
overseas p.a.
64 in 18 offices

post-qualification
Salary (2001) £48,000
% of trainees offered job
on qualification (as at
31/3/01) 98%
% of partners (as at
31/1/01) who joined as
trainees 63%

international offices
Amsterdam, Antwerp, Bangkok, Beijing, Brussels, Bratislava, Budapest, Dubai, Frankfurt, Hamburg, Hong Kong, Luxembourg, Madrid, Milan, Moscow, New York, Paris, Prague, Rome, Singapore, Tirana, Tokyo, Turin, Warsaw

Arnold & Porter

Tower 42, 25 Old Broad Street, London EC2N 1HQ
Tel: (020) 7786 6100 Fax: (020) 7786 6299
Website: www.arnoldporter.com

firm profile
With seven offices and over 650 lawyers practising in over 25 practice and industry areas Arnold & Porter is able to bring clients a sophisticated understanding of changing environments at the intersection of business, law and public policy. The firm was established in Washington DC in 1946 and the London office was initially opened in 1997, but has grown rapidly over the past two years. By the end of 2001 it is anticipated that there will be approximately 40 lawyers in the London office.

main areas of work
Arnold & Porter is a full service law firm providing legal services worldwide. In the London office the practice areas include litigation, telecommunications, information technology, intellectual property, competition, corporate and life sciences. The firm's clients include multinationals, UK and European concerns ranging from start-ups to Fortune 500 companies. Chambers and Partners presented the firm with the *Chambers Global 2001-2002* 'Antitrust Law Firm of the Year in North America' Award.

trainee profile
The firm's commitment to excellence means that it expects its trainees to be well-rounded individuals with an outstanding academic background.

training environment
The London office reflects the environment of the firm generally. It has a collegial and informal atmosphere which is enhanced by twice-weekly informal social gatherings and other events, a casual dress policy and team-based assignment policies. Trainees will be expected to work on several matters at once and to assume responsibility quickly. The office emphasises teamwork and trainees will be quickly exposed to working for a variety of partners and fee-earners throughout the office and the firm. In the US, the firm is rated as the number one choice for new associates. The London office is offering training contracts for the first time, to commence in 2004.

sponsorship & benefits
Sponsorship is provided for CPE/LPC. Private health insurance, season ticket loan, life assurance are amongst the benefits offered by the firm.

vacation placements
Summer vacation scheme, applications on the firm's application form to be received by 15 March 2002.

Partners 9
Assistant Solicitors 18
Total Trainees 0

contact
Sandra Felmingham
Director of Office Administration

method of application
Application on firm's application form

selection procedure
Interviews

closing date for 2004
31 August 2002

application
Training contracts p.a. 4-6
2004 will be the first year that Arnold & Porter takes trainees
Required degree grade 2:1

training
Salary Minimum £28,000
Holiday entitlement 22 days

post-qualification
Salary £59,000

overseas/regional offices
Washington DC, New York, Denver, Los Angeles, Century City, Northern Virginia

Andersen Legal

2 Arundel Street, London WC2R 3GA
Tel: (020) 7344 0344 Fax: (020) 7438 2518
Email: louise.constantinou@glegal.com
Website: www.andersenlegal.com/england

[handwritten: Dissolved 30th May]

firm profile
Andersen Legal is an international organisation of independent law firms sharing common methodologies, technology and standards of client service. Andersen Legal is represented in the UK by Garretts, a leading provider of first-rate, business-focused legal services to major corporates, financial institutions, governments and agencies, at home and internationally.

main areas of work
Legal services include mergers and acquisitions; banking and financial services; e-business; intellectual property and information technology; competition and trade; litigation and arbitration; real estate and labour law. The firm specialises in a number of industry sectors including healthcare; pharmaceuticals and biotechnology; hospitality; leisure and travel; technology; media and communications; financial services.

trainee profile
Successful candidates will have a strong academic background, outgoing personality, relevant work experience and an interest in extra curricular activities.

training environment
Trainees spend six months in four different seats, in a variety of departments. Formal training consists of a residential induction course, two day courses at the start of each new seat and professional in-house lectures. Social and sporting activities are encouraged.

benefits
The firm offers a flexible benefits package which enables the individual to tailor their benefit choices to meet their personal needs, ie BUPA, holiday allowance. Other benefits include subsidised gym membership and S.T.L.

vacation placements
Places for 2002: 60 throughout the UK; Duration: 3 weeks; Remuneration: £250 p.w. (2001 London); Closing Date: 8 February 2002.

sponsorship & awards
CPE and LPC fees paid, plus £4,500-£5,000 grant p.a.

Partners 51
Assistant Solicitors 129
Total Trainees 52

contact
Kate Calcutt
UK Graduate Recruitment Manager

method of application
Firm's application form (at the back of the graduate recruitment brochure)

selection procedure
1 hour interview in London, 2nd interview held in regional office of choice

application
Training contracts p.a. **40**
Applications p.a. **2,000**
% interviewed p.a. **c.20%**
Required degree grade **2:1**

training
Salary
1st year (2001)
£28,500 (London)
Holiday entitlement
20 days

secondment programme
There are opportunities to spend time abroad. Currently the firm has trainees on secondment to Andersen Legal in Sydney, Rajah & Tann in Singapore, Archibald Anderson in Paris & Studio di Consulenza Legale e Tributeria in Italy. The firm is actively looking into secondments to other countries

other offices
Birmingham, Cambridge, Manchester, Reading

Ashurst Morris Crisp

Broadwalk House, 5 Appold St, London EC2A 2HA
Tel: (020) 7638 1111 Fax: (020) 7859 1800
Email: gradrec@ashursts.com
Website: www.ashursts.com

firm profile
An international City practice, smaller than its principal competitors yet consistently ranked amongst the top few firms in the country in terms of the work in which it is involved and clients for whom it acts.

main areas of work
Company/commercial, real estate, international finance, litigation and tax, with specialist groups for competition, construction, employment, energy, transport and infrastructure, environment, insolvency, insurance, intellectual property, management buy-outs, sport and technology, media and telecommunications.

trainee profile
Candidates should want to be involved in the highest quality work that a City firm can offer. The firm is looking for high achievers academically as the work is intellectually challenging. Candidates should show common sense, good judgement, a willingness to take on responsibility, a sense of humour and an outgoing nature. Language skills and an international perspective on life will impress.

training environment
The training contract consists of four six month seats, one of which is a general corporate seat. Two seats are then spent in any two of the real estate, international finance and litigation departments. This will typically leave trainees with six months to choose one other department or specialist area of law in which they would like to gain experience. Trainees also have the opportunity to spend one of their seats abroad or in-house with a major client. The nature of a trainee's work varies from seat to seat but as trainees gain in experience and grow in confidence they can expect increased responsibility with much less direct supervision.

benefits
Benefits include private health insurance, pension, life assurance, interest-free season ticket loan, gym membership and 25 days holiday per year during training.

vacation placements
Places for 2002: 2 week Easter placement scheme for up to 30 non-law students. 3 week Summer placement scheme for up to 70 law students; Remuneration: £250 p.w.; Closing Date: 25 January 2002.

sponsorship & awards
CPE and LPC funding, plus £5,000 maintenance allowance p.a. (£4,500 outside London and Guildford). LPC Distinction award of £500. Language tuition bursaries.

Partners 124
Assistant Solicitors 390
Total Trainees 104

contact
Stephen Trowbridge
Graduate Recruitment

method of application
Online

selection procedure
Interviews with 1 assistant followed by interview with 2 partners

closing date for 2004
31 July 2002

application
Training contracts p.a. 50
Applications p.a. 3,500
% interviewed p.a. 15%
Required degree grade 2:1

training
(2001)
First six months
£28,000
Second six months
£29,000
Third six months
£31,000
Fourth six months
£32,000
Holiday entitlement
25 days
% of trainees with a non-law degree p.a. 45-50%
Number of seats abroad available p.a. 15

post-qualification
Salary £48,000
% of trainees offered job on qualification 97%

overseas offices
Brussels, Frankfurt, Madrid, Milan, Munich, New Delhi, New York, Paris, Singapore, Tokyo

Baker & McKenzie ✓

100 New Bridge Street, London EC4V 6JA
Tel: (020) 7919 1000 Fax: (020) 7919 1999
Email: london.graduate.recruit@bakernet.com
Website: www.ukgraduates.bakernet.com

firm profile
Baker & McKenzie is the law firm with the greatest global reach – 61 offices in 35 countries. The London office is a leading City practice with a domestic and foreign client base. It provides business and financial legal services to corporations, financial institutions, governments and entrepreneurs.

main areas of work
Corporate/finance/EC/tax/commercial 49%; litigation/construction 18%; employment/pensions/immigration 15%; intellectual property 12%; commercial property 6%.

trainee profile
Baker & McKenzie are looking for trainees who are stimulated by intellectual challenge and want to be 'the best' at what they do. Effective communication together with the ability to be creative but practical problem solvers, team players and to have a sense of humour are qualities which will help candidates stand out from the crowd. Language and IT skills are also valued. The firm encourages its trainees to take time out before commencing their training contract, whether just to travel or undertake further studies.

training environment
Four six-month seats which include corporate and litigation together with the possibility of a secondment abroad or with a client. During each seat you will have formal and informal reviews to discuss your progress as well as subsequent seat preferences. Your training contract commences with a highly interactive and practical induction programme which focuses on key skills including practical problem solving, interviewing, presenting and the application of information technology. The firm's training programmes include important components on management and other business skills, as well as seminars and workshops on key legal topics for each practice area. They run the Professional Skills Course in-house – two modules of which are undertaken at the start of your training contract. There is a Trainee Solicitor Liaison Committee which acts as a forum for any new ideas or problems which may occur during the training contract. Trainees are actively encouraged to participate in a variety of pro bono issues and outside of office hours there is a varied sporting and social life.

benefits
Permanent health insurance, life insurance, private medical insurance, group personal pension plan, gym membership, luncheon vouchers, interest-free season ticket loan.

Partners 68
Assistant Solicitors 208
Total Trainees 55

contact
Natalie Stacey

method of application
Letter & application form

selection procedure
Candidates to give a short oral & written presentation, interview with 2 partners, meeting with a trainee

closing date for 2004
Non-law **18 Feb 2002**
Law **28 July 2002**

application
Training contracts p.a. **30**
Applications p.a. **2,000**
% interviewed p.a. **10%**
Required degree grade **2:1**

training
Salary
1st year (2001) **£28,000**
2nd year (2001) **£32,000**
Holiday entitlement **25 days**
% of trainees with a non-law degree p.a. **Approx 50%**
No. of seats available abroad p.a. **Variable**

post-qualification
Salary (2001) **£50,000–£52,000**
% of trainees offered job on qualification (2001) **70%**
% of partners (as at 1/9/01) who joined as trainees **40%**

Baker & McKenzie continued

vacation placements
Places for 2002: 30; Duration: Summer (3 weeks); Remuneration: £250 p.w.; Closing Date: 31 January 2002

sponsorship & awards
CPE Funding: Fees paid plus £5,000 maintenance.
LPC Funding: Fees paid plus £5,000 maintenance.

additional information
As mentioned, trainees have the opportunity to spend three months working in one of the firm's overseas offices. Trainees have already been seconded to its offices in Sydney, Hong Kong, Frankfurt, Chicago and Riyadh. In addition the firm also operates an Associate Training Programme which enables lawyers with 18–24 months pqe to spend between 6–24 months working in an overseas office. In recent years the firm has had associates spend time in Palo Alto, Chicago, New York, Washington DC, Moscow, Hong Kong and Sydney. Baker & McKenzie has a very extensive know-how practice both in London and globally which is ably assisted by BakerWeb, the firm's intranet.

trainee comments
"Within a week of joining, I was liaising with our offices in six or seven jurisdictions on what was then the largest deal of its kind in Europe. Two months later I was attending the signing in Germany. The experience really gave me a feel for the international culture of B&M and the work we do here…and responsibility from day one!" (Elizabeth Shemming, first seat trainee, University of Leeds.)

"Being a trainee at B&M has been a very rewarding experience, both in terms of the work, and also meeting new people. I have worked on a wide range of projects, and in all of them the international aspect of the work and the level of responsibility I have enjoyed has been particularly fulfilling. It has been a great start to my legal career!" (Emily Carlisle, second seat trainee, Somerville College, Oxford.)

"When I accepted a training contract at B&M I never anticipated that I would be making legal history within months of joining the firm. It was a great honour for me to be asked to work on the Camelot judicial review against the National Lottery Commission and an experience I am unlikely to forget." (Richard Pike, third seat trainee, University of East Anglia.)

overseas offices
Almaty, Amsterdam, Bahrain, Baku, Bangkok, Barcelona, Beijing, Berlin, Bogotá, Brasilia, Brussels, Budapest, Buenos Aires, Cairo, Caracas, Chicago, Dallas, Düsseldorf, Frankfurt, Geneva, Guadalarjara, Hanoi, Ho Chi Minh City, Hong Kong, Houston, Hsinchu, Juarez, Kyiv, Madrid, Manila, Melbourne, Mexico City, Miami, Milan, Monterrey, Moscow, Munich, New York, Palo Alto, Paris, Prague, Rio de Janeiro, Riyadh, Rome, St Petersburg, San Diego, San Francisco, Santiago, São Paulo, Singapore, Stockholm, Sydney, Taipei, Tijuana, Tokyo, Toronto, Valencia, Warsaw, Washington DC, Zürich

Berwin Leighton Paisner

Adelaide House, London Bridge, London EC4R 9HA
Tel: (020) 7760 1000 Fax: (020) 7760 1111
Email: traineerecruit@berwinleightonpaisner.com
Website: www.berwinleightonpaisner.com

firm profile
Berwin Leighton Paisner is a top 15 City practice. It is a commercial law firm with expertise in many major industry and service sectors. The firm is a modern growing practice that puts a premium on commercial, as well as technical advice, client relations and transactional care. The firm is entrepreneurial and innovative.

main areas of work
Corporate finance; tech media; commercial; employment; commercial property; planning; regulatory; construction and engineering; banking and capital markets; property finance; PFI/projects; and litigation and dispute resolution.

trainee profile
The firm is looking for intelligent, energetic, positive and hard working team players who have an interest in business and gain a sense of achievement from finding solutions.

training environment
Training starts with an induction covering all the practical aspects of working in a law firm from billing to client care. Comprehensive technical education programmes have been developed for each department and trainees attend weekly seminars supplemented by trainee lunches and skills sessions. You will undertake a tailor-made Professional Skills Course which is run in-house. Trainees spend six months in four seats and your progress will be reviewed every three months. The office environment is relaxed and friendly and trainees can enjoy early responsibility secure in the knowledge that they are fully supervised.

benefits
Flexible benefits package including permanent health insurance, private medical insurance, subsidised conveyancing, subsidised gym membership, 25 days holiday a year.

vacation placements
Places for 2002: Open Days held during the Easter Vacation, application by CV and covering letter before 28 February 2002. Attendance at an Open Day could lead to a one week placement in the Summer Vacation. There are 180 places on the Open Days and 60 places on the summer placement scheme.

sponsorship & awards
CPE/PgDL and LPC fees paid and £4,500 maintenance p.a.

Partners 123
Assistant Solicitors 220
Total Trainees 67

contact
Claire Benson

method of application
Firm application form

selection procedure
Assessment day & partner interview

closing date for 2004
31 July 2002

application
Training contracts p.a. 35
Applications p.a. 2,000
% interviewed p.a. 5%
Required degree grade 2:1

training
Salary
1st year (2000) £28,000
2nd year (2000) £32,000
Holiday entitlement
25 days
% of trainees with a
non-law degree p.a. 40%
No. of seats available
abroad p.a. 4

post-qualification
Salary (2001) £48,000
% of trainees offered job
on qualification 93%
% of assistants who joined
as trainees 35%
% of partners who joined
as trainees 19%

european offices
Brussels, associated office in Paris

SJ Berwin

222 Gray's Inn Road, London WC1X 8XF
Tel: (020) 7533 2222 Fax: (020) 7533 2000
Email: graduate.recruitment@sjberwin.com
Website: www.sjberwin.com

firm profile
Since its formation in 1982, SJ Berwin has established a strong reputation in corporate finance. It also has a number of niche specialisms in areas such as film finance and private equity. Much work is international and clients range from major multinational business corporations and financial institutions to high net worth individuals.

main areas of work
Corporate 45%; property 20%; litigation 17%; EU and competition 8%; commercial media and IP 7%; tax 3%.

trainee profile
The firm wants ambitious, commercially-minded individuals who seek a high level of involvement from day one. Candidates must be bright and determined to succeed. They should be likely to achieve a 2:1 or first.

training environment
Four seats of six months each will be completed, and the seats are set, ideally, to the needs of the trainee. Two seats will be in the corporate finance arena, which includes Frankfurt and Madrid. The firm has a dedicated training department and weekly training schedules coupled with training designed specifically for trainees allow a good grounding in legal and non-legal skills and knowledge. Overseas seats are available in Paris, Frankfurt, Brussels and Madrid.

benefits
Corporate sports membership, free lunch, health insurance.

vacation placements
Places for 2002: 60; Duration: 2 weeks; Remuneration: £225 p.w.; Closing Date: 31 January 2002.

sponsorship & awards
CPE and LPC fees paid and £4,000 maintenance p.a.(£4,500 in London).

Partners 92
Assistant Solicitors 220
Total Trainees 70

contact
Graduate Recruitment Team

method of application
Letter & CV

selection procedure
Interview (early September)

closing date for 2004
31 July 2002

application
Training contracts p.a. **35**
Applications p.a. **3,000**
% interviewed p.a. **10%**
Required degree grade **2:1**

training
Salary
1st year (2001) **£28,000**
2nd year (2001) **£32,000**
Holiday entitlement
50 days over 2 years
% of trainees with a non-law degree p.a. **40%**
No. of seats available abroad p.a. **8**

post-qualification
Salary (2001) **£50,000**
% of trainees offered job on qualification (2001) **85%**
% of assistants (as at 1/9/01) who joined as trainees **26%**
% of partners (as at 1/9/01) who joined as trainees **12%**

overseas offices
Brussels, Frankfurt, Madrid, Berlin, Paris, Munich

Bevan Ashford

35 Colston Avenue, Bristol BS1 4TT
Tel: (0117) 918 8992 Fax: (0117) 929 1865
Email: j.brierley@bevanashford.co.uk
Website: www.bevanashford.co.uk and www.bevan-ashford.com

firm profile

Bevan Ashford is one of the largest regional practices in the UK with a network of seven offices in Bristol, Birmingham, Exeter, London, Plymouth, Taunton and Tiverton. With 81 experienced partners, each of whom is a specialist in their field, and a total staff of over 500, the firm is able to provide clients with an efficient, professional and cost-effective service. Its national reputation means that the firm's client base ranges from multinational corporations and institutions through to smaller businesses, partnerships and individuals. Its success in attracting and keeping quality clients is achieved by the firm's complete commitment to total client care. By recruiting, training and keeping top quality personnel the firm believes it can continue its culture of client care and offer its clients the individual standards of service they require.

main areas of work

Healthcare 27%; commercial property 20%; commercial litigation 15%; company and commercial 16%; private client 17%; other work 5%.

trainee profile

Bevan Ashford is only as strong as its people. The firm's success is achieved by attracting and keeping enthusiastic, bright people with sound common sense, plenty of energy and the ability to work and communicate well with others plus a sense of humour! Language and IT skills are also desirable.

training environment

The core of your training will be practical work experience in conjunction with an extensive education programme consisting of talks, lectures and a residential weekend seminar to back-up the practical work. The training is aimed at developing attitudes, skills and legal and commercial knowledge essential for your career success. Your practical work experience will be reviewed on a regular basis by your supervising partner and you will be encouraged to take on as much work, and responsibility, as you wish. The firm is friendly with an open door policy with a wide range of social, sporting and cultural activities plus an active social club.

vacation placements

Places for 2002: 80.

sponsorship & awards

Available for LPC and in some cases PgDL (CPE).

Partners 81
Assistant Solicitors 140
Total Trainees 42

contact
Jean Brierley

method of application
Application form (available from the firm's website) & covering letter

closing date for 2004
31 July 2002

application
Training contracts p.a. 25
Required degree grade 2:1

post-qualification
% of trainees offered job on qualification (2001)
100%

other offices
Bristol, Cardiff, Exeter, (London), Plymouth, Taunton, Tiverton

Bird & Bird

90 Fetter Lane, London EC4A 1JP
Tel: (020) 7415 6000 Fax: (020) 7415 6111
Website: www.twobirds.com

firm profile
Bird & Bird is an international commercial law firm with offices in London, Brussels, Paris, Stockholm and Hong Kong. The firm maintains a strong sectoral focus and has an enviable reputation in each of its key practice areas: e-commerce; communications; IT; IP; media; sports; pharmaceuticals and biosciences. Within these sectors, advice is also offered for corporate and commercial law, employment, banking and financial services, litigation and tax.

main areas of work
Company 55%; intellectual property 22%; litigation 14%; property 8%; private client 1%.

trainee profile
The firm looks for high calibre recruits – confident individuals capable of developing expert legal skills and commercial sense.

training environment
Following an introduction course, you will undertake four seats of six months, three of which are spent in company, litigation and property. The choice of final seat is yours. You will share an office with a partner or senior assistant who will guide and advise you. You will hone drafting and legal research skills and gain familiarity with legal procedures. The firm encourages you to make an early contribution to case work and to meet clients immediately. Internal seminars and external lectures are arranged to cover the PSC. Trainees are welcome to join the number of sports teams at the firm and to attend various social events and outings.

benefits
BUPA, season ticket loan, subsidised sports club membership, life cover, PHI.

vacation placements
Places for 2002: 12; Duration: 3 weeks; Remuneration: £185 p.w.; Closing Date: February 2002.

sponsorship & awards
LPC and CPE fees paid and a yearly maintenance grant of £3,500.

Partners 79*
Assistant Solicitors 200*
Total Trainees 26*
denotes world-wide figures

contact
Lynne Walters

method of application
Application form

selection procedure
Assessment mornings

closing date for 2004
July 2002

application
Training contracts p.a. **17**
Applications p.a. **1,500**
% interviewed p.a. **10%**
Required degree grade **2:1**

training
Salary
1st year (2001) **£25,000**
2nd year (2001) **£27,000**
Holiday entitlement
25 days
% of trainees with
a non-law degree p.a.
Varies

post-qualification
Salary (2001) **£43,000**
% of trainees offered job on qualification (2000) **100%**
% of assistants (as at 1/9/00) who joined as trainees **20%**
% of partners (as at 1/9/00) who joined as trainees **17%**

overseas offices
Brussels, Hong Kong, Paris, Sweden

Blake Lapthorn

Harbour Court, Compass Road, North Harbour, Portsmouth PO6 4ST
Tel: (023) 9222 1122 Fax: (023) 9222 1123
Website: www.blakelapthorn.co.uk

firm profile

Founded in 1869 and one of the largest and most progressive regional law firms in the south of England, the firm's main activities are centred in two large purpose-built out of town offices on the M27 – one providing commercial and litigation services and the other private client services. In addition there are offices in Southampton and London and all the offices are equipped with state of the art information technology. The size of the firm means that it is able to offer clients the same range and level of service expected from the best London firms. There are 46 partners, many of whom were trainees with the firm, and a total staff of over 400.

main areas of work

Company/commercial; commercial property; litigation; private client.

trainee profile

In addition to excellent academic achievements, the firm values previous experience, which has developed maturity and a wider perspective. Commercial awareness, team-working and well-developed communication skills are also an advantage as well as familiarity with the use of IT.

training environment

Five trainees are recruited each year and have a minimum of four placements lasting three or six months. Trainees' preferences are taken into account as far as possible, but the firm believes in providing well-rounded training supplemented with in-house education and regular appraisals and reviews with the Training Principal. Trainees are also allocated a 'mentor', normally a senior solicitor.

sponsorship & awards

LPC: Fees of up to £6,000; bursary of £4,000.

Partners 46
Assistant Solicitors 81
Total Trainees 15

contact
Ruth Little
Director of Personnel & Training

method of application
Firm's application form (on website) & CV

selection procedure
Interview with partners, including giving a presentation & group exercise

closing date for 2004
31 July 2002

application
Training contracts p.a. 5
Applications p.a. 750
% interviewed p.a. 8-10%
Required degree grade 2:1

training
Salary
1st year (2000) £15,000
2nd year (2000) £17,000
Holiday entitlement
22 days

post-qualification
Salary (2001) £28,000
% of trainees offered job on qualification (2001) 80%

Bond Pearce

Ballard House, West Hoe Road, Plymouth PL1 3AE
Tel: (01752) 266 633 Fax: (01752) 225 350
Email: thosken@bondpearce.com

firm profile
Bond Pearce's merger in July 2001 with Cartwrights consolidates its position as one of the UK's leading law firms and one of the fastest growing. Bond Pearce now has over 60 partners with a total staff in excess of 600.

main areas of work
The size of Bond Pearce and the full range of legal services provided ensures trainee solicitors gain unrivalled experience with training in four separate specialist seats. Specialist groups within Bond Pearce, backed up by effective support services, provide the highest quality of services to a broad range of clients: commercial group (corporate, banking and insolvency, commercial litigation); insurance group; property group (commercial property, planning and environment, private client); and personal injury.

trainee profile
Successful candidates may come from various backgrounds and enjoy a wide range of interests, but will have in common the desire to excel at their work and get the most out of life. Personal qualities are paramount. The firm looks for bright and enthusiastic individuals who can demonstrate initiative, commercial acumen, team working skills and a sense of humour.

training environment
Trainee solicitors have their own desks in the same office as the partner, associate or senior solicitor with whom they are working. They become an integral part of each team, closely involved in the diversity of their work and whilst fully supervised, trainees are encouraged to take on as much responsibility as possible. Technology plays a vital role in Bond Pearce. The firm's offices are linked by a networked computer system, the accounts and time recording systems are fully computerised and all staff, including trainee solicitors, are equipped with a fully networked PC on their desks. There are close links between the firm's offices and trainee solicitors join together in all training and many social activities. Bond Pearce has a thriving sports and social club.

vacation placements
Closing Date: Deadline for summer placement scheme is 31 March 2002.

sponsorship & awards
LPC financial assistance.

Partners 61
Assistant Solicitors 160
Total Trainees 41

contact
Tina Hosken

method of application
Application form, CV & photograph

selection procedure
Interviews & vacation placement scheme

closing date for 2004
31 July 2002

application
Training contracts p.a. **10-15**
Applications p.a. **500**
% interviewed p.a. **10%**

training
Salary
1st year (2000)
Depending on location
up to **£16,250**
Holiday entitlement
20 days
% of trainees with
a non-law degree p.a. **25%**

post-qualification
Salary (2000)
Depending on location
up to **£28,000**
% of trainees offered job
on qualification (2000) **93%**
% of assistants (as at 1/9/00) who joined as trainees **38%**
% of partners (as at 1/9/00) who joined as trainees **37%**

Boyes Turner

Abbots House, Abbey Street, Reading RG1 3BD
Tel: (0118) 959 7711 Fax: (0118) 957 3257
Email: hbarnett@boyesturner.com/lcassar@boyesturner.com
Website: www.boyesturner.com

firm profile
Boyes Turner is a leading Thames Valley practice, renowned for its insolvency and medical negligence work and well respected for corporate and commercial, commercial property, intellectual property, employment, personal injury, family law and private client. While the focus for growth has been commercial work, the firm retains a commitment to acting for individuals and also to civil legal aid.

main areas of work
Company/commercial (including employment) 20%; commercial property 20%; medical negligence/personal injury 20%; litigation 15%; insolvency 10%; family 5%; private client 10%.

trainee profile
Boyes Turner regards its trainees of today as its assistant solicitors and beyond of tomorrow and expects a high level of commitment, hard work and resourcefulness. Trainees must be responsive to the firm's mission to provide an excellent quality of service to both commercial and individual clients and also contribute to the team-working philosophy.

training environment
The programme is structured so that trainees spend six months in each of four areas: property, litigation, private client and commercial. Work covers both individual and commercial clients, with as much client contact as possible, supervised by a partner or a senior solicitor. The training principal oversees all aspects of the programme, while each trainee is assigned a tutor (one of the partners) who reviews their progress monthly. This is on two levels – first in assessing how the trainee is developing as a lawyer and secondly how the trainee is developing as an individual, including communication and negotiating skills.

benefits
Firm pension scheme.

sponsorship & awards
LPC loan of £3,000 and only one loan per applicant. Interest free and repaid over training contract.

Partners 16
Assistant Solicitors 15
Total Trainees 6

contact
Helen Barnett
Lisa Cassar

method of application
Letter & CV

selection procedure
2 interviews & 1 week work placement

closing date for 2004
1 June 2002

application
Training contracts p.a. **3/4**
Applications p.a. **2,200**
% interviewed p.a. **1%+**
Required degree grade **2:2**

training
Salary
1st year (2000) **£17,000**
2nd year (2000) **£18,000**
Holiday entitlement
22 days
% of trainees with
a non-law degree p.a.
Varies

post-qualification
Salary (2000) **£26,000**
% of trainees offered job on qualification (2000)
100%
% of assistants (as at 1/9/00) who joined as trainees **33%**
% of partners (as at 1/9/00) who joined as trainees **20%**

BP Collins

Collins House, 32-38 Station Road, Gerrards Cross SL9 8EL
Tel: (01753) 889 995 Fax: (01753) 889 851
Email: jacqui.symons@bpcollins.co.uk

firm profile
B P Collins was established in 1965, and has expanded significantly to become one of the largest and best known legal practices at the London end of the M4/M40 corridors. At its main office in Gerrards Cross, the emphasis is on commercial work, with particular strengths being company/commercial work of all types, commercial conveyancing and general commercial litigation. Alongside this there is a highly respected private client department specialising in tax planning, trusts, charities, wills and probates.

main areas of work
Company/commercial, employment, IP/IT, civil and commercial litigation, commercial conveyancing, property development, private client.

trainee profile
Most of the partners and other fee-earners have worked in London at one time or another but, tired of commuting, have opted to work in more congenial surroundings and enjoy a higher quality lifestyle. Gerrards Cross is not only a very pleasant town with a large number of high net worth private clients but is also a convenient location for serving the extremely active business community at the eastern end of the Thames Valley including West London, Heathrow, Uxbridge, Slough and Windsor. The firm therefore looks for trainees who are likely to respond to this challenging environment.

training environment
The firm aims to have five or six trainee solicitors at different stages of their training contracts at all times. Trainees serve five months in four separate departments of their choice. The final four months is spent in the department handling the sort of work in which the trainee intends specialising. The firm has a training partner with overall responsibility for all trainees and each department has its own training principal who is responsible for day to day supervision. There are regular meetings between the training principal and the trainee to monitor progress and a review meeting with the training partner midway and at the end of each departmental seat. The firm also involves its trainees in social and marketing events including golf and cricket matches, go-karting and racing and other sporting and non-sporting activities and has its own six-a-side football team.

sponsorship & awards
50% LPC costs refunded once trainee starts contract.

Partners 16
Assistant Solicitors 14
Total Trainees 5/6

contact
Mrs J J Symons

method of application
Handwritten covering letter & CV

selection procedure
Screening interview & selection half day

training
Salary
1st year £15,500
2nd year £16,500

Brabners

1 Dale St, Liverpool L2 2ET
Tel: (0151) 600 3000 Fax: (0151) 227 3185
7 Chapel Street, Preston
Tel: (01772) 823 921 Fax: (01772) 201 918
Email: vera.atkins@brabners.com
Website: www.brabners.com

firm profile
One of the top North West commercial firms, Brabners, in Liverpool and Preston, has the experience, talent and prestige of a firm that has a 200-plus-year history. Brabners is a dynamic, client-led specialist in the provision of excellent legal services to clients ranging from large plcs to private individuals.

main areas of work
The firm carries out a wide range of specialist legal services and Brabners' client base includes plcs, public sector bodies, banks and other commercial, corporate and professional businesses. Brabners is organised into five client-focused departments: corporate (including commercial law), employment, litigation (including media), property (including housing association and construction) and private client.

trainee profile
Graduates and those undertaking CPE or LPC who can demonstrate intelligence, intuition, humour, approachability and commitment and who have some connection with Liverpool or the North West.

training environment
The firm is one of the few law firms that holds Investors in People status, and has a comprehensive training and development programme. Trainees are given a high degree of responsibility and are an integral part of the culture of the firm. Seats are available in the firm's five departments and each trainee will have partner level supervision. Personal development appraisals are conducted at six monthly intervals to ensure that trainee progress is valuable and informed. The training programme is overseen by the firm's Trainee Partners, Mark Glenville (Liverpool) and Ross Shine (Preston). It is not all hard work and the firm has an excellent social programme.

sponsorship & awards
May be available for LPC.

Partners	28
Assistant Solicitors	37
Total Trainees	13

contact
Liverpool office:
Dr Tony Harvey
Director of Training & Development

method of application
Application form

selection procedure
Open day & interview

closing date for 2004
Apply by 31 August 2002 for training contracts commencing in September 2004

application
Required degree grade 2:1 or higher

training
Starting salary
£16,000 currently, & subject to review
Holiday entitlement 25 days

offices
Liverpool, Preston

Bristows

3 Lincoln's Inn Fields, London WC2A 3AA
Tel: (020) 7400 8000 Fax: (020) 7400 8050
Email: info@bristows.com
Website: www.bristows.com

firm profile
Bristows is a leading commercial practice in Central London, pre-eminent in intellectual property law including IT, e-business, brands and biotechnology. It has a substantial practice in company and commercial law and strong complementary practices in commercial litigation, employment, competition, tax, environmental and property law.

main areas of work
Intellectual property 54%; company/corporate finance/commercial/tax 15%; computer and IT 16%; commercial litigation 10%; commercial property 5%.

trainee profile
Bristows recruits graduates of all disciplines. As well as academic ability, the firm looks for practical intelligence, the capacity to communicate well and the ability to assimilate complex materials while still seeing the wood for the trees.

training environment
Trainees receive a high level of individual attention, spending each of their four or five seats with either a partner or senior solicitor. This, plus the opportunity of secondments to multinational clients, gives trainees closer involvement in cases and greater contact with partners and clients alike. Continuous and formal assessment by seat holders, regular review sessions with the training partner and a comprehensive in-house training programme all provide additional support for trainees to develop the skills gained from this excellent hands on experience. Working in small teams, with each team headed by a partner, trainees play an active role from very early on in their training, seeing assignments through from start to finish.

benefits
Excellent career prospects, a competitive package, firm pension scheme, life assurance and health insurance.

vacation placements
Places for 2002: 36; Duration: Summer – 2 weeks, Christmas/Easter – 1 week; Remuneration: £200 p.w.; Closing Date: Christmas –16 November; Easter/Summer – 28 February.

sponsorship & awards
CPE/LPC fees plus £5,000 maintenance grant for each.

Partners 28
Assistant Solicitors 55
Total Trainees 13

contact
Graduate Recruitment Officer

method of application
Application form

selection procedure
2 individual interviews

closing date for 2004
31 January 2002 for February interviews,
31 August 2002 for September interviews

application
Training contracts p.a. **10**
Applications p.a. **2,000**
% interviewed p.a. **6%**
Required degree grade **2:1 (preferred)**

training
Salary
1st year (2001) **£26,000**
2nd year (2001) **£28,000**
Holiday entitlement
4 weeks
% of trainees with
a non-law degree p.a. **75%**

post-qualification
Salary (2001) **£43,000**
% of trainees offered job on qualification (1999) **72%**
% of assistants (as at 1/9/99) who joined as trainees **50%**
% of partners (as at 1/9/99) who joined as trainees **47%**

Browne Jacobson

44 Castle Gate, Nottingham NG1 7BJ
Tel: (0115) 976 6000 Fax: (0115) 947 5246
Aldwych House, 81 Aldwych, London WC2B 4HN
Tel: (020) 7404 1546 Fax: (020) 7836 3882
102 Colmore Row, Birmingham B3 3AG
Tel: (0121) 237 3900 Fax: (0121) 236 1291
Email: info@brownej.co.uk
Website: www.brownej.co.uk

firm profile

Browne Jacobson is a substantial business and insurance services law firm, which has a practical approach providing a first class client service. Already acknowledged as a leading regional practice offering a comprehensive range of services, the firm has continued to develop a nationwide reputation for quality and has a growing international presence. It operates from Nottingham, London and Birmingham. International development is driven primarily through London and Paris where the firm has an associated office and through key relationships with selected US law firms.

main areas of work

Insurance Services: Personal injury litigation; professional indemnity; public authority and defendant medical negligence.
Business Services: Corporate and commercial; tax and financial planning; commercial property; commercial litigation and employment.

trainee profile

The firm's trainees are bright, have high academic ability and bring enthusiasm and commitment to its practice. Personable and practical, they are able to demonstrate an appropriate sense of humour and work as part of a team whilst accepting individual responsibility.

training environment

Training at Browne Jacobson is practical and structured. You will spend four periods of six months working in all practice areas of the firm to obtain an overview and experience many new challenges. The firm aims to develop rather than control its trainees; you will have a programme of skills training during which you will be strongly supported by Browne Jacobson's training team.

sponsorship & awards

PgDL, LPC.

Partners 47
Assistant Solicitors 82

contact
Carol King
Training Manager

method of application
CV & covering letter to
Carol King, or via website

selection procedure
Assessment Centre

closing date for 2004
31 July 2002

application
Training contracts p.a. 8
Applications p.a. 1,500
% interviewed p.a. 5%
Required degree grade 2:1

training
Salary £18,000
Holiday entitlement
20 days
% of trainees with a
non-law degree p.a. 5%

post-qualification
Salary Regional variations
Holiday entitlement
5 weeks

Burges Salmon

Narrow Quay House, Narrow Quay, Bristol BS1 4AH
Tel: (0117) 902 2725 Fax: (0117) 902 4400
Email: lisa.head@burges-salmon.com
Website: www.burges-salmon.com

Partners	50
Assistant Solicitors	170
Total Trainees	38

contact
Lisa Head
Graduate Recruitment & Development Manager

method of application
Employer's application form

selection procedure
Penultimate year law students, final year non-law students, recent graduates or mature candidates are considered for open days, vacation placements &/or training contracts

closing date for 2004
9 August 2002

application
Training contracts p.a. 20-25
Applications p.a. **1,000**
% interviewed p.a. **10%**
Required degree grade **2:1**

training
Salary
1st year (2001) **£20,000**
2nd year (2001) **£21,000**
Holiday entitlement
24 days
% of trainees with a non-law degree p.a. **40%**

post-qualification
Salary (2001) **£34,000**
% of trainees offered job on qualification (2001) **93%**
% of assistants (as at 1/9/01) who joined as trainees **45%**
% of partners (as at 1/9/01) who joined as trainees **20%**

firm profile
Burges Salmon is a leading regional law firm with a reputation for quality and an ability to attract people and clients normally regarded as the preserve of City firms. Some 75% of the firm's clients are situated outside its South West base and, over recent years, Burges Salmon has witnessed an extraordinarily high and sustainable rate of growth. This stems from a client-centric culture that pervades throughout the firm and is reflected in the acquisition of new clients as well as the secure relationships that continue to be maintained with them.

main areas of work
Based in Bristol, with a presence in London, the firm provides national and international clients with a full commercial service through four departments: company commercial, litigation, property, and tax and trusts. Specialist areas of the firm include: agribusiness, banking, competition, corporate finance, dispute resolution, e-commerce, environment, human resources, IP and IT, and transport.

trainee profile
Candidates must demonstrate strong academic ability, as well as high levels of analytical skills, interpersonal and communication skills, resilience and commercial awareness.

training environment
Attracting and retaining first class trainee solicitors is central to Burges Salmon's philosophy. The firm's excellent trainee retention rate on qualification is attributed in part to its Law Society accredited training programme. In preference to a traditional four seat training contract structure, Burges Salmon operates a six seat system. This allows trainees maximum exposure to all areas of the firm's work and the opportunity to revisit departments of particular interest or to opt for niche areas of their choice.

benefits
Annually reviewed competitive salary, annual bonus and pension scheme.

vacation placements
Places for 2002: 32; Duration: 2 weeks; Remuneration: £150 pw; Closing Date: 22 Feb 2002.

sponsorship & awards
The firm pays CPE and LPC fees at the institution of your choice, and maintenance grants of £4,500 are paid to LPC students and £5,000 to students studying for both the CPE and LPC (£2,500 p.a.).

Cadwalader, Wickersham & Taft

55 Gracechurch Street, London EC3V 0EE
Tel: (020) 7456 8573 Fax: (020) 7456 8600
Email: hrdept@cwt-uk.com
Website: www.cadwalader.com

firm profile
Cadwalader, Wickersham & Taft is a major New York based law firm, recognised for its innovative approach to legal and commercial matters. The London office, established in September 1997, is renowned for its expertise in capital markets, financial restructuring, corporate, project finance, litigation and real estate. The office services clients interested in capitalising on the European and worldwide markets, as well as those seeking US-style investment banking services and access to American capital markets.

main areas of work
Capital markets, financial restructuring, project finance, corporate, litigation and real estate.

trainee profile
Candidates need to demonstrate that they are intellectually bright and ambitious, have good communications skills and a commitment to the law. The firm looks for well-rounded individuals with a desire to succeed and a robust and resilient personality.

training environment
Training consists of four six month seats taking into account trainees' preferences. Responsibility and exposure to client meetings will take place at an early stage. Trainees share an office with a partner or associate, who supervise, review performance and provide feedback on a regular basis. Formal reviews will be carried out every six months. Elements of the PSC will occur at the start of the training contract; the remainder will take place over the following two years. The firm is friendly and supportive with an open door policy, operating a business casual dress down code all year round. There is also a varied sporting and social calendar.

benefits
Permanent health insurance, season ticket loan, BUPA (dental and health) and life assurance.

sponsorship & awards
CPE Funding: Fees paid plus £4,500 maintenance.
LPC Funding: Fees paid plus £4,500 maintenance.

Partners 7
Assistant Solicitors 32
Total Trainees 6

contact
HR Department

method of application
CV & covering letter

selection procedure
2 interviews

closing date for 2004
31 August 2002

application
Training contracts p.a. 4-6
Applications p.a. 500
% interviewed p.a. 10%
Required degree grade 2:1

training
Salary
1st year (2001) £30,000
2nd year (2001) £33,600
Holiday entitlement
24 days

post-qualification
Salary (2001) £65,000
% of trainees offered job on qualification (2001) 100%

overseas offices
New York, Washington, Charlotte

Campbell Hooper

35 Old Queen St, London SW1H 9JD
Tel: (020) 7222 9070 Fax: (020) 7222 5591
Email: humanresources@campbellhooper.com
Website: www.campbellhooper.com

firm profile
With over 200 years experience, Campbell Hooper is well equipped to face the requirements of today's ever changing market and adopts a modern and dynamic management style with high investment in IT, knowledge management and training. The firm's clients are involved in a variety of industries including information technology, telecoms, banking, advertising, construction, property investment and development, media, manufacturing, a number of service industries and local government and government departments. Membership of Proteus, a European network of independent law firms, provides an invaluable international aspect to the firm.

main areas of work
High standards of client service are delivered through four departments: company/commercial; commercial property; construction; private client. The principal areas of work are charities; company; construction; defamation; domestic conveyancing; employment; environmental; European; family; immigration; insurance; litigation; media; planning; property; rating; tax; trust and estate planning and wills and probate.

trainee profile
Applications are welcomed from those with a keen commercial focus complemented by a solid academic history. Motivation, enthusiasm and professional commitment are equally important.

training environment
You will develop your commercial acumen and legal flair through exposure in each of the four departments. Equal emphasis is placed on providing you with both professional and personal career support. This is facilitated through day to day coaching from either a partner or solicitor, constructive feedback on performance through mid and end of seat reviews and mentoring from the trainee partner who will take a personal interest in your professional development. In addition the firm is committed to continuous development and you will be encouraged to attend client seminars, be actively involved in practice development initiatives as well as participating in other training and development activities including the compulsory professional skills course.

sponsorship & benefits
LPC and CPE fees paid. Benefits include private medical insurance, pension scheme, life assurance, permanent health insurance and season ticket loan.

Partners	20
Assistant Solicitors	27
Total Trainees	6

contact
Annette Fritze-Shanks

method of application
CV with covering letter.
Brochures available on request

selection procedure
Interviews

closing date for 2004
31 July 2002

application
Training contracts p.a. 3-4
Applications p.a. c.1,000
% interviewed p.a. 4-5%
Required degree grade
2:1 any discipline

training
Salary
1st year (2001)
£21,000-£22,000 p.a.
2nd year (2001)
£23,000-£24,500 p.a.
Holiday entitlement
25 days

Capsticks

77-83 Upper Richmond Road, London SW15 2TT
Tel: (020) 8780 2211 Fax: (020) 8780 4811
Email: career@capsticks.co.uk
Website: www.capsticks.com

firm profile
Described as 'the legal experts on the NHS' in *Chambers 1999-2000* and rated as the leading NHS law firm in London by other leading directories, CAPSTICKS handles litigation, administrative law, commercial and property work for the full range of NHS bodies, as well as other public sector bodies, charities and regulatory bodies.

main areas of work
Clinical law 54%; commercial 6%; commercial property 15%; dispute resolution 7%; employment law 18%.

trainee profile
Successful candidates possess intellectual agility, good interpersonal skills and are capable of taking initiative.

training environment
Six four month seats, which may include clinical negligence/personal injury; commercial property; contract and commercial; employment law; commercial/property litigation. Trainees take responsibility for their own caseload and are involved in client meetings from an early stage. There are also opportunities to contribute to the firm's marketing and management processes. There are numerous in-house lectures for all fee-earners. There is an open door policy, and trainees receive informal feedback and supervision as well as regular appraisals. Despite the firm's rapid expansion, it has retained a friendly atmosphere and a relaxed working environment. There are numerous informal social and sporting activities.

benefits
Bonus scheme, pension, PHI, death in service cover, interest-free season ticket loan.

vacation placements
Places for 2002: Yes; Duration: 2 weeks; Closing Date: 28 February 2002.

sponsorship & awards
Scholarship contributions to CPE and LPC courses.

Partners	23
Assistant Solicitors	37
Total Trainees	11
Other Fee-earners	5

contact
Sue Laundy

method of application
Application form

selection procedure
Candidates are encouraged to participate in the firm's summer placement scheme. Final selection is by interview with the Training Principal & other partners

closing date for 2004
31 July 2002

application
Training contracts p.a. 6-8
Applications p.a. c.200
% interviewed p.a. c.3%
Required degree grade 2:1 or above

training
Salary
1st year £23,000 (as at 1/9/01)
2nd year £25,000 (as at 1/9/01)
Holiday entitlement
22 days p.a. (increased by 1 day p.a. to max 25 days)
% of trainees with a non-law degree p.a. 45%

post-qualification
Salary (2001) £36,000 + benefits
% of trainees offered job on qualification (2001) 100%
% of assistants (as at 1/9/01) who joined as trainees 100%
% of partners (as at 1/9/01) who joined as trainees 9%

Charles Russell

8–10 New Fetter Lane, London EC4A 1RS
Tel: (020) 7203 5000 Fax: (020) 7203 5307
Graduate Recruitment Line: (020) 7203 5353
Website: www.cr-law.com

firm profile
Charles Russell is a progressive City law firm with regional offices in Cheltenham and Guildford and a network of close professional contacts throughout the world. A rapidly growing law firm, it offers a wide range of legal services for both corporate and private clients. The firm recruits a small number of trainees for a firm of its size. This enables trainees to undergo the best possible training. The firm is committed to its clients and their demands. It also respects the fact that its staff need to have a life of their own. This ethos fosters a strong team spirit throughout the firm.

main areas of work
Whilst the commercial division offers the opportunity for involvement in major corporate transactions, the firm's commitment to private clients and charities remains unshaken. Charles Russell is particularly well known for media and communications, employment, charities, private client, family and corporate/commercial and offers clients specialist expertise in litigation, commercial property and insurance.

trainee profile
Trainees should be balanced, rounded achievers with a solid academic background. Outside interests are fundamental.

training environment
Trainees spend six months in four of the following training seats – litigation, company/commercial, property, private client, family, employment and intellectual property. Wherever possible the firm will accommodate an individual preference. You will be seated with a partner/senior solicitor. Regular appraisals are held to discuss progress and direction. Trainees are encouraged to attend the extensive in-house training courses. The PSC is taught both internally and externally. All trainees are expected to take on as much responsibility as possible. A social committee organises a range of activities from quiz nights through to sporting events.

benefits
BUPA immediately, PHI and life assurance after six months service, 25 days holiday.

sponsorship & awards
CPE and LPC fees paid and annual maintenance of £4,000 (under review).

Partners	75
Associates	11
Assistant Solicitors	123
Total Trainees	28

contact
Eileen Moran
Graduate Recruitment
Line: (020) 7203 5353

method of application
Handwritten letter & application form

selection procedure
Assessment days to include an interview & other exercises designed to assess identified performance criteria

closing date for 2004
31 May 2002

application
Training contracts p.a.
10–12
Applications p.a. Approx 2,000
% interviewed p.a. 3%
Required degree grade 2:1

training
Salary
1st year (2001) £26,500
2nd year (2001) £29,000
Holiday entitlement
25 days

post-qualification
Salary (2001) £43,500

regional offices
Also offers training contracts in its Cheltenham & Guildford offices. Applications are dealt with by the London office

Clarks

Great Western House, Station Rd, Reading RG1 1JX
Tel: (0118) 958 5321 Fax: (0118) 960 4611
Email: inmail@clarks-solicitors.co.uk
Website: www.clarks-solicitors.co.uk

firm profile
Founded in 1913, Clarks is a commercial law firm with a proven track record across the UK and overseas (with 15 partners and nine associates). Clients range from small to medium sized enterprises to multinational companies. Clarks is particularly recognised for the number of international FTSE 250 clients who have chosen to use its services. Based in 'Reading, Clarks has taken full advantage of the rapid commercial and professional expansion of this thriving 'capital' of the Thames Valley.

main areas of work
Commercial property; corporate and technology; litigation; employment; planning; insolvency; private client.

trainee profile
Candidates must have a consistently good academic record and should have effective interpersonal skills. Language skills are an advantage.

training environment
On joining Clarks, trainees will receive a full induction programme. Trainees immediately become part of a team and are encouraged to have direct involvement with clients and to play a part in building long-term relationships with them. Training usually consists of seats of six months in four of the following teams: property, corporate, litigation, employment and IP/IT. Within each seat you will have a mentor (a partner or an associate) who will have responsibility for guiding and encouraging you through that seat. In addition to training within a workgroup you are also encouraged to attend the firm's in-house weekly seminars. Clarks also supports you in your professional skills courses. Clarks is a classic yet innovative firm with an open, friendly culture. It retains a high number of trainees upon qualification and a significant number have progressed through the firm to become associates or partners.

benefits
Pension, free conveyancing.

vacation placements
Places for 2003: On application.

Partners	15
Assistant Solicitors	32
Total Trainees	10

contact
Sarah Moore
HR Manager

method of application
Application form (from brochure or website)

selection procedure
Open day/interview & second interview (with limited written tests)

closing date for 2004
No closing date

application
Training contracts p.a. 5-6
Applications p.a. 500-600
% interviewed p.a. 10%
Required degree grade
Usually 2:1 or above (but will consider lower grade subject to explanation)

training
Salary
1st year (2000) £17,000
2nd year (2000) £18,500
Holiday entitlement
20 days

post-qualification
% of trainees offered job on qualification (2000) 90%
% of assistants (as at 1/9/00) who joined as trainees 35%
% of partners (as at 1/9/00) who joined as trainees 40%

overseas offices
Affiliated to TagLaw worldwide - ability to second to foreign office possible, subject to appropriate language skills

Cleary, Gottlieb, Steen & Hamilton

City Place House, 55 Basinghall Street, London EC2V 5EH
Tel: (020) 7614 2200 Fax: (020) 7600 1698
Website: www.cgsh.com

firm profile
Founded in the United States in 1946, from its inception the firm has maintained a strong international presence. It now has over 630 lawyers in 10 offices worldwide with more than 250 lawyers in Europe, with offices in Paris (opened 1949), Brussels (1960), Frankfurt (1991) and Rome (1998) in addition to London (1971). It is common for lawyers to spend time in offices other than their home office.

main areas of work
Mergers and acquisitions (takeovers, cross-border mergers, joint ventures), securities (equity offerings, debt offerings, bond issues, privatisations, global offerings, private placements), banking and finance, tax, EU and competition law.

trainee profile
Candidates must have an excellent academic background including at least a 2:1 law degree from a top UK university and have an open and outgoing personality. IT and language skills are an advantage.

training environment
There are no departments. Trainees sit with partners and senior solicitors and will do a mix of M&A, capital markets, tax and regulatory work. Seats change every six months. One seat will be in Brussels and there will be opportunities to travel and work in other offices. Ongoing legal training is provided by regular training talks covering all areas of law practised at the firm. Trainees will be required to take the New York bar exam. Assistance will be given with this. Trainees will work on a wide range of matters, many governed by laws other than English law. Trainees will in most respects be fulfilling the same roles as first year lawyers do in its other offices.

benefits
Pension, health insurance, long-term disability insurance, health club, employee assistance programme.

sponsorship & awards
LPC Funding: Fees paid plus £4,500 maintenance award.

Partners 10
Assistants 37
Total Trainees 4

contact
Penny Cave

method of application
Letter & CV

selection procedure
2 interviews

closing date for 2004
30 Sept 2002

application
Training contracts p.a.
Up to 4
Required degree grade 2:1

training
Salary
1st year (2000) £33,000
2nd year (2000) £39,000
Holiday entitlement
20 days

post-qualification
Salary varies from office to office

overseas offices
Brussels, Frankfurt, Hong Kong, Moscow, New York, Paris, Rome, Tokyo, Washington DC

Clifford Chance

200 Aldersgate Street, London EC1A 4JJ
Tel: (020) 7600 1000 Fax: (020) 7600 5555
Email: graduate.recruitment@cliffordchance.com
Website: www.cliffordchance.com/grads

firm profile
Clifford Chance is one of the largest law firms in the world with 29 offices throughout Europe, Asia and America. It delivers legal services to powerful and influential businesses and financial institutions around the globe, working across international borders to shape the deals that make the news. As a trainee this means you will gain breadth and depth in your experiences.

main areas of work
Banking and finance; capital markets; corporate; litigation and dispute resolution; real estate; tax, pensions and employment.

trainee profile
Consistently strong academic profile (minimum 2:1 degree), a broad range of interpersonal skills and extra curricular activities and interests.

training environment
The Clifford Chance training contract has been devised to provide you with the technical skills and experience you need to contribute to the firm's success on a day-to-day basis, to achieve your professional qualification and to progress to a rewarding career. Your two year training contract consists of four six month seats. Most trainees will spend a seat on a secondment at an international office or with a client. In each seat you will be working alongside senior lawyers. Trainees are encouraged to use initiative to make the most of expertise and resources available to the firm. Three-monthly appraisals and monitoring in each seat ensure trainees gain a range of work and experience.

benefits
Prize for first class degrees and distinction in LPC, interest-free loan, private health insurance, subsidised restaurant, fitness centre, life assurance, occupational health service, and permanent health assurance.

vacation placements
Places for 2001-2002: Christmas, Easter and summer break. There is a strong social element to the programme; Duration: Approx 2 weeks; Remuneration: £240 pw; Closing Date: 2 November 2001 for Christmas scheme; 8 February 2002 for other schemes.

sponsorship & awards
CPE and LPC fees paid and currently £5,000 maintenance p.a. for London, Guildford and Oxford, £4,500 p.a. elsewhere.

London office
Partners 217
Lawyers 842
Trainees 225

contact
Louise McMunn
Graduate Recruitment

method of application
Application form.
Preferably apply online

selection procedure
Assessment day comprising an interview with a partner & senior solicitor, a group exercise & a verbal reasoning test

application
Training contracts p.a. **130**
Applications p.a. **2,000**
% interviewed p.a. **25%**
Required degree grade **2:1**

training
Salary
1st year £28,500 (Sept 2001)
2nd year £32,000
Holiday entitlement
25 days
% of trainees with a non-law degree p.a. 35%
No. of seats available abroad p.a. 90

post-qualification
Salary (Sept 2001) £50,000
% of trainees offered job on qualification (2001) 95%

overseas offices
Amsterdam, Bangkok, Barcelona, Beijing, Berlin, Brussels, Budapest, Dubai, Dusseldorf, Frankfurt, Hong Kong, Leipzig, Luxembourg, Madrid, Milan, Moscow, Munich, New York, Padua, Paris, Prague, Rome, Sao Paulo, Shanghai, Singapore, Tokyo, Warsaw, Washington DC

Clyde & Co

51 Eastcheap, London EC3M 1JP
Tel: (020) 7648 1580 Fax: (020) 7623 5427
Email: careers@clyde.co.uk
Website: www.clydeco.com

firm profile
A major international commercial firm with over 700 personnel worldwide and a client base spanning more than 100 countries. It is a leading practice in international trade, insurance, reinsurance, shipping and energy, and has experienced a high level of growth in corporate and finance. UK offices are in London, Guildford and Cardiff, with trainee solicitors recruited for London and Guildford.

main areas of work
Insurance/reinsurance 26%; banking, corporate commercial and tax 26%; marine and transport 21%; other commercial litigation 10%; property 7%; employment 3%.

trainee profile
The firm has no stereotypical trainee. Non-law graduates are welcome, especially those with modern languages or science degrees. The firm places as much importance on finding candidates with an outgoing, interesting personality as it does on academic credentials.

training environment
Trainees are immediately given as much responsibility as they can handle, and usually have their own office. They are also encouraged to take on as much client contact as possible, and are involved in developing business relationships. The PSC is run in-house and there is a full programme of lectures, seminars, courses, workshops and educational visits.

benefits
Subsidised sports club, interest free ticket loan, staff restaurant and weekly free bar (London); monthly staff lunch and monthly free bar (Guildford).

legal work experience
The firm runs two Legal Training Days during the Easter holidays and a Summer Vacation Placement scheme for 2 weeks in July. Closing Date: 28 February 2002.

sponsorship & awards
CPE and LPC fees paid and maintenance grant. Sponsorship provided where no LEA funding available.

Partners 120
Assistant Solicitors 170
Total Trainees 41

contact
Georgia de Saram
Graduate Recruitment & Development Officer

method of application
Application form & covering letter

selection procedure
Individual interview with Georgia de Saram followed by interview with 2 partners

closing date for 2004
31 August 2002

application
Training contracts p.a. 20
Applications p.a. 3,000 +
% interviewed p.a. 6%
Required degree grade 2:1

training
Salary (Under review)
1st year (2001) £24,000
2nd year (2001) £27,000
Holiday entitlement
25 days
% of trainees with a non-law degree p.a.
Varies
No. of seats available abroad p.a. Varies

post-qualification
Salary (2001) £46,000
% of trainees offered job on qualification (2001) 82%

overseas offices
Caracas, Dubai, Hong Kong, Paris, Piraeus, Singapore, St Petersburg*
* Associated office

CMS Cameron McKenna

Mitre House, 160 Aldersgate Street, London EC1A 4DD
Tel: (020) 7367 3000 Fax: (020) 7367 2000
Email: gradrec@cmck.com
Website: www.cmck.com/gradrec

Partners	180
Assistant Solicitors	460
Total Trainees	100

contact
Graduate Recruitment Team (0845) 3000 491

firm profile
CMS Cameron McKenna is a major full service UK and international commercial law firm advising businesses and governments on transactions and projects particularly in the UK, continental Europe, the Asia Pacific region, North America and Southern Africa. It has particular strengths in a number of industry sectors such as banking and international finance, corporate, construction, projects, energy, healthcare, bioscience, insurance and property. The firm is modern, entrepreneurial and innovative and is strong on achievement. (It believes the key to success is clear communication and entrepreneurial flair.)

method of application
Employer's application form

selection procedure
2 stage selection procedure. Initial interview followed by assessment centre

main areas of work
Banking; corporate; insurance; energy, projects and construction; property; commercial.

closing date
Continuous recruitment

trainee profile
The firm looks for high-achieving team players with good communication, analytical and organisational skills. You will need to show initiative and be able to accept personal responsibility, not only for your own work, but also for your career development. You will need to be resilient and focused on achieving results.

application
Training contracts p.a. **80**
Applications p.a. **1,500**
% interviewed p.a. **27%**
Required degree grade **2:1**

training
Salary
1st year (2001) **£28,000**
2nd year (2001) **£32,000**
Holiday entitlement
25 days + option of flexible holiday
% of trainees with
a non-law degree p.a. **40%**
No. of seats available
abroad p.a. **Currently 15**

training environment
The firm is friendly and supportive and puts no limits on a trainee's progress. It offers four six month seats, three of which will be in the firm's main area of practice. In addition you may gain experience of a specialist area or opt for a secondment to national or international clients. In each seat you will be allocated high quality work on substantial transactions for a range of government and blue-chip clients. Regular appraisals will be held with your seat supervisor to assess your progress, skills and development needs. The three compulsory modules of the PSC will be completed before joining, allowing trainees to become effective and participate on a practical level as soon as possible. The Professional Skills Course is complemented by a comprehensive in-house training programme that continues up to qualification and beyond.

post-qualification
Salary (2001) **£50,000**
% of trainees offered job on qualification (2000) **90%**

vacation placements
Places for 2002: 55; Duration: 2 weeks; Remuneration: £200 p.w.

sponsorship & awards
PgDL and LPC Funding: Fees paid and a maintenance grant of £5,000 (London, Guildford and Oxford), £4,500 (elsewhere).

CMS Cameron McKenna continued

additional information

Every trainee has a PC on their desk with email connection and access to legal and business databases. The firm financially supports trainees who wish to learn or improve a foreign language. There will be the opportunity to become involved in a number of sporting and social events.

trainee comments

"The firm has an incredibly wide base of areas to choose from, varying from healthcare and biotechnology to energy, projects and construction to the more traditional areas of banking, corporate and litigation. You'll find yourself in a pleasant and down to earth working environment where you'll be offered a variety of different opportunities, both in and out of work." (Trainee solicitor, Property).

"Compared to other firms where I have friends it's very friendly and unstuffy here. It has retained the smaller firm environment even though we're now a top ten firm. Some firms pay lip service to the 'open door' idea but it really happens here. My best moment so far was helping the team who pitched against four of the top ten City firms for one of two places to do work for the Post Office - and we were appointed." (Trainee solicitor, Commercial).

"The most rewarding thing about the international opportunities here, whether it's before or after qualification, is the sheer scope the firm can offer you. There is no doubt that an international perspective is a massive selling point for law firms. Clients don't want to be dealing with one firm in London and any number of others overseas. And that's great news when you're a trainee because you have more chance to travel during your training contract, and then after qualification. My overseas experience was an invaluable part of my contract. I completed a seat in Hong Kong in our Corporate Recovery Group and worked in Orissa, India on the restructuring of the electricity industry. I doubt I'd get those kind of opportunities elsewhere." (Solicitor, Corporate).

branch offices
Aberdeen, Amsterdam, Arnhem, Beijing, Berlin, Bristol, Brussels, Bucharest, Budapest, Capetown, Chemnitz, Dresden, Düsseldorf, Frankfurt, Hamburg, Hilversum, Hong Kong, Johannesburg, Kazakhstan, Leipzig, Moscow, Munich, Prague, Russia, Singapore, Slovakia, Stockholm, Stuttgart, Toronto, Utrecht, Vienna, Warsaw, Washington DC, Zürich

cameron mcKenna

Cobbetts

Ship Canal House, King Street, Manchester M2 4WB
Tel: (0161) 833 3333 Fax: (0161) 833 3030
Email: lawyers@cobbetts.co.uk
Website: www.cobbetts.co.uk

firm profile
Cobbetts is one of Manchester's most long-established firms with a staff of 270 including 50 partners. The firm has successfully managed to remain at the forefront of commercial law practice without sacrificing the professionalism by which it earned its reputation. The recent dual accreditation of Investors In People and Lexcel provide national recognition of the firm's outstanding commitment to quality.

main areas of work
The firm is divided into two main divisions. The corporate division deals with the following areas of work: corporate; commercial; intellectual property; IT; banking and private client. The commercial property division is one of the largest under one roof in the North and includes specialist expertise in environmental law, planning, licensing, property litigation, Housing Associations, and construction. Cobbett's client base includes both plcs and owner-managed businesses, banks and financial institutions, public-sector organisations, property companies and retail and licensed operators.

trainee profile
Law and non-law graduates.

training environment
Four six month seats are available. Typically, these include one property, one litigation and one commercial/corporate seat. There is an opportunity for one trainee each year to spend three months in Brussels.

benefits
Social club and LA Fitness pool and gym.

vacation placements
Places for 2002: 18 placements are available during July and August.

sponsorship & awards
CPE and LPC grant available.

trainee comments
"A challenging environment..."
"The training offered is hands on...the firm is renowned for being a friendly place to work, a reputation that is justly and richly deserved."

Partners	50
Fee-earners	71
Total Trainees	22

contact
Richard Webb
Trainee Partner

method of application
Application form (available on request/via Internet)

selection procedure
Half day assessments

closing date for 2004
31 July 2002

application
Training contracts p.a. 10
Applications p.a. 700
% interviewed p.a. 10%
Required degree grade 2:1

training
Salary
1st year Competitive rate
2nd year Reviewed each year
Holiday entitlement 20 days
% of trainees with a non-law degree p.a. 30%
No. of seats available abroad p.a. 1

post-qualification
% of trainees offered job on qualification (2001) 100%
% of assistants (as at 1/9/00) who joined as trainees 75%
% of partners (as at 1/9/01) who joined as trainees 60%

overseas offices
Brussels

Coffin Mew & Clover

17 Hampshire Terrace, Portsmouth PO1 2PU
Tel: (023) 9281 2511 Fax: (023) 9229 1847
Email: saralloyd@portsmouth.coffinmew.co.uk
Website: www.coffinmew.co.uk

firm profile
Founded more than a century ago, the firm has grown to become one of the larger legal practices in the South East with major offices located in the cities of Portsmouth and Southampton and just off the M27 Motorway at Fareham. The firm is in the enviable position of operating a balanced practice offering private client and business services in approximately equal volume and is particularly noted for a number of niche practices with national reputations.

main areas of work
The firm is structured through eight core departments: corporate/commercial; employment; commercial litigation; personal injury; commercial property; family/crime; residential property; trust/probate. Niche practices include intellectual property; finance and business regulation; social housing; medical negligence and mental health.

trainee profile
The firm encourages applications from candidates with very good academic ability who seek a broad-based training contract in a highly progressive and demanding but friendly and pleasant environment.

training environment
The training contract is divided into six seats of four months each which will include a property department, a litigation department and a commercial department. The remainder of the training contract will be allocated after discussion with the trainee concerned. The firm aims to ensure that the trainee spends the final four months of his or her training contract in the department in which he or she hopes to work after qualification.

benefits
CPE and LPC funding available by discussion with candidates.

vacation placements
Open week in July each year; application as per training contract.

Partners 20
Assistant Solicitors 22
Total Trainees 8

contact
Sara Lloyd
Director of HR

method of application
CV & covering letter

selection procedure
Interview

closing date for 2004
31 July 2002

application
Training contracts p.a. **4-5**
Applications p.a. **400+**
% interviewed p.a. **5%**
Required degree grade
2:1 (save in exceptional circumstances)

training
Salary
1st year
Competitive market rate
2nd year
Competitive market rate
Holiday entitlement **20 days**
% of trainees with a
non-law degree p.a. **25%**

post-qualification
Salary (2001) **£23,500**
% of trainees offered job
on qualification (2001)
100%
% of assistants who joined
as trainees **25%**
% of partners who joined
as trainees **50%**

Coudert Brothers

60 Cannon Street, London EC4N 6JP
Tel: (020) 7248 3000 Fax: (020) 7248 3001
Email: info@london.coudert.com
Website: www.coudert.com

firm profile
Founded in 1853, Coudert Brothers is a global partnership with 33 offices in 15 countries worldwide. In London the firm was one of the first English multinational partnerships of English solicitors and registered foreign lawyers. The firm advises on all aspects of national and international business law.

trainee profile
The quality and complexity of legal work undertaken by the firm demands that it recruits only individuals of the highest calibre. It is essential that trainees are enthusiastic, confident and outward going individuals, able to perform in a fast-moving and challenging environment. Early responsibility is routine and broad-based experience guaranteed. Coudert Brothers accepts law and non-law graduates. Applicants should have at least three A-level passes at grades A and B and a 2:1 degree. In view of the international nature of the firm's work and clients, language skills are an advantage, but not essential.

training environment
The training at Coudert Brothers comprises four six month placements. Three of these will be with the firm's core practices: corporate and commercial, banking and finance, litigation, and property. The fourth will be drawn from one of the firm's other disciplines: energy and utilities, telecommunications, tax and funds, and competition law. There is an opportunity for a secondment to one of the firm's foreign offices. Partners and senior assistants ensure that trainees gain practical experience in research, drafting, procedural and client-related skills by working closely with them during each placement. There are regular appraisals during the two year training contract. Legal and professional training is provided through an in-house training programme and external conferences.

benefits
Pension, health insurance, subsidised gym membership, season ticket loan.

sponsorship & awards
CPE Funding: Fees paid plus £4,000 p.a. maintenance.
LPC Funding: Fees paid plus £4,000 p.a. maintenance.

Partners 9
Assistant Solicitors 23
Total Trainees 6

contact
Simon Cockshutt

method of application
Letter & CV

selection procedure
2 interviews with partners

closing date for 2004
31 July 2002

application
Training contracts p.a. 4
Required degree grade 2:1

training
Salary (Subject to review)
1st year (2000) £25,000
2nd year (2000) £28,000
Holiday entitlement
20 days

post-qualification
Prospects are good as the firm only takes a small number of trainees each year

overseas offices
Almaty, Antwerp, Bangkok, Beijing, Berlin, Brussels, Denver, Frankfurt, Ghent, Hong Kong, Jakarta, Los Angeles, Milan, Montréal, Moscow, Munich, New York, Palo Alto, Paris, San Francisco, San José, Singapore, Stockholm, St Petersburg, Sydney, Tokyo, Washington DC

associated offices
Budapest, Prague, Mexico City, Rome

Cripps Harries Hall

Seymour House, 11-13 Mount Ephraim Road, Tunbridge Wells TN1 1EG
Tel: (01892) 506 006 Fax: (01892) 544 878
Email: aol@crippslaw.com
Website: www.e-cripps.co.uk

firm profile
Established almost 150 years ago, Cripps Harries Hall has progressed steadily towards being regarded as the leading law firm in the South East outside London. It is an innovative and young firm; most of the partners are in their thirties or forties and the atmosphere is friendly and outgoing. The firm achieved the Lexcel quality mark in January 1999, the first 'Top 100' firm to do so. In addition to its headquarters in Tunbridge Wells, there is an office in central London.

main areas of work
Commercial 30%; finance and investment 27%; dispute resolution 24%; private client 19%.

trainee profile
Cripps Harries Hall is looking for talented, confident, capable people who want to make a contribution during their period of training and who will want to stay with the firm as assistant solicitors and potential partners. You will be expected to integrate expert legal advice with a highly developed use of information technology.

training environment
The two year training contract is divided into six periods, spent in different departments where you receive a thorough grounding in the relevant practice and have frequent one-to-one reviews of your progress. You will usually share a room with a partner, and work as an integral member of a small team. The Director of Education will arrange your continuing education to include seminars, courses and training in business, presentation, IT and marketing skills.

sponsorship & awards
Discretionary LPC Funding: Fees – 50% interest free loan, 50% bursary.

Partners 31
Assistant Solicitors 39
Total Trainees 14

contact
Annabelle Lawrence,
Head of Human Resources

method of application
Handwritten letter & firm's application form available on website or directly via the website.

selection procedure
1 interview with Managing Partner & Head of Human Resources

closing date for 2004
31 July 2002

application
Training contracts p.a. **8**
Applications p.a. **Up to 750**
% interviewed p.a. **6%**
Required degree grade **2:1**

training
Salary
1st year (2001) **£15,500**
2nd year (2001) **£17,000**
Holiday entitlement
25 days
% of trainees with
a non-law degree p.a. **15%**

post-qualification
Salary (2001) **£28,000**
% of trainees offered job on qualification (2001) **90%**
% of assistants/associates (as at 1/9/01) who joined as trainees **35%**
% of partners (as at 1/9/01) who joined as trainees **20%**

associated firms
A network of independent law firms in 18 European countries

Cumberland Ellis Peirs

Columbia House, 69 Aldwych, London WC2B 4RW
Tel: (020) 7242 0422 Fax: (020) 7831 9081
Email: rogerhollinshead@cep-law.co.uk
Website: www.cep-law.co.uk

firm profile
A Central London firm of solicitors with a varied practice. The firm has a broad base of commercial and institutional clients including those involved in the media and information technology, quasi government councils, sporting associations, charities, City Livery companies, housing associations and landed estates, as well as having an established reputation for its private client services.

main areas of work
Company/commercial; commercial property; litigation and private client.

trainee profile
Law and non-law graduates who have a consistently strong academic record. Individuals who can work with and relate well to others; who are commercially aware, with an ability to think creatively and to make a contribution to the firm. The firm is looking for candidates who have presence and enthusiasm, who are outgoing and articulate and who have a broad range of outside interests. IT skills are important.

training environment
Trainees spend six months in each of the company commercial, litigation, private client and property departments under the supervision of a partner or senior assistant. Trainees are fully involved in all aspects of the work of the department. Client contact and early responsibility for handling your own caseload are encouraged, subject to necessary guidance and supervision. There are a number of social, sporting and marketing activities going on during the course of the year and life outside the office is encouraged. An open door policy applies and the firm has a friendly and informal environment. Where possible the firm aims to recruit its trainees at the end of the training contract. The PSC is taught externally at the College of Law.

benefits
Season ticket loan, luncheon vouchers.

sponsorship & awards
It is not the firm's policy to offer vacation placements or sponsorship.

Partners 11
Assistant Solicitors 9
Total Trainees 3

contact
Roger Hollinshead

method of application
Handwritten letter & covering CV (adding reference to 'Chambers')

selection procedure
2 interviews with partners

closing date for 2004
30 September 2002

application
Training contracts p.a.
1 or 2
Applications p.a. 500
% interviewed p.a. 4%
Required degree grade 2:1

training
Holiday entitlement
20 days

Davenport Lyons

1 Old Burlington Street, London W1S 3NL
Tel: (020) 7468 2600 Fax: (020) 7437 8216
Email: dl@davenportlyons.com
Website: www.davenportlyons.com

firm profile
Davenport Lyons is a leading entertainment and media law practice and combines this work with strong company/commercial (including IP/IT), litigation, property and private client departments. The firm adopts a keen commercial and practical partner-led approach and builds on long-term partnership with its clients.

main areas of work
Media/entertainment, music; litigation (defamation/IP/IT/property/general commercial/insolvency/entertainment licensing); company commercial (IP/IT); commercial property; tax and trust; matrimonial; employment.

Trainee Profile
Upper Second plus; interesting background; business acumen; practical and breadth of interest; sociable; knowledge of foreign languages an advantage.

training environment
Four seats of six months each. Three-monthly assessments. Supervision from within departments. Ongoing programme of in-house lectures and professional skills training. Davenport Lyons offers interesting hands-on training. Trainees are treated as junior fee-earners and are encouraged to develop their own client relationships and to handle their own matters under appropriate supervision.

benefits
Season ticket loans; client introduction bonuses; contribution to gym membership; discretionary bonuses; 23 days holiday.

vacation placements
Places for 2002: 14; Duration: 2 weeks; Remuneration: £175 p.w.; Closing Date: None fixed.

sponsorship & awards
The firm does not generally offer financial assistance other than in exceptional circumstances.

Partners 30
Assistant Solicitors 44
Total Trainees 9

contact
Ann Goldie
HR/Training Manager
Michael Hatchwell
Training Partner

method of application
Letter & CV

selection procedure
Interviews

closing dates
Closing date for 2002
October 2001
Closing date for 2003
March 2002

application
Training contracts p.a. **5**
Applications p.a. **1,500**
% interviewed p.a. **20%**
Required degree grade **2:1**

training
Salary:
1st year (2001) £24,500
2nd year (2001) £25,500
Holiday entitlement
23 days
% of trainees with a
non-law degree p.a. **50%**

post-qualification
Salary (2001) **£40,000**
% of trainees offered job
on qualification (2000)
100%
% of assistants (as at
2001) who joined as
trainees **15%**
% of partners (as at 2001)
who joined as trainees **3%**

DAVENPORT LYONS

Davies Arnold Cooper

6–8 Bouverie Street, London EC4Y 8DD
Tel: (020) 7936 2222 Fax: (020) 7936 2020
Email: daclon@dac.co.uk
Website: www.dac.co.uk

Partners	42
Total Fee-earners	169
Total Trainees	17
Total Staff	332

contact
Graduate Recruitment

method of application
DAC application form

selection procedure
Open day & individual interviews

closing date for 2004
31 July 2002

application
Training contracts p.a. **5**
Applications p.a. **1,000**
% interviewed p.a. **5%**
Required degree grade **2:1**
capability

firm profile
Davies Arnold Cooper is a leading practice in dispute resolution (including all forms of litigation, arbitration and alternative dispute resolution), corporate risk and commercial property services. The firm looks for the issues of the future and has recently been at the forefront of issues such as transnational litigation, rehabilitation, corporate governance/accountability, human rights, e-risks, occupational health and employee issues, reputation management and health and safety. It has taken a lead in its firm-wide usage of ADR and technological advances such as paperless litigation. The firm remains the number one choice for multi-party actions arising in the UK and internationally relating to product liability or physical disasters and accidents. Examples of high profile litigation include actions arising out of the collapse of the Maxwell empire, Barings, Polly Peck, Banesto, Piper Alpha, Haemophilia and Heathrow Tunnel collapse.

main areas of work
Insurance, financial services, construction, commercial property, pharmaceutical, healthcare, manufacturing and retailing.

trainee profile
Davies Arnold Cooper looks for people who can demonstrate a strong intellect combined with analytical and problem solving skills. Well organised, flexible and self motivated, you must be a strong communicator and able to work effectively with a variety of different people. You will thrive in a fast moving, commercial environment with plenty of opportunity for early responsibility. The firm welcomes applications from all age groups and backgrounds, from people who want to make a positive difference.

training environment
One of the only two law firms listed in the 'Britain's Best Employers' Directory. The firm's induction and training schemes are widely admired and trainees receive a comprehensive grounding in core legal skills. As a medium-sized firm it offers a flexible training programme with the opportunity for early responsibility within a supportive environment. The firm offers a career, not just a training contract, and sees its trainees as the future of its business.

sponsorship & awards
CPE and LPC: Grants covering course and examination fees. Discretionary interest-free loans for maintenance are available.

Davies Wallis Foyster

37 Peter Street, Manchester M2 5GB
Tel: (0161) 228 3702 Fax: (0161) 835 2407
5 Castle Street, Liverpool L2 4XE
Tel: (0151) 236 6226 Fax: (0151) 236 3088
Email: trainees@dwf-law.com
Website: www.dwf.co.uk

firm profile
Davies Wallis Foyster is one of the leading law firms in the North West, providing a full range of services for corporate and commercial clients and insurance clients. Over the years, the firm has recruited market leaders in all its service areas and has built substantial, multi-skilled teams around them. It is, therefore, capable of delivering a menu of world-class services to help clients achieve a competitive edge. The firm has a reputation for the quality, style and energy of its people and its willingness to provide client references. DWF is a member of EU-LEX, a network of international law firms handling cross-border work.

main areas of work
Services for corporate and commercial clients 65%. Services for insurance clients 35%.

trainee profile
DWF wants trainees to play a part in building on its success. The firm is looking for trainees who enjoy working as part of a busy team, who respond positively to a challenge and think they have what it takes to deliver results for clients. The firm is looking for its partners of the future.

training environment
All trainees commence life at DWF with a welcome programme designed to provide a clear picture of the firm and its services before moving to their first seat. The firm provides a flexible seat rotation including corporate, property, commercial litigation and insurance with agreed options which focus on post-qualification aspirations. This is supplemented by general training as well as specific training relevant to the particular seat which may be run in-house or using external courses. Appraisals are carried out during each seat to review progress and development. Trainees will have the opportunity to join in the busy social life within the office and with local trainee solicitors' groups.

benefits
Life assurance. Pension scheme to be introduced autumn 2001.

vacation placements
Open day events at each office.

sponsorship & awards
LPC funding for tuition fees.

Partners	53
Assistant Solicitors	70
Total Trainees	14

contact
Miss Vicki Holmes
Training Assistant
(Manchester address)

method of application
Handwritten letter & CV or DWF application form

selection procedure
2 stage interview/ selection process

closing date for 2004
2 August 2002

application
Training contracts p.a. **8**
Applications p.a. **c.1000**
% interviewed p.a. **5%**
Required degree grade **2:1 in any subject preferred**

training
Salary
1st year (2001) £16,000
Holiday entitlement
23 days p.a. minimum

post-qualification
% of trainees offered job on qualification (2001) **100%**

Dechert

2 Serjeants' Inn, London EC4Y 1LT
Tel: (020) 7583 5353 Fax: (020) 7775 7322
Email: info@dechertEU.com
Website: www.dechert.com

Partners	47
Assistant Solicitors	90
Total Trainees	26

contact
Lynn Muncey

method of application
Letter & application form

selection procedure
Written exercise & interviews with partners & associates

closing date for 2004
16 August 2002

application
Training contracts p.a. **20**
Applications p.a.
Over 1,000
% interviewed p.a. **12%**
Required degree grade
2:1 (or capability of attaining a 2:1)

training
Salary
1st year (2001) **£28,000**
2nd year (2001) **£32,000**
(to be reviewed in September 2002)
Holiday entitlement
20 days
% of trainees with a non-law degree p.a.
Varies
No. of seats available abroad p.a. **3 (plus shorter secondments to US offices)**

post-qualification
Salary (2001) c.**£50,000**
(to be reviewed July 2002)
% of trainees offered job on qualification (2001)
100%
% of partners (as at 1/9/01) who joined as trainees
30%

firm profile
Following a six year alliance Titmuss Sainer Dechert and Dechert Price & Rhoads merged on 1 July 2000 to form the international law firm, Dechert. The London office is organised into three core areas: business law, litigation and property. Within these areas there are specialist lawyers in areas such as banking and insolvency, commercial, customs and excise, defamation, employment, financial services, insurance, intellectual property, investigations, securitisation and tax. The London office has a total complement of 410 lawyers and supporting staff. In total, the firm has in the region of 700 lawyers in its 12 offices throughout Europe and the US. The offices are: Boston, Brussels, Harrisburg, Hartford, London, Luxembourg, Newport Beach, New York, Paris, Philadelphia, Princeton and Washington.

main areas of work – london
Commercial (including trademarks) 6%, corporate 20%, employment 3%, financial services 13%, litigation 27%, property 27% and tax 4%.

trainee profile
Candidates should be able to empathise with a wide range of people, as their clients come from all walks of life. Dechert looks for enthusiasm, intelligence, an ability to find a practical solution to a problem and for powers of expression and persuasion. Also wanted are those with a desire and ability to promote the firm's business at every opportunity. Dechert wants people who will remain on qualifying and make their careers with the firm.

training environment
Unusually training is divided into six four-monthly periods, giving trainees the chance to sample a wide range of work. Your supervisor will participate with you and a Trainee Panel Partner (who will be responsible for your well-being throughout your training contract) in a formal oral and written assessment of your work towards the end of each seat. Trainees have the opportunity to spend four months in the firm's office in Brussels and some trainees may now spend a period in their second year in one of the US offices. The greater number of seats makes it easier to fit in with any special requests to work in specific areas of the firm. Prior to the merger, the London office was the first English firm to appoint a training director in the early 1980s and their most recent appointee is a senior educator and the former director of the College of Law in London. The PSC is provided in a tailored format by the firm, with some modules taking place in-house. That apart there is an extensive training programme in which trainees are encouraged to participate (numerous aspects being particularly aimed at trainees).

Dechert continued

benefits
Free permanent health and life assurance, subsidised membership of local gym and interest-free season ticket loans.

vacation placements - 2 programmes
Date: 8 to 19 July 2002 and 22 July to 2 August 2002; Places for 2002: 16 (8 on each programme); Remuneration: no less than £225 p.w.; Closing Date: 28 February 2002.
Open day for law undergraduates: Date: 9 April 2002; Number of places: 20-30; Closing Date: 28 February 2002.
Open day for non-law graduates: Date: 2 July 2002; Places: 20-30.

sponsorship & awards
CPE/PgDL and LPC fees paid and £4,500 maintenance p.a. (where local authority grants unavailable).

trainee comments
"My training at Dechert has been first rate and thoroughly enjoyable. The firm's four month rotation system has provided me with hands on experience in each of the firm's main practice areas. Frequent lunchtime lectures and seminars mean you are always learning new skills and honing your skills as a lawyer." (Charles Carvell, newly qualified solicitor, read Law at Durham.)

"I think that there are three factors which have made my training with Dechert both enjoyable and rewarding: Firstly, having a specialist Director of Training in Bernard George has meant that the training contract has been organised, open and focused and I have always felt that I have been able to have some input into decisions affecting my job. Every effort is made to place people in departments which suit that individual, and once your career path is set, the aim has always been to hone your skills towards that goal. The four month seat rotation gives a broader perspective of the legal world and gives one the experience of six different departments rather than the standard four on a six month rotation. Finally, the open-door policy and excellent supervision provided by all the trainee supervisors makes learning on the job a painless experience and means there is the support there for you when you need it ." (Andrew McCormack, newly qualified solicitor, read Law at Manchester.)

"Since the merger we are now beginning to live up to our reputation as a transatlantic firm. This applies not only in the transactions we are instructed on but also in the secondment of trainees to our US offices as well as our Brussels office. This is a great way of familiarising oneself with the vast number of people in a firm like Dechert."(Kevin Ho, newly qualified solicitor, read Law at the School of Oriental and African Studies.)

overseas offices
Boston, Brussels, Harrisburg, Hartford, London, Luxembourg, Newport Beach, New York, Paris, Philadelphia, Princeton, Washington

Denton Wilde Sapte

Five Chancery Lane, Clifford's Inn, London EC4A 1BU
Tel: (020) 7242 1212 Fax: (020) 7320 6555
Email: trainingcontracts@dentonwildesapte.com
Website: www.dentonwildesapte.com

Partners	**202**
Assistant Solicitors	**445**
Total Trainees	**110**

contact
Emma Hooper

firm profile
Denton Wilde Sapte is a large international law firm with particular strengths in banking and finance, corporate, energy and infrastructure, technology, media and communications, property, retail and aviation as well as in construction, environment, financial services, insurance and reinsurance, local government, rail, roads, and shipping. The firm has offices in Europe, the CIS, Asia and the Middle East. In addition the firm is a founder member of Denton International, a network of leading law firms that covers 23 jurisdictions in total.

method of application
Application form

selection procedure
First interview; selection test; second interview

closing date for 2004
Law/non-law
2 August 2002

main areas of work
Corporate 35% (including tax, media, energy, employment and pensions); litigation 25%; banking and finance 23%; property 18%.

application
Training contracts p.a. **50**
Applications p.a. **2,500**
% interviewed p.a. **10%**
Required degree grade **2:1**

trainee profile
The firm looks for candidates from any degree discipline with a strong academic and extra curricular record of achievement. The firm looks for good team players with excellent interpersonal skills and the flexibility to grow with the firm. Languages are an advantage, but not essential.

training
Salary
1st year **£27,000-£28,000**
2nd year **£30,000-£31,000**
Holiday entitlement **23 days**
% of trainees with a non-law degree p.a. **40% max**
No. of seats available abroad p.a. **Currently 10**

training environment
Four six month seats, one of which may be spent in one of the firm's international offices. Two week induction at the beginning of contract. PSC core modules completed by October with remaining electives completed by the end of the first year. The firm has many social and sporting activities.

post-qualification
Salary (2001) **£48,000**
% of trainees offered job on qualification (2001) **100%**

benefits
Holiday entitlement commences at 23 days, meal away from home allowance, private health cover, season ticket loan, subsidised sports club membership, permanent health insurance, death in service cover.

overseas offices
Abu Dhabi, Almaty, Beijing, Cairo, Dubai, Gibraltar, Hong Kong, Istanbul, Moscow, Muscat, Paris, Singapore, Tashkent, Tokyo

vacation placements
Places for 2002: 80-90 places available on information weeks/open days during summer; Closing date for vacation placements is 15 March 2002 with interviews taking place during March/April 2002. Closing date for 2004 training contracts is 2 August 2002.

associated offices
Barcelona, Berlin, Budapest, Chemnitz, Cologne, Copenhagen, Dar es Salaam, Düsseldorf, Frankfurt, Gothenburg, Hamburg, Lusaka, Madrid, Malmö, Potsdam, Stockholm, Vienna

sponsorship & awards
CPE and LPC Funding: Fees and maintenance grant (less any local authority funding).

Dickinson Dees

St. Ann's Wharf, 112 Quayside, Newcastle upon Tyne NE99 1SB
Tel: (0191) 279 9000 Fax: (0191) 279 9100
Email: law@dickinson-dees.com
Website: www.dickinson-dees.com

firm profile
The largest firm in the North East, Dickinson Dees has developed a national reputation for both commercial and private client services. The firm has new premises on Newcastle's Quayside and in the Tees Valley. The firm has an associated office in Brussels with opportunities for trainees to spend time on secondment there.

main areas of work
Corporate 30%; property 30%; private client 20%; litigation 20%.

trainee profile
Good academic and analytical ability. Good commercial and business sense. Confident, personable and adaptable with good communication skills. Able to fit into a team.

training environment
Trainees are relatively few for the size of the practice. You are fully integrated into the firm and involved in all aspects of firm business. The training contract consists of four seats. One seat is spent in each of the commercial property, company/commercial and litigation departments. You are able to specialise for the fourth seat. This is encouraged so that personnel rise through the firm rather than being recruited from outside. Trainees sit with partners or associates and training is reviewed every three months. The firm has its own Training Manager. There are in-house induction courses on each move of department and opportunities for trainees to get involved in the in-house training programme. The professional skills course is run in conjunction with Northumbria University and the firm has played a key role in the development and implementation of this course. The working environment is supportive and friendly. You will lead a busy life with sporting and social events organised by the office.

vacation placements
Places for 2002: 36; Duration: 1 week; Remuneration: £125 p.w.; Closing Date: 28 February 2002. Application forms are available.

open days
Open days will be held in the Easter and Summer vacations in 2002. Application forms are available on request. Closing date: 28 February 2002 for Easter vacation open day; 30 April 2002 for Summer vacation open days.

Partners 57
Total Fee-earners 279
Total Trainees 27

contact
Jamie Pass

method of application
Application form & letter

selection procedure
Interview & in-tray exercise

closing date for 2004
31 July 2002

application
Training contracts p.a. **15**
Applications p.a. **700**
% interviewed p.a. **10%**
Required degree grade **2:1**

training
Salary
1st year (2001) **£18,000**
2nd year (2001) **£19,500**
Holiday entitlement
23 days
% of trainees with
a non-law degree p.a. **50%**
No. of seats available
abroad p.a. **1**

post-qualification
Salary (2001) **£30,000**
% of trainees offered job
on qualification (2001)
100%
% of assistants (as at
1/9/01) who joined as
trainees **60%**
% of partners (as at
1/9/01) who joined as
trainees **34%**

other offices
Tees Valley, Brussels

Dickinson Dees continued

sponsorship & awards
CPE/LPC fees paid and £4,000 interest free loan.

trainee comments
"I wanted to work for a leading commercial firm with a progressive outlook and an excellent training record; Dickinson Dees is the law firm that fulfils all their criteria." (Elizabeth Allen, first year trainee in 1998/99, read English at University of London and LLB at Northumbria University.)

"I was impressed at how everyone treated me as an important member of the team from the start, rather than just an extra pair of hands." (Robin Steel, first year trainee in 2000/01, read English Literature at Newcastle University.)

"After completing a week of work experience at Dickinson Dees I felt that I would get a thorough training at a leading commercial firm and great future prospects." (Sara Brody, second year trainee in 1999/2000, read law at Hull University.)

"Dickinson Dees offers trainees the highest level of training. Trainees are involved at all levels and have a high degree of client contact. Overall a great place to work in a friendly and relaxed environment." (Ian Hornby, second year trainee in 1999/2000, read Law at Newcastle University.)

"If you are looking for a leading commercial firm that provides nationally recognised training, and real longer term opportunities, Dickinson Dees cannot be overlooked." (Ben Butler, first year trainee in 1999/2000, read Ancient History at Newcastle University.)

D J Freeman

43 Fetter Lane, London EC4A 1JU
Tel: (020) 7583 4055 Fax: (020) 7353 7377
Email: annemellars@djfreeman.com
Website: www.djfreeman.com

firm profile
An innovative firm whose lawyers work in multidisciplinary teams concentrating on specific business sectors. It is one of the leading firms in the property, insurance and media/communications industries, and has a strong commercial litigation department. It also has more women partners than any other City law firm.

main areas of work
Property services 42%; insurance services 29%; commercial litigation 14%; media and communications 15%.

trainee profile
Clear and creative thinkers who work well under pressure and as part of a team.

training environment
Trainees spend six months in the firm's major practice areas, and once a month are able to discuss their progress in each seat with a partner. Believing supervised experience to be the best training, the firm soon gives trainees the chance to meet clients, be responsible for their own work and join in marketing and client development activities. Regular workshops in each seat help develop basic skills in the different departments. Any suggestions or concerns can be voiced at a trainee solicitors' committee. The firm has an active social committee which organises events from quiz evenings to wine tasting, as well as a theatre club.

benefits
Subsidised meals in staff restaurant; BUPA after three months; a variety of social and sporting events.

vacation placements
Places for 2002: 18; Duration: 3 weeks; Remuneration: £150 p.w.; Closing Date: 28 February 2002.

sponsorship & awards
CPE and LPC funding.

Partners 50
Assistant Solicitors 78
Total Trainees 28

contact
Anne Mellars
(020) 7556 4181

method of application
Application form

selection procedure
Interview

closing date for 2004
31 July 2002

application
Training contracts p.a. **12–15**
Applications p.a. **600**
% interviewed p.a. **10%**
Required degree grade **2:1**

training
Salary (2001)
1st six months £25,000
2nd six months £26,000
3rd six months £27,000
4th six months £28,000
Holiday entitlement
20 days

post-qualification
Salary (2001) £46,000

DLA

3 Noble Street, London EC2V 7EE
Tel: (020) 7796 6677 Fax: (0121) 262 5793
Email: recruitment.graduate@dla.com
Website: www.dla.com

firm profile
DLA is an ambitious and forward thinking firm with modern values and a clear strategy for the future. It has experienced a period of massive growth and is now the seventh largest law firm in the UK, with offices in Birmingham, Edinburgh, Glasgow, Leeds, Liverpool, London, Manchester and Sheffield. DLA has an annual fee income of £176 million and, unlike most national groupings, is managed as one partnership.

main areas of work
DLA has ten main practice groups. They are as follows: banking; business support and restructuring; commercial and projects; corporate; human resources; insurance; litigation; marine, aviation and reinsurance; real estate; technology, media and communications.

trainee profile
The firm wants exceptional people as good academic ability alone is no longer sufficient. DLA values individuality and wants to recruit people from different backgrounds with a wide range of skills. Successful candidates will believe in themselves, relate well to other people, have an appetite for life and a desire to succeed in business.

training environment
The firm deliberately takes on a relatively small number of trainees. This enables it to offer a broad range of experience, a high level of responsibility and excellent prospects on qualification. During their training contract, trainees complete four six month seats in different commercial areas, learning through observation and practice. Through-the-job training is complemented by an ongoing commercial skills training programme and by the Professional Skills Course, which is run in-house.

benefits
Contributory pension scheme, health insurance, life assurance, 25 days holiday, good sports and social facilities, car scheme and Lifeworks concierge service.

vacation placements
Places for 2002: 200; Duration: 1 week; Remuneration (2001 figures): £200 per week (London), £150 per week (Regions), £140 per week (Scotland); Closing Date: 28 February 2002.

sponsorship & awards
Payment of full fees during the CPE and LPC years, plus a maintenance grant in both years.

Partners	279
Associates	181
Assistant Solicitors	318
Total Trainees	139

contact
Sally Carthy
National Graduate Recruitment Manager

method of application
Application form

selection procedure
First interview, second interview assessment afternoon, including a second interview

closing date for 2004
31 July 2002

application
Training contracts p.a. 80+
Applications p.a. 2,000
% interviewed p.a. 15-20%
Required degree grade 2:1

training
Salary
1st year
£28,000 (London)
£20,000 (regions)
£16,000 (Scotland)
2nd year
£31,000 (London)
£22,000 (regions)
£18,000 (Scotland)
Holiday entitlement
25 days
% of trainees with a non-law degree p.a. 40%

post-qualification
Salary
£47,000 (London)
£33,000 (Birmingham)
£32,000 (Other regional offices)
£30,000 (Scotland)
% of trainees offered job on qualification 96%

DLA continued

trainee comments

"Having decided that I did not want to be based in London, but that I wanted to work for a firm with a City reputation, it may have seemed that I wanted to have my cake and be able to eat it, however DLA with its strong network of UK offices provided the natural solution. From the outset of my training I have been impressed by, and take great pride in, the achievements of DLA. High quality commercial work on an international playing field, an emphasis on teamwork and individual excellence and commitment to training and development make DLA an inspiring place in which to work." (Tim Lake, second year trainee at the Birmingham office, read Law and Business at Humberside University.)

"Having grown up in the area, I knew that Liverpool was a lively, friendly city, and was keen to return here to begin my career. At interview, it became obvious that DLA, as the largest law firm in Liverpool, was ideally placed to offer the quality of commercial work and standard of training which I was seeking. It was clear to me that the DLA training programme aimed to provide a framework within which trainees were actively encouraged to develop their legal skills both as individuals and as part of a highly successful team, providing trainees with hands on experience in a diverse range of legal areas. During my first 18 months in Liverpool, DLA has exceeded all of my expectations." (Lydia Plunkett, newly qualified in the Liverpool office, read Law at Newcastle University.)

"I had always harboured ambitions of working in London with a large City firm which does high quality commercial work. DLA offered this opportunity and it was clear at my interviews that the firm was highly ambitious and had an identifiable vision of where it wanted to be in the future. During my time at the firm it has matched and even exceeded this vision by continuing its rapid expansion. I was equally aware that I wanted to work in a firm where I would not be just another face in the crowd and where I would feel comfortable in my working environment. I was hugely impressed by the commitment DLA were willing to show towards both my training and my own personal development." (Paul Dineen, second year trainee in the London office, read Law at Leeds University.)

"Having undertaken work experience at a variety of firms, I decided upon two of the most important factors which would shape my career. I knew I would prefer not to live and work in London, but also became convinced that City type work was for me - a combination I thought would be difficult to achieve. However, after a friendly, honest and encouraging interview, DLA offered me the opportunity to combine the best quality work with a high quality of life here in Sheffield. DLA's dedicated approach to training and the value it places on each trainee were strikingly apparent at interview. DLA has proved an excellent choice both for my training contract and a succesful career upon qualification." (Anna Kelsey, second year trainee in the Sheffield office, read Law and German at Sheffield University.)

overseas offices
Brussels, Hong Kong, Singapore

associated offices (D&P)
Belgium, Denmark, France, Germany, Hong Kong, Italy, Netherlands, Norway, Singapore, Spain, Sweden

DMH

100 Queens Road, Brighton BN1 3YB
Tel: (01273) 329 833 Fax: (01273) 747 500
Email: jean.clack@dmh.co.uk
Website: www.dmh.co.uk

firm profile
DMH is an approachable and innovative firm with an open culture which encourages personal development and provides its personnel with a high level of support in order to achieve this. The firm offers expertise and service comparable to City firms to a range of commercial organisations, non-profit institutions and individual clients. By focusing on the client's needs DMH provides practical and creative solutions. DMH operates from offices in Brighton, Crawley, London and Worthing.

main areas of work
Corporate/commercial; land development (including commercial property, planning and commercial); employment, IP/IT; litigation; residential conveyancing; personal injury; private client.

trainee profile
The firm welcomes applications from motivated graduates from all backgrounds and age groups. Enthusiasm, a mature outlook and commercial awareness are as prized as academic ability, and good communication skills are a must. Ideal applicants are those with the potential to become effective managers or strong marketeers.

training environment
Usually four six month seats taken from the following areas: employment, innovation and media, corporate/commercial, planning and environmental, commercial property, commercial litigation, property litigation, personal injury, civil litigation, residential conveyancing and private client work. Trainees are closely supervised by the partner to whom they are attached but have every opportunity to work as part of a team and deal directly with clients. The majority of seats are in the Brighton and Crawley offices.

vacation placements
Places for 2002: Limited number, priority given to trainee interviewees and Sussex University; Duration: 1-2 weeks; Remuneration: £100 p.w. plus expenses; Closing Date: 31 January 2002.

Partners 33
Assistant Solicitors 24
Total Trainees 9

contact
Jean Clack

method of application
CV & covering letter

closing date for 2004
December 2002

application
Training contracts p.a. 4-6
Applications p.a. 350-450
% interviewed p.a. 3%
Required degree grade 2:1

training
Salary
1st year (2001) £16,000
2nd year (2001) £18,000
Holiday entitlement 23 days
% of trainees with a non-law degree p.a. 50%

post-qualification
Salary (2001) £27,500
% of trainees offered job on qualification (2001) 100%
% of assistants (as at 1/9/01) who joined as trainees 25%
% of partners (as at 1/9/01) who joined as trainees 54%

Edwards Geldard

Dumfries House, Dumfries Place, Cardiff CF10 3ZF
Tel: (029) 2023 8239 Fax: (029) 2023 7268
Email: info@geldards.com
Website: www.geldards.com

Partners	42
Assistant Solicitors	63
Total Trainees	25

contact
Owen Golding
Human Resources Manager

method of application
Application form

selection procedure
Interview

closing date for 2004
For summer placements end of February 2002, otherwise end of June 2002

application
Training contracts p.a. **12**
Applications p.a. **400**
% interviewed p.a. **20%**
Required degree grade **2:1 desirable**

training
Salary
1st year (2000) **£14,000**
2nd year (2000) **£15,200**
Holiday entitlement
20 days
% of trainees with a non-law degree p.a. **Varies**

post-qualification
Salary (2001) **Under review**
% of trainees retained (2001) **80%**

firm profile
Edwards Geldard is one of the leading regional law firms. In the United Kingdom the firm's offices are located in Cardiff, Derby and Nottingham. Whilst continuing to expand the traditional areas of work in the company and commercial, commercial property, dispute resolution and private client departments, the firm has acquired particular expertise in a variety of 'niche' areas of legal work. These include mergers and acquisitions, corporate finance and banking, intellectual property, public law, planning and environmental law, energy law, rail and transport law, construction contracts and building arbitration, employment law, insolvency, trusts and tax, secured lending, property litigation and clinical negligence. The firm's growth in recent years has been characterised by an expansion of its work for major Stock Exchange listed clients and for City of London based organisations and by the growing reputation of its work for public sector bodies.

main areas of work
Company/commercial 40%; property 25%; litigation 20%; other 15%.

trainee profile
Candidates should be motivated and hardworking with a strong academic background. A sense of humour is essential, as is involvement in extra curricular activities and interests which show evidence of a balanced and well-rounded individual.

training environment
Training is divided into six four month seats in the firm's main practice areas. Trainees are allocated to a particular team and are supervised by the lead partner or senior solicitors working within the team. An 'open door' policy applies and trainees are regarded very much as an integral part of the team to which they have been allocated. A dedicated partner within each office has responsibility for the trainees in that office. A senior partner monitors consistency, progress and development across the three offices. Training is reviewed every three months. Your formal training will be a combination of external courses and internal seminars. Early contact with clients is encouraged in both work and social environments, as is the acceptance of responsibility. The atmosphere is friendly and the firm encourages its own social and sporting functions outside the office.

benefits
Life assurance at three times salary, 20 days holiday entitlement per annum.

sponsorship & awards
£5,000 towards the LPC and £2,000 towards the CPE.

Eversheds

Senator House, 85 Queen Victoria Street, London EC4V 4JL
Tel: (020) 7919 4761 Fax: (020) 7919 4919
Application Form Hotline: (Freephone) (0500) 994 500
Email: gradrec@eversheds.com
Website: www.eversheds.com

firm profile
A global top three law firm, Eversheds has over 2,000 legal and business advisers based in 20 locations. Its distinctive approach gives clients access to a large team of lawyers who combine local market knowledge with an international perspective.

main areas of work
Corporate, commercial, litigation and dispute management, commercial property, employment and commoditised services. In addition to these core areas each office provides expertise in a further 30 business and industry sectors.

trainee profile
Eversheds' people are valued for being straightforward, enterprising and effective. The firm listens to its clients. It likes to simplify rather than complicate. It expects trainees to be business-like, unstuffy and down-to-earth. You will need to display commercial acumen, imagination and drive and, above all, you will need to be results-driven.

training environment
You will be encouraged to play a major part in the direction your training and development takes, with advice and supervision always available. In each department you will sit with a partner or a senior assistant and participate from an early stage in varied, complex and high-value work. Eversheds aims to retain as many trainees as possible on qualifying and many of the partners were trainees with the firm. A steep learning curve begins with a week of basic training followed by departmental seats – three of which will cover the firm's main practice areas. During your training you will also complete an Eversheds-designed Professional Skills Course and, on qualification, follow a progressive career structure.

benefits
Regional variations.

vacation placements
Places for 2002: 150; Duration: 2 weeks; Remuneration: regional variations; Closing Date: 31 January 2002.

sponsorship & awards
CPE/LPC fees and maintenance grants.

Partners 417
Assistant Solicitors 1223
Total Trainees 300

contact
Andrew M Looney
Graduate Recruitment Officer

method of application
EAF to be returned to London office, specifying the region you wish to work in

selection procedure
Selection days include group & written exercises, presentations & interview

closing date for 2004
31 July 2002

application
Training contracts p.a. **125**
Applications p.a. **3,000**
% interviewed p.a. **15%**
Required degree grade **2:1**

training
Salary
1st year London (2001) **£27,500**
2nd year London (2001) **£30,500**
Holiday entitlement **23 days**
% of trainees with a non-law degree p.a. **45%**
No. of seats available abroad p.a. **Up to 12**

post-qualification
Salary London (2001) **£48,000**
% of trainees offered job on qualification (2001) **90%**

offices
Amsterdam*, Birmingham, Brussels, Cambridge, Cardiff, Copenhagen*, Derby, Hong Kong*, Ipswich, Kuala Lumpur*, Leeds, London, Manchester, Monaco, Newcastle, Norwich, Nottingham, Paris, Singapore*, Sofia*   ** Associated office*

Farrer & Co

66 Lincoln's Inn Fields, London WC2A 3LH
Tel: (020) 7242 2022 Fax: (020) 7242 9899
Email: trainees@farrer.co.uk
Website: www.farrer.co.uk

firm profile
Farrer & Co is one of the UK's leading law practices. It provides a range of specialist advice to private, institutional and corporate clients.

main areas of work
The firm's breadth of expertise is reflected by the fact that it has an outstanding reputation in fields as diverse as matrimonial law, offshore tax planning, employment, heritage work, charity law and defamation.

trainee profile
Trainees are expected to be highly motivated individuals with keen intellects and interesting and engaging personalities. Those applicants who appear to break the mould – as shown by their initiative for organisation, leadership, exploration, or enterprise – are far more likely to get an interview than the erudite, but otherwise unimpressive, student.

training environment
The training programme involves each trainee in the widest range of cases, clients and issues possible in a single law firm. This provides a broad foundation of knowledge and experience and the opportunity to make an informed choice about the area of law in which to specialise. A high degree of involvement is encouraged under the direct supervision of solicitors and partners. Trainees attend an induction programme and regular internal lectures. The training principal reviews trainees' progress at the end of each seat and extensive feedback is given. The firm has a very friendly atmosphere and regular sporting and social events.

benefits
Health and life insurance, subsidised gym membership, season ticket loan.

vacation placements
Places for 2001: 18; Duration: 2 weeks at Easter, 3 weeks in summer; Remuneration: £210 p.w.; Closing Date: 31 January 2002.

sponsorship & awards
CPE Funding: Fees paid plus £4,000 maintenance. LPC Funding: Fees paid plus £4,000 maintenance.

Partners 51
Assistant Solicitors 51
Total Trainees 18

contact
Graduate Recruitment Manager

method of application
Firm's application form & covering letter

selection procedure
Interviews with Graduate Recruitment Manager & partners

closing date for 2004
31 July 2002

application
Training contracts p.a. **6**
Applications p.a. **1,500**
% interviewed p.a. **2.5%**
Required degree grade **2:1**

training
Salary
1st year (2001) **£24,000**
2nd year (2001) **£26,000**
Holiday entitlement
20 days
% of trainees with
non-law degrees p.a. **42%**

post-qualification
Salary (2001) **£37,000**
trainees offered job
on qualification (2000)
100%
% of assistants (as at 1/9/00) who joined as trainees **72%**
% of partners (as at 1/9/00) who joined as trainees **70%**

Fenners

15 New Bridge Street, London EC4V 6AU
Tel: (020) 7936 8000 Fax: (020) 7936 8100
Email: info@fenners.com

firm profile
Fenners is a City based firm specialising in company/commercial law, corporate finance, technology law, commercial property, town planning and banking law. The firm has a broad client base, including listed and unquoted companies, financial advisers, brokers, banks and other institutions.

main areas of work
Commercial property 40%; corporate/commercial 40%; banking 20%.

trainee profile
Candidates will demonstrate academic excellence combined with commitment and motivation to pursuing a career in a specialist City firm. In addition, extra curricular activities and interests are highly regarded as evidence of a balanced and well rounded candidate.

training environment
Training consists of seats within the firm's commercial property and corporate/commercial departments, with an option for a further contentious seat. You will sit with a partner or an experienced solicitor who will provide you with daily tasks and support. In addition, you will have an opportunity to receive feedback and discuss your progress with your training principal every three months. Fenners' trainees are highly valued and their development within the firm is encouraged by providing a challenging, supportive and enjoyable environment in which to work.

benefits
Health insurance, season ticket loan.

vacation placements
Places for 2002: 10; Duration: 2 weeks; Remuneration: competitive rates; Closing Date: 30 April 2002.

sponsorship & awards
CPE and LPC funding to be discussed with candidates.

Partners 6
Assistant Solicitors 6
Total Trainees 5

contact
Robert Fenner

method of application
Handwritten letter & CV.
Brochures available on request

selection procedure
2 interviews with partners.
The firm does not require completion of an application form.
Candidates should submit CVs

closing date for 2004
Applications should preferably be received by 1 September 2002

application
Training contracts p.a. 4
Applications p.a. 400
% interviewed p.a. 5%
Required degree grade 2:1

training
Salary
1st year Market for City
2nd year Market for City
Holiday entitlement
22 days
% of trainees with a non-law degree p.a.
Variable

post-qualification
Salary Market for City

Field Fisher Waterhouse

35 Vine Street, London EC3N 2AA
Tel: (020) 7861 4000 Fax: (020) 7488 0084
Email: kmd@ffwlaw.com
Website: www.ffwlaw.com

firm profile
Field Fisher Waterhouse is a progressive City law firm with a reputation for providing a quality service to an impressive list of UK and international clients. The firm has particular strengths in its core practice areas of finance, corporate, IP/IT and commercial property. It is also highly regarded for its expertise in commercial litigation, e-commerce, medical negligence and personal injury, communications and media, travel and tourism, employment and its professional regulatory group. The firm prides itself on its collegiate atmosphere, its creative and commercial approach to the law and its constructive approach to career development.

main areas of work
IP/IT 24%; property 21%; corporate 15%; litigation 14%; banking, finance and commercial 13%; professional regulation 7%; employment 3%; other 3%.

trainee profile
The firm is looking to recruit ambitious individuals with ability, enthusiasm and determination, who will be able to respond creatively and commercially to its clients' needs. It values strong personal qualities as well as academic achievement and welcomes applications from both law and non-law students.

training environment
Training will be split into five seats to enable you to gain the widest possible exposure to the firm's broad range of practice areas. In each seat you will work with several partners and assistants to gain a wide experience of the department. You will participate in a formal assessment at the end of each seat. The firm aims to develop your grasp of legal principles and to foster your commercial awareness. Your training will combine practical hands on experience and a comprehensive training programme of in-house lectures and external seminars. Staff enjoy the benefits of a busy sports and social committee which organises many trainee and FFW events throughout the year.

sponsorship & benefits
Tuition fees and maintenance grant paid for CPE and LPC. 25 days annual holiday, season ticket loans, health insurance, private medical healthcare.

vacation placements
Places for 2002: A summer vacation scheme will be run during July 2002. Application by CV and covering letter, by 28 February 2002.

Partners 70
Assistant Solicitors 106
Total Trainees 20

contact
Karen Danker

method of application
Firm's own application form & covering letter

selection procedure
Interview

closing date for 2004
31 August 2002

application
Training contracts p.a. **10-12**
Applications p.a. **2,000**
Required degree grade **2:1**

training
Salary
1st year (2001) **£25,000**
2nd year (2001) **£28,000**
Holiday entitlement
25 days
% of trainees with a non-law degree p.a. **50%**

post-qualification
Salary (2001) **£44,000**
% of trainees offered job on qualification (2000) **80%**
% of assistants (as at 1/9/01) who joined as trainees **40%**
% of partners (as at 1/9/01) who joined as trainees **40%**

Finers Stephens Innocent

179 Great Portland St, London W1N 6LS
Tel: (020) 7323 4000 Fax: (020) 7580 7069
Email: admin@fsilaw.co.uk
Website: www.fsilaw.co.uk

Partners	40
Assistant Solicitors	29
Total Trainees	12

contact
Personnel Director

firm profile
Finers Stephens Innocent was formed in 1999 by the merger of West End property and commercial practice Finers with City niche media and litigation practice Stephens Innocent. The environment of the firm is friendly and forward thinking, and it is known for being client focused and having an entrepreneurial and practical approach to its work. The firm is a member of the Network of Leading Law Firms and of LAWROPE, a European network of law firms.

method of application
CV & covering letter

selection procedure
2 interviews, each with 2 partners, usually including one of the Training Partners, Robert Craig & Carolyn Brown

main areas of work
Commercial property, litigation, media, family, defamation, company/commercial, private client. See the firm's website for further details.

closing date for 2004
31 July 2002

application
Training contracts p.a. 3-6
Applications p.a. **1,500**
% interviewed p.a. **5%**
Required degree grade **2:1**

trainee profile
The firm looks for academic excellence in applicants and prefers those with a law degree. It also looks for maturity, an interesting personality, strong communication skills, ability to think like a lawyer and an indefinable 'it' which shows that you have the potential to become a long-term member of the firm's team.

training
Salary
1st year **Highly competitive**
2nd year **Highly competitive**
Holiday entitlement
20 days
% of trainees with a non-law degree p.a.
0-33%

training environment
After your induction programme, you will complete four six month seats, sharing a room with either a Partner or Senior Assistant. The firm has two Training Partners who keep a close eye on the welfare and progress of trainees. There are regular group meetings of trainees and an appraisal process which enables you to know how you are progressing as well as giving you a chance to provide feedback on your view of your training.

post-qualification
Salary **Highly competitive**
% of trainees offered job on qualification (2000)
75%

benefits
20 days holiday, private medical insurance, life insurance, long-term disability insurance, subsidised gym membership, season ticket loan.

sponsorship & awards
Contribution of £3,000 towards LPC course fees.

Foot Anstey Sargent

21 Derry's Cross, Plymouth PL1 2SW
Tel: (01752) 675 000 Fax: (01752) 671 802
Email: training@foot-ansteys.co.uk
Website: www.foot-ansteys.co.uk

firm profile
A major regional practice with a growing national client base. Foot Anstey Sargent prides itself on providing a level of service and expertise which can be compared with the best in the country, but from a south west base and at regional rates.

main areas of work
The firm provides a comprehensive range of legal services, acting for businesses, individuals and institutions, and is particularly recognised nationally for banking, employment, insolvency, marine and media law.

trainee profile
A strong academic background and communication skills, with a practical approach. Selection is by interview and competitive assessment day including oral presentation, written test and individual interview followed by psychometric test.

training environment
The wide range of legal services offered by the firm gives trainee solicitors opportunities in many areas of the law. Four six month seats are chosen from banking litigation, commercial litigation, insolvency litigation, marine litigation, commercial property, planning and land use, employment, childcare, company/commercial, property litigation, civil agency, private client and criminal litigation. Trainees shadow their supervisors and sit near them, and are seen as an integral part of the team. Following an induction course, trainees attend an in-house seminar programme. The PSC is taught externally. Monthly meetings are held with supervisors (individually) and the training partner (together). Appraisals are conducted quarterly by supervisors. A non-partner acts as a confidential and objective counsellor. The atmosphere is open and friendly, encouraging trainees to learn as much as possible, and to take on responsibility. Investment in the latest technology and office facilities ensures an excellent working environment for all staff.

Partners 33
Assistant Solicitors 43
Total Trainees 6

contact
Richard Sutton
(01752) 675 000

method of application
Handwritten letter & CV, or online at www.foot-ansteys.co.uk

selection procedure
Interview & assessment day

application
Training contracts p.a. 4

post-qualification
Salary (2001) £26,500
% of trainees offered job on qualification (2001) 100%

Forbes

Marsden House, 28-32 Wellington Street (St. Johns), Blackburn BB1 8DA
Tel: (01254) 662 831 Fax: (01254) 681 104
Email: siobhanh@f-p.co.uk

Partners	23
Assistant Solicitors	44
Total Trainees	8

contact
Siobhan Hardy

firm profile
A leading North West practice with nine offices, including an office recently established in Leeds, and 290 staff, Forbes is progressive and forward looking in all aspects of its business. Underlying the practice is the strongest commitment to quality, both in its service to clients and as an employer, with strong emphasis being placed on staff training and career development – a fact confirmed by Forbes being one of the first firms to be recognised as an Investor in People. Offering a wide range of legal expertise, Forbes is noted, in particular, for excellence in company/commercial, civil litigation, defendant insurer, crime, family and employment services. Three partners are qualified Higher Court Advocates and the firm holds many Legal Aid franchises as well as ISO 9001 accreditation.

method of application
Handwritten letter & CV

selection procedure
Interview with partners

closing date for 2004
31 July 2002

main areas of work
Company/commercial, civil litigation, defendant insurer, crime, family and employment services.

application
Training contracts p.a. 3
Applications p.a. 350
% interviewed p.a. **Varies**
Required degree grade **2:1**

trainee profile
Forbes looks for high-calibre recruits with strong local connections and good academic records, who are keen team players.

training
Salary
1st year £12,000
Holiday entitlement
20 days

training environment
A tailored training programme involves six months in four of the following: crime, civil litigation, defendant insurer, matrimonial, and non-contentious/company commercial.

post-qualification
Salary (2000)
Highly competitive
% of trainees offered job on qualification (2000)
Usually 100%

Forsters

67 Grosvenor Street, London W1K 3JN
Tel: (020) 7863 8333 Fax: (020) 7863 8444
Email: ajfairchild@forsters.co.uk
Website: www.forsters.co.uk

firm profile
Forsters opened for business in 1998 with eleven of the 21 founding partners previously being partners of Frere Chomley Bischoff. It is a progressive law firm with a strong reputation for its property and private client work as well as thriving commercial and litigation practices. The working atmosphere of the firm is friendly and informal, yet highly professional. A social committee organises a range of activities from quiz nights to sporting events as Forsters actively encourages all its staff to have a life outside of work!

main areas of work
The firm has a strong reputation for all aspects of commercial and residential property work. The groups handle investment funding; development; planning; construction; landlord and tenant; property taxation and residential investment and development. Forsters is also recognised as one of the leading proponents of private client work in London with a client base comprising a broad range of individuals and trusts in the UK and elsewhere. The firm's commercial practice specialises in acquisitions and financing for technology, communication and media companies whilst its litigation group conducts commercial litigation and arbitration and advises on a broad spectrum of matters.

trainee profile
Successful candidates will have a strong academic background and either have attained or be expected to achieve a good second class degree. The firm considers that factors alongside academic achievements are also important. The firm is looking for individuals who give a real indication of being interested in a career in law and who the firm feels would readily accept and work well in its team environment.

training environment
The first year of training is split into three seats of four months in three of the following departments: commercial property, private client, company commercial or litigation. In the second year the four month pattern still applies, but the firm discusses with you whether you have developed an area of particular interest and tries to accommodate this. The training is very 'hands on' as you share an office with a partner or assistant who will give you real responsibility alongside supervision. At the end of each seat your progress and performance will be reviewed by way of an appraisal with a partner from the relevant department.

sponsorship & benefits
22 days holiday p.a., season ticket loan, permanent health insurance, life insurance, subsidised gym membership. No sponsorship for CPE or LPC courses is currently provided.

Partners 21
Assistant Solicitors 40
Total Trainees 7

contact
Alison Fairchild

method of application
Application form

selection procedure
First interview with HR Manager & Graduate Recruitment Partner; second interview with 2 partners

training
Salary
1st year (2001) £23,500
2nd year (2001) £25,500
Holiday entitlement 22 days

post-qualification
Salary (2001) £40,000
% of trainees offered job on qualification 100%

Freshfields Bruckhaus Deringer

65 Fleet Street, London EC4Y 1HS
Tel: (020) 7936 4000 Fax: (020) 7832 7001
Email: graduaterecruitment@freshfields.com
Website: www.freshfields.com

firm profile
Freshfields Bruckhaus Deringer is a leading international firm with a network of 29 offices in 19 countries. The firm provides first-rate legal services to corporations, financial institutions and governments around the world.

main areas of work
Corporate; mergers and acquisitions; banking; dispute resolution; joint ventures; employment, pensions and benefits; asset finance; real estate; tax; capital markets; intellectual property and information technology; project finance; private finance initiative; US securities; EC/competition and trade; communications and media; construction and engineering; energy; environment; financial services; restructuring and insolvency; insurance; international tax; investment funds.

trainee profile
Good academic qualifications, good record of achievement in other areas, common sense and creative thinking. Language and computer skills are also an advantage.

training environment
The firm's trainees receive a thorough professional training in a very broad range of practice areas, an excellent personal development programme and the chance to work in one of the firm's international offices or on secondment with a client in the UK or abroad. It provides the professional, technical and pastoral support necessary to ensure that you enjoy and make the most of the opportunities on offer – during your training contract and beyond.

benefits
Life assurance; permanent health insurance; group personal pension; interest-free loan; interest-free loan for a season travel ticket; free membership of the firm's private medical insurance scheme; subsidised staff restaurant; gym.

vacation placements
Places for 2002: 100; Duration: 2 weeks; Remuneration: £450; Closing Date: 14 February 2002 but apply as quickly as possible after 1 December 2001 as there may not be places left by the deadline.

sponsorship & awards
CPE and LPC fees paid and £5,000 maintenance p.a. for those studying in London and Oxford and £4,500 p.a. for those studying elsewhere.

Partners 475
Asst Solicitors 1,457
Total Trainees 169
(London-based)

contact
Maia Lawson

method of application
Application form

selection procedure
1 interview with 2 partners & written test

closing date for 2004
24 July 02 (final year undergrads or grads)
24 August 02 (penultimate year law undergrads)

application
Training contracts p.a. **100**
Applications p.a. **c.2,500**
% interviewed p.a. **c.10%**
Required degree grade **2:1**

training
Salary
1st year (2001) **£28,000**
2nd year (2001) **£32,000**
Holiday entitlement **25 days**
% of trainees with a non-law degree p.a. **c.40%**
No. of seats available abroad p.a. **c.44**

post-qualification
Salary (2001) **£50,000**
% of trainees offered job on qualification (01) **99%**

overseas offices
Amsterdam, Bangkok, Barcelona, Beijing, Berlin, Bratislava, Brussels, Budapest, Cologne, Düsseldorf, Frankfurt, Hamburg, Hanoi, Ho Chi Minh City, Hong Kong, Madrid, Milan, Moscow, Munich, New York, Paris, Prague, Rome, Shanghai, Singapore, Tokyo, Vienna, Washington DC

Goodman Derrick

90 Fetter Lane, London EC4A 1PT
Tel: (020) 7404 0606 Fax: (020) 7831 6407
Email: law@goodmanderrick.co.uk
Website: www.goodmanderrick.co.uk

firm profile
Founded in 1954 by Lord Goodman, the firm now has a broad commercial practice and is well known for its media and defamation work, particularly relating to television.

main areas of work
Media 24%; commercial and general litigation 18%; corporate 31%; property 15%; charities/private client 4%; employment 8%.

trainee profile
Candidates must show that they will quickly be able to handle responsibility and deal directly with clients. They must be suited to the firm's work environment, present themselves confidently and be quick thinking and practically-minded.

training environment
Training at the firm is based on direct and active involvement with the work of the practice. The PSC is partly carried out at the start of the training contract, with some courses taking place over the following two years, coupled with the firm's general training programme. Trainees are in addition expected to initiate personal research if specialist knowledge needs to be gained for a particular piece of work. Periods of six months are spent in four of the following departments: company/commercial, media, property, litigation, employment and private client. Work groups within these main departments allow trainees to experience further specialist fields. Trainees' own preferences and aptitude will be monitored by the supervising partner and discussed at monthly meetings and at three-monthly appraisals. The firm has a very friendly and informal environment.

benefits
Medical Health Insurance, season ticket loan, pension scheme.

sponsorship & awards
LPC fees plus maintenance grant.

Partners 20
Assistant Solicitors 9
Total Trainees 7

contact
Nicholas Armstrong

method of application
CV & covering letter

selection procedure
2 interviews

closing date for 2004
July 2002

application
Training contracts p.a. **3/4**
Applications p.a. **1,000**
% interviewed p.a. **3%**
Required degree grade
Min. **2:1**

training
Salary
1st year (2001) **£20,500**
2nd year (2001) **£21,750**
Holiday entitlement
20 days
% of trainees with a
non-law degree p.a. **60%**

post-qualification
Salary (2001) **£35,000**
% of trainees offered job
on qualification (2001) **66%**
% of assistants (as at 1/9/01) who joined as trainees **66%**
% of partners (as at 1/9/01) who joined as trainees **26%**

Gouldens

10 Old Bailey, London EC4M 7NG
Tel: (020) 7583 7777 Fax: (020) 7583 6777
Email: recruit@gouldens.com
Website: www.gouldens.com

firm profile
Gouldens is a leading commercial firm based in the City of London with a high quality client base in the UK and abroad. It provides a full range of legal services to major commercial clients from the UK and overseas.

main areas of work
Company/commercial (including tax) 42%; property (including planning) 27%; litigation (incl. IP) 20%; banking/capital markets 11%.

trainee profile
Candidates should have obtained or be predicted a 2:1 degree in any discipline. They should be willing to accept the challenge of responsibility in an atmosphere where not only technical expertise but flair, originality and enthusiasm are rewarded.

training environment
The firm operates a unique non-rotational system of training and trainees receive work simultaneously from all departments in the firm. The training is designed to provide freedom, flexibility and responsibility from the start. Trainees have their own office and are encouraged to assume their own workload which allows early responsibility, a faster development of potential and the opportunity to compare and contrast the different disciplines alongside one another. Work will vary from small cases which the trainee may handle alone (under the supervision of a senior lawyer as a mentor) to larger matters where they will assist a partner or an assistant solicitor. The firm runs a structured training programme with weekly seminars to support the thorough practical training and regular feedback trainees receive from the assistants and partners they work with. The firm looks to retain all trainees on qualification.

benefits
BUPA, season ticket loan, subsidised sports club membership, group life cover.

vacation placements
Places for 2002: Summer (law): 35; 2 weeks; £250; closing date 28 February;
Easter (non-law): 7; 2 weeks; £250; closing date 28 February;
Christmas (non-law): 14 ; 2 weeks; £250; closing date 31 October.

sponsorship & awards
CPE and LPC fees paid and £5,000 maintenance p.a.

Partners 37
Assistant Solicitors 53
Total Trainees 30

contact
Lisa Holmes

method of application
Letter & CV

selection procedure
2 interviews with partners

closing date for 2004
30 October 2002

application
Training contracts p.a. 20
Applications p.a. 2,000
% interviewed p.a. 10%
Required degree grade 2.1

training
Salary
1st year (2001) £32,000
2nd year (2001) £36,000
Holiday entitlement
5 weeks
% of trainees with
a non-law degree p.a. 40%

post-qualification
Salary (2001) £55,000
% of trainees offered job
on qualification (2001)
90%
% of assistants (as at
1/9/01) who joined as
trainees 60%
% of partners (as at 1/9/01)
who joined as trainees
45%

Halliwell Landau

St. James's Court, Brown St, Manchester M2 2JF
Tel: (0161) 835 3003 Fax: (0161) 835 2994
Email: pmrose@halliwells.com

firm profile
Halliwell Landau is the largest independent commercial law firm in the North West. Over the last few years the firm has increased substantially in both size and turnover and now has in excess of 200 fee-earners and 60 partners. This development leads to a continuing requirement for solicitors and has given rise to more internal promotions to partnerships.

main areas of work
Corporate/banking 24%; commercial litigation 20%; commercial property 17%; insolvency 12%; insurance litigation 12%; planning/environmental law 4%; trust and estate planning 4%; intellectual property 4%; employment 3%.

trainee profile
Candidates need to show a good academic ability but do not necessarily need to have studied law at university. They should demonstrate an ability to fit into a hardworking team. In particular Halliwell Landau is looking for candidates who will develop with the firm after their initial training.

training environment
Each trainee will spend six months in at least three separate departments. These will usually include commercial litigation, corporate and property. So far as possible if an individual trainee has a particular request for experience in one of the more specialist departments then that will be accommodated. In each department the trainee will work as a member of one of the teams within that department as well as being able to assist other teams. Specific training appropriate to each department will be given and in addition trainees are strongly encouraged to attend the firm's regular seminars on legal and related subjects. There is also a specific training programme for trainees. Each trainee will be assessed both mid-seat and at the end of each seat.

benefits
A subsidised gym membership is available.

vacation placements
Places for 2002: 24; Duration: 2 weeks; Remuneration: £100 p.w.; Closing Date: 31 March 2002.

sponsorship & awards
CPE and LPC fees will be paid in full.

Partners **57**
Assistant Solicitors **94**
Total Trainees **19**

contact
Paul Rose

method of application
CV & application form

selection procedure
Open days or summer placements

closing date for 2004
31 July 2002

application
Training contracts p.a. **10**
Applications p.a. **1,000**
% interviewed p.a. **5%**
Required degree grade **2:1**

training
Salary
1st year (2001) £18,000
2nd year (2001) £19,000

post-qualification
Salary (2000)
£26,000-£28,000
% of trainees offered job on qualification (2001) **100%**
% of assistants (as at 1/9/00) who joined as trainees **12%**
% of partners (as at 1/6/01) who joined as trainees **5%**

Hammond Suddards Edge

7 Devonshire Square, Cutlers Gardens, London EC2M 4YH
2 Park Lane Leeds LS3 1ES
Trinity Court, 16 Dalton Street, Manchester M60 8HS
Rutland House, 148 Edmund Street, Birmingham B3 2JR
Tel: (020) 7655 1000 Fax: (020) 7655 1001
Website: www.hammondsuddardsedge.com

firm profile

Hammond Suddards Edge is one of the top ten leading commercial law firms in the UK, with offices in London, Birmingham, Leeds, Manchester, Brussels, Paris, Berlin and Munich. The firm has nearly 2,000 staff, including 185 partners, 720 solicitors and 94 trainees, and is regarded as innovative, opportunistic and highly successful in the markets in which it operates.

main areas of work

Banking; corporate finance; commercial dispute resolution; construction; employment; financial services and corporate tax; business finance and recovery; intellectual property; commercial insurance; pensions; property.

trainee profile

Hammond Suddards Edge seeks applications from all disciplines for both vacation work and training contracts. It looks for three characteristics: strong academic performance, work experience in the legal sector and significant achievement in non-academic pursuits.

training environment

Around 45 trainee solicitors are recruited each year who each carry out six four month seats during their training contract. All trainees are required to move around a minimum of three offices during their training and subsidised trainee accommodation is provided in all locations to facilitate this process. Trainees can choose their seats as they progress through the training contract.

benefits

Subsidised accommodation in all locations. Flexible benefits scheme which allows trainees to choose their own benefits from a range of options.

vacation placements

Places for 2002: 60; Duration: 3 weeks; Remuneration: £230 p.w. (London), £180 p.w. (Leeds, Manchester and Birmingham); Closing Date: 28 February 2002.

sponsorship & awards

CPE and LPC fees paid and maintenance grant of £4,500 p.a.

Partners 197
Assistant Solicitors 550
Total Trainees 94

contact
Alison Archer
Graduate Recruitment Manager
(London office)

method of application
Application form

selection procedure
2 interviews

closing date for 2004
31 July 2002

application
Training contracts p.a. **45**
Applications p.a. **1,500**
% interviewed p.a. **3%**
Required degree grade **2:1**

training
Salary
1st year (2000) **£20,500** + accommodation
2nd year (2000) **£23,000** + accommodation
Holiday entitlement
23 days
% of trainees with
a non-law degree p.a. **25%**
No. of seats available
abroad p.a. **9**

post-qualification
Salary (2000)
London **£47,500**
Other **£33,000-£34,000**
% of trainees accepting job on qualification (2001)
95%

overseas offices
Brussels, Paris, Berlin and Munich

Harbottle & Lewis

Hanover House, 14 Hanover Square, London W1S 1HP
Tel: (020) 7667 5000 Fax: (020) 7667 5100
Email: kathy.beilby@harbottle.com
Website: www.harbottle.com

firm profile
Harbottle & Lewis is recognised for the unique breadth of its practice in the entertainment, media, travel (including aviation) and leisure industries. It undertakes significant corporate commercial and contentious work for clients within these industries including newer industries such as digital mixed media.

main areas of work
Music, film and television production, theatre, broadcasting, computer games and publishing, sport, sponsorship and advertising, aviation, property investment and leisure.

trainee profile
Trainees will have demonstrated the high academic abilities, commercial awareness, and initiative necessary to become part of a team advising clients in dynamic and demanding industries.

training environment
The two year training contract is divided into four six month seats where trainees will be given experience in a variety of legal skills including company commercial, litigation, intellectual property and real property, working within teams focused on the firm's core industries. The firm has a policy of accepting a small number of trainees to ensure they are given relevant and challenging work and are exposed to and have responsibility for a full range of legal tasks. The firm has its own lecture and seminars programme in both legal topics and industry know-how. An open door policy and a pragmatic entrepreneurial approach to legal practice provides a stimulating working environment.

benefits
Lunch provided; season ticket loans.

sponsorship & awards
LPC fees paid and interest-free loans towards maintenance.

Partners 17
Assistant Solicitors 60
Total Trainees 8

contact
Kathy Beilby

method of application
CV & letter

selection procedure
Interview

closing date for 2004
31 July 2002

application
Training contracts p.a. **4**
Applications p.a. **800**
% interviewed p.a. **5%**
Required degree grade **2:1**

training
Salary
1st year (2001) **£22,500**
2nd year (2001) **£24,000**
Holiday entitlement
in the first year **21 days**
in the second year **26 days**
% of trainees with
a non-law degree p.a. **40%**

post-qualification
Salary (2001) **£40,000**
% of trainees offered job
on qualification (2001) **80%**

Henmans

116 St. Aldates, Oxford OX1 1HA
Tel: (01865) 722181 Fax: (01865) 792376
Email: welcome@henmans.co.uk
Website: www.henmans.co.uk

firm profile
Henmans is a well-established Oxfordshire based practice with a strong national reputation serving business and private clients. Henmans' philosophy is to be extremely client focused and to deliver exceptional levels of service. The firm achieves this through an emphasis on teamwork to ensure clients always have access to a specific partner with specialist support, and through an ongoing program of training to guarantee clients optimum advice and guidance. The firm's policy of bespoke services and controlled costs ensures that both corporate and private clients benefit from City level litigation standards at competitive regional prices.

main areas of work
The firm's core service of litigation is nationally recognised. The personal injury and clinical negligence litigation is strong, as is professional negligence work. Personal injury 26%; professional negligence and commercial litigation 29%; corporate/employment 12%; property 17%; private client (including family) charities and trusts 16%.

trainee profile
Commercial awareness, sound academic accomplishment, intellectual capability, IT literacy, teamworking, good communication skills.

training environment
Trainees are introduced to the firm with a detailed induction and overview of its client base. Experience is likely to be within the PI, property, family, commercial litigation, and private client departments. The firm values commitment and enthusiasm both professionally and socially as an integral part of its culture. The firm provides an ongoing programme of in-house education and regular appraisals within its supportive and friendly environment.

Partners	21
Assistant Solicitors	30
Total Trainees	5

contact
Viv J Matthews MA FCIPD
Human Resources Manager

method of application
Handwritten letter & CV

selection procedure
Interview with HR Manager & partners

closing date for 2004
30 July 2002

application
Training contracts p.a. 3
Applications p.a. 500

training
Salary
1st year (2000) £14,000
2nd year (2000) £15,100
Holiday entitlement
20 days
% of trainees with a non-law degree p.a. 30%

post-qualification
Salary (2000) £24,000
% of assistants (as at 1/9/00) who joined as trainees 35%
% of partners (as at 1/9/00) who joined as trainees 15%

Herbert Smith

Exchange House, Primrose Street, London EC2A 2HS
Tel: (020) 7374 8000 Fax: (020) 7374 0888
Email: graduate.recruitment@herbertsmith.com
Website: www.herbertsmith.com

firm profile
A major City firm with an international dimension, Herbert Smith has particular strengths in international M&A, corporate finance and international projects with a strong profile in litigation and arbitration. The working environment is strongly team-orientated, friendly and informal, probably as a result of the diverse backgrounds of the firm's partners and staff.

main areas of work
International mergers and acquisitions; corporate finance and banking (including capital markets); energy; projects and project finance; competition; property; international litigation; arbitration.

trainee profile
Trainees need common sense, self-confidence and intelligence to make their own way in a large firm. They are typically high-achieving and intelligent, numerate and literate with general and legal work experience.

training environment
Structured training and supervision are designed to allow trainees to experience a unique range of both contentious and non-contentious work and take on responsibilities as soon as they can. You will work within partner-led teams and have your own role. Individual strengths will be monitored, developed and utilised. On-the-job training will be divided into four six month seats. One seat will be in the corporate division, one in the litigation division and you have a choice of specialist seats such as IP/IT or EU and competition, as well as an opportunity to go on secondment to a client or to an overseas office. Lectures and case studies will take up 30 days of the contract and the firm runs its own legal development programme. There are good social and sporting activities and a life outside work is positively encouraged.

sponsorship & benefits
CPE and LPC fees paid and £5,000 maintenance p.a. Benefits include profit share, permanent health insurance, private medical insurance, season ticket loan, life assurance, gym, group personal accident insurance and matched contributory pension scheme.

vacation placements
Places for 2002: 115. Christmas (non-law students only): 1x2 weeks, 10-21 December 2001. Easter (law and non-law): 1x2 weeks, 2-12 April 2002. Summer (law and non-law): 4x2 weeks, 24 June - 5 July 2002, 8-19 July 2002, 19 July - 9 August 2002 and 12-23 August 2002. Closing Date: Friday 23 November 2001 for Christmas scheme; Thursday 31 January 2002 for Easter and Summer scheme.

Partners 188
Assistant Solicitors 800
Total Trainees 180

contact
Kate Quail

method of application
Application form

selection procedure
Interview

closing date for 2004
31 August 2002

application
Training contracts p.a. **100**
Applications p.a. **1,750**
% interviewed p.a. **20%**
Required degree grade **2:1**

training
Salary
1st year (2001) £28,500
2nd year (2001) £32,000
Holiday entitlement
25 days, rising to 27 on graduation
% of trainees with a non-law degree p.a.
c.40%

post-qualification
Salary (2001) £50,000
% of trainees offered job on qualification (2001) 95%

overseas offices
Bangkok, Beijing, Brussels, Hong Kong, Moscow, Paris, Singapore, Tokyo

A-Z SOLICITORS

Hewitson Becke + Shaw

42 Newmarket Road, Cambridge CB5 8EP
Tel: (01604) 233 233 Fax: (01223) 316 511
Email: mail@hewitsons.com (for all offices)
Website: www.hbslaw.co.uk (for all offices)

firm profile
Established in 1865, the firm handles mostly company and commercial work, but has a growing body of public sector clients. The firm has three offices: Cambridge, Northampton and Saffron Walden.

main areas of work
Three sections: corporate technology, property and private client.

trainee profile
The firm is interested in applications from candidates who have achieved a high degree of success in academic studies and who are bright, personable and able to take the initiative.

training environment
The firm offers four six month seats.

benefits
The PSC is provided during the first year of the training contract. This is coupled with an extensive programme of Trainee Solicitor Seminars provided by specialist in-house lawyers.

vacation placements
Places for 2002: A few placements are available, application is by way of letter and CV to Caroline Lewis; Duration: 1-2 weeks.

sponsorship & awards
Funding for the CPE and/or LPC is not provided.

Partners 47
Assistant Solicitors 40
Total Trainees 18

contact
Caroline Lewis
7 Spencer Parade
Northampton NN1 5AB

method of application
Firm's application form

selection procedure
Interview

closing date for 2004
End of August 2002

application
Training contracts p.a. **15**
Applications p.a. **1,400**
% interviewed p.a. **10%**
Required degree grade
2:1 min

training
Salary
1st year (2001) £17,000
2nd year (2001) £18,000
Holiday entitlement
22 days
% of trainees with a
non-law degree p.a. **50%**

post-qualification
Salary (2000) **Under review**
% of trainees offered job
on qualification (2000) **63%**
% of assistants (as at
1/9/00) who joined as
trainees **48%**
% of partners (as at 1/9/00)
who joined as trainees
14%

Hill Dickinson

Pearl Assurance House, 2 Derby Square, Liverpool L2 9XL
Tel: (0151) 236 5400 Fax: (0151) 236 2175
Email: law@hilldicks.com
Website: www.hilldickinson.com

Partners	79
Assistant Solicitors	65
Total Trainees	20

contact
Ruth Lawrence
Partner

method of application
CV & passport-sized photograph with supporting letter

selection procedure
Assessment day

closing date for 2004
1 October 2002

training
Salary
1st year (2000) £16,500
2nd year (2000) £18,000
Holiday entitlement
4 weeks

post-qualification
% of trainees offered job on qualification (2000) 89%

firm profile
The firm is one of the largest in the North West, with offices in Liverpool, Manchester, Chester and London. It adopts a pragmatic and personal approach with clients on a local, national and international level.

main areas of work
Litigation (insurance/construction/professional negligence/commercial litigation/insolvency) 50%; commercial property, planning and environmental 15%; shipping 15%; health/medical negligence 10%; company, commercial, pensions, tax, intellectual property, PFI 10%.

trainee profile
Consistent achievers of a high intellectual calibre, possessing team skills, commercial acumen, resilience and a sense of humour. The firm recruits people who vary greatly in terms of personality and values outside interests.

training environment
Trainees spend six months in each of the four departments (insurance, marine and transit, health, and commercial) and will be given the chance to specialise in specific areas. You will be given the opportunity to learn and develop communication and presentation skills, legal research, drafting, interviewing and advising, negotiation and advocacy. Trainees are encouraged to accept responsibility and are expected to act with initiative. The practice has an active social committee and a larger than usual selection of competitive sporting teams.

vacation placements
Places for 2002: Yes; Duration: 1 week; Remuneration: No; Closing Date: 1 April 2002.

sponsorship & awards
LPC funding.

Hodge Jones & Allen

31-39 Camden Road, London NW1 9LR
Tel: (020) 7482 1974 Fax: (020) 7267 3476
Email: hja@hodge-jones-allen.co.uk
Website: www.hodge-jones-allen.co.uk

firm profile
Hodge Jones & Allen was founded in 1977 with the intention of providing high quality legal help for those who have suffered injustice. The firm has grown to 20 partners and one hundred and fifty staff and is led by senior partner Patrick Allen. It has been involved in a number of high profile and leading cases, notably personal injury cases arising from the King's Cross fire and the Marchioness disaster, and is also handling major group claims, including Gulf War Syndrome.

main areas of work
Personal injury 35%; crime 28.5%; family 21%; housing 7.5%; property and employment 7%.

trainee profile
Ideally candidates should have strong IT skills together with a proven commitment to and/or experience of working in Legal Aid/Advice sectors.

training environment
Trainees have a full induction on joining HJA covering the work of the firm's main departments, procedural matters and professional conduct. Training consists of four six month seats and trainees normally share an office with a partner who assists them and formally reviews their progress at least once during each seat.

benefits
Pension, life assurance, permanent health insurance, quarterly drinks, summer outing, Christmas party.

Partners	20
Assistant Solicitors	24
Total Trainees	10

contact
Sarah Firth
Personnel Manager

method of application
By application form only, 1 year in advance

selection procedure
Interview & selection tests in previous October

closing date for 2004
September 2002

application
Required degree grade
2:1 degree preferred

Holman Fenwick & Willan

Marlow House, Lloyds Avenue, London EC3N 3AL
Tel: (020) 7488 2300 Fax: (020) 7481 0316
Email: grad.recruitment@hfw.co.uk

firm profile
Holman Fenwick & Willan is an international law firm and one of the world's leading specialists in maritime transportation, insurance, reinsurance and trade. The firm is a leader in the field of commercial litigation and arbitration and also offers comprehensive commercial and financial advice. Founded in 1883, the firm is one of the largest operating in its chosen fields with a team of over 200 lawyers worldwide, and a reputation for excellence and innovation.

main areas of work
Their range of services include marine, admiralty and crisis management, insurance and reinsurance, commercial litigation and arbitration, international trade and commodities, energy, corporate and financial.

trainee profile
Applications are invited from commercially minded undergraduates and graduates of all disciplines with good A levels and who have, or expect to receive, a 2:1 degree. Good foreign languages or a scientific or maritime background are an advantage.

training environment
During your training period the firm will ensure that you gain valuable experience in a wide range of areas. It also organises formal training supplemented by a programme of in-house seminars and ship visits in addition to the PSC. Your training development as an effective lawyer will be managed by the Recruitment and Training Partner, Ottilie Sefton, who will ensure that your training is both successful and enjoyable.

benefits
Private medical insurance, permanent health and accident insurance, subsidised gym membership, season ticket loan.

vacation placements
Places for 2002: 12; Duration: 2 weeks. Dates: 24 June - 5 July / 15 July - 26 July; Remuneration (2001): £250 p.w.; Closing Date: Applications accepted 1 Jan - 14 Feb 2002.

sponsorship & awards
PgDL Funding: Fees paid plus £5,000 maintenance; LPC Funding: Fees paid plus £5,000 maintenance.

Partners	83
Other Solicitors & Fee-earners	124
Total Trainees	20

contact
Graduate Recruitment Officer

method of application
Handwritten letter & typed CV

selection procedure
2 interviews with partners & written exercise

closing date for 2004
31 July 2002

application
Training contracts p.a. 8
Applications p.a. 1,200
% interviewed p.a. 5%
Required degree grade 2:1

training
Salary (Sept 2001)
To be reviewed
1st six months £25,000
2nd six months TBA
3rd six months TBA
4th six months TBA
Holiday entitlement
22 days
% of trainees with
a non-law degree p.a. 50%

post-qualification
Salary (2000) £44,000
% of trainees offered job on qualification
(Sept 2001) 100%

overseas offices
Hong Kong, Nantes, Paris, Piraeus, Rouen, Shanghai, Singapore

Howes Percival

Oxford House, Cliftonville, Northampton NN1 5PN
Tel: (01604) 230 400 Fax: (01604) 620 956
Email: law@howes-percival.co.uk
Website: www.howes-percival.co.uk

firm profile
Howes Percival is a twenty-nine partner commercial law firm with offices in Leicester, Milton Keynes, Northampton and Norwich. The firm's working environment is young, progressive and highly professional and its corporate structure means that fee-earners are rewarded on merit and can progress to associate or partner status quickly. The type and high value of the work that the firm does places it in a position in which it is recognised as being a regional firm by location only. Howes Percival has the expertise, resources and partner reputation that match a city firm.

main areas of work
The commercial strength of the firm means that the practice is departmentalised and the breakdown of work is as follows: corporate 30%; commercial property 25%; commercial litigation 20%; insolvency 10%; employment 10%; private client 5%.

trainee profile
The firm is looking for six well-educated, focused, enthusiastic, commercially aware graduates with a minimum 2:1 degree in any discipline. Howes Percival welcomes confident communicators with strong interpersonal skills who share the firm's desire to be the best.

training environment
Trainees complete four six month seats, each one in a different department. Trainees joining the Norwich office will remain at Norwich for the duration of their training contract. In order to gain exposure to as much of the firm as possible, trainees in the East Midlands will, where possible, complete a seat in each of the three East Midlands offices. Trainees report direct to a partner and after three months and again towards the end of each seat they will be formally assessed by the partner training them. Trainees will be given every assistance by the fee-earners in their department to develop quickly and will be given responsibility as soon as they are ready.

benefits
Contributory pension scheme. Private health insurance. The firm will make discretionary LPC funding available to candidates.

vacation placements
The firm has a limited number of summer placements available in July and August. Please apply to Miss Katy Pattle at the above address for further details.

Partners 29
Assistant Solicitors 25
Total Trainees 10

contact
Miss Katy Pattle
HR Assistant

method of application
Letter, CV & firm's application form

selection procedure
Assessment centres including second interview with training principal & partner

closing date for 2004
31 July 2002

application
Training contracts p.a. **6**
Applications p.a. **300**
% interviewed p.a. **10%**
Required degree grade **2:1**

training
Salary
1st year (2001) **£16,500**
2nd year (2001) **£17,750**
Holiday entitlement
23 days p.a.

post-qualification
% of trainees offered job on qualification (2001)
100%
% of assistants (as at 1/9/01) who joined as trainees **30%**
% of partners (as at 1/9/01) who joined as trainees **7.5%**

Hugh James Ford Simey

Arlbee House, Greyfriars Rd, Cardiff CF10 3QB
Tel: (029) 2022 4871 Fax: (029) 2038 8222
Email: trainingcontracts@hjfs.co.uk
Website: www.hjfs.co.uk

firm profile
Hugh James Ford Simey is one of the UK's leading regional law firms. The firm has experienced phenomenal growth and success since it was formed in 1960 and has for many years been one of only a handful of firms to dominate the legal scene in Wales. As Hugh James Ford Simey, the firm is placed high in the table of the top 100 law firms in the UK. The firm offers its clients a comprehensive service covering the whole of South Wales and the West Country through its network of twelve offices.

main areas of work
The main areas covered by the firm are commercial litigation, commercial services, commercial property and private client. In response to demand for specific services, a number of specialist groups have been established which include construction, debt recovery, e-business, employment, head injury, housing associations, insurance, lender services and sports law. The breakdown of the main areas of work is as follows: claimant personal injury 30%; commercial and insurance litigation 25%; commercial services 13%; commercial property 12%; private client 10%; construction and professional indemnity 10%.

trainee profile
Hugh James Ford Simey welcomes applications from law and non-law undergraduates with a good class degree. Candidates must exhibit first class legal and practice skills and good interpersonal and IT skills are essential. The firm seeks to retain its trainees upon qualification and sees them as an integral part of the future of the firm. Hugh James Ford Simey is proud of the fact that the majority of the firm's present partners were trained at the firm.

training environment
Trainees generally undertake four seats of not less than six months which may be in any of the firm's offices. Broadly, experience will be gained in all four main work categories. The breadth of work dealt with by the firm enables it to ensure that over-specialisation is avoided.

benefits
Company pension scheme.

vacation placements
Places for 2002: Available.

Partners 60
Assistant Solicitors 51
Total Trainees 14

contact
Jane O'Rourke
HR Manager

method of application
Application form available from HR Manager

selection procedure
Assessment day

closing date for 2004
31 July 2002

application
Training contracts p.a. 7
Applications p.a. 350
% interviewed p.a. 30%
Required degree grade 2:2

training
Salary
1st year (2000)
Competitive & reviewed annually
Salary
2nd year (2000)
Competitive & reviewed annually

other offices
Cardiff, Merthyr Tydfil, Bargoed, Talbot Green, Blackwood, Treharris, Pontlottyn, Bristol, Exeter, Exmouth, Sidmouth

Ince & Co

Knollys House, 11 Byward Street, London EC3R 5EN
Tel: (020) 7623 2011 Fax: (020) 7623 3225
Email: claire.kendall@ince.co.uk

firm profile
Since its foundation in 1870, Ince & Co has specialised in international commercial law and is best known for its shipping and insurance work.

main areas of work
Shipping and aviation 39%; insurance/reinsurance/professional indemnity 25%; energy/construction/environment/pollution/personal injury 22%; corporate/private client/property 6%; international trade/commodities 4%; sale and purchase 4%.

trainee profile
Hard working competitive individuals with initiative who relish challenge and responsibility within a team environment. Academic achievements, positions of responsibility, sport and travel are all taken into account.

training environment
Trainees sit with four different partners for six months at a time throughout their training. Under close supervision, they are encouraged from an early stage to meet and visit clients, interview witnesses, liaise with counsel, deal with technical experts and handle opposing lawyers. They will quickly build up a portfolio of cases from a number of partners involved in a cross-section of the firm's practice and will see their cases through from start to finish. In the second year of their training contract there is the opportunity of a seat in the Piraeus office. They will also attend in-house and external lectures, conferences and seminars on practical and legal topics.

benefits
STL, corporate health cover, PHI, contributory pension scheme.

vacation placements
Places for 2002: 16; Duration: 2 weeks; Remuneration: £250 p.w.; Closing Date: 15 February 2002.

sponsorship & awards
LPC fees, £4,000 grant for study in London, £3,500 grant for study elsewhere. Discretionary sponsorship for CPE.

Partners 54*
Assistant Solicitors 65*
Total Trainees 22*
* denotes world-wide figures

contact
Claire Kendall

method of application
Typed/handwritten letter & CV with contact details of 2 academic referees

selection procedure
Interview with HR professional & interview with 2 partners from Recruitment Committee & a written test

closing date for 2004
3 September 2002

application
Training contracts p.a. 12
Applications p.a. 2,000
% interviewed p.a. 5%
Required degree grade 2:1

training
Salary
1st year (2001) £25,000
2nd year (2001) £28,000
Holiday entitlement
22 days
% of trainees with a non-law degree p.a. 55%

post-qualification
Salary (2001) £47,000
% of trainees offered job on qualification (2001) 100%. 100% accepted!
% of assistants (as at 2001) who joined as trainees 66%
% of partners (as at 2001) who joined as trainees 74%

overseas offices
Hong Kong, Singapore, Shanghai, Piraeus (consultancy)

Irwin Mitchell

St. Peter's House, Hartshead, Sheffield S1 2EL
Recruitment Line: (0114) 274 4580 Fax: (0114) 272 9346
Email: enquiries@irwinmitchell.co.uk
Website: www.imonline.co.uk

firm profile
Irwin Mitchell is a rapidly expanding 79 partner general practice with 1,500 employees and offices in Sheffield, Birmingham, Leeds and London. It is particularly well known for commercial law, commercial litigation, insurance law, business crime and claimant personal injury litigation. The firm's strong reputation for dealing with novel and complex areas of law and handling developmental cases (such as the vibration white finger and CJD cases and the Matrix-Churchill 'arms to Iraq' affair) means that it can offer a broad range of experience within each of its specialist departments, giving its trainees a high standard of training.

main areas of work
Corporate services 32%; claimant personal injury 25%; insurance litigation 32%; private client 11%.

trainee profile
The firm is looking for well motivated individuals with a real commitment to the law and who can demonstrate above average academic and social ability. It recruits law and non-law graduates. Foreign languages and IT skills are an asset. Irwin Mitchell believes that trainees are an investment for the future and as such it prefers to keep its trainees once they qualify.

training environment
The two year training contract consists of four seats. The firm's trainees also benefit from an induction programme, monthly training meetings and the Professional Skills Course which is organised and financed by the firm. Each trainee has a review every three months with their supervising partner. There are numerous other activities in which trainees are encouraged to participate, eg team skills challenges, conferences, mock trials.

vacation placements
Places for 2002: 30; Duration: 2 weeks; Remuneration: £75 p.w.; Closing Date: 1 March.

sponsorship & awards
CPE and LPC fees plus £3,000 maintenance grant.

Partners 79
Assistant Solicitors 149
Total Trainees 27

contact
Sue Lenkowski

method of application
Brochures & application forms are available from the Training Department. Call the recruitment line between 1 March & 31 July

selection procedure
Assessment centres & interviews are held in August & early September & successful candidates are invited to a second interview with 2 partners

closing date for 2004
31 July 2002

application
Training contracts p.a. **15**
Applications p.a. **1,000**
% interviewed p.a. **5%**

training
Salary
1st year £16,500
2nd year £18,500
Holiday entitlement
23 days
% of trainees with a non-law degree p.a. **25%**

post-qualification
% of trainees offered job on qualification (2001) **80%**
% of assistants (1/6/01) who joined as trainees **41%**
% of partners (1/6/01) who joined as trainees **19%**

Keoghs

2 The Parklands, Bolton BL6 4SE
Tel: (01204) 677 000 Fax: (01204) 677 111
Email: info@keoghs.co.uk

firm profile
Keoghs is one of the UK's leading insurance litigation firms offering national coverage to clients and acts for most of the UK's major insurance companies. The company and commercial team specialise in commercial business advice serving a client base ranging from the private individual to small growing businesses and national blue chip organisations. The high standard of service given to new and existing clients has enabled the firm to achieve ISO 9001 accreditation.

main areas of work
The main practice areas are personal injury litigation, commercial litigation and company commercial (which includes corporate, employment, intellectual property commercial property and private client).

trainee profile
The firm is looking to recruit the partners of the future and indeed many current partners and assistant solicitors joined the firm as trainees. Applicants should be able to demonstrate a high academic standard (at least a 2:1 degree but not necessarily in law), an ability to work in a team, and good communication and decision making skills. The firm welcomes commercially aware, enthusiastic and self motivated candidates with good IT skills and a sense of humour.

training environment
Trainees undertake a flexible programme of six month periods in each of the firm's three main practice areas of defendant personal injury litigation, commercial litigation and company commercial work. A final six months can then be spent in the department of the trainee's choice. The trainee will work as part of a specialist team, receiving specific training from their departmental supervisor. The supervisor will also assess the trainee during and at the end of their placement to review progress and development of their drafting, research, communication, advocacy and negotiation skills. The firm's Training and Development department runs a comprehensive programme of in-house training designed to complement the compulsory Professional Skills Course.

Partners 26
Trainees 9
Total Staff 320

contact
Mrs Frances Cross
Director of HR

method of application
Apply by sending a CV & covering letter

selection procedure
By 2 stage interview

closing date for 2004
August 2002

application
Training contracts p.a. 3 in Bolton, 1 in Coventry
Applications p.a. 800
% interviewed p.a. 3.5%
Required degree grade 2:1

training
Salary for each year of training
Currently under review (in excess of Law Society minimum)
Holiday entitlement
25 days + 8 statutory days

post-qualification
Salary £24,500
% of trainees offered job on qualification The firm aims for 100%

regional offices
Bolton, Coventry

KLegal

1-2 Dorset Rise, London EC4Y 8AE
Tel: (020) 7694 2500 Fax: (020) 7694 2501
Website: www.klegaltrainees.co.uk

firm profile
KLegal is the UK associated firm of KPMG and was founded in July 1999. The firm exists to provide legal services as part of KPMG's multidisciplinary approach to client service. The firm has a unique opportunity to help develop a top-quality legal practice on an international basis alongside one of the top global professional services providers.

main areas of work
The firm's focus is on developing its legal expertise in practice areas that complement the services offered by KPMG. These include banking and finance, corporate, commercial, e-commerce, IT and telecoms, employment, intellectual property, projects/PFI, property, tax litigation and dispute resolution.

trainee profile
KLegal is looking for top-quality candidates with ambition who share the firm's vision and who are capable of helping it to achieve it. The firm is a constantly changing environment and its rapid growth rate is set to continue apace. The firm is looking to those who see the opportunities this provides both for themselves as individuals and for their colleagues generally.

training environment
KLegal's training is based upon a conventional rotation of seats of six months in four main practice areas. The firm provides opportunities for its trainees to learn their legal skills as part of multidisciplinary teams and secondment opportunities within KPMG may also be available, enabling them to become amongst the best commercially minded lawyers in the City. And its personal development training is second to none. The firm's commitment is to provide an enjoyable experience, allowing individuals to maximise both their own personal and professional development.

benefits
Non-contributory pension, life assurance, free lunch, Flextra, 25 days holiday.

vacation placements
Places for 2002: 12; Duration: 5 weeks; Remuneration: £250 p.w.; Closing Date: 28 February 2002.

sponsorship & awards
CPE Funding: Fees paid plus maintenance of £4,500.
LPC Funding: Fees paid plus maintenance of £4,500.

Partners 17
Assistant Solicitors 61
Total Trainees 22

contact
Kate Hedstrom
Graduate Recruitment Officer

method of application
Online application. Visit www.klegaltrainees.co.uk

selection procedure
2 interviews & assessment exercises

closing date for 2004
31 July 2002

application
Training contracts p.a. 30
Applications p.a. c.750
Required degree grade 2:1

training
Salary (Reviewed annually)
1st year (October 2001) £28,000
2nd year (October 2001) £32,000

post-qualification
Salary (October 2000) £45,000

overseas offices
Member of KLegal International

Knight & Sons

The Brampton, Newcastle under Lyme ST5 0QW
Tel: (01782) 619 225 Fax: (01782) 717 260
Email: ttpc@knightandsons.co.uk
Website: www.knightandsons.co.uk

firm profile
Knight & Sons is a medium sized, commercially orientated firm with a strong private client department. The firm was founded in 1767 and it has 19 partners and approximately 130 members of staff.

main areas of work
The firm's main areas of work are commercial property 41%; litigation 23%; tax, trust and private client 21%; corporate and commercial 15%.

trainee profile
The firm is keen to recruit trainees who will stay on once they have qualified. Successful candidates are commercially aware, proactive and outgoing in character. Languages, computer literacy and outstanding academic achievement are desirable, as is some connection with North Staffordshire.

training environment
Trainees generally spend six months in each of the four main departments (litigation, commercial property, company commercial and tax, trusts and private client), but may also gain experience in the specialist units such as development planning and environmental, employment, personal injury, agriculture and charity. The firm runs in-house skills-based programmes designed to enhance business and client care skills for all fee-earners. The atmosphere is lively and a social committee organises events throughout the year ranging from a summer ball to a quiz night.

benefits
Subsidised gym membership.

vacation placements
Applications to be received by:
31 October for the following Christmas;
28 February for the following Easter;
30 April for the following Summer.

sponsorship and awards
Interest-free loans may be available but are strictly subject to individual negotiation.

Trainees	7
Partners	19

contact
Isabel Hancock

method of application
Please make a handwritten application supported by CV

closing date for 2004
By 31 July each year to begin 2 years hence

application
Training contracts p.a. 3-4

starting salary
Above Law Society minimum with a review each 6 months

minimum qualifications
2:1 degree

offices
Newcastle under Lyme

Lawrence Graham

190 Strand, London WC2R 1JN
Tel: (020) 7759 6694 Fax: (020) 7379 6854
Email: graduate@lawgram.com
Website: www.lawgram.com

firm profile
Lawrence Graham is a growing firm with a broad client base, which includes many UK and international public and private companies, pension funds, financial institutions, shipping companies, small businesses and private individuals. The firm's business is divided into four main practice areas: commercial property, company and commercial, litigation and tax and financial management. Each of the four main practice areas is organised into specialised teams. The firm has associations with many law firms throughout the world, including North America, Europe and the Far East. It also has an office in the Ukraine where the firm has had clients since the 1920s.

main areas of work
Property 35%; company and commercial 29; litigation (including shipping) 23%; tax and financial management 13%.

trainee profile
The firm purposely recruits a small number of trainees for its size to enable comprehensive, hands on training. Candidates, who are normally of 2:1 calibre, should demonstrate strong technical and interpersonal skills, the ability to understand a client's commercial priorities and objectives and the judgement to deal with complex problems.

training environment
Trainees are given the opportunity to learn both formally and practically. Seminars are regularly held throughout the two years. Training consists of four six month seats including a seat in each of the company and commercial, litigation and property departments. The fourth seat can be in either tax and financial management or back to one of the main departments. Each trainee is assigned a mentor. All work is supervised but independence and responsibility increases with experience. Social events including sporting events are also organised.

benefits
Season ticket loan, on-site gym.

vacation placements
Places for 2002: 40; Duration: 2 weeks during Easter break and 4 x 2 weeks between June and August; Remuneration: £225 p.w.; Closing Date: 31 January 2002.

sponsorship & awards
CPE Funding: Course fees and £3,750 maintenance grant.
LPC Funding: Course fees and £3,750 maintenance grant.

Partners 81
Assistant Solicitors 98
Total Trainees 30

contact
Cathy Butterworth
Human Resources Officer

method of application
Firm's application form.
For law **After 2nd year results**
For non-law **After final results**

selection procedure
Interview

closing date for 2004
31 July 2002

application
Training contracts **18**
Applications p.a. **1,000**
Required degree grade **2:1**

training
Salary
1st year (2001) **£28,000**
2nd year (2001) **£32,000**
% of trainees with a non-law degree p.a. **40%**

post-qualification
Salary (2001) **£48,000**
% of trainees offered job on qualification (2001) **98%**
% of assistants (as at 1/9/01) who joined as trainees **42%**
% of partners (as at 1/9/01) who joined as trainees **32%**

Laytons

Carmelite, 50 Victoria Embankment, Blackfriars, London EC4Y 0LS
Tel: (020) 7842 8000 Fax: (020) 7842 8080
Email: london@laytons.com
Website: www.laytons.com

firm profile
Laytons assigns a core legal team to each client who knows its business and can advise directly or by deploying the specialist skills of colleagues. The approach to legal issues is practical, creative and energetic, providing high quality advice founded on a range of complementary specialist skills relevant to the firm's primary fields of focus. The firm is a single national team operating through its four offices, each of which draws on the strengths of the whole with the benefit of excellent IT and communications.

main areas of work
Company/commercial 51%; commercial property/land development 19%; general litigation 12%; building litigation 2%; employment 10%; trusts, private client and private tax 4%; insolvency 2%.

trainee profile
All trainees have contact with clients from an early stage, working on a wide variety of transactions. Trainees will soon be responsible for their own files, although they are always supported and have regular appraisals throughout the training contract. The firm recruits with a view to retaining trainees to assistant level. Trainees are also encouraged to participate in the firm's business development activities.

training environment
Trainees are placed in four six month seats in each of the firm's principal departments: company commercial, property, litigation and private client.

vacation placements
Places for 2002: 6; Duration: 1 week; Closing Date: 31 March 2002.

sponsorship & awards
CPE Funding: Yes; LPC Funding: Yes.

Partners 32
Assistant Solicitors 42
Total Trainees 12

contact
Ian Burman

method of application
Application form

selection procedure
2 interviews

closing date for 2004
31 August 2002

application
Training contracts p.a. 8
Applications p.a. **2,000**
% interviewed p.a. **5%**
Required degree grade
1 or 2:1

training
Salary
1st year (2002) **Market rate**
2nd year (2002) **Market rate**
Holiday entitlement
22 days

post-qualification
Salary (2002) **Market rate**
% of trainees offered job on qualification (2000)
80%
% of assistants (as at 1/9/00) who joined as trainees **90%**
% of partners (as at 1/9/00) who joined as trainees **20%**

LeBoeuf, Lamb, Greene & MacRae

1 Minster Court, Mincing Lane, London EC3R 7AA
Tel: (020) 7459 5000 Fax: (020) 7459 5099
Email: traineelondon@llgm.com
Website: www.llgm.com

firm profile
LeBoeuf, Lamb, Greene & MacRae is an international law firm with some 750 lawyers worldwide in offices across Europe, the US, Africa and the Middle East. The London office, established as a multinational partnership in 1995, employs 60 lawyers and is the 'hub' office for the firm's European and international practice. The London office handles varied, interesting work and will suit people who want early responsibility in a relaxed but hard working environment.

main areas of work
General corporate, litigation, corporate finance, project finance, asset finance, insurance, insolvency, property, tax, intellectual property.

trainee profile
The firm wants outstanding people in the broadest possible sense, and welcomes applications from varied, non-traditional backgrounds. Inter-personal skills are very important: the firm is looking for bright, engaging people. The London office is very international: linguistic skills are useful (but not crucial). LeBoeuf needs proactive people who will contribute from day one.

training environment
Trainees spend six months in four seats. The firm's training programme is comprehensive and covers an induction programme, participation in internal seminars and training sessions and attendance at external courses, including the Professional Skills Course. Trainees are encouraged to act on their own initiative from an early stage. Trainees sit with a senior lawyer, often a partner, who can give ongoing feedback and guidance and progress is reviewed every six months.

benefits
Private medical insurance, season ticket loan, subsidised restaurant.

sponsorship & awards
The firm's policy is currently under review. Please ask about this at interview.

Partners 12
Assistant Solicitors 39
Total Trainees 8

contact
Hywel Jones

method of application
CV & covering letter

selection procedure
2 interviews

closing date for 2004
31 August 2002

application
Training contracts p.a. **4**
Applications p.a. **1,000**
% interviewed p.a. **3%**

training
Salary
1st year (2001) **£28,000**
2nd year (2001) **£32,000**
Holiday entitlement
20 days
% of trainees with a non-law degree p.a. **50%**

post-qualification
Salary (2001) £50,000

overseas offices
Albany, Almaty, Beijing, Bishkek, Boston, Brussels, Denver, Harrisburg, Hartford, Houston, Jacksonville, Johannesburg, Los Angeles, Moscow, New York, Newark, Paris, Pittsburgh, Riyadh, Salt Lake City, San Francisco, Tashkent, Washington

Le Brasseur J Tickle

Drury House, 34-43 Russell Street, London WC2B 5HA
Tel: (020) 7836 0099 Fax: (020) 7831 2215
Email: enquiries@lbjt.co.uk
6-7 Park Place, Leeds LS1 2RU
Tel: (0113) 234 1220 Fax: (0113) 234 1573
Windsor House, Windsor Lane, Cardiff CF10 3DE
Tel: (029) 2034 3035 Fax: (029) 2034 3045

firm profile
Le Brasseur J Tickle has an enviable reputation for tradition and excellence. The firm has 28 partners and approximately 100 members of staff. The firm is located in three major commercial and legal centres, London, Leeds and Cardiff, from which legal expertise is provided to all types of clients from multinational corporations to individuals.

main areas of work
Health care 55%; personal injury 5%; employment 12.5%; company commercial 15%; commercial property 7.5%; commercial litigation 5%.

trainee profile
Le Brasseur J Tickle looks to recruit trainees in the London and Leeds offices from a broad academic background with good intellectual ability and an assured outgoing personality who will prove to be responsive to the needs of the firm's clients. When recruiting trainees, the partners look to the future and to appointing trainees as assistant solicitors following qualification. Indeed a significant number of partners trained with the firm.

training environment
The firm provides an extensive legal and skills training programme for trainee solicitors and other qualified staff in addition to on-the-job training. Trainees are introduced to the firm with an induction programme covering the work of the firm's departments, the major clients, procedural matters and professional conduct. Training consists of four six month seats in the following areas: company commercial; commercial property; health care law; and litigation. Every endeavour is made to allocate the final seat, following discussion, in the area of law in which the trainee wishes to specialise after qualification. You will share an office with a partner, who will assist you and formally review your progress at the end of your seat. The PSC is taught externally. The firm is friendly with an open-door policy and there are various sporting and social events organised throughout the year.

Partners 28
Assistant Solicitors 26
Total Trainees 8

contact
Training Partner

method of application
Letter & CV

selection procedure
2 interviews

closing date for 2004
31 July 2002

application
Training contracts p.a. **3**
Applications p.a. **1,500**
% interviewed p.a. **2%**

training
Salary
1st year (2001)
(London) £19,000
(Leeds) £14,750
2nd year (2001)
(London) £21,000
(Leeds) £15,500
Holiday entitlement
4 weeks
% of trainees with a
non-law degree p.a. **50%**

post-qualification
Salary (2000)
(London) £32,500
(Leeds) £25,000
% of trainees offered job
on qualification (2001) **70%**
% of assistants (as at 1/9/00) who joined as trainees **50%**
% of partners (as at 1/9/00) who joined as trainees **45%**

Lee Bolton & Lee

1 The Sanctuary, Westminster, London SW1P 3JT
Tel: (020) 7222 5381 Fax: (020) 7222 7502
Email: enquiries@1thesanctuary.com
Website: www.leeboltonlee.com

firm profile
Founded in 1855, Lee Bolton & Lee is a successful medium sized firm based in Westminster. It is closely associated with parliamentary agents and solicitors, Rees and Freres, who provide a specialist service in parliamentary, public and administrative law.

main areas of work
Commercial; property; private client; litigation; charity; education work.

trainee profile
They seek to recruit trainees with a good degree (2:1 or above), first class communication skills, motivation, professionalism, initiative, enthusiasm, and a sense of humour.

training environment
Trainees spend six months in each of four seats: private client, property, litigation and commercial property, sitting with either a senior solicitor or a partner. Training is comprehensive and covers a full induction programme, participation in internal seminars and training sessions and attendance at external courses, including the Professional Skills Course. Trainees are given responsibility for their own files from the beginning, and whilst this might at first seem daunting, the firm operates an open door policy and help is never far away. Progress is reviewed monthly by your elected Supervisor and every three months by the Training Principal. There are various sporting and social events.

benefits
Season ticket loan, non-guaranteed bonus.

sponsorship & awards
A contribution towards LPC funding but dependent upon being offered a training contract.

Partners 14
Assistant Solicitors 10
Total Trainees 4

contact
Susie Hust

method of application
Letter & CV

selection procedure
Panel interview

closing date for 2004
End July 2002

application
Training contracts p.a. 2
Applications p.a. 800
% interviewed p.a. 3%
Required degree grade 2:1

training
Salary (2000)
1st year £18,500
2nd year £19,500
Holiday entitlement
22 days
% of trainees with a
non-law degree p.a. 50%

post-qualification
Salary (2000) £29,000
% of trainees offered job
on qualification (2000)
100%
% of assistants (as at
1/9/00) who joined as
trainees 40%
% of partners (as at 1/9/00)
who joined as trainees
15%

Lester Aldridge

Russell House, Oxford Road, Bournemouth BH8 8EX
Tel: (01202) 786 161 Fax: (01202) 786 110
Alleyn House, Carlton Crescent, Southampton SO15 2EU
Tel: (023) 8082 0400 Fax: (023) 8082 0410
Email: enquiries@lester-aldridge.co.uk
Website: www.lester-aldridge.co.uk

firm profile
LA is a dynamic business, providing both commercial and private client services. Based on the south coast (in Southampton and Bournemouth), it operates predominantly within central southern England, although it offers a number of renowned services on a national and international basis, including LA Marine and Asset Finance and Banking. LA is run as a business with a corporate-style management structure. The firm's vision is to be recognised as the best law firm within its region.

main areas of work
Litigation 34%; corporate, banking and finance 26%; private client services 19%; commercial property 15%; investment services 6%.

trainee profile
Candidates should have strong intellectual capabilities, be commercially aware, resourceful and able to relate easily to other people. IT skills and a team approach are also required.

training environment
Trainees receive an extended version of the firm's induction procedure which covers the firm's aims, values and structure, marketing, administration and support services. Training consists of four six month seats across the firm. About halfway through each seat, trainees discuss their preferences for the next seat and every attempt is made to match aspirations to the needs of the firm. Trainees have a training principal for the duration of the contract who will discuss progress every month. They receive a comprehensive formal appraisal from their team leader towards the end of each seat, and the managing partner meets all trainees as a group every three months.

benefits
Life assurance and pension schemes.

vacation placements
Places for 2002: 8; Duration: 2 weeks; Remuneration: £60 p.w.; Closing Date: March 2002.

sponsorship & awards
Discretionary.

Partners 35
Assistant Solicitors 19
Total Trainees 10

contact
Juliet Milne

method of application
Letter, CV & completed application form

selection procedure
Interview by a panel of partners

closing date for 2004
31 August 2002

application
Training contracts p.a. 5
Applications p.a. 300
% interviewed p.a. 5%
Required degree grade 2:1

training
Salary
1st year (2001) £16,500
2nd year (2001) £18,000
Holiday entitlement
22 days
% of trainees with
a non-law degree p.a. 20%

post-qualification
Salary (2001) £29,000
% of trainees offered job on qualification (2000) 100%
% of assistants (as at 1/9/01) who joined as trainees 30%
% of partners (as at 1/9/01) who joined as trainees 25%

Lewis Silkin

12 Gough Square, London EC4A 3DW
Tel: (020) 7074 8000 Fax: (020) 7832 1200
Email: train@lewissilkin.com

firm profile
Lewis Silkin places the highest priority on its relationship with clients, excellent technical ability and the commercial thinking of its lawyers. As a result, it is a profitable and distinctive firm, with a friendly and lively style.

main areas of work
The firm has a wide range of corporate clients and provides services through three main departments: corporate, litigation and property. The major work areas are: construction; corporate services, which includes company, commercial and corporate finance; commercial litigation and dispute resolution; employment; housing and project finance; marketing services, embracing advertising and marketing law; property; technology and communications, which includes IT, media and telecommunications.

trainee profile
The firm looks for trainees with keen minds and personality, who will fit into a professional but informal team. Law and non-law degrees considered.

training environment
Lewis Silkin provides a comprehensive induction and training programme, with practical 'hands-on' experience in four six month seats, three of which will be in one of the main departments. The fourth seat can be in one of the specialist areas. Trainees usually sit with a partner who can give ongoing feedback and guidance and progress is formally reviewed every three months. Trainees have the opportunity to get involved in the firm's social and marketing events and also to represent the firm at local trainee solicitors' groups and Law Centres.

benefits
Life assurance, critical illness cover, health insurance, season ticket loan, group pension plan.

vacation placements
Places for 2002: None.

sponsorship & awards
Full fees paid for LPC.

Partners 32
Assistant Solicitors 45
Total Trainees 12

contact
Ruth Willis
Head of Human Resources

method of application
Application form

selection procedure
Assessment day, including an interview with 2 partners & an analytical exercise

closing date for 2004
31 July 2002

application
Training contracts p.a. **6**
Applications p.a. **1,000**
Required degree grade **2:1**

training
Salary
1st year £25,000
2nd year £26,500
Holiday entitlement
25 days

post-qualification
Salary (2001) £40,000-£42,000

Linklaters

One Silk Street, London EC2Y 8HQ
Tel: (020) 7456 2000 Fax: (020) 7456 2222
Email: graduate.recruitment@linklaters.com
Website: www.linklaters.com

firm profile

Linklaters is one of the leading global law firms, with first-class corporate, finance and specialist practices operating throughout the world. Its lawyers work closely with leading corporates, investment banks and other major institutions, offering the highest quality advice and innovative use of technology to meet its clients' needs. Linklaters is a member of Linklaters & Alliance, which brings together five of Europe's premier law firms. It is one of the leading global legal practices, with lawyers and other professionals operating in combined teams from major financial and business centres worldwide.

main areas of work

There are three core practice areas: corporate, global finance and projects (includes capital markets, banking, projects and asset finance) and specialist groups (includes construction and engineering; corporate tax; employment, pensions and incentives; environment (including planning); EU and competition; financial markets; intellectual property; investment management; IT and communications; litigation and arbitration; real estate; restructuring and insolvency; trusts).

trainee profile

High academic achievers with outside interests, confidence and commitment to thrive in a strong client-centred, commercial environment. Desire for early involvement and responsibility. Language skills are advantageous. All degree disciplines considered.

training environment

All trainees gain experience in the core practice areas. There is one other seat of choice, and any can be spent overseas or on a client secondment. The exact seat plan will depend on your specific interests. After three months the firm discusses your progress with you – a key opportunity to confirm or change the direction of your training. At this point, it also works out with you the best mix of experience to gain during the rest of your training so you qualify with confidence.

sponsorship & benefits

CPE and LPC fees are paid in full, plus a maintenance grant of £4,500-£5,000 p.a. Language bursaries are also offered upon completion of LPC. PPP medical insurance, life assurance, pension, season ticket loan, in-house gym and corporate membership of Holmes Place, in-house dentist, doctor and physio, 24 hour subsidised restaurant.

vacation placements

Places for 2002: 120 places at Christmas, Easter and Summer. Opportunity for some summer students to spend time in one of our European offices. Remuneration: £250 p.w.

**Partners
(including local)** 357
Associates 1154
Trainees 405

contact
Sarah Emmott

method of application
Application form

selection procedure
2 interviews (same day)

application
Training contracts p.a. 150
Applications p.a. 2,500
% interviewed p.a. 20%
Required degree grade 2:1

training
Salary
1st year £28,500
2nd year £32,000
Holiday entitlement 25 days
% of trainees with a
non-law degree p.a. 40%
No. of seats available
abroad p.a. 80

post-qualification
Salary £48,000 + bonus
% of trainees offered job
on qualification 95%

overseas offices
Alicante, Amsterdam, Antwerp, Bangkok, Beijing, Berlin, Bratislava, Brussels, Bucharest, Budapest, Cologne, Frankfurt, The Hague, Hong Kong, London, Luxembourg, Madrid, Malmö, Milan, Moscow, Munich, New York, Padua, Paris, Prague, Rome, Rotterdam, São Paulo, Shanghai, Singapore, Stockholm, Tokyo, Warsaw, Washington DC

Lovells

65 Holborn Viaduct, London EC1A 2DY
Tel: (020) 7296 2000 Fax: (020) 7296 2001
Email: recruit@lovells.com
Website: www.lovells.com

firm profile
Lovells is one of the world's leading international law firms based in the City of London, with offices in Asia, Europe and North America. The firm's strength across a wide range of practice areas sets it apart from most of its competitors.

main areas of work
The firm's core areas of practice are corporate, litigation, commercial property and specialist groups (including EU/competition, intellectual property, media and telecommunications, employment, tax).

trainee profile
High calibre candidates who can demonstrate intelligence, lateral thinking, commercial awareness and personality.

training environment
Trainees spend six months in four different areas of the practice to gain as much experience as possible. They have the option of spending their third seat in an international office or on secondment to the in-house legal department of a major client. A comprehensive programme of skills training is run for trainees both in-house and externally, placing a particular emphasis on advocacy and communication. Trainees are offered as much responsibility as they can handle as well as regular reviews, six monthly appraisals and support when they need it.

benefits
PPP medical insurance, life assurance, PHI, season ticket loan, corporate gym membership of Holmes Place, staff restaurant, financial planning, in-house dentist, doctor and physiotherapist, discounts at local retailers.

vacation placements
Places for 2001: 90. Placements available at Christmas 2001 (closing date 16 November), Easter and Summer 2002 (closing date 15 February).

sponsorship & awards
CPE and LPC course fees are paid, and a maintenance grant is also provided of £5,000 for London, Guildford and Oxford and £4,500 elsewhere. In addition, £500 bonus on joining the firm; £1,000 advance in salary on joining; £500 prize for a First Class degree result; £250 for a Distinction in the LPC.

Partners 300
Assistant Solicitors 1,400
Total Trainees 140

contact
Clare Harris
Recruitment Manager

method of application
Application form

selection procedure
Assessment day: critical thinking test, group exercise, interview

closing date for 2004
31 August 2002

application
Training contracts p.a. 80
Applications p.a. 1,500
% interviewed p.a. 18%
Required degree grade 2:1

training
Salary
1st year (2001) £28,000
2nd year (2001) £32,000
Holiday entitlement
25 days
% of trainees with a non-law degree p.a. 40%
No. of seats available abroad p.a. 24

post-qualification
Salary
(2001) £50,000

international offices
Alicante, Amsterdam, Beijing, Brussels, Budapest, Chicago, Düsseldorf, Frankfurt, Hamburg, Ho Chi Minh City, Hong Kong, London, Milan, Moscow, Munich, New York, Paris, Prague, Rome, Singapore, Tokyo, Vienna, Warsaw, Washington DC, Zagreb

Mace & Jones

19 Water Street, Liverpool L2 0RP
Tel: (0151) 236 8989 Fax: (0151) 227 5010
Email: donal.bannon@maceandjones.co.uk
14 Oxford Court, Bishopsgate, Manchester M2 3WQ
Tel: (0161) 236 2244 Fax: (0161) 228 7285
Website: www.maceandjones.co.uk

firm profile
Mace & Jones is a leading regional practice in the North West and remains a full service firm while enjoying a national reputation for its commercial expertise, especially in employment, litigation/insolvency, corporate and property. The firm's clients range from national and multinational companies and public sector bodies to owner managed businesses and private individuals, reflecting the broad nature of the work undertaken. Sound practical advice is given always on a value for money basis.

main areas of work
Commercial litigation/insolvency 15%; commercial property 15%; company/commercial 15%; employment 35%; personal injury/private client/family 20%

trainee profile
The firm seeks to recruit highly motivated trainees with above average ability and the determination to succeed. The right calibre of trainee will assume responsibility early in their career. The firm provides a comprehensive internal and external training programme.

training environment
Trainees complete an induction course to familiarise themselves with the work carried out by the firm's main departments, administration and professional conduct. Training consists of four six month seats in the following departments: company/commercial, employment, commercial litigation/personal injury litigation, property law, family law. Strenuous efforts are made to ensure that trainees are able to select the training seat of their choice. A trainee will normally be required to share an office with a partner who will supervise their work and review the trainee's progress at the end of the seat. The PSC is taught externally. The firm operates an open door policy and has various social events.

Partners	29
Assistant Solicitors	45
Total Trainees	8

contact
Donal Bannon
Liverpool Office

method of application
Covering letter & typed CV which should indicate individual degree subject results

selection procedure
Interview with partners

closing date for 2004
31 March 2003

application
Training contracts p.a. **8**
Applications p.a. **1,500**
% interviewed p.a. **1%**
Required degree grade **2:1**

training
Salary
1st year (2001) **£13,000**
2nd year (2001) **£13,500**
Holiday entitlement
20 days
% of trainees with a non-law degree p.a. **40%**

post-qualification
Salary (2001) **Negotiable**
% of trainees offered job on qualification (2001) **75%**
% of assistants (as at 1/7/01) who joined as trainees **40%**
% of partners (as at 1/9/00) who joined as trainees **40%**

Macfarlanes

10 Norwich Street, London EC4A 1BD
Tel: (020) 7831 9222 Fax: (020) 7831 9607
Email: gs@macfarlanes.com
Website: www.macfarlanes.com

firm profile
A leading City firm serving national and international commercial, industrial, financial and private clients.

main areas of work
Corporate 49%; property 25%; litigation 13%; private client 13%.

trainee profile
Any degree discipline. Actual or predicted 2:1 or better.

training environment
Macfarlanes divides the training contract into four six month periods. You will usually spend time in each of the firm's four main departments (corporate; litigation; property; private client). There is an extensive in-house training programme. Trainees have responsibility for real work and make a contribution that is acknowledged and appreciated.

benefits
Twenty-one working days holiday in each calendar year (rising to 26 days upon qualification); interest free season ticket loan; pension; free permanent health insurance[*]; free private medical insurance[*]; subsidised conveyancing; subsidised health club/gym membership; subsidised firm restaurant; subscription paid to the City of London Law Society or the London Trainee Solicitors' Group.

[*]After 12 months service.

vacation placements
Places for 2002: 40; Duration: 2 weeks; Remuneration: £250 p.w.; Closing Date: 28 February 2002 but applications considered and places offered from the beginning of January 2002.

sponsorship & awards
CPE and LPC fees paid in full and a £5,000 maintenance allowance for courses studied in London, Guildford and Oxford and £4,500 for courses studied elsewhere. Prizes for those gaining distinction or commendation for the LPC.

Partners 56
Assistant Solicitors 115
Total Trainees 34

contact
Graham Stoddart

method of application
Application form & letter

selection procedure
Assessment day

closing date for 2004
31 July 2002

application
Training contracts p.a. **25**
Applications p.a. **1,500**
% interviewed p.a. **15%**
Required degree grade **2:1**

training
Salary
1st year (2001) **£28,000**
2nd year (2001) **£32,000**
Holiday entitlement
21 days
% of trainees with a non-law degree p.a. **40%**

post-qualification
Salary (2000) **£50,000**
% of trainees offered job on qualification (2000)
100%
% of assistants (as at 1/9/00) who joined as trainees **53%**
% of partners (as at 1/9/00) who joined as trainees **65%**

Manches

Aldwych House, 81 Aldwych, London WC2B 4RP
Tel: (020) 7404 4433 Fax: (020) 7430 1133
Email: sheona.clark@manches.co.uk
Website: www.manches.com

firm profile
Manches is a highly focused London and Oxford based commercial firm with strengths across a range of services and industry sectors. The firm's strategy for 2001 and beyond will see greater concentration and focus on its four core commercial industry sectors of technology, property, construction and retail, whilst continuing to be market leaders in family law.

main areas of work
Industry Sectors: Technology, property, construction and retail.
Legal Groups: Family, corporate finance (emphasis in technology), commercial property, construction, employment, commercial litigation, intellectual property, information technology and biotechnology (Oxford office).

trainee profile
The firm looks for candidates with a sound academic background, commercial acumen, enthusiasm and commitment. It wants engaging and outgoing personalities who will contribute to its development and help achieve its business goals. Clear and persuasive communication skills and tenacity are a must. The firm advises students to obtain a place on the summer vacation scheme.

training environment
The firm provides high quality, individual training. Training is generally divided into four periods of six months (usually one in a niche practice area). Its comprehensive in-house training programme enables trainees to take responsibility from an early stage ensuring that they become confident and competent solicitors. Trainees are also encouraged to participate in departmental meetings and briefings and receive regular appraisals.

benefits
Season ticket loan, BUPA after six months, permanent health insurance, life insurance, pension after six months.

vacation placements
Places for 2002: 24; Duration: 1 week; Remuneration: £175 p.w.; Closing Date: 31 January 2002.

sponsorship & awards
CPE and LPC Funding: Tuition fees and maintenance.

Partners	48
Assistant Solicitors	62
Total Trainees	18

contact
Sheona Clark
Tel: (020) 7872 8690
(Graduate Recruitment line)

method of application
Application form

selection procedure
Individual interview with 2 partners. Possible 2nd interview & assessments

closing date for 2004
31 July 2002

application
Training contracts p.a. **7-8**
Applications p.a. **1,000**
% interviewed p.a. **5%**
Required degree grade **2:1**

training
Salary (Under review)
1st year (2001)
London £23,100
2nd year (2001)
London £25,900
Holiday entitlement
22 days

post-qualification
Salary (Under review)
London £39,500 (2001)
% of trainees offered job on qualification (2001)
90%

Martineau Johnson

St. Philips House, St. Philips Place, Birmingham B3 2PP
Tel: (0121) 200 3300 Fax: (0121) 200 3330
Email: emily.dean@martjohn.co.uk
Website: www.graduates4law.co.uk

firm profile

Forward thinking and on the leading edge of commercial practice, Martineau Johnson is a substantial law firm with offices in Birmingham and London. As one of the most innovative and progressive commercial law firms, it is a recognised market leader in many areas of practice and has a high reputation. The firm recently strengthened its name and reputation by launching four brand values: Know-How, Plain Speaking, Passion and Done Deals. These encapsulate both the service provided to clients and the culture within the firm.

main areas of work

Corporate 18%; property 16%; litigation 20%; private client 15%; education 5%; intellectual property 5%; employment 4%; banking and insolvency 7%; trade and energy 10%.

trainee profile

Martineau Johnson seeks to recruit 14 trainees in the year 2004. Successful candidates must have a good degree, not necessarily in law, be motivated, outgoing, with commercial flair and business skills, and be capable of original and creative thought.

training environment

The firm is committed to the personal supervision and training of trainees. Each trainee has a personal mentor. There is a unique system of seat rotation – seats are of four months duration and can be combined so that time can be spent in six different seats or longer if preferred. The firm offers a structured training programme and, in addition to the above, trainees are encouraged to take part in the firm's varied sporting and social activities.

benefits

Pension; private health; life assurance; permanent health insurance; interest free travel loans; critical illness cover; Denplan; Birmingham Hospital Saturday Fund; gym membership; domestic conveyancing; will drafting and subscription fees.

open days

Open days (not vacation placements) held at Easter and during the summer months. Closing date for applications: 28 February 2002.

sponsorship & awards

CPE: Discretionary loan; LPC: Grant for fees and maintenance of £3,000.

Partners 41
Assistant Solicitors 100
Total Trainees 22

contact
Emily Dean

method of application
Online application form
www.graduates4law.co.uk

selection procedure
Assessment centre - half day

closing date for 2004
31 July 2002

application
Training contracts p.a. **14**
Applications p.a. **500**
% interviewed p.a. **10%**
Required degree grade **2:1**

training
Salary
1st year (2001) **£18,000**
2nd year (2001) **£19,500**
Holiday entitlement
23 days
% of trainees with a
non-law degree (2001)
40%

post-qualification
Salary (2001) **£33,000**
% of trainees offered job
on qualification (2001)
100%
% of assistants (as at
1/9/01) who joined as
trainees **66%**
% of partners (as at 1/9/01)
who joined as trainees
42%

Masons

30 Aylesbury Street, London EC1R 0ER
Tel: (020) 7490 4000 Fax: (020) 7490 2545
Email: graduate.recruitment@masons.com
Website: www.masons.com

firm profile
Masons is internationally recognised as one of the foremost legal advisers to the IT, construction and engineering, energy and infrastructure industries. Its strategy is to remain the premier legal adviser to these industries whilst remaining a leading provider of specialist skills. It has over 92 partners and more than 800 staff working in 11 offices worldwide, which share a national and international workload. The network operates as one team and the firm has a fluid approach to sharing resources and projects, always ensuring that the most appropriate people are selected for the job, regardless of where they are based. Its lawyers also regularly work in a range of jurisdictions across the world.

main areas of work
Training with Masons will give you access to first class training resources combined with hands on experience in a highly focused and exciting environment. You will be part of an expanding international team that is well known for its advice in the areas of information and technology, major projects and construction. It also has particular strength in finance, commercial property, planning, employment, specialist property litigation, company and commercial, environment, insolvency, commercial dispute resolution and pensions law.

trainee profile
Applications are welcome from both law and non-law students with a minimum 2:1 degree.

training environment
After inductions, your two year training contract will be divided into a number of 'seats'. Each seat will involve sharing an office with a partner or solicitor selected from one of the practice areas outlined above. Your rotation throughout the firm will ensure that you are exposed to a range of areas of law and to a variety of approaches. Wherever possible the firm tries to tailor the arrangement to meet individual needs.

benefits
Life assurance, private health care, subsidised restaurant and season ticket loan (London).

vacation placements
Places for 2002: 36 (London), 5 (Manchester); Duration: 2 weeks in 2 different departments, June to the end of August; Closing Date: 15 February 2002.

sponsorship & awards
Fees paid for CPE and LPC courses and maintenance grant which is currently under review.

Partners: 99*
Assistant Solicitors 290+*
Total Trainees: 51
denotes world-wide figures

contact
Kelcy Davenport

method of application
Firm's own application form

selection procedure
Assessment day followed by an interview

closing date for 2004
31 July 2002

application
Training contracts p.a. 32
Applications p.a. 2,000
% interviewed p.a. 10%
Required degree grade 2:1

training
Salary
1st year (currently under review) No less than £25,000
2nd year (currently under review) No less than £28,000
Holiday entitlement 23 days

post-qualification
Salary (under review) No less than £42,000
% of trainees offered job on qualification (2000) 94%
% of partners who joined as trainees 25%

overseas offices
Brussels, Dublin, Ghangzhou (PRC), Hong Kong, Singapore

branch offices
Bristol, Edinburgh (LSS), Glasgow (LSS), Leeds, Leeds, Manchester

May, May & Merrimans

12 South Square, Gray's Inn, London WC1R 5HH
Tel: (020) 7405 8932 Fax: (020) 7831 0011
Email: mmm@elawuk.com

firm profile
May May & Merrimans is an old established Inns firm with a broad-based practice which has a particularly strong reputation for its work with private clients, including landed estates and their related trusts.

main areas of work
Private client including tax and estate planning for UK and offshore clients; wills, settlements and probate; charity law; agricultural, commercial and residential property; civil litigation and family law; business law for private clients and unquoted companies.

trainee profile
The firm welcomes applications from law and non-law graduates with a first class academic record. The qualities it looks for in its trainees are initiative, enthusiasm, a practical turn of mind and good communication skills.

training environment
The firm's approach to training is to offer active involvement in good quality work and to maintain a careful balance between exercising supervision and encouraging trainees to accept as much responsibility as possible. The firm is not strictly departmentalised and trainees normally spend a few months of their training contract concentrating on litigation and family law and the remainder working on a variety of non-contentious matters, principally private client and property.

sponsorship & awards
Discretionary loans for LPC.

Partners 12
Assistant Solicitors 5
Total Trainees 2

contact
Alexandra Sarkis

method of application
Letter & CV

selection procedure
Interview

closing date for 2004
2 August 2002

application
Training contracts p.a. **1**
Applications p.a. **200**
% interviewed p.a. **3%**
Required degree grade **2:1**

training
Salary
Competitive with similar size/type firms
Holiday entitlement
20 days

post-qualification
% of trainees offered job on qualification (1998-2001) **100%**
% of assistants (as at 1/9/01) who joined as trainees **40%**
% of partners (as at 1/9/01) who joined as trainees **60%**

Mayer, Brown & Platt

Bucklersbury House, 3 Queen Victoria Street, London EC4N 8EL
Tel: (020) 7246 6200 Fax: (020) 7329 4465
Email: rrogers@mayerbrown.com
Website: www.mayerbrown.com

firm profile
Mayer, Brown & Platt is an international law firm headquartered in Chicago, with over 900 lawyers throughout offices across the United States, Mexico and Europe. MBP's London office, established in 1974, is the flagship of MBP's European network.

main areas of work
The principal practice areas of the firm's London offices comprise: conventional finance; project finance; leasing and asset finance; capital markets, securities and derivatives; mergers and acquisitions; and general corporate matters.

trainee profile
The firm seeks outstanding candidates with academic excellence and a flexible attitude with business acumen, along with a sense of humour, good judgement, common sense and motivation.

training environment
Trainees are inducted into the firm's culture and environment. Training seats are offered in the following departments: civil litigation; commercial; company; and banking. The litigation seat is covered by one of the firm's US international offices, usually New York or Chicago. Trainees usually move from seat to seat, sharing an office with a supervising senior associate. The Professional Skills Course is run externally and a programme of monthly in-house lectures is run for lawyers and trainees. At least three formal appraisals are carried out during the training contract, and ongoing progress is monitored at all times. MBP has a friendly, sociable environment with an open door policy. Regular evening social events are organised for all members of staff.

benefits
Private medical insurance, season ticket loan, life assurance (4 x basic salary), long term disability insurance, critical illness and pension.

vacation placements
Places for 2002: Not offered at present.

sponsorship & awards
100% funding for CPE and LPC plus maintenance grant.

Partners 8
Assistant Solicitors 15
Total Trainees 3

contact
Ricia Rogers

method of application
Application form

selection procedure
Two interviews with partners, associates & often a current trainee

closing date for 2004
31 August 2002

application
Training contracts p.a. 2
Applications p.a. 600
% interviewed p.a. 2%
Required degree grade
High 2:1

training
Salary
1st year (2001) £30,000
2nd year (2002) £35,000
Holiday entitlement
25 days
% of trainees with a non-law degree p.a. 50%

post-qualification
Salary (2000) £54,000
% of trainees offered job on qualification (2000) 100%

overseas offices
Chicago, Charlotte, Frankfurt, Houston, Köln, Los Angeles, New York, Palo Alto, Paris, Washington

representative offices
Ashgabat. Independent correspondent office: Mexico City

McCormicks

Britannia Chambers, 4 Oxford Place, Leeds LS1 3AX
Tel: (0113) 246 0622 Fax: (0113) 246 7488
Email: mccormicks@btinternet.com
Wharfedale House 37 East Parade Harrogate HG1 5LQ
Tel: (01423) 530 630 Fax: (01423) 530 709

Partners	**8**
Assistant Solicitors	**11**
Total Trainees	**8**

contact
Mark Burns
Training Partner

firm profile
McCormicks is a high profile, progressive and highly regarded firm offering a full range of legal services to both corporate and private clients. It is regarded as one of the leading firms in the North of England and has been described by the *Yorkshire Post* as 'a law firm in the top rank' and by Yorkshire Television as 'one of the region's top law firms'. The firm has a reputation for a vibrant and dynamic atmosphere.

method of application
Application form

selection procedure
Selection day & interview with Training Partner

closing date for 2004
31 July 2002

main areas of work
(In alphabetical order.) Charities; commercial litigation; company and commercial; corporate crime including VAT and Inland Revenue investigation work and tribunals; debt collection and mortgage repossessions; defamation; employment; family; general crime (especially road traffic); insolvency; intellectual property; media/entertainment; sports law; personal injury; private client – the firm is regarded as one of the leading commercial, litigation, fraud, media and sports law practices in the North.

application
Training contracts p.a. **4**
Applications p.a. **1,000**
% interviewed p.a. **10%**
Required degree grade **2:1**

training
Salary
1st year (2001)
Highly competitive

trainee profile
A McCormicks trainee will combine intellectual achievement, sense of humour, commitment to hard work and a pro-active disposition to achieving the best possible outcome for the firm and its clients.

post-qualification
Salary (2001)
Highly competitive
% of trainees offered job on qualification (2001)
75%
% of partners (as at 1/9/99) who joined as trainees
75%

training environment
You will be assigned to the appropriate department and will be supervised by a mentor. Your work and development will be constantly reviewed by your mentor together with regular file and progress reviews both by your team supervisor and by the Training Partner. This framework provides for your maximum development within a friendly, progressive and supportive environment. There is an open-door policy and a great team spirit.

vacation placements
Places for 2002: Available in summer vacation. Closing Date: Application forms by 1 January 2002.

McDermott, Will & Emery

7 Bishopsgate, London EC2N 3AQ
Tel: (020) 7577 6900 Fax: (020) 7577 6950
Website: www.mwe.com/london

firm profile
McDermott, Will & Emery was founded in 1934 and is now one of the largest international law firms, with more than 900 lawyers in 11 offices worldwide. The London office was opened in November 1998 and is quickly becoming a full-service practice providing comprehensive legal advice to a broad range of multinational and national corporate, institutional, governmental and private clients across Europe and elsewhere. The firm is unique amongst US law firms in London, as all but one of its lawyers are UK-qualified.

main areas of work
The London office is growing rapidly and has expertise in corporate finance; asset and project finance; securitisation and banking; capital markets; telecoms; IP/IT and e-business; pharmaceuticals and bio-tech; employment; pensions and employees benefits; litigation; taxation; broadcasting; insolvency; insurance; and commercial law.

trainee profile
Applications are invited from commercially aware candidates who have an outstanding academic record. The firm is also looking for a high degree of initiative and confidence.

training environment
Comprehensive in-house training in corporate and litigation, plus two other practice areas over two years. You will share an office with an experienced senior solicitor and be give a high level of responsibility and experience. The firm's trainees are considered to be part of the team immediately. MW&E is proud of its friendly and open working environment, whilst maintaining the highest levels of professional responsibility to clients. Scope exists for trainees to work on US secondment and on secondment to UK clients.

benefits
Private medical and dental insurance, life assurance, permanent health insurance, non-contributory pension, interest-free season ticket loan, gym membership.

sponsorship & awards
CPE and LPC funding and maintenance grant; Tuition for relevant courses.

Partners 498*
Associate Lawyers &
Other Fee-earners 439*
Total Trainees 2 in 2001
5 in 2003
denotes world-wide figures

method of application
Application form

closing date for 2004
31 July 2002

training
Salary
1st year (2001) £29,000

Mills & Reeve

Francis House, 3-7 Redwell Street, Norwich NR2 4TJ
Tel: (01603) 693 346 Fax: (01603) 693 248
Email: graduate.recruitment@mills-reeve.com
Website: www.mills-reeve.com

firm profile
Mills & Reeve is one of the largest UK commercial law firms and works for a range of household names. It operates throughout England and Wales from offices in Birmingham, Cambridge, London and Norwich.

main areas of work
The firm offers a full range of corporate, commercial, property, litigation and private client services to a mix of regional and national businesses. The firm is a regional leader in corporate and commercial work and a national specialist in the insurance, higher education, health, agriculture and hi-tech and bio-tech industries.

trainee profile
The firm seeks trainees with a strong academic background, maturity, energy and initiative. Strong candidates will be willing to accept responsibility and drive the business forward.

training environment
Trainees are based in the Birmingham, Cambridge or Norwich office and complete five seats. The first four seats last five months each and give the trainee a broad understanding of the nature of the firm's business. The remaining four month seat is arranged according to the interests of the trainee and their eventual specialisation. Each trainee is allocated a mentor who offers impartial guidance throughout their training contract. During each seat, trainees sit with a partner or experienced solicitor and their performance is reviewed via a mix of formal and informal appraisals. Staff at all levels are friendly and approachable and excellent support services allow trainees to concentrate on high-quality work. A full induction integrates trainees quickly into the firm and ongoing in-house lectures and training by Professional Support Lawyers support the PSC.

benefits
Life assurance at two times pensionable salary, a contributory pension scheme and 25 days holiday.

vacation placements
Applications for two week paid placements during the summer must be received before 1 March.

sponsorship & awards
The firm pays the full costs of the LPC fees and offers a maintenance grant for the LPC year. Funding for the CPE is discretionary.

Partners 60
Assistant Solicitors 176
Total Trainees 30

contact
Graduate Recruitment

method of application
Firm's application form

selection procedure
Normally one day assessment centre

closing date for 2004
15 August 2002 for training contracts
1st March 2002 for work placements

application
Training contracts p.a. 25-30
Applications p.a. **Approx 500**
% interviewed p.a. 13%
Required degree grade 2:1

training
Salary
1st year (2001) £17,000
2nd year (2001) £18,000
Holiday entitlement 25 days p.a.
% of trainees with a non-law degree 26%

post-qualification
Salary (2001) £30,000-£31,000
% of trainees offered job on qualification 84%
% of assistants (as at 1/9/01) who joined as trainees 48%
% of partners (as at 1/9/01) who joined as trainees 28%

Mishcon de Reya

21 Southampton Row, London WC1B 5HS
Tel: (020) 7440 7198 Fax: (020) 7404 5982
Email: graduate.recruitment@mishcon.co.uk
Website: www.mishcon.co.uk

firm profile
Mishcon de Reya is an unconventional commercial law firm, run by lawyers who understand business. Its lawyers have sound commercial knowledge and believe that the partnership with clients extends beyond office walls. Mishcon de Reya is an energetic and innovative practice committed to providing intelligent and creative legal advice. The practice has an open culture and many of its partners are young. Mishcon de Reya provides legal services to a wide range of corporate, entrepreneurial and individual clients and has a continuing commitment to a range of pro bono cases. Groups currently include: art, banking, financial services, technology, and communications, employment, fraud, retail and leisure, immigration and sport.

main areas of work
Litigation 30%, corporate and commercial 33%, property 28%, family 9%.

trainee profile
Those who read nothing but law books are probably not the right trainees for this firm. We want people who can meet the highest intellectual and business standards, while maintaining outside interests. Candidates should be cheerful, enterprising and ambitious - they should see themselves as future partners.

training environment
Trainees have four six month seats. Three of these are usually in the litigation, property and company commercial departments, with an opportunity to specialise in the fourth seat. Trainees share a room with an assistant solicitor or a partner and the firm style is friendly and informal. Computer literacy is encouraged and access to online legal and business databases is available. Trainees are encouraged to participate in voluntary work at Law Centres.

benefits
Medical cover, subsidised gym membership, season ticket loan, permanent health insurance, life assurance and pension.

vacation placements
Places for 2002: 12; Duration: 3 weeks; Expenses: £150 p.w.; Closing Date: 29 March 2002.

sponsorship & awards
CPE and LPC funding with bursary.

Partners 37
Assistant Solicitors 36
Total Trainees 16

contact
Human Resources Department

method of application
Application form

closing date for 2004
31 July 2002

application
Training contracts p.a. 8
Applications p.a. 800+
% interviewed p.a. 6%
Required degree grade 2:1

training
Salary
1st year £24,000
2nd year £26,000
Holiday entitlement
25 days p.a.
No. of seats available abroad p.a. Occasional secondments available

post-qualification
% of trainees retained 2001 75%
% of assistants (as at 1/8/01) who joined as trainees 38%
% of partners (as at 1/8/01) who joined as trainees 22%

Morgan Cole

Buxton Court, 3 West Way, Oxford OX2 0SZ
Tel: (01865) 262 699 Fax: (01865) 262 670
Email: louise.pye@morgan-cole.com
Website: www.morgan-cole.com

firm profile
Morgan Cole is one of the leading commercial law practices in the country, providing a comprehensive service to both individual and corporate clients in both the public and private sectors. The firm has a reputation for excellence and therefore attracts the highest quality of staff from all fields. The firm enjoys strong connections throughout the UK and the USA and is a founder member of the Association of European Lawyers, one of five leading UK law firms responsible for establishing a network of English speaking lawyers throughout Europe. The practice consists of five main divisions: business services, property, dispute management, insurance litigation and specialist insurance services. As a modern practice, it strives to meet the legal needs of clients in all sectors of industry and commerce. The firm's areas of work are acquisitions and disposals; commercial; corporate finance; employment; energy, European and competition; information technology; insolvency; intellectual property; joint ventures; management buy-outs and buy-ins; PFI; sports law; agricultural and commercial property; construction; environment/planning/health and safety; medical negligence; personal injury; professional indemnity; commercial litigation; licensing; family; alternate dispute resolution.

trainee profile
Successful candidates should be commercially aware, self motivated individuals with drive and initiative who are able to apply a logical and common-sense approach to solving client problems. The firm is seeking applications from graduates/undergraduates in both law and non-law subjects, preferably with at least a 2:1 degree.

training environment
Trainees spend not less than six months in at least three different divisions, and since each division handles a wide variety of work within its constituent teams, there is no danger of over-specialisation. Trainees also have the opportunity to be seconded to some of the firm's major clients for one of their business services seats.

vacation placements
Places for 2002: June to July; Duration: 1 week; Closing Date for Applications: 30 April 2002.

sponsorship & awards
The firm offers full funding of fees for attendance on the CPE/PgDL and LPC as well as making a contribution towards maintenance.

Partners	86
Lawyers	261
Total Trainees	40

contact
Paul Rippon
Training Principal

method of application
Firm's application form available from the HR department, Oxford

selection procedure
Assessment Centre & interview

closing date for 2004
31 July 2002

application
Required degree grade
Preferably 2:1

training
Salary
1st & 2nd year (2001)
Competitive for the London, Thames Valley and South Wales regions which are reviewed annually in line with market trends

other offices
Cardiff, Croydon, London, Reading, Swansea

Nabarro Nathanson

Lacon House, Theobald's Road, London WC1X 8RW
Tel: (0800) 056 4021 Fax: (020) 7524 6424
Email: graduateinfo@nabarro.com
Website: www.nabarro.com

firm profile
One of the UK's leading commercial law firms with offices in London, Reading and Sheffield. The firm is known for having an open but highly professional culture and expects its lawyers to have a life outside work.

main areas of work
Company and commercial law; commercial property; planning; pensions and employment; corporate finance; IP/IT; commercial litigation; construction; PFI; environmental law.

trainee profile
Nabarro Nathanson welcomes applications from law and non law undergraduates. Candidates will usually be expecting a minimum 2:1 degree. As well as strong intellectual ability graduates need exceptional qualities. These include: enthusiasm, drive and initiative, common sense, strong interpersonal skills and teamworking skills.

training environment
Trainees undertake six four-month seats which ensures maximum exposure to the firm's core practice areas (company commercial, commercial property and litigation). The firm aims to retain all trainees on qualification. In addition to the core seats, trainees have the opportunity to gain further experience by spending time in specialist areas (eg pensions, IP/IT, tax, employment), possibly in Paris or Brussels, or completing a further seat in a core area. In most cases trainees will return to the seat they wish to qualify into for the remaining four months of their contract. This ensures a smooth transition from trainee to qualified solicitor.

benefits
Trainees are given private medical insurance, 25 days holiday entitlement per annum, a season ticket loan, access to a subsidised restaurant and subsidised corporate gym membership. Trainee salaries are reviewed annually.

vacation placements
Places for 2002: 60; Duration: 3 weeks between mid-June and end of August; Closing Date: 28 February 2002.

sponsorship & awards
Full fees paid for CPE and LPC and a maintenance grant (London and Guildford: £5,000; elsewhere: £4,5l00).

Partners 107
Assistant Solicitors 219
Total Trainees 63

contact
Jane Drew

method of application
Application form

selection procedure
Interview & assessment day

closing date for 2004
31 July 2002

application
Training contracts p.a. 30
Applications p.a. 1,500
Required degree grade 2:1

training
Salary
1st year (2001)
London & Reading £28,000
Sheffield £20,000
2nd year (2001)
London & Reading £32,000
Sheffield £22,000
Holiday entitlement
25 days

post-qualification
Salary (2001)
London £48,000
(reviewed annually)

overseas offices
Brussels, Dubai*, Paris*
* Associated office

Nicholson Graham & Jones

110 Cannon Street, London EC4N 6AR
Tel: (020) 7648 9000 Fax: (020) 7648 9001
Email: info@ngj.co.uk
Website: www.ngj.co.uk

firm profile
A successful mid-sized practice, offering strength across a number of key disciplines to a broad range of corporate clients.

main areas of work
Company; commercial; litigation; property; construction and engineering; banking and insolvency; private client; intellectual property; planning and environmental; employment; sport; travel.

trainee profile
The firm recruits both law and non-law graduates with strong academic backgrounds and a practical approach.

training environment
Training is broad-based with six months in each of the main departments: company/commercial, litigation and property and a six month seat of your choice. The emphasis is on-the-job training with personal supervision from partners. There is also a comprehensive induction and in-house training programnme for each department and on a firmwide basis. The firm encourages individual development through early responsibility and client contact. Trainees participate in all activities including business development and marketing. The atmosphere is genuinely friendly and supportive and trainees' contributions are valued.

benefits
Life assurance, season ticket loan, subsidised gym membership, BUPA, 25 days holiday a year, salaries reviewed every year.

vacation placements
Eight two week placements during July 2002; Remuneration: £210 p.w.; Closing Date: 10 March 2002.

sponsorship & awards
CPE and LPC fees paid in full plus £4,000 maintenance allowance for each.

Partners 51
Assistant Solicitors 56
Total Trainees 19

contact
Gail Harcus

method of application
Application form

selection procedure
Interview & assessment

closing date for 2004
31 July 2002

application
Training contracts p.a. **10**
Applications p.a. **1,000**
% interviewed p.a. **5%**
Required degree grade **2:1**

training
Salary
1st year (2000) £25,000
2nd year (2000) £28,000
Holiday entitlement
25 days
% of trainees with a
non-law degree p.a. **Varies**

post-qualification
Salary (2000) £40,000
% of trainees offered job
on qualification (2001)
100%

overseas offices
Brussels

Norton Rose

Kempson House, Camomile Street, London EC3A 7AN
Tel: (020) 7283 6000 Fax: (020) 7283 6500
Email: grad.recruitment@nortonrose.com
Website: www.nortonrose.com

firm profile
A leading City and international law firm specialising in large-scale corporate and financial transactions. Strong in asset, project and ship finance. More than two thirds of the firm's work has an international element.

main areas of work
Corporate finance; banking; litigation; property, planning and environmental; taxation; competition; employment, pensions and incentives; intellectual property and technology.

trainee profile
Successful candidates will be commercially aware, focused, ambitious and team-orientated. High intellect and international awareness are a priority, and language skills are appreciated.

training environment
Norton Rose's seat system is innovative. In the first 16 months of the 24 month training contract, trainees will have a seat in each of the core departments of banking, commercial litigation and corporate finance, plus one in a more specialist area. The remaining time can be spent in one of three ways: all eight months in one chosen seat; or four months in one department and four months in the department in which they want to qualify; or four months abroad and four in their chosen department. In-the-field experience is considered as important as formal training at Norton Rose, and trainees are expected to learn by observing experienced lawyers at work, interacting with clients and solicitors, handling sensitive issues and organising their time as well as attending external courses. Internal competition among trainees is discouraged, as great store is placed on team-working.

benefits
Life assurance (25+), private health insurance (optional), season ticket loan, subsidised gym membership.

vacation placements
Places for 2002: 45 Summer, 15 Christmas; Duration: Summer: Three weeks, Christmas: Two weeks; Remuneration: £250 p.w.; Closing Date: 2 February 2002 for Summer, 3 November 2001 for Christmas. Five or six open days per year are also held.

sponsorship & awards
£1,000 travel scholarship, £800 loan on arrival, four weeks unpaid leave on qualification.

Partners 191*
Assistant Solicitors 668*
Total Trainees 110
* denotes world-wide figures

contact
Brendan Monaghan

method of application
Employer's application form

selection procedure
Interview & group exercise

closing date for 2004
3 August 2002

application
Training contracts p.a. **80-90**
Applications p.a. **2,500+**
% interviewed p.a. **10%**
Required degree grade **2:1**

training
Salary
1st year (2000) **£28,500**
2nd year (2000) **£32,000**
Holiday entitlement **25 days**
% of trainees with a non-law degree p.a. **40%**
No. of seats available abroad p.a. **15 (per seat move)**

post-qualification
Salary (2001) **£50,000**
% of trainees offered job on qualification (2000) **97%**

overseas offices
Athens*, Bahrain, Bangkok, Brussels, Cologne, Frankfurt, Jakarta*, London, Milan, Moscow, Munich, Paris, Piraeus*, Singapore, Warsaw
* Associated office

Olswang

90 Long Acre, London WC2E 9TT
Tel: (020) 7208 8888 Fax: (020) 7208 8800
Email: jeh@olswang.com
Website: www.olswang.com

firm profile
Forward thinking and progressive, Olswang is about realising the potential of its clients, of all of its people and the potential within every situation in which its clients find themselves. The firm's aim is simple. To be the preferred law firm of leading companies in the technology, media and telecommunications sectors. Olswang knows the players, knows the business and above all, understands the issues. This has brought rapid growth. Olswang is a 450+ strong team committed to providing innovative solutions through legal excellence.

main areas of work
Advertising; banking; commercial litigation; corporate and commercial; defamation; e-commerce; employment; EU and competition; film and TV (finance/production); information technology; intellectual property; music; private equity; property; sponsorship; sport; tax; telecommunications; TV/broadcasting.

trainee profile
Being a trainee at Olswang is both demanding and rewarding. The firm is interested in hearing from individuals with a 2:1 degree and above, exceptional drive and relevant commercial experience. In addition, it is absolutely critical that trainees fit well into the Olswang environment which is challenging, busy, energetic, individualistic, meritocratic and fun.

training environment
Olswang want to help trainees match their expectations and needs with those of the firm. Training consists of four six-month seats in the company, media and communications, litigation or property groups. You will be assigned a mentor, usually a partner, to assist and advise you throughout your training contract. In-house lectures supplement general training and six monthly appraisals assess development. Regular social events with the other trainees not only encourages strong relationship building but adds to the fun of work.

benefits
After six months: pension contributions, medical cover, life cover, dental scheme, season ticket loan, subsidised gym membership. After 12 months: PHI.

vacation placements
Places for 2002: 15 (June), 15 (July), 15 (August); Duration: 2 weeks; Remuneration: £250 p.w.; Closing Date: 1 March 2002.

Partners 58
Assistant Solicitors 117
Total Trainees 30

contact
James Hacking
Training & Graduate Recruitment Manager

method of application
CV & covering letter

selection procedure
Business case scenario, interview, psychometric test

closing date for 2004
29 July 2002

application
Training contracts p.a. **Up to 25**
Applications p.a. **Up to 3,000+**
% interviewed p.a. **2%**
Desired degree **2:1**

training
Salary
1st year (2001) **£26,500**
Holiday entitlement
23 days
% of trainees with a non-law degree p.a. **33%**

post-qualification
Salary (2001) **£46,000**

overseas offices
Brussels

Osborne Clarke

50 Queen Charlotte Street, Bristol BS1 4HE
Tel: (0117) 917 4322 Fax: (0117) 917 4323
Email: recruitment@osborneclarke.com
Website: www.osborneclarke.com

firm profile
Osborne Clarke will challenge your preconceptions about law firms. This is a firm that looks after its people, encourages individual thinkers and freedom of spirit. Its award winning management team has led the firm throught recent phenomenal growth and development. It also has 50% more people than two years ago and grew by 40% in turnover last year. For one of the UK's most forward thinking law firms it has two surprisingly simple objectives: to exceed its clients' expectations and, second only to that, to provide interesting and rewarding careers for all its people. No wonder over 90% of trainees stay on qualification.

main areas of work
Corporate (corporate finance, mergers and acquisitions, private equity), technology, media and telecoms, banking, real estate and construction, commercial, employment, pensions and incentives, litigation, tax.

trainee profile
Take it as read that candidates should have intelligence, commercial focus and strong communication skills. To succeed at Osborne Clarke they should also be down to earth, open minded and able to think outside the box.

training environment
Trainees can expect early responsibility. The firm takes an individual approach to ensure training is relevant to each trainee and offers a well structured programme. Trainees are encouraged to spend time in at least two of the firm's UK offices (London, Bristol and Thames Valley), in addition to which some international placements to Europe and the US, and client secondments are available.

benefits
Holiday entitlement of 21 days, employers' pension contributions, private healthcare cover, season ticket loan, permanent health insurance, group life assurance cover.

vacation placements
Places for 2002: 35-40. Easter or summer placements for 1-2 weeks; Closing Date: 31 January 2002; Remuneration: £150-200 p.w. depending on location .

sponsorship & awards
CPE and LPC fees and maintenance grant paid. (Some conditions apply.)

Partners 110
Assistant Solicitors 250
Trainee Solicitors 58
Total Staff 850

contact
Graduate Recruitment Team

method of application
Employer's application form, available on request or through the firm's website www.oc4jobs.com

selection procedure
Individual interviews, group exercises, selection testing

closing date for 2004
31 July 2002

application
Training contracts p.a. 30-35
Applications p.a. **1,000-1,200**
% interviewed p.a. **10%**
Required degree grade **2:1 preferred**

training
Salary (2001)
1st year **£25,000 London & Thames Valley, £19,000 Bristol**
Holiday entitlement **21 days**
% of trainees with a non-law degree p.a. Approx **40%**
No. of seats available abroad p.a. **6**

post-qualification
Salary (2001)
£34,000 Bristol, £47,500 London
% of trainees offered job on qualification **90%**

overseas offices
Barcelona, Brussels, Cologne, Copenhagen, Frankfurt, Helsinki, Madrid, Paris, Rotterdam, St Petersburg, Silicon Valley, Tallinn

Pannone & Partners

123 Deansgate, Manchester M3 2BU
Tel: (0161) 909 3000 Fax: (0161) 909 4444
Email: julia.jessop@pannone.co.uk
Website: www.pannone.com

firm profile
A high profile Manchester firm continuing to undergo rapid growth. The firm prides itself on offering a full range of legal services to a diverse client base which is split almost equally between personal and commercial clients. The firm was the first to be awarded the quality standard ISO 9001 and is a founder member of Pannone Law Group – Europe's first integrated international law group.

main areas of work
Commercial litigation 19%; personal injury 25%; corporate 13%; commercial property 8.5%; family 9.5%; clinical negligence 9%; private client 10%; employment 6%.

trainee profile
Selection criteria include a high level of academic achievement, teamwork, organisation and communication skills, a wide range of interests and a connection with the North West.

training environment
An induction course helps trainees adjust to working life, and covers the firm's quality procedures and good practice. Regular trainee seminars cover the work of other departments within the firm, legal developments and practice. Additional departmental training sessions focus in more detail on legal and procedural matters in that department. Four seats of six months are spent in various departments and trainees' progress is monitored regularly. Trainees have easy access to support and guidance on any matters of concern. Work is tackled with gusto here, but so are the many social gatherings that take place.

vacation placements
Places for 2002: 50; Duration: 1 week; Remuneration: None; Closing Date: 8 March 2002.

Partners 61
Assistant Solicitors 60
Total Trainees 20

contact
Julia Jessop

method of application
Application form & CV

selection procedure
Individual interview, second interview comprises a tour of the firm & informal lunch

closing date for 2004
9 August 2002

application
Training contracts p.a. **8**
Applications p.a. **500**
% interviewed p.a. **12%**
Required degree grade **2:2**

training
Salary
1st year (2000) **£16,500**
2nd year (2000) **£18,500**
Holiday entitlement
20 days
% of trainees with a
non-law degree p.a. **50%**

post-qualification
Salary (2001) **£27,000**
% of trainees offered job
on qualification (2001) **72%**
% of assistants who joined
as trainees **35%**
% of partners who joined
as trainees **33%**

Payne Hicks Beach

10 New Square, Lincoln's Inn, London WC2A 3QG
Tel: (020) 7465 4300 Fax: (020) 7465 4400
Email: apalmer@paynehicksbeach.co.uk
Website: www.paynehicksbeach.co.uk

firm profile
Payne Hicks Beach is a medium-sized firm based in Lincoln's Inn. It primarily provides specialist tax, trusts and probate advice to individuals and families. It also undertakes corporate and commercial work.

main areas of work
Private client 33%; commercial litigation 13%; commercial property 12%; matrimonial and family law/litigation 14%; residential/agricultural property 10%; tax (business and corporate) 10%; corporate/commercial 8%.

trainee profile
The firm looks for law and non-law graduates with a good academic record, a practical ability to solve problems, enthusiasm and an ability to work hard and deal appropriately with their colleagues and the firm's clients.

training environment
Following an initial induction course, trainees usually spend six months in four of the firm's departments. Working with a partner, they are involved in the day to day activities of the department, including attending conferences with clients, counsel and other professional advisers. Assessment is continuous and you will be given responsibility as you demonstrate ability and aptitude. To complement the PSC, the firm runs a formal training system for trainees and requires them to attend lectures and seminars on various topics.

benefits
Season travel ticket loan, life assurance 4 x salary, permanent health insurance.

sponsorship & awards
Fees for the CPE and LPC are paid.

Partners 24
Assistant Solicitors 17
Total Trainees 4

contact
Mrs Alice Palmer

method of application
Handwritten letter & CV

selection procedure
Interview

closing date for 2004
1 August 2002

application
Training contracts p.a. **2**
Applications p.a. **1,000**
% interviewed p.a. **3%**
Required degree grade **2:1**

training
Salary
1st year (2001) **£22,000**
2nd year (2001) **£24,500**
Holiday entitlement
4 weeks
% of trainees with a
non-law degree p.a. **50%**

post-qualification
Salary (2001) **£42,000**
% of trainees offered job
on qualification (2000) **67%**
% of assistants (as at
1/9/01) who joined as
trainees **35%**
% of partners (as at 1/9/01)
who joined as trainees
20%

Penningtons

Bucklersbury House, 83 Cannon Street, London EC4N 8PE
Tel: (020) 7457 3000 Fax: (020) 7457 3240
Website: www.penningtons.co.uk

firm profile
A London and South East law firm, with offices in the City, Basingstoke, Godalming, Newbury and Paris. There are four main departments. Specialist units cover industry sectors and key overseas jurisdictions, including North America, South Africa, Italy, France and India.

main areas of work
Property 37%; litigation (including shipping and family) 28%; corporate/commercial 21%; private client 14%.

trainee profile
Penningtons is looking for bright, enthusiastic, highly motivated and well rounded individuals with a keen interest in the practice of law.

training environment
Six month seats are provided in three or four of the following departments: corporate/commercial, property, litigation, and private client. Individual preference is usually accommodated in the second year. Trainees are given a thorough grounding in the law. International opportunities do arise. There are in-house lectures and reviews and appraisals occur regularly. The firm aims to utilise trainees' talents to their full, but is careful not to overburden them. All staff are supportive and the atmosphere is both professional and informal.

benefits
Subsidised sports and social club, life assurance, private medical, season ticket loan.

vacation placements
Places for 2002: 60 on London Open Days at Easter; Remuneration: Expenses; Closing Date: 15 February 2002. Some summer vacation placements out of London. Closing date: 30 April 2002.

sponsorship & awards
LPC funding is available. Awards are given for commendation or distinction in LPC.

Partners 53*
Assistant Solicitors 67*
Total Trainees 21
denotes world-wide figures

contact
Lesley Lintott

method of application
Handwritten letter, CV & application form

selection procedure
1 interview with a partner & director of studies

closing date for 2004
15 August 2002

application
Training contracts p.a. **10/11**
Applications p.a. **2,000**
% interviewed p.a. **5%**
Required degree grade **2:1**

training
Salary
1st year (2001)
£23,000 (London)
2nd year (2001)
£25,000 (London)
Holiday entitlement
23 days
% of trainees with a non-law degree p.a. **40%**

post-qualification
Salary (2000)
£38,000 (London)
% of trainees offered job on qualification (2000) **80%**
% of assistants (as at 1/9/00) who joined as trainees **45%**
% of partners (as at 1/9/00) who joined as trainees **49%**

overseas offices
Paris

Pinsent Curtis Biddle

Dashwood House, 69 Old Broad Street, London EC2M 1NR
Tel: (020) 7418 7097 Fax: (020) 7418 7050
3 Colmore Circus, Birmingham B4 6BH
Tel: (0121) 626 5731 Fax: (0121) 626 1040
1 Park Row, Leeds LS1 5AB
Tel: (0113) 244 5000 Fax: (0113) 244 8000
Email: maxine.jayes@pinsents.com
Website: www.pinsents.com

Partners	161
Assistant Solicitors	263
Total Trainees	69

contact
Ms Maxine Jayes
Recruitment Hotline:
(020) 7418 7097

method of application
Application form

selection procedure
Assessment centre including interview

closing date for 2004
31 July 2002

application
Training contracts p.a. 30+
Applications p.a. 4,000
Required degree grade 2:1

training
Salary
1st year (2001) £28,000
2nd year (2001) £30,000
Holiday entitlement
25 days

post-qualification
Salary (2001)
Approx £48,000
% of trainees offered job on qualification (2001) 80%

overseas offices
Brussels

firm profile
Pinsent Curtis Biddle is a major commercial firm. It has a first class reputation based on its work for a substantial list of quality corporate clients. The firm is ranked in the top 10 of named legal advisers to UK listed companies, spanning merchant banks to new technology businesses.

main areas of work
Corporate; commercial; employment; insolvency; litigation and professional indemnity; media and IT; pensions; property; tax.

trainee profile
The firm seeks applications from both law and non-law graduates with a good honours degree. However, not only is a good academic background required, but also personality, commitment and common sense. Given that the bulk of work is business oriented, trainees need to communicate with the business community, be interested in its problems and have the ability to give positive commercial advice.

training environment
Trainees sit in four seats of six months ranging from corporate, property, litigation, commercial, tax and employment. Hands-on experience is seen as an essential part of the learning process, so early responsibility and contact with clients are encouraged. Partners or associates oversee your work and are on hand to help and advise. The PSC is taught in-house, and there is an internal structured development programme to broaden your knowledge. The firm has an open-door policy and informal atmosphere, and there are many social and sporting activities for its staff.

vacation placements
Easter and Summer schemes.
Places for 2002: 140; Duration: 1 week; Closing Date: 28 February 2002.

sponsorship & awards
CPE/ LPC fees are paid. In addition to this, maintenance grants of £2,500 for CPE and £4,500 for LPC are offered.

Prettys

Elm House, 25 Elm Street, Ipswich IP1 2AD
Tel: (01473) 232 121 Fax: (01473) 230 002
Email: mail@prettys.co.uk
Website: www.prettys.co.uk

firm profile
Prettys is one of the largest and most successful legal practices in East Anglia. The firm is located in the centre of the East Anglian business community, with the expanding hi-tech corridor between Ipswich and Cambridge to the west, Felixstowe to the east and the City of London 60 minutes away to the south. The firm's lawyers are approachable and pragmatic. It provides expert advice to national and regional businesses – in particular owner managed enterprises. It has specialist expertise in shipping, insurance and agriculture. As members of Galaxy (a network of European firms) it has a recognised niche speciality, providing legal assistance to corporate and private clients travelling or working abroad.

main areas of work
Prettys' broad-based practice offers a full service to all its clients. Business law services: company, commercial, shipping, transport, construction, intellectual property, information technology, property, employment, insurance, professional indemnity and health and safety. Personal law services: French property, overseas litigation, personal injury, clinical negligence, financial services, estates, agriculture, conveyancing and family.

trainee profile
Prettys' trainees are the future of the firm. Applicants should be able to demonstrate a desire to pursue a career in East Anglia. Trainees are given considerable responsibility early on and the firm is therefore looking for candidates who are well motivated, enthusiastic and have a good common sense approach. IT skills are essential. Languages are valued – you will have a real opportunity to use them.

training environment
A two week induction program will introduce you to the firm, its IT and ISO 9001 procedures. You will receive continuous supervision and three monthly appraisals. Training is in four six month seats with some choice in your second year and the possibility of remaining in the same department for two seats. Trainees work closely with a partner, meeting clients and becoming involved in all aspects of the department's work. Frequent training seminars are provided in-house. The PSC is taken externally.

additional information
One day placements are available (apply to Angela Gage). A trainee brochure is available on request or online. Visit us at the career fairs at Nottingham, Leicester and UEA.

sponsorship & awards
Discretionary.

Partners 15
Total Trainees: 9

contact
Angela Gage

method of application
Handwritten application letter & CV

closing date for 2004
Apply by the end of August 2002 to begin 2004

application
Training contracts p.a. 4-5
Required degree grade
2:1 preferred in law or other relevant subject.
Good A Levels

training
Salary
1st year Above Law Society guidelines

Pritchard Englefield

14 New St, London EC2M 4HE
Tel: (020) 7972 9720 Fax: (020) 7972 9722
Email: po@pritchardenglefield.eu.com
Website: www.pritchardenglefield.eu.com

firm profile
A medium-sized City firm practising a mix of general commercial and non-commercial law with many German and French clients. Despite its strong commercial departments, the firm still undertakes family and private client work and is known for its clinical negligence and PI practice and its strong international flavour.

main areas of work
All main areas of commercial practice including litigation, company/commercial (UK, German and French) and employment, also estate and trusts, personal injury, clinical negligence and family.

trainee profile
Normally only high academic achievers with a second European language (especially German and French) are considered. However, a lower second degree coupled with exceptional subsequent education or experience could suffice.

training environment
An induction course acquaints trainees with the computer network, library and administrative procedures and there is a formal in-house training programme. Four six month seats make up most of your training. You can usually choose some departments, and you could spend two six month periods in the same seat. Over two years, you learn advocacy, negotiating, drafting and interviewing, attend court, use your language skills and meet clients. Occasional talks and seminars explain the work of the firm, and you can air concerns over bi-monthly lunches with the partners comprising the Trainee panel. PSC is taken externally over two years. Quarterly drinks parties, musical evenings and ten-pin bowling number amongst popular social events.

benefits
Some subsidised training, luncheon vouchers.

sponsorship & awards
£2,000.

Partners 25
Assistant Solicitors 11
Total Trainees 9

contact
Graduate Recruitment

method of application
Standard application form available from Graduate Recruitment

selection procedure
1 interview only in September

closing date for 2004
31 July 2002

application
Training contracts p.a. 3-4
Applications p.a. 300–400
% interviewed p.a. 10%
Required degree grade
Generally 2:1

training
Salary
1st year (2000) £19,000
2nd year (2000) £19,250
Holiday entitlement
25 days
% of trainees with a non-law degree p.a.
Approx 50%

post-qualification
Salary (2000)
Approx £30,000
% of trainees offered job on qualification (2000) 75%
% of assistants (as at 1/9/00) who joined as trainees 50-75%
% of partners (as at 1/9/01) who joined as trainees 50%

overseas offices
Hong Kong

Radcliffes

5 Great College Street, Westminster, London SW1P 3SJ
Tel: (020) 7222 7040 Fax: (020) 7222 6208
Email: marie.o'shea@radcliffes.com
Website: www.radcliffes.com

firm profile
A distinctive, highly accomplished law firm, Radcliffes combines traditional values like integrity and prompt response with a client-focused approach to everything it does. From its offices in the heart of Westminster, the firm handles commercial matters and private client work with equal skill, empathy and understanding of clients' individual needs.

main areas of work
The firm is organised into five departments: company/commercial, litigation and dispute resolution, commercial property, tax and private client, and family law. Experts within these departments integrate their knowledge in the firm's specialist groups: growing businesses, property investment and development, private client, charity and health.

trainee profile
Its aim is to recruit trainee solicitors who have a real prospect of becoming future partners. The firm seeks not just academic but also extra curricular activities, self-confidence, determination and a sense of humour.

training environment
Trainees are introduced to the firm with a full induction week.

benefits
Health insurance, season ticket loan, life assurance, PHI.

vacation placements
Places for 2002: 10; Duration: 2 weeks; Remuneration: £130 p.w.; Closing Date: 29 March 2002.

Partners **36**
Assistant Solicitors **20**
Total Trainees **13**

contact
Marie O'Shea
Administration Secretary

method of application
CV & covering letter or EAF

selection procedure
2 Interviews with partners

closing date for 2004
26 July 2002

application
Training contracts p.a. **4**
Applications p.a. **1016**
% interviewed p.a. **9%**
Preferred degree grade **2:1**

training
Salary
1st year (2000) **£20,000**
2nd year (2000) **£21,500**
Holiday entitlement
22 days p.a.

post-qualification
Salary (2000) **£37,000**
% of trainees offered job on qualification (2000) **100%**
% of assistants (as at 1/9/00) who joined as trainees **50%**
% of partners (as at 1/9/00) who joined as trainees **50%**

Reed Smith Warner Cranston

Pickfords Wharf, Clink St, London SE1 9DG
Tel: (020) 7403 2900 Fax: (020) 7403 4221
Email: tclaxton@reedsmith.co.uk
Website: www.reedsmith.co.uk

firm profile
Reed Smith Warner Cranston is a transatlantic law firm with two UK offices located in London and Coventry and a significant US presence. The UK is known for its international work and handles all types of commercial transactions for well-known clients.

main areas of work
The firms is divided into four core departments: business and finance, international litigation, real estate and employment.

trainee profile
Enthusiastic, proactive, bright, commercially-minded graduates who want to work in a friendly atmosphere where personality, a sense of humour and a hands-on approach are encouraged.

training environment
To help trainees build a strong career, the firm invests heavily in training (approximately one training session per week) covering a range of skills including advocacy, drafting and marketing. The firm provides an infomal but fast-paced working environment where trainees are immediately given access to clients and fulfilling work, often with an international bias. Trainees who are fluent French speakers will be given opportunities to develop these skills. The firm has four seats available in business and finance, international litigation, real estate and employment. Progress is reviewed regularly by a senior partner.

benefits
BUPA, IFSTL, life assurance, permanent health insurance, pension contributions (after qualifying period).

vacation placements
Places for Summer 2002: 12; Duration: 2 weeks; Remuneration: £400; Closing Date: 31 March 2002.

sponsorship & awards
CPE/LPC fees and maintenance grant plus interest-free loan.

Partners 27
Assistant Solicitors 29
Total Trainees 7

contact
Tassy Claxton
Recruitment Co-ordinator

method of application
Application form & covering letter

selection procedure
Assessment day:
2 interviews, aptitude test & presentation

closing date for 2004
31 July 2002

application
Training contracts p.a. **4**
Applications p.a. **1000**
% interviewed p.a. **3%**
Required degree grade **2:1**

training
Salary
1st year (2001) £26,500
2nd year (2001) £30,000
Holiday entitlement
25 days
% of trainees with
a non-law degree **25%**

post-qualification
Salary (2001) **£47,000**

Reynolds Porter Chamberlain

Chichester House, 278-282 High Holborn, London WC1V 7HA
Tel: (020) 7973 9270 Fax: (020) 7242 1431
Email: rpc@rpc.co.uk
Website: www.rpc.co.uk

firm profile
Reynolds Porter Chamberlain is a leading commercial law firm with approximately 200 lawyers. In addition to its main offices in Holborn, the firm has an expanding office at Leadenhall Street in the City which serves its insurance clients. Best known as a major litigation practice, particularly in the field of professional negligence, RPC also has thriving corporate, commercial property, private client and construction departments. Another rapidly expanding part of the firm is its media and technology unit. This handles major defamation actions and has dealt with some of the biggest internet deals to date.

main areas of work
Litigation 60%; corporate 10%; commercial property 10%; construction 10%; media and technology 5%; family/private client 5%.

trainee profile
The firm appoints ten trainees each year from law and non-law backgrounds. Although proven academic ability is important (they require a 2:1 or above), RPC also values flair, energy, business sense, commitment and the ability to communicate and relate well to others.

training environment
As a trainee you will receive first rate training in a supportive working environment. You will work closely with a partner and be given real responsibility as soon as you are ready to handle it. At least six months will be spent in each of the three main areas of the practice and the firm encourages trainees to express a preference for their seats. This provides a thorough grounding and the chance to develop confidence as you see matters through to their conclusion. In addition to the externally provided Professional Skills Course the firm provides a complimentary programme of in-house training.

benefits
Four weeks holiday, bonus schemes, private medical insurance, income protection benefits, season ticket loan, subsidised gym membership, active social calendar.

vacation placements
Places for July 2002: 12; Duration: 2 weeks; Remuneration: £200 p.w.; Closing Date: 28 February 2002.

sponsorship & awards
CPE Funding: Fees paid plus £4,000 maintenance; LPC Funding: Fees paid plus £4,000 maintenance.

Partners 54
Assistant Solicitors 135
Total Trainees 17

contact
Sally Andrews
Human Resources Director

method of application
Handwritten covering letter & application form

selection procedure
Assessment days held in September

closing date for 2004
16 August 2002

application
Training contracts p.a. **10**
Applications p.a. **600**
% interviewed p.a. **7.5%**
Required degree grade **2:1**

training
Salary
1st year (2001) **£25,000**
2nd year (2001) **£27,000**
Holiday entitlement
20 days
% of trainees with a non-law degree p.a. **25%**

post-qualification
Salary (2001) **£45,000**
% of trainees offered job on qualification (2001) **86%**
% of assistants (as at 1/9/01) who joined as trainees **50%**
% of partners (as at 1/9/01) who joined as trainees **35%**

Richards Butler

Beaufort House, 15 St. Botolph Street, London EC3A 7EE
Tel: (020) 7247 6555 Fax: (020) 7247 5091
Email: gradrecruit@richardsbutler.com

firm profile
Established in 1920, Richards Butler is noted for the exceptional variety of its work. It has acknowledged strengths in commercial disputes, commodities, competition, corporate finance, energy law, insurance, media/entertainment, property and shipping, in each of which it has international prominence.

main areas of work
Banking/commercial/corporate/finance 32%; insurance/international trade and commodities/shipping 29%; commercial disputes 23%; commercial property 16%.

trainee profile
Candidates should be players rather than onlookers, work well under pressure and be happy to operate as a team member or team leader as circumstances dictate. Candidates from diverse backgrounds are welcome, including mature students with commercial experience and management skills.

training environment
Four or five seat rotations enable Richards Butler to provide practical experience across as wide a spectrum of the law as possible. Trainees can also apply for secondment to one of the firm's overseas offices, Hong Kong, Paris, Abu Dhabi, São Paulo, or to one of their client in-house legal teams.

benefits
Performance related bonus, life insurance, BUPA, interest-free season ticket loan, subsidised staff restaurant, staff conveyancing allowance.

vacation placements
Places for 2002: 20; Duration: To be confirmed; Remuneration: £200 p.w.; Closing Date: 28 February 2002. In addition, the firm offers overseas scholarships to four students.

sponsorship & awards
CPE and LPC fees and maintenance paid.

Partners 109*
Fee earners 419*
Total Trainees 55*
denotes world-wide figures

contact
Jaqueline Senior

method of application
Online application form

selection procedure
Selection exercise & interview

closing date for 2004
31 July 2002

application
Training contracts p.a. **20**
Applications p.a. **2,000**
% interviewed p.a. **5%**
Required degree grade **2:1**

training
Salary
1st year (2000) **£25,000**
2nd year (2000) **£28,000**
Holiday entitlement
25 days
% of trainees with a
non-law degree p.a. **33%**
No. of seats available
abroad p.a. **10**

post-qualification
Salary (2001)
£48,000 plus bonus
% of assistants who
joined as trainees **59%**
% of partners who
joined as trainees **54%**

overseas offices
Abu Dhabi, Beijing, Brussels, Doha*, Hong Kong, Muscat*, Paris, Piraeus, São Paulo
Associated office

Rickerby Watterson

Ellenborough House, Wellington Street, Cheltenham GL50 1YD
Tel: (01242) 224 422 Fax: (01242) 518 428
Email: rw@rickerby.co.uk
Website: www.rickerby.co.uk

firm profile
One of the South West's growing law firms, advising a wide range of private and commercial clients. The firm has ambitious plans to develop the practice, so now is an exciting time to join the team.

main areas of work
Company/commercial (including e-commerce, information technology and intellectual property), commercial property, education, employment, family, insolvency, litigation, private client, residential property.

trainee profile
Rickerby Watterson regards its trainees as potential partners for the future. The firm has an excellent record of retaining trainees post-qualification and several of the firm's current equity partners trained with the firm. Successful candidates may come from various backgrounds but all must be team players that have a 'can do' attitude, strong communication and problem-solving skills, be self-motivated and have a sense of humour.

training environment
Rickerby Watterson deliberately takes on a relatively small number of trainees and works hard to ensure they are treated as individuals. Trainees spend six months in four placement areas, covering contentious and non-contentious law. Each trainee is allocated a training supervisor who oversees work and development. The firm's training is very hands-on. Under supervision trainees may conduct their own files and are often the first point of contact with clients. The firm has a thriving social committee that organises events for staff throughout the year.

benefits
Non-contributory pension, life assurance, 24 days holiday.

Partners 17
Assistant Solicitors 19
Total Trainees 4

contact
Lesley Szperling
Personnel & Training Manager

method of application
Application form & CV

selection procedure
Interview & assessment day

closing date for 2004
April 2003

application
Training contracts p.a. **3-4**
Applications p.a. **200**
% interviewed p.a. **10%**
Required degree grade **2:1**

training
Salary
1st year (2001) **£15,000**
2nd year (2001) **£16,000**
Holiday entitlement **24 days**

post-qualification
Salary
£25,000 (2001)
% of trainees offered job on qualification **100%**

Rowe & Maw

20 Black Friars Lane, London EC4V 6HD
Tel: (020) 7248 4282 Fax: (020) 7248 2009
Email: roweandmaw@roweandmaw.co.uk
Website: www.roweandmaw.co.uk

firm profile
Founded 100 years ago, Rowe & Maw is a leading commercial firm, with offices in London, including one at Lloyd's, Manchester and in Brussels. Its strength lies in advising companies and businesses on day-to-day work and special projects.

main areas of work
Corporate 34%, litigation 22%, property 11%, pensions 8%, intellectual property 8%, construction 7%, banking and projects 6%, employment 4%.

trainee profile
The firm is interested in students with a good academic record and a strong commitment to law. Commercial awareness gained through legal or business work experience is an advantage. Extra curricular activities are taken into consideration. Trainees are expected to remain with the firm upon qualification and to become future partners. The current senior partner trained with the firm.

training environment
There are September and March intakes. Training divides into four six month seats. All trainees spend time in the corporate, litigation and property departments, frequently working for blue chip clients. Secondments to Brussels or to clients in the UK or abroad are an option for some. The firm has a professional development and training programme which covers subjects like EU law and the workings of the City. Advocacy and drafting skills are also taught. Trainees are encouraged to join in the sports and social life and to be active members of the team from day one.

benefits
Interest-free season ticket loan, subsidised membership of sport clubs, private health scheme.

vacation placements
Places for 2002: 25; Duration: 2 weeks; Remuneration in 2000: £200 p.w.; Closing Date: 28 February 2002.

sponsorship & awards
CPE and LPC fees paid and £4,000 (£4,500 for London/Guildford) maintenance p.a. (in 2000).

Partners 80
Assistant Solicitors 150
Total Trainees 40

contact
Sophie Wood

method of application
Application form

selection procedure
Selection workshops including an interview, a business exercise & group exercise

closing date for 2004
15 August 2002

application
Training contracts p.a. **25**
Applications p.a. **1,000**
% interviewed p.a. **7%**
Required degree grade **2:1**

training
Holiday entitlement **25 days**
% of trainees with a non-law degree p.a. **50%**
No. of seats available abroad p.a. **2**

post-qualification
Salary (2001) **£48,000**
% of trainees offered job on qualification (2001) **85%**
% of assistants (as at 1/9/01) who joined as trainees **50%**
% of partners (as at 1/9/01) who joined as trainees **40%**

Russell-Cooke

2 Putney Hill, London SW15 6AB
Tel: (020) 8789 9111 Fax: (020) 8788 1656
Email: traineeapplications@russell-cooke.co.uk

firm profile
A medium-sized practice with three offices in the London area. The City office deals primarily with commercial and contentious property. The Putney office has a range of specialist departments including company/commercial, crime, judicial review, commercial and construction litigation, matrimonial, French property and tax, domestic and commercial conveyancing, personal injury litigation, private client and trusts. The Kingston-upon-Thames office runs a specialist childcare department plus matrimonial, domestic conveyancing and crime.

main areas of work
Commercial property 20%; company commercial 10%; commercial litigation 15%; public law 10%; private client 10%; domestic conveyancing 10%; matrimonial 10%; crime 10%; personal injury 5%.

trainee profile
Trainees will need at least two A grades and a B grade at A Level and a 2:1 degree, though not necessarily in law. You will also need to be good at the practical business of advising and representing clients. Intellectual rigour, adaptability and the ability, under pressure, to handle a diverse range of people and issues efficiently and cost-effectively are vital attributes.

training environment
Trainees are usually offered four seats lasting six months each. Photocopying and researching points of law will not take up all your time in the firm. You will have the chance to manage your own case work and deal directly with clients, with supervision suited to your needs and the needs of the department and clients. Internal training and an annual executive staff conference supplement the externally provided PSC. Social events include quiz nights, wine tasting, summer and Christmas parties and thriving cricket and netball teams.

Partners 26
Assistant Solicitors 37
Total Trainees 9

contact
Julie Brown

method of application
CV & covering letter

selection procedure
First & second interviews

closing date for 2004
11 August 2002

application
Training contracts p.a. **4**
Applications p.a. **500**
% interviewed p.a. **7%**
Required degree grade **2:1**

training
Salary
1st year (2001) **£19,500**
2nd year (2001) **£21,000**
Holiday entitlement
22 days
% of trainees with a
non-law degree p.a. **50%**

post-qualification
Salary (2000) **Market**
% of trainees offered job
on qualification (2000)
100%
% of assistants (as at
1/9/00) who joined as
trainees **40%**
% of partners (as at 1/9/00)
who joined as trainees
50%

Russell Jones and Walker

Swinton House, 324 Gray's Inn Road, London WC1X 8DH
Tel: (020) 7837 2808 Fax: (020) 7837 2941
Email: enquiries@rjw.co.uk
Website: www.rjw.co.uk

firm profile
Russell Jones and Walker was founded in London in the 1920s but has expanded in recent years to become one of the largest litigation practices in the country with more than 618 lawyers and support staff and offices in London, Leeds, Birmingham, Bristol, Manchester, Sheffield, Newcastle upon Tyne, Cardiff, Edinburgh and Northampton.

main areas of work
Personal injury/clinical negligence 66%; criminal 13%; commercial litigation 12%; employment 5%; family/probate 2%; commercial and domestic conveyancing 2%.

trainee profile
Russell Jones and Walker are looking for candidates who are motivated and hard-working with a sense of humour and the ability and confidence to accept responsibility in fee-earning work and client care.

training environment
Each trainee will spend six months in four different departments under the supervision of a partner or senior solicitor. Your supervisor will conduct a three-month assessment and six-month review. A full induction programme and IT training is provided, together with a comprehensive in-house education timetable. The training partner supervises all aspects of the training contract. The firm is extremely sociable and trainees are encouraged to participate in social and sporting events.

benefits
Season ticket loan, pension, private healthcare or gym membership, group life assurance, all subject to qualifying periods.

vacation placements
Unfortunately the firm does not offer vacation placements.

sponsorship & award
LPC Funding: Interest-free loan provided to assist with fees available.

Partners 49
Assistant Solicitors 95
Total Trainees 16
(London and regional)

contact
HR Officer (Recruitment)

method of application
Application form –
available from 1 April 2002

closing date for 2004
31 July 2002

application
Training contracts p.a. **10**
Applications p.a. **800**
% interviewed p.a. **5%**
Required degree grade **2:1**

training
Salary (in London)
1st & 2nd seat £19,500 & £20,750
3rd & 4th seat £21,250 & £22,500
Holiday entitlement
4 weeks
% of trainees with a
non-law degree p.a. **50%**

post-qualification
Salary (2001) c.£32,000 (London)
% of trainees offered job on qualification (2001) **65%**
% of assistants (as at 1/9/01) who joined as trainees c.**25%**
% of partners (as at 1/9/01) who joined as trainees **10%**

Salans Hertzfeld & Heilbronn HRK

Clements House, 14-18 Gresham Street, London EC2V 7NN
Tel: (020) 7509 6000 Fax: (020) 7726 6191
Email: london@salans.com

firm profile
Salans Hertzfeld & Heilbronn ('Salans') is a multinational law firm with full-service offices in the City of London, Paris and New York, together with further offices in Moscow, St Petersburg, Warsaw, Kyiv, Almaty and Baku. The firm has currently over 450 fee-earners, including over 100 partners.

main areas of work
London Office: Banking and finance/corporate 50%; litigation 25%; employment 15%; commercial property 10%.

trainee profile
Candidates need to have high academic qualifications and the ability to approach complex problems in a practical and commercial way. The firm looks to recruit those who demonstrate an ability and a willingness to assume responsibility at an early stage, possess common sense and good judgement. Language skills are also valued.

training environment
The firm operates an in-house training scheme for both trainees and assistant solicitors. In addition, trainees will be offered the opportunity to attend external courses wherever possible. Trainees are at all times supervised by a partner and encouraged to take an active part in the work of their department. The caseload of the trainee will, in each case, depend on the trainee's level of expertise and experience. Where possible the firm seeks to recruit its trainees at the end of the training periods.

benefits
Private healthcare, pension, season ticket loan.

sponsorship & awards
LPC tuition fees paid.

Partners 106
Assistant Solicitors 219
Total Trainees 7

contact
Alison Gaines
Partner

method of application
Handwritten letter & CV

selection procedure
2 interviews with partners

closing date for 2004
31 July 2002

application
Training contracts p.a.
3 or 4
Applications p.a. **500+**
% interviewed p.a. **5%**
Required degree grade **2:1**

training
Salary
1st year (2000) £22,500
2nd year (2000) £23,500
Holiday entitlement
25 days
% of trainees with a non-law degree p.a.
Variable
No. of seats available abroad p.a. **None at present**

post-qualification
Salary (2001) **Variable**
% of trainees offered job on qualification (2001)
75%

overseas offices
Almaty, Baku, Kyiv, Moscow, New York, Paris, St Petersburg, Warsaw

Shadbolt & Co

Chatham Court, Lesbourne Road, Reigate RH2 7LD
Tel: (01737) 226 277 Fax: (01737) 234 660
Email: sally_thorndale@shadboltlaw.co.uk
Website: www.shadboltlaw.co.uk

firm profile
Established in 1991, Shadbolt & Co is a dynamic, progressive firm committed to high quality work and excellence in its field both in the UK and internationally. The firm is well known for its strengths in major projects, construction and engineering and dispute resolution/litigation with expansion into corporate/commercial, employment, commercial property, IT/e-commerce, aviation and marine insurance. Most partners have City backgrounds and the firm includes lawyers who have both engineering and legal qualifications. The atmosphere is young and informal with various social and sporting activities.

main areas of work
Corporate and commercial disputes 40%; projects/non-contentious construction and engineering 30%; corporate and commercial 30%.

trainee profile
Mature self-starters with a strong academic background and outside interests. Enthusiasm, initiative and good interpersonal skills are essential as is the ability to play an active role in the future of the firm. Linguists are particularly welcome.

training
Four six month seats from construction and engineering, construction litigation and arbitration, disputes resolution/litigation, major projects, corporate/commercial, employment and commercial property. Where possible individual preference is noted. Work has an international bias. There are opportunities for in-house training by secondment to major clients and work in the overseas offices. Trainees are rapidly integrated and immediately take active roles and early responsibility. Trainees are treated as valued members of the firm and are encouraged to participate in all the firm's activities, including practice development. There is an in-house lecture programme; the PSC is taught externally.

sponsorship & benefits
LPC partly payable when trainee commences work. PSC fees payable. Permanent health insurance, death in service, preferential rates on private medical care, annual bonus and season ticket loan.

vacation placements
Places for 2002: 6; Duration: 2 weeks; Remuneration(2001): £170 p.w.; Closing Date: 16 March 2002; Interviews: April 2002.

Partners 26
Assistant Solicitors 20
Total Trainees 15
Total Staff 105

contact
Sally Thorndale

method of application
Handwritten letter & CV

selection procedure
Interviews

closing date for 2004
31 August 2002 (interviews September 2002)

application
Training contracts p.a. 6
Applications p.a. 200
% interviewed p.a. 10%
Required degree grade 2:1

training
Salary
1st year (2001) £21,000
2nd year (2001) £25,000
Holiday entitlement
22 days
% of trainees with a
non-law degree p.a. 50%
No. of seats available
abroad p.a. 2

post-qualification
Salary (2001) £35,000
% of trainees offered job
on qualification (2001) 100%
% of assistants (2001) who
joined as trainees 20%
% of partners (2001)
who joined as trainees 0%

locations
Reigate, London (x2), Hong Kong, Paris, new office opening shortly in Greece, associated offices in Germany and Tanzania

Shearman & Sterling

Broadgate West, 9 Appold Street, London EC2A 2AP
Tel: (020) 7655 5000 Fax: (020) 7655 5500

firm profile
Shearman & Sterling is one of New York's oldest legal partnerships, which has transformed from a New York-based firm focused on banking into a diversified global institution. Recognised throughout the world, the firm's reputation, skills and expertise are second to none in its field. The London office, established in 1972, has become a leading practice covering all aspects of English and European corporate and finance law. The firm employs over 120 English and US trained legal staff in London and has more than 850 lawyers in 16 offices worldwide.

main areas of work
Banking, leveraged finance and securitisation (primary and secondary structured debt, bridging facilities, debt trading and financial restructuring). Project finance (all aspects, in the power, oil, gas, telecommunications, mining and transport infrastructure sectors). M&A (public and private cross-border transactions on a pan-European scale). Global capital markets (structuring and execution of high-yield debt and equity-linked financing). International arbitration and litigation (international commercial law on a global scale). Tax (all direct and indirect tax aspects of structured finance and securitisations, domestic and international banking, capital markets issues, M&A and reorganisations). EU and competition (cross-border and UK M&A transactions, restrictive practices and abuse of dominance, competition litigation, state aid, public procurement and utility regulation).

trainee profile
The firm's successful future development calls for people who will relish the hard work and intellectual challenge of today's commercial world. You will be a self-starter, keen to assume professional responsibility early in your career and determined to become a first-class lawyer in a first-class firm. The firm's two year training programme will equip you with all the skills needed to become a successful commercial lawyer. You will spend six months in each of four practice areas, with an opportunity to spend six months in Hong Kong or Singapore. You will be an integral part of the London team from the outset, with your own laptop and mobile phone. The firm will expect you to contribute creatively to all the transactions you are involved in. The firm has an informal yet professional atmosphere. Your enthusiasm, intellect and energy will be more important than what you wear to work. The firm will provide you with a mentor, arrange personal and professional development courses and give you early responsibility. The firm wants to recruit people who will stay with it; people who want to become partners in its continuing success story.

sponsorship & awards
Sponsorship for the CPE and LPC courses, together with a maintenance grant of £4,500.

Partners 22
Assistant Solicitors 112
Total Trainees 6

contact
Ms Hina Malak
Tel: (020) 7655 5983

method of application
Application form

selection procedure
Interviews

closing date for 2004
31 July 2002

application
Training contracts p.a. 6
Required degree grade 2:1

training
Salary
1st year £30,000
2nd year £34,000
Holiday entitlement 24 days p.a.
% of trainees with non-law degree p.a. 50%
No of seats available abroad 3

post-qualification
Salary £55,000
% of trainees offered job on qualification 100%

overseas offices
Abu Dhabi, Bejing, Brussels, Düsseldorf, Frankfurt, Hong Kong, Mannheim, Menlo Park, New York, Paris, San Francisco, Singapore, Tokyo, Toronto, Washington DC

Sheridans

14 Red Lion Square, London WC1R 4QL
Tel: (020) 7404 0444 Fax: (020) 7831 1982
Email: general@sheridans.co.uk

firm profile
A Holborn firm specialising in litigation and the entertainment and media industry, and offering private client and commercial services including property and company work.

main areas of work
Commercial and other litigation including media, family and crime 35%; entertainment and media 40%; property and planning 15%; company/commercial 10%.

trainee profile
Candidates should be intelligent, ambitious and self-confident with excellent communication and interpersonal skills.

training environment
Trainees spend six to eight months in each department (litigation, company/commercial, property and planning). Working alongside senior partners or solicitors, you will be involved with a whole variety of work. There are regular trainee and department meetings. In the second year, trainees may be given a limited number of their own files. Early responsibility is encouraged. Trainees are not usually placed in media and entertainment (at least not until their last six months, due to its particularly specialised nature). The training programme is being expanded to include in-house seminars and video assisted learning schemes. Full computer and technology training is provided. Trainees are expected to work hard and think on their feet. The firm is friendly and informal and organises a range of social/sporting activities.

benefits
Life assurance.

sponsorship & awards
LPC funding is variable for those who have accepted training contracts.

Partners 17
Assistant Solicitors 8
Total Trainees 5

contact
Cyril Glasser

method of application
Letter & CV

selection procedure
2 interviews

application date for 2004
1–31 August 2002

application
Training contracts p.a. 2-3
Applications p.a. 700
% interviewed p.a. 8%
Required degree grade 2:1

training
Salary
1st year (2000) £20,000
2nd year (2000) £22,000
Holiday entitlement
20 days
% of trainees with a non-law degree 33%

post-qualification
Salary (2001) £34,000
% of trainees offered job on qualification (2000) 50%
% of assistants (as at 1/9/00) who joined as trainees 75%
% of partners (as at 1/9/00) who joined as trainees 36%

Shoosmiths

The Lakes, Bedford Road, Northampton NN4 7SH
Tel: (01604) 543 223 Fax: (01604) 543 430
Email: join.us@shoosmiths.co.uk
Website: www.shoosmiths.co.uk

firm profile
The firm operates in three divisions – commercial, financial institutions and personal injury, each with its own management structure designed to enable a responsive approach to the markets they serve. The firm has in excess of 1,200 members of staff and 74 partners.

main areas of work
Corporate/commercial, dispute resolution, employment, planning, commercial property, private client/family, personal injury, banking and financial institutions.

trainee profile
You will be confident, motivated and articulate with natural intelligence and the drive to succeed, thereby making a real contribution to the firm's commercial success. You will want to be a part of a winning team and will care about the kind of service you give to your clients, both internal and external.

training environment
Shoosmiths recognises that lawyers need more than just legal training to survive in today's challenging commercial environment. That is why every opportunity will be made available to you so that you can develop both personally and professionally. Trainees will be involved in 'real' work from day one. Sitting with a partner who will oversee your training and career development, you will have direct contact with clients and will draft your own letters and documents. Your experience will build through your daily practical workload, complemented by the training you would expect from a leading national law firm. In addition to the Professional Skills Course, the firm offers a comprehensive programme that includes managerial, organisational and IT training as standard. For example, over the two years you could receive development in the areas of intellectual property, business functions, e-commerce and advanced drafting skills. Social and sporting activities are organised regularly by local offices and the Shoosmiths group as a whole.

benefits
Life assurance, pension after 3 months, staff discounts on a range of products and services.

vacation placements
Places for 2002: 30; Duration: 2 weeks; Remuneration: £120 pw; Closing Date: 28 Feb 2002.

sponsorship & awards
Funding: £10,000 – split between fees and maintenance.

Partners 74
Assistant Solicitors 104
Total Trainees 26

contact
Claire Lewis

method of application
Application form

selection procedure
Assessment centre - half day

closing date for 2004
31 July 2002

application
Training contracts p.a. **10**
Applications p.a. **2,000**
% interviewed p.a. **10%**
Required degree grade **2:1**

training
Salary
1st year (2000) **£16,000**
2nd year (2000) **£17,250**
Holiday entitlement
23 days

post-qualification
Salary (2000) **Market rate**

offices
Northampton, Nottingham, Reading, Fareham, Banbury, Milton Keynes, Basingstoke

Sidley Austin Brown & Wood

1 Threadneedle Street, London EC2R 8AW
Princes Court 7 Princes Street London EC2R 8AQ
Tel: (020) 7360 3600 Fax: (020) 7626 7937
Email: jpage@sidley.com
Website: www.sidley.com

firm profile
Sidley Austin Brown & Wood is one of the world's largest full-service law firms combining the strengths of two exceptional law firms. With more than 1,300 lawyers practising in 13 offices on three continents (North America, Europe and Asia), the firm provides a broad range of integrated services to meet the needs of its clients across a multitude of industries. The firm has over 100 lawyers in London and is expanding fast.

main areas of work
Corporate securities; corporate finance; investment funds; tax; banking regulation; securitisation and structured finance; corporate reconstruction; property and property finance.

trainee profile
Sidley Austin Brown & Wood is looking for focused, intelligent and enthusiastic individuals with personality and humour who have a real interest in practising law in the commercial world. Trainees should have a 2:1 degree (not necessarily in law) and three A levels at A and B grades. Trainees would normally be expected to pass the CPE (if required) and the LPC at the first attempt.

training environment
Sidley Austin Brown & Wood is looking to recruit six to eight trainee solicitors to start in September 2004/March 2005. The firm is not a typical City firm and it is not a 'legal factory' so there is no risk of you being just a number. The team in London is young, dynamic and collegiate. Everyone is encouraged to be proactive and to create their own niche when they are ready to do so. Trainees spend a period of time in the firm's four specialist groups: international finance, corporate and commercial, tax and property. Sidley Austin Brown & Wood in London does not have a separate litigation department, although some litigation work is undertaken. In each group you will sit with a partner or senior associate to ensure that you receive individual training that is both effective and based on a real caseload. In addition, there is a structured timetable of training on a cross-section of subjects and an annual training weekend.

benefits
Healthcare, disability cover, life assurance, contribution to gym membership, interest-free season ticket loan.

sponsorship & awards
CPE and LPC fees paid and maintenance p.a.

Partners 25
Assistant Solicitors 54
Total Trainees 13

contact
Jo Page

method of application
Covering letter & employee application form - please call 0800 731 5015

selection procedure
Interview(s)

closing date for 2004
1 July 2002

application
Training contracts p.a. **6-8**
Applications p.a. **500**
% interviewed p.a. **15**
Required degree grade **2:1**

training
Salary
1st year (2000) £27,000
2nd year (2000) £30,000
Holiday entitlement
25 days
% of trainees with a non-law degree p.a. 50%

overseas offices
Beijing, Chicago, Dallas, Hong Kong, London, Los Angeles, New York, San Francisco, Seattle, Shanghai, Singapore, Tokyo, Washington DC

Simmons & Simmons

CityPoint, One Ropemaker Street, London EC2Y 9SS
Tel: (020) 7628 2020 Fax: (020) 7628 2070
Email: recruitment@simmons-simmons.com
Website: www.simmons-simmons.com

firm profile
Simmons & Simmons is a world class law firm providing advice to financial institutions, corporates, public and international bodies and private individuals through its international network of offices. It provides a comprehensive range of legal services with strength and depth. The ability to provide technically excellent, commercial and high quality advice is expected of leading law firms. Simmons & Simmons aims to provide an additional dimension by focusing on the way it works with its clients and by shaping its services to fit the clients' needs.

main areas of work
Corporate (corporate finance, M&A, private equity); finance (capital markets, structured securities, financial services); dispute resolution; competition and trade; employment; IP; major projects; real estate; tax; private capital. Main industry sector focus: finance; asset management; transport; energy; TMT; pharmaceuticals and biotechnology.

trainee profile
While a good academic record and sound commercial judgement is important, strength of character and outside interests are also taken into consideration.

training environment
Trainees sit with a partner or senior lawyer and are given the best work to help them become world class lawyers. Whilst the firm has its requirements, it places great emphasis upon trainees being able to discuss their progress and develop their professional interests. As well as having a supervisor and dedicated personnel professional they are each assigned a principal who acts as mentor and provides advice on developing as a solicitor in a City law firm.

benefits
Season ticket loan, fitness loan, group travel insurance, group accident insurance, death in service, medical cover, staff restaurant.

vacation placements
Places for 2002: 40-50; Duration: 2-4 weeks; Remuneration: £225 p.w.; Closing Date: 22 February 2002.

sponsorship & awards
In the absence of local authority funding LPC fees and PgDL/CPE fees are paid, plus a maintenance grant of £5,000 for London, Oxford or Guildford and £4,500 elsewhere.

Partners 153
Assistant Solicitors 366
Total Trainees 154

contact
Katharyn White

method of application
Application form, CV & covering letter

selection procedure
Assessment day: Document exercise, interview & written exercise

closing date for 2004
16 August 2002

application
Training contracts p.a. 50-60
Applications p.a. 2,700
% interviewed p.a. 10%
Required degree grade 2:1

training
Salary
1st year (2001) £28,000
2nd year (2001) £32,000
Holiday entitlement 25 days
% of trainees with a non-law degree p.a. 50%
No. of seats available abroad p.a. 25

post-qualification
Salary (2001) £50,000
% of trainees offered job on qualification (2001) 90%

overseas offices
Abu Dhabi, Brussels, Düsseldorf, Hong Kong, Lisbon, Madrid, Milan, New York, Paris, Rome, Shanghai

Sinclair Roche & Temperley

Royex House, 5 Aldermanbury Square, London EC2V 7LE
Tel: (020) 7452 4000 Fax: (020) 7452 4001

firm profile
Sinclair Roche & Temperley is a major international law firm specialising in international trade and transportation. The firm was founded in the City of London in 1934 and provides high quality, specialised legal advice to the international business community.

main areas of work
Litigation, arbitration and ADR; corporate and commercial advice; asset, project and trade finance; commercial property; insolvency and corporate restructuring, marine casualty and insurance; oil and gas; commodities and trade finance; new technology; EU law.

training environment
Four six month seats. Trainees sit with a partner, associate or a senior solicitor. As well as gaining the requisite skills, business development and management skills will be covered. Client contact is encouraged. A thorough programme of continuing professional training through lectures, seminars and external courses is provided.

benefits
Private health cover, pension scheme, discretionary bonus, PHI, accident insurance, subsidised sports club membership.

vacation placements
Places for 2002: 10-12; Duration: 2 weeks; Remuneration: TBA; Closing Date: 28 February 2002, subject to availability.

sponsorship & awards
CPE and LPC fees paid and £4,500 maintenance p.a.

Partners 29
Fee-earners 62
Total trainees 16

contact
David Shufflebotham

method of application
Firm's application form

selection procedure
Interview

closing date for 2004
31 October 2002 (subject to availability)

application
Training contracts p.a. 6-8
Applications p.a. **1,000**
% interviewed p.a. **Varies**
Required degree grade **2:1**

training
Salary
1st year (2001) **£25,000**
2nd year (2001) **£26,000**
Holiday entitlement
23 days p.a.
% of trainees with a non-law degree p.a. **Varies**
No. of seats available abroad p.a. **Varies**

post-qualification
Salary (2001)
£43,000-£45,500
% of trainees offered job on qualification (Sept 2001)
87.5%
% of fee-earners (as at Sept 2001) who joined as trainees **20%**

overseas offices
Bucharest, Hong Kong, Shanghai

Slaughter and May

35 Basinghall Street, London EC2V 5DB
Tel: (020) 7600 1200 Fax: (020) 7600 0289
Website: www.slaughterandmay.com

firm profile
One of the leading law firms in the world, Slaughter and May enjoys a reputation for quality and expertise. The corporate and financial practice is particularly strong and lawyers are known for their business acumen and technical excellence. International work is central to the practice and lawyers travel widely. No London partner has ever left the firm to join a competing practice.

main areas of work
Corporate and financial 66%; commercial litigation 11%; tax 7%; property (commercial) 6%; pensions and employment 5%; competition 3%; intellectual property 2%.

trainee profile
The work is demanding and the firm looks for intellectual agility and the ability to work with people from different countries and walks of life. Common sense, a mature outlook and the willingness to accept responsibility are all essential. The firm expects to provide training in everything except the fundamental principles of law, so does not expect applicants to know much of commercial life. Trainees are expected to remain with the firm on qualification.

training environment
Four or five seats of three or six months duration. Two seats will be in the corporate and financial department with an option to choose competition or financial regulation, a property seat is optional, and one seat in either litigation, intellectual property, tax or pensions and employment. In each seat a partner is responsible for monitoring your progress and reviewing your work. There is an extensive training programme which includes the PSC. There are also discussion groups covering general and specialised legal topics.

benefits
BUPA, STL, pension scheme, subsidised membership of health club, 24 hour accident cover.

vacation placements - summer 2002
Places: 60; Duration: 2 weeks; Remuneration: £250 p.w.; Closing Date: 8 February 2002 for penultimate year (of first degree) students only.

sponsorship & awards
CPE and LPC fees and maintenance grants are paid; some grants are available for postgraduate work.

Partners 121
Assistant Solicitors 390
Total Trainees 147

contact
Charlotte Houghton

method of application
Covering letter & CV to include full details of all examination results

selection procedure
Interview

application
Training contracts p.a.
Approx 85
Applications p.a. **3,000**
% interviewed p.a. **20%**
Required standard
Good 2:1 ability

training
Salary (May 2001)
1st year **£29,000**
2nd year **£32,500**
Holiday entitlement
25 days p.a.
% of trainees with a non-law degree **50%**
No. of seats available abroad p.a. **Approx 30**

post-qualification
Salary (May 2001) **£50,000**
% of trainees offered job on qualification (2000)
100%

overseas offices
Brussels, Hong Kong, New York, Paris, Singapore

Speechly Bircham

6 St Andrew Street, London EC4A 3LX
Tel: (020) 7427 6400 Fax: (020) 7427 6600
Email: trainingcontracts@speechlys.com
Website: www.speechlybircham.com

firm profile
Speechly Bircham is an independent mid-sized City law firm with an excellent client base including a number of well-known corporate and institutional clients. Speechly Bircham's strong commercial focus is complemented by a highly regarded private capital practice. The firm handles major transactions as well as commercial disputes and has a good reputation for several specialist advisory areas, notably personal and corporate tax.

main areas of work
Corporate 30%; property 20%; litigation 25%; private capital 25%.

trainee profile
Both law and non-law graduates who are capable of achieving a 2:1. The firm seeks intellectually dynamic individuals who enjoy a collaborative working environment where they can make an impact.

training environment
Speechly Bircham divides the training contract into four six month seats. Emphasis is given to early responsibility and supervised client contact providing trainees with a practical learning environment.

benefits
Season ticket loan, private medical insurance, life assurance.

vacation placements
Places for 2002: 10. The firm's summer placement scheme for students gives them the chance to experience a City legal practice. In a three-practice placement, students will be asked to research and present on a legal issue at the end of their placement; Duration: 3 weeks; Remuneration: £250 p.w.; Closing Date: 14 February 2002.

sponsorship & awards
CPE and LPC tuition fees are paid in full plus a maintenance grant of £4,000 (£4,500 for London/Guildford) p.a.

Partners 36
Assistant Solicitors 50
Total Trainees 10

contact
Nicola Swann
Human Resources Director

method of application
Application form

selection procedure
Interview

closing date for 2004
15 August 2002

application
Training contracts p.a. 5
Applications p.a. 1,000
% interviewed p.a. 5%
Required degree grade 2:1

training
Salary
1st year (2001) £26,000-£27,000
2nd year (2001) £28,000-£29,000
Holiday entitlement 20 days
% of trainees with a non-law degree p.a. 50%

post-qualification
Salary (2001) £45,000

Steele & Co

2 Norwich Business Park, Whiting Rd, Norwich NR4 6DJ
Tel: (01603) 274 700 Fax: (01603) 274 728
Email: personnel@steele.co.uk
Website: www.steele.co.uk

firm profile
Steele & Co is an innovative and progressive commercial firm with an increasingly national client base. It is recognised in particular for the strength of its commercial practitioners and for the range and quality of its services to local authorities and the commercial sector.

main areas of work
The firm offers a full range of corporate, property, litigation and public sector services. The firm is dedicated to delivering high quality value for money services to its clients regardless of location.

trainee profile
Candidates will be highly motivated, with a strong academic record and previous legal work experience.

training environment
The aim is to ensure that every trainee will wish to continue their career with the firm. The training programme consists of four six month seats in the following departments: company commercial, commercial property, civil litigation, commercial disputes, employment, family and public sector. You will have some choice in the order of your seats. Trainees are encouraged to take on as much responsibility as possible with considerable client contact early on in their training contract. Bi-monthly meetings provide a forum for discussion of topical issues. The offices are open-plan, providing a supportive and learning environment which reflects the firm's accreditation to both ISO 9001 and Investor in People. Trainee solicitors are appraised at the end of each seat and are part of the firm's mentor scheme. There is an active sports and social life.

benefits
Pension, accident insurance, legal services, interest-free season ticket loan, gym membership loan.

vacation placements
Places for 2002: Places offered throughout the Easter and Summer vacation.

Partners 14
Assistant Solicitors 18
Total Trainees 10

contact
Ann Chancellor
Human Resources Manager

method of application
Handwritten letter & CV

selection procedure
Interview

application
Training contracts p.a. **6**
Applications p.a. **300-400**
Required degree grade **2:1**

post-qualification
% of trainees offered job on qualification (2000)
100%

Stephenson Harwood

One St Paul's Churchyard, London EC4M 8SH
Tel: (020) 7329 4422 Fax: (020) 7606 0822
Email: sharon.green@shlegal.com

firm profile
Established in the City of London in 1828, Stephenson Harwood has developed into a large international practice, with a commercial focus and a wide client base.

main areas of work
Corporate; litigation; property; private capital; shipping.

trainee profile
The firm looks for high calibre graduates with excellent academic records and an outgoing personality.

training environment
As the graduate intake is relatively small, the firm gives trainees individual attention, coaching and monitoring. Your structured and challenging programme involves four six month seats in both contentious and non-contentious areas across the firm. These seats include 'on the job' training, as well as sharing an office and working with a partner or senior solicitor. In-house lectures complement your training and there is continuous review of your development. You will have the opportunity to spend six months abroad and have language tuition where appropriate. You will be given your own caseload and as much responsibility as you can shoulder. The firm plays a range of team sports, has its own gym, subsidised membership of health clubs and has privileged seats for concerts at the Royal Albert Hall and the London Coliseum and access to private views at the Tate Gallery.

benefits
Subsidised membership of health clubs, private health insurance, BUPA membership, season ticket loan and 25 days paid holiday per year.

vacation placements
Places for 2002: 21; Duration: 2 weeks; Remuneration: £200 p.w.; Closing Date: 15 February 2002.

sponsorship & awards
£7,400 fees paid for CPE and LPC and £4,700 maintenance p.a.

Partners 79*
Assistant Solicitors 115*
Total Trainees 44
denotes world-wide figures

contact
Graduate Recruitment

method of application
Application form only

selection procedure
Interview with 2 partners

closing date for 2004
31 July 2002

application
Training contracts p.a. 18
% interviewed p.a. 10%
Required degree grade 2:1

training
Salary
1st year (2001) £26,000
2nd year (2001) £29,000
Holiday entitlement
25 days
% of trainees with a non-law degree p.a. 46%
No. of seats available abroad p.a. 10

post-qualification
Salary (2001) £48,000
% of trainees offered job on qualification (2001) 95%
% of assistants (as at 1/9/01) who joined as trainees 37%
% of partners (as at 1/9/01) who joined as trainees 46%

overseas offices
Brussels, Guangzhou, Hong Kong, Madrid, Piraeus, Singapore

Tarlo Lyons

Watchmaker Court, 33 St John's Lane, London EC1M 4DB
Tel: (020) 7405 2000 Fax: (020) 7814 9421
Email: trainee.recruitment@tarlolyons.com
Website: www.tarlolyons.com

firm profile
Tarlo Lyons is recognised as one of the leading law firms in the country for its expertise in information technology and related areas. The firm has expanded at 30% per annum over the past three years and nearly two-thirds of the firm's turnover now derives from IT, telecommunications and Internet-related projects and advice, including e-commerce. The firm holds Investors in People accreditation.

main areas of work
Technology and communications; media; company and commercial; commercial property; dispute resolution; employment.

trainee profile
Applicants should have a sound academic record and a natural inquisitiveness and intellectual curiosity. An interest or background in information technology or commercial ventures is an advantage, as is a gap year or work undertaken outside of law. Applicants should also have common sense, resourcefulness and a good sense of humour.

training environment
Trainees will gain work experience in all the main areas of the practice. The PSC is taught externally and trainees also attend internal seminars. Trainees meet regularly with both a supervisor and the Training Partner and formal reviews are conducted every two months. The firm has a friendly, open-door policy and trainees are encouraged to take part in a wide range of marketing, sporting and social events.

benefits
Tarlo Lyons offers competitive compensation and salary may be enhanced by an annual discretionary bonus. The firm offers membership of a private health scheme, participation in a pension plan and subsidised membership of a nearby health club.

sponsorship & awards
LPC fees paid.

Partners 24
Assistant Solicitors 35
Total Trainees 6

contact
Trainee Recruitment Co-ordinator

method of application
Application form available from website

selection procedure
2 interviews with partners & skills assessment

closing date for 2004
10 August 2002

application
Training contracts p.a. 3
Applications p.a. 500
% interviewed p.a. 5%
Required degree grade 2:1

training
Salary
1st year (2001) £23,000 on average
2nd year (2001) £26,000 on average
Holiday entitlement 22 days
% of trainees with a non-law degree p.a. 50%

post-qualification
Salary (2001) £42,000
(Salary levels may increase subject to market conditions)

Taylor Joynson Garrett

Carmelite, 50 Victoria Embankment, Blackfriars
London EC4Y 0DX
Tel: (020) 7300 7000 Fax: (020) 7300 7100
Website: www.tjg.co.uk

firm profile
Taylor Joynson Garrett is a major City and international law firm, with an impressive UK and international client base. The firm, which has offices in London, Brussels and Bucharest, has recognised expertise in its corporate and intellectual property practices, as well as strength in depth across the full range of commercial disciplines.

main areas of work
Corporate 26%; dispute resolution 17%; intellectual property 21%; private client 7%; commercial property 13%; finance and projects 9%; employment 7%.

trainee profile
Academic achievement is high on the firm's list of priorities, and a 2:1 or better is expected. It wants individuals who have good communication skills and will flourish in a competitive environment. Strength of character, determination and the ability to think laterally are also important.

training environment
Trainees will have six month seats in four different departments, with the possibility of a placement in Brussels. You will be supervised by a partner or assistant and appraised both three months into and at the end of each seat. There will be plenty of opportunity to take early responsibility. The firm works closely with external training providers to meet the needs of the PSC. The course is tailored to suit the firm's needs, and most of the training is conducted in-house. A full sports and social calendar is available.

benefits
Private medical care, permanent health insurance, STL, subsidised staff restaurant, non-contributory pension scheme on qualification.

vacation placements
Places for 2002: 30; Duration: 2 weeks; Remuneration: £200 p.w.; Closing Date: 22 February 2002.

sponsorship & awards
CPE and LPC fees paid and £4,000 maintenance p.a.

Partners 91
Assistant Solicitors 135
Total Trainees 45

contact
Graduate Recruitment Department

method of application
Firm's application form

selection procedure
2 interviews, 1 with a partner

closing date for 2004
9 August 2002

application
Training contracts p.a. 25
Applications p.a. **1,600**
% interviewed p.a. **10%**
Required degree grade **2:1**

training
Salary
1st year (2000) £24,000
2nd year (2000) £27,000
Holiday entitlement
25 days
% of trainees with a non-law degree p.a. **40%**
No. of seats available abroad p.a. **2**

post-qualification
Salary (2000) £41,000
% of trainees offered job on qualification (2000) **90%**
% of assistants (as at 1/9/00) who joined as trainees **51%**
% of partners (as at 1/9/00) who joined as trainees **31%**

overseas offices
Brussels, Bucharest

Taylor Vinters

Merlin Place, Milton Rd, Cambridge CB4 0DP
Tel: (01223) 423 444 Fax: (01223) 426 523
Email: joanne@taylorvinters.com
Website: www.taylorvinters.com

firm profile
One of the largest firms in East Anglia, based in the university city of Cambridge. The largest single office firm in Cambridge.

main areas of work
Company commercial; commercial litigation; commercial property; claimant personal injury; private client.

trainee profile
Candidates should have energy, enthusiasm, intelligence, common sense, a friendly nature and a good sense of humour. Non-law degree graduates are welcomed.

training environment
The training contract comprises four seats: commercial, property/planning, claimant personal injury and commercial litigation. Opportunities exist for exchanges with European Network firms. Trainees' progress is reviewed and assessed every three months. There is an extensive in-house training programme within all departments and firmwide. The PSC is also organised in-house.

benefits
Benefits include private medical insurance, life insurance and pension. Many social activities are actively encouraged, from a theatre club to karaoke. Cambridge of course now has the largest pub in Europe.

vacation placements
Places for 2002: Places available; Duration: 1 week; Closing Date: 31 March 2002.

Partners	26
Assistant Solicitors	52
Total Trainees	10

contact
Paul Tapner/Jo Douglas

method of application
Application form

selection procedure
Single interview with 1 partner & the HR Manager

closing date for 2004
31 August 2002

application
Training contracts p.a. 5
Applications p.a. 300
Required degree grade 2:2

training
Salary
1st year (2001) £15,500
2nd year (2001) £17,100
Holiday entitlement
25 days
% of trainees with a non-law degree p.a. 40%

post-qualification
Salary (2001) £31,500 + benefits

Taylor Walton

28-44 Alma Street, Luton LU1 2PL
Tel: (01582) 731 161 Fax: (01582) 457 900
Email: luton@taylorwalton.co.uk
Website: www.taylorwalton.co.uk

firm profile
Strategically located in Luton, Harpenden, St Albans and Hemel Hempstead, Taylor Walton is a major regional law practice advising both businesses and private clients. Its strengths are in commercial property, corporate work and commercial litigation, whilst maintaining a strong private client side to the practice. It has a progressive outlook both in its partners and staff and in its systems, training and IT.

main areas of work
Company/commercial 15%; commercial property 20%; commercial litigation 15%; employment 5%; personal injury 5%; family 5%; private client 10%; residential property 20%; relocation 5%.

trainee profile
Candidates need to show excellent intellectual capabilities, coupled with an engaging personality so as to show that they can engage and interact with the firm's clients as the practice of law involves the practice of the art of communication. Taylor Walton sees its partners and staff as business advisers involved in clients' businesses, not merely stand-alone legal advisers.

training environment
The training consists of four six month seats. The training partner oversees the structural training alongside a supervisor who will be a partner or senior solicitor in each department. The firm does try to take trainees' own wishes in relation to seats into account. In a regional law practice like Taylor Walton you will find client contact and responsibility coupled with supervision, management and training. There is an in-house training programme for all fee-earning members of staff. At the end of each seat there is a post seat appraisal conducted by the training partner, the trainee and the supervisor. The PSC is taught externally. The firm is friendly with an open door policy and there are various sporting and social events.

vacation placements
Places for 2002: 4; Duration: Up to 4 weeks; Remuneration: Agreed with trainee; Closing Date: 30 April 2002.

Partners	22
Assistant Solicitors	39
Total Trainees	8

contact
Jim Wrigglesworth

method of application
CV with covering letter

selection procedure
First & second interview with opportunity to meet other partners

closing date for 2004
30 September 2002

application
Required degree grade 2:1 or above

Teacher Stern Selby

37-41 Bedford Row, London WC1R 4JH
Tel: (020) 7242 3191 Fax: (020) 7242 1156
Email: r.raphael@tsslaw.com
Website: www.tsslaw.com

firm profile
A central London-based general commercial firm, with clientele and caseload normally attributable to larger firms. It has a wide range of contacts overseas.

main areas of work
Commercial litigation 25%; commercial property 39%; company and commercial 15%; secured lending 11.5%; residential conveyancing/probate 4.5%; clinical negligence/education/judicial review 5%.

trainee profile
Emphasis falls equally on academic excellence and personality. The firm looks for flexible and motivated individuals, who have outside interests and who have demonstrated responsibility in the past. Languages an advantage.

training environment
Trainees spend six months in three departments (company commercial, litigation and property) with, where possible, an option to return to a preferred department in the final six months. Most trainees are assigned to actively assist a partner who monitors and supports them. Trainees are expected to fully immerse themselves and take early responsibility. After a short period you will conduct your own files. Trainees are welcome to attend in-house seminars and lectures for continuing education. The atmosphere is relaxed and informal.

vacation placements
Places for 2002: Possibly to those that have accepted or applied for training contracts.

sponsorship & awards
CPE Funding: None; LPC Funding: Unlikely.

Partners 16
Assistant Solicitors 22
Total Trainees 6

contact
Russell Raphael

method of application
Letter & application form

selection procedure
2 interviews

closing date for 2004
31 October 2002

application
Training contracts p.a. **6**
Applications p.a. **1,000**
% interviewed p.a. **5%**
Required degree grade
2:1 (not absolute)

training
Salary
1st year (2004) **£22,000**
Holiday entitlement
4 weeks
% of trainees with a
non-law degree p.a. **50%**

post-qualification
Salary (2001) **£33,000**
% of trainees offered job
on qualification (2001) **33%**
% of assistants (as at
1/9/01 who joined as
trainees **39%**
% of partners (as at 1/9/01)
who joined as trainees
44%

Theodore Goddard

150 Aldersgate Street, London EC1A 4EJ
Tel: (020) 7606 8855 Fax: (020) 7606 4390
Email: recruitment@theodoregoddard.co.uk
Website: www.theogoddard.com

firm profile
Theodore Goddard is a long-established City firm which supports clients not only in the traditional legal specialisations expected of a City firm but also in the media and communications sector. It is distinctive in that it punches above its weight in the size of the transactions it handles. With a reputation for having a friendly, unstuffy atmosphere, trainees are given early responsibility and are viewed as an integral part of the firm from day one. This is demonstrated by the offer of a permanent contract from the outset.

main areas of work
Corporate, corporate finance and corporate tax; banking; PFI; commercial litigation; commercial property; employment; intellectual property and music; film; audio-visual; e-commerce; advertising; sport.

trainee profile
The firm seeks graduates from all disciplines who can demonstrate academic excellence. In an increasingly global, technology-driven market, the firm is looking for those who think they will enjoy a fast-paced, intellectually demanding working environment.

training environment
Theodore Goddard's training is exceptional; it has won five awards both from within the legal profession and across all sectors of employment. Trainees spend six months in four practice areas with the option of three months in Paris, Brussels, or at a client. All trainees are consulted about seat preferences.

benefits
Pension, profit-related bonus, permanent health insurance, private medical insurance, subsidised health and fitness club membership and firm restaurant.

vacation placements
Places for 2002: 20 in the Summer vacation (70 open day places in the Easter vacation); Duration: 2 weeks; Remuneration: £200 p.w.; Closing Date: For summer placements and Easter open days – end of February 2002.

sponsorship & awards
CPE and LPC fees paid in full. £4,200 maintenance paid for London and South East, £3,750 elsewhere.

Partners 68
Assistant Solicitors 190
Total Trainees 33

contact
Recruitment Manager

method of application
Firm's application form

selection procedure
Initial interview followed by second interview

closing date for 2004
31 August 2002

application
Training contracts p.a. 20
Applications p.a. 3,000
% interviewed p.a. 5-10%
Required degree grade 2:1+

training
Salary
1st year £27,500 (2001)
2nd year £30,000 (2001)
Holiday entitlement
25 days
% of trainees with a non-law degree p.a. 40%
No. of seats available abroad p.a. 8

post-qualification
Salary (2001) £48,000
% of trainees offered job on qualification (2000) 100%

overseas offices
Brussels (associated offices worldwide)

Thomson Snell & Passmore

3 Lonsdale Gardens, Tunbridge Wells TN1 1NX
Tel: (01892) 510 000 Fax: (01892) 549 884
Email: solicitors@ts-p.co.uk
Website: www.ts-p.co.uk

firm profile
Established in 1570, Thomson Snell & Passmore continues to be regarded as one of the premier law firms in the South East. The firm has a reputation for quality and a commitment to deliver precise and clear advice which is recognised and respected by its clients, contacts and competitors. It has held the Lexcel quality mark since January 1999. The firm is vibrant and progressive and enjoys an extremely friendly atmosphere. Its offices are located in the centre of Tunbridge Wells and attract clients both locally and nationally.

main areas of work
Commercial litigation 25%; corporate and commercial property 17%; private client 21%; personal injury/clinical negligence 15%; residential property 14%; family law 8%.

trainee profile
Thomson Snell & Passmore regards its trainees from the outset as future assistants, associates and partners. The firm is looking for people not only with strong intellectual ability, but enthusiasm, drive, initiative, strong interpersonal and team-working skills, together with good IT skills.

training environment
The firm's induction course will help you to adjust to working life. As a founder member of Law South your training is provided in-house with trainees from other member firms of Law South who are all leading law firms in the South of England. Your two year training contract is divided into four periods of six months each. You will receive a thorough grounding and responsibility with early client exposure. You will be monitored regularly, receive advice and assistance throughout and appraisals every three months. The Training Partner will co-ordinate your continuing education in the law, procedure, commerce, marketing, IT and presentation skills. Trainees enjoy an active social life which is encouraged and supported.

sponsorship & awards
Grant and interest free loan available for LPC.

Partners	35
Assistant Solicitors	35
Total Trainees	8

contact
Ms Chantal Warner
Personnel Manager
Tel: (01892) 510 000

method of application
Handwritten letter & firm's application form available from website

selection procedure
1 interview with Training Partner & 2 other partners

closing date for 2004
31 July 2002

application
Training contracts p.a. 4
Applications p.a. Approximately 500
% interviewed p.a. 5%
Required degree grade 2:1 (any discipline)

training
Salary for each year of training
1st year £15,000 (Sept 2001)
2nd year £16,000 (Sept 2001)
Holiday entitlement 20 days

post-qualification
Salary £24,000 (Sept 2001)
% of trainees offered job on qualification 75%-100%

overseas/regional offices
Network of independent law firms throughout Europe

TLT Solicitors

One Redcliff St, Bristol BS99 7JZ
Tel: (0117) 917 7777 Fax: (0117) 917 7778
Email: lbevan@TLTsolicitors.com
Website: www.TLTsolicitors.com

firm profile
TLT is the third largest firm in Bristol and one of the top 100 in the country. The firm has over 100 lawyers, a total complement of over 280 people and a turnover of £10m plus.

main areas of work
Commercial and corporate 25%; property and planning 20%; litigation 10%; family 6%; banking and lender services 30%; employment 9%.

TLT has very strong corporate/commercial teams which undertake a wide range of work including acquisitions and disposals, joint ventures and OFEX work. The property and planning teams undertake a range of work including planning and advocacy, advice to regulatory authorities, and building and construction claims. TLT has one of the leading dispute resolution practices in the region. Particular emphasis is on insolvency, professional indemnity and negligence, mortgage possession proceedings and general commercial matters. The family team is consistently acknowledged as the best in the region. The private client team handles conveyancing, wills, trusts and probate as well as other less traditional financial services.

trainee profile
A strong academic background is preferred and a resourceful personality is also a consideration.

training environment
Trainees indicate their preference for three or four seats of six months each, which the firm tries to match. All trainees sit with another lawyer, but in every case their work is drawn from all parts of the team or department so that they gain as much experience as possible. Review meetings are held regularly. TLT strives to give you a high level of responsibility and involvement, while ongoing lectures are designed to extend your knowledge. Sports and social activities are available.

benefits
Subsidised health insurance, subsidised sports and health club facility, pension.

vacation placements
Places for 2002: A minimum of six places each year.

sponsorship & awards
See TLT's website.

Partners 33
Assistant Solicitors 33
Total Trainees 14

contact
Liz Bevan
Human Resources

method of application
Firm's application form

selection procedure
Assessment day

closing date for 2004
16 August 2002

application
Training contracts p.a. **8**
Applications p.a. **1,000**
% interviewed p.a. **1.5%**
Required degree grade **N/A**

training
Holiday entitlement
25 days
% of trainees with a
non-law degree p.a. **50%**

post-qualification
Salary (2001) **Market rate**

Travers Smith Braithwaite

10 Snow Hill, London EC1A 2AL
Tel: (020) 7295 3000 Fax: (020) 7295 3500
Email: graduate.recruitment@traverssmith.com
Website: www.traverssmith.com

firm profile
A leading medium-sized corporate, financial and commercial law firm with the capability to advise on a wide range of business activities. The practice offers small, closely-knit teams providing consistent service to clients.

main areas of work
Corporate; litigation; property; banking; tax; pensions; employment.

trainee profile
Applications are welcome from both law and non-law graduates. The firm looks for people who combine academic excellence with plain common sense; who are articulate – on their feet and on paper; who are tenacious, self-motivated and have a healthy dose of humour.

training environment
Training consists of four six month seats taken from the corporate, commercial, banking, corporate recovery, employment, litigation, property, pensions, financial services, and corporate tax departments. There is no crowd to get lost in; trainees quickly get to know each other and everyone else in the firm. They are treated as individuals and given immediate responsibility for handling deals and clients. Formal training includes a comprehensive programme of in-house training and seminars, a weekly technical bulletin to keep staff abreast of changes in the law. Trainees sit with partners. Social and sporting activities are enjoyed by the whole firm.

benefits
Private health insurance, permanent sickness cover, life assurance cover, season ticket loans, refreshment credit, subsidised sports club membership.

vacation placements
Places for 2002: Summer.

sponsorship & awards
LPC and CPE fees paid and between £4,500 and £5,000 maintenance p.a.

Partners 49
Assistant Solicitors 107
Total Trainees 39

contact
Germaine VanGeyzel

method of application
Handwritten letter & CV

selection procedure
Interviews

closing date for 2004
September 2002

application
Training contracts p.a. **25**
Applications p.a. **1,600**
% interviewed p.a. **15%**
Required degree grade **2:1**

training
Salary
1st year (2001) **£28,000**
2nd year (2001) **£32,000**
Holiday entitlement
20 days
% of trainees with a
non-law degree p.a.
Approx 50%

post-qualification
Salary (2001) **£50,000**
% of trainees offered job
on qualification (2001)
100%
% of assistants (as at
1/9/00) who joined as
trainees **58%**
% of partners (as at 1/9/01)
who joined as trainees
40%

Trowers & Hamlins

Sceptre Court, 40 Tower Hill, London EC3N 4DX
Tel: (020) 7423 8000 Fax: (020) 7423 8001
Email: gradrecruitment@trowers.com
Website: www.trowers.com

firm profile
Trowers & Hamlins is a substantial international firm. A leader in housing and public sector law, the firm also has a strong commercial side. The firm has regional offices in the UK, offices in the Middle East and links with Jordan, Yemen, Singapore, USA and Europe.

main areas of work
Property (housing, public sector, commercial) 35%; company and commercial/construction 32%; litigation 27%; private client 6%.

trainee profile
Personable, enthusiastic candidates with a good academic record and wide-ranging outside interests. The ability to work under pressure and with others, combined with versatility, are essential characteristics.

training environment
Trainees will gain experience in four seats from: company/commercial, construction, property, international, litigation, employment and private client. Trainees are encouraged to learn from direct contact with clients and to assume responsibility. The training programme is flexible and, with reviews held every three months, individual preferences will be considered. A training officer assists partners with the training programme and in-house lectures and seminars are held regularly. There are opportunities to work in Manchester, Exeter and the Middle East. The firm encourages a relaxed atmosphere and blends traditional qualities with contemporary attitudes. Activities are organised outside working hours.

benefits
Season ticket loan, private health care after six months service, Employee Assistance Programme and discretionary bonus, Death in Service.

vacation placements
Places for 2002: 25-30; Duration: 2 weeks; Remuneration: £175 p.w.; Closing Date: 1 March (Summer). Open Day: Date to be confirmed.

sponsorship & awards
CPE and LPC fees paid and £4,000-£4,250 maintenance p.a.

Partners 65
Assistant Solicitors 86
Total Trainees 27

contact
Graduate Recruitment Office

method of application
Letter, application form & CV

selection procedure
Interview(s), essay & practical test

closing date for 2004
1 August 2002

application
Training contracts p.a. **12-15**
Applications p.a. **1,600**
% interviewed p.a. **4%**
Required degree grade **2:1+**

training
Salary
1st year (2000) **£24,000**
2nd year (2000) **£26,000**
Holiday entitlement
20 days (1st year)
22 days (2nd year)
% of trainees with a non-law degree p.a. **40%**
No. of seats available abroad p.a. **Between 4 and 6**

post-qualification
Salary (2001) **£40,000**
% of trainees offered job on qualification (2000) **90%**
% of assistants (as at 1/9/00) who joined as trainees **40%**
% of partners (as at 1/9/00) who joined as trainees **45%**

overseas offices
Abu Dhabi, Dubai, Oman, Bahrain, Cairo

UK branch offices
Manchester, Exeter

Walker Morris

Kings Court, 12 King Street, Leeds LS1 2HL
Tel: (0113) 283 2500 Fax: (0113) 245 9412
Email: traineerecruit@walkermorris.co.uk
Website: www.walkermorris.co.uk

firm profile
Based in Leeds, Walker Morris is one of the largest commercial law firms in the North, providing a full range of legal services to commercial and private clients. It is increasingly gaining an international reputation.

main areas of work
Commercial litigation 32%; commercial property 30%; company and commercial 22%; building societies 12%; private clients 4%.

trainee profile
Bright, articulate, highly motivated individuals who will thrive on early responsibility in a demanding yet friendly environment.

training environment
Trainees commence with an induction programme, before spending four months in each main department (commercial property, corporate and commercial litigation). Trainees can choose in which departments they wish to spend their second year. Formal training will include interactive role plays, interactive video, lectures, workshops and seminars. The PSC covers personal work management, advocacy and professional conduct. Individual IT training is provided. An option exists for a four month trainee exchange programme with a leading Parisian law firm. Emphasis is placed on teamwork, inside and outside the office. The firm's social and sporting activities are an important part of its culture and are organised by a committee drawn from all levels of the firm. A trainee solicitors' committee also organises events and liaises with the Leeds Trainee Solicitors Group.

vacation placements
Places for 2002: 45 over 3 weeks; Duration: 1 week; Remuneration: £120 p.w.; Closing Date: 28 February 2002.

sponsorship & awards
PgDL and LPC fees plus maintenance of £4,000 (both PgDL and LPC) or £3,500 (LPC only).

Partners 37
Assistant Solicitors 73
Total Trainees 23

contact
Nick Cannon

method of application
Application form

selection procedure
Telephone & face-to-face interviews

closing date for 2004
31 July 2002

application
Training contracts p.a. **15**
Applications p.a. **Approx 600**
% interviewed p.a.
Telephone **16%**
Face to face **10%**
Required degree grade **2:1**

training
Salary
1st year (2000) **£17,250**
2nd year (2000) **£18,500**
Holiday entitlement **24 days**
% of trainees with a non-law degree p.a. **30% on average**
No. of seats available abroad p.a. **1**

post-qualification
Salary (2001) **£31,000**
% of trainees offered job on qualification (2001) **80%**
% of assistants (as at 1/9/00) who joined as trainees **60%**
% of partners (as at 1/9/00) who joined as trainees **47%**

Ward Hadaway

Sandgate House, 102 Quayside, Newcastle upon Tyne NE1 3DX
Tel: (0191) 204 4000 Fax: (0191) 204 4001
Email: personnel@wardhadaway.com
Website: www.wardhadaway.com

firm profile
Ward Hadaway is one of the most progressive commercial law firms in the North of England. The firm is firmly established as one of the North East region's legal heavyweights.

main areas of work
Litigation 35%; property 32%; company/commercial 26%; private client 7%.

trainee profile
The usual academic and professional qualifications are sought. Sound commercial and business awareness are essential as is the need to demonstrate strong communication skills, enthusiasm and flexibility. Candidates will be able to demonstrate excellent interpersonal and analytical skills.

training environment
The training contract is structured around four seats (property, company/commercial, litigation and private client) each of six months duration. At regular intervals, and each time you are due to change seat, you will have the opportunity to discuss the experience you would like to gain during your training contract. The firm will always try to give high priority to your preferences. You will share a room with a partner or associate which will enable you to learn how to deal with different situations. Your practical experience will also be complemented by an extensive programme of seminars and lectures. All trainees are allocated a 'buddy', usually a second year trainee or newly qualified solicitor, who can provide as much practical advice and guidance as possible during your training. The firm has an active Social Committee and offers a full range of sporting and social events.

benefits
23 days holiday (26 after five years service), death in service insurance, pension.

vacation placements
Places for 2002, duration 1 week.

sponsorship & awards
LPC fees paid and £2,000 interest-free loan.

Partners 41
Assistant Solicitors 60
Total Trainees 16

contact
Carol Todner
Personnel Manager

method of application
Application form & handwritten letter

selection procedure
Interview

closing date for 2004
31 July 2002

application
Training contracts p.a. 10
Applications p.a. 400
% interviewed p.a. 10%
Required degree grade 2:1

training
Salary
1st year (2000) £16,000
2nd year (2000) £17,000
Holiday entitlement
23 days
% of trainees with a non-law degree p.a. Varies

post-qualification
Salary (2001) Minimum £27,500
% of trainees offered job on qualification (2001) 100%

Watson, Farley & Williams

15 Appold Street, London EC2A 2HB
Tel: (020) 7814 8000 Fax: (020) 7814 8141/2
Website: www.wfw.com

firm profile
Established in 1982, Watson, Farley & Williams has its strengths in corporate, banking and asset finance, particularly ship and aircraft finance. The firm aims to provide a superior service in specialist areas and to build long-lasting relationships with its clients.

main areas of work
Shipping; ship finance; aviation; banking; asset finance; corporate; litigation; e-commerce; intellectual property; EC and competition; taxation; property; insolvency; telecoms; project finance.

trainee profile
Outgoing graduates who exhibit energy, ambition, self-assurance, initiative and intellectual flair.

training environment
Trainees are introduced to the firm with a comprehensive induction course covering legal topics and practical instruction. Seats are available in at least four of the firm's main areas, aiming to provide trainees with a solid commercial grounding. There is also the opportunity to spend time abroad, working on cross-border transactions. Operating in an informal, friendly and energetic atmosphere, trainees will receive support whenever necessary. You will be encouraged to take on early responsibility and play an active role alongside a partner at each stage of your training. The practice encourages continuous learning for all employees and works closely with a number of law lecturers, producing a widely-read 'digest' of legal developments, to which trainees are encouraged to contribute. All modules of the PSC are held in-house. The firm has its own sports teams and organises a variety of social functions.

benefits
Life assurance, PHI, BUPA, STL, pension, subsidised gym membership.

vacation placements
Places for 2002: 30; Duration: 2 weeks; Remuneration: £200 p.w.; Closing Date: 31 March 2002.

sponsorship & awards
CPE and LPC fees paid and £4,500 maintenance p.a. (£4,000 outside London).

Partners 60
Assistant Solicitors 150
Total Trainees 24

contact
Graduate Recruitment Officer

method of application
Handwritten letter & application form

selection procedure
Interview & assessment

closing date for 2004
31 July 2002

application
Training contracts p.a. **12**
Applications p.a. **1,000**
% interviewed p.a. **5%**
Required degree grade **2:1 ideally**

training
Salary
1st year (2000) **£25,000**
2nd year (2000) **£28,000**
Holiday entitlement **22 days**
% of trainees with a non-law degree p.a. **50%**
No. of seats available abroad p.a. **12**

post-qualification
Salary (2001) **Not less than £48,000 at the time of writing**
% of trainees offered job on qualification (2001) **80%**
% of assistants (as at 1/9/01) who joined as trainees **40%**
% of partners (as at 1/9/01) who joined as trainees **4%**

overseas offices
Moscow, New York, Paris, Piraeus, Singapore

Wedlake Bell

16 Bedford Street, Covent Garden, London WC2E 9HF
Tel: (020) 7395 3000 Fax: (020) 7836 9966
Email: recruitment@wedlakebell.com
Website: www.wedlakebell.com

firm profile
Wedlake Bell is a medium-sized law firm providing legal advice to businesses and high net worth individuals from around the world. The firm's services are based on a high degree of partner involvement, extensive business and commercial experience and strong technical expertise. The firm has over 80 lawyers in central London and Guernsey, and affiliations with law firms throughout Europe and in the United States.

main areas of work
For the firm's business clients: Banking and asset finance; corporate finance; commercial property; media, IP and commercial; Internet and e-business; employment services; pensions and share schemes; construction; litigation and dispute resolution.
For private individuals: Tax, trusts and wealth protection; offshore services.

trainee profile
In addition to academic excellence, Wedlake Bell looks for commercial aptitude, flexibility, enthusiasm, a personable nature, confidence, mental agility and computer literacy in its candidates. Languages are not crucial.

training environment
Trainees have four seats of six months across the following areas: corporate finance, banking, construction, media and IP/IT, employment, litigation, property and private client. As a trainee the firm encourages you to have direct contact and involvement with clients from an early stage. You will work within highly specialised teams and have a high degree of responsibility. You will be closely supervised by a partner or senior solicitor and become involved in high quality and varied work. The firm is committed to the training and career development of its lawyers and many of its trainees continue their careers with the firm often through to partnership. Wedlake Bell has an informal, creative and co-operative culture with a balanced approach to life.

sponsorship & benefits
LPC and CPE fees paid where local authority grant not available. During training contract: pension. On qualification: pension, life assurance, medical insurance, PHI, subsidised gym membership and travel loans.

vacation placements
Places for 2002: 6; Duration: 3 weeks in July; Remuneration: £150 p.w.; Closing Date: End of February.

Partners 33
Assistant Solicitors 33
Total Trainees 10

contact
Natalie King

method of application
CV & covering letter

selection procedure
Interviews in September

closing date for 2004
End August 2002

application
Training contracts p.a.
4 or 6
Applications p.a. 800
% interviewed p.a. 3%
Required degree grade 2:1

training
Holiday entitlement
20 days
% of trainees with a
non-law degree p.a. 25%

post-qualification
% of trainees offered job
on qualification (2001)
50%
% of assistants (as at
1/9/00) who joined
as trainees 50%

overseas offices
Guernsey

Weightmans

Richmond House, 1 Rumford Place, Liverpool L3 9QW
Tel: (0151) 227 2601 Fax: (0151) 227 3223
Email: info.liv@weightmans.com
Website: www.weightmans.com

firm profile
Weightmans is one of the country's largest defendant-based insurance practices. It also has a thriving commercial division. With over 400 staff in Liverpool, Manchester, Birmingham and Leicester, Weightmans is renowned as a responsive, consistent, solution-driven firm which offers genuine value for money. Weightmans is committed to the development of its employees and to the highest standards of client care. The firm is committed to harnessing new IT developments to reduce the cost of service delivery. The firm is developing new and innovative systems which will offer its clients full access to all case information, costs to date and other vital case related information.

main areas of work
Insurance litigation; professional indemnity; clinical negligence; employment; commercial; commercial property; licensing.

trainee profile
Weightmans looks to recruit individuals who can enhance its high professional standards and contribute to the solution-driven culture of the practice as a whole. Applications from a wide variety of academic backgrounds are considered, with a preference to those whose academic record demonstrates an ability to study with discipline and common sense to achieve results.

training environment
Weightmans provides quality training split into four seats, each of six months. There are regular appraisals and opportunities to discuss progress of meeting of objectives.

Partners 57
Assistant Solicitors 64
Total Trainees Varies

contact
Lyn Ryan
HR Information Adviser
Bill Radcliffe
Training Principal

method of application
Application forms & brochures are available from Lyn Ryan, HR Information Adviser in Liverpool

closing date for 2004
31 July 2002

other offices
Birmingham, Leicester, Manchester

Weil, Gotshal & Manges

One South Place, London EC2M 2WG
Tel: (020) 7903 1000 Fax: (020) 7903 0990
Email: uktrainingcontracts@weil.com
Website: www.weil.com

firm profile
Weil, Gotshal & Manges was founded in New York in 1931. The London office, established in 1996, has grown rapidly to become the second largest office of the firm and is now the hub of the European practice. With more than 120 lawyers, it is one of the largest US-based international law firms in London, with one of the widest ranging practices. The London office provides its clients with full dual capability in US, UK and German law.

main areas of work
The firm advises some of the world's leading international corporations and financial institutions. Its practice bridges the traditional divide between US and UK corporate and finance law and encompasses acquisition finance, asset finance and leasing, banking, biotechnology and pharmaceuticals, commercial litigation and arbitration, competition, corporate restructurings and workouts, derivatives, environmental, financial services, mergers and acquisitions, pensions, private equity, project finance, real estate, securitisation, structured finance, taxation and technology.

trainee profile
The firm is looking for trainees with the commercial acumen and energy to become legal experts providing high quality client service and advice to complex international transactions. It needs people who have a genuine contribution to make to the continued success in the development of the London office. It aims to recruit down-to-earth people with the intelligence, personality and drive to be happy and successful in an entrepreneurial environment.

training environment
Trainees who join the firm in 2004 will usually complete four six month seats, one of which may be in an overseas office. In order to ensure its trainees receive adequate support and on-the-job training, they each work closely with a senior associate or partner. The practical experience gained through exposure to client work is enhanced by regular internal seminars and attendance at external conferences. Legal staff are also assisted by an excellent team of support staff. The firm aims to keep all trainees on qualification.

benefits
Pension, permanent health insurance, private health cover, life assurance, subsidised gym membership, season ticket loan. The firm will pay tuition fees and a maintenance allowance for CPE and LPC.

vacation placements
Places for 2002: 12 in summer vacation. Closing date for applications by EAF: 14 Feb 2002.

Partners 23
Assistant Solicitors 83
Total Trainees 17

contact
Cathy McDonagh
Graduate Recruitment Assistant

method of application
Employer's application form

closing date for 2004
31 July 2002

application
Training contracts p.a. 10
Required degree grade 2:1

training
Salary
1st year (2001) £35,000
Holiday entitlement
23 days

overseas offices
Brussels, Budapest, Dallas, Frankfurt, Houston, Silicon Valley, Miami, New York, Prague, Warsaw, Washington DC

affiliated offices
Paris, Singapore, Cairo

White & Case

7-11 Moorgate, London EC2R 6HH
Tel: (020) 7600 7300 Fax: (020) 7600 7030
Email: efalder@whitecase.com
Website: www.whitecase.com

firm profile
White & Case is a law firm with over 1,400 lawyers in 39 offices worldwide. It works with financial institutions, multinational corporations and governments on major international corporate and financial transactions and complex disputes.

main areas of work
In the London office: acquisition finance; asset finance; banking; capital markets; corporate finance; commercial real estate; construction; dispute resolution; EU and competition law; intellectual property; M&A; project finance; tax; telecommunications.

trainee profile
Trainees should be enthusiastic, be able to show initiative and have a desire to be involved with innovative and high profile legal matters. You should have an understanding of international commercial issues.

training environment
The firm's trainees are important and valued members of the London office and frequently work on multijurisdictional matters requiring close co-operation with lawyers throughout the firm's established overseas network. You will spend six months in each seat and cover the majority of work dealt with in the London office during the course of the two year training contract. You will be sitting with an associate or partner and hands-on experience will be supplemented by formal internal training sessions. You are encouraged to spend six months in one of the firm's overseas offices to gain a fuller understanding of the global network. The Professional Skills Course is run throughout the contract.

benefits
BUPA, gym membership contribution, life insurance, pension scheme, permanent health scheme, season ticket loan, bonus scheme.

vacation placements
Places for 2002: 30; Duration: 2 weeks; Remuneration: £250; Closing Date: End of February 2002.

sponsorship & awards
CPE and LPC fees paid and £5,500 maintenance p.a. Prizes for commendation and distinction in the LPC.

Partners 27
Assistant Solicitors 70
Total Trainees 16

contact
Ms Emma Falder

method of application
EAF, CV & covering letter

selection procedure
Interview

closing date for 2004
31 July 2002

application
Training contracts p.a. 20-25
Applications p.a. **1,500**
Required degree grade **2:1**

training
Salary (2001) £33,000, rising by £1,000 every six months
Holiday entitlement 25 days

All trainees are encouraged to spend a seat abroad

post-qualification
Salary (2001) £57,500

overseas offices
Almaty, Ankhara, Bahrain, Bangkok, Berlin, Bombay, Bratislava, Brussels, Budapest, Dresden, Düsseldorf, Frankfurt, Hamburg, Helsinki, Ho Chi Minh City, Hong Kong, Istanbul, Jakarta, Jeddah, Johannesburg, London, Los Angeles, Mexico City, Miami, Milan, Moscow, New York, Palo Alto, Paris, Prague, Riyadh, Rome, São Paulo, Singapore, Shanghai, Stockholm, Tokyo, Warsaw, Washington DC

Wiggin and Co

95 The Promenade, Cheltenham GL50 1WG
Tel: (01242) 224 114 Fax: (01242) 224 223
Email: law@wiggin.co.uk

firm profile
Based in Cheltenham, with offices in London and Los Angeles, Wiggin and Co is a 'city-type' niche practice. It specialises in media, communications, technology and entertainment and in the tax and company/commercial fields.

main areas of work
Private client 28%; media and entertainment 50%; litigation 13%; property 9%.

trainee profile
Candidates will have a strong academic background, be personable and show a willingness to work hard individually or as part of a team.

training environment
The training is divided into six seats. Trainees will spend time in all five departments, namely the company/commercial, media, property, litigation and private client departments. You will be encouraged to take an active role in transactions, assume responsibility and deal directly with clients. In-house lectures and seminars are held regularly and training reviews are held every four months. The firm offers the attraction of Cheltenham combined with technical ability and experience akin to a large City firm. Its relatively small size encourages a personal approach towards staff and client relations.

benefits
Life assurance, private health cover, pension scheme, permanent health insurance.

sponsorship & awards
CPE and LPC fees and £3,000 maintenance p.a. Brochure available on request.

Partners 13
Assistant Solicitors 11
Total Trainees 6

contact
Simon Baggs

method of application
Letter & CV

selection procedure
2 interviews

closing date for 2004
21 August 2002

application
Training contracts p.a. **3**
Applications p.a. **1,700**
% interviewed p.a. **2%**
Required degree grade **2:1**

training
Salary
1st year (2000) **£21,900**
2nd year (2000) **£27,000**
Holiday entitlement
20 days
% of trainees with a
non-law degree p.a. **60%**

post-qualification
Salary (2000) **£36,700**
% of trainees offered job on qualification (2001) **100%**
% of assistants (as at 2000) who joined as trainees **17%**
% of partners (as at 2000) who joined as trainees **17%**

overseas offices
Los Angeles

Withers

16 Old Bailey, London EC4AM 7EG
Tel: (020) 7597 6160 Fax: (020) 7597 6543
Email: mailto@withers.co.uk
Website: www.withers.co.uk

firm profile

Withers gives individuals pragmatic and commercial advice; it gives companies personal attention; it has a business-like approach to charities. The exciting mix of work creates a diverse and interesting training for the small number of trainees employed. Withers' status as the largest private client team in Europe and its outstanding reputation in family law set it apart from other city firms. Not only does it have the UK's leading Italian commercial practice, the growth in its commercial areas is astounding. The firm's clients range from large companies and individuals to successful entrepreneurs and individuals with substantial inherited wealth.

main areas of work

Private client and charities 42%; family 15%; litigation 17%; corporate, company and commercial 13%; property 13%.

training environment

Trainees spend six months in four of the firm's five departments. On the job training is supplemented by the firm's departmental and trainee-specific training. Buddy and mentor systems ensure that trainees are fully supported from the outset.

benefits

Interest-free season ticket loan, private medical insurance, life assurance, social events, subsidised café facilities.

vacation placements

Easter and Summer vacation placements are available. Students spend two weeks in two different departments of their choice. The closing date for applications is 8 February 2002. The firm has 20 places available during Summer and six at Easter.

sponsorship & awards

CPE/PgDL and LPC fees and £4,500 maintenance p.a. are paid. A cash prize is awarded for a distinction or commendation in the CPE/PgDL and/or LPC.

Partners 50
Legal Staff 105
Total Trainees 21

contact
Graduate Recruitment Officer

method of application
Application form & covering letter

selection procedure
2 interviews

closing date for 2004
31 July 2002

application
Training contracts p.a. **12**
Applications p.a. **1,500**
% interviewed p.a. **15%**
Required degree grade **2:1**

training
Salary
1st year **£26,500**
2nd year **£29,000**
Holiday entitlement
20 days
% of trainees with a non-law degree p.a. **40%**

post-qualification
Salary (2001) **TBA**

overseas offices
Milan

withers

Wragge & Co

55 Colmore Row, Birmingham B3 2AS
Tel: (0800) 096 9610 Fax: (0121) 214 1099
Email: gradmail@wragge.com
Website: www.wragge.com

Partners	109
Assistant Solicitors	290
Total Trainees	46

contact
Julie Cox
Graduate Recruitment & Training Manager

method of application
Application form & online

selection procedure
Telephone interview & assessment day

closing date for 2004
31 July 2002

application
Training contracts p.a. **25**
Applications p.a. **1,000**
% interviewed p.a. **10%**
Required degree grade **2:1**

training
Salary
1st year **£21,000**
2nd year **£24,000**
Holiday entitlement
23 days
% of trainees with a non-law degree p.a. **Varies**

post-qualification
Salary (2001) **£33,000**
% of trainees offered job on qualification (2001)
95%
% of assistants (as at 1/9/01) who joined as trainees **30%**
% of partners (as at 1/9/01) who joined as trainees **47%**

firm profile
Wragge & Co is a leading law firm providing a full range of quality legal services to clients in commerce, finance and industry, including over 200 listed companies. The firm is renowned for its strategy of having successfully and distinctively developed a national firm from its base in the Midlands. As a result of this strategy, Wragge & Co won the 'Regional Law Firm of the Year 2000 Award', and was also awarded 14th place in the 'Best Companies to Work For in the UK' by *The Sunday Times*, and was also the number one law firm to work for.

main areas of work
The firm enjoys a national reputation in areas such as corporate, dispute resolution, insurance litigation, property, employment, corporate tax, information technology, EU/competition, transport and utilities, project finance and banking. The firm has also built 'top five' reputations in selected niche areas such as construction, intellectual property and pensions. The quality of the firm's work is reflected in the organisations included in its client list – Bank of Scotland, Bass, Beazer Homes, Birmingham International Airport, British Airways, Carlton UK TV, DVLA, H J Heinz, HMV, Lloyds TSB and PowerGen. Whilst Wragge & Co's base remains in Birmingham, it also has offices in Brussels, supporting the EU/competition team, and in London dealing solely with intellectual property matters. The firm has a substantial number of international connections, regularly represents UK clients doing business overseas and acts as project managers on international transactions. Around 25% of the firm's work is international.

trainee profile
Graduates should be of a 2:1 standard at degree level, with some legal and/or commercial work experience gained either via holiday jobs or a previous career. Candidates should be practical with a common-sense approach to work and problem solving, and be able to show adaptability, enthusiasm and ambition on their applications.

training environment
Wragge & Co places considerable emphasis on transforming trainees into high quality, commercially-minded lawyers. You will spend six months in four different practice areas (usually corporate, property and litigation, with a chance to specialise in a final seat of your choice). There is also an opportunity for trainees to spend six months in Brussels and London. From day one, you will work on live files with direct contact with clients, other solicitors and also be responsible for the management of the transaction and its ultimate

Wragge & Co continued

billing. The more aptitude you show, the greater the responsibility you will be given. You will be supported by a monitoring partner and a second year trainee who will be assigned to 'mind' you. Introductory courses are provided at the start of each seat in addition to the Professional Skills Course training requirements. This formal training complements 'on the job' learning and it is more than likely that the firm's commitment to your development will extend well past the number of days recommended by the Law Society. Some of the courses will be residential, allowing you to reflect on your work practices away from the office environment and forge relationships and compare notes with your colleagues without the disturbances of your daily work.

benefits

Benefits include tuition fees for CPE and LPC and maintenance grant of £4,500 for each year of study, £1,000 interest free loan, prize for 1st class degree and LPC distinction, pension scheme, life assurance, 23 days holiday per annum, travel schemes, sports and social club, permanent health insurance, independent financial adviser, Christmas gift and access to private medical insurance at corporate rates.

vacation placements

Places for 2002: 20 (Easter) 40 (Summer); Duration: 1 week (Easter) 2 weeks (Summer); Remuneration: £170 p.w.; Closing Date: 31 January 2002.

Wragge&Co

Blackstone Chambers (P Baxendale QC and C Flint QC)

Blackstone House, Temple, London EC4Y 9BW DX: 281
Tel: (020) 7583 1770 Fax: (020) 7822 7350
Email: clerks@blackstonechambers.com
Website: www.blackstonechambers.com

chambers profile
Established at its old site 2 Hare Court for many years, Blackstone Chambers recently moved to new purpose built fully networked premises in the Temple.

type of work undertaken
Chambers' formidable strengths lie in three principal areas of practice: commercial, employment and public law. Commercial law includes financial/business law, international trade, conflicts, sport, media and entertainment, intellectual property and professional negligence. All aspects of employment law, including discrimination, are covered by chambers' extensive employment law practice. Public law incorporates judicial review, acting both for and against central and local government agencies and other regulatory authorities, human rights and other aspects of administrative law.

pupil profile
Chambers looks for articulate and intelligent applicants who are able to work well under pressure and demonstrate high intellectual ability. Successful candidates usually have at least a 2:1 honours degree, although not necessarily in law.

pupillage
Chambers offers four 12 month pupillages to those wishing to practice full-time at the Bar normally commencing in October each year. Pupillage is divided into three or four sections and every effort is made to ensure that pupils receive a broad training. The environment is a friendly one; pupils attend an induction week introducing them to the chambers working environment. Chambers prefers to recruit new tenants from pupils wherever possible. Chambers subscribes to OLPAS; applications should be made for the summer season.

mini pupillages
Assessed mini pupillages are available and are an important part of the application procedure. Applications for mini pupillages must be made by 30 June; earlier applications are strongly advised and are preferred in the year before pupillage commences.

funding
Awards of £30,000 per annum are available. The pupillage committee has a discretion to consider applications for up to £7,500 of the pupillage award to be advanced during the BVC year.

No of Silks 27
No of Juniors 36
No of Pupils 4 (current)

contact
Ms Julia Hornor
Practice Manager

method of application
OLPAS

pupillages (p.a.)
12 months 4
Required degree grade
Minimum 2:1
(law or non-law)

income
Award £30,000
Earnings not included

tenancies
Junior tenancies offered in last 3 years 100%
No of tenants of 5 years call or under 9

Essex Court Chambers (Gordon Pollock QC)

24 Lincoln's Inn Fields, London WC2A 3EG DX: 320
Tel: (020) 7813 8000 Fax: (020) 7813 8080
Email: clerksroom@essexcourt-chambers.co.uk
Website: www.essexcourt-chambers.co.uk

chambers profile
Essex Court Chambers is one of London's leading commercial sets. In *Chambers 2000-2001*, Essex Court Chambers appeared in nine categories as a 'leading set': arbitration (international); commercial (litigation); insurance; shipping; banking; energy; media and entertainment; aviation; and employment. Fifteen of its silks were recognised as 'leading' in one or more fields with Head of Chambers Gordon Pollock QC leading the 'Stars at the Bar'. 22 Juniors were recommended; 14 in two or more areas of specialisation.

type of work undertaken
Barristers advise on a wide range of international and domestic commercial law and appear as Counsel in litigation and commercial arbitration worldwide. In addition to the 'leading' areas of specialisation above, the set has expertise in the following areas of law: administrative/judicial review; agriculture/farming; Chinese; company/insolvency; construction; engineering; commodities; computer; employment; sports; environmental; European; financial services; human rights; injunctions/arrests; fraud; international trade and transport; professional negligence; public international; product liability; and VAT. For further information see the website; a detailed brochure is also available on request.

pupil profile
The best candidates are required for this set's intellectually demanding work.

pupillage
Up to four 12 month funded pupillages are offered each year for an October start. The set welcomes applications through OLPAS in 2002 for pupillage in October 2003 and for deferred pupillage in October 2004.

mini pupillages
Chambers offers up to 30 mini pupillages during June and July. Applicants, who should have completed at least one year of a law degree or have passed or be in the course of studying for the CPE, should contact Miss Lucy Paterson, the Secretary to the Pupillage Committee, by letter, fax or email (lpaterson@essexcourt-chambers.co.uk) for an application form. Forms will be issued and applications considered between 1 February and 31 May.

funding
£27,500 per annum, payable in two instalments. Applications to advance part are considered for the BVC year; interest-free loans are also available in cases of need.

No of Silks 19
No of Juniors 42
No of Pupils 4

contact
Pupillage Secretary

method of application
OLPAS (pupillage);
Application form (mini-pupillage)

pupillages (p.a.)
12 months 4
Required degree grade
2:1 or higher preferred

income
£27,500 p.a.

tenancies
Junior tenancies offered in last 3 years 7

4 Essex Court (Nigel Teare QC)

4 Essex Court, Temple, London EC4Y 9AJ
DX: 292 London (Chancery Lane)
Tel: (020) 7653 5653 Fax: (020) 7653 5654
Email: clerks@4sx.co.uk
Website: www.4sx.co.uk

chambers profile
4, Essex Court is one of the foremost and longest-established sets of chambers specialising in commercial law. Chambers has remained in Essex Court although it moved from No 2 to No 4 some ten years ago. Chambers has kept abreast of the latest technological advances in information and computer technology. 4, Essex Court offers a first class service at sensible fee rates and has a staff renowned for their openness and fairness.

type of work undertaken
The challenging and rewarding work of chambers encompasses the broad range of commercial disputes embracing arbitration, aviation, banking, shipping, international trade, insurance and reinsurance, professional negligence, entertainment and media, environmental and construction law. Over 70% of chambers' work involves international clients.

pupil profile
4, Essex Court seeks high calibre pupils with good academic qualifications (at least a 2:1 degree) who exhibit good written and verbal skills.

pupillage
Chambers offers a maximum of four funded pupillages of 12 months duration (reviewable at six months). Pupils are moved amongst several members of chambers and will experience a wide range of high quality commercial work. Outstanding pupils are likely to be offered a tenancy at the end of their pupillage.

mini pupillages
Mini pupillages are encouraged in order that potential pupils may experience the work of chambers before committing themselves to an application for full pupillage.

funding
Awards of £28,000 p.a. are available for each funded pupillage - part of which may be forwarded during the BVC, at the Pupillage Committee's discretion.

No of Silks 8
No of Juniors 31

contact
Secretary to Pupillage Committee

method of application
Chambers' application form

pupillages (p.a.)
1st 6 months 4
2nd 6 months 4
12 months
(Reviewed at 6 months)
Required degree
Good 2:1+

income
1st 6 months
£14,000
2nd 6 months
£14,000
Earnings not included

tenancies
Current tenants who served pupillage in chambers 21
Junior tenancies offered in last 3 years 6
No of tenants of 5 years call or under 7
Income (1st year)
c.£40,000

3 Hare Court (Mark Strachan QC)

3 Hare Court, Temple, London EC4Y 7BJ DX: 212
Tel: (020) 7415 7800 Fax: (020) 7415 7811

chambers profile
Whilst individual practices within chambers differ significantly, most members of chambers specialise in the field of commercial and business law. This includes everything from international arbitration to sale of goods and employment law. Members of chambers frequently appear in the Privy Council undertaking constitutional, human rights cases and other appellate work. The work of chambers also includes most areas of non-specialist civil litigation such as personal injury and landlord and tenant work. There is also work in the field of public and administrative law.

pupil profile
Chambers seeks to have three or four pupils at any time and offer 12 month pupillages. Chambers are well aware that the aim of most pupils is to secure a tenancy and to this end seek to recruit one tenant of sufficient calibre every year. Pupils will be reviewed after five months and given an indication of whether they have any prospect of becoming a tenant at the end of the year.

mini pupillages
Mini pupillages and student visits are available. Application by letter and CV to Michael Oliver.

funding
It is chambers' policy to offer finance to two pupils for 12 months. There are two awards of up to £25,000, being £12,500 for the first six months and £12,500 from earnings and/or chambers' funds in the second six months.

No of Silks 4
No of Juniors 19
No of Pupils 3

contact
James Dingemans
Michael Oliver
(Chambers Manager)

method of application
OLPAS

pupillages (p.a.)
12 months 3

tenancies
Junior tenancies offered in last 3 years 3
No of tenants of 5 years call or under 5

Old Square Chambers (John Hendy QC)

1 Verulam Buildings, Gray's Inn, London WC1R 5LQ
DX: 1046 Chancery Lane/London
Tel: (020) 7269 0300 Fax: (020) 7405 1387
Email: moor@oldsquarechambers.co.uk
Website: www.oldsquarechambers.co.uk

chambers profile
A highly specialised, forward thinking set committed to expansion.

type of work undertaken
Employment, personal injury, product liability and environmental law. Public law and human rights issues are encompassed within these areas. There is some business and mercantile work and some medical negligence. There is much use of European jurisprudence. In employment law, members of chambers have been involved in many of the ground-breaking cases of the past 20 years. Chambers' profile in personal injury law is excellent; particular strengths are disaster and multi-party litigation. Environmental law work is predominantly on large 'toxic tort' litigation - damage caused by pollution. Fields of practice are organised around special interest groups in chambers enabling the sharing of information and effective marketing.

pupil profile
Chambers look for intelligent candidates who have the potential to be excellent advocates. You must be motivated to come to the Bar and wish to practise in at least one of chambers' specialist fields. You must have ability to cope with hard work and deal with many different people. Chambers is committed to equal opportunities. Chambers' recruitment methods are designed to avoid discrimination on the grounds of race, gender, disability, sexuality or religion.

pupillage
Chambers offer high quality training, generously funded. Pupils spend three months with each pupil supervisor. Preferences for fields of work will be considered. There is the opportunity to undertake work for silks on complex and sometimes high profile work.

mini pupillages
Mini pupillages are available but in demand. Preference is given to final year students. Send Philip Mead your CV and a letter explaining your interest in chambers.

funding
2002 grant: between £18,000 and £20,000 for 12 months in London, £14,000 in Bristol. Second six pupils undertake a great deal of work on their own account.

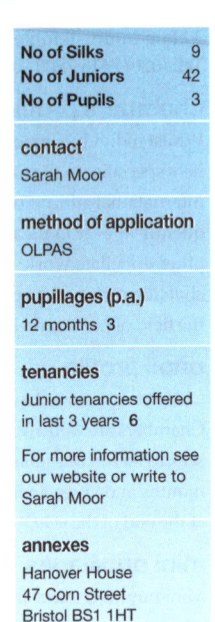

No of Silks 9
No of Juniors 42
No of Pupils 3

contact
Sarah Moor

method of application
OLPAS

pupillages (p.a.)
12 months 3

tenancies
Junior tenancies offered in last 3 years 6

For more information see our website or write to Sarah Moor

annexes
Hanover House
47 Corn Street
Bristol BS1 1HT
Tel: (0117) 927 7111
Fax: (0117) 927 3478

18 Red Lion Court (Anthony Arlidge QC)

18 Red Lion Court, London EC4A 3EB DX: 478 LDE
Tel: (020) 7520 6000 Fax: (020) 7520 6248/9
Email: stephen.requena@18rlc.co.uk

chambers profile
Chambers operate from a spacious listed building off Fleet Street near the Temple. Comprising 19 silks and 50 juniors, chambers offer one of the most comprehensive cross-sections of expertise in the field of criminal law.

type of work undertaken
18 Red Lion Court covers the whole range of crime, defending and prosecuting at all levels. Particular strengths are commercial fraud, Inland Revenue and VAT offences, money laundering, corruption, drugs and drug trafficking and sex cases, including child abuse and obscene publications. Individual members are involved in international human rights cases from Rwanda to Santa Monica. Others have written well respected practitioners texts on a wide range of topics. Chambers' work is centred primarily on the South Eastern circuit with an emphasis on London and East Anglia. Much of the East Anglian work is serviced by the set's annexe in Chelmsford.

pupil profile
Chambers look for pupils with potential to develop into first class advocates. Pupils are selected for a combination of marked intellectual ability, together with good judgement and independent personalities.

pupillage
Chambers offer four funded twelve months pupillages. Pupils will receive £15,000, made up of £9,000 award, £6,000 guaranteed earnings. Chambers' pupils receive excellent training. In addition to experiencing a broad range of work, all pupils participate in an in-house advocacy programme. Nearly all chambers' pupils get tenancies with chambers or elsewhere. Chambers do not offer second or third six pupillages. Sponsored pupils are accepted.

pupillage applications
Requests for an application form should be made to Stephen Requena. Please contact chambers for application deadline for entry 2003.

mini pupillages
Available subject to numbers all year round. Applications with CV should be made to Louis-Peter Moll.

Chambers operate an equal opportunities policy.

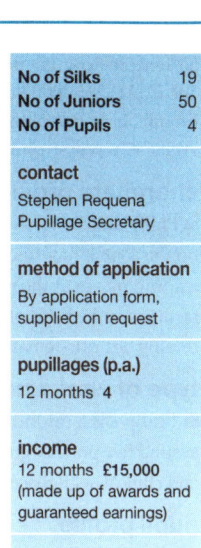

No of Silks 19
No of Juniors 50
No of Pupils 4

contact
Stephen Requena
Pupillage Secretary

method of application
By application form, supplied on request

pupillages (p.a.)
12 months 4

income
12 months £15,000
(made up of awards and guaranteed earnings)

tenancies
Junior tenancies offered in last 3 years 5

annexes
Chelmsford

St Philip's Chambers

55 Temple Row, Birmingham B2 5LS
Tel: (0121) 246 7000 Fax: (0121) 246 7001
Email: clerks@st-philips.co.uk
Website: www.st-philips.co.uk

chambers profile
St Philip's Chambers is one of the largest barristers chambers in the country. Since formation in 1998 it has quickly gained a reputation for innovative change and has become a leading player at the regional and national bar. The recent relocation to state of the art facilities at the heart of Birmingham's commercial centre has underlined St Philip's continuing desire to remain on the front foot as legislative and competitive pressures increase.

type of work undertaken
St Philip's is a multidisciplinary chambers. Its individual specialisations are focused around five practice groups - commercial, crime, employment, family, and personal injury and clinical negligence.

pupil profile
The set is looking for exceptional and well-rounded individuals with good intellectual ability and a practical approach to problem solving. It is more interested in potential than background.

pupillage
The set expects to offer three 12 month pupillages to commence in October 2003. All pupillages are offered with a view to a tenancy and attract funding of £10,000 for the first six months and an income guarantee for the second six. Pupils gain experience in the work of all of the practice groups.

mini pupillages
Mini pupillages are available by agreement. Please contact Elizabeth Hodgetts.

funding
See under pupillage.

No of Silks	7
No of Juniors	86
No of Pupils	3

contact
John de Waal
Tel: (0121) 246 7000

method of application
On chambers' own application form - please don't send CVs

pupillages (p.a.)
Three twelve month pupillages offered every year

tenancies
Pupils are selected with a view to tenancy

annexes
None

3 Verulam Buildings (Christopher Symons QC/John Jarvis QC)

3 Verulam Buildings, Gray's Inn, London WC1R 5NT DX: LDE 331
Tel: (020) 7831 8441 Fax: (020) 7831 8479
Email: chambers@3vb.com
Website: www.3vb.com

chambers profile

3 Verulam Buildings is a large commercial set with a history of expansion by recruitment of tenants from amongst pupils. Over the past ten years two of its pupils have become tenants every year. Chambers occupies recently refurbished, spacious offices overlooking Gray's Inn Walks with all modern IT and library facilities. Chambers prides itself on a pleasant, friendly and relaxed atmosphere.

type of work undertaken

A wide range of commercial work, in particular banking and financial services, insurance and reinsurance, commercial fraud, professional negligence, company law, entertainment, insolvency, public international law, EU law, arbitration/ADR, building and construction as well as other general commercial work. Members of chambers regularly appear in high profile cases and a substantial amount of chambers' work is international.

pupil profile

Chambers looks for intelligent and ambitious candidates with strong powers of analysis and reasoning, who are self confident and get on well with others. Candidates should normally have at least a 2:1 grade in an honours subject which need not be law.

pupillage

Chambers seeks to recruit four funded twelve months pupils every year through OLPAS. Each pupil spends three months with four different members of chambers to gain experience of different types of work. Chambers also offers pupillages to pupils who do not intend to practise at the Bar of England and Wales.

mini pupillages

Mini pupillages are available for one week at a time for university, CPE or Bar students who are interested in finding out more about chambers' work. Chambers considers mini-pupillage to be an important part of the recruitment process. Candidates should have, or expect to obtain, the minimum requirements for a funded 12 month pupillage. Applications are accepted throughout the year and should be addressed to Ian Wilson.

funding

In the year 2002-2003 the annual award will be at least £27,000 payable monthly.

No of Silks 13
No of Juniors 39
No of Pupils 4

contact
Mr Peter Ratcliffe (Pupillage)
Mr Ian Wilson (Mini pupillage)
Pupillage Committee

method of application
OLPAS, or for unfunded pupillage & mini pupillage CV & covering letter stating dates of availability

pupillages (p.a.)
12 months 4
Required degree grade 2:1

income
At least £27,000 per annum.
Earnings not included

tenancies
Current tenants who served pupillage in chambers 33
Junior tenancies offered in last 3 years 5
No of tenants of 5 years call or under 8

notes

notes

notes